Business Law
in Canada
Casebook

THIRD EDITION

D'ANNE DAVIS

MARIA KORONEOS

Prentice
Hall

Toronto

DEDICATION

To Brennan and Erin
D.D.

To my parents, Stamatios and Vasilia.
M.K.

National Library of Canada Cataloguing in Publication Data

Davis, D'Anne
        Business law in Canada casebook

3rd ed.
To accompany Business Law in Canada by Richard Yates.
ISBN 0-13-093652-9

Commercial law – Canada – Cases. I. Koroneos, Maria. II. Yates, Richard. Business law in Canada. III. Title.

KE918.5.D3 2002   346.71'07C2001-930494-3
KF888.D3 2002

0-13-093652-9

Vice President, Editorial Director: Michael Young
Marketing Manager: Deborah Merry
Developmental Editor: Suzanne Schaan
Production Editor: Gillian Scobie
Copy Editor: Gail Marsden
Production Coordinator: Deborah Starks
Page Layout: Carol Magee
Art Director: Mary Opper
Cover and Interior Design: Lisa Lapointe
Cover Image: PhotoDisk, Inc.

1 2 3 4 5   06 05 04 03 02

Printed and bound in the United States of America.

TABLE OF CONTENTS

TABLE OF CASES

An asterisk (*) following the case indicates it is a decision of the Supreme Court of Canada (S.C.C.) or it was upheld by the S.C.C. or the S.C.C. refused permission to appeal.

LIST OF SOURCES

A.C.	Appeal Cases (British)
A.P.R.	Atlantic Provinces Reports
B.C.L.R.	British Columbia Law Reports
C.C.C.	Canadian Criminal Cases
C.C.L.I.	Canadian Cases on the Law of Insurance
C.C.L.T.	Canadian Cases on the Law of Torts
C.E.L.R. (N.S.)	Canadian Environmental Law Reports (New Series)
C.P.R.	Canadian Patent Reporter
D.L.R.	Dominion Law Reports
E.R.	English Reports
F.C.	Canada Law Reports, Federal Court
K.B.	King's Bench (British)
Man. R.	Manitoba Reports
Nfld. and P.E.I.R.	Newfoundland and Prince Edward Island Reports
O.A.C.	Ontario Appeal Cases
O.R.	Ontario Reports
R.P.R.	Real Property Reports
S.C.R.	Supreme Court Reports
Sask. R.	Saskatchewan Reports
W.W.R.	Western Weekly Reports
	Alberta: http://www.albertacourts.ab.ca/
	British Columbia: http://www.courts.gov.bc.ca/
	Ontario: http://www.ontariocourts.on.ca/
	Supreme Court of Canada: http://www.lexum.umontreal.ca/
	Federal Court: http://www.fja.gc.ca/

Edupage is a service of EDUCAUSE, an international nonprofit association dedicated to transforming education through information technologies. LISTSERV@LISTSERV.EDUCAUSE.EDU

TABLE OF CORRESPONDENCE

This table shows cases in this casebook that correspond to *Business Law in Canada*, Sixth Edition, by Yates, and to *The Law and Business Administration in Canada*, Ninth Edition, by Smyth, Soberman, and Easson.

PREFACE

In order to play the game, you need to know the rules. Your ability to conduct your business successfully is necessarily enhanced by learning about our legal system: the fundamental principles of tort and contract law; the basic terms of the contracts between buyer and seller, debtor and creditor, employer and employee; and the law of partnerships, corporations, and property.

Knowledge of these principles and an appreciation for judicial reasoning, which you gain from reading the court decisions, also equips you for your role as a lawmaker. Humans, intrinsically complex, often perverse, adjusting to a multiplicity of events, inventions and discoveries, provide us with more than good entertainment — they force us, the ultimate lawmakers, to create new rules to cover the unexpected. We do that not only through our legislators but also through our judges, who every day must decide between opposing views and must justify those decisions. The law from both sources, legislation and court decisions, incorporates the community standard of what is right. When the court, especially the Supreme Court of Canada, responds to new questions, it makes frequent and explicit reference to our collective conscience. Directly and indirectly, your opinions count, and your opinion is more informed when you appreciate the complexity of issues and how the courts strive to balance legitimate but competing interests.

The study of law should also give you respect for human achievement. Our adoption of rule by law rather than by whim is impressive in itself. Our constant effort to apply and create rules to curb our worst human tendencies and to create a just and good society is worthy of admiration, even of reverence.

Because we find the study of law both practical and honourable, we have tried to bring you a collection of cases that are both authoritative and memorable. The most notable changes in this edition reflect the courts' attempt to apply existing laws, or to create law, to bring order where new technology and global commerce seem to invite chaos. Also, this edition includes new Supreme Court of Canada decisions in the fields of administrative law, negligence, secured transactions, employment, intellectual property, and insurance.

As in the last edition, the casebook contains three types of entries: (1) the main cases — extracts from the court decision itself, (2) cases primarily summarized from the court decision or from secondary sources, and (3) short statements of relevant cases or stories.

The casebook was written to accompany the sixth edition of *Business Law in Canada* by Richard Yates. It also complements the ninth edition of *The Law and Business Administration in Canada* by Smyth, Soberman, and Easson, and can be used with other business law texts.

ACKNOWLEDGMENTS

We wish to express our gratitude to Craig Davis and Howard Cherniack, without whose computer skills this project may well have been abandoned; to colleagues Catherine Ryan and Bill Hooker and to the production team of our publisher — Suzanne Schaan, Gillian Scobie, and Gail Marsden — for their help. We are also grateful for the support of our families and for the patience of friends. Thanks also to Toshiko Nasu for services rendered. Special thanks to Craig and C.H.

I

THE LEGAL SYSTEM

A. PHILOSOPHICAL BASIS OF THE LAW

- *T*he age-old discourse about the legitimacy of man-made law by the supporters of natural law theory goes on. The news account of M.P. Svend Robinson petitioning the House of Commons, on behalf of his Humanist constituents, to remove the reference to God in the preamble of the Constitution, prompted a letter to the editor in which the writer quoted the Italian philosopher and theologian Thomas Aquinas (1225–74): "an unjust law is a human law that is not rooted in eternal law and natural law."[1]

B. CONSTITUTIONAL MATTERS

Q u e s t i o n s

When does a case involve a "constitutional issue"?
How does a constitutional issue get before the courts?

---

1. ALLOCATION OF POWERS

R. *v.* *Hydro-Québec*

http://www.lexum.umontreal.ca/
SUPREME COURT OF CANADA
SEPTEMBER 18, 1997

La Forest, J. :...

[85] This Court has in recent years been increasingly called upon to consider the interplay between federal and provincial legislative powers as they relate to environmental protection. Whether viewed positively as strategies for maintaining a clean environment, or negatively as measures to combat the evils of pollution, there can be no doubt that these measures relate to a public purpose of superordinate importance, and one in which all levels of government and numerous organs of the international community have become increasingly engaged. ...

[87] This latest case in which this Court is required to define the nature of legislative powers over the environment is of major significance. The narrow issue raised is the extent to and manner in which the federal Parliament may control the amount of and conditions under which Chlorobiphenyls (PCBs) — substances well known to pose great dangers to humans and the environment generally — may enter into the environment. However, the attack on the federal power to secure this end is not really aimed at the specific provisions respecting PCBs. Rather, it puts into question the constitutional validity of its enabling statutory provisions. What is really at stake is whether Part II ("Toxic Substances") of the Canadian Environmental Protection Act, R.S.C., 1985, c. 16 (4th Supp.), which empowers the federal Ministers of Health and of the Environment to determine what substances are toxic and to prohibit the introduction of such substances into the environment except in accordance with specified terms and conditions, falls within the constitutional power of Parliament.

FACTS

[88] The case arose in this way. The respondent Hydro-Québec allegedly dumped polychlorinated biphenyls (PCBs) into the St. Maurice River in Quebec in early 1990. On June 5, 1990, it was charged with ... two infractions under order, P.C. 1989-296 (hereafter "Interim Order"), which was adopted and enforced pursuant to ss. 34 and 35 of the Canadian Environmental Protection Act: ...

On July 23, 1990, the respondent pleaded not guilty to both charges before the Court of Québec.

[89] On March 4, 1991, the respondent Hydro-Québec brought a motion before Judge Michel Babin seeking to have ss. 34 and 35 of the Act as well as s. 6(a) of the Interim Order itself declared *ultra vires* the Parliament of Canada on the ground that they do not fall within the ambit of any federal head of power set out in s. 91 of the Constitution Act, 1867. The Attorney General of Quebec intervened in support of the respondent's position. Judge Babin granted the motion on August 12, 1991 [that these provisions of the legislation were *ultra vires*] ([1991] R.J.Q. 2736), and an appeal to the Quebec Superior Court was dismissed by Trottier J. on August 6, 1992 ([1992] R.J.Q. 2159). A further appeal to the Court of Appeal of Quebec was dismissed on February 14, 1995 [1995] R.J.Q. 398, 67 Q.A.C. 161, 17 C.E.L.R. (N.S.) 34, [1995] Q.J. No. 143 (QL). Leave to appeal to this Court was granted on October 12, 1995: [1995] 4 S.C.R. vii. ... [La Forest reviews the judicial history of the case.]

Constitutional Questions

[97] On December 21, 1995, Lamer C.J. framed the following constitutional question: Do s. 6(a) of the Chlorobiphenyls Interim Order, P.C. 1989-296, and the enabling legislative provisions, ss. 34 and 35 of the Canadian Environmental Protection Act, [CEPA] R.S.C., 1985, c. 16 (4th Supp.), fall in whole or in part within the jurisdiction of the Parliament of Canada to make laws for the peace, order and good government of Canada pursuant to s. 91 of the Constitution Act, 1867 or its criminal law jurisdiction under s. 91(27) of the Constitution Act, 1867 or otherwise fall within its jurisdiction?

[98] As can be seen, the constitutional question first raises the constitutionality of s. 6(a) of the Interim Order. ... It is clear that the Interim Order will be of no force or effect if the enabling provisions pursuant to which it was adopted are themselves found to be *ultra vires*. ... [La Forest reviews the legislative structure of CEPA.]

[108] In this Court, the appellant Attorney General of Canada seeks to support the impugned provisions of the Act on the basis of the national concern doctrine under the peace, order and good government clause of s. 91 or under the criminal law power under s. 91(27) of the Constitution Act, 1867. The respondent Hydro-Québec and the *mis en cause* Attorney General of Quebec dispute this. In broad terms, they say that the provisions are so invasive of provincial powers that they cannot be justified either under the national dimensions doctrine or under the criminal law power. The attack on the validity of the provisions under the latter power is also supported, most explicitly by the intervener the Attorney General for Saskatchewan, on the ground that they are, in essence, of a regulatory and not of a prohibitory character. Finally, I repeat that while the Interim Order precipitated the litigation, there is no doubt that the re-spondent and *mis en cause* as well as their supporting interveners are after bigger game — the enabling provisions.

[110] ... [I]n my view, the impugned provisions are valid legislation under the criminal law power — s. 91(27) of the Constitution Act, 1867. It thus becomes unnecessary to deal with the national concern doctrine, which inevitably raises profound issues respecting the federal structure of our Constitution which do not arise with anything like the same intensity in relation to the criminal law power. ...

ANALYSIS

Introduction

[112] In considering how the question of the constitutional validity of a legislative enactment relating to the environment should be approached, this Court in *Oldman River, supra*, made it clear that the environment is not, as such, a subject matter of legislation under the Constitution Act, 1867. As it was put there, "the Constitution Act, 1867 has not assigned the matter of 'environment' sui generis to either the provinces or Parliament" (p. 63). Rather, it is a diffuse subject that cuts across many different areas of constitutional responsibility, some federal, some provincial (pp. 63–64). Thus Parliament or a provincial legislature can, in advancing the scheme or purpose of a statute, enact provisions minimizing or preventing the detrimental impact that statute may have on the environment, prohibit pollution, and the like. In assessing the constitutional validity of a provision relating to the environment, therefore, what must first be done is to look at the catalogue of legislative powers listed in the Constitution Act, 1867 to see if the provision falls within one or more of the powers assigned to the body (whether Parliament or a provincial legislature) that enacted the legislation (ibid. at p. 65). If the provision in essence, in pith and substance, falls within the parameters of any such power, then it is constitutionally valid.

[113] Though pith and substance may be described in different ways, the expressions "dominant purpose" or "true character" used in *R. v. Morgentaler*, [1993] 3 S.C.R. 463, at pp. 481–82, or "the dominant or most important characteristic of the challenged law" used in *Whitbread v. Walley*, [1990] 3 S.C.R. 1273, at p. 1286, and in *Oldman River* ... appropriately convey the meaning to be attached to the term. ...

THE CRIMINAL LAW POWER

[118] Section 91(27) of the Constitution Act, 1867 confers the exclusive power to legislate in relation to criminal law on Parliament. ...

[119] What appears from the analysis in *RJR-MacDonald* is that as early as 1903, the Privy Council, in *Attorney-General for Ontario v. Hamilton Street Railway* Co., [1903] A.C. 524, at pp. 528–29, had made it clear that the power conferred on Parliament by s. 91(27) is "the criminal law in its widest sense" (emphasis added). Consistently with this approach, the Privy Council in *Proprietary Articles Trade Association v. Attorney-General for Canada*, [1931] A.C. 310 (hereafter PATA), at p. 324, defined the criminal law power as including any prohibited act with penal consequences. As it put it, at p. 324: "The criminal quality of an act cannot be discerned ... by reference to any standard but one: Is the act prohibited with penal consequences?" This approach has been consistently followed ever since and, as *RJR-MacDonald* relates, it has been applied by

the courts in a wide variety of settings. Accordingly, it is entirely within the discretion of Parliament to determine what evil it wishes by penal prohibition to suppress and what threatened interest it thereby wishes to safeguard. ...

[120] ... This power is, of course, subject to the "fundamental justice" requirements of s. 7 of the Canadian Charter of Rights and Freedoms ... but that is not an issue here.

[121] The Charter apart, only one qualification has been attached to Parliament's plenary power over criminal law. The power cannot be employed colourably. Like other legislative powers, it cannot, as Estey J. put it in *Scowby v. Glendinning*, [1986] 2 S.C.R. 226, at p. 237, "permit Parliament, simply by legislating in the proper form, to colourably invade areas of exclusively provincial legislative competence." To determine whether such an attempt is being made, it is, of course, appropriate to enquire into Parliament's purpose in enacting the legislation. As Estey J. noted in *Scowby*, at p. 237, since the *Margarine Reference*, it has been "accepted that some legitimate public purpose must underlie the prohibition." ...

[123] ... But I entertain no doubt that the protection of a clean environment is a public purpose ... sufficient to support a criminal prohibition. It is surely an "interest threatened" which Parliament can legitimately "safeguard," or to put it another way, pollution is an "evil" that Parliament can legitimately seek to suppress. Indeed, as I indicated at the outset of these reasons, it is a public purpose of superordinate importance; it constitutes one of the major challenges of our time. It would be surprising indeed if Parliament could not exercise its plenary power over criminal law to protect this interest and to suppress the evils associated with it by appropriate penal prohibitions. ...

[131] ... [T]he use of the federal criminal law power in no way precludes the provinces from exercising their extensive powers under s. 92 to regulate and control the pollution of the environment either independently or to supplement federal action. The situation is really no different from the situation regarding the protection of health where Parliament has for long exercised extensive control over such matters as food and drugs by prohibitions grounded in the criminal law power. This has not prevented the provinces from extensively regulating and prohibiting many activities relating to health. The two levels of government frequently work together to meet common concerns. The cooperative measures relating to the use of tobacco are fully related in *RJR-MacDonald*. ... It is also the case in many other areas. ...

[133] The respondent, the *mis en cause* and their supporting interveners primarily attack ss. 34 and 35 of the Act as constituting an infringement on provincial regulatory powers conferred by the Constitution. This they do by submitting that the power to regulate a substance is so broad as to encroach upon provincial legislative jurisdiction. ...

[The court considers the argument that the power to regulate encroaches upon provincial legislative jurisdiction. He examines the scheme established in Part II of the Act and concludes it is not too broad as it doesn't deal with environmental protection generally, but "simply" with the control of toxic substances.]

[159] I should say that the respondent and *mis en cause* do not contest the toxicity of PCBs but simply argue that their control should not fall exclusively within federal competence. ... I have already discussed the issue of concurrency. ...

[160] I conclude, therefore, that the Interim Order is also valid under s. 91(27) of the Constitution Act, 1867.

DISPOSITION

[161] I would allow the appeal. ... I would answer the constitutional question as follows:

> Q. Do s. 6(a) of the Chlorobiphenyls Interim Order, P.C. 1989-296, and the enabling legislative provisions, ss. 34 and 35 of the Canadian Environmental Protection Act, R.S.C., 1985, c. 16 (4th Supp.), fall in whole or in part within the jurisdiction of the Parliament of Canada to make laws for the peace, order and good government of Canada pursuant to s. 91 of the Constitution Act, 1867 or its criminal law jurisdiction under s. 91(27) of the Constitution Act, 1867 or otherwise fall within its jurisdiction?

> A. Yes. They fall wholly within Parliament's power to enact laws under s. 91(27) of the Constitution Act, 1867. It is not necessary to consider the first issue.

Appeal allowed with costs   [5–4]

R. v. Sobey's Inc.

NOVA SCOTIA COURT OF APPEAL
[1998] N.S.J. NO. 467 (Q.L.)
DECEMBER 4, 1998

[1] Cromwell J.A. (orally):— Sobey's Incorporated was acquitted by Cole, Prov. Ct. J. on a charge that it ... sold tobacco or a tobacco product to a person under the age of 19 years contrary to s. 5(1) of the Tobacco Access Act, S.N.S. 1993, c. 14.

[2] .... The issues at trial, and on this appeal, involve the constitutionality of the Act and the defence of due diligence.

[3] The trial judge found that the Tobacco Access Act was *ultra vires* the Legislature. He reasoned that federal legislation had "occupied the field" with the Tobacco Act, S.C. 1997, c. 13, that it "cannot stand side by side with the provincial legislation", and that the federal legislation therefore prevails. Having found the legislation under which the accused was charged to be unconstitutional, an acquittal was entered. The Crown appeals from that finding.

[4] The trial judge also ... thought the relevant consideration [in determining due diligence] was whether the employee who sold the tobacco product had been duly diligent rather than

whether the accused, Sobey's, had been duly diligent. ...

[7] As submitted by the Crown, the proper method of analysis in this case has three steps. First, it is necessary to determine "the matter", or the "pith and substance" of each of the federal and provincial laws. We are satisfied that the Province's Tobacco Access Act is legislation in relation to the health of young persons. As for the federal legislation, it has been assumed by both parties that it is in pith and substance criminal law as was decided in relation to its predecessor statute by a majority of the Supreme Court of Canada in *RJR-Macdonald Inc. v. Attorney General of Canada,* [1995] 3 S.C.R. 199; (1995), 127 D.L.R. (4th) 1. ...

[8] The second step requires that the matter of each of the laws be assigned to one or more of the classes of subjects in respect of which the federal and provincial governments have legislative authority under the Constitution Act, 1867. The "matter" of the provincial Statute, the health of young persons, is within provincial legislative competence under section 92(16). As the Supreme Court of Canada noted in *R. v. Morgentaler,* [1993] 1 S.C.R. 462; (1993), ... that section gives the provinces "...general jurisdiction over health matters within the province..." The matter of the federal Act is assumed to fall under s. 91 (27) setting out the power to legislate in relation to criminal law.

[9] The third step in the analysis is to determine whether there is conflict between the federal and the provincial laws. ... If there is conflict, the federal law prevails under the doctrine of paramountcy.

[10] The test for determining whether there is conflict was set out by the Supreme Court of Canada in *Multiple Access v. McCutcheon,* [1982] 2 S.C.R. 161 and [others]. ... In *Multiple Access,* Dickson, J., as he then was, said at page 191:

> In principle, there would seem to be no good reasons to speak of paramountcy and preclusion except where there is actual conflict in operation as where one enactment says "yes" and the other says "no"; "the same citizens are being told to do inconsistent things"; compliance with one is defiance of the other.

[11] There is no conflict here in this sense between the federal and provincial legislation. It follows that the two Acts can operate side by side and that the trial judge erred in finding the provincial Act unconstitutional. ...

[12] Turning to the due diligence issue raised on the cross-appeal, the trial judge also erred in concluding that the onus on Sobey's was to show that its employee was duly diligent rather than that it was duly diligent. ...

[13] In the result, the appeal is allowed, the judgment of the trial judge is set aside and the matter is remitted to a differently constituted Provincial Court for trial. ...

Unanimous

- *T*he Supreme Court of British Columbia held that it was *ultra vires* the jurisdiction of the province to pass the *Tobacco Damages and Health Care Costs Recovery Act* because the statute improperly imposed liability on foreign companies, namely it tried to reach the parent companies not just the Canadian subsidiaries operating in British Columbia.

  The legislature rewrote the statute in an effort to eliminate this legal problem.[2]

- *T*he court ruled that a municipal bylaw that made it an offence under the B.C. *Offence Act* for a female over the age of eight to be topless in the park was invalid as being beyond the power of the municipality. The "pith and substance" of the bylaw was a matter of criminal law, which section 91 of the *Constitution Act* allocates exclusively to the federal government.[3]

2. CHARTER OF RIGHTS AND FREEDOMS

Q u e s t i o n s

If the Charter of Rights and Freedoms was entrenched in the Constitution to curb the power of the government, what is the government? For example, does the Charter bind the conduct of hospitals, universities, and other government bodies like the CBC?

Adbusters Media Foundation *v.* *Canadian Broadcasting Corporation*

http://www.courts.gov.bc.ca/
BRITISH COLUMBIA SUPREME COURT
NOVEMBER 8, 1995

Holmes, J.: — [1] The Adbusters Media Foundation ("Adbusters") is a non-profit society which provides educational services to the media and promotes environmental awareness and media literacy.

[2] Adbusters believes the media is too commercial and hence they seek to "re-define" it through social marketing of their ideas.

[3] The defendant Canadian Broadcasting Corporation ("CBC") is a federal corporation established under the *Broadcasting Act,* S.C. 1991, c.11 which provides a national television and radio network facility.

[4] Adbusters and Greenpeace International devised, financed and produced a 30-second television advertisement they title *"Autosaurus."* It uses animated dinosaurs to convey a message that the automobile is becoming obsolete and the automotive age coming to an end.

[5] Adbusters wished to have the advertisement shown in the commercial television market.

[6] The CBC carried a commercially sponsored television program called *"Driver's Seat."* The basic format was for journalistic reports on the analytic testing and review of new cars and related products. The program also offered automotive consumer advice and safety messages of interest to car owners or prospective purchasers.

[7] The program was co-produced by an independent producer, Mr. Waldin, and the CBC. The CBC provided facilities and the "hardware" for production, Mr. Waldin's company provided the creative talent and administration. The program contained six minutes of advertising of which the independent producers sold and received the proceeds from two minutes and the CBC sold and retained the proceeds of the other four minutes. The advertising of the independent producer was melded into the show as it was produced. The advertisers were related to the automotive product and service industry.

[8] Adbusters considered the *"Driver's Seat"* viewing audience to be an ideal market to deliver its "anti-auto" message. They contacted the CBC sales office to place *"Autosaurus"* on *"Driver's Seat"* and also submitted the advertisement to the Advertising Standards Branch of the CBC for review.

[9] Adbusters was aware that the CBC had a written Advertising Standard with which they must comply. In particular within those Standards was an Advocacy Advertising policy. The preamble to the policy read:

> The purpose of this policy is to permit access to the airwaves for advertisements that advocate a point of view or particular course of action on issues of public interest or concern. It is based on the principle that the democratic rights of Canadians will best be served by policies promoting freedom of speech.

[10] The CBC under the written policy would accept advertisements subject to, *inter alia*:

(d) Advocacy advertisements will not be aired within news programs, programs whose regular mandate is to report on controversial public issues, or programs in which the CBC does not schedule advertising.

[11] Through a translation error from the French to English version the italicised words "... and information ..." were omitted in the English version as it existed and was known to the plaintiff in early 1993. The sub-section should therefore have read:

(d) Advocacy advertisements will not be aired within news *and information* programs. ...

[12] The advertisement as submitted for review as to Advertising Standards was approved for broadcast. February 4, 1993 Adbusters and the CBC contracted in writing for the broadcast of *"Autosaurus"* on the February 27, 1993 and March 6, 1993 showing of *"Driver's Seat"*.

[13] The cost of the advertising was paid in full in advance as required. The CBC broadcast *"Autosaurus"* on the February 27, 1993 date as contracted. On March 2, 1993 the CBC however advised Adbusters the March 6, 1993 *"Driver's Seat"* program was preempted and that it had erred in application of its Advertising Standards and was not willing to permit future broadcast of the advertisement within the *"Driver's Seat"* program.

[14] Alternate scheduling of the advertisement was offered including the time period immediately preceding or following the show. Adbusters refused the offers of alternative broadcast placement and the CBC returned its payment.

[15] Adbusters as a result of the cancellation of its advertisement on *"Driver's Seat,"* and the refusal of the CBC to permit the advertisement future access to that program, brought this action claiming damages for a breach of contract, coupled with claims for relief by way of declarations, damages and injunctive relief for breaches of the Canadian *Charter of Rights and Freedoms ("Charter")*. In particular the plaintiff claims the defendant breached the plaintiff's right to freedom of expression under Section 2(b) and discriminated against the plaintiff in violation of s. 15, of the Charter. ... [The judge finds that CBC did breach its contract with Adbusters when it refused to proceed with the second scheduled showing of the advertisement. He further observes that the contract claim was being used "as a platform to launch a Charter challenge" and finds that there were no apparent damages resulting from the breach and makes no award of damages, not even a nominal sum.]

[26] In the event damages at law must be presumed the award should in the circumstances be the minimal or token amount that the law requires.

CHARTER

[27] 1. Does the *Charter* apply to the CBC?
   2. If so, was there a violation of Section 2(b) or Section 15?

[28] The plaintiff contends the CBC is amenable to the Charter specifically because it is a governmental body; alternatively, because the *Charter* in the existing circumstances would apply to all broadcasters.

[29] The Charter provides the individual with protection from the coercive power of the State. Section 32(l) of the Charter provides that it applies:

(a) To the Parliament and government of Canada in respect of all matters within the authority of Parliament. ...

[30] As Mr. Justice Campbell in *Trieger v. Canadian Broadcasting Corp. et al* (1988), 54 D.L.R. (4th) 143 said, the *Charter* "... represents a curb on the power of government, not a fetter on the rights of organizations or individuals independent of government which do not exercise the functions of government."

[31] The CBC does have several of the indicia of a governmental body. The test however is conduct based. It must therefore be found that the conduct in issue of the entity in question is governmental in nature to give rise to Charter application. ...

[34] Although the CBC was created by Parliament, it is an agent of the Crown, and remains ultimately responsible through the Minister to Parliament, this form of "ultimate or extraordinary" control is not determinative of operational, routine or regular control... .

[35] In a trilogy of cases decided by the Supreme Court of Canada as to whether entities such as universities and hospitals were subject to the Charter in respect of mandatory retirement policies ..., the entities were found to be *not* subject to the *Charter* in respect of the activity in question. The judgments of members of the court differ as to factors to be considered in deciding if the entity is governmental in nature but it would appear fair to conclude that a court should give weight to factors indicative of the entity in question being independent or autonomous of governmental control. ...

[37] It is overall control of programming that lays at the base of the issue here. ...

[38] The *Broadcasting Act* makes clear that the CBC in pursuing its objects and in the exercise of its powers enjoys "... freedom of expression and journalistic, creative and programming independence" [Section 46(5)].

[39] The *Broadcasting Act* provides to both the CBC specifically and to broadcasters generally the protection of this independence through directed interpretation of the statute and strongly indicates the importance placed by Parliament upon the preservation of those freedoms from governmental influence or control. [The judge reviews relevant sections of the *Broadcasting Act* and also shows that the CBC is not subject to control under the *Financial Administration Act*. After citing relevant cases he concludes.]

[46] The Advocacy Advertising policy has not been shown to have either government input, influence, or its formulation interfered with in any way. It is a policy clearly appropriate and incidental to the CBC's carefully protected mandate to exercise power and enjoy freedom of expression and journalistic, creative and programming independence under the *Broadcasting Act*.

[47] The conduct of the CBC in the classification of the "Autosaurus" advertisement cannot fairly be said to be a decision of government, nor is there evidence that the government influenced, interfered, or participated in any sense in the impugned decision-making process. The advertiser complaints brought to light the embarrassing error or omission that occurred regarding the Advocacy Advertising policy during review of the *"Autosaurus"* advertisement under the Advertising Standards.

[48] I do not find the Charter has application to the CBC as contended either specifically or generally as a broadcaster, viewed in the context of the circumstances and conduct of its dealing with the plaintiff in issue here. I find it unnecessary therefore to deal with the issue of breach of specific Charter sections.

[49] The claims for Charter relief are dismissed. In the circumstances of the finding that the CBC was in breach of its contract, but with no damages being shown; and the failure of the plaintiff on its Charter claims, I find it appropriate that each party bear its separate costs.

[Claim for Charter relief dismissed.]

Note: This decision was affirmed by the Court of Appeal. The Supreme Court of Canada refused to hear an appeal from the Court of Appeal.

S. 1 AND S. 2

▶▶ For a discussion of ss. 1 and 2 see *U.F.C.W. Local 1518 v. KMart Canada Ltd.* (Supreme Court of Canada) on p. 180 below.

The *Tobacco Products Control Act*, a federal statute, came into force on January 1, 1989 purportedly to address a national public health problem. The Act, among other things, banned advertisement of tobacco products. Cigarette manufacturers challenged the statute, alleging that the statute was unconstitutional. Judge Chabot of the Quebec Superior Court agreed; he struck it down by holding that it was *ultra vires* the federal government.

The judge held that the effect of the law was to eliminate advertising and that such commercial activities were within the jurisdiction of the provinces—covered by *The Constitution Act*

s. 92(13) [property and civil rights] or 92(16) [matters of a local or private nature]. He rejected the argument of the lawyers for the Attorney General that the federal government had the right to create the statute under its residual power to pass laws for the "peace, order, and good government of Canada." Furthermore, the judge held that, even if the purpose of the legislation was to protect the public health, such matters came within the jurisdiction of the provinces. The judge also found the legislation offended against the *Charter of Rights and Freedoms* because it violated s. 2(b), the freedom of expression. Nor could it be saved by s.1, as an infringement that could be justified in a free and democratic society.

Imperial Tobacco Ltd. v. Le Procureur General du Canada
Summarized from The Lawyers Weekly, *August 23, 1991, p. 9*

This decision was reversed by the Cour d'appel du Québec, District of Montreal. The Supreme Court of Canada gave the tobacco companies leave to appeal.

In 1995, on the question of the Parliament's authority to pass the statute, the majority of Supreme Court of Canada concluded that the legislation was validly enacted under the criminal law power given to the federal Parliament in the constitution, because its essence was to protect Canadians from the injurious effects of tobacco. The court, however, held that the Act's broad prohibition on advertising violated the Charter rights of the tobacco companies, namely the right of freedom of expression. Five of the nine judges found that the violation of the Charter rights could not be saved by s. 1 of the Charter, that is, the government failed to demonstrate that the Act's ban on advertising was justified. The four dissenting judges felt the Charter infringement on free expression was demonstrably justified. Thus, several sections of the Act were struck down as unconstitutional.[4]

RJR-MacDonald Inc. et al. v. Canada (Attorney General) et al.
http://www.lexum.umontreal.ca/
Supreme Court of Canada
September 21, 1995

Note: Subsequent to the court's decision on the Tobacco Products Control Act, Parliament passed the Tobacco Act, the preponderance of which was given Royal Assent on April 25, 1997.

- *I*n July of 1999 the Chinese government outlawed the Falun Gong, a spiritual movement blending ideas from Buddhism, Taoism, and traditional meditative exercises. The government crackdown on what it terms the "evil cult" includes the murder of several adherents, the detention of as many as "tens of thousands" to re-education camps, labour camps, insane asylums, or prisons. Some of those detained have committed suicide. Despite the government's effort to repress the movement, which it declared the most serious threat to its rule since the 1989 democracy demonstrations, members have been protesting "nearly every day" according to a "stunning" admission by the official press agency.[5]

- *O*nce again, Archbishop John Yang Shudao (of the outlawed Roman Catholic Church) was taken into custody by the Chinese police. First arrested in 1955 and sentenced to life imprisonment for refusing to denounce the authority of the Pope, he was imprisoned until 1981. Arrested again in 1988, he served another three years. He was most recently arrested in February 2000, at the age of 80, by 150 Chinese police.[6]

- *T*he courts in Iran shut down the sixteen newspapers that favoured reform; seven dailies with acceptable religious content remain.[7]

- *A* case was summarized as follows: "While there might be an expressive quality to lap dancing which could be protected under s. 2(b), an impugned by-law which prohibited such a performance was saved under s. 1."[8]

- *M*r. Thompson, ticketed for failing to wear his seat belt, contrary to the *Motor Vehicle Act*, argued that the provincial seat belt law conflicted with his religious freedom guaranteed by s. 2(a) of the Charter, namely his belief in free will and that he "creates his own reality." He lost.[9]

- *T*he ruling mullahs of Iran have banned Abdelkarim Soroush, a philosopher, from teaching, speaking or writing because he challenged the core concept of the late Ayatullah Khomeini, namely, that the "holy men have a God-given right to rule." Soroush maintains that religion is interpreted by imperfect humans so one infallible interpretation is not possible, not even that of the Supreme Leader.[10]

s. 3

- *I*n February of 1999 the people of Iran elected local councils, ending 2500 years of centralized rule.[11]

- *O*n July 1, 1997, the British government handed over to China the control of Hong Kong. The Beijing government disbanded the elected representatives and replaced them with an appointed legislature. During its first meeting, the appointed legislature voted to deport children who entered Hong Kong to join their parents. The new law, which required them to first obtain a certificate of entitlement from the government, was criticized as contrary to the "Basic Law" referred to as the mini-constitution of Hong Kong. "Vanquished former legislators looked on powerless from the public gallery and protesters outside played funeral music."[12]

s. 7

- *S*ection 7? 8? 9? or none of the above? While play was under way between the Pakistani and Afghan soccer clubs, Afghanistan's religious police ran onto the field and caught and arrested 12 members of the Pakistani soccer team. While being detained, the captured players had their heads shaved. Their crime? Wearing shorts, contrary to the Taliban strict dress code. The governor of the city apologized.[13]

s. 8 AND s. 24(2)

R. v. T.L.

THE DISTRICT COURT OF ONTARIO
FILE NO: YOA 2/89 COBURG, ONTARIO
MAY 9, 1990

Background facts: A Crime Stoppers tip led to the search of a teenager, who was found to have a vial of hash oil and a stolen wallet. He was arrested, read his *Charter* rights and charged with possession of stolen property. He was found guilty by the trial court. The conviction was appealed on the grounds that the police, by acting on a Crime Stoppers tip, had breached his rights under s. 8 of the *Charter* to be free from unreasonable search and seizure.

Kerr, D.C.J.:

... It appears that the trial judge took the view that the police have the right, solely on the basis of an anonymous tip, to conduct a search of the accused. While I am sure that anonymous tips are useful tools in enabling police to initiate criminal investigations, I do not accept the proposition that they are entitled to conduct warrantless searches on members of

the public without anything further. Constable Dunn at the time of conducting the search of the accused had nothing but a suspicion based on the anonymous call to his fellow officer. There was no evidence of the caller's identity, reputation or motivation. No subsequent investigation by Constable Dunn was conducted which would provide him with reasonable and probable grounds for suspecting the commission of an offence and under these circumstances he could not, in my view, have obtained a search warrant. If such warrantless searches by the police were condoned by the courts the right sought to be protected by Section 8 of the Charter would be meaningless. I conclude that there was a breach of the accused's Charter Rights under these circumstances.

In fact, on the argument of this appeal it was conceded by the Crown that the police had breached Section 8 in searching the accused, but the Crown submitted that the evidence being "real" evidence ought to be admitted notwithstanding the breach and that I ought not to apply Section 24(2) of the Charter to exclude the evidence obtained on the search. He relies on *Collins vs. R.* (1987) 33 C.C.C. 3rd, 1 (S.C.C.). However I am of the view that the appellant has met the onus upon him to establish on the balance of probabilities that the admission of this evidence would bring the administration of justice into disrepute when one considers the long term consequences of the regular admission of such evidence on the repute of the administration of justice. If the evidence obtained by Officer Dunn under the circumstances of this particular case were extended into a general policy to admit such evidence it would become readily apparent that the right of a private citizen to be secure from an unreasonable search and seizure would evaporate whenever real evidence was found. It is my view that Section 8 of the Charter has been in place for a sufficiently long period of time so that any competent and conscientious officer should realize that he does not have the right to conduct such a search without something more than a mere suspicion. A malicious or mischievous informant protected by anonymity could well create havoc with the rights and reputation of a well-respected, honest, average citizen. It was to protect the security of such citizens against a search of this type that Section 8 was enacted. Accordingly, the appeal succeeds on that ground...

Note: The evidence obtained after an illegal detention is not always inadmissible. In *R. v. Manolikakis,* the Ontario Court of Appeal followed the directions of the Supreme Court of Canada in *R. v. Collins* (the case cited in *R. v. T.L.* above), and held that, among other things, the reputation of the administration of justice would not be brought into disrepute by allowing evidence of the kilo of cocaine and the handgun. See [1997] O.J. No. 3284 (Q.L.) or Docket: C19123, Ontario Court of Appeal, August 12, 1997.

s. 9

Green *v.* Her Majesty the Queen

QUEEN'S BENCH, JUDICIAL CENTRE OF WEYBURN
REGISTRY NO. Q. 129
MAY 16, 1995

Matheson J.:—The appellant has appealed from his conviction, in Provincial Court, on a charge that on March 29, 1994, at Weyburn, he did, having consumed alcohol in such quantity that the concentration thereof in his blood exceeded 80 milligrams of alcohol in 100 mlliliters of blood, operate a motor vehicle, contrary to ss. 253(b) and 255(1) of the Criminal Code, R.S.C. 1985, c. C-46, as am. S.C. 1994, c 44.

It has been alleged, firstly, that the trial judge erred in not ruling that the appellant was arbitrarily detained within the meaning of s. 9 of the *Canadian Charter of Rights and Freedoms,* Part I of the Constitution Act, 1982, being Schedule B of the Canada Act 1982 (U.K.), c. 11 and in not thereby excluding the breathalyzer test results ...

FACTS

A police officer stopped the truck being operated by the appellant at approximately 2:35 a.m. on March 29, 1994. After being asked to do so, the appellant produced both his operator's licence and vehicle registration certificate. The police officer testified that he could smell liquor. The appellant was thereupon asked to go to the police vehicle. A demand for an Alcometer test was read to the appellant. The appellant complied with the demand. A 'fail' reading resulted. [Green was informed about his right to retain counsel, spoke with a lawyer, and consented to undergo a breathalyzer test.]

ARBITRARY DETENTION

Section 9 of the *Charter* states that "Everyone has the right not to be arbitrarily detained or imprisoned."

The Supreme Court of Canada has, in a series of decisions, considered the legality of the random stopping of motorists by police officers: *R. v. Dedman,* [1985] 2 S.C.R. 2; *R. v. Hufsky,* [1988] 1 S.C.R. 621; *R. v. Ladouceur,* [1990] 1 S.C.R. 1257; *R. v. Duncanson,* [1992] 1 S.C.R. 836; and *R. v. Mellenthin,* [1992] 3 S.C.R. 615. [A review of each of those decisions follows]...

The police officer who detained the appellant, Lyle Rodney Green, was alone in a patrol car in the City of Weyburn just prior to the stopping of the appellant's vehicle. ... [In cross-examination the police officer explained the reason for the detention:]

...

A. ... I just checked it to see who it was driving around that time of the night and kind of — and I didn't recognize the vehicle from being around town.

Q. Okay. What would be the significance of it being on the Weyburn Inn lot then? Like if it's parked in the Weyburn Inn lot, so what? I mean that's a place where people would come and stay and spend the night and —

A. Yeah, there was no significance really. I just saw it drive onto the lot. ...

Q. Yeah. And again I'm asking — you were kind enough to send me disclosure, and I notice in the disclosure statement that I got, "I decided I would try and stop the vehicle as I had previously seen it drive onto the Weyburn Inn lot." and I'm just wondering what — why that would be significant?

A. Just the idea that it was kind of hanging around downtown. I just wanted to see who it was basically. ...

It is clear from the foregoing that the detention of the appellant was arbitrary. But was it nevertheless a legally valid detention?

In response to the submission on behalf of the appellant that the detention of the appellant was not legally justified, the trial judge concluded:

The reason for stopping the vehicle, which he gave in evidence on cross-examination ... was that it was a strange vehicle. And although Mr. Fox has argued that it's questionable whether he should have stopped it, the — I relate this as good police work. When you see a strange vehicle in town driving around at two thirty in the morning, one would — the reasonable person would expect that the police officers on duty that evening would make inquiries as to what was about. So I interpret it as good police work. He was simply doing what he is trained to do.

There was no evidence before the trial judge that ascertaining the identity of a 'stranger in town' was within the scope of the police officer's duties or responsibilities, which might have justified the detention pursuant to the decision in *Duncanson*.

The detention of the appellant was arbitrary and, therefore, an infringement of the appellant's right, guaranteed by s. 9 of the *Charter*, not to be arbitrarily detained. It could only be justified if it could be established, pursuant to s. 1 of the Charter, that the limitation on the guaranteed right was demonstrably justified in a free and democratic society. Crown counsel, quite properly, did not seriously suggest that the identification of a 'stranger in town' was sufficient justification, in a free and democratic society, to override a guaranteed *Charter* right. ...

As was clearly stated in *Mellenthin*, the random stopping of motorists should not be extended beyond checks for sobriety, licences, ownership, insurance and the mechanical fitness of the motor vehicles. Random stopping must not be permitted to be turned into a means of conducting an unfounded general inquisition.

EXCLUSION OF EVIDENCE

...The evidence obtained from the appellant, Green, after his detention, and which resulted in his conviction, consisted, firstly, of his 'fail' reading following the administration of the Alcometer test, which provided the police officer with reasonable and probable grounds to demand a breathalyzer test and, secondly, the results of the breathalyzer test. It was not 'real' evidence. But for the arbitrary detention, the evidence would not have been available. ... [I]f it should be concluded that the breathalyzer evidence was properly admitted, notwithstanding the Charter violation, police officers would be entitled, in the future, to arbitrarily detain motorists, merely to ascertain the identity of strangers, with the knowledge that any evidence of an offence, derived from the arbitrary detention in violation of a guaranteed Charter right, would be admissible. The guarantee would thereupon be meaningless. Thus, the breathalyzer evidence should have been excluded. ...

There will be an order setting aside the conviction of the appellant and substituting therefore a verdict of acquittal. If the appellant has paid the fine imposed on him, it shall be repaid to him forthwith.

---

s. 15 AND s. 24

Law *v.* Canada

http://www.lexum.umontreal.ca/
SUPREME COURT OF CANADA
MARCH 25, 1999

Background facts: Canada Pension Plan (CPP) rules disallowed survivor's benefits to a 30-year-old woman without dependent children or disability. The claimant argued that the rules discriminated against her on the basis of age and they were therefore contrary to s. 15(1) of the Charter of Rights and Freedoms. She lost her appeals before the Minister of National Health and Welfare, the Pension Plan Review Tribunal and then the Pension Appeals Board, all of which held that the age distinctions did not violate her equality rights. The majority on Pension Appeals Board held that if the rules did infringe s. 15(1) of the Charter they were justified under s. 1 of the Charter. The complainant's appeal to the Federal Court of Appeal was also dismissed.

The issue before the Supreme Court of Canada was: Do ss. 44(1)(d) and 58 of the Canada Pension Plan infringe s. 15(1) of the Charter on the ground that they discriminate on the basis of age against widows and widowers under the age of 45 and if so, whether the infringement is saved by s. 1, i.e., it is demonstrably justified in a free and democratic society?

Iacobucci J.—

E. SUMMARY OF GUIDELINES

[88] Before moving on to apply the principles that I have just discussed to the facts of this case, I believe it would be useful to summarize some of the main guidelines for analysis under s. 15(1) to be derived from the jurisprudence of this Court, as reviewed in these reasons. As I stated above, these guidelines should not be seen as a strict test, but rather should be understood as points of reference for a court that is called upon to decide whether a claimant's right to equality without discrimination under the *Charter* has been infringed. ... It goes without saying that as our s. 15 jurisprudence evolves it may well be that further elaborations and modifications will emerge.

General Approach

(1) It is inappropriate to attempt to confine analysis under s. 15(1) of the Charter to a fixed and limited formula. A purposive and contextual approach to discrimination analysis is to be preferred, in order to permit the realization of the strong remedial purpose of the equality guarantee, and to avoid the pitfalls of a formalistic or mechanical approach. ...

(3) ... [A] court that is called upon to determine a discrimination claim under s. 15(1) should make the following three broad inquiries:

(A) Does the impugned law (a) draw a formal distinction between the claimant and others on the basis of one or more personal characteristics, or (b) fail to take into account the claimant's already disadvantaged position within Canadian society resulting in substantively differential treatment between the claimant and others on the basis of one or more personal characteristics?

(B) Is the claimant subject to differential treatment based on one or more enumerated and analogous grounds? and

(C) Does the differential treatment discriminate, by imposing a burden upon or withholding a benefit from the claimant in a manner which reflects the stereotypical application of presumed group or personal characteristics, or which otherwise has the effect of perpetuating or promoting the view that the individual is less capable or worthy of recognition or value as a human being or as a member of Canadian society, equally deserving of concern, respect, and consideration?

Purpose

(4) In general terms, the purpose of s. 15(1) is to prevent the violation of essential human dignity and freedom through the imposition of disadvantage, stereotyping, or political or social prejudice, and to promote a society in which all persons enjoy equal recognition at law as human beings or as members of Canadian society, equally capable and equally deserving of concern, respect and consideration.

(5) The existence of a conflict between the purpose or effect of an impugned law and the purpose of s. 15(1) is essential in order to found a discrimination claim. The determination of whether such a conflict exists is to be made through an analysis of the full context surrounding the claim and the claimant.

Comparative Approach

(6) The equality guarantee is a comparative concept, which ultimately requires a court to establish one or more relevant comparators. The claimant generally chooses the person, group, or groups with whom he or she wishes to be compared for the purpose of the discrimination inquiry. However, where the claimant's characterization of the comparison is insufficient, a court may, within the scope of the ground or grounds pleaded, refine the comparison presented by the claimant where warranted. Locating the relevant comparison group requires an examination of the subject-matter of the legislation and its effects, as well as a full appreciation of context.

Context

(7) The contextual factors which determine whether legislation has the effect of demeaning a claimant's dignity must be construed and examined from the perspective of the claimant. The focus of the inquiry is both subjective and objective. The relevant point of view is that of the reasonable person, in circumstances similar to those of the claimant, who takes into account the contextual factors relevant to the claim.

(8) There is a variety of factors which may be referred to by a s. 15(1) claimant in order to demonstrate that legislation demeans his or her dignity. The list of factors is not closed. ...

(9) Some important contextual factors influencing the determination of whether s. 15(1) has been infringed are, among others:

(A) Pre-existing disadvantage, stereotyping, prejudice, or vulnerability experienced by the individual or group at issue. The effects of a law as they relate to the important purpose of s. 15(1) in protecting individuals or groups who are vulnerable, disadvantaged, or members of "discrete and insular minorities" should always be a central consideration. Although the claimant's association with a historically more advantaged or disadvantaged group or groups is not *per se* determinative of an infringement, the existence of these pre-existing factors will favour a finding that s. 15(1) has been infringed.

(B) The correspondence, or lack thereof, between the ground or grounds on which the claim is based and the actual need, capacity, or circumstances of the claimant or others. Although the mere fact that the impugned legislation takes into account the claimant's traits or circumstances will not necessarily be sufficient to defeat a s. 15(1) claim, it will generally be more difficult to establish discrimination to the extent that the law takes into account the claimant's actual situation in a manner that respects his or her value as a human being or member of Canadian society, and less difficult to do so where the law fails to take into account the claimant's actual situation.

(C) The ameliorative purpose or effects of the impugned law upon a more disadvantaged person or group in society. An ameliorative purpose or effect which accords with the purpose of s. 15(1) of the Charter will likely not violate the human dignity of more advantaged individuals where the exclusion of these more advantaged individuals largely corresponds to the greater need or the different circumstances experienced by the disadvantaged group being targeted by the legislation. ... and

(D) The nature and scope of the interest affected by the impugned law. The more severe and localized the consequences of the legislation for the affected group, the more likely that the differential treatment responsible for these consequences is discriminatory within the meaning of s. 15(1). ...

F. APPLICATION TO THE CASE AT BAR

(1) Differential Treatment

[89] The preliminary issue in this case is whether the questioned law draws a distinction, on the basis of one or more personal characteristics, between the claimant and some other person or group of persons, resulting in unequal treatment. ... [A]s a result of the ages specified under the CPP, a clear distinction is drawn between claimants over and under age 35, and also between claimants who are over age 45 and those between the ages of 35 and 45. In my view, both the delay in the receipt of benefits and the reduced entitlement to benefits constitute a denial of equal benefit of the law under the first step of the equality analysis.

(2) Distinction on the Basis of Enumerated or Analogous Grounds

[91] Age is one of the enumerated grounds of discrimination in s. 15(1) of the *Charter*. ...

(3) Discrimination

[95] The central question in the present case is whether the age distinctions drawn by ss. 44(1)(d) and 58 of the CPP impose a disadvantage upon the appellant as a younger adult in a manner which constitutes discrimination under s. 15(1) of the *Charter*. ...

[107] ... I would also note that people in the position of the appellant are not completely excluded from obtaining a survivor's pension, although it is delayed until the person reaches age 65 unless they become disabled before then. ...

[108] In these circumstances, recalling the purposes of s. 15(1), I am at a loss to locate any violation of human dignity. The impugned distinctions in the present case do not stigmatize young persons, nor can they be said to perpetuate the view that surviving spouses under age 45 are less deserving of concern, respect or consideration than any others. Nor do they withhold a government benefit on the basis of stereotypical assumptions about the demographic group of which the appellant happens to be a member. I must conclude that, when considered in the social, political, and legal context of the claim, the age distinctions in ss. 44(1)(d) and 58 of the CPP are not discriminatory.

[109] ... My analysis herein is not meant to suggest that young people do not suffer following the death of a loved one, but only that the impugned CPP provisions are not discriminatory between younger and older adults within the purpose and meaning of s. 15(1) of the *Charter*.

[110] I conclude, then, that this is one of the rare cases ... in which differential treatment based on one or more of the enumerated or analogous grounds in s. 15(1) is not discriminatory.

Appeal dismissed.

Vriend v. *Alberta*

http://www.lexum.umontreal.ca/
SUPREME COURT OF CANADA
APRIL 2, 1998

Background facts: The plaintiff Vriend was dismissed from his job solely on the basis of his homosexuality, but he could not proceed with a complaint under the Alberta *Individual's Rights Protection Act* (IRPA) because it did not include sexual orientation as a protected ground against discrimination. He therefore attacked the statute as unconstitutional, at variance with s. 15 of the Charter of Rights and Freedoms. The court concluded that to comply with the Charter the Alberta statute should be read as including "sexual orientation" as a prohibited ground of discrimination.

In the words of Iacobucci, J.:
[129] Having found the exclusion of sexual orientation from the IRPA to be an unjustifiable violation of the appellants' equality rights, I now turn to the question of remedy under s. 52 of the Constitution Act, 1982. ...

[145] Once the Charter inconsistency has been identified, the next step is to determine which remedy is appropriate. In *Schachter*, [*Schachter v. Canada* (1992) 10 C.R.R. (2nd) 1] this Court noted that, depending upon the circumstances, there are several remedial options available to a court in dealing with a Charter violation that was not saved by s. l. These include striking down the legislation, severance of the offending sections, striking down or severance with a temporary suspension of the declaration of invalidity, reading down, and reading provisions into the legislation. ...

[150] As I discussed above, the purpose of the IRPA is the recognition and protection of the inherent dignity and inalienable rights of Albertans through the elimination of dis-

criminatory practices. It seems to me that the remedy of reading in would minimize interference with this clearly legitimate legislative purpose and thereby avoid excessive intrusion into the legislative sphere whereas striking down the IRPA would deprive all Albertans of human rights protection and thereby unduly interfere with the scheme enacted [by] the Legislature.

[151] I find support for my position in *Haig,* [86 D.L.R. (4th) 617] ... where the Ontario Court of Appeal read the words

"sexual orientation" into s. 3(1) of the Canadian Human Rights Act, R.S.C., 1985, c. H-6. At p. 508, Krever, J.A., writing for a unanimous court, stated that it was

> ... inconceivable ... that Parliament would have preferred no human rights Act over one that included sexual orientation as a prohibited ground of discrimination. To believe otherwise would be a gratuitous insult to Parliament.

Note: Following this case and the Supreme Court of Canada case *M v. H*, which held that the *Family Law Act* of Ontario offended the Charter by not allowing spousal support on the breakdown of a same-sex relationship, Ontario in its *M v. H Act* amended over 65 provincial statutes to eliminate discrimination against same-sex couples.[14] Such amendments have also been taken by British Columbia, Quebec, and the Federal Government.[15]

M of *M v. H* alleged that Ontario failed to honour the court's ruling because the term "spouse" was reserved for opposite-sex partners; "same-sex partners" defined same-sex couples. The Supreme Court of Canada refused to review Ontario's response.[16]

- *T*he discriminatory laws by the ruling group of Afghanistan against females in education and employment has led to more than 100,000 refugees asking permission to stay in Iran, where women have greater rights and are not required to wear a full face veil. The U.N. high commissioner for refugees, Dadako Ogata, visited Afghanistan and urged the Taliban officials to change the policies towards women. The officials blamed tradition for the suppression of women but insisted they have made headway by banning some tribal customs, e.g., forcing widows to marry male relatives and selling girls to settle tribal disputes.[17]

s. 33

- *F*ollowing the *Vriend* decision (supra p. 12) the Alberta Government has, for the first time, used the "notwithstanding clause" to protect its definition of marriage in its *Marriage Amendment Act*. The definition limits marriage to heterosexual couples.

- *D*ue to public outcry, the Alberta government did not proceed to pass proposed legislation to limit the compensation to those who were sterilized without consent under a government policy from 1928 to 1972. The legislators planned to use s. 33, the notwithstanding clause, because the proposed legislation clearly would have been in violation of s. 15 of the Charter of Rights and Freedoms.[18]

- *I*n 1989 the Supreme Court of Canada struck down, as unconstitutional, Quebec legislation that banned English from all signs. The Quebec government responded by invoking s. 33 of the Charter of Rights and Freedoms, the "notwithstanding" clause, to save the French-only law for the 5-year period allowed by the Charter. At that time, although the legislature could have invoked the "notwithstanding" clause, it decided to amend its Charter of the French Language to allow bilingual signs provided that the lettering in French was twice the size of the lettering in English or other language. In April 2000, the owners of an antique store were charged because the lettering in French and English was of equal size. Successful at trial, the owners lost at the Quebec Superior Court, which held that the French language still needed protection in Quebec.[19]

C. CIVIL LITIGATION

1. THE THEORY OF PRECEDENT

Novak v. *Bond*

http://www.courts.gov.bc.ca/
COURT OF APPEAL FOR BRITISH COLUMBIA
JUNE 24, 1998

Southin, J.:

[1] [This appeal concerning medical negligence raises] the vexing question of the meaning of s. 6(4)(b) of the *Limitation Act*, R.S.B.C. 1996, c. 266. ...

[6] The facts are sad.

[7] The appellant, Mrs. Novak, consulted the respondent, the defendant below, in October 1989, concerning a lump in her breast. In the ensuing year she saw the respondent at least six times concerning the lump. The respondent did not diagnose cancer. She says that he has admitted to her that he made a mistake.

[8] On 3rd October, 1990, upon, I think, the respondent's referral, she consulted a surgeon who recommended an immediate biopsy. That biopsy disclosed cancer.

[9] On 9th October, she underwent a radical mastectomy which disclosed heavy lymph node involvement. Thereafter, she received chemotherapy and radiation. From April 1991 to May 1995, she exhibited no clinical signs of cancer, but in May 1995, she was diagnosed as having cancer of the spine, lung and liver said to be a recurrence of the cancer of the breast. She is now gravely ill.

[10] I must not be taken as saying that a misdiagnosis is *ipso facto* negligence or a breach of the contractual duty of care which a physician owes his patient or that there is a causal connection between the misdiagnosis, if such there was, and Mrs. Novak's present condition. Those issues are not before us and were not before the learned judge below.

[11] She brought this action on the 9th April, 1996.

[12] Her reasons for delaying [past the two year limitation period] were explained in her affidavit sworn 4th August, 1997, and in her examination for discovery. ...

[14] Upon discovery, she put it this way: I remember distinctly thinking, I'm not going to worry about litigation until I get my treatment. It was very profound, I was extremely ill for about a year, and I started to get back on my feet and — so it was after my chemo, probably the summer of '90, and then my father died and I was dealing with my dad's death. So it would have been the late summer maybe early fall of '91, somewhere around there, and I tossed it about and tossed it about and thought, well do I have the strength to really go through this at this stage of the game? And I talked to my parish priest about it and thought, well I'm well, I have to believe that I'm well, I have to believe that I've been cured, if I go for litigation it brings back all the horrible memories and I won't at this point, we'll wait to see for a few years what's going to happen down the road.

[15] ... [The] Statute of Limitations, 1623, a statute which, despite its ... archaic language, had at least the beauty of simplicity, was repealed. ...

[After Judge Southin reviews and interprets the relevant subsections of the current Limitations Act and the case law, she concludes that she would dismiss the plaintiff's action as being too late. However, she felt bound by the authority of the case law which] postponed the running of the limitation period on sympathetic, compassionate, or other grounds based upon the personal preferences of the plaintiff.

[30] If the matter were res integra [a new point of law], I would dismiss this appeal. I cannot accept that the Legislature could have intended postponement founded on "sympathetic, compassionate, or other grounds based upon the personal preferences of the plaintiff", to use the words of my lord the Chief Justice. To so construe the legislation is to make limitation issues depend on the personal predilection of the judge hearing the case "to bring into operation what a former colleague called the Sympathy (Deep Pockets) Act" the plaintiff's plight must engage one's sympathy and the defendant must have deep pockets. This is not a sound foundation for determining legal rights.

[31] I am satisfied that this appellant considered, not unreasonably, that it was in her own interest not to sue but to devote herself to recovering her health and that is sufficient, on the authorities, to take her out of the two year limitation.

[32] I would allow the appeal accordingly.

Newbury, J.:

[33] I am in full agreement with the reasons of Madam Justice Southin and in particular record my view that if we were not bound by authorities of this court, I would have dismissed the appeal. As it is, unless and until those authorities are modified or overruled, we are bound to allow the appeal.

Hall, J.:

[After reviewing statute, case law, and the appellant's personal circumstances, he concludes]

[38] ... It appears to me that this plaintiff was truly in the position of an individual who was not, having regard to her interests in preserving and maintaining her health, an individual who "ought, in the person's own interests and taking the person's circumstances into account, to be able to bring an action", prior to the time that she commenced this action. This quoted portion in the previous sentence is language found in s. 6(4)(b) of the Limitation Act, R.S.B.C. 1996, c. 266.

[39] It is because I take this view of the case that I reach the conclusion that this appeal ought to be allowed. ...

Appeal allowed [Action allowed to proceed.]

2. The Burden of Proof in a Civil Action

Q u e s t i o n

Who must prove what to win a civil action?

In his reasons for judgment, Judge Bouck began as follows: "On the afternoon of 7 July 1985, Richard Robert Krusel suffered a tragic accident and became a quadriplegic. He alleges he came down a swimming pool slide head first into the water and struck his head on the bottom of the pool. He says the slide was improperly placed at the side of the pool since it was too close to the shallow end. He also contends the slide lacked adequate warning labels." The plaintiff named seventeen defendants including the owners of the pool, the manufacturers, and distributors of the water slide. After reviewing the evidence of sixty-five witnesses who gave testimony over a thirty-five-day trial, the judge concluded that "the plaintiff did not prove the slide theory on a balance of probabilities. There are any number of reasons as to how the plaintiff suffered this tragic injury. First, he could have been pushed in. Second, while standing near the slide and close to the edge of the pool, he could have lost his balance and started to fall into the pool. Instead of just letting himself collapse into the water on his back or stomach, he may have unthinkingly converted the fall into a dive at the shallow end of the pool. Third, the same manoeuvre could have occurred if, as he argues, he was at the bottom of the slide at one time splashing water up onto the dry slide. Fourth, inadvertently, he could have just dived into the shallow end and struck his head on the bottom of the pool. Etc. ... Over all, the proof offered by the plaintiff does not reach that degree of certainty where I can find he proved negligence on the part of any defendant on a balance of probabilities.

"Evidence on the issue of damages illustrated the enormous loss suffered by the plaintiff as a result of this accident. On the morning of 7 July 1985, a bright future lay ahead of him. He was engaged to be married. He just purchased a new house. His employers spoke glowingly of his work skills. He was upgrading his qualifications as an electrician by taking a course at B.C.I.T. The accident took all of that promising future away from him. A catastrophe is the only word that comes close to his situation.

"But, he is not a person who gives up easily. Since the accident he has acquired computer skills. He is optimistic by nature. He is not a quitter. He lives in a group home with 2 or 3 other people with similar kinds of handicaps. Government and community assistance make his life as comfortable as possible.

"This judgment will undoubtedly cause him great anguish and disappointment. The law is sometimes a blunt instrument. Often, a judge is left with two unpalatable choices. Both are before me in stark contrast. Based upon the evidence, the law compels me to dismiss the action as not proven.

"The action is dismissed as against all defendants."

Krusel v. Firth, et al.
Supreme Court of British Columbia
Vancouver Registry No. C862311
August 23, 1993

3. Class Actions

• *G*eorge W. Harris, a Winnipeg social worker and activist, was permitted by the Federal Court of Appeal to proceed with a class-action lawsuit on behalf of taxpayers. Challenging a Revenue Canada[20] tax ruling that allowed a trust with a value of $2.2 billion to leave the country without being taxed,

Harris will ask the court for a declaration that the ruling was a preferential treatment of a taxpayer and thus illegal and for a second declaration that Revenue Canada should follow the trust and collect the tax.[21] The Supreme Court of Canada dismissed Revenue Canada's request to stay the proceeding. This ruling may encourage more citizens to seek "public interest standing," that is, the right to take legal action although they are not one of the parties directly involved.[22]

- *T*he "Fudge-it Budget" scandal in B.C. resulted in legal action that climbed to the Supreme Court of Canada. In January of 2000 the Supreme Court ruled that a group of voters could proceed in a class action suit against three NDP MLAs for breach of the *Election Act* and fraud.[23] The case was based on the voters' allegation that the government announced an $87 million surplus, called an election and within a month after the election announced a $200 million deficit.[24]

  Help B.C., the group that launched the action, lost its case; the judge ruled that budgets were more like forecasts, not financial statements, and that the finance minister was wrong but not fraudulent. On the bright side, the case and a report by the auditor-general damning the NDP's budgeting practices, led to the legislature passing laws "requiring budgets to be 'transparent' and balanced."[25]

4. EXAMINATION FOR DISCOVERY

- *I*vana Sharp, was sentenced to 89 days in jail for lying during the examination for discovery. During the cross-examination at trial case she admitted the truth. Sharp, a seller of a restaurant business, was sued for fraudulent misrepresentation, for misrepresenting its financial situation.[26]

Q u e s t i o n

What is the scope of the questions that a judgment creditor can ask the judgment debtor at the examination in aid of execution?

Lauzier v. Ranger

[1995] O.J. No. 1943 (Q.L.)
ONTARIO COURT OF JUSTICE (GENERAL DIVISION)
JUNE 23, 1995

Charron J.: — Pierre Ranger is a judgment creditor of Jocelyne Lauzier as a result of several orders for costs made against her in these proceedings. He brings this motion seeking various relief with respect to the judgment debtor examination of Ms. Lauzier. He also seeks a declaration that Ms. Lauzier's assets are not exempt from seizure pursuant to section 8(l) of the Execution Act, R.S.O. 1990, Ch. E.24. Finally, Mr. Ranger seeks an order for the payment of [certain] monies. ...

THE EXAMINATION IN AID OF EXECUTION

A dispute has arisen between the parties as to the scope of the examination in aid of execution to which Ms. Lauzier must be subjected. Rule 60.18(2) of the Rules of Civil Procedure governs in this respect:

60.18(2) A creditor may examine the debtor in relation to,

(a) the reason for nonpayment or nonperformance of the order;
(b) the debtor's income and property;
(c) the debts owed to and by the debtor;

(d) the disposal the debtor has made of any property either before or after the making of the order;
(e) the debtor's present, past and future means to satisfy the order;
(f) whether the debtor intends to obey the order or has any reason for not doing so; and
(g) any other matter pertinent to the enforcement of the order.

It is evident from the language of the Rule that the scope of the examination is wide. It is equally evident from a reading of the transcripts of two aborted examinations that Ms. Lauzier has been generally uncooperative in providing the requested information. For example, during the course of the examination of May 17, 1995 the first seven pages of transcript are spent in an attempt to confirm Ms. Lauzier's name. She then categorically refuses to provide her social insurance number; her counsel intercedes and points out that the number is noted on the income tax return and Ms. Lauzier then concedes that it is her social insurance number. Next comes an objection to producing a list of her assets on the basis that this information is already available to Mr. Ranger as it is contained in various affidavits filed during the course of these proceedings. She then refuses to disclose where some of the assets mentioned in those affidavits are located. All of these examples are taken from the first 27 pages of a 144 page transcript. A perusal of the balance of the transcript reveals that, although some information was provided to Mr. Ranger, the tone of the examination did not improve appreciably over its course. The continuation of the examination on June 2, 1995 proved to be disastrous. Ms. Lauzier was generally uncooperative and belligerent and at times abusive — often swearing at Mr. Ranger and eventually throwing styrofoam cups at him.

Nevertheless, substantial productions have been made to Mr. Ranger through counsel for Ms. Lauzier and some particular issues were raised with respect to the scope of the examination.

a) *Disclosure as to matters preceding the debtor's liability*

Counsel for Ms. Lauzier contends that there is no basis in law for going behind the time his client's liability was incurred. Mr. Ranger argues that the very language of the Rule says otherwise. Both parties rely on the same jurisprudence in support of their respective positions.

I agree with Mr. Ranger's position. Subsections (d) and (e) of Rule 60.18 make express reference to the time preceding the order from which liability arises and subsection (g) obliges the debtor to disclose any other matter pertinent to the enforcement of the order without limiting the scope as to time. The case of *The Ontario Bank v. Mitchell* (1881), 32 U.C.C.P. 73 (Ont. C.A.), cited by both parties as authoritative, supports Mr. Ranger's position …

> … The chief object is to shew what property the debtor has at the time of the examination which can be made available to the creditor, and it is material in making or in the attempt to make out present property, to shew that at some anterior time, no matter how far back, the debtor [knows] where that property is, or what has been done with it.
>
> It is not a sufficient account of property acquired before the judgment debt was incurred to say it all had been disposed of before the debt was incurred. The debtor must shew how, when, and to whom, and for what it was disposed of, as he is able to do it.
>
> If the rule were as the defendants contend it is, the examination would be a farce.

The same rationale applies today and furthermore, the language of the present rule expressly widens the scope of the examination to a period of time prior to the time when liability was incurred. Of course, the information sought must be reasonably relevant to the enforcement of the order. …

b) *Joint assets*

Ms. Lauzier also refused to answer any questions pertaining to assets she owns jointly with another person. Counsel for Ms. Lauzier refers to a decision of the Ontario Divisional Court in support of his client's position: *Director of Support and Custody Enforcement, for Gardiner v. Jones; Bank of Nova Scotia* … [1991] 5 O.R. (3d) 499. While this case reaffirms the common law position that joint assets are not exigible, in no

way does it serve to exclude joint assets from the scope of the examination in aid of execution. Nothing in Rule 60.18 can or should be interpreted to so restrict the examination. …

The scope of the examination in this case therefore extends to joint assets and Ms. Lauzier's objection in this respect is not valid. Any objection which may be raised with respect to assets which may be statutorily exempted from execution is likewise not valid. Even though an asset may not be exigible, it can still form the subject-matter of an examination in aid of execution.

c) *Examination of third parties*

Mr. Ranger seeks an order permitting him to examine four individuals pertaining to Ms. Lauzier's dealings with her assets since December 14, 1993. He maintains that he needs to examine these parties since he is unable to obtain the relevant information from Ms. Lauzier. Provision for such an examination is found in Rule 60.18(6). …

Counsel for Ms. Lauzier takes the position that a creditor must exhaust all other means of obtaining the information from the debtor before an order for the examination of a third person can be made. I do not agree. The rule simply requires that any difficulty arise concerning the enforcement of an order. A reading of the transcripts of the aborted examination in this case leads to the inescapable conclusion that much difficulty has already been encountered. The evidence from the sheriff's representatives who indicate they were told by Ms. Lauzier to "take a hike," when they first appeared at her residence to enforce the Writ of Seizure and Sale and the subsequent removal of many assets from the residence prior to execution provide additional evidence that enforcement is very difficult in this case.

However I am concerned by the lack of notice to the named persons. This aspect of the motion is dismissed without prejudice to Mr. Ranger's right to bring a new motion with service on the appropriate persons with material in support clearly indicating the basis upon which it is believed relevant information would likely be in their possession.

    ….

MS. LAUZIER'S STATE OF HEALTH

A medical report dated June 12, 1995 has been filed from Ms. Lauzier's family physician. He states that his patient's mental condition is frail and he recommends she avoid excessive stress for at least one month. In his opinion his patient is physically and psychologically unfit to attend court proceedings for at least one month. Ms. Lauzier's counsel asked that his client be permitted to provide her information by way of affidavit instead of having to appear personally at an examination. He maintains that his client appears unable to withstand the stress of finding herself in the same room as Mr. Ranger. The transcript of the aborted examinations certainly seem to substantiate counsel's views in this respect. I should point out that the transcripts do not reveal any inappropriate behaviour on the part of Mr. Ranger or of Mr. Max.

In the interest of avoiding the cost of further unproductive sessions before a reporter, I am prepared to accede to this request.

CONCLUSION

Consequently, there will be an order [as per my findings above].

D. ENFORCEMENT OF JUDGMENTS

Q u e s t i o n s

What can you do if someone owes you money but won't pay?
Do you have to have judgment against the person before you take such steps?

---

1. GARNISHMENT

• *I*ncome Tax legislation allows Revenue Canada to garnishee refunds for outstanding delinquent student loans and unemployment insurance overpayments.[27]

Dishonest as to why she needed the funds, Miriam Grant persuaded her co-worker at Canada Customs to guarantee repayment of a $15,000.00 loan she and her husband were seeking from the Civil Service Co-Operative Society. The co-worker did sign the documents as a guarantor.

Subsequently the Grants defaulted on the loan, left the country, and left the co-worker to repay the balance of the loan. In an effort to collect the money owed to her, the co-worker discovered that the Grants had sold their house for $240,000 and that Miriam Grant was entitled to a retroactive pay equity payment from their employer, the federal government. She sought and was granted an order to have the pay equity payment paid into court. She then obtained default judgment against the Grants. The government, employer, did not comply with the order. The co-worker also served the government with a Notice of Garnishment.

On appeal, the court faced two issues. With regard to issue #1: whether the Crown can be ordered to pay the monies owed to the defendant Ms. Grant into Court, the court agreed with the submissions of the Crown that it was immune from such orders both in common law and by statute. However, with regard to issue #2: whether the retroactive pay equity payment can be garnished, the court reviewed the wording of the relevant statutes and commentary and found that the Crown was bound by provincial garnishment law (the debt being owed by a private debtor, not by the Crown itself) and that the pay equity payment was a garnishable form of payment as it was simply back payment of wages. Furthermore, the court ordered that the typical exemption from garnishment of 80% of Grant's wages be reduced to 0%. The court concluded:

> [66]... An order will issue that Her Majesty the Queen in Right of Canada as Represented by Canada Customs and Revenue Agencies (Canada Customs) garnish any and all monies otherwise payable to the defendant Miriam Grant pursuant to the Notice of Garnishment issued April 12, 2000 to a total of $24,968.97 and pay such amount to the plaintiff's counsel in trust for the plaintiff.
>
> [67] This amount of $24,968.97 includes the default judgment of $14,174.33 (inclusive of $1,500.00 costs), subsequent further costs payable to the plaintiff on a solicitor and client scale which I fix at $9,801.89 and order against the two defendants on a joint and several basis, plus postjudgment interest at 7% per annum from June 17, 1999 to July 7, 2000 of $992.75.

Gumbs v. Grant
[2000] O.J. No. 2601 (Q.L.)
Ontario Superior Court of Justice
July 7, 2000

2. EXECUTION

• *I*n a California court Mr. Kroll sued the Soviet Union and *Izvestia* for libel. *Izvestia* had called him a spy, which allegation caused him to lose his business license after 15 years of selling medical supplies from a Moscow office. The plaintiff was awarded $413,000. In his effort to collect the award of damages, the plaintiff's lawyer seized a manual Russian-language typewriter used by an *Izvestia* correspondent in Washington.

The article quotes the lawyer for the plaintiff as saying "The typewriter is just the start.... We had a writ to seize everything in the apartment that belongs to *Izvestia*.... There are also three desks, three metal filing cabinets, some bookshelves and a big color television set. I'm going back for all that tomorrow with a truck."[28]

Mortil *v.* **International Phasor Telecom Ltd.**

23 B.C.L.R. (2D) 354
BRITISH COLUMBIA COUNTY COURT
FEBRUARY 16, 1988

Wong, C.C.J.

Secrets are easier heard than kept: Jewish Proverb

This is an application by the defendant judgment debtor, International Phasor Telecom Ltd., for a declaration that its rights in the Phasor Code 1000 Computer Software and instruction manual for same are not liable under s. 49 of the *Court Order Enforcement Act*, R.S.B.C. 1979, C. 75, to seizure and sale under a writ of execution.

At issue is whether a computer software program incorporating a trade secret is exigible for execution purposes.

On 4th May 1987 the plaintiff judgment creditor, Mortil, obtained default judgment against the defendant, inclusive of interest and costs, in the amount of $6,946.11. On 4th December 1987, pursuant to a writ of seizure and sale, one copy of the defendant's two copies of Phasor Code 1000 Computer Software System and one instruction manual were seized by the sheriff.

...

[I]n January 1987 the master software copy, from which copies are made for subsequent sale, was stolen and never recovered.

There is a concern by the defendant that if the copy seized by the sheriff is sold, under writ of seizure and sale, the secret nature of the Phasor Code 1000 Computer Software System will be lost.

I think it is established law as outlined by Professor Dunlop in his book, *Creditor-Debtor Law in Canada* (1981), at pp. 152-53, that s. 49 of the *Court Order Enforcement Act* and analogous sections of execution statutes in other provinces have been restrictively interpreted by the court to disallow writs of fi. fa. to reach trademarks, patents or industrial design rights because under common law incorporeal or intangible property was not subject to seizure and sale. Section 52 of the same Act, however, extended the common law somewhat by permitting seizure of specified categories of intangible property—which does not include intellectual property rights.

Counsel for the plaintiff submitted that what was seized by the sheriff was only the physical computer software—clearly tangible property and therefore "goods and chattels"—which are expressly exigible assets under s. 49 of the *Court Order Enforcement Act*. Provided the purchaser of the seized computer software does not infringe the trademark or copyright of the defendant, the purchased software is no different than the purchase of any brandname product. She also submitted that if Phasor Code 1000 System was indeed a trade secret, it was no longer such when the master copy was stolen and never recovered.

There is no reported Canadian judicial decision as to whether a tangible asset with a non-divulged trade secret is exigible to a writ of seizure and sale.

After consideration, I have concluded that this tangible property, like any other corporeal asset, is exigible under s. 49 of the *Court Order Enforcement Act*. However, to safeguard the secret process of the Phasor Code, I direct that its sale be subject to terms. The terms of sale will be a requirement that the purchaser enter into a trust agreement with the defendant concerning non-disclosure and prohibition of unauthorized use of the Phasor Code System, similar to the terms of the licence agreement required by the defendant in its ordinary sale to others.

...

As this was a novel point of argument with divided success, there will be no order as to costs.

Order accordingly

3. LIMITATION PERIODS

Novak **v.** *Bond*

http://www.lexum.umontreal.ca/
SUPREME COURT OF CANADA
MAY 20, 1999

Background facts: In a 4 to 3 decision, the SCC dismissed an appeal from the B.C. Court of Appeal decision to allow Novak's action to proceed, (see page 14 above). The court did, however, agree on the approach to be taken by the court in its interpretation of s. 6(4)(b) of the *Limitation Act.*

McLachlin J.: ...

I. SUMMARY

[34] This appeal requires the Court to consider the proper interpretation to be given to s. 6(4)(b) of the *Limitation Act*, R.S.B.C. 1996, c. 266 (the "Act"). This subsection allows the running of a limitation period for certain actions to be postponed until a reasonable person would consider that the plaintiff "ought, in the person's own interests and taking the person's circumstances into account, to be able to bring an action". The meaning of this obscure provision has been a longstanding source of frustration in British Columbia.

[35] The respondent, Mrs. Novak, went to see the appellant, Dr. Bond, about a lump she had discovered in her breast. Between October 18, 1989 and October 1, 1990, she saw him at least six times. Dr. Bond advised Mrs. Novak not to worry. On October 4, 1990, a specialist diagnosed Mrs. Novak with breast cancer. She had a partial radical mastectomy, and it was discovered that the cancer had spread to at least twelve of her thirteen lymph nodes.

[36] After recovering from a year of illness, Mrs. Novak considered suing Dr. Bond and even discussed the matter with her parish priest. She decided not to sue at that time, preferring to concentrate on maintaining her health and a positive belief that she had been cured. Four years later, in May 1995, Mrs. Novak's cancer recurred, spreading to her spine, liver and lung. She and her husband started this action on April 9, 1996. Section 3(2)(a) of the Act provides that this type of personal injury action is subject to a two-year limitation period. Therefore, for it to have been brought in time, Mrs. Novak must establish that s. 6(4)(b) postponed the running of time until at least April 9, 1994.

[37] Before trial, Dr. Bond sought an order dismissing this action as statute-barred. The motions judge granted the application and dismissed the action. The Court of Appeal held, however, that the motions judge had not given proper attention to s. 6(4)(b) and, holding that this provision allows the running of time to be postponed on the basis of compassionate or sympathetic factors that are personal to the plaintiff, allowed the appeal. Dr. Bond now appeals to this Court. ...

[39] The scheme and purpose of the Act leads me to conclude that ... the proper interpretation of s. 6(4)(b) may be summarized as follows: Section 6(4)(b) requires the court to adopt the perspective of a reasonable person who knows the facts that are within the plaintiff's knowledge and has taken the appropriate advice a reasonable person would seek on those facts. Time does not begin to run until this reasonable person would conclude that someone in the plaintiff's position could, acting reasonably in light of his or her own circumstances and interests, bring an action. The question posed by s. 6(4)(b) therefore becomes: "in light of his or her own particular circumstances and interests, at what point could the plaintiff reasonably have brought an action?" The reasonable person would only consider that the plaintiff could not have brought an action at the time the right to do so first arose if the plaintiff's own interests and circumstances were serious, significant, and compelling. Purely tactical concerns have no place in this analysis.

[40] This approach recognizes the special problems injured persons may encounter and the intense stresses and strains involved in litigation. It recognizes that in some cases, the plaintiff's own circumstances and interests may be so compelling that it cannot be reasonably said that he or she could bring an action within the prescribed limitation period. Finally, it makes practical sense. People ought to be encouraged to take steps short of litigation to deal with their problems. They should not be compelled to sue when to do so runs counter to a vital interest, such as the need to maintain their health in the face of a life-threatening disease.

[41] Applying this test to the facts of this case, I would dismiss the appeal and permit the action to proceed.

ENDNOTES

1. *The Vancouver Sun*, June 9, 1999, p. A17.

2. For a more detailed account see *The Vancouver Sun*, January 16, 2001, p. A3.

3. For a more detailed account see *The Lawyers Weekly*, June 23, 2000, p. 17.

4. *Maclean's*, October 25, 1993, p. 11. Also see *The New York Times*, September 22, 1995.

5. The *National Post*, December 3, 1999, A16; *The International Herald Tribune*, April 21, 2000, p.1; *The Globe and Mail*, January 2, 2001, A8 *inter alia*.

6. See *The Vancouver Sun*, February 14, 2000, A4.

7. *Time*, May 8, 2000, p. 13.

8. For a more complete summary of the Court of Appeal's decision in *Ontario Adult Entertainment Bar Assn. v. Metropolitan Toronto (Municipality)* see *The Lawyers Weekly*, October 17, 1997, p. 15.

9. See *R. v. Thompson* 30 C.C.C. (3d) 125, British Columbia Court of Appeal, September 29, 1986.

10. For a more detailed account see *Time Magazine*, June 23, 1997, p. 38 which reports that the followers of Soroush have a home-page on the Internet. The Council of Foreign Relations in New York has a 56-page study on Soroush's political thought.

11. *The Vancouver Sun*, April 30, 1999, p. A16.

12. For a more detailed account see *The Herald Tribune*, July 10, 1997, pp. 1, 4.

13. For a more detailed account of this incident and other Taliban rules, e.g., banning women from most work and school, see *The Vancouver Sun*, July 18, 2000, p. 1.

14. For a more detailed discussion of this issue see *Law Now*, June/July 2000, paragraph 16.

15. *Modernization of Benefits and Obligations Act* is the federal law amending 68 statutes to extend benefits and obligations now available to common-law opposite-sex couples to same-sex couples. (*The Lawyers Weekly,* November 3, 2000, p. 8.)

16. For a more detailed account see *The Lawyers Weekly*, June 9, 2000, p. 22.

17. See the *Wall Street Journal*, June 17, 1998, p. 1 and the *Washington Post* article reprinted in *The Vancouver Sun*, September 22, 2000, p. A8.

18. For a more detailed account see *The Globe and Mail*, March 12, 1998, p. 1.

19. For a more detailed account see *The Lawyers Weekly*, April 28, 2000, p. 7.

20. Now Canada Customs and Revenue Agency (CCRA).

21. For a more detailed account of *Harris v. Canada* (Federal Court of Appeal, June 2, 2000) see *The Lawyers Weekly*, June 16, 2000, p. 1.

22. *The Vancouver Sun*, October 20, 2000, p. A2.

23. *The Vancouver Sun*, January 29, 2000, p. A2.

24. *The Globe and Mail,* September 29, 1997, p. A4.

25. *The Vancouver Sun,* August 5, 2000, p. A8.

26. For a more detailed account of the trial *Morrison v. Sharp*, see *The Lawyers Weekly*, January 7, 1994, p. 2. The award of damages, $278,000 for losses and $20,000 as punitive damages, was appealed. The parties settled at $160,000. For a more detailed account of the settlement and perjury action, see *The Lawyers Weekly*, March 22, 1996, p. 19.

27. Summarized from *The Globe and Mail*, March 10, 1992, p. A8.

28. A more detailed account is given in *The Vancouver Sun*, November 14, 1986.

II

GOVERNMENT REGULATION AND ADMINISTRATIVE TRIBUNALS

A. GOVERNMENTAL REGULATION

Question

In what ways can government affect your business plans and practices?

- *I*f a law bans your squeegee business, is it an infringement of your constitutional rights? Ontario's *Safe Streets Act* imposes fines for aggressively soliciting and this includes cleaning a person's windshield. The hearing challenging the constitutionality of what has been called the Squeegee Kids Bill was to begin in January 2001. A group of Ontario lawyers have promised to take the question "all the way to the Supreme Court of Canada."[1]

Fraser v. *Saanich (District)*

[1999] B.C.J. No. 3100 (Q.L.)
BRITISH COLUMBIA SUPREME COURT
MAY 31, 1999

Background facts: The owner and her company operated a nursing home since the 1930s. When they applied to redevelop the facilities, the Ministry of Health told them that they needed to demonstrate the financial viability of the project and receive the approval from the District of Saanich. In turn the District told them that the redevelopment of the property would largely be determined by the position of the neighbourhood residents.

The residents petitioned that the hospital property be down zoned to single-family residential zone. A few months later the neighbourhood residents and the District of Saanich tried to have the nursing home designated as a heritage building. Subsequently they recommended it be rezoned and downsized to a new Personal Care Zone with limitations on height and floor space ratio. The owner of the property sued the Saanich District and the residents involved for bad faith, collusion, negligence, breach of fiduciary duty, interference with contractual relations and conspiracy which resulted in collapse of all offers and contracts for the property. The excerpts below begin with the judge reviewing the plaintiff's Statement of Claim.

Singh, J.: ...

[27] Finally, paragraphs 64, 65, 67 and 68 allege that as a result of the defendants' negligence, conspiracy, bad faith, breach of fiduciary duty and interference of contractual relations, the plaintiffs have suffered and continue to suffer loss, economic harm, damages, injury, special damages and punitive and aggravated damages. ...

[29] In order for this claim to be dismissed under Rule 19(24)(a) the court must be satisfied, absolutely, beyond a doubt, that the claim discloses no cause of action. The court must proceed on the premise that the allegations of fact contained in the Statement of Claim are true.

[30] In *Carey Canada Inc. et al v. Hunt*, [1990] 2 S.C.R. 959, the Supreme Court of Canada ... held that the test to be applied is whether it is "plain and obvious" that a plaintiff's Statement of Claim discloses no reasonable claim. ...

[The judge reviews the law with regard to the torts alleged by Fraser. With regard to inducing breach of contract, the judge says:]

[35] ... in order to make out the tort of inducing breach of contract the plaintiff must establish five propositions—first, the existence of a valid and enforceable contract; second, awareness by the defendant of the existence of the contract; third, breach of the contract procured by the defendant; fourth, wrongful interference; and fifth, damage suffered by the plaintiff. ...

[The judge found no evidence to support the plaintiff's claims. He then addresses the issue of neighbourhood participation.]

[43] While neighbourhood participation in municipal politics often places an almost adversarial atmosphere into land use questions, this participation is a key element to the democratic involvement of said citizens in community decision making. Signing petitions, making submissions to municipal councils and even the organization of community action groups are sometimes the only avenues for community residents to express their views on land use issues. The solicitation of public opinion is specifically mandated in the Municipal Act. This type of activity often produces unfavourable results for some parties involved. However, an unfavourable action by local government does not, in the absence of some other wrongdoing, open the doors to seek redress on those who spoke out in favour of that action. To do so would place a chilling effect on the public's participation in local government.

[44] If the process itself here was flawed, or disclosed bad faith on the part of the District of Saanich, the plaintiffs can take appropriate action against the District of Saanich. However, to place blame on the community group involved is doomed

to failure where there has been no, and I repeat, no pleading of any material facts that could support any such claim of wrongdoing. If the plaintiffs wish to support such a claim surrounding the democratic activities of others, it would be necessary to provide at least some factual underpinning. The plaintiffs have not done so, as yet, at all.

[45] What I am faced with is the bald assertion that the neighbourhood residents were negligent, that they colluded, conspired, breached fiduciary duty, acted in bad faith, and as well, interfered with breached contractual relations. There is no allegation that during this process the neighbourhood residents breached any proper procedure set out by the District or made any false statements. Nor is there any allegation that the neighbourhood residents ever had any direct dealings with the plaintiffs or any prospective purchasers of the hospital property.

[46] I have no difficulty, therefore, in finding that it is "plain and obvious" that the plaintiffs' Statement of Claim discloses no reasonable claim and contains radical defects. ... It has no merit against those defendants. The action against the neighbourhood residents is dismissed.

[47] I now deal with the defendants' claim for special costs.

[48] Counsel for the neighbourhood residents has argued that the claim against his clients is in the nature of a SLAPP suit, an acronym for Strategic Lawsuit Against Public Participation. He forcefully submits that what the plaintiffs are attempting to do here is to stifle free statement by characterizing lawful conduct as a conspiracy. He has referred the court to [academic articles and various cases, including] *Everywoman's Health Centre Society (1988) et al v. Bridges et al* (1991), 47 C.P.C. (2d) 97, a decision of our Court of Appeal, where the court held that special costs are available, either in the circumstances giving rise to the cause of action, or in the proceedings, which makes such costs desirable as a form of chastisement.

[49] A SLAPP suit is a claim for monetary damages against individuals who have dealt with a government body on an issue of public interest or concern. It is a meritless action filed by a plaintiff whose primary goal is not to win the case but rather to silence or intimidate citizens who have participated in proceedings regarding public policy or public decision making. ...

[52] I find ... that this action not only contains an unreasonable claim, is meritless and devoid of any factual foundation, but also has been used as an attempt to stifle the democratic activities of the defendants, the neighbourhood residents. I find the plaintiffs' conduct reprehensible and deserving of censure by an award of special costs.

[53] ... [After hearing the submissions of counsel, the court awarded special costs in the sum of $2,500 plus disburse-

---

The purchasers bought property zoned for industrial use. They planned to have the property rezoned to allow for the construction of residential condominiums. This intended use was not made known to the seller. The purchasers were later informed by the Ministry of the Environment that the soil was contaminated. The existence of contaminants, later classified as hazardous waste, prevented the purchasers from developing the property as planned. The purchasers took court action for rescission of the contract and damages.

The court found that the purchasers "got just what they bargained for—industrial land."

Their undisclosed intention to use the property for residential purposes does not alter the bargain the appellants made, or create a latent defect in the industrial property. ...

> If I am wrong and the presence of the contaminant was a defect, ... [that defect] was a patent one. It would have been readily discoverable by the appellants had they exercised reasonable vigilance. ... [T]he appellants chose not to disclose their intended use of the property and to take no steps to satisfy themselves that the property could be used for that purpose. ...
>
> The purchasers' failure to examine the property or to take reasonable steps to determine if the law would allow the intended use of the land, were costly mistakes; the price paid for the property was $1,250,000.

Tony's Broadloom & Floor Covering Ltd. v. NMC Canada Inc.
[1996] O.J. No. 4372 (Q.L.)
Court of Appeal for Ontario
December 12, 1996

- *A*fter a 15-year court battle, Little Sister's Book and Art Emporium no longer has to prove that its materials should be allowed into Canada. In its decision, the Supreme Court of Canada shifted the onus of proving that material is obscene from the importer to Canada Customs officers, who had routinely seized material addressed to the bookstore.[2]

- *N*eighbourhood residents sought and were granted an injunction prohibiting FedEx from their usual practice of loading and unloading between 3:00 a.m. and 4:00 a.m. The court found the company was in breach of the City of North Bay's Noise By-law.[3]

- *I*n *R. v. Bata Industries,* two former directors of the company involved with the day-to-day operations were convicted under environmental protection legislation for *not* taking steps to prevent the release of pollutants by the company. Furthermore, the court order against the convicted company prohibited the company from indemnifying the convicted directors.[4]
  On appeal the court upheld the order that prohibited the company from indemnifying the directors.[5]

B. CHALLENGES TO DECISIONS OF MUNICIPALITIES OR ADMINISTRATIVE TRIBUNALS

PRIVATIVE CLAUSES

Q u e s t i o n

Does a privative clause in the legislation creating the tribunal prevent a judicial review of a tribunal's decision?

Pasiechnyk et al. v. *Saskatchewan (Workers' Compensation Board)*

http://www.lexum.umontreal.ca/
SUPREME COURT OF CANADA
AUGUST 28, 1997

Sopinka, J.:

FACTS

[2] On May 25, 1990 a crane owned by Procrane fell over onto a trailer in which employees at a Saskatchewan Power Corporation construction site were taking their morning coffee break. Two workers died and six others suffered serious and debilitating injuries. The injured workers and the dependents of the deceased workers qualified for and received Workers' Compensation Benefits.

[3] In January 1991, the respondents launched an action against SaskPower, Procrane, and the Saskatchewan Government. The claim against the government alleged that it failed to meet its duties under *The Occupational Health and Safety Act*, R.S.S. 1978, c. O-1, by failing adequately to inspect the crane. ...

[4] The Board held that the government, Procrane and SaskPower were "employers" within the meaning of the Act, and accordingly the actions were barred by the Act. The Saskatchewan Court of Queen's Bench dismissed the respondents' application for judicial review. The Saskatchewan Court of Appeal allowed the respondents' appeal with respect to the action against the government but not with respect to the actions against Procrane and SaskPower. This appeal involves only the action against the Government of Saskatchewan.

[The issue before the court was whether the Board was patently unreasonable in barring the action against the government. However, the court had to determine if there was a privative clause barring its review.]

RELEVANT STATUTORY PROVISIONS

[5] *The Workers' Compensation Act*, 1979, S.S. 1979, c. W-17.1 ...

> 22.—(1) The board shall have exclusive jurisdiction to examine, hear and determine all matters and questions arising under this Act and any other matter in respect of which a power, authority or discretion is conferred upon the board and, without limiting the generality of the foregoing, the board shall have exclusive jurisdiction to determine: ...
>
> (h) whether any industry or any part, branch or department of any industry is within the scope of this Act and the class to which it is assigned;
>
> (2) The decision and finding of the board under this Act upon all questions of fact and law are final and conclusive and no proceedings by or before the board shall be restrained by injunction, prohibition or other proceeding or removable by certiorari or otherwise in any court.
>
> ...

> 44. No employer and no worker or any dependent of a worker has a right of action against an employer or a worker with respect to an injury sustained by a worker in the course of his employment.
>
> ...
>
> 167. The right to compensation provided by this Act is in lieu of all rights of action, statutory or otherwise, to which a worker or his dependants are or may be entitled against the employer of the worker for or by reason of any injury sustained by him while in the employment of the employer.
>
> ...
>
> 180. Except as otherwise provided in this Act, all rights of action against the employers for injuries to workers, either at common law or under The Workmen's Compensation Act, are abolished. ...

ANALYSIS

Standard of Review

[16] To determine the standard of review, I must first decide whether the subject matter of the decision of the administrative tribunal was subject to a privative clause having full privative effect. If the conclusion is that a full privative clause applies, then the decision of the tribunal is only reviewable if it is patently unreasonable or the tribunal has made an error in the interpretation of a legislative provision limiting the tribunal's powers. In either circumstance the tribunal will have exceeded its jurisdiction. These principles are summarized in *U.E.S., Local 298 v. Bibeault*, [1988] 2 S.C.R. 1048. ...

[17] A "full" or "true" privative clause is one that declares that decisions of the tribunal are final and conclusive from which no appeal lies and all forms of judicial review are excluded. ... Where the legislation employs words that purport to limit review but fall short of the traditional wording of a full privative clause, it is necessary to determine whether the words were intended to have full privative effect or a lesser standard of deference. ...

[18] ... Factors such as the purpose of the statute creating the tribunal, the reason for its existence, the area of expertise and the nature of the problem are all relevant in arriving at the intent of the legislature. ... See *Bibeault* ...

HISTORY AND PURPOSE OF WORKERS' COMPENSATION

[23] The history and purpose of workers' compensation supports the proposition that the Board in this case had exclusive jurisdiction to decide the question of whether the statutory bar applies, because this question is intimately related to one side of the historic trade-off embodied in the system.

[24] Workers' compensation is a system of compulsory no-fault mutual insurance administered by the state. [The judge summarizes the history of our legislation and the "historic trade off]... by which workers lost their cause of action against their

employers but gained compensation that depends neither on the fault of the employer nor its ability to pay. Similarly, employers were forced to contribute to a mandatory insurance scheme, but gained freedom from potentially crippling liability. …

[26] The importance of the historic trade off has been recognized by the courts. …

[28] The cases also support the conclusion that the legislature intended to commit exclusively to the Board the question of whether the statutory bar applied. …

[There follows a thorough review of the purpose, role and expertise of the Board.]

[38] The composition, tenure, and powers of the Board demonstrate that it has very considerable expertise in dealing with all aspects of the workers' compensation system. Not only does the Board have day-to-day expertise in handling claims for compensation, in setting assessment rates and promoting workplace safety; but it also has expertise in ensuring that the purposes of the Act are not defeated. …

[42] There can be no question that the question of eligibility for compensation is one that is within the Board's exclusive jurisdiction. It is also clear upon examination that the issue of whether an action is barred is equally within the Board's exclusive jurisdiction. It would undermine the purposes of the

scheme for the courts to assume jurisdiction over that question. It could lead to one of the problems that workers' compensation was created to solve, namely, the problem of employers becoming insolvent as a result of high damage awards. The system of collective liability was created to prevent that, and thus to ensure security of compensation to the workers. Individual immunity is the necessary corollary to collective liability. The interposition of the courts could also lead to uncertainty about recovery. …

[43] In view of the above, the issue as to whether the proposed action is barred is one that is committed to the Board for final decision and is not reviewable unless it is patently unreasonable.

IS THE DECISION PATENTLY UNREASONABLE?

[After reviewing the procedure by which the Board held the government to be an "employer" and after considering the argument of the Court of Appeal, the judge concluded:]

Applying the standard which I have determined is appropriate, I conclude that clearly the decision of the Board is not patently unreasonable.

Appeal allowed.

Question

How can you challenge government decisions that interfere with your business?

IS THE DECISION ULTRA VIRES?

IS THE INTRA VIRES *RESOLUTION PATENTLY UNREASONABLE?*

Nanaimo (City) v. *Rascal Trucking Ltd.*

http://www.lexum.umontreal.ca/
SUPREME COURT OF CANADA
MARCH 2, 2000

[1] Major, J.:— This appeal engages an interpretation of s. 936 of the *Municipal Act,* R.S.B.C. 1979. … As well, it raises the standard of judicial review applicable to municipal bodies. …

I. FACTUAL BACKGROUND

[2] The respondent, Rascal Trucking Ltd. ("Rascal"), leased a parcel of land located within the City of Nanaimo ("Nanaimo" or the "City") from Kismet Enterprises Inc. ("Kismet"). In April 1996, Rascal applied for and received a permit from the appellant Nanaimo to deposit approximately 15,000 cubic yards of soil on its site with the intent to conduct soil processing operations, an activity permitted by the applicable zoning classification.

[3] Shortly after Rascal started delivering soil to the site, neigh-

bouring residents raised complaints about dust and noise emissions. A City inspector inspected the site and recommended that an order be issued compelling the owner to remove the pile of soil.

[4] On July 3, 1996, Nanaimo held a public meeting where it heard from local residents and the respondent. It received a professional engineer's report analysing the noise emissions from the property, and an opinion from its legal counsel. The Nanaimo council deliberated and ultimately passed a resolution declaring the pile of soil a nuisance pursuant to s. 936 of the Municipal Act, and ordered Kismet to remove it within 30 days. It did not comply.

[5] On August 19, 1996, Nanaimo passed a second resolution ordering the respondent to remove the topsoil within 15

days, in default of which it would be removed by the city at the respondent's or owner's cost. Neither the owner Kismet nor the respondent Rascal obeyed. On September 6, 1996, Rascal denied access for removal purposes to agents of the City.

[6] These events precipitated two applications before the Supreme Court of British Columbia. Nanaimo brought the first, asking for a declaration that it was entitled to access the property and remove the offending pile of soil. Maczko J. granted the petition on the basis that Nanaimo had the jurisdiction both to declare the dirt pile a nuisance and order its removal.

[7] Kismet and Rascal brought the second petition, requesting that the resolutions be quashed. Rowan J. dismissed the petition.

[8] The British Columbia Court of Appeal allowed Rascal's appeal, set aside the orders and quashed the July 3rd and August 19th resolutions: . ...

[The court reviews the relevant provisions of the Municipal Act, Interpretation Act and the Statutory Revision Act.]

IV. ISSUES

[13] This appeal raises two issues:

(1) Did s. 936 of the Municipal Act empower the appellant to pass the resolutions declaring the pile of soil a nuisance and ordering its removal?

(2) If so, upon what standard must the appellant's decision be reviewed?

V. ANALYSIS

(1) Did s. 936 of the Municipal Act empower the appellant to pass the resolution declaring the pile of soil a nuisance and ordering its removal?

[The court reviews the arguments of the parties on the proper interpretation of the relevant sections of the Municipal Act].

[17] The first step is to consider the approach the courts should take when construing municipal legislation. As noted by Iacobucci J. in *R. v. Sharma*, [1993] 1 S.C.R. 650, at p. 668:

> ...as statutory bodies, municipalities "may exercise only those powers expressly conferred by statute, those powers necessarily or fairly implied by the expressed power in the statute, and those indispensable powers essential and not merely convenient to the effectuation of the purposes of the corporation".

[18] The process of delineating municipal jurisdiction is an exercise in statutory construction. There is ample authority, on the interpretation of statutes generally and of municipal statutes specifically, to support a broad and purposive approach. ...

[20] This ... [approach] follows recent authorities dictating that statutes be construed purposively in their entire context and in light of the scheme of the Act as a whole with a view to ascertaining the legislature's true intent. ...

[The court reviews the wording of the Municipal Act and cases on interpretation.]

[26] It is my opinion that s. 936 empowered the appellant to issue resolutions declaring Rascal's pile of soil a nuisance and ordering its removal. As a result of that conclusion the second question requires review.

(2) Upon what standard must the appellant's decision be reviewed? ...

[28] In this case we are considering the standard of review applicable to a municipality's adjudicative function as opposed to its policy making. The decision in question was clearly adjudicative as it involved an adversarial hearing, the application of substantive rules to individual cases and a significant impact on the rights of the parties. ... In *U.E.S., Local 298 v. Bibeault*, [1988] 2 S.C.R. 1048, and subsequent cases, this Court adopted what was described as a "pragmatic and functional" approach to discerning the standards of review applicable to administrative tribunals, be they delegates of federal or provincial jurisdiction. As municipalities are also delegates of provincial jurisdiction, there is harmony in applying the pragmatic and functional approach in ascertaining the standard of review applicable to municipalities exercising an adjudicative function.

[29] As recently noted in *Pushpanathan v. Canada (Minister of Citizenship and Immigration)*, [1998] 1 S.C.R. 982, at paras. 29-38, several factors must be weighed in determining whether to afford an administrative tribunal curial deference. The approach is a contextual one that must be adapted to the body in question. It considers, where relevant, the existence of a privative clause, if any, the body's expertise, the purpose of the body's enabling legislation and whether the question at issue is one of law or fact. Here, s. 936 requires the municipal council to apply principles of statutory interpretation in order to answer the legal question of the scope of its authority. On such questions, municipalities do not possess any greater institutional competence or expertise than the courts so as to warrant a heightened degree of deference on review. The test on jurisdiction and questions of law is correctness.

[30] A consideration of the nature of municipal government and the extent of municipal expertise further militates against a deferential standard on the question of jurisdiction. Furthermore, these factors reflect the institutional realities that make municipalities creatures distinct and unique from administrative bodies.

[31] First, in contrast to administrative tribunals, that usually adjudicate matters pertaining to a specialized and confined area, municipalities exercise a rather plenary set of legislative and executive powers, a role that closely mimics that of the provincial government from which they derive their existence. ... Municipalities essentially represent delegated government.

[32] Second, municipalities are political bodies. Whereas tribunal members should be and are, generally, appointed because they possess an expertise within the scope of the agency's authority, municipal councillors are elected to further a political platform. Neither experience nor proficiency in municipal law and municipal planning, while desirable, is required to be elected a councillor. ... Finally, [... to] a large extent council decisions are necessarily motivated by political considerations and not by an entirely impartial application of expertise.

[33] The fact that councillors are accountable at the ballot box is a consideration in determining the standard of review for *intra vires* decisions. ...

[35] In light of the conclusion that Nanaimo acted within its jurisdiction in passing the resolutions at issue, it is necessary to consider the standard upon which the courts may review those *intra vires* municipal decisions. Municipal councillors are elected by the constituents they represent and as such are more conversant with the exigencies of their community than are the courts. The fact that municipal councils are elected representatives of their community, and accountable to their constituents,

is relevant in scrutinizing *intra vires* decisions. The reality that municipalities often balance complex and divergent interests in arriving at decisions in the public interest is of similar importance. In short, these considerations warrant that the *intra vires* decision of municipalities be reviewed upon a deferential standard.
[36] *Kruse v. Johnson*, [1898] 2 Q.B. 91 (Div. Ct.), has long been an authority in Canadian courts for scrutinizing the reasonableness of municipal by-laws. ... Or as more recently expressed in *Shell*, supra, per McLachlin J., at p. 244:

> Recent commentary suggests an emerging consensus that courts must respect the responsibility of elected municipal bodies to serve the people who elected them and exercise caution to avoid substituting their views of what is best for the citizens for those of municipal councils. ... Whatever rules of construction are applied, they must not be used to usurp the legitimate role of municipal bodies as community representatives.

[37] I find these comments equally persuasive in the scrutiny of municipal resolutions. The conclusion is apparent. The standard upon which courts may entertain a review of *intra vires* municipal actions should be one of patent unreasonableness. [39] We are left to consider whether Nanaimo was patently unreasonable in declaring this specific pile of soil a nuisance. The pile of soil had serious and continuing effects upon the neighbouring community. It was an annoyance and a source of pollution. Nanaimo's decision to declare Rascal's pile of soil a nuisance was not patently unreasonable. I would allow the appeal. ...

Unanimous

The facts were stated by Judge Grange of the Court of Appeal for Ontario as follows:

"An exotic dancer at Jilly's Tavern in the east end of Toronto performed her act with the assistance of a declawed Siberian tiger. The tiger, when not required for the act, was sometimes kept on a leash behind the tavern. There were no incidents of harm, either to persons or the tiger, but a city councilor for the area, spurred on by animal rights groups, brought the matter before City Council."

A city by-law was passed and later amended to regulate the keeping of animals. The inclusive language of the by-law prohibited circuses and similar shows from using exotic animals unless the performance related to certain films or education. The circus companies challenged the by-law as being, among other things, *ultra vires*. The court agreed in these words:

"... In my view the Legislature in enacting s. 210(1) [of the Municipal Act] did not intend the City to use it to control the conduct of circuses. What was intended instead was that the by-laws passed under the section would control the keeping of exotic animals such as, perhaps, the tiger associated with the dancer at Jilly's Tavern and would restrain the activities of persons who fancied boa constrictors or barracudas as domestic pets.

For these reasons, I am of the opinion that council of the city exceeded its powers in attempting to prohibit the use of exotic animals in circuses visiting the city. ...

I would allow the appeal, set aside the order of the Divisional Court and grant judgment ordering a declaration that the prohibition against the keeping of animals used in live public entertainment in the city of Toronto under City of Toronto By-law No. 212-86 as amended is *ultra vires* the legislative authority of the city of Toronto and is therefore of no force or effect."...

Stadium Corporation of Ontario Ltd. v. City of Toronto
Registry No. C13313
Court of Appeal for Ontario Court
April 1993

Johnson **v.** *Athletics Canada and International Amateur Athletics Federation*

[1997] O.J. No. 3201 (Q.L.)
ONTARIO COURT OF JUSTICE (GENERAL DIVISION)
JULY 25, 1997

[1] Caswell J.:— The applicant Benjamin Johnson has applied to the court for the following relief:

1. a declaration that the life-time ban issued by the respondents, Athletics Canada (A.C.) and the International Amateur Athletics Federation (I.A.A.F.), preventing him from participating in amateur athletic events governed by the respondents is contrary to the common law doctrine of restraint of trade;

2. an order reinstating Mr. Johnson's eligibility to participate in all activities governed by the respondents; and

3. costs on a solicitor and client basis.

FACTS

...

[11] At the Seoul Olympics in 1988, Mr. Johnson tested positive for the use of stanozolol, a prohibited substance. He was stripped of his gold medal and ultimately was banned from competition for two years. In 1990 he was re-instated as a member of A.C. He competed thereafter at various events and at the 1992 Olympics in Barcelona as a member of the Canadian team. Subsequent to his re-instatement Mr. Johnson was tested after every event in which he participated. ...

[13] On January 17, 1993 Mr. Johnson participated in an I.A.A.F. competition held in Montreal. At the conclusion of the race he provided a urine sample for testing. The sample was collected and sent to INRS-Sant, for analysis in accordance with the approved scientific protocols as set out in I.A.A.F. Procedural Guidelines 4.8–4.11. The urine sample was divided between two containers and they were labelled "A" and "B". ...

[14] Sample "A" was tested between January 19 and January 25 and the results revealed a testosterone to epitestosterone ratio of 10.3:1 [where 6:1 constitutes an offence]. ...

[15] ... The testing and analysis of sample "B" occurred on February 15 and 16, 1993. Mr. Johnson's lawyer, Terrence O'Sullivan, and his expert, Dr. David Black, President and Laboratory Director of Aegis Analytical Laboratories in Nashville, Tennessee were present on both days. Mr. Johnson's representatives examined the integrity of the "B" sample and agreed that there was no evidence of tampering, improper sealing of the "B" sample or any difficulties as to the coding of the sample bottles. The results of the testing [of] ... sample "B" had a ratio of testosterone to epitestosterone identical to sample "A", namely 10.3:1. ...

[17] ... Mr. Johnson [was informed] ... that the I.A.A.F. Doping Commission had ruled that the positive test contravened I.A.A.F. Rules 55 and 60 and constituted a doping offence. Since this was a second doping offence under I.A.A.F. Rule 60 2(a)(ii), pursuant to Rule 59.1 and 59.2, he was suspended from competition. The letter further stated ... [that he had the right to appeal the ruling, but Johnson did not appeal].

[22] On April 21, 1993 A.C. again wrote to Mr. Johnson to advise that the period had expired within which he could launch his appeal from the finding of the I.A.A.F. Doping Commission. The letter stated that since the deadline for return of the notice of application for a hearing expired as of midnight April 1, 1993, Mr. Johnson was declared ineligible for competition for life.

THE LAW

Restraint of Trade

[23] Competition among world class "amateur" athletes provides the successful athlete with considerable financial rewards including support from his national body as a carded athlete and payments from companies whose products he endorses. In order to preserve the athlete's amateur status, the monies that the athlete earns are deposited in an athlete reserve trust fund. In the 1980's and even after the Seoul Olympics, Mr. Johnson continued to be considered a world class athlete with lucrative endorsement contracts.

[24] It is the position of the applicant that the court should find that the life-time ban from competition is in restraint of Mr. Johnson's common law rights to carry on the trade or business from which he earns his livelihood: running. ...

[25] There is no "bright line" test with respect to the categories to which the doctrine of restraint of trade applies. ...

[26] In the English case of *Gasser v. Stinson et al.*, unreported, June 15, 1988 (Ch. Div.), Scott J., ... on the issue of restraint of trade, found as follows:

> The policy underlying restraint of trade law is that people should be free to exploit for their financial gain the talents and abilities that they may have. I would accept that restraint of trade law would not be applicable to activities that were undertaken for no financial reward at all (for example, school sport). ... But, in a sport which allows competitors to exploit their ability in the sport for financial gain and which allows that gain to

be a direct consequence of participation in competition, a ban on competition is, in my judgment, a restraint of trade.

[27] I adopt Scott J.'s reasoning and I find that the life-time ban imposed on Mr. Johnson is in restraint of trade.

Justification for the Restraint

[28] In *Nordenfelt v. Maxim Nordenfelt Guns & Ammunition Co. Ltd.*, [1894] A.C. 535 (H.L.) Lord Macnaghten stated at p. 565:

The public have an interest in every person's carrying on his trade freely: so has the individual. All interference with individual liberty of action in trading, and all restraints of trade of themselves, if there is nothing more, are contrary to public policy, and therefore void. That is the general rule. But here are exceptions: restraints of trade and interference with individual liberty of action may be justified by the special circumstances of a particular case. It is a sufficient justification, and indeed it is the only justification, if the restriction is reasonable—reasonable, that is, in reference to the interests of the parties concerned and reasonable in reference to the interests of the public, so framed and so guarded as to afford adequate protection to the party in whose favour it is imposed, while at the same time it is in no way injurious to the public. That, I think, is the fair result of all the authorities.

[29] I am persuaded that this statement represents the present state of the law in Canada: *Connors v. Connors Brothers Limited et al.*, [1939] S.C.R. 162. A.C. and the I.A.A.F. have argued that the life-time ban after a second doping offence is reasonable for many reasons. I agree that the ban is reasonable and is not an illegal restraint of trade. It is necessary to protect Mr. Johnson for the sake of his own health from the effects of consistently using prohibited substances. It is necessary to protect the right of the athlete, including Mr. Johnson, to fair competition, to know that the race involves only his own skill, his own strength, his own spirit and not his own pharmacologist. [30] The public has an interest in the protection of the integrity of the sport. Governments around the world subsidize their elite athletes through carding systems. The public pays to attend the events. The elite athlete is viewed as a hero and his influence over the young athlete cannot be underestimated. Mr. Johnson became both rich and famous during his athletic career as a result of his athletic performances. In at least some of the races he has admitted that he was cheating. Most major sports impose a life-time ban after an athlete has been caught for a second time using banned substances. ...

[32] This court is required to extend a measure of deference to the justifications advanced by the I.A.A.F. as the world governing body for amateur athletes when considering the reasonableness of the ban. It is not this court's function to serve as a court of appeal on the merits of decisions reached by tribunals exercising jurisdiction over specialized fields. The I.A.A.F. has special expertise not only in regulating amateur athletics but also in regulating, detecting and preventing drug abuse. ...

Denial of Natural Justice

[34] The position of Mr. Johnson is that the actions and proceedings of the I.A.A.F. and A.C. in 1993 were inherently unfair and as a result he was denied natural justice. The requirements of natural justice are set out by the Supreme Court

of Canada in many cases including *Lakeside Colony of Hutterian Brethren v. Hoffer,* [1992] 3 S.C.R. 165 Gonthier J. at p. 195:

The content of the principles of natural justice is flexible and depends on the circumstances in which the question arises. However, the most basic requirements are that of notice, opportunity to make representations, and an unbiased tribunal.

[35] ... Mr. Johnson now raises the issue of apprehension of bias as the reason for his failure to initiate appeal proceedings during the 28-day period following March 5, 1993. Mr. Johnson claims that this bias was revealed in certain statements reported in the press that were made by Dr. Ljungqvist [Chairman of the Doping Control Commission] and by Mr. Dupr [President of A.C.]. The statements suggested the futility of any appeal by Mr. Johnson in view of the findings of the Doping Commission. When Mr. Johnson announced his resignation on March 7, 1993, however, he stated that he did not wish to appeal the ban for three reasons; his age, the potential cost of an appeal, and the obligations that he felt to spare his family any further trauma. He did not at that time mention any apprehension of bias by A.C.'s and/or I.A.A.F.'s appellate panels.

[36] Both A.C. and I.A.A.F. referred to the procedures open to Mr. Johnson, after the Doping Commission confirmed his suspension, as being appeal procedures. ... These procedures were really in the nature of hearings "de novo," that is new hearings. Mr. Johnson was entitled notice of the hearing(s) to be represented by counsel, to be present personally and to present further evidence including witnesses. The panels were required to consider existing and additional evidence and to hear submissions from counsel. It is important to note that Mr. Johnson was represented at the time by Terrence O'Sullivan, a very experienced and capable counsel. The pleadings in this application contain voluminous correspondence between Mr. O'Sullivan and A.C. and the I.A.A.F.

[37] There is insufficient evidence before me that any appeal panel would have been biased against Mr. Johnson, in order to justify Mr. Johnson's failure to enforce his rights at the time. While I consider the remarks of Mr. Ljungqvist and Mr. Dupr, to be most improper given their positions, I have no evidence that either person would have affected the decision of an appeal panel. [38] Even if I were to find that on March 5, 1993, the Doping Commission should have heard from Mr. Johnson's counsel and should have considered any additional evidence, I am faced with the fact that Mr. Johnson did not avail himself of any of the several opportunities that were available to him for further hearings on the merits. Such hearings were capable of curing any perceived lack of fairness at the Doping Commission hearing and it must be assumed that they would do so: *Grey v. Canadian Track and Field and Association* (1986), 39 A.C.W.S. (2d) 483 (Ont. H.C.) ... [and others].

[39] Mr. Johnson failed to exhaust the remedies that were available to him without sufficient justification. The procedures in place in 1993 complied with the requirements of natural justice and were procedurally fair. In my view there was no violation of the rules of natural justice.

DISPOSITION

[40] The application is therefore dismissed.

- *I*n a criminal action, the judge charged the accused with "complete nincompoopery." This comment with others was sufficient to raise an apprehension of bias. The accused was successful in obtaining a prohibition and his case was assigned to a different judge.[6]

C. CHALLENGES TO DECISIONS OF ARBITRATORS

- *T*he Court of Arbitration for Sport overturned a decision of the International Weightlifting Federation that had banned the entire Bulgarian weightlifting team from competing in the 2000 Olympics because three lifters had tested positive for banned diuretics.[7]

When the National Ballet of Canada gave notice that her contract of employment would not be renewed, the ballerina, Kimberly Glasco, believing her contract was not being renewed because of positions she had taken as the dancers' representative on the Ballet's Board of Directors, responded with an array of legal proceedings including a grievance under the collective agreement. Both sides agreed to submit all the matters to private binding arbitration. The arbitrator made an interim order that the company reinstate her until the dispute was settled. The dance company made an application to stay the order. It argued that the arbitrator had only the powers granted by the Ontario *Labour Relations Act*, which explicitly prohibits orders requiring an employer to reinstate an employee. The court found, however, that the arbitrator did have the power to reinstate an employee under the provisions of the *Arbitration Act*. The Court, on the question of whether or not the order of reinstatement should be stayed, analyzed the question on the basis of the "balance of convenience."

> [20] Where lies the balance of convenience? Which will suffer the greater harm, Ms. Glasco if I stay the order for her reinstatement, or the National Ballet of Canada [Ballet] if I allow the order to stand?

After reviewing the arguments of the parties, the court concluded:

> [23] Glasco is a mature artist in the final stages of her career, performing at the highest level. Any further hiatus in her dancing is likely to prevent her from being able to resume her career. Such a loss to her is impossible to measure and cannot be adequately compensated for by monetary damages.

> [24] The National Ballet of Canada will not suffer a fatal blow if the order for reinstatement stands but Ms. Glasco's dancing career will likely be finished if she is kept from dancing any longer.

> [25] Ballet loses on the balance of convenience test. Ms. Glasco will suffer a far greater loss if a stay is ordered than Ballet will experience if the reinstatement order stands. . . .

> [26] I therefore refuse the request for a stay of the reinstatement order made by the arbitrator.

The motion was dismissed.

National Ballet of Canada v. Glasco
[2000] O.J. No. 1071 (Q.L.)
Ontario Superior Court of Justice (Divisional Court)
March 31, 2000

National Ballet of Canada v. *Glasco*

[2000] O.J. No. 2083 (Q.L.)
ONTARIO SUPERIOR COURT OF JUSTICE
JUNE 6, 2000

Background: Within months of the court's refusal to stay the arbitrator's reinstatement order, the matter came before the court again, but this time, under the provisions of the *Arbitration Act*.

Swinton, J.

...

[13] ... [T]he appellant/applicant decided that the appropriate method to challenge the award was under the procedures set out in the *Arbitration Act*, rather than by way of application for judicial review. ...

THE REVIEW PROVISIONS OF THE *ARBITRATION ACT, 1991*

[15] The *Arbitration Act, 1991* sets out provisions governing the judicial role in the enforcement and review of arbitration awards. ...

THE APPLICATION TO SET ASIDE

[17] The Ballet seeks to set aside the award pursuant to s. 46(1), para. 6 on the basis that the arbitrator did not treat the Ballet fairly and did not give it an opportunity to present its case or respond to the other party's case, because it was denied the opportunity to cross-examine on the affidavits filed by Ms. Glasco. ...

[21] ... [T]he claim is, in effect, a denial of fairness or natural justice. ...

[23] The content of the concept of natural justice varies with the tribunal and the circumstances. Most importantly, a refusal to allow cross-examination is not necessarily a denial of natural justice. ... It is where the refusal of cross-examination interferes with the ability of a party to address key issues or essential elements of its case that the courts have found a denial of fairness or natural justice by an administrative tribunal. ...

[30] In accordance with ss. 19(2) and 46(1), para. 6 of the *Arbitration Act*, my concern is with the fairness of the procedure and whether the Ballet was denied an opportunity to make its case. With respect to some of the factual matters said to be in dispute, there is no denial of fairness in the refusal to allow cross-examination, since the Ballet could have filed its own affidavit material to contradict statements of Ms. Glasco. ... However, the Ballet submitted no affidavits to contradict Ms. Glasco's statements despite the opportunity to do so during the arbitration hearing. ...

[34] In the circumstances, the Ballet was not prevented from presenting its case on essential points ... The Ballet, having agreed to remove these disputes from the courts, can not now complain that the arbitration procedure which they accepted differs from the procedure which might have been available in the courts.

JURISDICTION TO HEAR THE MOTION FOR LEAVE TO APPEAL

[35] Pursuant to s. 3 of the *Arbitration Act*, the parties may expressly or by implication vary or exclude the right to appeal an arbitrator's award on a question of law, with leave. The Ontario Court of Appeal has held that it is the parties' intention that is paramount as to whether there is a right to appeal in an individual case, and "[a]n examination of the language of the agreement and the circumstances surrounding its making is necessary in order to determine the parties' intention" with respect to the right to appeal. ...

[37] The parties here have used the term "binding", but not the words "final and binding" with respect to the submission to arbitration. ... [Furthermore,] I do not read the arbitration agreement as impliedly expressing the intention to exclude the right to appeal. ...

[39] Therefore, I interpret the agreement as not excluding the right to seek leave to appeal a question of law. ... Therefore, leave to appeal is granted.

APPEAL UNDER S. 45

[40] An appeal under s. 45(1) can only be with respect to a question of law. The appellant makes three arguments that the arbitrator erred in law: first, he granted an order of reinstatement in the absence of mutual confidence between the parties; second, that the order of interim reinstatement is contrary to Charter values; and third, that the arbitrator erred in ordering reinstatement when a court would not have done so, thus violating the choice of law provisions in s. 32 of the *Arbitration Act*. ...

[43] ... [T]he standard of review [in this case] is correctness. ...

MUTUAL CONFIDENCE

[49] ... [T]he essence of the argument is that there can be no mutual confidence when the Artistic Director [Mr. Kudelka] has expressed his lack of confidence in a dancer's abilities or her compatibility with his vision.

[50] It is important to emphasize the scope of my role here. I have jurisdiction only with respect to errors of law. I do not have any jurisdiction to review findings of fact or findings of mixed fact and law. A careful reading of the arbitration award indicates that the arbitrator applied the correct principles of law to the facts as he found them. While it is unusual for a court to order specific performance of an employment con-

tract or a contract of personal service, there is no absolute rule against this, and the appellant conceded this. ...

[51] In determining whether to make such an interlocutory order, a court considers a number of factors, of which the element of mutual confidence is one. It is not, however, a "condition precedent" or threshold. ...

[52] ... [The] element of confidence is one factor to be considered within the balance of convenience. Moreover, the concept of confidence is one of "sufficient confidence". ... It is to be expected that where an employer has dismissed an employee, there will be some degree of resistance in having that employee return to the workplace, even on an interim basis, and other employees may be averse to having the employee return. The issue is whether there is such a problem of lack of confidence or antipathy that it outweighs other considerations in determining the balance of convenience.

[53] Arbitrator Albertyn considered a number of factors in determining where the balance of convenience lay in this case. He was well aware of Mr. Kudelka's opposition [to Ms. Glasco]... [He made no errors in law.]

[55] The Ballet's real quarrel is with the findings of fact made by the arbitrator, and his conclusions when he applied the legal principles to those facts and exercised his discretion to award interlocutory relief under s. 41 of the Act. The Ballet agreed to give him jurisdiction to make such findings of fact or mixed fact and law, and did not obtain an agreement to allow appeals on such questions of fact or mixed fact and law. Therefore, this ground of appeal fails.

CHARTER VALUES

[56] The Canadian Charter of Rights and Freedoms does not apply directly to the arbitration award, as it is the result of private, consensual arbitration and the Charter does not apply to private action. ... However, the Ballet relies on the principle espoused in *Hill v. Church of Scientology*, [1995] 2 S.C.R. 1130, 126 D.L.R. (4th) 129 that while the Charter does not apply directly to private action, it can be used to influence the development of the common law — that is, common law rules should evolve in a manner consistent with Charter values. The Ballet argues that the order to reinstate Ms. Glasco, with the potential for the arbitrator to require that she perform certain roles, is a violation of Mr. Kudelka's freedom of statement, guaranteed in s. 2(b) of the Charter. ...

[58] ... As stated by Cory J. in *Hill*: "It is up to the party challenging the common law to bear the burden of proving not only that the common law is inconsistent with Charter values but also that its provisions cannot be justified" (pp. 1171-72). There has been no effort to satisfy that onus here. Therefore, this ground of appeal fails as well.

THE CHOICE OF LAW ARGUMENT

[59] ... [The appellant takes the position that the *Labour Relations Act* does not confer jurisdiction on either a grievance arbitrator or the labour board to reinstate an employee on an interim basis and in fact expressly removes the power to order interim reinstatement from these tribunals.] Therefore, argues the Ballet, the arbitrator should apply the rules that a court would apply in these circumstances. ...

[60] ... [The arbitrator] correctly concluded that as an arbitrator under the *Arbitration Act*, he had the express power to order interim relief, including an injunction — a power that the parties did not remove from him. ...

[62] ... [T]he Ballet errs in assuming that the arbitrator must act in the same way as a court. While he has been given the powers of a court to deal with aspects of the parties' dispute, he is not a court. Rather, he acts as an arbitrator appointed under the *Arbitration Act, 1991*, with all the powers available to him under that Act. It is true that he must act according to law, and he did so, applying the correct legal principles respecting interlocutory injunctions. ...

[65] Thus, the arbitrator did not err in law in exercising his discretion to order reinstatement here, nor did he apply the law incorrectly. ...

CONCLUSION

[67] The parties to this appeal and application made an agreement to refer their dispute to arbitration with the hope that there would be an expeditious resolution. Sadly, the parties are far from a resolution of the merits of the dispute.

[68] The regime of private arbitration which they have chosen gives a limited supervisory role to the courts. In exercise of that role, I have found no error of law nor breach of procedural fairness on the part of the arbitrator in the interlocutory award. Therefore, the application to set aside the award and the appeal are dismissed. ...

Appeal and application dismissed[8]

- *T*he dispute between the student association and B.C.I.T. (British Columbia Institute of Technology) over the use of leased premises was submitted to arbitration. When the arbitrator ruled in favour of B.C.I.T., the student association sought leave to appeal pursuant to the *Commercial Arbitration Act*. The B.C. Court of Appeal gave the Student Association of B.C.I.T. permission to appeal the decision of an arbitrator.[9]

- *W*hat if? What if Darryl Neudorf had taken his dispute with Sarah McLachlan to arbitration? What if he had accepted the pre-trial settlement offer of the equivalent of 20 years of his present income? Clearly he could not have fared worse than he did taking the case to court, which rejected his case and also ordered him to pay a significant portion of McLachlan's legal fees.[10]

D. Remedies

Prerogative Writs

Mandamus

A community association, to block a development on land zoned multiple dwelling, requested the city to rezone the area. The city complied and passed a resolution to have the city solicitor prepare the necessary by-law. The next day, the Cheungs, the owners of the property, were told by the city that under s. 981(2) that they had seven days to apply for the building permit or they would be caught by the new zoning bylaw. The Cheungs filed their application for a building permit within six days. The city purported to freeze all building permit applications under s. 981(1).

The Cheungs sought an order of *mandamus* to force the city to issue the building permit. It was granted. The court of appeal reviewed the statutory provisions and concluded:

"The purpose of subs. (2) of s. 981 was explained by Esson C.J.S.C. in *Taina Developments (Blackford) Ltd. v. New Westminster (City)* (28 February 1990), Vancouver Registry A900370 (B.C.S.C.), as follows … : (At pp. 8-9)

> The broad purpose of s. 981 is to provide machinery to block developments, which comply with existing zoning but will be in conflict with proposed zoning, from being pressed ahead during the time required to enact the bylaw that is "under preparation". The purpose of s. 981(2), in my view, is not to give an opportunity to developers who hear of the intention to amend the law to crystallize their position under existing law by advising the city's officials of a concept which meets the requirements of that law. *Rather it is, as Mr. de Villiers suggests, to provide relief to those who at the time preparation commences are ready to build and who take the step of applying for a building permit within 7 days.* For a building of any substantial size and complexity, the application could be ready within 7 days of the resolution only if it was in an advanced state of readiness at the date of the resolution. (Emphasis added.)

Sections 981(1) and 981(2)] are necessarily linked and must work together. To hold otherwise would allow a municipality to both approbate and reprobate s. 981. …

Section 981(1) is not applicable here as the application for a building permit, complete in all its essentials, was made within 7 clear days from the City Council's December 9, 1993 resolution to instruct the City solicitor to prepare the down-zoning by-law. …

… The Cheungs were rightly entitled to the order made in their favour.

Appeal dismissed; mandamus granted."

Cheung v. Victoria (City)
100 B.C.L.R. (2d) 235
British Columbia Court of Appeal
December 22, 1994

Injunction

▶▶ To understand how the court proceeds to determine whether or not an injunction should be granted, see *Ethical Funds Inc. v. Mackenzie Financial Corporation,* p. 234 or 1267623 *Ontario Inc. et al. v. Nexx Online, Inc.,* p. 122.

- **W**hen protesters blocked the efforts of International Forest Products and its contractors to log in the Elaho Valley of B.C., the company was granted an injunction ordering the protesters to stop their interference. When the protesters disobeyed the court order they were found in contempt of court and two were given one-year jail terms, perhaps some of the harshest judgments in our history.[11]

Sue Rodriguez was afflicted with Amyotrophic Lateral Sclerosis (known as Lou Gehrig's Disease) which causes a person to lose control of muscle functions. Death is ultimately caused by the inability to swallow and breathe because of the failure of the requisite muscles. The disease, however, does not affect the mind.

Unwilling to endure such a death, Ms. Rodriguez wanted to end her life when it became unbearable, but was physically unable to do it without assistance. Because s. 241 of the *Criminal Code* makes it a crime to assist anyone in committing suicide, she commenced a court action in which she asked for a declaration that s. 241 of the *Criminal Code* violates her rights under s. 7 of the *Charter* which reads:

> Everyone has the right to life, liberty and security of the person and the right not to be deprived thereof except in accordance with the principles of fundamental justice.

Her application was dismissed by the B.C. Supreme Court.

She appealed to the B.C. Court of Appeal. The three justices who heard the appeal agreed that s. 241 of the *Criminal Code* did violate her rights under s. 7 of the *Charter*; nevertheless, the appeal was dismissed. Justice Hollinrake held that the violation was not contrary to the principles of fundamental justice; Justice Proudfoot held that the declaration sought would establish a bad precedent in that it would exempt unnamed persons from future criminal liability. Justice McEachern, dissenting, interpreted s. 7 of the *Charter* as ensuring individual control and held that s. 241 of the *Criminal Code* denied her rights, and those rights were not deprived in accordance with the principles of fundamental justice. He would not have struck down s. 241, but instead would have allowed a doctor-assisted suicide, for Ms. Rodriguez only, if she would follow certain prescribed rules.[12]

Ms. Rodriguez appealed to the Supreme Court of Canada which heard argument on May 20, 1993 in a nationally televised session.[13]

The reserved judgment, released in October, held against her. By a 5-to-4 vote, the court rejected her argument that the ban on assisted suicide should be struck down. The majority felt, *inter alia*, that society had not reached a consensus on the issue of assisted suicides and that allowing assisted suicides could lead to abuse affecting the more vulnerable members of society.[14]

On February 12, 1994, Sue Rodriguez died. It was determined that it was an assisted suicide. The response has ranged from cries to prosecute, to the full extent of the law, the person who assisted her to calls for a bill to be presented to Parliament to legalize assisted suicide.

Rodriguez v. British Columbia (Attorney General)
http://www.lexum.umontreal.ca
May 20, September 30, 1993

Question

If the court orders a person or company to stop polluting a water system or stop blocking the roads, what can be done if they don't obey the court order?

E. CONTEMPT OF COURT

The lower court found Jetco Manufacturing Ltd. in contempt of court when it continued to discharge excessive amounts of nickel, cadmium, and cyanide into the water system after the court had ordered the company to stop. Because the company had 69 convictions for violating anti-water pollution bylaws and because the president of the company admitted treating the fines as a cost of doing business, the judge doubled the fine to a further $200,000 and sentenced the president of the company to one year in jail. The court of appeal overturned the decision on the grounds that the trial judge erred in finding the company had notice of the prohibition order.

Regina v. Jetco Manufacturing Ltd. et al.
57 O.R. (2d) 776
Ontario Court of Appeal
January 16, 1987

When the government of British Columbia made a decision to allow some logging in Clayoquot Sound on Vancouver Island, protesters began a blockade. Those who ignored a court order against disrupting the logging were arrested in the "largest mass arrest in B.C. history" for contempt of court.[15]

By November 11, 1993 more than 800 protesters had been arrested.[16]

The following are excerpts from Justice Bouck's decision reprinted by the *Times-Colonist* of Victoria, B.C.:

"Before fixing the actual sentences, something must be said about the legal concept of contempt of court. …[D]emocracy allows a society to govern itself by the rule of law and not by the rule of the individual…Some Canadians take democracy for granted. It is easy to forget that democracies have failed. It can happen to us unless we as a people co-exist by the rule of law. If we do not, Canada could collapse into a form of tyrannical rule. Our country will ultimately deteriorate if people feel they are entitled to abuse the rights of others when they are unable to convince the majority of the rightness of their cause. …[T]he right to peacefully protest brings with it the responsibility of avoiding interfering with the rights of others. …

Preserving the dignity of the court is only a minor part of contempt proceedings. The fundamental issue is much deeper. Underneath it all, contempt proceedings are taken primarily to preserve the rule of law. Without the rule of law democracy will collapse. Individuals will then decide which laws they will obey and which ones they won't. Government by the rule of law will disappear. People will then be controlled by the rule of the individual. The strongest mob will rule over the weak. Anarchy will prevail.

Most of you have indicated that you prefer to follow the law of God. No doubt encouraged by submissions of your counsel, who ought to have known better, some of you have invited me to apply the law of God. This court does not apply the law of God, irrespective of whose interpretation of that law is offered for consideration. This court applies the law as it is determined to be by the legislators of this country and by the decisions of this court, which have accumulated now for 700 years. …

The rule of law exists in this society only because the overwhelming majority of citizens, irrespective of their different views on religion, morality, or science, agree to be bound by the law. That agreement, which cannot be found recorded in a conventional sense, has survived the deepest and most profound conflicts of religion, morality and science. In that sense it might be thought that its strength is overwhelming and its future secure. But that is not the case at all, for the continued existence of that agreement is threatened by its own inherent fragility. That fragility was described by former Chief Justice Farris of this court in the celebrated case of *Canadian Transport Co. Ltd. v. Alsbury* (1952), 6 W.W.R. (N.S.) 473 (B.C.S.C.), to which counsel have referred, I quote from p. 478:

> Once our laws are flouted and orders of our courts treated with contempt the whole fabric of our freedom is destroyed. We can then only revert to conditions of the dark ages when the only law recognized was that of might. One law broken and the breach thereof ignored, is but an invitation to ignore further laws and this, if continued, can only result in the breakdown of the freedom under the law which we so greatly prize. …

[In response to the contention that the actions of the protesters followed the path of Ghandi, Martin Luther King and the suffragettes, Judge Bouck said:] But here, the elected representative of the people of this province made the law allowing MacMillan Bloedel Ltd. to log the timber in Clayoquot Sound. It was not decreed. … Except for the out-of-province defendants, the others have the right to vote. They were simply unable to persuade the elected representatives of the people to adopt their point of view. Unlike Mr. Gandhi, Mr. King and the suffragettes, they could attempt to change the law through their vote and the votes of others whom they could persuade. Unlike Mr. Gandhi, Mr. King and the suffragettes, they infringed a legal right: the right of MacMillan Bloedel Ltd. to cut timber in Clayoquot Sound. Their behavior in no way follows the noble ideals of Mr. Gandhi, Mr. King or the suffragette movement. …

I turn now to fix the sentence for each of the defendants found guilt of contempt of the court orders made 20 July 1992 and 16 July 1993. It is not a pleasant duty. I take no joy in the task. …

Despite repeated comments by various judges concerning the necessity of working within the democratic system, and despite relatively modest sentences, disobedience of court orders continues. Many people do not seem to get the message. …

The only way the law can deal with continuous breaches of court orders is to increase the penalty in the hope it will dissuade others from committing the same kinds of acts.

The sentences I am about to impose should reflect a degree of penalty for their unlawful behaviour. Mostly, it should serve as a deterrent to others who contemplate undermining the rule of law."

[The sentences imposed ranged from fines of $1,000 to $3,000 and jail terms from 45 to 60 days.]

MacMillan Bloedel Limited v. Simpson
Times-Colonist
October 15, 1993 p. A5

F. GOVERNMENT CHALLENGES AND EFFORTS TO REGULATE MODERN BUSINESS

Q u e s t i o n

What challenges face the government in trying to regulate E-Commerce?

- *T*he "Love Bug" virus, released May 4, 2000, circled the globe in just two hours and may have caused $10 billion in damages. The virus, (also a worm as it bored into e-mail programs and sent copies of itself to those listed in one's address book), targeted .jpgs and MP3s and thus destroyed archives of digital pictures and music. If this were prosecuted in the U.S., the creator could receive a sentence of five years in prison and a $250,000 fine under the *U.S. Computer Fraud and Abuse Act* of 1986.[17]

The person accused of releasing the virus was not successfully prosecuted under the existing law of the Philippines. The Philippines did not have a law covering electronic commerce or computer hacking until June and the law could not be applied retroactively.[18]

"The Council of Europe has drawn up a treaty that would require nations to pass computer-crime legislation and cooperate on enforcement."[19]

- *A* computer hacker, known on the Internet as Mafiaboy, accused of causing approximately $1.7 billion in damages by paralyzing, among others, CNN Web site, Yahoo.com, Amazon.com and eBay, has pled guilty to 56 charges of unauthorized access to computer and mischief relating to data. The court ordered him not to use a computer until further sentencing. The teenager is quoted as saying after entering his plea "I'm a bit relieved. It's a load off my mind."[20]

- *I*f you would like to be part of the second coming of Jesus, you could send your money, all of it if you wish, to some post office box in Berkeley, California. Your contribution would go toward the cloning of Jesus by taking a cell from some relic. This scheme was one cited in an article about the RCMP's difficulty in fighting securities fraud and other rackets.[21]

- *T*he Canadian Internet Registration Authority (CIRA) plans to adopt a policy that provides an alternative dispute resolution service to assist with the regulation of any dispute that would arise among entities having domain names ending with dot-ca. CIRA's ADR process will be in addition to rights available through the court system. Only Canadian law will be recognized with the hopes that the ADR process will produce decisions similar to those of the Canadian courts.[22]

- *P*resently, at the international level, ICANN (Internet Corporation for Assigned Names and Numbers) requires that any individual or company that registers in the dot-com, dot-net or dot-org domains agree to a policy that domain name disputes must be resolved by agreement, court action, or arbitration (ADR) before the registrar will cancel, suspend, or transfer the name. ADR on-line services have been approved.[23]

- *T*he Business Software Alliance (BSA), a nonprofit group of computer software companies fighting software piracy, received $2.4 million when it settled with 20 companies that unlawfully copied programs or used unlicensed programs. A spokesperson for the Alliance said, "When most people hear about software piracy, they think of some guy selling disks at a flea market. The biggest problem ... is with businesses."[24]

ENDNOTES

1. For a more detailed account see *The Vancouver Sun,* February 4, 2000, p. A1 and June 14, 2000, p. A12, and *Canadian Lawyer,* June 2000, p. 8.

2. For a more detailed account see *The Vancouver Sun,* December 16, 2000, p. A1.

3. See *Campbell et al. v. Federal Express Canada Ltd.* [1997] O.J. No. 3510 (Q.L.) Ontario Court of Justice (General Division) August 27, 1997.

4. *The Lawyers Weekly,* May 1, 1992, pp. 1, 13.

5. See *The Lawyers Weekly,* August 20, 1993, p. 9.

6. For a more detailed account see the summary of *R. v. Gerlach* in *The Lawyers Weekly,* July 15, 1994.

7. For a more detailed account see *The Vancouver Sun,* September 25, 2000, p. C3.

8. For an opinion that there was an unfortunate fallout from this reinstatement—the tense working environment that resulted from Glasco's demands that conflicted with the casting decisions of the artistic director and the aspirations of the other dancers—see "The Glasco fiasco (Act XVII)" in *The Globe and Mail,* July 4, 2000, p. A15.

9. For a summary of *B.C. Institute of Technology (Student Assn.) v. B.C. Institute of Technology,* see *The Lawyers Weekly,* November 3, 2000, p. 19.

10. For a more detailed account see *The Vancouver Sun*, August 28, 2000, p. A1.

11. *The Vancouver Sun*, September 16, 2000, p. B1 and September 19, 2000, p. A3.

12. *The Lawyers Weekly*, March 26, 1993, pp. 1, 22; April 9, 1993, p. 16.

13. Summarized from *The Globe and Mail*, May 21, 1993, p. A1.

14. For a more detailed account see *Maclean's*, October 11, 1993, p. 27.

15. Summarized from *Maclean's*, August 23, 1993, p. 13 and October 25, 1993, p. 11.

16. *The Globe and Mail*, November 11, 1993, p. A6.

17. For a detailed account see *Time*, May 15, 2000, p. 37.

18. *The Globe and Mail,* August 22, 2000, p. B7.

19. *Time,* May 22, 2000, p. 34.

20. For a more detailed account see the *National Post,* January 19, 2001, p. A6.

21. See *The Lawyers Weekly,* October 27, 2000, p. 8.

22. For a more detailed account see *The Globe and Mail,* September 26, 2000, p. E15.

23. *LawNow*, August/September 2000, p. 27.

24. *Associated Press*, June 26, 2000, reprinted in Edupage.

III

THE LAW OF TORT

A. DISTINCTION BETWEEN CRIMINAL AND CIVIL ACTIONS

Q u e s t i o n s

What is the difference between a criminal and a civil action?
Can the same incident attract both types of action?

- "Mr. McSorley, I must find you guilty as charged" were words concluding *R. v. McSorley*, the criminal trial in which Marty McSorley, the NHL "enforcer," was charged with assault with a weapon, viz. slashing the head of Donald Brashear with his hockey stick in the final seconds of a game between the Vancouver Canucks and the Boston Bruins. Brashear was knocked unconscious and sustained a serious concussion. He, and his family, also suffered from the misconception by many that the trial was a civil action instigated by him.[1] McSorley did not appeal the decision.[2]

THE EXAMPLES BELOW ILLUSTRATE BEHAVIOUR THAT DID OR COULD LEAD TO BOTH A CRIMINAL AND A CIVIL ACTION.

- *O*.J. Simpson, U.S. football star and T.V. and movie personality, was charged with the criminal offence of the murder of his ex-wife, Nicole Simpson, and her friend Ronald Goldman. In the criminal trial in Los Angeles the prosecutors failed to prove beyond a reasonable doubt that Simpson had committed the murders.[3] In a subsequent civil trial taken by the victims' families, Simpson was found liable for the deaths. The court of appeal affirmed the decision and did not reduce the award of damages, the equivalent of Cdn. $47 million.[4]

- *A* beer fight at Koo Koo Bananas in Whitby, Ontario resulted in charges of common assault being laid against Eric Lindros, a hockey player with the Philadelphia Flyers. The judge, finding the Crown had failed to prove its case beyond a reasonable doubt, dismissed the charge after a four-day trial.[5]

- *A* funeral director in Halifax had bodies transferred from the chosen expensive caskets into cheap pressboard boxes before cremation.[6]

B. Intentional Torts

Questions

When will the loss suffered by the plaintiff be shifted to the defendant?
When is the defendant at fault in law?

---

1. Abuse of Process

Dykun **v.** *Odishaw et al.*

[2000] A.J. No. 915 (Q.L.)
Alberta Court of Queen's Bench
August 3, 2000

Background facts: Dykun retained lawyer Daniel Rogers to commence an action on his behalf against Canada Post for wrongful dismissal. The action was settled for $96,000. Displeased, Dykun retained Odishaw to sue Rogers for negligence for his handling of the case and recommending settlement. After an eight-day trial the action was dismissed. An appeal from that decision was dismissed. Dykun then sued Odishaw for negligence in the negligence suit against Rogers. Years of litigation followed all involving the same grievance. At one point Dykun declares bankruptcy. The judge reviews this history and the Plaintiff's new statement of claim based on conspiracy.

Lee, J.: ...

[35] The Court has jurisdiction to strike the Statement of Claim pursuant to Rule 129 of the Alberta Rules of Court on the ground that it is frivolous and vexatious or that it constitutes an abuse of the Court's process. The impugned Statement of Claim is frivolous and vexatious and is an abuse of the Court's process.

(a) The Statement of Claim is an Abuse of the Court's Process

...

[38] It is an abuse of the process of the Court to attempt to re-litigate a matter already decided against the party advancing the matter ... or to collaterally attack a decision of a court of competent jurisdiction. ...

[39] The very matters raised by the Plaintiff in this Statement of Claim have already been decided against him. ... This latest action is a collateral attack on the previous decisions of the Court.

[40] The Statement of Claim in the present action constitutes a clear case of abuse of process.

(b) The Statement of Claim is Frivolous and Vexatious

[41] When one analyses all the allegations against the Defendants, in essence the Plaintiff complains that the Defendants did something which ultimately had the effect of denying the Plaintiff the right to sue Mr. Odishaw. However, Costigan, J. ruled that there was no claim against Mr. Odishaw in any event, and the Plaintiff exhausted his full rights of appeal from this decision, twice being denied leave to the Supreme Court of Canada.

[42] The Ontario High Court has determined that a proceeding is vexatious if it satisfies any of the following tests:

(a) the bringing of one or more actions to determine an issue which has already been determined by a court of competent jurisdiction constitutes a vexatious proceeding;

(b) where it is obvious that an action cannot succeed, or if the action would lead to no possible good, or if no reasonable person can reasonably expect to obtain relief, the action is vexatious;

(c) vexatious actions include those brought for an improper purpose, including the harassment and oppression of other parties by multifarious proceedings brought for purposes other than the assertion of legitimate rights;

(d) it is a general characteristic of vexatious proceedings that grounds and issues raised tend to be rolled forward into subsequent actions and repeated and supplemented, often with actions brought against the lawyers who have acted for or against the litigant in earlier proceedings;

(e) in determining whether proceedings are vexatious, the court must look at the whole history of the matter and not just whether there was originally a good cause of action;

(f)   the failure of the person instituting the proceedings to pay the costs of unsuccessful proceedings is one factor to be considered in determining whether proceedings are vexatious;

(g)   the respondent's conduct in persistently taking unsuccessful appeals from judicial decisions can be considered vexatious conduct of legal proceedings.

...

[43] The history of litigation brought by the Plaintiff set out above demonstrates that this Statement of Claim fulfils all seven criteria indicative of vexatious proceedings. The Plaintiff refuses to accept the determinations of the Courts. He rolls forward claims against solicitors involved in the preceding actions. Almost every decision is appealed; all appeals have been unsuccessful. Not only has the Plaintiff failed to pay costs awarded against him, he now seeks those same costs as damages from these Defendants.

IV. DISPOSITION

[54] I grant the following relief to the Defendants:

1.   A Declaration that the within action is an abuse of this Court's process and is frivolous and vexatious.

2.   An Order striking the within Statement of Claim.

3.   An Order directing John Dykun to deposit $20,000.00 with the Clerk of the Court of Queen's Bench of Alberta, to be held as security for costs, prior to instituting any legal proceedings or process, or commencing any action, in Alberta, against either Joseph B. Brumlik, Vivian R. Stevenson or James H. Odishaw. ...

• *I*n South Carolina, Ms. Martin sued a Bi-Lo store. She alleged that she suffered back injuries after slipping on a wet floor in the store. A witness claimed that the plaintiff herself poured water on the floor and then sat in it. This fraudulent behaviour resulted in a criminal action against her. It could have also resulted in an action by Bi-Lo against Ms. Martin for the tort of abuse of process.[7]

2. Assault

In 1348 a man irritated by a pubkeeper's refusal to open the pub threw a hatchet at her head. He missed. She sued and won. The case, *I de S et Ux*, established the principle that creating in another apprehension of an imminent hit was wrong. In 1994 Nova Scotia gave us a variation.

Freeman, J.A. (orally): — In the course of a heated argument with his companion Sandra Thibodeau, the appellant produced a double-bitted axe he took from under a bed and, in his version of events, threatened to cut the house down around her because she was blocking a doorway, refusing to let him leave because she said she feared he would drive while impaired by alcohol.

He has appealed his conviction by Judge John Nichols of the Provincial Court on a charge of using a weapon to commit an assault, contrary to s. 267(1)(a) of the Criminal Code... .

An axe produced in the circumstances of an angry domestic dispute can only be considered a weapon and its use for the purpose of threatening or intimidating can be inferred. The appellant's expressed intention to use the axe to damage the house rather than to harm Ms. Thibodeau does not overcome the inference that the axe was used for the purpose of intimidation. The appeal is dismissed.

R. v. Lowe
[1994] N.S.J. No. 36 (Q.L.)
The Nova Scotia Court of Appeal
January 26, 1994

3. Battery

Malette **v.** *Shulman*

37 O.A.C. 281
Ontario Court of Appeal
March 30, 1990

Background facts: Mrs. Malette, seriously injured in an automobile accident, arrived at the emergency ward unconscious. The doctor gave her a blood transfusion even after it was brought to his attention that she was carrying a card indicating her unwillingness to have such treatment. She sued. The only defendant (of many) found liable at the trial level was the doctor; liable for the tort of battery. The plaintiff was awarded $20,000. The following is an excerpt from the decision of the court hearing his appeal.

Robins, J.A.: …
[12] I should perhaps underscore the fact that Dr. Shulman was not found liable for any negligence in his treatment of Mrs. Malette. The judge held that he had acted "promptly, professionally and was well-motivated throughout" and that his management of the case had been "carried out in a confident, careful and conscientious manner" in accordance with the requisite standard of care. His decision to administer blood in the circumstances confronting him was found to be an honest exercise of his professional judgment which did not delay Mrs. Malette's recovery, endanger her life or cause her any bodily harm. Indeed, the judge concluded that the doctor`s treatment of Mrs. Malette "may well have been responsible for saving her life."
[13] Liability was imposed in this case on the basis that the doctor tortiously violated his patient's rights over her own body by acting contrary to the Jehovah's Witness card and administering blood transfusions that were not authorized. His honest and even justifiable belief that the treatment was medically essential did not serve to relieve him from liability for the battery resulting from his intentional and unpermitted conduct. …
[22] On the facts of the present case, Dr. Shulman was clearly faced with an emergency. He had an unconscious, critically-ill patient on his hands who, in his opinion, needed blood transfusions to save her life or preserve her health. If there were no Jehovah's Witness card, he undoubtedly would have been entitled to administer blood transfusions as part of the emergency treatment and could not have been held liable for so doing. In those circumstances he would have had no indication that the transfusions would have been refused had the patient then been able to make her wishes known and, accordingly, no reason to expect that, as a reasonable person, she would not consent to the transfusions.
[23] However, to change the facts, if Mrs. Malette, before passing into unconsciousness, had expressly instructed Dr. Shulman, in terms comparable to those set forth on the card, that her religious convictions as a Jehovah's Witness were such that she was not to be given a blood transfusion under any circumstances and that she fully realized the implications of this position, the doctor would have been confronted with an obviously different situation. Here, the patient, anticipating an emergency in which she might be unable to make decisions about her health care contemporaneous with the emergency, has given explicit instructions that blood transfusions constitute an unacceptable medical intervention and are not to be administered to her. Once the emergency arises, is the doctor nonetheless entitled to administer transfusions on the basis of

his honest belief that they are needed to save his patient's life?
[24] The answer, in my opinion, is clearly no. A doctor is not free to disregard a patient's advance instructions any more than he would be free to disregard instructions given at the time of the emergency. The law does not prohibit a patient from withholding consent to emergency medical treatment, nor does the law prohibit a doctor from following his patient's instructions. While the law may disregard the absence of consent in limited emergency circumstances, it otherwise supports the right of competent adults to make decisions concerning their own health care by imposing civil liability on those who perform medical treatment without consent. …
[26] The distinguishing feature of the present case — and the one that makes this a case of first impression — is, of course, the Jehovah's Witness card on the person of the unconscious patient. What then is the effect of the Jehovah's Witness card?
[27] In the appellant's submission, the card is of no effect and, as a consequence, can play no role in determining the doctor's duty toward his patient in the emergency situation existing in this case. …
[29]… He argues that it could properly be doubted whether the card constituted a valid statement of Mrs. Malette's wishes in this emergency …
[30] … I share the trial judge's view that, in the circumstances of this case, the instructions in the Jehovah's Witness card imposed a valid restriction on the emergency treatment that could be provided to Mrs. Malette and precluded blood transfusions. …
[36]… The doctor is bound in law by the patient's choice even though that choice may be contrary to the mandates of his own conscience and professional judgment. If patient choice were subservient to conscientious medical judgment, the right of the patient to determine her own treatment, and the doctrine of informed consent, would be rendered meaningless. …
[37] In sum, it is my view that the principal interest asserted by Mrs. Malette in this case — the interest is the freedom to reject, or refuse to consent to, intrusions of her bodily integrity — outweighs the interest of the state in the preservation of life and health and the protection of the integrity of the medical profession. …
[41] At issue here is the freedom of the patient as an individual to exercise her right to refuse treatment and accept the consequences of her own decision. Competent adults, as I have sought to demonstrate, are generally at liberty to refuse medical treatment even at the risk of death. The right to determine what shall be done with one's body is a fundamental right in our society. The

concepts inherent in this right are the bedrock upon which the principles of self-determination and individual autonomy are based. Free individual choice in matters affecting this right should, in my opinion, be accorded very high priority. I view the issues in this case from that perspective. …

Appeal dismissed.

Note: This case illustrates the value society places on the individual's right to the integrity of his or her body even if that right collides with the conscience of a physician and the interest of the state to preserve life. These dramatic life and death incidents may now decline as the Elders of the Jehovah's Witnesses have decreed that blood transfusions in life/death situations will no longer lead to excommunication.[8]

For a recent case showing the extreme difficulty in making a right decision given the principles set out in *Malette v. Shulman* and the duty to take care of an injured person see the summary of *Fortey (Guardian ad Litem) v. Canada (A.G.)* below or the full 1999 case at the B.C. Court of Appeal site: http://www.courts.gov.bc.ca/.

The Court of Appeal unanimously upheld the lower court's decision that found police officers negligent in not overriding the refusals of a man ("drunk, angry, aggressive, profane and obstinate") to receive medical attention. The attending police officers who "walk the line between committing the tort of battery by compelling him to be treated against his will, and the tort of negligence by failing to realize that he is intoxicated to such a degree that he has lost the capability of rational decision" knew that the plaintiff had suffered a potentially serious head injury. The court, therefore, found the police negligent in not making sure he received medical attention even though they were very concerned about Fortey and repeatedly urged him to let them take him to the hospital.

Fortey (Guardian ad Litem) v. Canada (A.G.)
Court of Appeal for British Columbia
May 10, 1999

- "I don't want to die, but I would rather die than have the transplant and have someone else's heart." These are the words of a teen who refused consent but was forced to have a heart transplant by order of the court on the grounds that she was not able to "come to terms with" the gravity of her situation.[9]

- "When a fist-fight broke out Monday between two surgeons performing an operation in a northern English hospital, a junior doctor stepped in to finish the operation."[10]

- Mr. Umpierrez, a 26-year old Uruguayan man, bit several passengers aboard a jetliner on its flight from Costa Rica to Rio de Janeiro. The crew members reported that his teeth had been filed down to sharp points.[11]

- The pie-in-your-face expression of voter disapproval, which has been on the increase, could clearly lead to a civil action for battery by the victimized politicians.

- After the Chicago Bears lost to the San Francisco 49ers 41-0, an unidentified woman among a crowd taunting the Bears coach Mike Ditka alleged that Ditka tossed a wad of gum at her and hit her on the head. "Police officer Richard Galliani said the gum 'was found and booked as evidence. What we have is just a basic assault or battery.'"[12]

- *A*fter a dispute with a customer, Ms. Carson, a cake decorator in Arkansas, gave the customer a cake. The cake was laced with laxatives; seventeen people were made ill.[13]

- *A* cyclist landed on the pavement on the left side of his head and on his shoulders after an attack by motorists with a powerful squirt gun. The pranksters were liable for all the consequent damage caused by their "assault and battery."[14]

DEFENCE OF CONSENT

The court found that a consent form signed by a university student who had submitted to a medical experiment at the University Hospital was not valid in law because the doctors failed to give him a fair and reasonable explanation of the proposed treatment and probable effect or risks so that he could make an informed consent. The doctors did not inform him that they were testing an anaesthetic or that a catheter would be advanced to and through his heart. The student, therefore, succeeded in his action for "trespass to the person." He had suffered a complete cardiac arrest during the treatment and was resuscitated by the manual massage of his heart.

Halushka v. the University of Saskatchewan et al.
53 D.L.R. (2d) 426
Saskatchewan Court of Appeal
May 4, 1965

- *I*n 1996 Evander Holyfield won the World Boxing Association title by an upset victory over the reigning champion Mike Tyson. The rematch in Las Vegas on June 28, 1997 illustrates the limits to the defence of consent often used against plaintiffs injured in contact sports. Holyfield had of course consented to bodily contact, but not to the damage inflicted by Tyson. Tyson bit off a chunk of Holyfield's ear.[15]

- *A*fter learning he was infected with the HIV virus, he did not warn his sexual partner and continued the relationship with her. She later tested HIV-positive and initiated a criminal action against him. The criminal action was successful. The court found he endangered her life and that there was no true consent to unprotected sex because he had failed to tell her he was HIV positive.[16]

4. CONVERSION (TRESPASS TO CHATTELS)

▶▶ See *von Bismark v. Sagl* on p. 183 for an example of conversion that the judge described as "despicable."

- *I*n London, Ontario, Mr. McMahon testified that he had warned his sister's pet budgie that if it did not quit biting his hand he would bite its head off. The budgie paid no heed and continued to bite; Mr. McMahon "followed through with the threat."[17]

5. DECEIT

Note: The tort of deceit is also known as a "fraudulent misrepresentation" when a deceitful representation is used to induce a person to enter a contract. Therefore, see *Sidhu Estate v. Bains* on p. 106.

- *I*nvestors may have lost as much as $6 billion when the price of shares in Bre-X Minerals Ltd. collapsed after an independent study found *no* gold at its Busang gold site. It was revealed that the bags of core samples from that site, which had caused investor excitement, had been salted with bought flakes of gold. The company subsequently hired Forensic Investigative Associates Inc. whose report traces the chronology of the fraud and asserts it has evidence that the exploration manager, Michael de Guzman, and others carried out the salting. De Guzman apparently jumped to his death from a helicopter when the fraud was exposed. This massive fraud has resulted in several lawsuits.

- *A*lan Eagleson, the founder of the National Hockey League Players' Association, and its executive director from 1967 to 1991, pleaded guilty to "defrauding Labatt Brewing Co. and three sports organizations." As a result of a plea bargain with both U.S. and Canadian authorities, the Ontario Court of Appeal sentenced Eagleson to 18 months in the Mimico Correctional Institute located not far from where he grew up "for frauds that had the effect of skimming thousands of dollars from hockey players' pensions." In addition, it was alleged that he deceived Bobby Orr by failing to disclose to him that Orr had received an offer from the Boston Bruins that included part ownership of the club.[18]

- *I*n California, Allstate Insurance Co. took action against 45 individuals, including doctors and lawyers, who conspired to defraud the insurance company by staging false collisions. The insurance company sought $107 million in statutory damages.[19]

  On the other hand, in Illinois, the State Farm Mutual Automobile Assurance Co. was ordered to pay $456 million in damages for using inferior generic repair parts, instead of the brand name parts available from the manufacturer, when its policy promised to restore the cars to their pre-accident condition.[20]

- *L*loyd's (formerly Lloyd's of London), the world's most renowned insurance organization, is being sued by some of its investors (known as "Names"). The suit claims that the Names, required to risk their entire personal fortunes for a share of profit, were recruited fraudulently; Lloyd's suppressed information about its sizable losses and altered the financial reports to show a profit.[21]

- *T*he lawyer, the accountant, the businessman, and the nuns—the players in this sordid tale. The first three conspired to falsify nearly 800 legal documents to swindle the nuns of their pension funds. The $25 million pocketed by the three, and hidden in Swiss bank accounts to foil the tax man, was not the total loss suffered by The Sisters of the Good Shepherd and Les Soeurs de Notre Dame; they have little chance of realizing any of the $80 million they were persuaded to invest in a now bankrupt shopping mall.

  The lawyer, agreeing to cooperate with the authorities in all the criminal and civil actions, has been ordered to pay $5 million in restitution to the nuns and has received a five-and-a-half year sentence.[22]

- *A* Hasidic fundraising group pleaded guilty to tax evasion and was fined $400,000. The Orthodox Jewish organization gave tax receipts for donations to the charity but then surreptitiously returned "upwards of two-thirds of the contribution in cash."[23]

6. DEFAMATION

Hill *v.* Church of Scientology of Toronto

http://www.lexum.umontreal.ca/
SUPREME COURT OF CANADA
JULY 20, 1995

CORY J.—On September 17, 1984, the appellant Morris Manning, accompanied by representatives of the appellant Church of Scientology of Toronto ("Scientology"), held a press conference on the steps of Osgoode Hall in Toronto. Manning, who was wearing his barrister's gown, read from and commented upon allegations contained in a notice of motion by which Scientology intended to commence criminal contempt proceedings against the respondent Casey Hill, a Crown attorney. The notice of motion alleged that Casey Hill had misled a judge of the Supreme Court of Ontario and had breached orders sealing certain documents belonging to Scientology. The remedy sought was the imposition of a fine or the imprisonment of Casey Hill.

[2] At the contempt proceedings, the allegations against Casey Hill were found to be untrue and without foundation. Casey Hill thereupon commenced this action for damages in libel against both Morris Manning and Scientology. On October 3, 1991, following a trial before Carruthers J. and a jury, Morris Manning and Scientology were found jointly liable for general damages in the amount of $300,000 and Scientology alone was found liable for aggravated damages of $500,000 and punitive damages of $800,000. Their appeal from this judgment was dismissed by a unanimous Court of Appeal: …

III. ANALYSIS

(a) Application of the Charter

(1) Section 32: Government Action

[The court rejects the argument that Hill's actions were government action and thus open to Charter scrutiny and focuses on the assertion that the common law must be interpreted in light of Charter values.]

(2) Section 52: Charter Values and the Common Law …

[91] It is clear from [case law] that the common law must be interpreted in a manner which is consistent with Charter principles. This obligation is simply a manifestation of the inherent jurisdiction of the courts to modify or extend the common law in order to comply with prevailing social conditions and values.…

[92] Historically, the common law evolved as a result of the courts making those incremental changes which were necessary in order to make the law comply with current societal values. The Charter represents a restatement of the fundamental values which guide and shape our democratic society and our legal system. It follows that it is appropriate for the courts to make such incremental revisions to the common law as may be necessary to have it comply with the values enunciated in the Charter. …

[95] Private parties owe each other no constitutional duties and cannot found their cause of action upon a Charter right. The party challenging the common law cannot allege that the common law violates a Charter right because, quite simply, Charter rights do not exist in the absence of state action. The most that the private litigant can do is argue that the common law is inconsistent with Charter values. It is very important to draw this distinction between Charter rights and Charter values. …

[96] Courts have traditionally been cautious regarding the extent to which they will amend the common law. Similarly, they must not go further than is necessary when taking Charter values into account. Far-reaching changes to the common law must be left to the legislature. …

[99] With that background, let us first consider the common law of defamation in light of the values underlying the Charter.

(b) The Nature of Actions for Defamation: The Values to Be Balanced

[100] There can be no doubt that in libel cases the twin values of reputation and freedom of expression will clash. As Edgerton J. stated in *Sweeney v. Patterson*, 128 F.2d 457 (D.C. Cir. 1942), at p. 458, cert. denied 317 U.S. 678 (1942), whatever is "added to the field of libel is taken from the field of free debate." The real question, however, is whether the common law strikes an appropriate balance between the two. Let us consider the nature of each of these values.

(i) Freedom of Expression

[101] Much has been written of the great importance of free speech. Without this freedom to express ideas and to criticize the operation of institutions and the conduct of individual members of government agencies, democratic forms of government would wither and die. See, for example, *Reference re Alberta Statutes*, [and others]…. More recently, in *Edmonton Journal*, supra, at p. 1336, it was said:

> It is difficult to imagine a guaranteed right more important to a democratic society than freedom of expression. Indeed a democracy cannot exist without that freedom to express new ideas and to put forward opinions about the functioning of public institutions. The concept of free and uninhibited speech permeates all truly democratic societies and institutions. The vital importance of the concept cannot be over-emphasized.

[102] However, freedom of expression has never been recognized as an absolute right. Duff C.J. emphasized this point in *Reference re Alberta Statutes*, supra, at p. 133:

> The right of public discussion is, of course, subject to legal restrictions; those based upon considerations of decency and public order, and others conceived for the protection of various private and public interests with which, for example, the laws of defamation and sedition are concerned. In a word, freedom of discussion means … "freedom governed by law." [Emphasis added.] …

[103] Similar reasoning has been applied in cases argued under the Charter. Although a Charter right is defined broadly, generally without internal limits, the Charter recognizes, under s. 1, that social values will at times conflict and that some limits must be placed even on fundamental rights. As La Forest J. explained in *United States of America v. Cotroni*, [1989] 1 S.C.R. 1469, at p. 1489, this Court has adopted a flexible approach to measuring the constitutionality of impugned provisions wherein "the underlying values [of the Charter] must be sensitively weighed in a particular context against other values of a free and democratic society ...".

[104] In *R. v. Keegstra*, [1990] 3 S.C.R. 697, for example, s. 319(2) of the Criminal Code was found to be justified as a reasonable limit on the appellant's freedom to spread falsehoods relating to the Holocaust and thus to promote hatred against an identifiable group. Dickson C.J. adopted the contextual approach to s. 1 and concluded that, since hate propaganda contributed little to the values which underlie the right enshrined under s. 2(b), namely the quest for truth, the promotion of individual self-development, and participation in the community, a restriction on this type of expression might be easier to justify than would be the case with other kinds of expression. ...

[106] Certainly, defamatory statements are very tenuously related to the core values which underlie s. 2(b). They are inimical to the search for truth. False and injurious statements cannot enhance self-development. Nor can it ever be said that they lead to healthy participation in the affairs of the community. Indeed, they are detrimental to the advancement of these values and harmful to the interests of a free and democratic society. This concept was accepted in *Globe and Mail Ltd. v. Boland*, [1960] S.C.R. 203, at pp. 08–9, where it was held that an extension of the qualified privilege to the publication of defamatory statements concerning the fitness for office of a candidate for election would be "harmful to that 'common convenience and welfare of society.'" Reliance was placed upon the text *Gatley on Libel and Slander in a Civil Action: With Precedents of Pleadings* (4th ed. 1953), at p. 254, wherein the author stated the following:

> It would tend to deter sensitive and honourable men from seeking public positions of trust and responsibility, and leave them open to others who have no respect for their reputation. ...

(ii) The Reputation of the Individual

[107] The other value to be balanced in a defamation action is the protection of the reputation of the individual. ...

[108] Democracy has always recognized and cherished the fundamental importance of an individual. That importance must, in turn, be based upon the good repute of a person. It is that good repute which enhances an individual's sense of worth and value. False allegations can so very quickly and completely destroy a good reputation. A reputation tarnished by libel can seldom regain its former lustre. A democratic society, therefore, has an interest in ensuring that its members can enjoy and protect their good reputation so long as it is merited.

[109] From the earliest times, society has recognized the potential for tragic damage that can be occasioned by a false statement made about a person. This is evident in the Bible, the Mosaic Code and the Talmud. As the author Carter-Ruck, in *Carter-Ruck on Libel and Slander* (4th ed. 1992), explains at p. 17:

> The earliest evidence in recorded history of any sanction for defamatory statements is in the Mosaic code. In Exodus XXII 28 we find "Thou shalt not revile the gods nor curse

the ruler of thy people" and in Exodus XXIII 1 "Thou shalt not raise a false report: put not thine hand with the wicked to be an unrighteous witness." There is also a condemnation of rumourmongers in Leviticus XIX 16 "Thou shalt not go up and down as a talebearer among thy people."

[110] To make false statements which are likely to injure the reputation of another has always been regarded as a serious offence. During the Roman era, the punishment for libel varied from the loss of the right to make a will, to imprisonment, exile for life, or forfeiture of property. In the case of slander, a person could be made liable for payment of damages.

[111] It was decreed by the Teutons in the *Lex Salica* that if a man called another a "wolf" or a "hare," he must pay the sum of three shillings; for a false imputation of unchastity in a woman the penalty was 45 shillings. In the Normal Costumal, if people falsely called another "thief" or "manslayer," they had to pay damages and, holding their nose with their fingers, publicly confess themselves a liar.

[112] With the separation of ecclesiastical and secular courts by the decree of William I following the Norman conquest, the Church assumed spiritual jurisdiction over defamatory language, which was regarded as a sin. The Church "stayed the tongue of the defamer at once *pro custodia morum* of the community, and *pro salute anim\ae* of the delinquent." See V.V. Veeder, "The History and Theory of the Law of Defamation" (1903), 3 Colum. L. Rev. 546, at p.551.

[113] By the 16th century, the common law action for defamation became commonplace. This was in no small measure due to the efforts of the Star Chamber to eradicate duelling, the favoured method of vindication. The Star Chamber even went so far as to punish the sending of challenges. However, when it proscribed this avenue of recourse to injured parties, the Star Chamber was compelled to widen its original jurisdiction over seditious libel to include ordinary defamation.

[114] The modern law of libel is said to have arisen out of the case *De Libellis Famosis* (1605), 5 Co. Rep. 125a, 77 E.R. 250. There, the late Archbishop of Canterbury and the then Bishop of London were alleged to have been "traduced and scandalized" by an anonymous person. As reported by Coke, it was ruled that all libels, even those against private individuals, ought to be sanctioned severely by indictment at common law or in the Star Chamber. The reasoning behind this was that the libel could incite "all those of the same family, kindred, or society to revenge, and so tends per consequens to quarrels and breach of the peace" (p. 251). It was not necessary to show publication to a third person and it made no difference whether the libel was true or whether the plaintiff had a good or bad reputation. Eventually, truth was recognized as a defence in cases involving ordinary defamation.

[115] It was not until the late 17th century that the distinction between libel and slander was drawn by Chief Baron Hale in *King v. Lake* (1679), Hardres 470, 145 E.R. 552, where it was held that words spoken, without more, would not be actionable, with a few exceptions. Once they were reduced to writing, however, malice would be presumed and an action would lie.

[116] The character of the law relating to libel and slander in the 20th century is essentially the product of its historical development up to the 17th century, subject to a few refinements such as the introduction and recognition of the defences of privilege and fair comment. From the foregoing we can see that a central theme through the ages has been that the reputation of the individual is of fundamental importance. As

Professor R. E. Brown writes in *The Law of Defamation in Canada* (2nd ed. 1994), at p. 1–4:

"(N)o system of civil law can fail to take some account of the right to have one's reputation remain untarnished by defamation." Some form of legal or social constraints on defamatory publications "are to be found in all stages of civilization, however imperfect, remote, and proximate to barbarism."

[117] Though the law of defamation no longer serves as a bulwark against the duel and blood feud, the protection of reputation remains of vital importance... .This sentiment was eloquently expressed by Stewart J. in *Rosenblatt v. Baer*, 383 U.S. 75 (1966), who stated at p.92:

The right of a man to the protection of his own reputation from unjustified invasion and wrongful hurt reflects no more than our basic concept of the essential dignity and worth of every human being — a concept at the root of any decent system of ordered liberty. ...

[120] Although it is not specifically mentioned in the Charter, the good reputation of the individual represents and reflects the innate dignity of the individual, a concept which underlies all the Charter rights. It follows that the protection of the good reputation of an individual is of fundamental importance to our democratic society.

(c) The Proposed Remedy: Adopting the New York Times v. Sullivan "Actual Malice" Rule

[122] In *New York Times v. Sullivan*, supra, the United States Supreme Court ruled that the existing common law of defamation violated the guarantee of free speech under the First Amendment of the Constitution. It held that the citizen's right to criticize government officials is of such tremendous importance in a democratic society that it can only be accommodated through the tolerance of speech which may eventually be determined to contain falsehoods. The solution adopted was to do away with the common law presumptions of falsity and malice and place the onus on the plaintiff to prove that, at the time the defamatory statements were made, the defendant either knew them to be false or was reckless as to whether they were or not. ...

(e) Conclusion: Should the Law of Defamation be Modified by Incorporating the Sullivan Principle?

[137] *The New York Times v. Sullivan* decision has been criticized by judges and academic writers in the United States and elsewhere. It has not been followed in the United Kingdom or Australia. I can see no reason for adopting it in Canada in an action between private litigants. The law of defamation is essentially aimed at the prohibition of the publication of injurious false statements. It is the means by which the individual may protect his or her reputation which may well be the most distinguishing feature of his or her character, personality and, perhaps, identity. I simply cannot see that the law of defamation is unduly restrictive or inhibiting. Surely it is not requiring too much of individuals that they ascertain the truth of the allegations they publish. ...

(f) Should the Common Law Defence of Qualified Privilege be Expanded to Comply with Charter Values?

[143] Qualified privilege attaches to the occasion upon which the communication is made, and not to the communication itself. As Lord Atkinson explained in *Adam v. Ward*, [1917] A.C. 309 (H.L.), at p. 334:

... a privileged occasion is ... an occasion where the person who makes a communication has an interest or a duty, legal, social, or moral, to make it to the person to whom it is made, and the person to whom it is so made has a corresponding interest or duty to receive it. This reciprocity is essential. ...

[144] The legal effect of the defence of qualified privilege is to rebut the inference, which normally arises from the publication of defamatory words, that they were spoken with malice. Where the occasion is shown to be privileged, the bona fides of the defendant is presumed and the defendant is free to publish, with impunity, remarks which may be defamatory and untrue about the plaintiff. However, the privilege is not absolute and can be defeated if the dominant motive for publishing the statement is actual or express malice. See *Horrocks v. Lowe*, [1975] A.C. 135 (H.L.), at p. 149.

[145] Malice is commonly understood, in the popular sense, as spite or ill-will. However, it also includes, as Dickson J. (as he then was) pointed out in dissent in *Cherneskey*, supra, at p. 1099, "any indirect motive or ulterior purpose" that conflicts with the sense of duty or the mutual interest which the occasion created. ...

[147] In other words, the information communicated must be reasonably appropriate in the context of the circumstances existing on the occasion when that information was given. ...

[149] The principal question to be answered in this appeal is whether the recitation of the contents of the notice of motion by Morris Manning took place on an occasion of qualified privilege. If so, it remains to be determined whether or not that privilege was exceeded and thereby defeated... .

[155] ... It is my conclusion that Morris Manning's conduct far exceeds the legitimate purposes of the occasion. The circumstances of this case called for great restraint in the communication of information concerning the proceedings launched against Casey Hill. As an experienced lawyer, Manning ought to have taken steps to confirm the allegations that were being made. This is particularly true since he should have been aware of the Scientology investigation pertaining to access to the sealed documents. In those circumstances he was duty bound to wait until the investigation was completed before launching such a serious attack on Hill's professional integrity. Manning failed to take either of these reasonable steps. As a result of this failure, the permissible scope of his comments was limited and the qualified privilege which attached to his remarks was defeated.

[156] The press conference was held on the steps of Osgoode Hall in the presence of representatives from several media organizations. This constituted the widest possible dissemination of grievous allegations of professional misconduct that were yet to be tested in a court of law. His comments were made in language that portrayed Hill in the worst possible light. This was neither necessary nor appropriate in the existing circumstances. While it is not necessary to characterize Manning's conduct as amounting to actual malice, it was certainly high-handed and careless. It exceeded any legitimate purpose the press conference may have served. His conduct, therefore, defeated the qualified privilege that attached to the occasion. ...[The issue of damages was reviewed at length and the $1.6 million award was upheld.]

The appeal is dismissed with costs.

- *C*BC was successfully sued by a cardiologist interviewed for a news program, *the fifth estate*. The producers had taken his words out of context in a way that depicted him as a villain, namely as a doctor who knowingly "pushed" a dangerous drug thereby endangering thousands.[24]

   The CBC was also successfully sued by another cardiologist who was portrayed as the "bad guy," uncaring, even foolish, about the negative effects of the drug nifedipine.[25]

Q u e s t i o n

In defamation actions, what constitutes "malice" and what is the effect of the court finding the libel was made with malice?

Hodgson v. Canadian Newspapers Co. Ltd.

http://www.ontariocourts.on.ca/
ONTARIO COURT OF APPEAL
JUNE 22, 2000

Sharpe, J.A.

OVERVIEW

[1] On March 22, 1991, The Globe and Mail (the appellant) published a front-page story reporting on the purchase of certain lands from a developer by the Region of York. The Region paid a substantial sum for the lands. The story stated that the respondent, the Engineering Commissioner of York Region, had recommended the purchase, but that planning documents indicated that the Region was entitled to acquire the lands at no cost and that the respondent had not disclosed that fact to the Regional Council. It was also reported that the developer who received the money was a long-time friend of the respondent. These allegations were repeated in several subsequent articles.

[2] The respondent brought this action for defamation. After a 78-day trial, Lane J., sitting without a jury, rejected the defences of justification, fair comment and qualified privilege and found that the appellant Jock Ferguson, the journalist who wrote the articles, had acted with express malice. The respondent was awarded $880,000 for special, general, and punitive damages. ...

ANALYSIS

Issue 1: Did the trial judge err in finding that the appellants had failed to establish justification? [The court answers "No."]
...
Issue 2: Did the trial judge err in finding that the appellant Ferguson was guilty of actual malice?

[33] The issue of malice is relevant to both the defences of fair comment and qualified privilege and to the assessment of damages. In *Hill v. Church of Scientology of Toronto*, ... Cory J. described malice in the following terms:

> Malice is commonly understood, in the popular sense, as spite or ill-will. However, it also includes ... "any indirect motive or ulterior purpose" that conflicts with the sense of duty or the mutual interest which the occasion created. ... Malice may also be established by showing

that the defendant spoke dishonestly, or in knowing or reckless disregard for the truth.

[35] Malice, then, relates to the state of mind of the defendant. As it is usually difficult to prove spite or ill-will, malice is ordinarily established through proof that the defendant knew that the statement complained of was untrue, was reckless with respect to its truth or that the defendant had some improper motive or purpose. It has also been held that malice is shown where the defendant did not believe the truth of the statements published. ...

[45] ... There was ample evidence to support the trial judge's finding that Ferguson's purpose was not to report the facts but rather to create a sensational story. ... In the end, the trial judge's findings amount to this: Ferguson was, above all, intent on writing a sensational story and engaged in "systematic reporting of one side and non-reporting of the other." In view of the trial judge's detailed and explicit rejection of Ferguson as a credible witness and the high degree of deference the court must accord to finding of facts, I see no basis for interference with these findings. They provide an adequate foundation for a finding of malice ... The trial judge found that, whatever he meant to say, and whatever his belief, Ferguson was on a mission to write a sensational story without regard for the facts.

Issue 3: Did the trial judge err in rejecting the defence of fair comment?

Issue 4: Did the trial judge err in rejecting the defence of qualified privilege?

[46] In the face of the findings related to malice that I have just reviewed, I cannot accept the appellant's attempt to characterize the articles they published as an honest attempt to present the true facts on an important issue of public concern. The finding of malice is fatal to the defences of fair comment and qualified privilege. ...

Issue 5: Did the trial judge err with respect to damages?

(a) Special Damages ...

[50] In my view, there was evidence to support the trial judge's finding that there was a sufficient causal link between the

defamatory articles and the respondent's termination to justify an award of damages. ...

[51] Accordingly, I would not interfere with the award of special damages.

(b) General Damages ...

[52] The trial judge also awarded $400,000 for general and aggravated damages. The appellants submit that the trial judge erred in awarding aggravated damages.

[53] In *Hill v. Church of Scientology*, [. . . Cory J. referred to the words of] Robins J.A. in *Walker v. CFTO Ltd.,* [(1987), 59 O.R. (2d) 104 (C.A.)]: ...

> Where the defendant is guilty of insulting, high-handed, spiteful, malicious or oppressive conduct which increases the mental distress – the humiliation, indignation, anxiety, grief, fear and the like – suffered by the plaintiff as a result of being defamed, the plaintiff may be entitled to what has come to be known as 'aggravated damages'.

...

(c) Punitive Damages

[63] Punitive damages are rarely awarded and are only appropriate in limited circumstances. In *Hill v. Church of Scientology*, supra at p. 1208, Cory J. stated:

> Punitive damages may be awarded in situations where the defendant's misconduct is so malicious, oppressive and high-handed that it offends the court's sense of decency. Punitive damages bear no relation to what the defendant should receive by way of compensation. Their aim is not to compensate the plaintiff, but rather to punish the defendant. It is the means by which the jury or judge expresses its outrage at the egregious conduct of the defendant. They are in the nature of a fine which is meant to act as a deterrent to the defendant and to others from acting in this manner. It is important to emphasize that punitive damages should only be awarded in those circumstances where the combined award of general and aggravated damages would be insufficient to achieve the goal of punishment and deterrence. (Emphasis added.)

[64] In my view, the trial judge erred in awarding punitive damages in the present case. I do not agree that an award of punitive damages was required to achieve the goal of punishment and deterrence in view of the other damages awarded. The award of $780,000 imposes upon the appellants a heavy price for the wrong they have committed. This is a very substantial award. ...

[65] Accordingly, I would set aside the award of punitive damages. ...

CONCLUSION

[77] For these reasons I would allow the appeal, but only to the extent of varying the judgment by deleting paragraph 3 awarding punitive damages. Otherwise the appeal is dismissed.

The Supreme Court refused to hear an appeal.

The newspaper reporter, David Baines, a reporter for *The Vancouver Sun*, frequently wrote articles critical of some companies that were members of the Vancouver Stock Exchange. He became the victim of vicious taunting, inflammatory and continuous libel (some of it distributed world-wide) and slander by the writings and words of the defendant Chelekis whose campaign was to ruin Baines' credibility. The trial court found Chelekis and his publishers liable and awarded Baines $250,000 in damages, which included aggravated and punitive damages against Chelekis.

Two of the defendants appealed from the assessment of damages. The court of appeal quoted extensively from the decision of the lower court and after reviewing the facts and the law dismissed the appeal.

> [27] It may be that these compensatory damages are on the generous side but, in my opinion, when one considers that Baines is a journalist with his professional interest in stock markets, the enormity of the libel, the conduct of the appellants ... and the finding of the trial judge that they "willingly participated in the distribution of Chelekis' material" leading to a finding of joint liability, I do not think it can be said that these damages are "inordinately high," "wholly out of proportion to the injury," or a "wholly erroneous estimate of the damage suffered." See Southin J.A. in *Cole v. Brown*, [[1999] 7 W.W.R. 703 (B.C.C.A.)].

Southam Inc. et al. v. Chelekis et al.
http://www.courts.gov.bc.ca/
Court of Appeal of British Columbia
February 14, 2000

> **Note:** The Supreme Court of Canada refused to hear a further appeal. Baines announced that he will donate $64,000 of the award to the Sing Tao School of Journalism at the University of B.C.[26]

7. FALSE IMPRISONMENT

Parlee (Guardian ad Litem of) v. Port of Call Holdings Ltd.

http://www.courts.gov.bc.ca/
BRITISH COLUMBIA SUPREME COURT
MARCH 30, 2000

Background facts: In the words of the trial judge and repeated in the decision of the appeal court: "[S]ubstantially what I find as a fact is that Mr. Parlee, Myles Parlee, was returning this chocolate milk product to the dairy cooler and was observed by store employees to be acting in a manner that aroused their suspicion when he placed it back in the cooler. It was the manner in which he looked at them, the manner in which he left the scene which excited their suspicion. Immediately one of the employees asked another to go and check the carton of milk product that he had seen Mr. Parlee place back in the dairy cooler. That second employee noticed that the product was unsealed, open, and that some of the contents had been removed. At that time it was determined that Mr. Parlee, Myles Parlee, would be stopped, detained, questioned, and that is subsequently what happened."

The trial judge had "no hesitation in finding on the facts that the store employees were well within their rights to stop and arrest, under the circumstances, Myles Parlee. In fact, this is a case — not even a close case, in my view, of reasonable and probable grounds. This is, in my view, a clear case where the employees had an obligation to their employer and perhaps an obligation to the public to effect the arrest. There were ample grounds for so doing." In addition to awarding the defendants their costs and expenses, the trial judge awarded each defendant a penalty; the total penalty amounted to $4,000.

The decision was appealed to the British Columbia Supreme Court which reviewed the legal history on the issue of when a citizen can legally detain a person.

Davis, J.

[9] Section 9 of the Canadian Charter of Rights and Freedoms recognizes that "everyone has the right not to be arbitrarily detained or imprisoned." ... The Newfoundland Court of Appeal in *Sears Canada Inc. v. Smart* (1987), 36 D.L.R. (4th) 756 quoted Sir Rufus Isaacs C.J. in *Walters v. W. H. Smith & Son Ltd.*, [1914] 1 K.B. 595 at p. 602 who said:

> Interference with the liberty of the subject, and especially interference by a private person has ever been most jealously guarded by the common law of the land. At common law a police constable may arrest a person if he has reasonable cause to suspect that a felony has been committed although it afterwards appears that no felony has been committed, but that is not so when a private person makes or accuses the arrest, for to justify his action he must prove, among other things, that a felony has actually been committed ....

Gushue, J.A. then went on to say at p. 758 in *Sears* (supra):

> Thus, at common law, an arrest by a private person could only be justified if the arresting person could establish that a crime was committed and that there were "reasonable grounds of suspicion" that the person arrested had committed that crime. In more modern terms, "reasonable grounds of suspicion" may be translated as "reasonable and probable cause for his belief".

> In Canada, the circumstances in which private persons, including owners of property and their employees, may effect an arrest without first obtaining a warrant to do so are now governed by the Criminal Code. This, in my view, is as it should be because arrest is an act of governmental authority and, if it is to be carried out by other than persons representing the state, such as police officers, the circumstances under which it may be done must be determined and sanctioned by that authority.

[The court then reviewed cases that had different interpretations of the relevant sections in the Criminal Code and stated its preferred interpretation and its conclusion.]

[11] ... [A] private person who arrests an individual must satisfy the court on a balance of probabilities:

(a) that someone committed an indictable offence, and

(b) that the private person effecting the arrest had reasonable grounds for believing and did believe the person arrested had committed that indictable offence.

[12] There is ample authority to support the conclusion that the person who makes the arrest must subjectively believe the person arrested committed the offence, and that those grounds must be objectively reasonable: *Regina v. Storrey* (1990), 53 C.C.C. (3d) 316 (S.C.C.), *Regina v. Klimchuk* (1991), 8 C.R. (4th) 327 (B.C.C.A.), *Swansburg v. Smith* (1996), 141 D.L.R. (4th) 94. This subjective and objective test is also of application in civil matters. ...

[13] In this case I am satisfied there was sufficient evidence before the trial judge upon which he, or any trier of fact, could be satisfied on a balance of probabilities that someone com-

mitted the indictable offence of theft. Mr. Taylor testified that he had worked in the dairy department at Thrifty Foods and he had never experienced a defective carton that arrived at the store opened. This evidence, coupled with the evidence that some of the contents of the carton were gone, establishes the first requirement noted above. ...

[15] [However] the evidence of Mr. Taylor who detained Mr. Parlee does not support a finding on a balance of probabilities that he subjectively believed Mr. Parlee had committed theft. ...

[20] ... [I]n my view, the evidence specific to Mr. Taylor's belief regarding Myles Parlee at the moment he was detained ... mandates a finding that Mr. Taylor did not subjectively believe Myles Parlee had committed the offence. He was detaining Master Parlee to investigate only. An arrest only for the purpose of investigation is unlawful: *Regina v. Storrey* (supra), *Swansberg v. Smith* (supra), *Regina v. Duguay* (1985), 18 C.C.C. (3d) 289 (Ont. C.A.) and *Regina v. Roberge*, [1983] 1 S.C.R.312 (S.C.C.).

[21] I must therefore conclude that the learned trial judge erred in dismissing the claimant's claim.

[22] As to damages, I defer to the learned trial judge's finding of fact in this regard. I agree, however, with the submission of learned counsel for the appellant that "damages for false arrest and imprisonment flow directly from the false arrest and imprisonment as an unjustified interference with the liberty of the person without proof of other damages." Mr. Taylor and the other employees did not act maliciously. They tried to prevent embarrassment to Master Parlee. The detention was brief. In the circumstances, I assess nominal damages in the amount of $500, recognizing this to be a significant sum for an individual of the appellant's age. That sum is to be paid to the Public Trustee to be released after Master Parlee attains the age of majority. ...

[27] The appeal is allowed. Damages in the amount of $500 are awarded. The order as to costs, expenses and penalties are set aside. The appellant is entitled to the costs of this appeal and disbursements in the court below.

---

8. Inducing Breach of Contract

 See *Fraser v. Saanich (District)* p. 22, especially paragraph 35.

9. Injurious Falsehood (Trade Libel)

- *I*n a 314-day trial, McDonald's won its lawsuit against environmentalists who accused McDonald's, among other things, of destroying the environment, promoting disease, and contributing to starvation. McDonald's was awarded $136,000; its legal expenses may have exceeded $20 million.[27]

- *T*exas ranchers, in a class action suit, failed to prove to the courts that Oprah Winfrey was liable under the U.S. *False Disparagement of Perishable Food Products Act* for losses caused by her exclaiming, "It has just stopped me cold from eating another burger!" after a discussion of the U.S. beef industry's practice of feeding cows other cows that may have been infected with mad cow disease.[28]

- *S*cientist Mr. Zanakis tried to extort $5 million from McDonald's by claiming that there was a rat's tail in his son's fried potatoes. He was convicted of fraud in a U.S. federal court when evidence was submitted that the tail matched the type of albino rat used in Zanakis' lab.[29]

10. Intentional Infliction of Nervous Shock

Over several years, a female RCMP officer was harassed by the actions of her male colleagues and their sarcastic and sexist remarks, which led to their desired result — her resignation due to depression and anxiety. The court found the Crown liable for the intentional infliction of nervous shock and also for the negligence of her supervisor who consistently breached the standard of care owed her by not stopping the offensive behaviour and by condoning it by his own improper behaviour.

Clark v. Canada
[1994] 3 F.C. 323 (T.D.)
Federal Court (T.D.)
April 26, 1994

11. BREACH OF PRIVACY/MISAPPROPRIATION

Note: In some provinces this tort may be codified; for example, see the *Privacy Act,* R.S.B.C.

- *T*ony Twist, former NHL tough guy who played for the St. Louis Blues, successfully sued Todd McFarlane of Spawn Comic Books for using the name Antonio Twistelli for a seriously evil Mafia kingpin. The jury awarded Twist $24.5 million.

     The appeal court, overturning the lower court's decision, found that the comic book character had not hurt Twist financially or otherwise "except, perhaps, in the plaintiff's imagination."[30]

- *S*alli Pateman's Vancouver restaurant previously named "De Niro's" has been renamed "Section 3," after s. 3 of the *Privacy Act* of British Columbia with which she was threatened by Robert De Niro's lawyers to change the name or risk a lawsuit.[31]

- *N*orm and Cliff are at the airport bar, "Cheers." Norm and Cliff are robots. George Wendt and John Ratzenberger (the actors who portrayed Norm and Cliff respectively in the TV sitcom *Cheers*) are not pleased. Although Paramount allowed the chain of bars to use the name "Cheers," the actors had not given consent to use their likeness.[32] The issue of who owns the rights to a fictitious character, the studio or the actor who played that character, began in the California courts and has now reached the U.S. Supreme Court, which will decide whether it or a California court should hear the case.[33]

- *A*skJeeves.com, the popular and profitable search engine, has attracted the attention of the literary agents of the late P.J. Wodehouse who created the fictional character of Jeeves, the erudite and problem-solving manservant. Will there be a court action? Ask Jeeves.[34]

- *D*ustin Hoffman in a dress, again? But this time, unlike when he portrayed a cross-dresser in the film *Tootsie*, it was without his permission. A magazine, by computer-generated image, showed him wearing a dress to promote a fashion line. Dustin Hoffman successfully sued for $1.5 million U.S.[35]

- *K*areem Abdul-Jabbar (basketball guy) sued Karim Abdul-Jabbar (football guy) alleging Karim appropriated his name.[36] The dispute was settled; Karim uses only the name "Abdul" on his football jersey.[37]

- *M*ichael Costanza's rights were not infringed by the creators of *Seinfeld* who developed the "neurotic and nutty" character of George Costanza. Dismissing the $100 million law suit, the judge of the appeal court in New York wrote, "While a program about nothing can be successful, a lawsuit must have more substance."[38]

An "unknown trouble" call is the name given to a 911 call that has been disconnected before the caller has spoken. When such a call is received, do the police have the right to breach the privacy of your home and investigate?

     In the words of Lamer C.J. for a unanimous court:

     "While there is no question that one's privacy at home is a value to be preserved and promoted, privacy cannot trump the safety of all members of the household. If our society is to provide an effective means of dealing with domestic violence, it must have a form of crisis response. The 911 system provides such a response. Given the wealth of experience the police have in such matters [domestic violence], it is unthinkable that they would take the word of the person who answers the door without further investigation. Without making any comment on the specific facts of this case, it takes only a modicum of common sense to realize that if a person is unable to speak to a 911 dispatcher when making a call, he or she may likewise be unable to answer the door when help arrives. Should the police then take the word of the person who does answer the door, who might well be an abuser and who, if so, would no doubt pronounce that all is well inside? I think not. ...

As I have already discussed, the privacy interest of the person at the door must yield to the interests of any person inside the apartment. A threat to life and limb more directly engages the values of dignity, integrity and autonomy underlying the right to privacy than does the interest in being free from the minimal state intrusion of police entering an apartment to investigate a potential emergency. Once inside the apartment, the police heard the appellant's wife crying. They had a duty to search the apartment and find her. In my view, Finlayson J.A. for the Court of Appeal correctly concluded that the police conduct was a justifiable use of their powers."

> ### R. v. Godoy
> *Supreme Court of Canada*
> *http://www.lexum.umontreal.ca/*
> *February 4, 1999*

- *The E-Commerce Times* reported that Alibris, an online bookseller, was charged with breaching the *U.S. Electronic Communications Privacy Act* by intercepting more than 4,000 Amazon.com internal e-mails to determine how to improve its competitive advantage. Alibris settled the matter out of court by admitting guilt and paying a fine of $250,000.[39]

12. TRESPASS

- *R*eported as a first-of-its-kind case, a California court held that a barrage of e-mail sent to the employees of Intel by a disgruntled former employee was an illegal form of trespass. The judge compared borders between computer networks to property boundaries; he saw Intel's computer system as the company's private property. "The mere connection of Intel's e-mail system with the Internet does not convert it into a public forum."[40]

C. NEGLIGENCE

Q u e s t i o n s

What must the plaintiff prove in order to win an action for negligence?

If the plaintiff proves that the defendant owed the plaintiff a duty of care, fell below the standard of care owed and caused the plaintiff foreseeable damage, does the defendant have any other arguments that may result in the court dismissing the claim, or forcing the plaintiff to absorb some of his or her loss?

---

1. DUTY OF CARE

Q u e s t i o n

Did the defendant owe the plaintiff a duty to be careful?

M'Alister (or Donoghue) v. Stevenson

[1932] A.C. 562
HOUSE OF LORDS

By action brought in the Court of Session the appellant, who was a shop assistant, sought to recover damages from the respondent, who was a manufacturer of aerated waters, for injuries she suffered as a result of consuming part of the contents of a bottle of ginger-beer which had been manufactured by the respondent, and which contained the decomposed remains of a snail. The appellant by her condescendence [pleadings] averred [stated as a fact] that the bottle of ginger-beer was purchased for the appellant by a friend in a cafe at Paisley, which was occupied by one Minchella; that the bottle was made of dark opaque glass and that the appellant had no reason to suspect that it contained anything but pure ginger-beer; that the said Minchella poured some of the ginger-beer out into a tumbler, and that the appellant drank some of the contents of the tumbler; that her friend was then proceeding to pour the remainder of the contents of the bottle into the tumbler when a snail, which was in a state of decomposition, floated out of the bottle; that as a result of the nauseating sight of the snail in such circumstances, and in consequence of the impurities in the ginger-beer which she had already consumed, the appellant suffered from shock and severe gastro-enteritis. The appellant further averred that the ginger-beer was manufactured by the respondent to be sold as a drink to the public (including the appellant); that it was bottled by the respondent and labelled by him with a label bearing his name; and that the bottles were thereafter sealed with a metal cap by the respondent. She further averred that it was the duty of the respondent to provide a system of working his business which would not allow snails to get into his ginger-beer bottles, and that it was also his duty to provide an efficient system of inspection of the bottles before the ginger-beer was filled into them, and that he had failed in both these duties and had so caused the accident.

The respondent objected that these averments were irrelevant and insufficient to support the conclusions of the summons.

Lord Atkin. My Lords, the sole question for determination in this case is legal: Do the averments made by the pursuer [plaintiff] in her pleading, if true, disclose a cause of action? I need not restate the particular facts. The question is whether the manufacturer of an article of drink sold by him to a distributor, in circumstances which prevent the distributor or the ultimate purchaser or consumer from discovering by inspection any defect, is under any legal duty to the ultimate purchaser or consumer to take reasonable care that the article is free from defect likely to cause injury to health. I do not think a more important problem has occupied your Lordships in your judicial capacity. … The law of both countries [Scotland and England] appears to be that in order to support an action for damages for negligence the complainant has to show that he has been injured by the breach of a duty owed to him in the circumstances by the defendant to take reasonable care to avoid such injury. In the present case we are not concerned with the breach of the duty; if a duty exists, that would be a question of fact which is sufficiently averred and for present purposes must be assumed. We are solely concerned with the question whether, as a matter of law in the circumstances

alleged, the defender owed any duty to the pursuer to take care.

At present I content myself with pointing out that in English law there must be, and is, some general conception of relations giving rise to a duty of care, of which the particular cases found in the books are but instances. The liability for negligence, whether you style it such or treat it as in other systems as a species of "culpa," is no doubt based upon a general public sentiment of moral wrongdoing for which the offender must pay. But acts or omissions which any moral code would censure cannot in a practical world be treated so as to give a right to every person injured by them to demand relief. In this way rules of law arise which limit the range of complainants and the extent of their remedy. The rule that you are to love your neighbour becomes in law, you must not injure your neighbour; and the lawyer's question, Who is my neighbour? receives a restricted reply. You must take reasonable care to avoid acts or omissions which you can reasonably foresee would be likely to injure your neighbour. Who, then, in law is my neighbour? The answer seems to be—persons who are so closely and directly affected by my act that I ought reasonably to have them in contemplation as being so affected when I am directing my mind to the acts or omissions which are called in question. This appears to me to be the doctrine of *Heaven v. Pender* (1), as laid down by Lord Esher (then Brett M.R.) when it is limited by the notion of proximity introduced by Lord Esher himself and A.L. Smith L.J. in *Le Lievre v. Gould*. (1) Lord Esher says: "That case established that, under certain circumstances, one man may owe a duty to another, even though there is no contract between them. So A.L. Smith L.J.: "The decision of *Heaven v. Pender* (2) was founded upon the principle, that a duty to take due care did arise when the person or property of one was in such proximity to the person or property of another that, if due care was not taken, damage might be done by the one to the other." I think that this sufficiently states the truth if proximity be not confined to mere physical proximity, but be used, as I think it was intended, to extend to such close and direct relations that the act complained of directly affects a person whom the person alleged to be bound to take care would know would be directly affected by his careless act.

There will no doubt arise cases where it will be difficult to determine whether the contemplated relationship is so close that the duty arises. But in the class of case now before the court I cannot conceive any difficulty to arise. A manufacturer puts up an article of food in a container which he knows will be opened by the actual consumer. There can be no inspection by any purchaser and no reasonable preliminary inspection by the consumer. Negligently, in the course of preparation, he allows the contents to be mixed with poison. It is said that the law of England and Scotland is that the poisoned consumer has no remedy against the negligent manufacturer. If this were the result of the authorities, I should consider the result a grave defect in the law, and so contrary to principle that I should hesitate long before following any decision to that effect which had not the authority of this House. I would point out that, in the assumed state of the authorities, not only would the consumer have no remedy against the manufacturer, he would have none against any one else, for in the circumstances alleged there would be no evidence of negligence against any one other than the manufacturer; and, except in the case of a consumer who was also a purchaser, no contract and no warranty of fitness, and in the case of the purchase of a specific article under its patent or trade name, which might well be the case in the purchase of some articles of food or drink, no warranty protecting even the purchaser-consumer. There are other instances than of articles of food and drink where goods are sold intended to be used immediately by the consumer, such as many forms of goods sold for cleaning purposes, where the same liability must exist. The doctrine supported by the decision below would not only deny a remedy to the consumer who was injured by consuming bottled beer or chocolates poisoned by the negligence of the manufacturer, but also to the user of what should be a harmless proprietary medicine, an ointment, a soap, a cleaning fluid or cleaning powder. I confine myself to articles of common household use, where every one, including the manufacturer, knows that the articles will be used by other persons than the actual ultimate purchaser—namely, by members of his family and his servants, and in some cases his guests. I do not think so ill of our jurisprudence as to suppose that its principles are so remote from the ordinary needs of civilized society and the ordinary claims it makes upon its members as to deny a legal remedy where there is so obviously a social wrong.

In my opinion several decided cases support the view that in such a case as the present the manufacturer owes a duty to the consumer to be careful. …

It is always a satisfaction to an English lawyer to be able to test his application of fundamental principles of the common law by the development of the same doctrines by the lawyers of the Courts of the United States. In that country I find that the law appears to be well established in the sense in which I have indicated. The mouse had emerged from the ginger-beer bottle in the United States before it appeared in Scotland, but there it brought a liability upon the manufacturer. I must not in this long judgment do more than refer to the illuminating judgment of Cardozo J. in *MacPherson v. Buick Motor Co.* in the New York Court of Appeals (2), in which he states the principles of the law as I should desire to state them, and reviews the authorities in other States than his own.

My Lords, if your Lordships accept the view that this pleading discloses a relevant cause of action you will be affirming the proposition that by Scots and English law alike a manufacturer of products, which he sells in such a form as to show that he intends them to reach the ultimate consumer in the form in which they left him with no reasonable possibility of intermediate examination, and with the knowledge that the absence of reasonable care in the preparation or putting up of the products will result in an injury to the consumer's life or property, owes a duty to the consumer to take that reasonable care.

It is a proposition which I venture to say no one in Scotland or England who was not a lawyer would for one moment doubt. It will be an advantage to make it clear that the law in this matter, as in most others, is in accordance with sound common sense. I think that this appeal should be allowed.

Note: Justice Taylor, a retired judge of the B.C. Court of Appeal, who refers to this case as the "most famous case of all time," "the most celebrated victory in the entire 800-year history of our common law," has written a film script on the case to help students understand it and its significance in the common law world.[41]

 See *Stewart v. Pettie*, p. 58, for a current approach for determining a duty of care.

- ***A*** deli owner was successfully sued for negligence when a woman broke her tooth on an olive pit in a deli sandwich. The tooth had to be extracted and the treatment recommended was the placement of a dental implant supporting a crown. She underwent lengthy and painful treatment (unfinished at the time of trial).

  As the sandwich was bought by her friend, this case presents a contemporary fact pattern analogous to that of *Donoghue v. Stevenson*.[42]

2. STANDARD OF CARE

Question

Was the defendant's behaviour below the standard of care owed?

- ***F***rench investigators of the crash of an Air France Concorde suspect the tire of the jet was punctured by a strip of metal on the runway. Air France is suing Continental Airlines after the company admitted that the metal piece resembled one from its DC-10, which took off minutes before the Concorde.[43]

- *A*t the Kingston General Hospital, a food tube, filled with pureed food, was accidentally attached to an intravenous line and the food passed directly into a patient's veins, blocked an artery bringing blood from his lungs to his heart, and killed the patient by causing cardiac and pulmonary arrest.

- *D*onald Parkes, a 41-year-old man, was brought to the emergency ward of the Cambridge Memorial Hospital unconscious from an overdose of anti-depressant drugs. In an effort to revive him, the nurses hooked up an oxygen line directly from a wall outlet through an endotracheal tube to his lungs. The nurses failed to use a device that would have allowed the patient to exhale as well as to receive the oxygen. Consequently the patient was killed by having his lungs "blown up."

  Although a defence was entered, the court found "gross, wanton negligence." The case was interesting to the legal community because of the court's reduction of damages due to the deceased's particular background. He had a history of mental illness which led to two suicide attempts. The court concluded that his life expectancy was lower than that of the average man.[44]

- *T*he driver of a garbage truck in Melville, New York failed to see a sunbathing couple and drove over their faces. The couple suffered tire bruises and jaw injuries. The court found more serious damage was averted probably by their having used a sand pillow which gave way under the weight of the truck. The matter was eventually settled out of court for $150,000.[45]

COMMERCIAL HOSTS

Stewart v. *Pettie*

http://www.lexum.umontreal.ca/
SUPREME COURT OF CANADA
JANUARY 26, 1995

[1] Major J.:—On December 8, 1985, Gillian Stewart, her husband Keith Stewart, her brother Stuart Pettie, and his wife Shelley Pettie went to the Stage West, a dinner theatre in Edmonton for an evening of dinner and live theatre. Before the evening was finished tragedy had struck. After leaving Stage West at the conclusion of the evening a minor single vehicle accident left Gillian Stewart a quadriplegic. Among others, she sued Mayfield Investments Ltd. (Mayfield), the owner of Stage West claiming contribution for her injuries. This appeal is to decide whether on the facts of this case the principles of commercial host liability, first established by this Court in *Jordan House Ltd. v. Menow*, [1974] S.C.R. 239, apply to impose liability on Mayfield. … [The trial court, The Aberta Court of Queen's Bench found for the defendant, that is, the commecial host was not liable. The Alberta Court of Appeal allowed the appeal and found the commercial host liable.]

III. ISSUES

[18] … The main issue is:
1. Did Mayfield Investments Ltd. meet the standard of care required of a vendor of alcohol, or was it negligent in failing to take any steps to ensure that Stuart Pettie did not drive after leaving Stage West?

IV. ANALYSIS

1. Was Mayfield Investments Ltd. negligent in failing to take any steps to ensure that Stuart Pettie did not drive after leaving Stage West?
[20] This Court has not previously considered a case involving the liability of a commercial host where the plaintiff was not the person who became inebriated in the defendant's establishment. In both *Jordan House Ltd. v. Menow*, supra, and *Crocker v. Sundance Northwest Resorts Ltd.*, [1988] 1 S.C.R. 1186, it was the plaintiff who became drunk and as a consequence was unable to look after himself.
…
[22] The present appeal is one in which a third party is claiming against the commercial host. This raises the question of whether the establishment owed any duty of care to that third party. If a duty of care is found to exist, then it is necessary to consider what standard of care was necessary and whether that standard was met.
[23] Another consideration is whether there was a causal connection between the defendant's allegedly negligent conduct and the damage suffered by the plaintiff.

A. *Duty of Care*
[24] The "modern" approach to determining the existence of a duty of care is that established by the House of Lords in *Anns*

v. Merton London Borough Council, [1978] A.C. 728, and adopted by this Court in *City of Kamloops v. Nielsen*, [1984] 2 S.C.R. 2, at pp. 10–11. This test, as established by Wilson J. in Kamloops, paraphrasing Anns is:

(1) is there a sufficiently close relationship between the parties … so that, in the reasonable contemplation of the authority, carelessness on its part might cause damage to that person? If so,

(2) are there any considerations which ought to negative or limit (a) the scope of the duty and (b) the class of persons to whom it is owed or (c) the damages to which a breach of it may give rise?

[25] This approach has been approved in *Just v. British Columbia*, [1989] 2 S.C.R. 1228, and *Hall v. Hebert*, [1993] 2 S.C.R. 159. The basis of the test is the historic case of *Donoghue v. Stevenson*, [1932] A.C. 562, which established the "neighbour principle": that actors owe a duty of care to those whom they ought reasonably have in contemplation as being at risk when they act.

[26] In *Jordan House Ltd. v. Menow*, supra, it was established that a duty of care exists between alcohol-serving establishments and their patrons who become intoxicated, with the result that they were unable to look after themselves. The plaintiff, who was a well-known patron of that bar, became intoxicated and began annoying customers. He was ejected from the bar, even though the waiters and employees of the bar knew that, in order to get home, he would have to walk along a busy highway. While doing so, he was struck by a car. …

[28] It is a logical step to move from finding that a duty of care is owed to patrons of the bar to finding that a duty is also owed to third parties who might reasonably be expected to come into contact with the patron, and to whom the patron may pose some risk. …

[29] In this case, there was a sufficient degree of proximity between Mayfield Investments Ltd. and Gillian Stewart that a duty of care existed between them. The more difficult question is what was the standard of care and whether or not it was breached.

[30] … The duty of care arises because Gillian Stewart was a member of a class of persons who could be expected to be on the highway. It is this class of persons to whom the duty is owed.

…

B. Standard of Care

[34] Laskin J. said in *Jordan House Ltd. v. Menow*, supra, at p. 247, "The common law assesses liability for negligence on the basis of breach of a duty of care arising from a foreseeable and unreasonable risk of harm to one person created by the act or omission of another." The respondents argued, and the Court of Appeal agreed, that Mayfield was negligent because they (a) served Stuart Pettie past the point of intoxication, and (b) failed to take any steps to prevent harm from coming to himself or a third person once he was intoxicated.

[35] I doubt that any liability can flow from the mere fact that Mayfield may have over-served Pettie. To hold that over-serving Pettie *per se* is negligent is to ignore the fact that injury to a class of persons must be foreseeable as a result of the impugned conduct. I fail to see how the mere fact that an individual is over-imbibing can lead, by itself, to any risk of harm

to third parties. …

[36] … Without a reasonably foreseeable risk of harm to him or a third party, the fact of over-serving Pettie is an innocuous act. Therefore, liability on the part of Mayfield, if it is to be found, must be in their failure to take any affirmative action to prevent the reasonably foreseeable risk to Gillian Stewart.

[37] Historically, the courts have been reluctant to impose liability for a failure by an individual to take some positive action. This reluctance has been tempered in recent years where the relationship between the parties is such that the imposition of such an obligation has been warranted. In those cases, there has been some "special relationship" between the parties warranting the imposition of a positive duty. *Jordan House Ltd. v. Menow*, supra, was such a case.

…

[39] … Canadian courts have been willing to expand the kinds of relationships to which a positive duty to act attaches. …

[41] … [T]here are two questions to be answered. The first is whether the defendant was required, in the circumstances, to take any positive steps at all. If this is answered in the affirmative, the next question is whether the steps taken by the defendants were sufficient to discharge the burden placed on them.

[42] There is no dispute that neither the appellant nor anyone on its behalf took any steps to ensure that Stuart Pettie did not drive. … Therefore, if Mayfield is to avoid liability, it will have to be on the basis that, on the facts of this case, Mayfield had no obligation to take any positive steps to ensure that Stuart Pettie did not drive. …

[49] The existence of this "special relationship" will frequently warrant the imposition of a positive obligation to act, but the *sine qua non* of tortious liability remains the foreseeability of the risk. Where no risk is foreseeable as a result of the circumstances, no action will be required, despite the existence of a special relationship. …

[50] … Tort law does not require the wisdom of Solomon. All it requires is that people act reasonably in the circumstances. The "reasonable person" of negligence law was described by Laidlaw J.A. in this way in *Arland v. Taylor*, [1955] O.R. 131 (C.A.), at p. 142:

He is not an extraordinary or unusual creature; he is not superhuman; he is not required to display the highest skill of which anyone is capable; he is not a genius who can perform uncommon feats, nor is he possessed of unusual powers of foresight. He is a person of normal intelligence who makes prudence a guide to his conduct. He does nothing that a prudent man would not do and does not omit to do anything a prudent man would do. He acts in accord with general and approved practice. His conduct is guided by considerations which ordinarily regulate the conduct of human affairs. His conduct is the standard "adopted in the community by persons of ordinary intelligence and prudence."

[51] Obviously, the fact that tragedy has befallen Gillian Stewart cannot, in itself, lead to a finding of liability on the part of Mayfield. The question is whether, before 11:00 p.m. on December 8, 1985, the circumstances were such that a reasonably prudent establishment should have foreseen that Stuart Pettie would drive, and therefore should have taken steps to prevent this.

[52] I agree with the Court of Appeal that Mayfield cannot escape liability simply because Stuart Pettie was apparently not

exhibiting any visible signs of intoxication. The waitress kept a running tab, and knew that Pettie had consumed 10 to 14 ounces of alcohol over a five-hour period. On the basis of this knowledge alone, she either knew or should have known that Pettie was becoming intoxicated, and this is so whether or not he was exhibiting visible symptoms.

[53] However, I disagree with the Court of Appeal that the presence of the two sober women at the table cannot act to relieve Mayfield of liability. ... Had Pettie been alone and intoxicated, Mayfield could have discharged its duty as established in *Jordan House Ltd. v. Menow* by calling Pettie's wife or sister to take charge of him. How, then, can Mayfield be liable when Pettie was already in their charge, and they knew how much he had had to drink? While it is technically true that Stuart Pettie was not "put into" the care of his sober wife and sister, this is surely a matter of semantics. He was already in their care, and they knew how much he had to drink. It is not reasonable to suggest in these circumstances that Mayfield had to do more. ...

[58] On the facts of this case I conclude that Mayfield Investments Ltd. did not breach the duty of care they owed to Gillian Stewart. On this basis I would allow the appeal.

C. Causation

[59] An equally compelling reason to allow this appeal flows from the absence of proof of causation.

[60] The plaintiff in a tort action has the burden of proving each of the elements of the claim on the balance of probabilities. This includes proving that the defendant's impugned conduct actually caused the loss complained of.

...

[[66] ... There is nothing unusual or difficult in this case about proving causation. Nor do the facts lie particularly within the knowledge of the defendant. The person who had the obligation and could have provided some evidence, if such existed, on whether intervention by Mayfield would have made any difference was the injured Gillian Stewart. She testified at the trial, but not on this point. This leaves the inference that had she been asked if Mayfield's had intervened, that is to advise her of facts already known to her that would have made any difference to her decision to have Pettie drive, her answer would have been no.

[67] That answer would accord with the circumstances. The respondent Stewart, in the company of an equally sober sister-in-law, concluded that Pettie was competent to drive. The courts should not interfere in such decisions freely made.

[68] This is ... a case where there is no evidence to indicate that Gillian Stewart and Shelley Pettie would have reached any other conclusion than the one they reached even if Mayfield had intervened.

[69] I would therefore also allow this appeal on the basis that the plaintiffs have failed to discharge the onus placed on them to show that Mayfield's failure to intervene actually caused Gillian Stewart's injuries.

[70] Given the fact that I do not find any liability on the part of Mayfield Investments Ltd., it is unnecessary to address the issues relating to Gillian Stewart's contributory negligence, or whether the fact that Stuart Pettie drove while intoxicated could be said to be, in itself, gross negligence.

Appeal allowed with costs; cross-appeal dismissed.

EMPLOYERS

Nineteen-year-old Michael Jacobsen worked a 16-hour shift as a warehouseman with Nike Canada Ltd., during which he and his co-workers drank a substantial amount of beer provided by the company. After work he drank more beer with his friends. Unfortunately, on his way home in the morning he lost control of his vehicle and the injuries that he sustained rendered him a quadriplegic.

Following the same analysis as that in *Stewart v. Pettie*, (but distinguishing the facts of that case), the court found Nike 75% at fault for the damages suffered by Jacobsen. The company owed its employee a duty of care and fell below the standard of care "by providing a large quantity of alcohol, not monitoring its consumption and not preventing the plaintiff from driving."

Jacobsen v. Nike Canada Ltd.
Vancouver Registry No. C918359
Supreme Court of British Columbia
February 22, 1996

The employer did not supply the alcohol as in the *Nike* case, but knew its nightshift employee, Flynn, was an alcoholic and drank in the parking lot during his breaks. One morning after work, but after a stop at his house, Flynn struck and injured Claude John. His blood alcohol level was twice the legal limit. The issue was the liability of the employer. In the words of the court:

[11] At the end of the work shift it was apparent that Flynn was about to drive. Eaton Yale [the employer] took no steps to prevent the obvious. Eaton Yale took no precautions to curtail Flynn's drinking either by monitoring him or the parking area where he was known to drink. It was open to Eaton Yale to send Flynn home from work by taxi, to take his car keys, to take custody of his car, to place him in the charge of a union official or other responsible person. Eaton Yale did nothing in a situation demanding something beyond passivity. ...

[13] Flynn drank for eight hours preceding his work shift; he drank at every opportunity while at work. It was readily foreseeable that he would continue that established pattern, and that upon leaving work he would drive his car. Foreseeability is the foundation of liability. At page 378 in *Cotic v. Gray* (1981), 33 O.R. (2d) 356 (Ont. C.A.), Lacourciere J.A. states the general rule:

> A break in the line of causation is subject to the qualification that if the intervening act is such that it might reasonably have been foreseen as anticipated, as the natural and probable result of the original negligence, then the original negligence will be regarded as the proximate cause of the injury, notwithstanding the intervening event.

[14] The arrival at his home did not represent the outer limit of Eaton Yale's liability. The natural and probable result of the negligence was that Flynn would drive his car. It was reasonably foreseeable that Flynn would come to harm on the highway. Eaton Yale failed to act in the face of obvious risk. Forty minutes later that risk became reality. ...

[15] In those circumstances Eaton Yale owed a duty of care to Flynn, and by logical extension, to other highway users. ...

[16] There was no break in the chain of causation to relieve the duty of care. ...

[17] The application is dismissed."

John v. Flynn
[2000] O.J. No. 128
Ontario Superior Court
January 14, 2000

OCCUPIERS OF PREMISES

- *M*r. Faust stopped at a rural canyon construction site to use the outhouse. He fell through a plywood covering into a 12-metre-deep cesspool and, according to the UPI news release, "spent 13 hours fighting off a nasty gopher who fell in with him."[46]

- *S*moking can be hazardous. A tenant of a building, out on the fire escape to smoke a cigarette, was locked out and attempted to use the fire escape ladder. When it didn't move, he put his full weight on the ladder and the ladder—with him on it—dropped, causing him to fracture both his ankles. The court held that the owner of the building was an "occupier" within the meaning of the *Occupiers' Liability Act* and the owner fell below the standard of care owed the tenant by not instructing tenants on it use. The owner, however, was only 40% at fault as the tenant's method of dislodging the ladder was not the act of a "reasonably prudent person."[47]

CITY

Ingles v. Tutkaluk Construction Ltd. et al.

http://www.lexum.umontreal.ca/
SUPREME COURT OF CANADA
MARCH 2, 2000

Bastarache J. —

I. INTRODUCTION

[1] The issue to be resolved in this appeal is the liability of a public authority for breach of its duty of care in the exercise of a function that it has undertaken pursuant to a policy decision to that effect.

II. FACTUAL BACKGROUND

... [With the knowledge of the owners of the house, renovations were begun before the contractor had obtained a building permit. The inspectors were unable to easily see if the underpinnings were installed properly. One inspector relied on the assurances of the contractor that the width of the underpinnings were in accordance with the plans.]

[7] Within weeks of the completion of the project, the appellant [the owner] began to experience flooding in his basement. He hired another contracting company to remedy the drainage problems. In the course of their work, the contractors discovered that the initial underpinning construction was completely inadequate. The underpinning was only 6 inches wide, instead of the 24 inches specified in the permit. In several places, the underpinning had not been installed to the depth stated in the plans. In fact, neither the width, nor the depth of the underpinning was in accordance with the specifications, and neither met the requirements of the *Building Code Act*, R.S.O. 1980, c. 51. ....

[The trial judge found that the city owed a duty of care, fell below the standard of care owed and apportioned the loss Tutkaluk 80%, the city 14% and the owner 6%. The court of appeal reversed this decision holding that owners were not owed a duty of care by the city because they allowed the construction to proceed without a permit.] ...

IV. ANALYSIS

A. Duty of Care

[16] This Court recently affirmed ... that the test set in *Anns v. Merton London Borough Council*, [1977] 2 All E.R. 492 (H.L.), adopted by this Court in *Kamloops v. Nielsen* (the "*Anns/Kamloops*" test) is the appropriate test for determining whether a private or public actor owes a duty of care. ... To determine whether a private law duty of care exists, two questions must be asked. These questions are set out by Wilson J. ... of the decision in *Kamloops v. Nielsen* as follows:

(1) is there a sufficiently close relationship between the parties (the local authority and the person who has suffered the damage) so that, in the reasonable contemplation of the authority, carelessness on its part might cause damage to that person? If so,

(2) are there any considerations which ought to negative or limit (a) the scope of the duty and (b) the class of persons to whom it is owed or (c) the damages to which a breach of it may give rise? ...

[18] ... To determine whether an inspection scheme by a local authority will be subject to a private law duty of care, the court must determine whether the scheme represents a policy decision on the part of the authority, or whether it represents the implementation of a policy decision, at the operational level. True policy decisions are exempt from civil liability to ensure that governments are not restricted in making decisions based upon political or economic factors. It is clear, however, that once a government agency makes a policy decision to inspect, in certain circumstances, it owes a duty of care to all who may be injured by the negligent implementation of that policy. ...

(1) <u>Did the City Owe the Appellant a Duty of Care?</u>

[21] Both the trial judge and the Court of Appeal found that the city owed the appellant a *prima facie* duty of care in these circumstances. I agree with their finding in this respect. It is certainly foreseeable that a deficient inspection of the underpinnings of a home could result in damage to the property of the homeowners, or injury to the homeowners or others. ... The first stage of the *Anns/Kamloops* test has been met.

[22] Having found that the city owed the appellant a *prima facie* duty of care, I now turn to the legislative scheme which governs municipal inspections in Ontario to determine whether there is any policy reason to limit the *prima facie* duty of care. ... [The judge reviews the relevant provisions of the *Building Code Act*, R.S.O. 1990, c. B.13].

[23] ... The purpose of the building inspection scheme is clear from these provisions: to protect the health and safety of the public by enforcing safety standards for all construction projects. The province has made the policy decision that the municipalities appoint inspectors who will inspect construction projects and enforce the provisions of the Act. Therefore, municipalities owe a duty of care to all who it is reasonable to conclude might be injured by the negligent exercise of their inspection powers.

[24] ... Here, the evidence is that the city had made a policy decision to inspect construction, even if the permit was issued after the construction had begun. ...

[25] Following the *Anns/Kamloops* test, the city owed Mr. Ingles a duty of care to conduct an inspection of the renovations on their home and to exercise reasonable care in doing so, despite the fact that the building permit was obtained late. Therefore, the city could be found negligent if it ignored its own scheme and chose not to inspect the renovations. It could also be found negligent for conducting an inspection of the renovations without adequate care.

(2) The Negligent Owner-Builder ...

[32] There are several passages in the reasons of La Forest J. in *Rothfield v. Manolakos* which make it clear that the negligent conduct of an owner-builder should not absolve a municipality of its duty to take reasonable care in its inspection. ...

[39] To summarize, ... it is clear that La Forest J. created a complete defence for municipalities that could be used to militate against a finding of negligence only in the rarest of circumstances, namely, when the owner-builder's conduct was such that a court could only conclude that he or she was the sole source of his or her own loss. ...

B. Standard of Care ...

[47] The trial judge applied the correct principles in determining that the inspector failed to conduct a reasonable inspection in the circumstances. He recognized that in the circumstances, especially in light of the importance of the underpinning to the structural safety of the home, a more vigilant inspection was required. The Act granted the power to the inspector to conduct such an inspection. By failing to exercise those powers to ensure that the underpinning met the specifications in the plan, the inspector failed to meet the standard of care that would have been expected of an ordinary, reasonable and prudent inspector in the circumstances. ...

C. The Negligent Owner-Builder

[48] Having found that the city owed a duty to the appellant to conduct a reasonable inspection, and that its inspector failed to conduct a reasonable inspection in the circumstances, I must now examine whether the conduct of the appellant in this case was negligent, absolving the city of some of its liability for its insufficient inspection. The appellant's conduct may even have been such as to justify absolving the city of all liability for its negligence. ...

[51] The contributory negligence bar, where a plaintiff was denied any means of recovery once he or she was seen to have contributed to his or her own loss, is no longer a part of our system of tort law. It has been replaced by statutory schemes which apportion liability between negligent defendants and contributorily negligent plaintiffs. ... In the case at bar, the liability will also be apportioned in accordance with the appellant's

negligence. In the rarest of circumstances, such as those described in *Rothfield v. Manolakos*, a defendant may be absolved of all liability because it is shown that the owner-builder is entirely responsible for the damage and did not rely on the inspection.

[52] ... Certainly, an owner-builder who submitted false plans and documents to receive a permit would be mocking the scheme. Similarly, an owner-builder who never contacted an inspector to conduct an inspection would show a lack of respect for the inspection scheme and certainly no reliance on it. However, in this case the appellant did not act in these ways. He certainly acted negligently. The trial judge, however, found that he did not participate in a conscious effort to undermine the building code regime. In my view, such conduct does not amount to a "flouting" of the building code. As a result, I find that the Court of Appeal erred in absolving the city of all liability.

D. Damages ...

[58] The city also argues that it should not be held to be jointly and severally liable with the contractor and that it should be liable only for its portion of the fault. To support this contention, the city relies on authorities from British Columbia that have held that where the plaintiff is contributorily negligent, multiple tortfeasors will only be liable to the extent of their fault. ... I do not find these authorities to be applicable in this case. The legislation in British Columbia differs significantly from the legislation in Ontario. ...

[59] The Ontario legislation has been interpreted differently, and joint and several judgments have been awarded to contributorily negligent plaintiffs. ... The purpose of a regime which imposes joint and several liability on multiple defendants is to ensure that plaintiffs receive actual compensation for their loss. ...

[60] In light of the foregoing analysis, I would allow the appeal and restore the apportionment of fault by the trial judge. ... [Tutkaluk 80%, the city 14% and the owner 6%.]

[62] I would accordingly allow the appeal, set aside the judgment of the Court of Appeal and restore the decision of the trial judge. ...

Unanimous

RESTAURATEURS

- *S*tella Liebeck bought a cup of coffee at the drive-through window at McDonald's. Holding the cup between her knees and attempting to take off the lid to add cream and sugar, she spilled the coffee causing third-degree burns, which necessitated her undergoing skin grafts. She sued McDonald's Corp. for negligence, namely, for serving coffee too hot. To meet the preference of its customers, McDonald's purposely brews and serves its coffee at high temperatures. After a seven-day jury trial in the U.S. the court concluded McDonald's was liable; serving coffee at that temperature was below the standard of care owed its customers. For compensatory damages the jury awarded Liebeck $200,000; (less $40,000 as the jury found Liebeck 20% at fault); for punitive damages, $2.7 million.[48]

SOCIAL HOSTS

- *A*lthough David Stringer was warned not to crawl through a window and dive from a roof into a pool, he continued to do so until, on his fourth dive, he broke his neck and was rendered a quadriplegic.

He sued the hosts of the party under an Ontario home liability statute and succeeded. An insurer commented that the statute placed a standard of care on hosts that is higher than that expected of a reasonable person.[49]

BROKERS/FINANCIAL ADVISORS

LaFlamme Inc. *v.* Prudential-Bache Commodities Canada Ltd.

http://www.lexum.umontreal.ca/
SUPREME COURT OF CANADA
MAY 3, 2000

[1] Gonthier J. — The issue in this case relates to the extent of the liability of a securities dealer acting as a portfolio manager. More specifically, the case relates to the point in time when that liability ceases.

1. FACTS

[2] In June 1987, when he was about 60 years of age, Armand Laflamme and his brother sold the door and window business they owned. Armand Laflamme's share of the proceeds was $2,200,000, which he transferred to the appellant company, Placements Armand Laflamme Inc., 98 percent of the shares of which he owned. . . . The appellant is a company established for tax purposes to receive the proceeds of the sale of Armand Laflamme's shares.

[3] In April 1987, Armand Laflamme, accompanied by his son Benoît, met with the respondent, Jules Roy, who was at that time a securities dealer ... to discuss investments. The purpose of these investments was primarily to provide him with a retirement fund. Armand Laflamme had only a grade four education, and his son Benoît had no experience in portfolio management. ...

[4] ... [T]he Laflamme family were stunned to learn from their auditor ... that Roy was managing the portfolio on margin without their knowledge and that a number of the investments were speculative. However, the primary purpose of the investments was supposed to have been to provide Armand Laflamme with a retirement fund.

[5] On July 15, 1988, Suzanne Laflamme, Armand's daughter, wrote to Roy advising him to limit stock market investments to $500,000 — [TRANSLATION] "not all in high risk" — and to invest the rest of the money in safe investments. She stated that [TRANSLATION] "[n]aturally, we will no longer use the line of credit". Over the next few months, the position of the portfolio deteriorated, while interest on the line of credit, and Roy's commissions, increased. On November 10, 1988, another letter was sent to Roy setting the amount to be invested. ...This letter repeated the intention to stop using the line of credit and asked that the shares be sold when it was possible to do so without a loss, in order to reinvest the proceeds in safe investments.

[6] On May 3, 1989, the Laflamme family and Roy met at Le Bouvier restaurant to discuss the management of the portfolio. ...

[7] In the fall of 1989, the price of the shares held by the appellant fell, with the result that the value of the portfolio dropped significantly. On March 2, 1990, the appellant closed its account with the respondent Prudential-Bache, and sustained major losses at that time.

[8] The appellant and Armand Laflamme then commenced an action for damages against the respondents, claiming that these losses had been sustained as a result of their fault.

2. DECISIONS

Superior Court of Quebec, [1996] R.J.Q. 2694
[9] Lebrun J. of the Superior Court found that the respondents Roy and Prudential-Bache were entirely liable. ...
Court of Appeal of Quebec, [1998] R.J.Q. 765
[15] On March 16, 1998, the Court of Appeal allowed the respondents' appeal in part and reduced the total damages awarded to the appellant company. ...
[16] On the issue of the respondents' liability, Letarte J.A., writing for the Court of Appeal, expressed the view that the trial judge had instructed himself properly as regards the nature of the faults committed by Roy. However, in the opinion of Letarte J.A., the Laflamme family had gradually become capable of managing their portfolio ...

3. ANALYSIS ...

A. Law

[23] A securities dealer may perform a variety of functions. First, in his most common role, the dealer is an intermediary. He buys and sells securities on behalf of his client, in accordance with the client's instructions. The dealer is in no way involved in the management of his client's portfolio and has no discretion regarding its content and the transactions to be carried out. In this situation, the client's account is sometimes referred to as "non-discretionary".

[24] Second, a dealer may also be responsible for managing the portfolio. In addition to his function as a dealer, he is also a portfolio manager with responsibility for making decisions with respect to the management and make up of the portfolio. ...This kind of account is referred to as a "discretionary" account. ...

[25] The functions of a manager and the powers granted to the manager may be quite extensive. ...Beaudoin, *supra*, describes them as follows at pp. 25-26:

> [TRANSLATION] Authorized management of a portfolio results from delegation by the client of his decision-making authority. This task covers the intellectual, tactical and strategic activities performed in respect of a portfolio. The manager acts

in accordance with the investment objectives set with the client. His decisions are essentially guided by the concept of maximizing return on the portfolio, having regard to the risks that this involves. The manager determines the portfolio's make up and the investments to make. On behalf of the client, he forwards orders to a securities dealer to buy or sell securities ...

[26] Thus, the manager makes most of the decisions relating to the portfolio and the make up of the portfolio. The scope of his management authority and the exercise of his discretion will, however, depend on any restrictions that are imposed by law or agreement. ...

[27] For the most part, the legal relationship between the client and the securities dealer is governed by the rules of mandate. ...

[29] The content of the obligations that rest on the manager will vary with the object of the mandate and the circumstances. One of the most fundamental of these obligations is that the manager exercise reasonable skill and all the care of a prudent administrator (art. 1710 *C.C.L.C.*). The conduct expected is not that of the best of managers, nor the worst. Rather, it is the conduct of a reasonably prudent and diligent manager performing similar functions in an analogous situation. ...He must also deal in good faith, honestly and fairly with his clients (s. 234.1).

[30] The mandate also imposes an obligation for the manager to inform his client and, in certain circumstances, a duty to advise him. ...

[31] A professional mandatary also has a duty to provide advice. ...

[32] For the same reasons, a securities portfolio manager is also subject to this duty.

[33] The duty to provide advice requires that the manager make his knowledge and expertise available to the client, and that he use them better to serve the client's interests in light of the client's objectives. ...The manager being subject to an ongoing obligation to manage, this duty continues as long as the object of the mandate given by the client to the manager remains unchanged and could even survive the termination of the mandate (art. 1709 *C.C.L.C.*; art. 2182 *C.C.Q.*).

[34] The scope and nature of this duty will vary with the circumstances. Specifically, we note the importance of the client's personality. ...

B. Application to the Facts

[35] ... [T]he actual liability of the respondents is not in issue. The Superior Court and the Court of Appeal agree that they have incurred liability through their actions. The respondents have not appealed those findings to this Court.

[36] I agree with the findings of the trial judge in that regard. The faults committed by the respondent Roy are apparent from the record. He failed to comply with the conduct required of a prudent and diligent manager, in that he failed to construct an organized and diversified portfolio, carried out transactions that were inconsistent with the client's general instructions, acquired speculative securities and failed to have regard to his client's investment objectives. As a mandatary, the respondent Roy also failed to deal fairly and honestly with his client, as he was expected to do. There could be no clearer illustration of that breach than his failure to comply with the Laflamme family's instructions concerning the amounts to be invested in the stock market and the immediate cessation of transactions on margin.

[37] The issue which arises is the point in time when the respondents' liability ceased. ...

(i) <u>Change in Object of the Mandate</u>

[39] ... [Reviewing the facts, the court differed from the Court of Appeal and held that the family had not changed its mandate, but that even if it had changed the mandate from discretionary to non-discretionary management, Roy would still be responsible for the injury resulting from the faults he committed.]

(ii) <u>Mitigation of Damages</u>

[51] The Court of Appeal and the respondents also state that the Laflamme family ought to have acted earlier to mitigate the damages resulting from mismanagement of the portfolio. ...

[52] Civil law imposes an obligation on a creditor to mitigate damages. ...

[The court considered the trust the family had in a professional manager, the complexity of the portfolio (shares, warrants, call options, put options, mutual funds, debentures and government bonds) and concluded that an average investor faced with similar circumstances would have also been indecisive and hesitant in taking further measures to minimize the losses.]

[56] ... Those losses were sustained as a result of mismanagement by the respondents, which, as the trial judge found, continued until the account was closed. ...

[64] For these reasons, I would allow the appeal, ... [and] find the respondents jointly and severally liable to pay to the appellant the amount of $924,374, plus interest. ...

Unanimous

- *E*lton John, concerned about $14 million unaccounted for, has sued his accountants, PriceWaterhouseCoopers, and Gordon Pollock, the managing director of John Reid Enterprises which managed his business affairs. John Reid has settled out of court, paying Elton John U.S. $5 million.[50]

OTHERS

- *T*he gas fitter, who incompetently installed a furnace causing an explosion that destroyed twenty-eight homes, was not solely liable for negligence. The court also held the defendant gas company negligent for listing the fitter as qualified when in fact his licence had expired.[51]

- *J*udge Geatros of the Court of Queen's Bench in Prince Albert, Saskatchewan held that Constable Hunter, "dogmaster," was not negligent by allowing his police dog, Max, to subdue the plaintiff who was pursued after a break-in. The plaintiff, having tried to escape the police three times, was "taken down" by Max.[52]

3. CAUSATION

Question

Did the defendant's act or omission cause the injury suffered?

The tenant plaintiff, complained to the landlord defendants, that a ground floor window was loose and could easily be removed — a temptation to an intruder. Subsequently an intruder did break in—not by lifting out the loose window, but by breaking the window. The tenant returning home saw the broken window, entered through it cautiously, surveyed the situation and returned to the window to call to a friend when he slipped on the broken glass and cut himself severely. He sued the landlords for negligence.

Although the plaintiff advanced several arguments, the main issue fell to the question of causation. In the words of Judge Edwards:

[13] [T]he defendants' failure to secure the window made it less likely it would be broken by a thief tempted to effect entry because it was loose. That is it made it less likely if a break-in occurred that it would result in the very risk which was created.

[14] In other words the loose window may have made a break-in more likely but it made the creation of a risk of broken glass less likely than if a secure window had been broken to gain entry. ...

[16] ... I conclude the defendants' failure cannot be characterised as the cause of the accident which befell the plaintiff. Failure to secure the window did not make it more likely that accident would occur than would have been the case if the window had been secure.

[18] ... [The plaintiff failed] to maintain a proper lookout for his own safety in circumstances he himself had recognized as dangerous. I conclude the plaintiff has failed to prove on a balance of probabilities that the failure of the defendant to secure the window, whether it be characterized as negligence or a breach of contract or statutory duty, was the cause of the tragic accident which befell the plaintiff. ...

[32] In summary, I find the plaintiff has not proved causation and his action fails. ...

Hendry v. Chiang and Chao
http://www.courts.gov.bc.ca/
Supreme Court of British Columbia
November 27, 1996

Arndt *v.* Smith

http://www.lexum.umontreal.ca/
SUPREME COURT OF CANADA
JUNE 26, 1997

Background facts: The plaintiff contracted chicken pox while pregnant; the baby was born disabled. The mother sued the doctor for negligence, namely, failure to warn her of the risks to the fetus from her chicken pox and claimed for the costs of rearing the disabled child. The trial judge held that the plaintiff proved a breach of duty but failed to prove the breach caused her loss. That is, she failed to prove that if she had been told of the risk she would have aborted the pregnancy. The plaintiff appealed. The Court of Appeal directed a new trial on the basis that the trial judge had applied the wrong test for determining causation.

The issue before this court is: What is the proper test to determine whether or not the loss claimed by the plaintiff was caused by the doctor's failure to advise of the risk?

Cory J.:

... [2] The starting point for this question must be *Reibl v. Hughes*, [1980] 2 S.C.R. 880, which set out the basic principles for assessing causation in cases involving allegations of negligence by doctors. Reibl involved an action by a patient against a surgeon for failing to warn him of the risk of paralysis associated with the elective surgery performed by that surgeon. One of the defences raised was that even if the surgeon had disclosed all of the risks of the procedure, the plaintiff would nonetheless have gone ahead with the operation. In other words, the physician disputed whether his negligent failure to disclose had, in fact, caused the plaintiff's loss.

[3] The question presented to the Court was how to determine whether the patient would have actually chosen to decline the surgery if he had been properly informed of the risks. ... In trying to craft the appropriate test, Laskin C.J. for a unanimous Court quoted with approval an article from the New York University Law Review, entitled "Informed Consent — A Proposed Standard for Medical Disclosure" (1973), 48 N.Y.U.L. Rev. 548. The article distinguished between a subjective test, which asks whether the particular patient would have foregone treatment if properly informed, and an objective test, which asks whether the average prudent person in the patient's position would have foregone treatment if informed of all material risks. The authors preferred the objective test, since the subjective standard suffered from what they deemed to be a "gross defect": "[I]t depends on the plaintiff's testimony as to his state of mind, thereby exposing the physician to the patient's hindsight and bitterness." (p. 550) ...

[6] To balance the two problems [of the subjective test which places undue emphasis on the evidence of the plaintiff and the objective test which places too much emphasis on the medical evidence], Laskin C.J. opted for a modified objective test for causation. ... The test enunciated relies on a combination of objective and subjective factors in order to determine whether the failure to disclose actually caused the harm of which the plaintiff complains. It requires that the court consider what the reasonable patient in the circumstances of the plaintiff would have done if faced with the same situation. The trier of fact must take into consideration any "particular concerns" of the patient and any "special considerations affecting the particular patient" in determining whether the patient would have refused treatment if given all the information about the possible risks.

[7] This Court recently had occasion to reconsider the modified objective test in *Hollis v. Dow Corning Corp.* [1995] 4 S.C.R. 634... .

[8] ... The decision in *Hollis* is a very strong and recent affirmation of the *Reibl* test and should not be lightly disregarded... .

[15] *Reibl v. Hughes* is a very significant and leading authority. It marks the rejection of the paternalistic approach to determining how much information should be given to patients. It emphasizes the patient's right to know and ensures that patients will have the benefit of a high standard of disclosure. At the same time, its modified objective test for causation ensures that our medical system will have some protection in the face of liability claims from patients influenced by unreasonable fears and beliefs, while still accommodating all the reasonable individual concerns and circumstances of plaintiffs. The test is flexible enough to enable a court to take into account a wide range of the personal circumstances of the plaintiff, and at the same time to recognize that physicians should not be held responsible when the idiosyncratic beliefs of their patients might have prompted unpredictable and unreasonable treatment decisions.

[16] The *Reibl v. Hughes* test ... strikes a reasonable balance, which cannot be obtained through either a purely objective or a purely subjective approach. A purely subjective test could serve as an incitement for a disappointed patient to bring an action. The plaintiff will invariably state with all the confidence of hindsight and with all the enthusiasm of one contemplating an award of damages that consent would never have been given if the disclosure required by an idiosyncratic belief had been made. This would create an unfairness that cannot be accepted. It would bring inequitable and unnecessary pressure to bear upon the overburdened medical profession. On the other hand, a purely objective test which would set the standard by a reasonable person without the reasonable fears, concerns

and circumstances of the particular plaintiff would unduly favour the medical profession. ...

[17] ... In short, I see no reason to abandon the modified objective test to causation set down in *Reibl v. Hughes*, a test which asks whether a reasonable person in the circumstances of the plaintiff would have consented to the proposed treatment if all the risks had been disclosed.

[18] Turning now to this appeal, it is appropriate to infer from the evidence that a reasonable person in the plaintiff's position would not have decided to terminate her pregnancy in the face of the very small increased risk to the fetus posed by her exposure to the virus which causes chicken pox. [The court reviews the evidence.] I agree with the trial judge that the failure to disclose some of the risks to the fetus associated with maternal chicken pox did not affect the plaintiff's decision to continue the pregnancy to term. It follows that the failure to disclose did not cause the financial losses for which the plaintiff is seeking compensation.

[19] I would allow this appeal, set aside the judgment of the Court of Appeal and reinstate the judgment of the trial judge. The defendant should have her costs of the proceedings in this Court and the courts below.

Appeal allowed   [7–2]

---

4. INJURY AND FORESEEABILITY

Q u e s t i o n

Was there injury, and was that injury or type of injury foreseeable?

Mortimer v. Cameron et al.

[1992] O.J.No. 764 (Q.L.)
ONTARIO COURT OF JUSTICE (GENERAL DIVISION)
APRIL 13, 1992

McDermid J.: —

1. THE ACTION:

After writing an intermediate accounting examination on the morning of July 17, 1987, Stephen Mortimer made the fateful decision to go to a party at the apartment of a classmate, Sandra Hunt. The apartment she shared with Marijo Kale was on the second floor of a home owned by Stingray Investments Limited.

People there were drinking and relaxing. The mood was convivial but subdued. No one was boisterous or unruly. After a time, Mortimer engaged another classmate, John Cameron, in some friendly conversation and horseplay in the hall of the apartment. From the hall, they travelled down the interior stairs, pushing each other back and forth until they reached the interior landing. Both had been drinking but neither was angry nor hostile.

Mortimer, who was moving backwards, tripped over the raised threshold to the apartment. He fell back and pulled Cameron toward him. Together, they tumbled onto an exterior landing, through its exterior wall and plunged to the ground about 10 feet below.

Cameron picked himself up, but Mortimer could not move. As a result of the fall, he sustained a permanent spinal cord injury at the C4-5 level that rendered him a complete quadri-plegic without any motor function or sensation below the site of the injury.

This tragic event has spawned complex issues of liability and damages.

Mortimer sues Cameron on the basis of assault, battery, trespass to the person and negligence. He claims that Cameron applied force to him without due care and attention for his safety and caused him to trip and fall through the exterior wall of the stairway.

[In an exhaustive review of the facts, the arguments and the law, the judge, in a 209-page decision, found the City and the owners of the building at fault. With regard to the fault of the young men, the judgment was as follows:]

7. THE ISSUE OF CAMERON'S NEGLIGENCE:

Stairs in residential buildings are potentially dangerous. They connect two different levels, usually about 8 or more feet apart. Stair treads provide a relatively small surface area upon which to place one's foot. Unless one uses a handrail, one has to balance all one's weight first on one foot and then on the other when ascending or descending stairs. If one is not careful, one is liable to fall and sustain injury, which is sometimes serious. Therefore, generally, one ought not to engage in horseplay on a stairway because, in an already potentially dangerous situation, there is an increased risk of harm from falling.

In these potentially dangerous circumstances, Cameron was under a correspondingly high duty to act so as not to cause harm to Mortimer. With respect to the issue of Mortimer's contributory negligence, Mortimer was under a similar duty to act so as not to cause harm to himself. Mortimer and Cameron travelled down the stairway in a controlled manner. The force used by each against the other was measured and not excessive. Each had hold of the other. They managed to traverse the stairs without falling or losing their balance and reached the interior landing safely. At that point, the risk of harm from falling on the interior stairs had expired.

After they had traversed the interior stairs, the action that then set in motion the immediately ensuing chain of circumstances that resulted in Mortimer's injury was the push Cameron gave Mortimer that caused him to trip over the threshold. When he had entered the apartment, Cameron had noticed he had to step over the threshold and he was aware it was 3 or 4 inches high. When Cameron pushed Mortimer, he created the risk that Mortimer might trip over the threshold and fall through the open doorway onto the exterior landing or against the exterior wall of that landing and injure himself. A reasonable and prudent person would not have pushed Mortimer on the interior landing as Cameron did. Therefore, Cameron was in breach of his duty of care to Mortimer when he pushed him.

In Fridman, *The Law of Torts in Canada* (1989), Vol. 1 at pp. 320 to 329, the learned author deals with the issues of "causal connection" and "causation and remoteness." ... He refers first to the "directness approach" to causation, as set forth in *Re Polemis*, (1921) 2 K.B. 560 (C.A.), which in effect held that a defendant is liable for the direct consequences of his or her negligence, whether or not those consequences are foreseeable. ...

At p. 327, he states " ... the directness approach to causation, as stipulated in *Re Polemis*, was rejected" in *The Wagon Mound (No. 1)*, (1961) A.C. 388, which held that a

... defendant would only be liable for foreseeable consequences. Anything which could not be foreseen by the reasonable man in advance of his acts or omissions as being the probable outcome would be too remote and could not be attributed to his negligence.

The law in this area was further qualified by *The Wagon Mound (No. 2)*, (1967) 1 A.C. 617, which held that, " ... as long as what happened was within the realm of what was reasonably foreseeable, the defendant did not have to foresee the precise manner in which it came about." ...

Mortimer's injury was caused from hitting the ground. He would not have hit the ground if P1 [the plywood exterior wall] had held . ...

Even though there was a failure on Cameron's part to exercise the care that the circumstances demanded, his failure of care was not the proximate cause of Mortimer's injury. The damage ensuing to Mortimer was too remote a consequence of Cameron's breach of his duty to render him liable for its occurrence. ...

...[I]t was not reasonably foreseeable when Cameron pushed Mortimer on the interior landing that P1 would give way and permit Mortimer to fall from the landing to the ground below. It was not reasonably foreseeable when Cameron pushed Mortimer that Mortimer would be rendered a quadriplegic or even that he would be seriously injured. The probability of the sequence of actual events occurring was extremely remote, though obviously possible. In other words, what actually happened was not within the realm of what was reasonably foreseeable. ...

Accordingly, no liability should attach to Cameron's acts or omissions and the claim against him should be dismissed.

8. THE ISSUE OF MORTIMER'S NEGLIGENCE:

... [In summary], [e]ven though Mortimer initiated the horseplay and was modestly intoxicated, his legal position is not substantially different from that of Cameron, who had also been drinking and whose level of intoxication, according to Dr. LeBlanc, was probably close to Mortimer's. The same reasoning applies in the case of Mortimer as in Cameron's case. If exactly the same sequence of events had occurred, including Mortimer's initiation of the horseplay and his level of intoxication, but P1 had not given way, Mortimer would not be a quadriplegic today, nor would he have been seriously injured. Given the raised threshold and the fact he was going backwards, Mortimer probably would have tripped over it and lost his balance whether he had been sober or intoxicated to the degree he was. Neither his action in initiating the horseplay nor his level of intoxication was the proximate cause of his injury, nor, as in Cameron's case, was what happened to him within the realm of what was reasonably foreseeable. If P1 had held, he and Cameron probably would have picked themselves up from the exterior landing and returned to the party. Accordingly, no liability should attach to Mortimer's acts or omissions.

[With regard to issue of the liability of Cameron and Mortimer at the *appellate level*:]

COURT OF APPEAL 111 D.L.R. (4TH) 428 AT PP. 440 AND 441

There is no basis for disturbing this conclusion. ... Here, neither Cameron's negligence nor Mortimer's contributory negligence entailed an unreasonable or foreseeable likelihood of the risk or hazard that actually befell Mortimer. It was reasonable for them to assume that what purported and appeared to be a properly constructed wall was in fact a properly constructed wall. In regulating their conduct and having regard for their own safety, they were entitled to rely on the wall providing them reasonable protection. The risk to which they exposed themselves was the risk of being injured by falling down the stairs or onto the exterior landing or by hitting the exterior wall. The risk that materialized was of a different nature. ... The accident that in fact occurred was, in sum, beyond the reasonable contemplation of these parties; it was not within the scope of the risk created by their horseplay, no matter how imprudent that conduct may be considered.

Note: The Supreme Court of Canada refused to hear an appeal from the Ontario Court of Appeal.

In a bizarre Ontario case, the plaintiff's claim was for damages for nervous shock. A 14-year-old high school boy, Snider, out with his friends, got very drunk. At one point the police told Alford and Berard, both 16, to take Snider home or they'd put him in jail. They agreed; Snider got into Alford's car. On the way, Snider wanted out. They let him out and drove off. They returned once, saw Snider staggering but went on without him. A passing motorist, Stroud, tried to help Snider, but Snider walked on and collapsed on the road. Stroud pulled over and walked back to help him. As he did an oncoming car struck and killed Snider. The driver of the car, Nespolon, sued for damages for negligence causing post-traumatic stress disorder. (Nespolon showed 20 of 21 symptoms of post-traumatic stress disorder when only 7 are sufficient for a diagnosis.)

The trial court found for Nespolon and found the fault fell equally on Alford, Berard and the victim Snider.

On appeal, in a 2-1 split, the court overturned the decision. On the legal basis that "the *sine qua non* of tortious liability remains the forseeability of risk," the majority felt that it "was simply too remote and unreasonable to expect that Alford and Berard would foresee that dropping Snider off where they did could lead to Nespolon's nervous shock"; that "Nespolon's nervous shock is too remote from any relationship with or behaviour of Alford, Berard and Snider to be compensated in damages from any of them."

Nespolon v. Alford
http://www.ontariocourts.on.ca/
Court of Appeal For Ontario
June 24, 1998

- *I*n a U.S. case a woman, who was not pregnant at the time of the accident in which her pelvis was broken, later gave birth to a child with head and facial injuries related to the damage to her pelvis. The court held that injury to a child not yet conceived was not foreseeable.[53]

- *T*he Court of Appeal found the Mental Health Centre was not negligent in its treatment of Stephen Czupor, a paranoid schizophrenic, who stabbed his sister Anna in the back with a hunting knife rendering her partially paralyzed. The court assumed the centre owed a duty of care to the sister, but found that it had not breached its duty to her as the staff neither knew nor ought to have known that Stephen would commit a violent act remotely similar to that attack.[54]

- *A*fter the judge found that the accused was guilty of the criminal charges against him, the accused jumped from the window of the courtroom to his death. The widow sued the lawyer representing her husband for negligence in his duties as the legal representative. At the trial the plaintiff's action was dismissed. The court held that the accused's jumping out the window was not foreseeable.[55]

D. Negligent Misstatement

1. Financial Advisors

Deraps *v.* Coia et al.

http://www.ontariocourts.on.ca
Court Of Appeal For Ontario
September 13, 1999

Abella, J.A.:
[1] The issue in this appeal is the scope of a pension counsellor's duty in communicating information to potential beneficiaries of a pension plan. The pension plan advisor in this case failed to inform a union member and his wife in express terms that if the wife signed a spousal waiver, she would receive no benefits when her husband died.

[2] The question to be decided is whether or not the failure to provide this specific information breached a duty of care owed by the pension advisor to the wife. ...

BACKGROUND:

[Gabriel Deraps was suffering from terminal lung cancer when he requested information with regard to his disability benefits from the pension plan advisor, Ms. Hickey. Later, he attended her office and Ms. Hickey showed him his options: the first was to receive a lower monthly disability pension, with his wife receiving 60% of his benefits when he died; the second was that if his wife signed a spousal waiver, Mr. Deraps would receive a higher monthly amount for disability benefits while he was alive. The calculations did not show that the result of Mrs. Deraps signing a spousal waiver would be that she would receive "zero" when her husband died. Mr. Deraps checked the box indicating that he and his wife wished to waive the 60% joint and survivor annuity.]

[19] It is clear from this evidence that Ms. Hickey was of the view that in the absence of any questions, she was neither required to provide any explanation about the waiver to Mr. and Mrs. Deraps, nor under any obligation to be satisfied that they understood it. ...

[21] Mr. Deraps was the only source of income Mrs. Deraps had, and Mrs. Deraps thought he had less than a year to live.

[22] Gabriel Deraps died on April 22, 1991, 8 months after the August 23, 1990 meeting with Ms. Hickey. A week before he died, he called Ms. Hickey to ask her what benefits his wife would receive upon his death. She told him that his wife would not receive any benefits.

[23] Monique Deraps did not learn that by signing the waiver she had lost her benefits until around the time of her husband's death. ...

[24] ... [The trial judge found she thought that she would be entitled to a reduced pension on the death of her husband.]

ANALYSIS ...

(b) Negligent Misrepresentation

[42] The tort of negligent misrepresentation arises when there is a duty of care based on a special relationship; when information has been provided which is inaccurate, or misleading, or untrue; when the person giving the information was negligent in providing the information; when the recipient of the information relied on the negligent misrepresentation; when the reliance was reasonable; and when the reliance resulted in damages to the person receiving the information. (See *Hedley Byrne Ltd. v.Heller & Partners Ltd.*, [1963] 2 All E.R. 575 (H.L.), *Fletcher*, supra, *Hercules Management Ltd. v. Ernst & Young*, [1997] 2 S.C.R. 165, and *Queen v. Cognos Inc.*, [1993] 1 S.C.R. 87).

[43] In *Cognos*, Iacobucci J., discussed the standard of care to be applied in cases involving allegations of negligent misrepresentation:

> The applicable standard of care should be the one used in every negligence case namely the universally accepted, albeit hypothetical, "reasonable person". The standard of care required by a person making representations is an objective one. It is a duty to exercise such reasonable care as the circumstances require to ensure that representations made are accurate and not misleading: see *Hedley Byrne*, supra, at p. 486, per Lord Reid; ... Klar, supra, at pp. 159-60. Professor Klar provides some useful insight on this issue.:
>
>> An advisor does not guarantee the accuracy of the statement made, but is only required to exercise rea-

sonable care with respect to it. As with the issue of standard care in negligence in general, this is a question of fact which must be determined according to the circumstances of the case. Taking into account the nature of the occasion, the purpose for which the statement was made, the foreseeable use of the statement, the probable damage which will result from an inaccurate statement, the status of the advisor and the level of competence generally observed by others similarly placed, the trier of fact will determine whether the advisor was negligent. (at pp. 121-22)

[44] A special relationship giving rise to a duty of care was defined in *Hedley Byrne* as follows:

> A reasonable man, knowing that he was being trusted or his skill and judgment were being relied on, would, I think, have three courses open to him. He could keep silent or decline to give the information or advice sought: or he could give an answer with a clear qualification that he accepted no responsibility for it or that it was given without that reflection or inquiry which a careful answer would require: or he could simply answer without any such qualification. If he chooses to adopt the last course he must, I think, be held to have accepted some responsibility for his answer being given carefully, or to have accepted a relationship with the inquirer which requires him to exercise such care as the circumstances require. ...

[46] In *Hercules Managements*, La Forest J. said that the plaintiff and the defendant can be said to be in a "special relationship" when the following exists:

> In negligent misrepresentation actions, ... the plaintiff's claim stems from his or her detrimental reliance on the defendant's (negligent) statement, and it is abundantly clear that reliance on the statement or representation of another will not, in all circumstances, be reasonable. ...
>
> ... determining whether "proximity" exists on a given set of facts consists in an attempt to discern whether, as a matter of simple justice, the defendant may be said to have had an obligation to be mindful of the plaintiff's interests in going about his or her business. ...

[47] He summarized the reliance issue by setting out what he considered to be the two issues implicit in this analysis:

> In cases of negligent misrepresentation, the relationship between the plaintiff and the defendant arises through reliance by the plaintiff on the defendant's words.
>
> (a) the defendant ought reasonably to foresee that the plaintiff will rely on his or her representation; and
>
> (b) reliance by the plaintiff would, in the particular circumstances of the case, be reasonable....

CONCLUSIONS: . . .

[54] Ms. Hickey's failure to advise Monique Deraps at all, let alone in a clear way, that she would receive nothing when her husband died if she signed the waiver, was misleading and a misrepresentation.

[55] Because she had a responsibility to provide complete and clear information, Ms. Hickey's failure to do so amounts to a breach of her duty of care. ...

[57] ... It was reasonably foreseeable that Monique Deraps would rely on any information Ms. Hickey provided, and that the implication of not giving full information could be devastating to someone in Mrs. Deraps' circumstances. ...

[61] Any damages caused to Monique Deraps were a direct result of her reliance on Ms. Hickey's failure to provide relevant and complete information which Ms. Hickey knew or ought to have known would be relied on, and was in fact relied on by both Mr. and Mrs. Deraps.

[62] Accordingly, I would allow the appeal [and] grant judgment in favour of the appellant, Monique Deraps, for damages representing the pension earnings she would have received had the spousal waiver form not been signed. ...

After reviewing the facts, the court found it was reasonably foreseeable that the client would think that she could continue to withdraw $2,471, if not $3,000 per month, without diminishing the capital of her investment. The failure of the investment advisors to warn their client that her taking that much money per month could only be at the expense of reducing her capital constituted a breach of the duty of care that they owed to her. The court found that duty was required both by the law relating to fiduciary relationships and by the law relating to negligence.

Turcotte v. Global Securities Corp.
http://www.courts.gov.bc.ca/
British Columbia Supreme Court
August 14, 2000

Hercules Managements Ltd. et al. v. *Ernst & Young et al.*

http://www.lexum.umontreal.ca/
SUPREME COURT OF CANADA
MAY 22, 1997

[1] LA FOREST J.—This appeal arises by way of motion for summary judgment. It concerns the issue of whether and when accountants who perform an audit of a corporation's financial statements owe a duty of care in tort to shareholders of the corporation who claim to have suffered losses in reliance on the audited statements. It also raises the question of whether certain types of claims against auditors may properly be brought by shareholders as individuals or whether they must be brought by the corporation in the form of a derivative action.

FACTS

[2] Northguard Acceptance Ltd. ("NGA") and Northguard Holdings Ltd. ("NGH") carried on business lending and investing money on the security of real property mortgages. The appellant Guardian Finance of Canada Ltd. ("Guardian") was the sole shareholder of NGH and it held non-voting class B shares in NGA. The appellants Hercules Managements Ltd. ("Hercules") and Max Freed were also shareholders in NGA. At all relevant times, ownership in the corporations was separated from management. The respondent Ernst & Young (formerly known as Clarkson Gordon) is a firm of chartered accountants that was originally hired by NGA and NGH in 1971 to perform annual audits of their financial statements and to provide audit reports to the companies' shareholders. ...

[3] In 1984, both NGA and NGH went into receivership. The appellants, as well as [other] shareholders or investors in NGA ... brought an action against the respondents in 1988 alleging that the audit reports for the years 1980, 1981 and 1982 were negligently prepared and that in reliance on these reports, they suffered various financial losses. ...

ISSUES

[14] The issues in this case [with regard to the action for negligent misstatement] may be stated as follows:

    (1) Do the respondents owe the appellants a duty of care with respect to

    (a) the investment losses they incurred allegedly as a result of reliance on the 1980–82 audit reports; and

    (b) the losses in the value of their existing shareholdings they incurred allegedly as a result of reliance on the 1980–82 audit reports? ...

ANALYSIS ...

Issue 1: Whether the Respondents owe the Appellants a Duty of Care

(i) *Introduction*

[19] It is now well established in Canadian law that the exis-

tence of a duty of care in tort is to be determined through an application of the two-part test first enunciated by Lord Wilberforce in *Anns v. Merton London Borough Council*, [1978] A.C. 728 (H.L.), at pp. 751–52:

> First one has to ask whether, as between the alleged wrongdoer and the person who has suffered damage there is a sufficient relationship of proximity or neighbourhood such that, in the reasonable contemplation of the former, carelessness on his part may be likely to cause damage to the latter — in which case a prima facie duty of care arises. Secondly, if the first question is answered affirmatively, it is necessary to consider whether there are any considerations which ought to negative, or to reduce or limit the scope of the duty or the class of person to whom it is owed or the damages to which a breach of it may give rise. …

> While the House of Lords rejected the Anns test … the basic approach that test embodies has repeatedly been accepted and endorsed by this Court. …

(ii) The Prima Facie Duty of Care

[22] The first branch of the Anns/Kamloops test demands an inquiry into whether there is a sufficiently close relationship between the plaintiff and the defendant that in the reasonable contemplation of the latter, carelessness on its part may cause damage to the former. The existence of such a relationship — which has come to be known as a relationship of "neighbourhood" or "proximity" — distinguishes those circumstances in which the defendant owes a prima facie duty of care to the plaintiff from those where no such duty exists. In the context of a negligent misrepresentation action, then, deciding whether or not a prima facie duty of care exists necessitates an investigation into whether the defendant-represensor and the plaintiff-representee can be said to be in a relationship of proximity or neighbourhood. …

[24] … The label "proximity", as it was used by Lord Wilberforce in *Anns*, supra, was clearly intended to connote that the circumstances of the relationship inhering between the plaintiff and the defendant are of such a nature that the defendant may be said to be under an obligation to be mindful of the plaintiff's legitimate interests in conducting his or her affairs. Indeed, this idea lies at the very heart of the concept of a "duty of care," as articulated most memorably by Lord Atkin in *Donoghue v. Stevenson*, [1932] A.C. 562, at pp. 580–81. In cases of negligent misrepresentation, the relationship between the plaintiff and the defendant arises through reliance by the plaintiff on the defendant's words… . To my mind, proximity can be seen to inhere between a defendant-representor and a plaintiff-representee when two criteria relating to reliance may be said to exist on the facts: (a) the defendant ought reasonably to foresee that the plaintiff will rely on his or her representation; and (b) reliance by the plaintiff would, in the particular circumstances of the case, be reasonable… .

(iii) Policy Considerations

[31] As Cardozo C.J. explained in *Ultramares Corp. v. Touche*, 174 N.E. 441 (N.Y.C.A. 1931), at p. 444, the fundamental policy consideration that must be addressed in negligent misrepresentation actions centres around the possibility that the defendant might be exposed to "liability in an indeterminate amount for an indeterminate time to an indeterminate class." This potential problem can be seen quite vividly within the framework of the *Anns/Kamloops* test. …

[32] The general area of auditors' liability is a case in point. In modern commercial society, the fact that audit reports will be relied on by many different people (e.g., shareholders, creditors, potential takeover bidders, investors, etc.) for a wide variety of purposes will almost always be reasonably foreseeable to auditors themselves. Similarly, the very nature of audited financial statements — produced, as they are, by professionals whose reputations (and, thereby, whose livelihoods) are at stake — will very often mean that any of those people would act wholly reasonably in placing their reliance on such statements in conducting their affairs. …[The judge reviews the work of several authors writing on the topic.]

[36] As I have thus far attempted to demonstrate, the possible repercussions of exposing auditors to indeterminate liability are significant. In applying the two-stage *Anns/Kamloops* test to negligent misrepresentation actions against auditors, therefore, policy considerations reflecting those repercussions should be taken into account. … In the general run of auditors' cases, concerns over indeterminate liability will serve to negate a prima facie duty of care. But while such concerns may exist in most such cases, there may be particular situations where they do not. … This needs to be explained.

…

[40] [For example, t]his Court's decision in *Haig*, supra, can be seen to rest on precisely the same basis. There, the defendant accountants were retained by a Saskatchewan businessman, one Scholler, to prepare audited financial statements of Mr. Scholler's corporation. At the time they were engaged, the accountants were informed by Mr. Scholler that the audited statements would be used for the purpose of attracting a $20,000 investment in the corporation from a limited number of potential investors. The audit was conducted negligently and the plaintiff investor, who was found to have relied on the audited statements in making his investment, suffered a loss. While Dickson J. was clearly cognizant of the potential problem of indeterminacy arising in the context of auditors' liability (at p. 476), he nevertheless found that the defendants owed the plaintiff a duty of care. In my view, his conclusion was eminently sound given that the defendants were informed by Mr. Scholler of the class of persons who would rely on the report and the report was used by the plaintiff for the specific purpose for which it was prepared… . On the facts of *Haig*, then, the auditors were properly found to owe a duty of care because concerns over indeterminate liability did not arise. I would note that this view of the rationale behind *Haig*, supra, is shared by Professor Feldthusen. …

(iv) Application to the Facts

[42] In my view, there can be no question that a prima facie duty of care was owed to the appellants by the respondents on the facts of this case. …

[44] Having found a prima facie duty to exist, then, the second branch of the *Anns/Kamloops* test remains to be considered. It should be clear from my comments above that were auditors such as the respondents held to owe a duty of care to plaintiffs in all cases where the first branch of the *Anns/Kamloops* test was satisfied, the problem of indeterminate liability would normally arise. It should be equally clear, however, that in certain cases, this problem does not arise because the scope of potential liability can adequately be circumscribed on the facts. An investigation of whether or not indeterminate liability is truly a concern in the present case is, therefore, required. …

With respect to the present case, then, the central question is whether or not the appellants can be said to have used the 1980–82 audit reports for the specific purpose for which they were prepared. The answer to this question will determine whether or not policy considerations surrounding indeterminate liability ought to negate the prima facie duty of care owed by the respondents. ...

[48] What, then, is the purpose for which the respondents' audit statements were prepared? ...

[49] ... Thus, the directors of a corporation are required to place the auditors' report before the shareholders at the annual meeting in order to permit the shareholders, as a body, to make decisions as to the manner in which they want the corporation to be managed, to assess the performance of the directors and officers, and to decide whether or not they wish to retain the existing management or to have them replaced. On this basis, it may be said that the respondent auditors' purpose in preparing the reports at issue in this case was, precisely, to assist the collectivity of shareholders of the audited companies in their task of overseeing management.

[50] ...

To my mind, ... despite the appellants' submissions, the respondents did not, in fact, prepare the audit reports in order to assist the appellants in making personal investment decisions or, indeed, for any purpose other than the standard statutory one.

[The judge reviews the claims of the appellants for investment losses and loss in value of shares.] ... Whether the reports were relied upon in assessing the prospect of further investments or in evaluating existing investments, the fact remains that the purpose to which the respondents' reports were put, on this claim, concerned individual or personal investment decisions. Given that the reports were not prepared for that purpose, I find for the same reasons as those earlier set out that policy considerations regarding indeterminate liability inhere here and, consequently, that no duty of care is owed in respect of this claim.

[55] As regards ... the appellants' claim concerning the losses they suffered in the diminution in value of their equity, the analysis becomes somewhat more intricate. The essence of the appellants' submission here is that the shareholders would have supervised management differently had they known of the (alleged) inaccuracies in the 1980–82 reports, and that this difference in management would have averted the demise of the audited corporations and the consequent losses in existing equity suffered by the shareholders. At first glance, it might appear that the appellants' claim implicates a use of the audit reports which is commensurate with the purpose for which the reports were prepared, i.e., overseeing or supervising management. ...

[56] ... On the appellants' argument, however, the purpose to which the 1980-82 reports were ostensibly put was not that of allowing the shareholders as a class to take decisions in respect of the overall running of the corporation, but rather to allow them, as individuals, to monitor management so as to oversee and protect their own personal investments. Indeed, the nature of the appellants' claims (i.e. personal tort claims) requires that they assert reliance on the auditors' reports qua individual shareholders if they are to recover any personal damages. In so far as it must concern the interests of each individual shareholder, then, the appellants' claim in this regard can really be no different from the other "investment purposes" discussed above, in respect of which the respondents owe no duty of care.

[57] This argument is no different as regards the specific case of the appellant Guardian, which is the sole shareholder of NGH. The respondents' purpose in providing the audited reports in respect of NGH was, we must assume, to allow Guardian to oversee management for the better administration of the corporation itself. If Guardian in fact chose to rely on the reports for the ultimate purpose of monitoring its own investment it must, for the policy reasons earlier set out, be found to have done so at its own peril in the same manner as shareholders in NGA. Indeed, to treat Guardian any differently simply because it was a sole shareholder would do violence to the fundamental principle of corporate personality. I would find in respect of both Guardian and the other appellants, therefore, that the prima facie duty of care owed to them by the respondents is negated by policy considerations in that the claims are not such as to bring them within the "exceptional" cases discussed above.

Appeal dismissed.

Question

Does an auditor avoid liability by following the Generally Accepted Accounting Principles?

The Supreme Court of Canada refused to hear an appeal from the B.C. Court of Appeal, which held in a 2-1 decision that the auditing firm of Touche Ross & Co. was liable for damages for negligent misstatement although its preparation of the financial statements accorded with the then Generally Accepted Accounting Principles (GAAP).

The plaintiffs had purchased debentures after the issue of a prospectus by Victoria Mortgage Corporation Ltd., whose primary business was providing loans secured by mortgages on real property. In the notes to its financial statements in the prospectus, it was stated that the company's policy was to "capitalize" accrued interest on mortgages in default if the management believed those amounts were adequately secured. Thus, "where mortgage payments were in arrears, the unpaid interest was added to the principal value of the mortgage. The uncollected interest was included in the company's statement of income."

When the company failed, the investors claimed damages by alleging that the auditors were negligent by, among other things, failing to disclose that the company had $4.9 million worth of mortgage loans in default. The defendant held that it did not have an obligation to state that the financial statements presented fairly the financial position of the company, but only that they presented fairly the financial position according to GAAP.

On the question of whether or not the standards set by a profession would satisfy the standard of care demanded by law, Judge Finch of the Appeal Court cited the following passage from *ter Neuzen v. Korn* [Supreme Court of Canada (1995), 11 B.C.L.R. (3d) 201 at para. 51]:

> I conclude from the foregoing that, as a general rule, where a procedure involves difficult or uncertain questions of medical treatment or complex, scientific or highly technical matters that are beyond the ordinary experience and understanding of a judge or jury, it will not be open to find a standard medical practice negligent. On the other hand, as an exception to the general rule, if a standard practice fails to adopt obvious and reasonable precautions which are readily apparent to the ordinary finder of fact, then it is no excuse for a practitioner to claim that he or she was merely conforming to such a negligent common practice. ...

He continued:

> In my view, therefore, while professional standards would normally be a persuasive guide as to what constitutes reasonable care, those standards cannot be taken to supplant or to replace the degree of care called for by law. A professional body cannot bind the rest of the community by the standard it sets for its members. Otherwise, all professions could immunize their members from claims of negligence ...
>
> ... Touche had actual knowledge that a simple application of GAAP would omit material information and lead to financial statements that could not be said to have fairly presented the financial position of VMCL. Given this actual knowledge, Touche fell below the required standard of care when it made its auditor's report. ...
>
> I conclude that the plaintiffs have made out a successful claim for negligent misrepresentation. The defendant owed the plaintiffs a duty of care, a material misrepresentation was negligently made, and the plaintiffs relied upon this misrepresentation to their detriment.

Kripps v. Touche Ross Co. et al.
http://www.courts.gov.bc.ca/
Court of Appeal of British Columbia
April 25, 1997

---

2. BANKS

The 1964 House of Lords decision in *Hedley Byrne & Co. v. Heller and Partners Ltd.* established the principle that a person could be sued for carelessly giving inaccurate information which caused a financial loss. This principle was adopted in Canada in *Haig v. Bamford*. In *Hedley Byrne*, although the bank gave inaccurate information about the credit-worthiness of its customer, the court found the bank not liable for the loss because it had explicitly disclaimed liability.

In a recent British Columbia case, the general contractor and the bank of a subcontractor (Micron Construction Ltd.) wanted assurances that the owner had sufficient funding to complete the construction project. They requested information from the owner's bank, the Hongkong Bank, which assured them that the company had negotiated a multi-million dollar loan when, in fact, the loan money was not secure. The bank included its standard disclaimer. The owner ran out of money, the building was not completed, and Micron was owed $916,000. Micron sued the bank for negligent misstatement; the bank relied on its standard disclaimer clause.

The B.C. Court of Appeal in a 2-1 split decision found the bank liable despite its disclaimer because it was reasonable for the bank to foresee that the contractors would rely on the bank's letter and it was reasonable for the contractors to rely on the bank's assurances. Furthermore, the bank knew the contractors had no alternative way to determine if the financing was adequate.

The court reasoned that *Hedley Byrne* had been rejected by the Supreme Court in *Hercules Management Ltd. v. Ernst & Young* (see p.72), which stressed "reasonable reliance." The court found that the question to be answered is: If the plaintiff's reliance would have been reasonable without a disclaimer, was the plaintiff's reliance on the assurances reasonable even with knowledge of the disclaimer? The court answered yes.

Micron Construction Ltd. v. Hongkong Bank of Canada
British Columbia Court of Appeal
Summarized from the Lawyers Weekly
March 17, 2000, p. 1, April 7, 2000, p. 17

Note: The Supreme Court of Canada refused to hear an appeal.

3. EMPLOYERS

Queen *v.* *Cognos*

SUPREME COURT OF CANADA
99 D.L.R. (4TH) 626
JANUARY 21, 1993

Background facts: Mr. Queen, a chartered accountant, was interviewed for a position as manager, financial standards, for the development of accounting software. He was not told in the interview that the funding for the project was not guaranteed nor that it was subject to budgetary approval by senior management. He left a secure position to join Cognos, Inc. A few months after he signed the employment contract he was told there would be reassignments because of cuts in research and development. Within two years he had received an effective termination notice; the employment contract had allowed for the termination of his employment at any time.

Mr. Queen sued the employer for negligent misstatement. He won at the trial level, but the decision was reversed by the Ontario Court of Appeal. Below are excerpts from the decision of the Supreme Court.

Per Iacobucci J.: — This appeal involves the application of the tort of negligent misrepresentation to a pre-employment representation made by an employer to a prospective employee in the course of a hiring interview. Specifically, the court is being asked to determine in what circumstances a representation made during a hiring interview becomes, in law, a "negligent misrepresentation". A subsidiary question deals with the effect of a subsequent employment agreement signed by the plaintiff, and its provisions allowing termination "without cause" and reassignment, on a claim for damages for negligent misrepresentation. ...

This appeal involves an action in tort to recover damages caused by alleged negligent misrepresentation made in the course of a hiring interview by an employer (the respondent), through its representative, to a prospective employee (the appellant) with respect to the employer and the nature and existence of the employment opportunity. Though a relatively recent feature of the common law, the tort of negligent misrepresentation relied on by the appellant and first recognized by the House of Lords in *Hedley Byrne, supra,* [*Hedley Byrne & Co. Ltd. v. Heller & Partners Ltd.* [1964] A.C. 465] is now an established principle of Canadian tort law. This court has confirmed on many occasions, sometimes tacitly, that an action in tort may lie, in appropriate circumstances, for damages caused by a misrepresentation made in a negligent manner: . ...

While the doctrine of *Hedley Byrne* is well established in Canada, the exact breadth of its applicability is, like any common law principle, subject to debate and to continuous development. At the time this appeal was heard, there had only been a handful of cases where the tort of negligent misrepresentation was used in a pre-employment context such as the one involved here: … Without question, the present factual situation is a novel one for this court.

Some have suggested that it is inappropriate to extend the application of *Hedley Byrne*, *supra*, to representations made by an employer to a prospective employee in the course of an interview because it places a heavy burden on employers. As will be apparent for my reasons herein, I disagree in principle with this view. …

[T]his appeal may be disposed of simply by considering whether or not the required elements under the *Hedley Byrne* doctrine are established in the facts of this case. In my view, they are.

The required elements for a successful *Hedley Byrne* claim have been stated in many authorities, sometimes in varying forms. The decisions of this court cited above suggest five general requirements:

(1) there must be a duty of care based on a "special relationship" between the representor and the representee;

(2) the representation in question must be untrue, inaccurate, or misleading;

(3) the representor must have acted negligently in making said misrepresentation;

(4) the representee must have relied, in a reasonable manner, on said negligent misrepresentation; and

(5) the reliance must have been detrimental to the representee in the sense that damages resulted.

In the case at bar, the trial judge found that all elements were present and allowed the appellant's claim. …

[After a lengthy review of the decisions of the lower courts, the relevant case law and the facts, the justice concluded.] In my view, the appellant has established all the required elements to succeed in his action. The respondent and its representative, Mr. Johnston, owed a duty of care to the appellant during the course of the hiring interview to exercise such reasonable care as the circumstances required to ensure that the representations made were accurate and not misleading. This duty of care is distinct from, and additional to, the duty of common honesty existing between negotiating parties. The trial judge found, as a fact, that misrepresentations — both express and implied — were made to the appellant and that he relied upon them, reasonably I might add, to his eventual detriment. In all the circumstances of this case, I agree with the trial judge that these misrepresentations were made by Mr. Johnston in a negligent manner. While a subsequent contract may, in appropriate cases, affect a Hedley Byrne claim relying on pre-contractual representations, the employment agreement signed by the appellant is irrelevant to this action. In particular, cls.13 and 14 of the contract [regarding reassignment and termination] are not valid disclaimers of responsibility for the representations made during the interview.

For the foregoing reasons, I would allow the appeal, set aside the judgment of the Ontario Court of Appeal, and restore the judgment of White J., finding the respondent liable and granting the appellant damages in the amount of $67,224. The appellant should have his costs here and in the courts below.

Appeal allowed

E. Voluntary Assumption of Risk / Contributory Negligence

Poirier et al. v. *Murphy et al.*

36 C.C.L.T. 160
British Columbia Supreme Court
February 17, 1986

MacKinnon J.: — On June 24, 1982 the plaintiff Peter Albert Poirier (Poirier) and the defendant John Anthony Murphy (Murphy), each 18 years of age, agreed to perform and in fact did carry out a "stunt" which resulted in Poirier being injured by the car driven by Murphy. With Poirier and Murphy, as passengers, were three girls and two boys, all around 17 years of age. They had been driving around with no particular destination and were looking for something to do. A conversation took place between Poirier and Murphy about doing a "stunt." The passengers were unaware of what this meant. However, they did hear Murphy asking Poirier to do it and Poirier refusing twice and then agreeing. The stunt was done in an underground parking lot of the Lougheed Mall in Coquitlam where Poirier would stand underneath a water sprinkler pipe and Murphy, as the driver of the car, from a position about 100 feet away, would drive towards Poirier and at the last moment Poirier would jump up, grab the pipe, do a chin-up, and swerve his hips and legs to one side, and thereby allow the

car to pass under him. The expected clearance between Poirier's body and the car would be approximately 4 to 6 inches. It was intended to be thrilling to the participants and anybody watching. It was certainly a dangerous act. In the past, and on the occasion of the accident, the signal indicating that Poirier was ready for the stunt to commence was a slight nod by Poirier. It was to be seen only by Murphy. On observing the signal (the slight nod by Poirier) Murphy would drive the car toward Poirier and expect him to escape any impact. …

[After reviewing the testimony of the witnesses, the Judge continued:] Thus, on the first run, it would appear the stunt performance went as planned with one exception. It almost failed. Even though Poirier signalled to Murphy his readiness for the commencement he was not able to completely escape contact with the car. His foot or part of his body was hit by the car. That impact did not release his grip on the pipes so as to cause a fall but it was of a sufficient force to be perceived by two of the passengers.

On the second run there are different stories as to what occurred. I do not accept Murphy's evidence that on the second run he backed up and performed the second stunt in the same way as the first. Other witnesses testified that he made a U-turn, headed at Poirier with his back facing Murphy. I have concluded that, after completing his first run, Murphy turned the car around in some manner and immediately commenced his run from the opposite direction. At this time Poirier was still hanging from the pipe. I find Poirier did not signal his readiness for Murphy to start the second run. Notwithstanding Mark Anderson's cry to stop, Murphy proceeded ahead in the belief that Poirier would pull himself up and avoid the impact. [He did not. He was struck and suffered serious brain injury.]

The issues

1. Does the maxim of *volenti non fit injuria* apply to the circumstances of this case?
2. If not, was there contributory negligence?
3. Damages.

Volenti non fit injuria
The defendant submits the plaintiff knew, or ought to have known, the real risk involved in carrying out the stunt and that, when he agreed to do it, he impliedly exempted the defendant from liability. The defendant says that Poirier consented to assume the risk without compensation, and he absolved Murphy from the duty to take care.

Cartwright J., in delivering the majority judgment of the Supreme Court of Canada in *Stein v. Lehnert*, [1963] S.C.R. 38, 40 W.W.R. 616, 36 D.L.R. (2d) 159 said, at p. 620 [W.W.R.]:

> "The decision of this court in *Seymour v. Maloney; Car and Gen. Insur. Corpn. (Third Party)* [1956] SCR 322,...establishes that where a driver of a motor vehicle invokes the maxim *volenti non fit injuria* as a defence to an action for damages for injuries caused by his negligence to a passenger, the burden lies upon the defendant of proving that the plaintiff, expressly or by necessary implication, agreed to exempt the defendant from liability for any damage suffered by the plaintiff occasioned by that negligence, and that, as stated in *Salmond on Torts*, 13th ed., p.44:
>
> > 'The true question in every case is: did the plaintiff give a real consent to the assumption of the risk without compensation; did the consent really absolve the defendant from the duty to take care?' "

In *Lackner v. Neath* (1966), 57 W.W.R. 496, 58 D.L.R. (2d) 662 (Sask. C.A.) Culliton C.J.S., quoted the excerpt from *Stein v. Lehnert*, supra, and then stated at p. 489 [W.W.R.]:

> Clearly, then, to admit the defence of *volenti non fit injuria* there must be established, either by direct evidence or by inference, that the plaintiff: (a) Voluntarily assumed the physical risk; and (b) Agreed to give up his right for negligence, or, to put it more briefly, that the plaintiff accepted both the physical and legal risk. ...

In *Deskau v. Dziama; Brooks v. Dziama*, [1973] 3 O.R. 101, 36 D.L.R. (3d) 36, the plaintiff agreed to assume the risk of riding with the defendant driver whom he knew was driving the car over hills at high speeds so that the car would fly from the crest of the hill with all four wheels off the ground. Keith J. found the nature of the risk voluntarily assumed by the plaintiff was unlimited. He said at p. 106 [O.R.]:

> I respectfully agree with the following statement from Fleming, *Law of Torts*, 4th ed. (1971), pp. 243-4:
>
> > 'Formerly it mattered nothing whether a plaintiff was defeated on the ground of voluntary assumption of risk or contributory negligence. Now, however, the distinction has become critical, since the relevant legislation does not purport to extend apportionment to voluntary assumption of risk. All the more reason therefore for the courts to have taken an ever more restrictive view of the defence (*volenti no fit injuria*) in order to avoid the distasteful consequence of having to deny the plaintiff all recovery instead of merely reducing his award. In the result, the defence is nowadays but rarely invoked with success.' ...

The defendant submits, and I agree, that had Poirier been injured in the first run the authorities would support the application of the doctrine of *volens*, and his claim would be dismissed. ...

He did not give such approval on the second run. Unlike the first stunt, Poirier was not ready for the second. He did not expect Murphy from that direction. After the first run he may have remained swinging from the water pipes so as to stay out of the way as Murphy was to (but did not) return to the starting position for the second stunt. Had Murphy done so, Poirier could have indicated or withheld his signal to commence the second stunt.

Accordingly, I have concluded that Poirier had not assumed the physical risk of the second stunt and the defence of *volens* does not succeed.

Contributory negligence
Murphy was negligent. As the driver of a motor vehicle, he owed a duty to drive it in a manner different than he did in the underground parking lot where the accident occurred. He was negligent in doing the stunt. He was negligent in failing to hear the noise in the first stunt (Poirier's foot), in failing to pay heed to the passenger's cry to stop, and in failing to recognize that Poirier was not ready for the second stunt. His negligence caused or contributed to the damages suffered by Poirier.

Poirier contributed to his own fate. He failed to take reasonable care for himself. He clearly was negligent in agreeing to the stunt. Though he may not have agreed to the second stunt being done in the manner it was, he placed himself in a hazardous position and failed to remove himself from the risk.

In my view Poirier and Murphy were equally negligent in the first run, and both were negligent in the second. In the second run I attach more blame to Murphy. I apportion the liability two-thirds on the shoulders of Murphy and one-third on Poirier. ...

The plaintiff is entitled to two-thirds of the damages together with court order interest.

Action allowed.

Q u e s t i o n

If you cause an accident, can you be held 100% liable even if the driver of the other vehicle had failed to buckle his seat belt?

Labbee v. Peters

[1999] A.J. No. 939 (Q.L.)
ALBERTA COURT OF APPEAL
AUGUST 11, 1999

[1] THE COURT:— This is an appeal from a finding that a driver who suffered fatal injuries in a motor vehicle accident was not contributorily negligent for failing to wear his seat belt. The trial judge found as a fact that the deceased's disregard for his own safety did not cause or contribute to the consequences of the defendant driver's negligence as the harm would have occurred even if the deceased had been restrained. ...
[3] Labbee was not using his lap seat belt. He was thrown laterally from the cab of the truck through the door on the driver's side which had opened 180 degrees as a result of the impact. He landed on the ground facing upward and while in that position was struck on the head by the roof rail of the truck cab as it rolled over. He died two days later from massive head injuries. ...
[11] It was conceded that Labbee was not wearing his seat belt. He was obliged by law to wear it and his failure to do so was a breach of the duty of care he owed for his own safety. The issue at trial was one of causation. The test of causation in contributory negligence is stated as follows in Fleming, *The Law of Torts*, (9th ed., 1998) at 313-314:

> Thus a plaintiff's own negligence will not prejudice him at all, any more than it would a defendant, unless it was causally relevant to his injury in the sense that "but for it" he would not have been hurt.

And with particular reference to the failure to employ a seat belt, the author says at 315-316:

> [F]ailure to use an available seat belt is relevant only if, and to the extent that, the injury would have been sig-

nificantly less serious if it had been worn. Accordingly, apportionment may be applied only to that extent of the injury which could have been avoided.

...
[12] The trial judge had to decide, therefore, on the basis of the expert evidence, whether the appellant had established that but for Labbee's lack of care in not wearing his belt he would have avoided sustaining fatal injuries. ...
[14] In our opinion, the trial judge applied the correct test for contributory negligence in the circumstances of this case and in view of the evidence before him. Although it was clear that Labbee's fatal head injury was the direct result of his failure to wear the available seat belt, the trial judge held that that did not constitute contributory negligence where there was also evidence, which he accepted, showing that Labbee would have sustained equally severe injuries had he been restrained. The trial judge was simply not persuaded on a balance of probabilities that there was a causal link between Labbee's failure to wear his belt and serious injury that would have, in any case, resulted in his death. ...
[19] ... Where a trial judge is presented with competing explanations or conclusions from expert witnesses, there is no reversible error when he makes a reasoned choice between the two. ...
[23] We dismiss the appeal.

Unanimous

Note: For the curious, the full case has the details of the accident and the evidence of how he would have died if the seat belt had been worn.

- *A*lthough the defendants were found negligent for failing to have a reasonable system for keeping the premises free from ice, the plaintiff who fell and sued was found 25% contributorily negligent for wearing high-heeled dress shoes instead of "safe footgear for winter conditions."[56]

F. VICARIOUS LIABILITY

- *B*ecause a caretaker's duties did include controlling the conduct of tenants in the rooming house, the owner of the house, as employer of the caretaker, was found vicariously liable for the actions of the caretaker who chose to solve one disturbance by taking a three-foot board "described as a portion of a handrail with the word 'truth' marked on it" and striking a tenant in the face with it.[57]

Bazley v. Curry

http://www.lexum.umontreal.ca/
SUPREME COURT OF CANADA
JUNE 17, 1999

McLachlin, J.:—

I. INTRODUCTION

[1] It is tragic but true that people working with the vulnerable sometimes abuse their positions and commit wrongs against the very people they are engaged to help. The abused person may later seek to recover damages for the wrong. But judgment against the wrongdoer may prove a hollow remedy. This raises the question of whether the organization that employed the offender should be held liable for the wrong. The law refers to such liability as "vicarious" liability. It is also known as "strict" or "no-fault" liability, because it is imposed in the absence of fault of the employer. The issue in this case is whether such liability lies for an employee's sexual abuse of children in his care. ...

[41] Reviewing the jurisprudence, and considering the policy issues involved, I conclude that in determining whether an employer is vicariously liable for an employee's unauthorized, intentional wrong in cases where precedent is inconclusive, courts should be guided by the following principles:

(1) They should openly confront the question of whether liability should lie against the employer, rather than obscuring the decision beneath semantic discussions of "scope of employment" and "mode of conduct".

(2) The fundamental question is whether the wrongful act is sufficiently related to conduct authorized by the employer to justify the imposition of vicarious liability. Vicarious liability is generally appropriate where there is a significant connection between the creation or enhancement of a risk and the wrong that accrues therefrom, even if unrelated to the employer's desires. Where this is so, vicarious liability will serve the policy considerations of provision of an adequate and just remedy [for the victim] and deterrence. Incidental connections to the employment enterprise, like time and place (without more), will not suffice. Once engaged in a particular business, it is fair that an employer be made to pay the generally [page 560] foreseeable costs of that business. In contrast, to impose liability for costs unrelated to the risk would effectively make the employer an involuntary insurer.

(3) In determining the sufficiency of the connection between the employer's creation or enhancement of the risk and the wrong complained of, subsidiary factors may be considered. These may vary with the nature of the case. When related to intentional torts, the relevant factors may include, but are not limited to, the following:
(a) the opportunity that the enterprise afforded the employee to abuse his or her power;
(b) the extent to which the wrongful act may have furthered the employer's aims (and hence be more likely to have been committed by the employee);
(c) the extent to which the wrongful act was related to friction, confrontation or intimacy inherent in the employer's enterprise;
(d) the extent of power conferred on the employee in relation to the victim;
(e) the vulnerability of potential victims to wrongful exercise of the employee's power.

...

[57] The appropriate inquiry in a case such as this is whether the employee's wrongful act was so closely connected to the employment relationship that the imposition of vicarious liability is justified in policy and principle. From the point of view of principle, a prime indicator is whether the employer, by carrying on its operations, created or materially enhanced the risk of the wrong that occurred, such that the policy considerations of fair recovery and deterrence are engaged. In answering this question, the court must have regard to how the employer's enterprise increased opportunity to commit the wrong, and how it fostered power-dependency relationships that materially enhanced the risk of the harm. There is no special rule for non-profit corporations.

[58] Applying these considerations to the facts in the case at bar, the Foundation is vicariously liable for the sexual misconduct of Curry. ...

VI. CONCLUSION

[59] I would dismiss the appeal with costs and remit the matter to trial.

Unanimous

G. Strict Liability

Q u e s t i o n

Should we ever make the defendant pay when he is not at fault?

Methane gas, generated by the decomposition of organic material in a land-fill, escaped to the neighbouring areas, and entered the plaintiff's garage. When the plaintiff turned on the ignition of his car, the resulting explosion destroyed the garage, damaged his car, and injured him.

The plaintiff successfully sued the municipalities. Affirming the rule of *Fletcher v. Rylands* [(1866), L.R. 1 Ex. 265], the court found the municipalities which developed and used the land-fill strictly liable: the project was a non-natural use of the land and the subsequent escape of the methane gas caused damage to the neighbouring residents.

In this case, the court also found the defendants liable for nuisance and negligence.

Gertsen et al. v. Municipality of Metropolitan Toronto et al.
41 D.L.R. (3D) 646
Ontario High Court
August 21, 1973

H. Remedies

The Thin Skull Rule

A school bus driver was attacked and threatened by an irate father. The incident resulted not only in physical injury, but also severe emotional problems. A psychiatrist gave evidence that the driver was an emotionally vulnerable person.

In assessing damages, the judge relied on the thin skull rule and quoted the following from the 1996 Supreme Court of Canada case *Athey v. Leonati:*

> "the well-known 'thin skull' rule ... makes the tortfeasor liable for the plaintiff's injuries even if the injuries are unexpectedly severe owing to a pre-existing condition. The tortfeasor must take his or her victim as the tortfeasor finds the victim, and is therefore liable even though the plaintiff's losses are more dramatic than they would be for the average person".

Dunne v. Gauthier
Summarized from The Lawyers Weekly *January 12, 2001, p. 18*

Punitive Damages

 See *Whiten v. Pilot Insurance Co. et al.* on page 249.

- *I*n the first class action suit against the tobacco industry, a Miami jury found the defendants liable and awarded punitive damages of $145 billion (that's billion with a "b"), an amount that exceeded the value of the companies. A judge may lower that figure in his final judgment; also, the five defendant tobacco companies will appeal. Because each ailing plaintiff in the class action suit, representing 500,000 Florida residents, will have to prove damages, a lawyer for one of the five defendant tobacco companies estimated that those trials would take decades.[58]

- *T*he U.S. Supreme Court refused to hear an appeal from Exxon on the amount of the punitive damage award. A jury had awarded $5 billion as punitive damages against Exxon for the losses caused by the Exxon Valdez oil spill in Alaska.[59]

ENDNOTES

1. For the details and discussion of the court's decision see *The Vancouver Sun*, October 7, 2000, pp. 1 and 3.

2. *The Vancouver Sun*, Nov. 7, 2000, B1.

3. For a more detailed account see *The Vancouver Sun*, September 18, 1996, p. A10.

4. *The Vancouver Sun*, January 27, 2001, p. A18.

5. *The Globe and Mail*, February 9, 1993, p. A12.

6. A more detailed account is given in the *National*, April, 1986.

7. For a more detailed account see *The Lawyers Weekly*, January 19, 1996, p. 11.

8. See *The Vancouver Sun*, June 14, 2000, p. 1.

9. For a more detailed account see *The Vancouver Sun*, July 16, 1999, p. A9.

10. A more detailed account is given in *The Vancouver Sun*, December 1, 1987.

11. A more detailed account is given in *The Vancouver Sun*, October 24, 1989.

12. A more detailed account is given in *The Vancouver Sun*, January, 1984.

13. A more detailed account is given in *The Globe and Mail*, August 11, 1992, p. A2.

14. See *Vinthers v. Dumont*, British Columbia Supreme Court, http://www.courts.gov.bc.ca/.

15. For an account of the match, the bite, and subsequent events, see *Newsweek*, July 14, 1997, p. 58.

16. For a more detailed account of *R. v. Williams* see *The Lawyers Weekly*, June 2, 2000, p. 20.

17. *National*, July, 1988.

18. For a more detailed account see *The Globe and Mail*, January 17, 1998, p. A8. Subsequently Eagleson, faced with the possibility of expulsion, resigned from Canada's Hockey Hall of Fame. See *The Globe and Mail*, March 26, 1998, p. A15.

19. For a more detailed account see *The Lawyers Weekly*, March 27, 1998, p. 8.

20. *The Lawyers Weekly*, October 15, 1999, p. 2.

21. For a more detailed account with the specifics of Lloyd's enormous losses, the resulting personal tragedies (including many suicides) and the intervention of Parliament to limit Lloyd's liability see *Time*, February 28, 2000.

22. For more detailed accounts see *The Bottom Line*, October 2000, p.1; mid-October 2000, p. 3.

23. For more detailed accounts see *The Bottom Line*, November 2000, p.7.

24. For a more detailed account see *The Lawyers Weekly*, December 12, 1999, p. 1, for a summary of *Myers v. Canadian Broadcasting Corporation*.

25. For a summary of *Leenen v. Canadian Broadcasting Corp* see *The Lawyers Weekly*, May 26, 2000, p. 16.

26. *The Vancouver Sun*, October 7, 2000, p. B2.

27. For more details see *The Lawyers Weekly*, July 11, 1997, p. 5 and July 18, 1997, p. 3.

28. For more information see *Time*, February 2, 1998, p.96 and *The Lawyers Weekly*, Feb. 27, 1998, p. 3.

29. *The Lawyers Weekly*, January 30, 1998, p. 3.

30. *The Vancouver Sun*, November 2, 2000, p. A20.

31. *The Vancouver Sun*, August 10, 1999, B1.

32. *Playback* April 5, 1999, p. 15.

33. *The Vancouver Sun*, September 26, 2000, p. B10.

34. *The Vancouver Sun*, February 4, 2000, p. A5.

35. *Playback*, April 5, 1999, p.15.

36. *The Vancouver Sun,* March 24, 1998.

37. *Time*, April 24, 2000, p. 14.

38. *The Globe and Mail*, January 6, 2001, p. E18.

39. *E-Commerce Times*, November 23, 1999. Reprinted by Edupage.

40. Summarized from *Los Angeles Times*, April 29, 1999. Reprinted by Edupage.

41. For the story that would warm the heart of a lawyer see *The Vancouver Sun*, November 1, 1996, p. A12.

42. See *Hanna v. Olivieri* http://www.courts.gov.bc.ca/ Supreme Court of British Columbia, October 29, 1999.

43. *Time*, October 9, 2000, p. 10.

44. *Ontario Lawyers Weekly*.

45. A more detailed account is given in *The Vancouver Sun*.

46. A more detailed account is given in *The Vancouver Sun*, January 1985.

47. See *The Lawyers Weekly*, May 5, 2000, p. 21.

48. For a more detailed account see *The Globe and Mail*, September 2, 1994, pp. B1, B15. (The warning on the insulating sleeve of Starbucks coffee cups now states: "Careful, the beverage you're about to enjoy is extremely hot.")

49. For a more detailed account see *The Vancouver Sun*, February 2, 1994, A6.

50. For a more detailed account see *The Vancouver Sun*, October 31, 2000, p. C5 and *Time Magazine*, November 27, 2000, p. 79.

51. For a case dealing with negligence, allocation of fault, and statutory interpretation see *Aiello v. Centra Gas Ontario Inc. et al.*, October 8, 1999 [1999] O.J. No. 3777 (Q.L.) Ontario Superior Court of Justice.

52. See *Arnault v. The Board of Police Commissioners of the City of Prince Albert et al.*, Case No. Q.B. No. 356, September 25, 1995.

53. *The Lawyers Weekly*, January 30, 1998, p. 2.

54. If you have the heart for a very tragic tale see *Molnar v. Her Majesty the Queen in Right of the Province of British Columbia*, Vancouver Registry CA015514, June 24, 1993.

55. See *The Lawyers Weekly*, April 21, 1981, p. 20.

56. See *Britt v. Zagio Holdings Ltd.*, Ontario Court of Justice (General Division) [1996] O.J. No. 1014 (Q.L.) DRS 96-08791 File No. 12941/92 February 23, 1996.

57. See *Fagnan v. Monaghan,* Court of Queen's Bench of Manitoba, Suit No.: CI 93-01-70599, September 15, 1995.

58. For a more detailed account of the case *Engles v. R. J. Reynolds et al.* see *The Vancouver Sun*, July 15, 2000, p. A6. In *Time* magazine, July 24, 2000, p. 34, it was stated that before this tobacco case, the highest punitive damage award was $5 billion awarded in connection with the *Exxon-Valdez* oil spill.

59. *The Vancouver Sun,* October 3, 2000, p. A11.

IV
THE LAW OF CONTRACT

A. FREEDOM OF CONTRACT

Question

What kind of deals are we allowed to make?

- *J*apan's Mitsui Real Estate Ltd. learned through its agent that the asking price for the Exxon Building in New York was $375 million. The agent advised Mitsui that Exxon would probably take less. Mitsui instructed its agent to offer $610 million. The agent tried to dissuade it. Lawyers acting for Exxon did not want to accept it; $375 million would be sufficient. Eventually the $610 million offer was formally made and accepted. Why did Mitsui pay $235 million over the asking price? To break the record in the *Guinness Book of World Records* of the top price ever paid for a single building.[1]

- *T*he rock group Guns N' Roses insists that reporters and photographers sign a contract which provides that the interviewer must "acknowledge that [the band] shall own all right, title and interest, including, without limitation, the copyright, in and to the interview and all transcriptions or summaries thereof ..." and that the interviewer be considered an employee. Furthermore, the interview had to be submitted to the band for its written approval which could be withheld for any reason. The contract stipulates that any party in breach of the agreement will pay them $100,000 as damages.[2]

- *N*o matter how long you try to negotiate the term into the contract, U.S. Airways will probably hang tough and not let you bring your pig on board even if you're willing to buy it a first class seat. The "enormous, brown, angry and honking" pig, which was allowed on when the owners brought a doctor's note saying it was a therapeutic companion pet, was too disruptive and rude during the six-hour flight from Philadelphia to Seattle.[3]

B. FORMATION OF CONTRACTS

Question

A contract is often defined as an agreement the law will enforce, but that is not too helpful. What elements in particular must be present before the law will enforce an agreement?
---

1. GENERAL DUTY OF GOOD FAITH

In 1967, Gateway Realty Ltd. (Gateway), the owner of a shopping centre, rented space to Zellers, a retail chain. The lease gave Zellers the right to assign or sublet. The store was successful with annual sales over $14 million by the late 1980s. Mr. Hurst, the owner of a rival shopping centre, Bridgewater Mall, persuaded Zellers to leave those premises and to open a store in the new mall. Zellers did and assigned the remainder of its lease in the shopping centre to another of Mr. Hurst's companies, Arton Holdings and LaHave Developments (Arton). When Gateway Realty learned that its lessee had assigned its premises to its competitor it met with Hurst; Arton signed an agreement to use its best efforts to lease the space to suitable tenants. Gateway received inquiries about the space, but despite notices to Arton from Gateway, Arton did not follow up on any leads. Gateway took possession and eventually leased the space to K-mart.

Gateway took an action against Arton for a declaration that Zeller's assignment to Arton was invalid because Zellers had breached its duty of good faith by assigning the remainder of the lease to Gateway's main competitor; or a declaration that Gateway was entitled to terminate the lease with Arton because it had breached its duty of good faith to find a suitable replacement tenant. Arton defended by relying on the lease, which gave an unrestricted right to assign and by claiming that, in Canada, there was no duty of good faith in the performance of contracts. Justice Kelly of the N.S.S.C. found that "the law requires that parties to a contract exercise their rights under the agreement honestly, fairly and in good faith." The duty is breached if a party acts contrary to community standards of honesty, reasonableness or fairness.

On the evidence of Arton's actions, the judge concluded there was a breach of its duty of good faith and that the breach was serious enough to allow Gateway the right to terminate the lease. As an alternative reason for his decision, the Judge found that Gateway's agreement with Arton was an amendment to the Zellers lease, and that agreement was breached in such a way to justify Gateway's termination of the lease. He issued the declaration that the leasehold interest of Arton was terminated.

Gateway Realty Ltd. v. Arton Holding Ltd.
Nova Scotia Supreme Court
Summarized from The Lawyers Weekly
October 4, 1991 p. 1

Note: About three years later, in another contract case, Justice Kelly cited *Gateway* and also cases from New Zealand and Australia that he maintained affirmed a doctrine of good faith. In his words: "A party breaches its obligation to act in good faith if, without reasonable justification, the party acts in relation to the contract in a manner which substantially nullifies the bargained for benefits or defeats legitimate expectations of the other party."[4]

Note: In the 1997 Supreme Court case, *Wallace v. United Grain Growers* (p. 172), C.J. McLachlin in the dissent encouraged the adoption by the court of an implied term of good faith in employment contracts. For her argument for the inclusion of such a term, see the entire dissent at http://www.lexum.umontreal.ca/.

2. OFFER AND ACCEPTANCE

A. OFFER

Question

What test does the court apply to determine if there has been an offer and acceptance?

Campbell v. Sooter Studios Ltd.

MANITOBA QUEEN'S BENCH
AUGUST 22, 1989
UNREPORTED

Background facts: The lease between the plaintiff lessor and the defendant lessee expired on June 30, 1987. After that date, the lessor sent over a draft of a new lease which provided for a significant increase in the rent and for a three-year term commencing July 1, 1987 and ending June 30, 1990. The president of Sooter Studios, the lessee, not satisfied with the document, altered the term of the lease to make it a one-year lease ending June 30, 1988, and changed the rent. He then signed it and sent it back to the lessor with no letter or conversation indicating that the terms were changed. The lessor signed it without noticing the alterations, sent it back to the lessee for affixation of the corporate seal. The lessee did affix the seal and returned the lease to the lessor.

The lessor then noticed the changes and argued that there was no new lease; that the lessee should give up possession or pay double rent as an overholding tenant. The lessee maintained there was a lease and it remained in possession until June 30, 1988.

The lessor sued for double rent, for the cost of certain repairs, and for a share of realty taxes.

Jewers, J. … Counsel for the plaintiffs submitted that there was no concluded contract of lease between the parties…that the plaintiffs were never aware of the alterations made to the draft lease by the defendant, and that there was, therefore, never a true meeting of minds between the parties.

In *Chitty on Contracts* 25th Ed. p. 25 it is stated:

The normal test for determining whether the parties have reached agreement is to ask whether an offer has been made by one party and accepted by the other. In answering this question, the courts apply an objective test: if the parties have to all outward appearances agreed in the same terms upon the same subject-matter neither can generally deny that he intended to agree. Hence an unexpressed qualification or reservation on the part of one party to an apparent agreement will not normally prevent the formation of a contract. The theory, popular in England in the nineteenth century, that there can be no contract without a meeting of the minds of the parties, has been largely discredited as it would tend to produce commercially inconvenient results.

The question then is: objectively considered, was there an accepted offer? In my opinion, there was. The original offer was, of course, the draft lease prepared and sent by the plain-tiffs to the defendant; this offer was not accepted; the defendant made a counter offer by altering some of the essential terms of the lease, signing the document and then resubmitting it to the plaintiffs for their consideration; the plaintiffs then (objectively at least) accepted the counter offer by executing the lease and returning it to the defendant so that the defendant's seal could be affixed; the contract was finally concluded when the defendant affixed the seal and sent the lease back to the plaintiffs. The defendant had no way of knowing and did not know that the plaintiffs had not noticed the alterations and had not assented to them. The plaintiffs had not agreed to the alterations, but, to all outward appearances, they had. They had signed the document after it had been altered by the defendant and had returned it to the defendant without comment or dissent, except to ask that the defendant's corporate seal be affixed. Subjectively, there was no true meeting of minds, but objectively there was and that is the test. …

I therefore hold that the defendant did enter into a valid and binding lease of the premises expiring on June 30th, 1988: that the defendant was not an overholding tenant; and that the plaintiffs are not entitled to charge double rent.

[The judge awarded the plaintiffs an amount for a share of the taxes and the cost of repairs to a plate glass window.]

The plaintiffs have been partially successful, but the greater victor has been the defendant. …

When Alan Eagleson was acting as the executive director of the National Hockey League Players' Association, his company Rae-Con represented Michael Gillis. In 1984, Gillis, playing with the Boston Bruins, fractured his right ankle. Eagleson was instrumental in obtaining a settlement between Gillis and the insurer Lloyd's of London. Eagleson, through Rae-Con, sent Gillis a bill for $41,250 U.S. Gillis paid it but he thought the work was done by Eagleson as director of the NHLPA; Eagleson maintained he acted as the lawyer for Gillis and that was the agreed on fee. Justice O'Brien of the Ontario Court (General Division) found there was no fee arrangement between Eagleson and Gillis and ordered the return of the money.

Gillis v. Eagleson
Ontario Court (G.D.)
Summarized from The Lawyers Weekly
January 10, 1997 p. 2

- "If you pay, the story rolls. If you don't, the story folds."[5] This unusual announcement was made by the novelist Stephen King who began posting his unpublished novel, *The Plant*, in monthly installments on his Web site. He said he would continue to post installments if 75% of the people who download his work would send him a dollar for each copy downloaded. By the middle of the first day of the posting, 41,000 copies of the first 20 pages were downloaded and about 78% paid the $1 fee.[6]

  By the fourth installment the freeloaders were more numerous than the payers, only 46% paid the fee. King suspended posting, but not, he claims, due to the drop in payers. More than 500,000 had paid. He announced the 6th part of the story would be posted later for free.[7]

  Does this arrangement constitute a contract? Where is the offer? The acceptance? Is this just an honour system?

B. Revocation of Offer

Question

When is the revocation of an offer effective?

Mlodzinska et al. v. *Malicki et al.*

63 O.R. (2d) 180
Ont. High Court of Justice, Divisional Court
January 26, 1988

Hughes J. (orally):—The order in appeal was made by the Honourable Mr. Justice O'Brien in the course of a case involving a will. It discloses an interesting confrontation having occurred in court in the absence of the learned judge in which the validity of a withdrawal of an offer to settle is in question, and I cannot improve on his concise account in describing what happened.

He says:

The settlement now in issue occurred following a discussion between counsel. ...

It appears there had been offers of settlement made by both sides. The defence made one offer on April 2, 1987, which had not formally been withdrawn. ...

During an intermission of trial counsel for the defendants obtained further instructions from his client. Pursuant to those instructions, he wrote a formal notice indicating any offer of settlement had been withdrawn and formally withdrawing the offer of April 2, 1987.

He walked into the court-room indicating with thumb and forefinger the gesture of a zero, said words to the effect "Now, it's zero," took a few steps to counsel table, where plaintiffs' counsel was sitting, and handed to him the handwritten notice. As he did so, plaintiffs' counsel handed him a typewritten notice purporting to accept the offer April 2, 1987.

The position of counsel for the defence is, while there may have been a very short period of time between his action and that of plaintiff's counsel, there was a time differential, and counsel's position is "first in time, first in right" and the defendants' settlement offer was withdrawn prior to acceptance.

The position of counsel for the plaintiffs is that there has been ongoing settlement discussions, the gesture and statement made by defence counsel as he walked into the court-room was not unequivocal and the exchange of his acceptance and withdrawal was virtually simultaneous.

Plaintiff's counsel also urges it is unseemly to encourage "races" of this type between counsel during the course of a trial.

[I]n my view (and I am advised that my brother Austin will develop the point), [there was] an undisputed priority in time, however slight of the presentation of the withdrawal by counsel for the appellants before the handing over of the acceptance by counsel for the respondent.

Nonetheless, the learned judge came to the conclusion that because of the apparent unseemliness of this cut and thrust delivery of papers not, albeit, in his presence, and what Carruthers J. had to say about the policy of the rules being to prevent gamesmanship, that a settlement had been concluded, and he made an order to that effect ... I am more concerned with an aspect other than seemliness involved in this matter,

and that is the real purpose, I would have thought, of the rules, in respect of reaching a just result. ...

... To hold on such tenuous grounds that a settlement had been made would, I think, be unfair to the defendants in the case and the appellants here, and produce an unjust result.

In response to the concern of O'Brien J. that he should be given some direction, I am of the opinion that his order should be set aside and that he should continue with the trial.

Austin J. (orally):—It was apparent that, by virtue of the matters set out in the reasons of my brothers, the learned trial judge was in a very difficult position. In his reasons he said:

> It seems to me the purported acceptance and withdrawal were virtually simultaneous. I accept submissions of plaintiffs' counsel it is unseemly for courts to encourage the type of race which might result in gamesmanship in the exchange of paper during the course of trial.
>
> I conclude, therefore, the settlement offer was accepted by the plaintiffs and this litigation is ended.

No one disputes the desirability of settlement. In reaching the result he did, however, the trial judge must have concluded either that the acceptance was given first, or that the exchange was for all intents and purposes simultaneous. In my view, neither conclusion is supported by the evidence.

Counsel for the plaintiffs conceded that counsel for the defendants, "put his piece of paper down on my book prior to me handing mine to him." Leaving aside completely the gesture and oral statement of counsel for the defendants, the uncontradicted evidence is that the defendants delivered their notice of withdrawal before the plaintiffs delivered their notice of acceptance.

The time lapse between the two events may have been very short. Counsel for the plaintiffs described it as a split second. Whatever the length of the period, the withdrawal was first and the acceptance second. In those circumstances it does not seem to me that any offer remained available for the plaintiffs to accept.

...

I would allow the appeal and set aside the order of O'Brien J., dated April 24, 1987.

Appeal allowed.

Note: The Court of Appeal affirmed the decision.

C. REJECTION AND COUNTER OFFER

Question

What is the effect on the offer if the offeree makes a counter offer?

Hyde v. *Wrench*

1840 49 E.R. 132

The Defendant being desirous of disposing of an estate, offered, by his agent to sell it to the Plaintiff for £1200, which the Plaintiff, by his agent, declined: and on the 6th of June the Defendant wrote to his agent as follows:—"I have to notice the refusal of your friend to give me £1200 for my farm; I will only make one more offer, which I shall not alter from; that is, £1000 lodged in the bank until Michaelmas, when the title shall be made clear of expenses, land tax, &c. I expect a reply by return, as I have another application." This letter was forwarded to the Plaintiff's agent, who immediately called on the Defendant; and, previously to accepting the offer, offered to give the Defendant £950 for the purchase of the farm, but the Defendant wished to have a few days to consider.

On the 11th of June the Defendant wrote to the Plaintiff's agent as follows:—"I have written to my tenant for an answer to certain enquiries, and, the instant I receive his reply, will communicate with you, and endeavour to conclude the prospective purchase of my farm; I assure you I am not treating with any other person about said purchase."

The Defendant afterwards promised he would give an answer about accepting the £950 for the purchase on the 26th of June; and on the 27th he wrote to the Plaintiff's agent, stating he was sorry he could not feel disposed to accept his offer for his farm at Luddenham at present.

This letter being received on the 29th of June, the Plaintiff's agent on that day wrote to the Defendant as follows:—"I beg to acknowledge the receipt of your letter of the 27th instant, informing me that you are not disposed to accept the sum of £950 for your farm at Luddenham. This being the case, I at once agree to the terms on which you offered the farm, *viz.*, £1000 through your tenant Mr. Kent, by your letter of the 6th instant. I shall be obliged by your instructing your solicitor to communicate with me without delay, as to the title, for the reason which I mentioned to you."

[The defendant vendor alleged there was no contract. The plaintiff said there was a contract and] charged that the Defendant's offer for sale had not been withdrawn previous to its acceptance. …

Mr. Kindersley and Mr. Keene, in support [of the defendant vendor] . … To constitute a valid agreement there must be a simple acceptance of the terms proposed. *Holland v. Eyre* (2 Sim. & St. 194). The Plaintiff, instead of accepting the alleged proposal for sale for £1000 on the 6th of June rejected it, and made a counter proposal; this put an end to the Defendant's offer, and left the proposal of the Plaintiff alone under discussion; that has never been accepted, and the Plaintiff could not, without the concurrence of the Defendant, revive the Defendant's original proposal.

Mr. Pemberton and Mr. Freeling, *contra*. So long as the offer of the Defendant subsisted, it was competent to the Plaintiff to accept it; the bill charges that the Defendant's offer had not been withdrawn previous to its acceptance by the Plaintiff; there, therefore, exists a valid subsisting contract. *Kenney v. Lee* (3 Mer. 454), *Johnson v. King* (2 Bing. 270), were cited. …

The Master of the Rolls [Lord Langdale]… I think there exists no valid binding contract between the parties for the purchase of the property. The Defendant offered to sell it for £1000, and if that had been at once unconditionally accepted, there would undoubtedly have been a perfect binding contract; instead of that, the Plaintiff made an offer of his own, to purchase the property for £950, and he thereby rejected the offer previously made by the Defendant. I think that it was not afterwards competent for him to revive the proposal of the Defendant, by tendering an acceptance of it; and that, therefore, there exists no obligation of any sort between the parties. …

D. CONDITION PRECEDENT

Questions

Is there a contract if the acceptance is conditional upon the happening of an event?

Drabinsky v. *Heffel Gallery Limited*

http://www.courts.gov.bc.ca/
SUPREME COURT OF BRITISH COLUMBIA
MARCH 21, 2000

Holmes, J.
[1] The plaintiff's application is for summary judgment pursuant to Rule 18A for the amount of the loss incurred upon the resale of an Alex Colville painting resulting from the alleged breach by the defendant of a contract for its purchase.
[2] The defendant's position is it did not breach the contract; rather, the plaintiff failed to fulfil a condition precedent to the contract. …

THE FACTS:

[5] In the late fall of 1998 the plaintiff decided to sell an Alex Colville painting titled "French Cross" (the "Painting"), from his personal collection.

[6] In February 1999 David Heffel ("Heffel"), an owner of the defendant gallery, inquired through a Toronto gallery of which the plaintiff was part owner about the availability and price of the Painting. ...

[8] On April 24, 1999 the defendant made an unsolicited written offer to the plaintiff to purchase the Painting.

[9] The offer was for $165,000 and was "... subject to the following conditions for the sole benefit of the Heffel Gallery:

[1] The work is in condition acceptable to Heffel, and Heffel is given an opportunity to physically view and inspect the work at their premise of business.

[2] Heffel is given confirmation that they can purchase the work free and clear of any encumbrances, and Heffel agrees with the confirmation."

...

[11] The encumbrance condition was imposed by Heffel because of concerns he had that resulted from serious allegations reported at the time in the print and electronic media of alleged financial wrongdoing by the plaintiff in regard to his former company, Livent Inc.

[12] Heffel and the plaintiff discussed the initial offer to purchase by telephone and as a result the defendant increased its offer to $180,000 plus GST. The date for waiver of the condition precedent was set at May 5, 1999. All other conditions remained the same.

[13] The revised offer was presented to the plaintiff April 28, 1999 and he accepted.

[14] The Painting was immediately shipped to the defendant in Vancouver. The defendant inspected the Painting and was well satisfied as to its condition.

ENCUMBRANCE CONDITION:

[15] The plaintiff purported to satisfy the encumbrance condition by having Mr. Perelman, a Toronto solicitor with the firm of Goodman & Carr, provide a letter to the defendant dated April 28, 1999. ...

[The judge reviews the correspondence between Mr. Perelman and the solicitors for the defendant gallery. As Heffel had not received what he considered acceptable confirmations that the painting was free and clear of any encumbrances, the plaintiff promised a clear two line opinion from another law firm, Smith Lyons.]

[30] The letter was not the "two clear line opinion" the plaintiff had promised. The plaintiff appears to have obtained and provided the letter with a view to bullying Heffel into accepting the sufficiency of the material Mr. Perelman had forwarded.

[31] The plaintiff followed up the letter by phoning Heffel on May 7, 1999. This call was also recorded. He warned Heffel that if the purchase of the Painting was not concluded he would become "very aggressive".

[32] The plaintiff promised "massive litigation", unfavorable publicity, embarrassment to the defendant by the plaintiff reporting him to his professional dealers association, and he

promised immediately to institute legal action for specific performance and damages. ...

[34] The plaintiff served a Writ and Statement of Claim May 11, 1999 claiming specific performance or damages.

[35] On May 24, 1999 the plaintiff commenced a Rule 18A proceeding for summary judgment seeking only specific performance.

[36] The plaintiff however sold the Painting on June 24, 1999 together with a sketch by the artist for $170,000. The plaintiff values the sketch at $10,000.

[37] The plaintiff now seeks summary judgment for damages consisting of a $20,000 loss on the sale of the Painting together with the legal accounts of the two Toronto law firms he enlisted to provide confirmation of the absence of encumbrances.

THE LAW:

[38] The parties are agreed as to the principles concerning the interpretation of conditions precedent to contract.

[39] The Court of Appeal in *Mark 7 Development Ltd. v. Peace Holdings Ltd.*, [1991] BCJ No. 239 (C.A.), adopted Lambert J.A.'s three category analysis outlined in the appellate decision in *Wiebe v. Bobsien* (1984), 59 B.C.L.R. 183 (B.C.S.C.), upheld on appeal (1985), 64 B.C.L.R. 295.

[40] The three categories for analysis of conditions precedent to contract are:

(a) the conditions are imprecise or entirely subjective;
(b) the conditions are clear, precise and objective; and
(c) the conditions are mixed and contain both objective and subjective features.

[41] If the condition is within category (a) there is no contract and the beneficiary of the contract is not bound in any way.

[42] A binding contract will exist where the condition comes within category (b).

[43] When the condition is within category (c) there may be a binding contract and the Court will imply a term that the beneficiary of the condition is to act reasonably.

[44] Here the condition precedent to be fulfilled is that "...Heffel is given confirmation that they can purchase the work free and clear of any encumbrances, and Heffel agrees with the confirmations". This is both a subjective and objective condition. It comes within category (c) and there is a binding contract with a term implied that Heffel will act reasonably in considering the confirmation of the Painting being capable of purchase free and clear of encumbrances.

[45] The defendant was bound not to withhold its satisfaction unreasonably. [*Griffin v. Martens* (1988), 27 B.C.L.R. (2d) 152 (B.C.C.A.)].

[46] On the authority of T*au Holdings Ltd. v. Alderbridge Development Corp.*, [1991] BCJ No. 2957 (C.A.), the defendant must review the confirmation material provided by the plaintiff and not reject the material arbitrarily but only upon reasonable specified grounds.

[47] In my view the standard to be applied to Heffel's considering if he "agrees" with the "confirmation" provided would be that of a "... reasonable person with all the subjective but reasonable standards of the particular purchaser ..." which is the third of the four rational alternative meanings of the term "satisfactory" outlined by the Court in *Griffin, supra*, at p.154.

ANALYSIS:

... [The judge reviews the various letters, documents and telephone calls received by Heffel.]

[74] I conclude the defendant did consider all information supplied by the plaintiff to satisfy the condition precedent that the Painting was free and clear of all encumbrances. It did so in a timely and businesslike manner. The defendant, or its solicitors, responded promptly to all communications from the plaintiff or his solicitors.

[75] The defendant did not reject information arbitrarily. It did so only upon reasonable grounds and the defendant ar-

ticulated its concerns to the plaintiff or his counsel throughout.

[76] The plaintiff did not fulfill the condition precedent to the contract within the time he himself limited. The defendant did not waive fulfillment of the condition, either within the time limited, or at all.

[77] The plaintiff's failure to meet the condition precedent by May 6, 1999 relieved the defendant of its contractual obligation to complete the purchase of the Painting.

[78] The plaintiff's action is dismissed. ...

E. ACCEPTANCE

Q u e s t i o n s

When is the acceptance effective? Can a message by fax constitute a legal acceptance? How does the court determine which law governs the contract when the parties live in different jurisdictions?

Eastern Power Limited *v.* **Azienda Communale Energia and Ambiente**

http://www.ontariocourts.on.ca/
COURT OF APPEAL FOR ONTARIO
SEPTEMBER 9, 1999

Macpherson, J.A.:

INTRODUCTION

[1] This is an appeal from the judgment of Juriansz J. dated November 26, 1998 in which he set aside service in Italy of a statement of claim by an Ontario company and stayed the company's action in Ontario on *forum non conveniens* grounds. In addition to the standard *forum non conveniens* factors that need to be addressed, the appeal poses the interesting question of where a contract is formed when the acceptance of an offer is communicated by facsimile transmission. Is the contract formed, in accordance with the general rule of contract law, in the place where the acceptance is received? Or should the postal exception to the general rule, which says that a contract is formed when and where an acceptance is placed in the mail, apply to acceptances communicated by facsimile transmission?

A. FACTUAL BACKGROUND

[2] The appellant, Eastern Power Limited ("EP"), is a corporation organized under the laws of Ontario with its principal place of business in Toronto. Its business is the generation of power from non-conventional sources of energy such as landfill gas.

[3] Azienda Communale Energia and Ambiente ("ACEA") is a corporation under the laws of Italy with its principal place of

business in Rome. ACEA provides power to the City of Rome. ...

[4] In September 1994 representatives of ACEA came to Toronto to learn about EP's operations and to explore the possibility of developing power from non-conventional sources in Rome. In order to facilitate these discussions, a confidentiality agreement was prepared and signed. ...

[5] In December 1994 EP met with ACEA in Italy. The parties drafted a Co-Operation Agreement. ACEA signed the agreement on December 9 and faxed it to EP in Ontario. EP signed the agreement in Ontario and faxed it to ACEA in Rome on December 21. It was an express term of the agreement that the two companies would co-operate and use their best efforts to enter into a project agreement. This agreement, relating to the implementation of the alternative energy project, would be based on proposals to be developed by EP and submitted to ACEA for approval. The project was described as "an electricity generating plant fueled by landfill gas, sewage sludge and fossil fuel(s) located near Rome, Italy."

[6] On January 29, 1996 ACEA signed a Letter of Intent relating to the project. The Letter of Intent was faxed by ACEA to EP in Ontario. On February 14 EP accepted and signed the Letter of Intent in Ontario and faxed it back to ACEA in Rome. The Letter of Intent indicated that the parties wanted to proceed with the project and set out how EP would structure itself in order to be permitted to carry out its work in Italy. The Letter of Intent contained these two provisions:

6. The terms of reference between the parties of the new company are governed according to the Joint Venture Agreement which will be later signed by the parties.

7. The intended contents of the present letter are subject to conditions such as:
   a) The acquisition of a favourable written opinion from the Ministry of Industry regarding the award of CIP 6 subsidy to the plant to be built, and also in relation to the Italian Law N. 481 dated 14.11.95 and every subsequent change and integrations. ...

[7] The parties worked to conclude a Joint Venture Agreement. Many drafts were prepared. However, none was ever signed. During these further negotiations EP was concerned that ACEA was not diligently pursuing the important CIP 6 subsidy. On January 24, 1997 the Ministry of Industry amended the subsidy program in a way that made it inapplicable to the proposed joint venture.

[8] On February 14, 1997, ACEA wrote to EP and effectively terminated their relationship. ...

[9] On March 19, 1997 EP forwarded an invoice to ACEA for $478,547 for development and legal costs relating to the project. The time frame for this invoice was stated to be October 1994 – March 1997.

[10] On September 11, 1997 ACEA filed a summons with the Rome Civil Court. The summons essentially seeks a declaration that ACEA has no liability whatsoever to EP. ...

[11] In December 4, 1997 EP commenced its action against ACEA in Ontario. EP sought damages of $750,000 for development costs incurred and $160,000,000 for loss of profits as a result of the alleged negligence and breach of contract by ACEA with respect to the Co-operation Agreement. ...

[13] Juriansz J. ... stayed EP's action in Ontario on *forum non conveniens grounds.*

[14] EP appeals ...

B. ISSUES

[15] The issues on this appeal [include the following question]

Was the motions judge correct to stay EP's action in Ontario on the basis of *forum non conveniens?* ...

C. ANALYSIS

(1) *Forum non conveniens*

[17] On a motion to stay a proceeding on the basis of *forum non conveniens*, the test is whether there is clearly a more appropriate jurisdiction in which the case should be tried than the domestic forum chosen by the plaintiff: ...

[18] In determining which forum, domestic or foreign, is the more appropriate forum, the courts will look at a wide range of factors. The general approach was enunciated by Arbour J.A. in *Frymer v. Brettschneider*, at p. 79:

> The choice of the appropriate forum is designed to ensure that the action is tried in the jurisdiction that has the closest connection with the action and the parties. All

factors pertaining to making this determination must be considered.

[19] What, then, are the relevant factors? [The judge enumerates the factors and then commences to consider each of them.] ...

(a) Location where the contract was signed

[21] The contract which forms the basis of EP's action in contract and tort against ACEA is the Co-operation Agreement ... The motions judge found that the Co-operation Agreement was made in Italy because "acceptance was communicated to Italy." Since EP's acceptance was communicated by facsimile transmission, this raises the interesting question of the legal relationship between a faxed acceptance of an offer and the place where a contract is formed.

[22] The general rule of contract law is that a contract is made in the location where the offeror receives notification of the offeree's acceptance: see Fridman, *The Law of Contract in Canada*, 3rd ed., (1994), at p. 65; and *Re Viscount Supply Co.*, [1963] 1 O.R. 640 (S.C.). However, there is an exception to this general rule. It is the postal acceptance rule. As expressed by Ritchie J. in *Imperial Life Assurance Co. of Canada v. Colmenares*, [1967] S.C.R. 443 at 447:

> It has long been recognized that when contracts are to be concluded by post the place of mailing the acceptance is to be treated as the place where the contract was made.

See also: Fridman, *The Law of Contract in Canada*, supra, at pp. 67–68.

[23] EP contends that the rule with respect to facsimile transmissions should follow the postal acceptance exception. With respect, I disagree. EP has cited no authority in support of its position. There is, however, case authority for the proposition that acceptance by facsimile transmission should follow the general rule, which would mean that a contract is formed when and where acceptance is received by the offeror.

[24] In *Brinkibon Ltd. v. Stahag Stahl G.m.b.H.*, [1983] 2 A.C. 34 (H.L.), a contract was concluded when the buyer in London transmitted its acceptance to the seller in Vienna. The mode of acceptance was a message sent by telex, a form of instantaneous communication like the telephone. The law lords were unanimous in concluding that the contract was formed in Vienna where the acceptance was received by the offeror. Lord Brandon of Oakbrook analyzed the issue [and followed *Entores Ltd. v. Miles Far East Corporation* which held that when an offer is accepted by telex, the contract is made at the place where the telex was received.] ...

[25] In my view, this analysis is equally applicable to facsimile transmissions, another form of instantaneous communication. ...

[27] ... I would hold that in contract law an acceptance by facsimile transmission should follow the general rule of contract formation, not the postal acceptance exception.

[28] I do not say that this rule should be an absolute one; like Lord Wilberforce in his separate speech in *Brinkibon*, "I think it a sound rule, but not necessarily a universal rule." (p. 42). Lord Wilberforce discussed some of the factors that might suggest caution about applying the general rule to telex commu-

nications in all cases, including the many variants in such communications and whether the message was sent and received by the principals to the contemplated contract. However, he concluded, at p. 42:

> The present case is ... the simple case of instantaneous communication between principals, and, in accordance with the general rule, involves that the contract (if any) was made when and where the acceptance was received.

[29] In my view, the present appeal is also "the simple case." The acceptance was faxed by the principals of EP in Ontario to the principals of ACEA in Italy. There is nothing to suggest that the communication between these principals was not instantaneous. Hence, applying the general rule, the contract was formed in Italy.

(b) The applicable law of the contract

[30] The Co-operation Agreement contained no provision specifying which system of law, Ontario or Italy, was to govern issues arising under it. In such a situation, a court must infer which jurisdiction should be the proper law of the contract. In reaching a conclusion on the proper law, the court will consider a number of direct and contextual factors. ...

[31] In my view, the motions judge was alive to the full range of factors as he determined the proper law. ...He made a full and careful analysis of the factors. ...

[32] ... They point overwhelmingly to the conclusion [that] ...: the proper law of the contract was Italian law.

[The court then considers]
(c) Location where the majority of witnesses reside (Italy);
(d) Location of key witnesses (neutral);
(e) The location where the bulk of the evidence will come from (no conclusion)
(f) The jurisdiction in which the factual matters arose (favours Italy)
(g) The residence or place of business of the parties (neutral)
(h) Loss of juridical advantage [EP will suffer no juridical loss].

CONCLUSION

[50] Of the eight factors I have considered, five tell in favour of ACEA. Four of the five strike me as particularly important factors—the location where the contract was formed, the law of the contract, the jurisdiction in which factual matters arose, and the absence of a loss of juridical advantage for EP. The other three factors are neutral. No factors favour EP's position. Accordingly, the motions judge was correct to stay EP's action in Ontario on *forum non conveniens* grounds. ...

DISPOSITION

[56] I would dismiss the appeal with costs.

Unanimous

Note: The Supreme Court of Canada has refused to hear an appeal.

- *A* resident of Ontario vacationing on an American cruise line was injured on a tour bus in Grenada. Where should the plaintiff's action be heard? The court held that Ontario was the convenient forum for the action because it would be reasonable for the tour operators to assume that injured tourists would most likely return home to sue.[8]

- *A* purchaser in Manitoba bought computer software from a company in Ontario by credit card over the telephone. The packet was wrapped in a license agreement which stated that the contract would be governed by the laws of Ontario. The software was defective. The purchaser began an action in the Manitoba courts and argued that Manitoba was the proper jurisdiction because the contract was completed over the telephone and the license agreement on the package could not add terms to the contract.

    The court held that the seller could not have been expected to read all of the terms over the telephone and the seller had made it clear that opening the package had legal consequences. Therefore the terms were part of the contract and thus the matter was governed by the laws of Ontario and outside the jurisdiction of the Manitoba courts.[9]

- *Y*our electronic signature will have legal force when it complies with "e-sign" legislation already in force in some provinces. This legislation is augmented by a service provided by Juricert Services Inc., incorporated by the Law Society of British Columbia, which allows lawyers to affix an electronic "seal" to an e-mail message that assures the receiver of the identity of the sender and the authenticity of the document.[10]

3. CONSIDERATION

Degoesbriand v. Radford

SASKATCHEWAN COURT OF APPEAL
SEPTEMBER 16, 1986
UNREPORTED

Gerwing, J.A. (Orally)

The appellant appeals from a judgment dismissing her claim against the respondent, a shareholder in the company by which she was formerly employed, for a declaration that she was entitled to 5% of the shares owned by him in that company, on the alternate basis of either contract or constructive trust. ...

The appellant had worked for two companies, in which the respondent was interested, between 1979 and 1982. She testified that the respondent had promised to give to her 5% of his shares in the business when he either sold out or retired. Although the respondent denied this the learned trial judge accepted that such promises were made. He said:

> I conclude after considering the testimony of the witnesses, and particularly the evidence of Mr. Wall and Mr. Thomson, that the defendant did indeed state to the plaintiff he would give her five per cent of the shares of the business he was then involved in at some time in the future. I am not satisfied, however, this statement occurred as often as the plaintiff claims and I cannot [accept] her evidence it was made within one week of her becoming employed by the defendant.

The learned trial judge also found that the appellant had worked in excess of reasonable overtime, but then quoted from her examination for discovery [in which she admitted she would have worked just as hard even if she had not been promised the five percent of the company.]

The learned trial judge concludes that the promise was made after the relationship of employer-employee was already in existence, and also that the promise was not made to induce the appellant to work extra overtime. He concludes that there was no action by the appellant in reliance on, or in consideration for this promise. He also found as a fact that the appellant did not intend any promise he made to create a legal obligation.

This conclusion, however, falls short of holding a legally enforceable contract existed between the parties. The defendant on no occasion stated his promise was contingent on the plaintiff's continuing to work more than reasonable overtime nor did the plaintiff perform these duties as a result of the promise being made. It was only after their cordial relationship cooled, did the plaintiff claim the defendant was legally obliged to give her the shares in return for the hours of extra overtime she provided. The defendant may owe some moral obligation to the plaintiff, however, I am not satisfied the obligation arises from a contract between them.

On the facts as found by the learned trial judge, we are of the view that he was correct to dismiss the contractual claim. He found a bare promise by the respondent to the appellant, with no consideration requested or received by him from the appellant. The suggestion that in some way he made this conditional on performance of extra overtime by the appellant, and that performance of this overtime was a method of accepting this offer, was found by the learned trial judge to be only in the mind of the appellant, arising at a later time after the relationship had terminated.

Further, her services as an employee were already the subject of an employment contract which required her to work a reasonable amount of overtime. There was no evidence she did anything that she was not already contractually obliged to do, or that she was not prepared to do in any event, to do her job properly, in reliance on the promise of the respondent. There was nothing to provide consideration or raise the doctrine of estoppel, and the bare promise remained just that and was unenforceable as a contract. In light of the lack of consideration, it is not necessary to comment on the question of lack of congruence between the offer and acceptance or the question of intention to create a contract.

... In the result, the appeal is dismissed with costs. ...

- *A* woman in Kansas was charged with "criminal solicitation to commit murder." In exchange for the killing of her common-law husband she offered to give the killers his baseball card collection. She gave them ten cards as a down payment.[11]

- *I*f you get a parking ticket in Vancouver, you cannot pay your fine in Mexican pesos. Charles Jefferson's attempt to pay a $25 parking ticket in Mexican pesos, in coin, was refused. Nor did he win when he took his argument to the justice of the peace, or to the B.C. Supreme Court, or to the B.C. Court of Appeal which refused to hear his appeal.[12]

PROMISSORY ESTOPPEL

Central London Property Trust Limited	*v.*	**High Trees House Limited**

[1947] 1 K.B. 130

Denning J.

By a lease under seal made on September 24, 1937, the plaintiffs, Central London Property Trust Ld., granted to the defendants, High Trees House Ltd., a subsidiary of the plaintiff company, a tenancy of a block of flats for the term of ninety-nine years from September 29, 1937, at a ground rent of £2,500 a year. The block of flats was a new one and had not been fully occupied at the beginning of the war owing to the absence of people from London. With war conditions prevailing, it was apparent to those responsible that the rent reserved under the lease could not be paid out of the profits of the flats and, accordingly, discussion took place between the directors of the two companies concerned, which were closely associated, and an arrangement was made between them which was put into writings. On January 3, 1940, the plaintiffs wrote to the defendants in these terms, "we confirm the arrangement made between us by which the ground rent should be reduced as from the commencement of the lease to £1,250 per annum," and on April 2, 1940, a confirmatory resolution to the same effect was passed by the plaintiff company. On March 20, 1941, a receiver was appointed by the debenture holders of the plaintiffs and on his death on February 28, 1944, his place was taken by his partner. The defendants paid the reduced rent from 1941 down to the beginning of 1945 by which time all the flats in the block were fully let, and continued to pay it thereafter. In September, 1945, the then receiver of the plaintiff company looked into the matter of the lease and ascertained that the rent actually reserved by it was £2,500. On September 21, 1945, he wrote to the defendants saying that rent must be paid at the full rate and claiming that arrears amounting to £7,916 were due. Subsequently, he instituted the present friendly proceedings to test the legal position in regard to the rate at which rent was payable. In the action the plaintiffs sought to recover £625, being the amount represented by the difference between rent at the rate of £2,500 and £1,250 per annum for the quarters ending September 29, and December 25, 1945. ... [Accepting that the lessors promised to forgive half the rent during the war years, the court considers whether] they had waived their rights in respect of any rent, in excess of that at the rate of 1,250£, which had accrued up to September 24, 1945. ...

There has been a series of decisions over the last fifty years which, although they are said to be cases of estoppel are not really such. In each case the court held the promise to be binding on the party making it, even though under the old common law it might be difficult to find any consideration for it. The courts have not gone so far as to give a cause of action in damages for the breach of such a promise, but they have refused to allow the party making it to act inconsistently with it. It is in that sense, and that sense only, that such a promise gives rise to an estoppel. The decisions are a natural result of the fusion of law and equity: for the cases of *Hughes v. Metropolitan Ry. Co.* (6) *Birmingham and District Land Co. v. London & Northwestern Ry. Co.* (7) and *Salisbury (Marquess) v. Gilmore* (8), afford a sufficient basis for saying that a party would not be allowed in equity to go back on such a promise. In my opinion, the time has now come for the validity of such a promise to be recognized. The logical consequence, no doubt is that a promise to accept a smaller sum in discharge of a larger sum, if acted upon, is binding notwithstanding the absence of consideration: and if the fusion of law and equity leads to this result, so much the better. That aspect was not considered in *Foakes v. Beer* (1). At this time of day however, when law and equity have been joined together for over seventy years, principles must be reconsidered in the light of their combined effect. It is to be noticed that in the Sixth Interim Report of the Law Revision Committee, pars. 35, 40, it is recommended that such a promise as that to which I have referred, should be enforceable in law even though no consideration for it has been given by the promisee. It seems to me that, to the extent I have mentioned, that result has now been achieved by the decisions of the courts.

I am satisfied that a promise such as that to which I have referred is binding and the only question remaining for my consideration is the scope of the promise in the present case. ...

I prefer to apply the principle that a promise intended to be binding, intended to be acted on and in fact acted on, is binding so far as its terms properly apply. Here it was binding as covering the period down to the early part of 1945, and as from that time full rent is payable.

Judgment for plaintiffs.

Note: Judgment is for full rent from early 1945 but not for the rent forgiven during the war years.

When the corporate tenant, Med-Chem, was assigned into bankruptcy, the landlord filed proofs of claim for the rent in arrears on three premises rented by the tenant. The lease showed a rent higher than the tenant actually paid. The Registrar determined that the landlord could file a Proof of Claim for $232,571.71—the difference between the rents paid by the tenant and the amounts set out in the leases. The following are the excerpts from the court hearing the appeal from the Registrar's decision.

[10] Having reviewed the evidence, I am satisfied that the doctrines of promissory estoppel and waiver apply here. There was a course of conduct over an extended period that showed an intention by the landlord not to rely on the strict terms of the lease with respect to the amount of the rent. There was also reliance by the tenant, shown by its payment of the rents specified in the schedule provided to its controller. More precisely, according to the evidence before the Registrar, the same rents had been paid by Med-Chem from November, 1996—a period of more than two years before the bankruptcy. These rents were always the same and never those prescribed in the offers to lease. Dr. Alvi was the principal of both the landlord company and the tenant, and it was his personal assistant who had instructed the tenant's controller as to the amounts of rent to be paid. Not only were those amounts paid without protest for two years by Med-Chem; the same amounts had been paid by MSL, another Alvi company, before that . ... At the time that Med-Chem purchased the assets of MSL, Dr. Alvi signed a document, in his capacity as landlord, stating that there was no outstanding breach of any obligation of the tenant under the lease. Therefore, the landlord is estopped from claiming the higher rent at this time.

[11] Closely connected to the doctrine of promissory estoppel is the doctrine of waiver. The Registrar concluded that this doctrine could not apply because the landlord was mistaken with respect to its legal rights. However, a review of the evidence shows that there is no evidence of what the landlord thought in respect of the amount of rent. ... In the circumstances, the logical inference to be drawn from those facts and the lengthy course of conduct between the landlord and tenant was that the acceptable rent was the amount actually paid by the tenant, not that set out in the written offers to lease.

[12] Moreover, even where parties are mistaken with respect to their rights, the courts have at times applied the doctrine of estoppel. ... On the facts here, both the landlord and the tenant have conducted themselves as if the correct rents were those actually paid by Med-Chem. In these circumstances, it would be inequitable to revert to the terms of the written leases now, given their course of conduct. ...

[15] The appeal is allowed, and the Registrar's order is set aside.

Med-Chem Health Care Inc. (Re)
[2000] O.J. No. 4009 (Q.L.)
Ontario Superior Court
October 24, 2000

4. Capacity

Re Collins

Supreme Court of British Columbia
Vancouver Registry # A913069
October 21, 1991

Holmes, J.: The Petitioner Andrea Collins ("Ms. Collins") is the mother of the Petitioner [S.] Collins, an infant aged 15. S and his sister [J] Collins, 19 years of age, are parties to a contract dated December 11, 1989 with Ms. Collins the subject matter of which involves the infants interest in a residential property in Vancouver which is owned by a trust created irrevocably by their father Philip Collins. The contract was unenforceable from inception as both S and J (collectively hereafter referred to as "the children") were minors at that date. A letter of August 9, 1991 purportedly affirming the contract and stated to be pursuant to Section 16.2 (1) (b) of the *Infants Act* was signed by J the day after she reached the age of majority. As S remains an infant the contract is unenforceable against him and the purpose of the Petition is to make the contract enforceable by obtaining an Order under Section 16.4 (1) (b) of the *Infants Act* granting to S: "capacity to enter into a contract. …specified in the order."

Counsel for Philip Collins and the Public Trustee both are opposed to the Court granting the Order. …

THE FACTS:

Ms. Collins married Philip Collins in England in September 1975, they separated in 1979, and were divorced in August 1980. … As a consequence of her divorce from Philip Collins the Petitioner received a lump sum settlement of £100,000 and spousal support of £8,000 per annum. … Ms. Collins wished to move to Vancouver. … The cost of houses the Petitioner considered suitable were beyond her means and she was " … also concerned about the lack of financial security afforded her by the terms of the previous Orders." Discussions ensued with Philip Collins regarding his possible contribution towards the purchase of a residential property. The Petitioner located a suitable house and Philip Collins paid the $750,000 purchase price and created an irrevocable trust "Collins Children's Trust" to hold title with the Canada Trust Company as Trustee. The purpose of the Trust was to provide a home for J, S and Ms. Collins until S (the youngest child) reached age 20 at which time S and J would receive the property absolutely as tenants in common. Ms. Collins signed a License Agreement requiring her to pay property taxes and cost of maintenance repairs.

… Ms. Collins and the children moved into the house in September 1987 and Ms. Collins remains unhappy about what she considers was a misunderstanding as to the ownership interest she felt was promised in the house. … The unhappiness and insecurity of Ms. Collins in respect of the property became known to J and S. I am uncertain precisely how that occurred but assume she told them and the three of them discussed the matter. … [After visiting both a psychologist who assessed the children's' state of mind and a lawyer, the children signed the contract.]

The contract of December 11, 1989 provides that the children transfer their beneficial interest in the Collins Children's Trust to Ms. Collins when their interest vests. In return Ms. Collins agrees to provide financial support for their reasonable maintenance, care, education and benefit until they are age 25. … Ms. Collins also agrees to create a trust in favour of the children which will see the property, or its remainder, returned to them if she should remarry or die. Ms. Collins is Trustee under the Agreement with extremely wide and unfettered powers, including a power:

3.01 (b) "until the Material DATE (her death or remarriage)…in her absolute discretion, encroach upon the capital of the Trust Property and pay or transfer any amount or amounts of the capital…to or for the benefit of Andrea Collins…as the Trustee, in her absolute discretion, shall determine.

(c) Notwithstanding the generality of clause 3.01 (b), the Trustee may encroach upon the Trust Property to such an extent that the Trust Property is completely distributed and used up.

THE LAW

The relevant provision of the *Infants Act* is Section 16.4(1)(b) and (2):

The court may, on an application on behalf of an infant, make an order granting to the infant…capacity to enter into a contract…(but the Court must be) satisfied that it is for the benefit of the infant and that having regard to the circumstances of the infant, he is not in need of the protection offered by law to infants in matters relating to contracts.

It is obvious that the court's power is discretionary, but to grant the infant capacity to contract it is mandatory that:

(a) the contract be for his benefit, and
(b) considering the infant's circumstances does not need the protection accorded by the law to infants relating to contracts.

Counsel advised that they knew of no case law concerning this section which would be of assistance. Counsel also agree that the phrase "…for the benefit of the infant…" is to be given the same meaning at law as "…in the best interests of the infant…". Counsel for the Public Trustee argues there is a presumption in law that an infant is under the influence of a parent or guardian. I agree there is such a presumption however I concur with Petitioner's counsel that is a rebuttable presumption, and the opinion and evidence of Dr. Elterman [the psychologist] and Mr. Martin [the lawyer] supports the view there was no undue influence or pressure by Ms. Collins and both children fully understood the agreement and wished to enter into it.

I accept S is an intelligent young man who does understand the legal implication of his intended contract. He is not under direct compulsion, duress, or undue influence in respect of his agreement to sign. It is my view however that it was Ms. Collins who set a chain of events in motion by in some manner making it known to S and J how unhappy and insecure she felt because Philip Collins had not given her an ownership interest in the property. The inference has to be that in some manner the children received what she was promised and entitled to. I have no concern as to whether she is right in a moral context, I do have concern that the remedy for her insecurity has involved the children.

I view the contract of December 11, 1989 as a thinly disguised attempt to vary the trust set up by Philip Collins. … In my view the Court's discretionary power should not be exercised on a pretext of being for the benefit of the infants when in essence it is to have Ms. Collins achieve financial security.

The consequence of the agreement of December 11, 1989 is essentially that S would be giving up to Ms. Collins an interest in property which will vest in him within 5 years that has a present market value in excess of $700,000. Ms. Collins would have the ability to encroach upon that property for her exclusive benefit so there might be no reversion to him at all … In my view it is in the circumstances here insulting to suggest that this contract is of any financial benefit to S.

It is suggested that the emotional well being of S is best served by Ms. Collins being happy and secure, and that he genuinely wishes that to be so. I am sure that is true, as it would be in any family relationship. I cannot justify S giving away his interest in the trust to purchase that feeling of security for Ms. Collins. I see no benefit to S in the contract in question. I am of the opinion it is not in his best interest.

The decision to give up as substantial an asset as his interest in this trust is one to be reserved until he reaches the age of majority. Should he feel then, as he does now, he is free to make that gift. If his view, or the circumstances, change in the next five years he is not bound to an improvident contract.

The Petition is dismissed with costs. ...

---

5. LEGALITY

Question

In what ways is a contract or a provision of a contract illegal?

A. IF THE PURPOSE OF THE CONTRACT IS TO DEFRAUD

Cerilli v. *Klodt*

(1984) 48 O.R. (2D) 260
ONTARIO HIGH COURT
OCTOBER 17, 1984

Southey J. (orally): — This is an action for specific performance of an agreement for the sale by the defendants to the plaintiff of a house property at 242 Ester St. in Sudbury, owned by the defendants as joint tenants....

On [the] evidence, I find as a fact that the plaintiff Cerilli was party to a scheme with the male defendant Robert Klodt whereby a false price of $45,200 would be stated in the agreement of purchase and sale and other formal documents relating to the transaction so that the female defendant Sheila Klodt would be deceived into thinking that Mr. Cerilli was paying only $45,200. The balance of $4,800 was to be paid by the plaintiff directly to the male defendant without the knowledge of Mrs. Klodt, in the hope that Mr. Klodt could thereby avoid her obtaining any portion of that $4,800.

This scheme, in my judgment, was clearly fraudulent, and the result in law is that the agreement between the plaintiff and Robert Klodt is void and unenforceable in the courts. I think it is necessary to refer only to the passage from the decision of the Court of Appeal in England in *Alexander v. Rayson*, [1936] 1 K.B. 169, which was quoted and applied by the Supreme Court of Canada in *Zimmermann v. Letkeman*, [1978] 1 S.C.R. 1097 at p. 1101, 79 D.L.R. (3d) 508 at p. 519, [1977] 6 W.W.R. 741. Mr. Justice Martland, delivering the judgment of the court, quoted from the decision of Lord Justice Romer in the *Alexander v. Rayson* case as follows:

> It is settled law that an agreement to do an act that is illegal or immoral or contrary to public policy, or to do any act for a consideration that is illegal, immoral or contrary to public policy, is unlawful and therefore void. But it often happens that an agreement which in itself is not unlawful is made with the intention of one or both parties to make use of the subject matter for an unlawful purpose, that is to say a purpose that is illegal, immoral or contrary to

public policy. The most common instance of this is an agreement for the sale or letting of an object, where the agreement is unobjectionable on the face of it, but where the intention of both or one of the parties is that the object shall be used by the purchaser or hirer for an unlawful purpose. In such a case any party to the agreement who had the unlawful intention is precluded from suing upon it. *Ex turpi causa non oritur actio.** The action does not lie because the Court will not lend its help to such a plaintiff. Many instances of this are to be found in the books. ...

...[W]hen the fact that Mr. Cerilli had agreed to pay a total of $50,000 became known, Mrs. Klodt, through her solicitor, Mr. Rivard, confirmed that she was prepared to sell her one-half interest in the matrimonial home to Mr. Cerilli on a basis of a purchase price of $50,000. ...

It is clear from the authorities to which Mr. Humphrey referred, however, that the court is under an obligation to refuse to give effect to an illegal agreement whenever the illegality comes to the attention of the court, even though the parties do not raise it. See the judgment of Mr. Justice Krever in *Menard et al. v. Genereux et al.* (1982), 39 O.R. (2d) 55 at p. 64, 138 D.L.R. (3d) 273 at p. 283, where he quotes from a decision of the Court of Appeal of Saskatchewan in *Williams v. Fleetwood Holdings Ltd. et al.* (1973), 41 D.L.R. (3d) 636 at p. 640 [quoting from *Alexander v. Rayson, supra*, at p. 190]:

> The moment that the attention of the Court is drawn to the illegality attending the execution of the lease, it is bound to take notice of it, whether such illegality be pleaded or not. ...

Action dismissed.

*This clause means that from an illegal matter no action can arise.

Note: This decision was affirmed by the Ontario Court of Appeal.

B. *IF THE PERSON WAS ENGAGED IN AN ILLEGAL ACTIVITY*

Boyd v. *Newton*

NEW WESTMINSTER REGISTRY NO. C900402
SUPREME COURT OF BRITISH COLUMBIA
NOVEMBER, 1991

Selbie, J. (In Chambers) This action is for negligence in the operation of a motor-vehicle or, in the alternative, damages for assault and battery. I.C.B.C. applies under Rule 18A that the action be dismissed against it on the basis that the claim is barred by the application of the defense *ex turpi causa non oritur actio* [out of an illegal consideration no action can arise].

This action is about a drug "rip-off." The plaintiff, Boyd, was trafficking in marijuana at a local billiards arcade in Coquitlam. As usual, while waiting for buyers he was playing the video games. He had been there for about five hours. As well as selling the drug he was performing another function for other traffickers—"I just sit there and play video games all day and so people that deal dope up there used to put their drugs on top of the video games. So I got paid a gram for watching drugs." About nine o'clock a stranger approached him about buying some "grass." Boyd told him he had a gram he could have and the price was settled at $10. The driver of the buyer's car was to pay. Boyd gave over the gram of marijuana and both proceeded outside to a car driven by the defendant Newton. The buyer entered the passenger's seat and Boyd approached the open driver's door to get his $10. He stood in the gap between the door and the car frame waiting for his money. Newton suddenly pushed Boyd away and tried to drive off. Boyd, for the purpose of detaining Newton and getting his money, grabbed Newton by his coat and then grabbed the door frame to keep his balance as the car was driven away. He suffered injuries as he was dragged down the street. In effect, in fighting over the closing of an illegal transaction, he was injured. … This is not a situation, for instance, where, after a deal was closed, the car in leaving negligently ran over the trafficker's foot. There it could be argued that the injury had no causal connection with the drug deal and the maxim would, arguably, not apply. Here the injuries were directly caused by the action of Boyd in trying to detain Newton in order to complete the transaction.

"No Court will lend its aid to a man who founds his action upon an immoral or an illegal act"—Lord Mansfield in *Holman v. Johnson* (1775) 1 Cowp 342 as quoted by Gibbs JA in *Hall v. Hebert* B.C.C.A., (unreported), Vancouver Registry #CA010498, February 1, 1991. The principle is founded upon public policy.

Gibbs JA in *Hall v. Hebert* (supra), in discussing the maxim, said at p. 12 of the judgment:

> … the principle underlying *ex turpi causa* is not limited to circumstances where the injuries were sustained during the course of a joint criminal enterprise. The compass of the defence is much broader. It will be available wherever the conduct of the plaintiff giving rise to the claim is so tainted with criminality or culpable immorality that as a matter of public policy the court will not assist him to recover. The joint criminal enterprise ground is merely an example, and perhaps the most common example, of public policy at work.

In the instant case the injuries *were* "sustained during the course of a joint criminal enterprise" and not "after" as is argued. This then is one of those common examples spoken of by his Lordship which give rise to the maxim as a defense.

Speaking of the doctrine of *ex turpi causa* Taylor J. (as he then was) in *Mack v. Enns* (1981) 30 B.C.L.R. 337 at 344 said:

> The purpose of the rule to-day must be to defend the integrity of the legal system, and the repute in which the court ought to be held by law-abiding members of the community. It is properly applied in those circumstances in which it would be manifestly unacceptable to fair-minded, or right-thinking, people that a court should lend assistance to a plaintiff who has defied the law.

It is proper to apply it here. The application of the Third Party, the Insurance Corporation of British Columbia, is allowed and the action is dismissed as against it.

- *M*r. Andres sued his brother for breach of contract for failing to oversee the reconstruction of his house damaged by fire and to perform the necessary carpentry work in a workmanlike manner. The contract provided that in exchange for this work Andres would provide him with room and board and $10 per hour. Unfortunately for his case, Andres knew this arrangement would facilitate the brother's ability to wrongfully receive workers' compensation payments and to avoid paying income tax.[13]

C. *IF THE CONTRACT IS CONTRARY TO STATUTE*

- "Dynamite Donny Lalonde," later featured as "Golden Boy," was able to have an agreement declared unenforceable because it was not in writing, signed by the parties and approved as being "fair and reasonable" by the Boxing Commission contrary to the provisions of the *Boxing and Wrestling Commission Act*, R.S.M. The alleged contract allowed the defendant to take 50% of the net proceeds from ten fights which he was to promote and produce and 30% of the "total purse" earned by Lalonde even if he did nothing. The wisdom of the legislators is apparent.[14]

D.   *IF THE CONTRACT OR A PROVISION IS IN RESTRAINT OF TRADE*

 See the Ben Johnson case on p. 29 for a concise statement of the law on restraint of trade.

6. THE WRITING REQUIREMENT

Questions

Do all contracts have to be in writing? If there is an oral agreement that the parties want to put in writing, is the written document the contract or just evidence of the earlier oral contract?

Gendis Inc. **v.** *Richardson Oil & Gas Ltd.*

[2000] M.J. No. 328 (Q.L.)
MANITOBA COURT OF APPEAL
JUNE 19, 2000

[1] Monnin J.A.:— The issue in this appeal is whether or not the trial judge was in error in finding that the parties had negotiated a valid contract for the sale of shares in a privately held company. ...

[3] Since January 1, 1989, the appellant (Richardson) and the respondent (Gendis) had each held 50 per cent of the shares in Tundra Oil and Gas Ltd. (Tundra), a privately held company. ...

[7] ... Allan MacKenzie [for Gendis] and George Richardson ... agreed that Richardson would purchase the shares of Gendis for $39 million, plus two incentive payments of up to $1 million each if oil prices averaged $27 in the last six months of 1999 and $28 in the last six months of 2000. Upon reaching this agreement George Richardson told Allan MacKenzie that "we have a deal" and the two men then shook hands. Both businessmen further agreed that Gendis would provide Richardson with a written document to confirm and detail the transaction that they had agreed upon on that day.

[8] On the Monday following this meeting Allan MacKenzie sent to Richardson a document that, in his words, purported to structure the agreement reached. The document included three clauses which Richardson maintains changed the agreement that had been reached and which justified Richardson's refusal to complete the deal. ...

[The judge reviews the additional clauses inserted in the written document and finds that they were not part of the oral agreement but their inclusion was not a legal basis for refusing to complete the deal.]

[13] On the issue of the validity of the agreement itself the trial judge reached the following conclusions at paras. 27–29:

> The authorities generally show circumstances where essential terms had not been agreed upon or where the oral agreement was on condition that a formal document would be prepared and signed. I conclude that all of the cases cited can be distinguished on the facts. I

am satisfied, based on Mr. Richardson's evidence, that the written document to be prepared by the plaintiff was not a prerequisite to the contract being consummated. The written document was only for the purpose of identifying the terms of the agreement made between the parties on February 26 and 27, 1998.

The general principle of law with regard to finding whether the parties have entered into a binding contract is discussed by Lord Maugham in the case of *G. Scammell & Nephew Ltd. v. Ouston et al.*, [1941] A.C. 251 at p. 255:

> In order to constitute a valid contract the parties must so express themselves that their meaning can be determined with a reasonable degree of certainty. It is plain that unless this can be done it would be impossible to hold that the contracting parties had the same intention; in other words the consensus ad idem would be a matter of mere conjecture. This general rule, however applies somewhat differently in different cases. In commercial documents connected with dealings in a trade with which the parties are perfectly familiar the court is very willing, if satisfied that the parties thought that they made a binding contract, to imply terms and in particular terms as to the method of carrying out the contract. ...

In my opinion, the circumstances of this case are such that the above principle is applicable to the contract entered into by the parties in this trial.

I find that the contract (agreement) entered into by Mr. Richardson for the plaintiff's shares in Tundra identifies the parties and the price of $39 million in cash plus the incentive clause as set forth in the written agreement. The closing date requested by Mr. Richardson was two to three weeks after February 27, 1998, namely, any date between March 20 and March 31, 1998. The court will supply the closing date as March 31,1998.

[14] On this appeal Richardson argues that the trial judge erred in finding that the agreement reached by George Richardson with Allan MacKenzie on February 26, 1998 was a valid and binding final agreement. Richardson argues that the understanding arrived at on February 26, 1998 could not be binding as it was to be followed up by a written agreement, which written agreement, as the facts demonstrate, was never executed. Furthermore, Richardson argues that Gendis, by including clauses 3, 6 and 9 in the agreement, was still in the process of negotiating the terms of the contract and therefore the parties never reached an agreement. ...

[The court reviews the arguments and case law relied on by Richardson and the evidence regarding the subject matter in the unexpected clauses.]

[21] I do not take issue with the principles established in these decisions which Richardson relies upon. What, however, must not be forgotten is that all of these principles find their roots in factual situations. The case before us is no different. There are contract cases that make their way before the courts in which great and sometimes innovative principles of law are established. This is not such a case. The determination of this case is to be found on the facts, and absent an overriding and palpable error by a trial judge, an appellate court should not interfere with factfindings of a trial judge. . . .

[22] In *G. Scammell & Nephew Ltd. v. Ouston et al.,* [supra] Lord Wright puts into succinct language the circumstances in which a court should interfere and find that a contract between two parties did not exist:

There are in my opinion two grounds on which the court ought to hold that there was never a contract. The first is that the language used was so obscure and so incapable of any definite or precise meaning that the court is unable to attribute to the parties any particular contractual intention. The object of the court is to do justice between the parties, and the court will do its best, if satisfied that there was an ascertainable and determinate intention to contract, to give effect to that intention, looking at substance and not mere form. It will not be deterred by mere difficulties of interpretation. Difficulty is not synonymous with ambiguity so long as any definite meaning can be extracted. But the test of intention is to be found in the words used. If these words, considered however broadly and untechnically and with due regard to all the just implications, fail to evince any definite meaning on which the court can safely act, the court has no choice but to say that there is no contract. Such a position is not often found. ...

But I think the other reason, which is that the parties never in intention nor even in appearance reached an agreement, is a still sounder reason against enforcing the claim. In truth, in my opinion, their agreement was inchoate and never got beyond negotiations.

[26] ... In the words of Lord Wright in *Scammell,* there existed an ascertainable and determinative intention to contract between Richardson and Gendis and that intention was clear, precise and fixed. The trial judge made no error in finding that a valid and binding contract existed. ...

[32] I would, therefore, dismiss the appeal on all grounds, with costs to Gendis.

Unanimous

THE STATUTE OF FRAUDS

Q u e s t i o n

What is the significance of the Statute of Frauds?

Hoffer v. *Verdone*

[1994] O.J. No. 1967 (Q.L.)
ONTARIO COURT OF JUSTICE — GENERAL DIVISION
AUGUST 12, 1994

[1] Salhany J.:— Over two centuries ago Mr. Justice Wilmot decried that "Had the Statute of Frauds been always carried into execution according to the letter, it would have done ten times more mischief than it has done good, by protecting, rather than preventing fraud:" *Simon v. Motivos* (1766) 97 E.R. 1170. In this action the plaintiff claims that the defendant John Verdone promised to convey to her a condominium unit in exchange for marketing services rendered on behalf of the defendants. The defendant denies that there was any such agreement. But he also says that if he did agree to do so, that agreement is barred by the Statute of Frauds because it was an oral agreement with respect to an interest in land. At issue

in this action is whether the invocation of the Statute of Frauds by the defendant will protect or prevent fraud. ...

FINDINGS

[11] The first issue that has to be determined is whether there was an agreement between the plaintiff and John Verdone that the plaintiff be given unit 37 of the Treetops Project in exchange for marketing services rendered by her to the project. As I have already said, it was conceded by the defence that the plaintiff and Mr. Verdone contemplated moving into two units side by side at Crabtree Keys Project. I am satisfied that Mr. Verdone led the plaintiff to believe that she would get one of the units in exchange for her marketing services and that they discussed how this could be done in view of the fact that the condominiums were legally owned by VHL Construction Ltd. and that Angelo Verdone was a one-half owner of the company. It would seem natural to me that he, planning to marry the plaintiff, or at least giving her the impression that he intended to do so, would lead her to believe that they would set up living arrangements side by side and that he would find a way to ensure that she would have a unit in exchange for her marketing services. The defendant conceded that they discussed putting a door between the units so that they could go back and forth. Moreover, I am also satisfied that after the Crabtree Keys project was abandoned and the Treetops initiated, John Verdone continued to make the same promises to the plaintiff with respect to unit 13 and later unit 37. ...

DECISION

[13] Mr. Thomson, [counsel for the defendants] relying on the Statue of Frauds, argued that if there was any agreement, it was unenforceable. ...

[14] The agreement between the plaintiff and Mr. Verdone was, understandably, not reduced to writing because of their relationship and because of the difficulties that Mr. Verdone would have to eventually face in transferring title from the corporate defendant to the plaintiff. There is no memorandum relied upon by the plaintiff that would satisfy the requirements of the Statute of Frauds.

[15] The plaintiff relied upon the doctrine of part performance. The theory of part performance is that it tends to show that the contract really was made and is thus within the spirit of the Statute: See Waddams, *The Law of Contract*, 2nd ed. at p. 173. However, the law is clear that the acts relied upon as part performance must tend to corroborate proof of the agreement. To corroborate proof of the agreement, Canadian authorities have insisted that the acts of performance must not merely show, on balance, that there is an underlying contract between the parties but that "the acts are unequivocally or necessarily referable to some dealing with the land in question:" *Dealman v. Guaranty Trust Co. of Canada* [1954], 3 D.L.R. 785 (S.C.C.).

[16] [The judge reviews the facts submitted by the plaintiff.]

I am not satisfied that any of these acts relied upon by the plaintiff were necessarily referable to a contract between her and John Verdone. Moreover, the marketing services which she performed on behalf of VHL Construction Ltd. were for the purpose of selling condominiums for which she received $1,000 per unit upon occupancy and later in July, 1987, an agreed monthly fee of $5,000. They were not necessarily referable to their agreement. Thus in my view; the Statute of Frauds bars the plaintiff from recovery on her agreement with the plaintiff.

[17] On the eve of trial, the plaintiff abandoned her claim for specific performance because unit 37 had been already sold and sought damages alternatively for failure to perform the agreement. Counsel for the plaintiff indicated that this damage claim was for the work which she had performed on behalf of the defendants on a *quantum meruit* basis. Mr. Thomson's position was that if the enforcement of the contract was statute barred, there could be no alternative recovery of damages. He also said that a *quantum meruit* should not be entertained because it was not specifically pleaded. Although, the statement of claim did not specifically claim recovery on a *quantum meruit* basis, the general claim for damages did alert the defendant to the fact that this was an issue to be pursued. I am not convinced that the defendant has been prejudiced by this claim.

[18] I am satisfied that the plaintiff is entitled to recover on a *quantum meruit* basis for all of her preparatory work to make the project a successful one and for obtaining a number of reservation agreements. Indeed, Mr. Verdone admitted that it was one of their more successful projects. The work which she performed for the defendants was set out in her letter of November 27, 1987 which was marked as exhibit 1 in this action. I assess the value of her work and services on a *quantum meruit* basis at $25,000.00. ...

Note: In some provinces the Statute of Frauds has been repealed. In some jurisdictions it has been replaced with legislation giving more discretion to the court.

C. Challenges to Contracts

Question

In what instances will the court allow a party to an agreement to avoid his or her obligations?

1. MISTAKE

Marvco Color Research Ltd. v. *Harris et al.*

141 D.L.R. (3D) 577
SUPREME COURT OF CANADA
DECEMBER 6, 1982

Summary of the facts: Mr. and Mrs. Harris were induced by Johnston, a man living with their daughter, to sign a mortgage in favour of Marvco Color Research Ltd. Johnston led them to believe that the document was an unimportant amendment to an existing mortgage when it was, in reality, a second substantial mortgage. Although Mr. and Mrs. Harris did not sign at the same time, neither read the document nor questioned it. When the payments were in arrears, the mortgagee took this action for foreclosure. The sole defence was *non est factum*.

The trial court and the Ontario Court of Appeal held that the plea was effective, that their carelessness did not defeat the defence. The courts were following a precedent set by the S.C.C. in *Prudential Trust Co. Ltd. v. Cugnet et al.* (1956) 5 D.L.R. (2d), *(Prudential Trust)*. This appeal to the Supreme Court of Canada forced a re-examination of the legal principle set out in *Prudential Trust* in light of an English case, *Saunders v. Anglia Building Society* [1971] A.C. 1004 which held that carelessness would defeat the plea of *non est factum*.

Estey J.:—The decision of the House of Lords in *Saunders* has been considered by a number of Canadian courts. In *Commercial Credit Corp. Ltd. v. Carroll Bros. Ltd.* (1971), 20 D.L.R. (3d) 504*n* (Man. C.A.), the question of whether the principles laid down in *Saunders* are good law in Canada was left open by the court. In a number of more recent decisions, however, the reasoning of the House of Lords has been directly applied. ...

In my view, with all due respect to those who have expressed views to the contrary, the dissenting view of Cartwright J. (as he then was) in *Prudential, supra*, correctly enunciated the principles of the law of *non est factum*. In the result the defendants-respondents are barred by reason of their carelessness from pleading that their minds did not follow their hands when executing the mortgage so as to be able to plead that the mortgage is not binding upon them. The rationale of the rule is simple and clear. As between an innocent party (the appellant) [the mortgagee] and the respondents, the law must take into account the fact that the appellant was completely innocent of any negligence, carelessness or wrongdoing, whereas the respondents by their careless conduct have made it possible for the wrongdoers to inflict a loss. As between the appellant and the respondents, simple justice requires that the party, who by the application of reasonable care was in a position to avoid a loss to any of the parties, should bear any loss that results when the only alternative available to the courts would be to place the loss upon the innocent appellant. In the final analysis, therefore, the question raised cannot be put more aptly than in the words of Cartwright J. in *Prudential, supra*, at p. 5 D.L.R., p. 929 S.C.R.: "...which of two innocent parties is to suffer for the fraud of a third." The two parties are innocent in the sense that they were not guilty of wrongdoing as against any other person, but as between the two innocent parties there remains a distinction significant in the law, namely, that the respondents, by their carelessness, have exposed the innocent appellant to risk of loss, and even though no duty in law was owed by the respondents to the appellant to safeguard

the appellant from such loss, nonetheless the law must take this discarded opportunity into account.

In my view, this is so for the compelling reason that in this case, and no doubt generally in similar cases, the respondents' carelessness is but another description of a state of mind into which the respondents have fallen because of their determination to assist themselves and/or a third party for whom the transaction has been entered into in the first place. Here the respondents apparently sought to attain some advantage indirectly for their daughter by assisting Johnston in his commercial venture. In the *Saunders* case, *supra*, the aunt set out to apply her property for the benefit of her nephew. In both cases the carelessness took the form of a failure to determine the nature of the document the respective defendants were executing. Whether the carelessness stemmed from an enthusiasm for their immediate purpose or from a confidence in the intended beneficiary to save them harmless matters not. This may explain the origin of the careless state of mind but is not a factor limiting the operation of the principle of *non est factum* and its application. The defendants, in executing the security without the simple precaution of ascertaining its nature in fact and in law, have nonetheless taken an intended and deliberate step in signing the document and have caused it to be legally binding upon themselves. In the words of *Foster v. Mackinnon* this negligence, even though it may have sprung from good intentions, precludes the defendants in this circumstance from disowning the document, that is to say, from pleading that their minds did not follow their respective hands when signing the document and hence that no document in law was executed by them.

This principle of law is based not only upon the principle of placing the loss on the person guilty of carelessness, but also upon a recognition of the need for certainty and security in commerce. This has been recognized since the earliest days of the plea of *non est factum*. In *Waberly v. Cockerel* (1542), 1 Dyer 51a, 73 E.R. 112, for example it was said that:

…although the truth be, that the plaintiff is paid his money, still it is better to suffer a mischief to one man than an inconvenience to many, which would subvert a law; …

More recently in *Muskham Finance Ltd. v. Howard, supra,* at p. 912, Donovan L.F. stated:

> Much confusion and uncertainty would result in the field of contract and elsewhere if a man were permitted to try to disown his signature simply by asserting that he did not understand that which he had signed.

The appellant, as it was entitled to do, accepted the mortgage as valid, and adjusted its affairs accordingly. …

I wish only to add that the application of the principle that carelessness will disentitle a party to the document of the right to disown the document in law must depend upon the circumstances of each case. This has been said throughout the judgments written on the principle of *non est factum* from the earliest times. The magnitude and extent of the carelessness, the circumstances which may have contributed to such carelessness, and all other circumstances must be taken into account in each case before a court may determine whether estoppel shall arise in the defendant so as to prevent the raising of this defence. The policy considerations inherent in the plea of *non est factum* were well stated by Lord Wilberforce in his judgment in *Saunders, supra,* at pp. 1023-4:

> …the law…has two conflicting objectives: relief to a signer whose consent is genuinely lacking…protection to innocent third parties who have acted upon an apparently regular and properly executed document. Because each of these factors may involve questions of degree or shading any rule of law must represent a compromise and must allow to the court some flexibility in application. …

[Appeal allowed; the plaintiff lender wins.]

• r. Copperfield bid on a Batmobile; his bid of $189,500 won. He learned that that car was not the actual car used in the film *Batman*, but one of five cars used to promote the film. He sued the seller, Mr. Eisenberg who "has returned the favor."[15]

▶▶ For a case relying on the interpretation of terms see *Manulife Bank of Canada v. Conlin*, page 149.

2. MISREPRESENTATION

A. INNOCENT

Mr. Chorkawy co-signed a promissory note for $57,200 with his friend Welch. When Welch went bankrupt the bank looked to Chorkawy for payment. He refused to pay on the basis of misrepresentations made to him in response to his inquiries. The court summarized his position as follows:

> "It is Chorkawy's position that the execution of the promissory note was procured by the bank's misrepresentation of Welch's other financial obligations to Chorkawy, and, accordingly, ought to be entitled to rescission."

Despite the bank's denial, the court accepted Chorkawy's testimony that he had been assured by representatives of the bank that Welch had no other indebtedness and that the loan was secure when, in fact, Welch had other debts—a term loan of $46,500, a mortgage of $85,000 and arrears with Revenue Canada of $33,000.

The bank then argued the parol evidence rule: that evidence of an innocent misrepresentation was inadmissible because it contradicted the terms of a written guarantee.

Justice Mykle concluded:

> "On the strength of [the] authorities, it is clear that such evidence is admissible. I find that, on Chorkawy's testimony, which I accept, there was a misrepresentation to him by the bank, which misrepresentation directly induced him to sign the promissory note."
>
> In these circumstances, the note cannot bind Chorkawy, and accordingly the bank's claim is dismissed."

Royal Bank of Canada v. Chorkawy
[1994] M.J. No. 561 (Q.L.)
Manitoba Court of Queen's Bench
October 20, 1994

• *T*he National Consumer Council and the Plain English Campaign, which promote the use of clear, straightforward English, gave the 1986 "Golden Bull booby prize for gobbledegook" to a firm which used the following in their share prospectus: "[the signers] agree that without prejudice in any other rights to which you may be entitled, you will not be entitled to exercise any remedy of rescission for innocent misrepresentation at any time after acceptance of your application."

B. FRAUDULENT

B.C. Hydro, the defendant, had decided to contract out the construction of transmission lines in a rugged area of British Columbia. B.C. Hydro advertised for tenders. The trial court found as a fact that the defendant had deliberately omitted information from the tender documents about the condition of the right-of-way. The judge stated that the deliberate omission of words of warning amounted to "a form of tender by ambush." In his opinion, the defendant had a duty to make full disclosure of all information relevant to the project, to give the bidders information that accurately reflected the nature of the work to be done so they could prepare a proper bid. He held that the defendant had fraudulently induced the plaintiff to enter the contract and awarded the plaintiff $2.6 million, "the total loss suffered by the plaintiff as a result of being fraudulently induced to enter into this contract."[16]

B.C. Hydro appealed. After examining the contractual terms relevant to the case, the majority on the B.C. Court of Appeal concluded that the contract meant that the clearing was to have been completed and thus the words constituted a negligent, but not a fraudulent, misrepresentation that induced the plaintiff to enter into a contract at a price less than it would have if it had known the true facts. It reduced the award to $1,087,730 for negligence and remitted the breach of contract issue and the consequent damages back to the trial court.

With regard to the claim of fraudulent misrepresentation, the court agreed that fundamental principles still apply, namely, the plaintiff must prove the defendant's intention to deceive. It concluded that the evidence in the case did not show that any of the twelve members of the committee which prepared the tender documents did so with such an intention.

Judge Southin, although dissenting on the finding of negligent misrepresentation, agreed that the plaintiff failed to prove fraudulent misrepresentation. "[I]n my opinion, in the whole of his judgment, the learned judge never came to grips with the issue of who was fraudulent. To say, as the learned judge does, that the defendant did this or that is to ascribe to the defendant a soul which it does not possess. … I am persuaded that no one had a guilty mind." [At page 189][17]

B.C. Hydro appealed to the Supreme Court of Canada, which dismissed its appeal. All the judges agreed that B.C. Hydro had breached the contract and the majority held that the plaintiff, Checo, could also sue in tort for negligent misrepresentation even though the representations were also stated expressly in the contract. It sent the matter back to the trial court for the assessment of damages and stated that the law should move to reduce the significance of suing in tort rather than in contract. [In tort, the wronged is to be compensated for all the reasonably foreseeable loss that was caused by the tort; in contract the wronged is entitled to damages that would put him in the position he would have been in if there had been no breach.][18]

BG Checo International Ltd. v. B.C. Hydro and Power Authority
Summarized from The Lawyers Weekly
February 12, 1993, p.1

Note: This case will be remembered less for its finding of negligent rather than fraudulent misrepresentation than for the proposition that a person can bring an action in contract and tort, even if the duty in tort is also an express term of the contract, subject only to the limitations set out in the contract.

By Silence

Questions

Can silence be a misrepresentation?
If so, what has to be proved and by whom?

Sidhu Estate v. Bains, Bristow, Third Party

http://www.courts.gov.bc.ca/
COURT OF APPEAL FOR BRITISH COLUMBIA
JUNE 7, 1996

Background facts: Mr. Bhandar was induced to invest $134,000 in a company by the fraudulent misrepresentations of a Mr. Bristow who told Bhandar that he, Bristow, had invested $600,000 and that Bhandar's good friend Bains had invested $380,000 in cash when in fact neither had invested anything. Mr. Bains permitted Bristow to mislead Bhandar to induce him to invest in the project. Some time later, when Bristow asked Bhandar if he knew of any other investors, Bhandar said his sister might be interested. In the presence of Mr. Bains, Bhandar called his sister, Ms. Sidhu, and innocently relayed the misinformation to her. She invested $80,000.

The sister, Ms. Sidhu, died about three years after she invested in the company and four years before the action on behalf of her estate began. The action by her estate failed at trial on the basis that she had not relied on the misrepresentations; she invested because her brother had invested.

This case is an appeal from that decision.

---

1 Finch J: . . .

[3] The plaintiffs allege that Ms. Sidhu was induced to invest the sum of $80,000 in IPC in reliance upon representations made to her in a telephone conversation on 18 June 1987 by Mr. Bhandar, who believed the representations to be true, but which, to the knowledge of Mr. Bains, were false. Mr. Bains was present with Mr. Bhandar at the time the latter spoke with his sister by telephone. The plaintiffs allege that in standing silent, and in failing to correct the false information he knew Mr. Bhandar was conveying to Ms. Sidhu, Mr. Bains committed a fraudulent non-disclosure of material facts. The plaintiffs say Mr. Bains is liable for damages in deceit because Ms. Sidhu relied upon the representations, which she would not have done had Mr. Bains disclosed the truth.

[The judge reviewed the conflicting evidence as to what was said to Ms. Sidhu on the telephone and the findings of the trial judge.]

[28] I am therefore satisfied the only reasonable inference to be drawn in the circumstances was that Mr. Bains had the necessary fraudulent intention [and it was a material misrepresentation that induced Ms. Sidhu to invest.] . . .

[30] As to the trial judge's conclusion that a misrepresentation could be made by silence, I respectfully agree. . . .

[31] The circumstances required for silence to be actionable misrepresentation are articulated in *Spencer Bower & Turner, The Law of Actionable Misrepresentation*, 3d ed. (London: Butterworths, 1974) at 101:

A misrepresentation may be made by silence, when either the representee, or a third person in his presence, or to his knowledge, states something false, which indicates to the representor that the representee either is being, or will be, misled, unless the necessary correction be made. Silence, under such circumstances, is either a tacit adoption by the party of another's misrepresentation as his own, or a tacit confirmation of another's error as truth.

[32] And see also Halsbury's Laws of England, 4th ed., Vol. 31 at 639–40; *Hardman v. Booth* (1863), 1 H. & C. 803, 158 E.R. 1107; and *Howse v. Quinnel Motors Ltd.* (1949), [1952] 2 D.L.R. 425 (B.C.C.A.). . . .

[33] The fact that Mr. Bains was present at the time of the communication by Mr. Bhandar to his sister and the fact that Mr. Bains had the opportunity to correct the information that he knew to be false are essential to my conclusion that silence could, in law, constitute a misrepresentation. In the particular circumstances of this case, and on the findings of the learned trial judge, Mr. Bains's silence can only be seen as confirmation of the misinformation which Mr. Bhandar passed on to Ms. Sidhu.

[34] That brings one to the issues most actively addressed in this appeal, namely, whether the learned trial judge erred in finding that the plaintiffs had failed to prove reliance by Ms. Sidhu on the false representations; and whether liability for fraudulent misrepresentation can be found where there are, or may have been, additional representations or factors which induced the representee to act. . . .

[35] Given his acceptance of Mr. Bhandar's testimony as to what was said, I interpret … the trial judge's reasons to mean that both Mr. Bhandar's and Mr. Bains's investment in IPC were factors which induced Ms. Sidhu to follow suit. However, the learned trial judge appears to have held the view that the plaintiffs could only succeed by proving that those representations were the sole inducements upon which Ms. Sidhu relied. In so directing himself, in my respectful view, the learned trial judge erred in law. Fleming in *The Law of Torts*, 7th ed. (Sydney: Law Book, 1987), says at 604:

> Besides being intended to rely on the misrepresentation, the plaintiff must have actually done so. … At the same time, a defendant cannot excuse himself by proving that his misrepresentation was not the sole inducing cause, because it might have been precisely what tipped the scales, …

…

[36] It is therefore sufficient in my view to found liability in deceit if the fraudulent representation is a material inducement upon which the representee relied, even if that representation is only one of several factors contributing to her decision.

[37] I am also of the view that the learned trial judge erred in concluding that the plaintiffs had failed to discharge the onus of proving Ms. Sidhu's reliance on the fraudulent misrepresentation. There are two lines of authority on the nature of this onus. …

[42] I think the preferred view of the law in Canada is that once intention, materiality and causation of loss are proven, the burden of proving non-reliance shifts to the defendant. The antecedent elements are not in question in this case. The burden of proving that Ms. Sidhu did not rely on the statements therefore shifts to the defendant, as it did in *Parallels Restaurant.* Taking the trial judge's reasons as a whole, I am of the view that he did not find that the defendant had proven conclusively that Ms. Sidhu did not rely at all on the statements. He found only that she probably relied on other information as well. As I have observed, this is not enough.

[43] However, even if the other view of the law regarding the burden of proof is the correct one [i.e. that the plaintiff must prove all the elements], the plaintiffs should still succeed. … The only reasonable inference in all the circumstances is that Ms. Sidhu did rely on the representations made to her by Mr. Bhandar and uncorrected by Mr. Bains and that Mr. Bains has failed to rebut this inference by proving that she did not so rely.

[44] In my respectful view all of the elements of a successful claim in deceit have been proven or are reasonably to be inferred from the proven facts. I would allow the appeal.

Appeal allowed. Unanimous

Note: The Supreme Court of Canada refused to hear an appeal.

3. DURESS

As reported in *The Advocate:* Mr. and Mrs. B, aged 78 and 72, signed a contract to transfer certain real property to their son Jim. The contract had been prepared by a solicitor. When Jim brought an action for a declaration that he was the beneficial owner of this property, Mr. B testified that he and Mrs. B had only signed because Jim had threatened to blow his brother Bill's head off if a family money dispute was not settled. The parents heard this threat through a third brother. Mr. B said that he and his wife, who was very ill at the time and died not long afterwards, were terrified Jim would act on his threat and were prepared to do almost anything to prevent it. Their lawyer had been consulted on how to settle a tangle of money disputes among the members of the family, and he advised that this agreement seemed to be the only way to obtain peace.

Held: the agreement was void for Jim's duress or, alternatively, should be set aside for unconscionability. It was enough if the threat of harm was a reason for executing the document, albeit that the signer might well have done the same if the threat had not been made: *Barton v. Armstrong*, [1976] A.C. 104 (P.C.). A threat of harm to a third party, if acted on by the signer, was duress: *Saxon v. Saxon*, [1976] 4 W.W.R. 300 (B.C. Co. Ct.). Although Mr. and Mrs. B had independent legal advice and chose to sign the agreement, they did so because they feared that Jim would harm Bill unless they signed the agreement. This was a coercion of their will so as to vitiate their consent. Unconscionability was found because through the duress and their lack of understanding of the transaction the parents were in a weak position compared with Jim, and because the agreement was unfairly one-sided.

Byle v. Byle et al.
Vancouver S.C. Registry No. C854743 Legg, J.
August 5, 1988[19]

> **Note:** The Court of Appeal, after a thorough discussion of the law, upheld the judge's conclusion that there was duress, found that there was no affirmation of the agreement, and confirmed that the agreement was void. The court then found it unnecessary to consider whether the agreement was also voidable for unconscionability. It was a unanimous decision.

- *A* bank applied for summary judgment against a guarantor who pled duress and *non est factum*. The guarantor alleged that she signed the document unaware that it was a guarantee secured by a mortgage on her home because her husband threatened, among other things, "to open up your belly and drink your blood." The judge concluded a summary judgment was inappropriate. *TD Bank v. Nabmiache*[20]

4. UNDUE INFLUENCE

Tannock v. *Bromley*

10 B.C.L.R. 62
SUPREME COURT OF BRITISH COLUMBIA
JANUARY 24, 1979

Bouck J.:—

SYNOPSIS OF CLAIM AND DEFENCE

Between approximately July 1974 and January 1977 the plaintiff received treatment from the defendant through the medium of hypnosis. He now says that while he was under her influence he conveyed real estate to her, bought her a car and gave her many other items such as coins, a stereo set, etc. In this action he asks for return of the real property and judgment for the money value of the additional articles transferred to her.

There is not much of a contest over the fact the conveyances occurred and the chattels were given, but the defendant alleges all of this happened by way of gift from the plaintiff to her and so none of the property need be restored. ...

ISSUE

Must the defendant return to the plaintiff the property or its value?

LAW

Where the parties to a contract do not stand upon an equal footing the law has frequently intervened to set aside the contract on the grounds of undue influence by one towards the other. This principle has been applied with particular emphasis in circumstances where there is a fiduciary relationship between the parties. Such a bond has been held to exist between solicitor and client, principal and agent, doctor and patient, priest and penitent, etc.

The main theory of the law is that, when a person who because of his state of mind is incapable of exercising his free will and is induced by another to do an act which may be to his detriment, the other shall not be allowed to derive any benefit from his improper conduct. Conveyances or transfers by the victim are not set aside because of folly or want of prudence but to protect the weak from being forced, tricked or misled into parting with their property.

Once the relationship between the parties is established so that it is clear one has maintained dominion over the other, then a presumption of law arises where a gift is made by the servient to the dominant party. The onus of proof then shifts to the dominant party to uphold the validity of the gift. This presumption is to the effect that the dominant party used undue influence over the servient party and consequently the transaction should be set aside unless the dominant party can show the conveyance or gift was a spontaneous act of the donor performed under circumstances which enabled the donor to exercise an independent will.

The authorities on this branch of the law are not altogether consistent and so the textbook discussions of the cases tend to vary from author to author. Nonetheless, in broad outline the principles I have recited seem to be generally accepted: see for example the following texts and cases cited therein: ...

On the facts there is no question the defendant controlled the plaintiff in much the same way a solicitor may dominate his client or a doctor his patient. Her position was that of a fiduciary in relation to the plaintiff. Indeed, the influence she held is more profound than in the examples of other situations I have mentioned because of the nature of hypnotism and its method of manipulating the mind through suggestion. The plaintiff was incapable of resisting the defendant's influence and became her obedient servant. She either abused her position of trust or took advantage of the inequality which existed between them. As hypnotist and subject a presumption therefore arose that everything given by the plaintiff to her ought to be set aside unless she could prove the plaintiff's acts were spontaneous and done by him through the exercise of his independent will.

I could not find any solid evidence to support the defendant's cause by way of rebutting the presumption. The conveyances and gifts were voluntary in the sense there was no consideration moving from the defendant to the plaintiff. Furthermore the plaintiff did not receive independent advice so that one could say he was acting outside the influence of the defendant. Because of this the transfers must be set aside. ...

JUDGMENT

By way of summary the plaintiff will recover judgment against the defendant in the following terms:

(a) An order directing the defendant to sign a conveyance of her interest in the Wellington Street farm and in default of her so doing the district registrar of Nanaimo may sign on her behalf;

(b) An order directing that an account be taken as between the plaintiff and the defendant with respect to the moneys received by the defendant on the sale of the Amsterdam house;

(c) An order directing that the plaintiff has a charge against the car in question proportionate to his contribution and that the car be sold;

(d) An order directing the defendant to deliver up the stereo to the plaintiff:

(e) An order that there be an accounting between the plaintiff and the defendant with respect to any loss suffered by the plaintiff as a consequence of the sale of the car, and the value of the rent the defendant must pay to the plaintiff for her use of the car and the stereo;

(f) Costs to follow the event;

(g) Liberty to apply.

Action allowed in main.

- *A*n accountant prepared financial statements for a family business and saw the business was in difficulty. The accountant refused to release the statements to an investor intending to buy the company unless the investor signed an agreement to guarantee payment of his accounting fees. The court held the guarantee was obtained by undue influence and the investor was relieved of his obligation.[21]

5. UNCONSCIONABILITY

Turner Estate *v.* *Bonli Estate*

77 SASK. R. 49
SASK. COURT OF QUEEN'S BENCH
JUNE 2, 1989

[1] Sirois, J.: The plaintiff sues for specific performance of an option to purchase farmland entered into between the purchaser Gordon Turner and the vendor Oli Bonli on the 2nd day of May A.D. 1975. One of the difficulties encountered herein is that both of the main actors are now deceased and their personal representatives stand in their place. … The defendant resists the claim mainly on the basis that the alleged option agreement should be set aside as the entire transaction was unconscionable in that the purchase price of the land and the method of payment of purchase price by installments are gravely inequitable and constitute equitable fraud on the part of the plaintiff. The evidence must be carefully scrutinized. The sole issue is the validity of the option to purchase.

[2] At the time the lease agreements and option to purchase were entered into, Gordon Turner was 47 years of age and Oli Bonli was 88 years of age. Gordon Turner likely typed out the agreement at his residence on the previous night leaving the land description to be filled out later at his office where he had a municipal map to consult. It was executed bright and early around 7 o'clock in the morning. Oli Bonli who lived at the hotel walked over to Turner's office. Alan Pederson who worked at his brother's service station across the road was hailed to come over and sign as a witness. In five minutes or less the deed was done. This is the text of the agreement entered into:

May 2, 1975

TO WHOM IT MAY CONCERN:

I Oli Bonli do hereby rent all of my land to Gordon A. Turner for the period of five years starting as of today

May 2nd 1975. At the end of this time being May 2nd 1980 he may purchase this land for the sum of one hundred thousand dollars, this sum to be paid in twenty equal payments of five thousand dollars each year. This payment to cover principal and interest and there will be no further charges made to him.

If I should decease before the rental agreement is fulfilled, he may purchase the land from my estate under the same terms. The rentor may seed up to four hundred and fifty acres per year and must farm the land in a husbandly manner.

I will receive one third of the crop each year and will pay the taxes on all of this land.

The rentor will haul all my grain to the graneries (sic) and elevator for me at no cost to me, and I in return will let him use any of my machinery that he desires for farming any land at no cost to him.

The rentor will be allowed to store grain in any of my granaries (sic) that I am not using in that crop year at no cost to him.

The legal description of the said land is as follows:. …

I have clear titles to the above land in the Toronto Dominion Bank.

'Alan Pederson'	'Oli Bonli'
WITNESS	Oli Bonli

'G.A. Turner'
Gordon A. Turner"

[3] Gordon Turner was in the fuel business all his life. He drove fuel trucks for Texaco, B.A. Oil and finally Gulf. He was also involved in farming. In 1966-67 he purchased one-half section of land; in 1972 he purchased a further three quarter sections. There was further trading along the way so that by 1975 he owned five quarters of land, besides the Bonli land— the subject of the action. But he had his eyes on this land too. He was very involved in the community. He served on the Town Council for nine years, mayor for two terms and the Elks representative for eight years. In the wintertime he curled for a pastime. From all accounts, he was a mover and doer. He was well-liked and respected in the community. He was married with three children—all boys, with whom he got along well. He enjoyed people and his work. For the last six months of his life his nerves were bad and he suffered from arthritis. He took anti-depressants but finally succumbed, a victim of suicide on the 30th of September 1975.

[4] Oli Bonli appears to have been an entertaining person, always nice, friendly, with a twinkle in his eye. But as a bachelor he kept to himself quite often. He lived on the farm until the winter of 1973-74. He spent his summers on the farm and his winters at the hotel in Kyle. ...

In 1974 and 1975 age was catching up to Oli Bonli. He had good days and bad days when he was very confused. Finally, unable to care for himself properly at the hotel in Kyle, the Social Services Department intervened and he was taken to a nursing home in Langham in the month of November of 1976. In 1980, Oli Bonli was examined by psychiatrists to ascertain the state of his mental condition. In March of 1982 he was declared to be a mentally disturbed person, incapable of managing his affairs through mental infirmity arising from age and the Montreal Trust Company of Canada was appointed Committee of his estate under the *Mentally Disordered Persons Act*, R.S.S. 1978, c. M-4, ss. 5 and 42. He died on the 18th day of February, A.D. 1985 at the age of 98. ...

[13] The leading Canadian case appears to be *Waters v. Donnelly* (1884), 9 O.R. 391, where Fergus, J., held at 409:

The law which I think applicable to a case of this sort appears to be clearly and briefly stated in a case mentioned by the Chancellor. *Slater v. Nolan* Ir. R. 11 Eq. 386, by the Master of the Rolls, and the decision was afterwards affirmed in appeal. The learned Judge said:—'If two persons, no matter whether a confidential relation exists between them or not, stand in such a relation to each other that one can take undue advantage of the other whether by reason of distress, or recklessness, or wildness, or want of care, and when the facts show that one party has taken undue advantage of the other by reason of the circumstances I have mentioned, a transaction resting upon such unconscionable dealing will not be allowed to stand; and there are several cases to show, even where no confidential relation exists, that where the parties are not on equal terms, the party who gets a benefit cannot hold it without proving that everything has been right, and fair and reasonable on his part.' This decision does not, I think, lay down any new law but rather appears to state concisely what the law was and is. ...

[15] In *Black v. Wilcox*, (1976) 70 D.L.R. (3d) 192; 12 O.R. (2d) 759, at pp. 195-196, Evans, J.A., said:

In order to set aside the transaction between the parties, the Court must find that the inadequacy of the consideration is so gross or that the relative positions of the parties is so out of balance in the sense that there is a gross inequality of bargaining power or that the age or disability of one of the controlling parties places him at such a decided disadvantage that equity must intervene to protect the party of whom undue advantage has been taken. In considering whether a Court should intervene, it is necessary to look at all the circumstances surrounding the transaction but it is not necessary to find any intentional fraud. The question is whether the transaction reveals a situation existing between the parties which was heavily balanced in favour of the defendant and of which he knowingly took advantage.

[16] If the bargain is fair the fact that the parties were not equally vigilant of their interest is immaterial. Likewise, if one was not preyed upon by the other, an improvident or even grossly inadequate consideration is no ground upon which to set aside a contract freely entered into. It is the consideration of inequality and improvidence which alone may involve this jurisdiction. Then the onus is placed upon the party seeking to uphold the contract to show that his conduct throughout was scrupulously considerate of the other's interests. ...

[17] In the case at bar the 47 year old Turner and the 88 year old Oli Bonli were certainly not par or of equal bargaining power. Turner drew the agreement himself. ...When questioned by Tony Sander [long time friend, neighbour and helper] about the rumours that his land had been rented to Gordon Turner early in May 1975, Oli Bonli denied that he had either rented or sold any land. On the contrary he declared that he had bought land from Gordon Turner and that Sander would have more work to do for him that spring than he had ever done in the past. Now Oli Bonli was not a liar; he was a nice old man and trickery was not part of his arsenal. I have serious doubts that he really knew all that was contained in Exhibit P-1 or D-2.

[18] Let us look at the agreement itself between this 47 year old active businessman and this failing 88 year old gentleman. The evidence is that he was failing with good days and bad days. One year down the road he could not adequately take care of himself and was taken to a nursing home. This document drawn up by Gordon Turner provides for a five year lease at the end of which, he or his estate could exercise the option to buy. At that time the rentor, Oli Bonli, would be 93 years of age. Then, on the option being exercised over a 20 year period, Oli Bonli would be 113 years of age by the time it was all paid out. The price was $100,000.00 at a time when the land was worth $167,000.00, or was one third more than the purchase price, and at a time when the price of land was ascending rapidly. Furthermore, the agreement makes no provision for interest on the unpaid portion of the purchase price; the five thousand per year would comprise both principal and interest. Gordon Turner knew very well what land prices were doing at this time; this man was world wise and knew what he was after. The agreement moreover provides that the lessee can use any of the rentor's machinery to farm any land free of

charge. And again, the lessee reserves the right to use any of the rentor's granaries to store his grain that the rentor was not using at any relevant time.

[19] Can one honestly conceive a more one-sided or improvident agreement than this? To ask the question is to beg the answer. It was all one-sided in favour of Gordon Turner at the expense of Bonli.

[20] Here, there was no independent legal advice given to Oli Bonli; given the respective ages and state of health of both parties there was inequality of bargaining power; the consideration

was grossly inadequate and the terms of purchase were very unfair in the light of all circumstances. The transaction resting upon such unconscionable dealing cannot stand. The plaintiff has failed to discharge the onus that rests upon her to show that everything has been fair, right and reasonable on her part. Equity must intervene to protect the defendant's estate when undue advantage was taken of the deceased. The transaction is set aside and specific performance is refused. In effect, the action is dismissed with costs to the defendant. ...

Action dismissed.

Note: This decision was affirmed on appeal.

D. PRIVITY OF CONTRACT AND EXCEPTIONS

Two employees of Kuehne & Nagel International Ltd. caused extensive damage ($33,955.41 worth) to a transformer owned by London Drugs Ltd. They dropped it attempting to lift it with two fork lifts, contrary to the method advised. The storage contract included an exclusion clause limiting liability of Kuehne & Nagel on any one package to $40. London Drugs Ltd. sued the defendant in bailment, contract and tort (negligence); it sued the employees personally for the tort of negligence.

At trial the employees were found liable for the full amount of the damage while the liability of their employer company was limited to $40.

The B.C. Court of Appeal found it unreasonable to hold the employees responsible for the full amount of the loss when their employer's liability was limited to $40. The court reduced the employees' liability to $40. Justice Southin dissented with "regret" because the result is "in a moral sense, unjust," but, she concluded, "it is for judges to state the law and for the legislature to reform it."

London Drugs Ltd. v. Kuehne & Nagel International Ltd. et al.
70 D.L.R. (4th) 51
British Columbia Court of Appeal
March 30, 1990

On appeal, the Supreme Court of Canada focused on the issues of whether or not the employees owed a duty of care to their employer's customers and whether or not the liability clause contained in the contract between the employer company and the customer could afford any protection to the employees.

The court held that the employees did owe a duty of care to the employer's customer, but found the employees beneficiaries of the exemption clause in the contract between the employer and customer. Thus, the court added an exemption to the privity of contract rule: when a service contract between an employer and its customer contains a clause limiting liability, that clause, if it expressly or impliedly covers the employees, should protect the employees charged with performing the contract. The customer should not be able to circumvent the terms of the contract by suing the employees directly in tort.

London Drugs Ltd. v. Kuehne & Nagel International Ltd. et al.
S.C.C.
Summarized from The Lawyers Weekly
November 13, 1992, p. 1

E. Assignment of Contractual Rights

- *A* contract by which William Millard borrowed $250,000 from a venture-capital firm, Marriner & Co., allowed the lender to convert the note into 20 percent of the company's stock. The contract was sold to Mr. Martin-Musumeci, who, as the assignee of the contract, claimed the 20 percent of the company, ComputerLand. Millard resisted by claiming he had an oral agreement with Marriner that it could not transfer the right to convert the note. The matter went to court.

  The court held that Millard must give 20 percent of his stock to Martin-Musumeci plus punitive damages of $125 million. Twenty percent of ComputerLand, at that time, was estimated to be worth $50 million to $400 million. To appeal, Millard would have to post a cash bond equal to $1\frac{1}{2}$ times the award.[22]

EQUITABLE ASSIGNMENT

Question

What are the consequences of ignoring a valid assignment?

Bitz, Szemenyei, Ferguson & MacKenzie v. *Cami Automotive Inc.*

[1997] O.J. No. 2463
ONTARIO COURT (GENERAL DIVISION)
MAY 30, 1997

Background facts: This case was very complicated. The court had to determine whether or not the assignment was a matter of contract law, tort law, whether it needed to satisfy the *Conveyancing and Law of Property Act*, and whether it was invalid by the *Wages Act*. In the end it was held to be a valid assignment.

Cavarzan J.:—The plaintiff law firm successfully represented one James Mastronardi, an employee of the defendant corporation, in a grievance arbitration. The arbitrator found that James Mastronardi (hereinafter referred to as J.M.) had been wrongfully dismissed and that he was entitled to be compensated for his losses. Prior to the conclusion of negotiations to settle the amount of the compensation, J.M. executed an "irrevocable direction" to the defendant to pay from the settlement proceeds the sum of $15,120.91 to the plaintiff and the balance to himself.

Although the defendant had intended to comply with the terms of the irrevocable direction, the entire proceeds of the settlement were paid out to J.M. ...

The plaintiff now seeks summary judgment for the amount specified in the direction. Counsel advised me that the facts are not in dispute. They submitted, and I agree, that the only genuine issues are questions of law which should be determined by the court pursuant to rule 20.04(4) of the Rules of Civil Procedure. ...

THE ISSUES

In addition to the grounds alleged in the amended statement of claim, Mr. Mackenzie argued that the "irrevocable direction"

amounted to an equitable assignment which was binding upon the defendant and enforceable. ...

WAS THERE AN EQUITABLE ASSIGNMENT?

The following statements from *Halsbury* ... support the position of the plaintiff in this case:

> An engagement or direction to pay a sum of money out of a specified debt or fund constitutes an equitable assignment, though not of the whole debt or fund; but it is necessary to specify the debt or fund.

...

Although the precise amount of the award had yet to be calculated, the defendant became a debtor as of the date of the award. ... (*Halsbury, supra*, at para. 37):

> Consideration is not required to support the equitable assignment of an existing legal chose in action, provided that the assignor has done everything required to be done by him to make the assignment complete in equity.

...

I conclude … The irrevocable direction was a binding equitable assignment. …

Finally, I note that the parties before the court in this dispute are the innocent victims of what appears to be fraudulent behaviour by J.M. He retained the full amount of the arbitration award knowing that one week earlier he had executed an assignment of a major portion of that award. The defendant is by this judgment required to pay twice.

CONCLUSION

The plaintiff is entitled to summary judgment against the defendant . …

F. TERMINATION OF CONTRACTS

1. PERFORMANCE

Question

Is everybody happy?

- *M*r. Mateo of New York City bought fifty $100 gift certificates from Toys 'Я' Us and offered one certificate for each gun turned in to the police station. Over a few days, 375 weapons had been turned in—"almost 40 times as many as the precinct has collected in the past year under the department's amnesty program which pays up to $75 a gun." Donations from others allowed the programme to continue.[23]

- *S*omeone paid $1.26 million for the dress worn by Marilyn Monroe when she sang Happy Birthday to U.S. President John F. Kennedy in 1962.[24]

- *E*lton John was paid $800,000 to sing at a wedding.[25]

- *T*he Ontario housing ministry ordered a landlord to rebate $2,308.80 to his tenant. The tenant received that amount in change that filled two blue recycling boxes. The tenant said he may use the change to pay his rent.[26]

2. AGREEMENT

- *W*e ordered Thai green curry with pork, but we got chicken instead. We agreed to accept the substitution. No lawsuit.

3. FRUSTRATION

- *L*imp Bizkit cancelled the Vancouver show of its Anger Management Tour due to the lead singer being unable to perform because of a sore throat.[27]

Question

Has some unforeseen event beyond the control of either party happened after the contract was formed that makes it impossible or meaningless to perform?

KBK No. 138 Ventures Ltd.   *v.*   Canada Safeway Limited

http://www.courts.gov.bc.ca/
COURT OF APPEAL FOR BRITISH COLUMBIA
MAY 9, 2000

Background facts: After Safeway concluded a contract for the sale of its property to KBK for $8.8 million, or $38 multiplied by the number of square feet of floor area permitted by the city, the city re-zoned the property thereby drastically reducing the allowable floor space. KBK, which could no longer develop a mixed commercial and residential condominium project, requested the return of its first installment of $150,000. Safeway refused to do so. Ultimately Safeway sold the property for $5.4 million, which reflected the new restrictions imposed by the re-zoning.

The trial court found the contract between Safeway and KBK had been frustrated pursuant to the *Frustrated Contract Act* and ordered Safeway to return the $150,000.

Braidwood, J.: ...

DISCUSSION ...

[1] The Test for Frustration
[13] The leading case on the doctrine of frustration is *Davis Contractors Ltd. v. Fareham U.D.C.*, [1956] A.C. 696, [1956] 2 All E.R. 145 (H.L.), in which the House of Lords articulated the so-called "radical change in the obligation" test. Lord Radcliffe stated at p. 728-9 (A.C.):

So perhaps it would be simpler to say at the outset that frustration occurs whenever the law recognizes that without default of either party a contractual obligation has become incapable of being performed because the circumstances in which performance is called for would render it a thing radically different from that which was undertaken by the contract. *Non haec in foedera veni.* It was not this that I promised to do.

[....] In the nature of things there is often no room for any elaborate inquiry. The court must act upon a general impression of what its rule requires. It is for that reason that special importance is necessarily attached to the occurrence of any unexpected event that, as it were, changes the face of things. But, even so, it is not hardship or inconvenience or material loss itself which calls the principle of frustration into play. There must be as well such a change in the significance of the obligation that the thing undertaken would, if performed, be a different thing from that contracted for. [Emphasis added]

In a concurring judgment, Lord Reid stated at p. 723 that a finding of frustration depends "on the true construction of the terms which are in the contract read in light of the nature of the contract and of the relevant surrounding circumstances when the contract was made."
[14] The test for frustration was neatly summarized by Mr. Justice Sigurdson in *Folia v. Trelinski* (1997), 14 R.P.R. (3d) 5 (B.C.S.C.). He stated at paragraph 18:

In order to find that the contract at issue has been frustrated the following criteria would have to be satisfied. The event in question must have occurred after the formation of the contract and cannot be self-induced. The contract must, as a result, be totally different from what the parties had intended. This difference must take into account the distinction between complete fruitlessness and mere inconvenience. The disruption must be permanent, not temporary or transient. The change must totally affect the nature, meaning, purpose, effect and consequences of the contract so far as concerns either or both parties. Finally, the act or event that brought about such radical change must not have been foreseeable. [Emphasis added]

[15] There is no doubt that the *Davis Contractors* decision is the law in Canada. The Supreme Court of Canada applied this test as early as 1960: *Peter Kiewit Sons' Co. of Canada v. Eakins Construction Ltd.*, [1960] S.C.R. 361. What is important for the purpose of this appeal is that the "radical change in the obligation" test has also been applied to real estate contracts in Canada. ...
[16] In her reasons for judgment, the trial judge also referred to the English Court of Appeal decision of *Krell v. Henry*, [1903] 2 K.B. 740. I do not find there to be a necessary inconsistency in the "radical change in the obligation" test set out in the *Davis Contractors* case and the principles set out in the well-known case of Krell.
[17] The court in *Krell* laid down three conditions to be satisfied for the doctrine of frustration to apply. These are:

1. What, having regard to all the circumstances, was the foundation of the contract?

2. Was the performance of the contract prevented?

3. Was the event which prevented the performance of the contract of such a character that it cannot reasonably be said to have been in the contemplation of the parties at the date of the contract?

[18] The learned trial judge found that each of these conditions was satisfied and I agree with that result. ...

[The court examines the advertising and contract to determine the purpose of the contract. It then reviews the trial judge's finding that the change in zoning was not foreseen by the parties.]

SUMMARY AND DISPOSITION

[28] In all the circumstances, I agree with the conclusion of the trial judge. ... [T]here is an intervening event and change of circumstances so fundamental as to be regarded as striking at the root of the agreement and as entirely beyond what was contemplated by the parties when they entered into the agreement. The [re-zoning] "radically altered" the contract between the parties within the meaning of the test set out in *Davis Contractors* and the above cases. The change in zoning and the consequent reduction in FSR from 3.22 to 0.3, which meant a change in the allowable buildable square footage from 231,800 square feet to 30,230 square feet, did not amount to a mere inconvenience but, rather, transformed the contract into something totally different than what the parties intended.

[29] Accordingly, I would dismiss this appeal.

Unanimous

---

4. BREACH OF CONTRACT

- *I*n 1994, the New York Rangers won the Stanley Cup under coach Mike Keenan. When the Rangers were a day late with a playoff bonus (of $840,000), he maintained that the Rangers had breached their contract and declared himself a free agent. Within days he signed a five-year $7 million contract with the St. Louis Blues. The Rangers sued him for breach of contract with the argument that their late payment of the bonus did not constitute a material breach.

  Negotiations led to Keenan being free to coach and manage the St. Louis Blues but the NHL commissioner suspended him for 60 days, fined him $138,000 and ordered him to return most of a $691,000 earlier signing bonus.[28]

- *J*ohn Fogerty, former member of the successful band Creedence Clearwater Revival, did not record for almost ten years partly because of a bitter and protracted legal battle. He is reported as saying "I haven't been paid properly in 17 years." When he did record, the title and lyrics of one song referred to these contract disputes: "Zanz Kan't Danz." "Zanz can't dance/But he'll steal your money/Watch him or he'll rob you blind."[29]

- *H*unter Tylo, seductress on the TV soap *Melrose Place*, successfully sued Spelling Entertainment for breach of contract when she was fired after disclosing that she was pregnant. The defence unsuccessfully argued that it was not a case about pregnancy, but that the gain of 46 pounds made her unsuitable for the part and her contract explicitly stated that she could not undergo any material change in her appearance.[30]

- *U*niversal Pictures sued Mike Myers for failing to continue in the making of *Dieter*, a movie based on Myers' German character developed for skits on *Saturday Night Live*. Myers admitted trying to delay production because he found the script, his own, unsatisfactory and did not want to "cheat moviegoers who pay their hard-earned money."[31]

- *A* summary of the facts would rob you of the gross details of an outrageous "cruise" with Captain Higginbotham, whom the court appropriately found had "fundamentally breached the contract." The plaintiff paid over $20,000 for a luxury 28-day cruise between the mainland and Vancouver Island. To appreciate the reasons for the complete refund of the amount paid, plus special and general damages, go to http://www.courts.gov.bc.ca for the story of *Litner and Litner v. Delta Charter Inc. et al.* decided by the Supreme Court of British Columbia on April 16, 1997.

In *Lalonde v. Coleman*, the court held that the boxer was not bound by the agreement, not only on the grounds that the agreement was illegal (see pp. 99) but also on the grounds that Coleman's breach of the agreement entitled Lalonde to terminate the contract. Judge Scott wrote: "In this case, in my opinion, in light of the magnitude of the defendant's inability to perform, we are dealing with such a fundamental breach as to entitle the plaintiff to treat the contract as being at an end. ... What occurred was a total nonperformance or benefit to the plaintiff. What resulted was something totally different from that which the parties must have contemplated and in my opinion, the plaintiff was quite entitled to walk away from the agreement. ..."

Lalonde v. Coleman
67 Man. R. (2d) 187 at p. 195

ANTICIPATORY BREACH

Q u e s t i o n

What is an "anticipatory breach" and what are the choices of the person faced with such a breach?

The bank occupied premises in a shopping center under the terms of an offer to lease accepted by the owner of the premises. The agreement provided the bank sign a formal lease satisfactory to both parties. Such a lease was never signed. The bank had been a tenant for six years of a ten-year term when the owner, frustrated by years of negotiation, sent a letter from its lawyer that read in part: "...that the Lease is either to be executed in the form negotiated between our two respective offices or the Toronto Dominion Bank is to vacate the premises."

The letter was intended to be a bluff but the bank answered that it would vacate the premises, which it did. The owner sued for breach of the contract.

In the words of the judge: "The issue was whether the tenant improperly terminated the lease or whether it was entitled to do so by reason of the doctrine of anticipatory breach or repudiation." The judge continues:

> ... [T]he issue was whether there was an anticipatory breach or repudiation of the existing lease by the respondent [owner], followed by an election by the appellant [bank] to accept the repudiation, thereby terminating the contract.
>
> Anticipatory breach occurs when a party by express language or conduct, or by implication from his actions, repudiates his contractual obligations. There must be conduct which evidences an intention not to be bound by the terms of the contract and absence of justification for such conduct. The innocent party may then elect either to preserve the contract and seek to enforce its terms, or to accept the repudiation and terminate the contract. In the latter case, the innocent party is freed from his future obligations under the contract, but may pursue such remedies as would have been available to him if the breach had taken place when performance was due. ...
>
> The letter ... demanded that the appellant either sign a new lease or vacate the premises, at the same time foreclosing any further discussion of the matter. Even against the background of four years of fruitless negotiation toward a formal lease, the letter amounted to a clear and unequivocal statement of intention not to be bound by the terms of the existing lease. ... No other conclusion is possible because neither of the alternatives given in the letter contemplated continuation of the existing lease. The ... [bank] accepted the second of the two alternatives given, that is, to vacate the premises. It was an election to accept the repudiation and to terminate the contract.

The court allowed the appeal by the bank against the trial judge's decision, which treated the bank as being in breach of a ten-year lease.

Homer et al. v. Toronto Dominion Bank
(1990) 83 Sas. R. 300
Saskatchewan Court of Appeal
May 28, 1990

G. REMEDIES

1. LACHES

"I say that equity will not leap across an eight-year gulf of acquiescence in what, as a matter of contract, is a clear breach thereof. The right here has been slept on too long; it smacks of a stale claim, and the court will not enforce it." These are the words of Judge Anderson, quoting from the reasons for judgment of Judge Drake of the lower court which held that a husband's action, commenced in December of 1987 to set aside a separation agreement breached by his wife in December of 1979, was barred by laches. The Court of Appeal agreed with the lower court's decision.

Logan v. Williams (Logan)
41 B.C.L.R. (2d) 34
B.C.C.A. at p. 39

• *A*lna de Bodisco began an action seeking $2 million from the fashion designer Oscar de la Renta based on an agreement to give her half his wealth. De la Renta admitted signing a letter making the promise. The promise was made on June 22, 1956; the lawsuit was filed April 1979. The court held that the suit was barred by the *Statute of Limitations*.

• *A* cyst removed from a Ms. Argue contained a four-faceted diamond one-third of a centimetre across, which apparently was dropped into her by a careless doctor or nurse during the Caesarean birth of her daughter 52 years previously.

2. EXEMPTION CLAUSES

Q u e s t i o n s

A party to a contract has the right to ask the court for a remedy if the other party is in breach. That is the essence of contract law. How does the court help a person if a clause in the contract states that he agrees not to seek a remedy if the other party is in breach?

Do these exemption clauses illustrate the freedom of contract or are they contrary to the essence of contract law?

AN EXEMPTION CLAUSE FAILS TO BE EFFECTIVE:

a. *when on its true construction (interpretation) the clause does not cover the incident;*

The defendant courier company promised delivery within four hours of request. The plaintiff bank called the courier company at 12:08 requesting delivery of municipal tax payments due that day. The driver arrived for the envelopes about 1:30, but they were not ready until 2:00. Three of six deliveries were made by 4 p.m. but at that time the driver was erroneously told by the dispatcher that it was too late to deliver the rest of the cheques. The driver delivered them the following morning. Two of the municipalities did not accept late payment without penalty and assessed fines of $54,089 and $39,407.

After the court concluded that the defendant courier was in breach of contract, the defendant argued, *inter alia*, that the regulations to the *Motor Carrier Act* limited its liability for "any loss or damage" to "$2.00 per pound unless a higher value declared."

In a unanimous decision, the B.C. Court of Appeal upheld the trial judge's interpretation that the regulations only applied to loss or damage to the goods themselves and did not apply to damages arising from delay. The court concluded that the courier must pay the $93,000 penalties which were reasonably foreseeable damages.

Bank of Montreal v. Overland Freight Lines Ltd. *(unreported)*
Summarized from The Lawyers Weekly
April 21, 1989, p. 2; June 1, 1990, p. 19

---

b. *when there was no reasonable notice of the term;*

c. *when there was a fundamental breach and on the true construction of the contract it wasn't meant to cover such a breach;*

Aurora TV and Radio v. *Gelco Express*

65 Man. R. (24) 145
MANITOBA'S QUEEN'S BENCH
MAY 10, 1990

OVERVIEW

Oliphant, J.: The plaintiff owns and operates an audio and video sales and service outlet at Brandon, Manitoba.

The defendant is a national courier company.

The plaintiff's action is for the recovery from the defendant of the value of a videocassette recorder. The defendant contracted to transport the videocassette recorder for the plaintiff. The videocassette recorder was either lost by or stolen from the defendant.

The defendant does not deny liability. It says its liability is limited by virtue of the contract between it and the plaintiff.

THE ISSUES

There are two issues to be resolved:

(1) Is there a clause in the contract between the plaintiff and the defendant which limits the liability of the defendant for the loss of the videocassette recorder?

(2) If so, is the defendant entitled to rely upon the clause?

[After reviewing the facts and the case law, the judge concluded as follows.]

CONCLUSIONS

On the question of notice of the limitation clause, I agree with and adopt the principles set forth in *Firchuk, supra*. The court must carefully scrutinize any clause in a contract which purports to limit the liability of a party, especially where a limitation clause appears in a standard form contract and purports to limit the liability of the drawer of the contract. Before a party can rely upon a clause which purports to limit his liability, reasonable notice of that clause must be given to the other party to the contract. Also the loss must come within the four corners of the limitation clause.

Here, on the face of the bill of lading, there is a reference to the limitation of the carrier's liability. However, the clause which purports to limit that liability appears on the reverse side of the bill of lading in very small print, buried amongst other words under a heading which is not indicative of a limitation clause.

Notice cannot be said to be reasonable, in my view, if the clause is neither legible nor capable of comprehension.

The clause utilized in the case before me was printed in such a manner that it is difficult, if not impossible, to read without the aid of magnification.

The limitation clause becomes incomprehensible in its attempt to cover almost every possibility in terms of limiting the carrier's liability. The wording of the clause is neither plain nor unambiguous. It is unclear. It is, quite simply, legal gobbledygook.

Even if one accepts the proposition that the requirement of notice is met if the nondrawing party to the contract is given the opportunity to read it, the notice cannot, in my opinion, be said to be reasonable if the clause is unintelligible because of its complexity.

I am not persuaded that any notice of the limitation clause was given to the plaintiff here. If notice were given, then I find that such notice in all the circumstances, was not reasonable.

Accordingly, the defendant is not able to rely upon the clause limiting its liability.

Even if it could be said that reasonable notice of the limitation clause had been given, I would still allow the plaintiff's claim.

The essence of the contract here was that the defendant was to carry certain goods being shipped by the plaintiff from Brandon to Calgary and to deliver the goods to an address in Calgary.

In a contract for carriage, the unexplained disappearance of the goods which are the subject of the contract is in my opinion a fundamental breach of the contract.

Where the goods which are the subject of the contract inexplicably disappear, the possibility of theft is real. As stated by Cory, J. A., in *Punch, supra*, a carrier is liable for loss where theft is a possibility unless there is a clause which clearly exempts the carrier from loss occasioned by theft.

I agree that whether an exclusionary or exception clause is applicable where there is a fundamental breach is to be determined according to the true construction of the contract.

Looking at the contract as a whole and bearing in mind the factual circumstances here, I am not able to say that it is fair and reasonable to attribute to the parties the intention that the limitation clause should survive notwithstanding a fundamental breach by the party in whose favour it was drawn. That is the test applied by Grange, J. A., in *Cathcart, supra*. Is my view it is the correct test.

Cathcart, supra, is also authority for the proposition that in a contract for the delivery of goods, the failure to deliver, though not deliberate, is a fundamental breach. I agree with the correctness of that proposition as well.

I disagree with the reasons for judgment given by Rowbotham, J., in *Lotepro Engineering and Construction Ltd., supra*. He took the view that a failure to deliver does not constitute a breach of the fundamental term of a contract for delivery, rather, it is negligent performance of a contract. I respectfully disagree.

Here, we have a contract for the carriage and delivery of goods. The goods were not delivered and there is no explanation for the disappearance of same. The defendant is liable for the fundamental breach of the contract and because of the lack of clarity in the limitation clause, it cannot, in my opinion, rely upon that clause to escape the consequences of the loss of the goods.

For the reasons stated, then, there will be judgment for the plaintiff in the sum of $699.95.

The plaintiff is entitled to its costs in the court below in the sum of $88.99. I award the plaintiff costs here in the sum of $250.00.

Additionally, the plaintiff is entitled to interest as is provided for under Part XIV of the *Court of Queen's Bench Act*, S.M. 1988-89, c. 4; C.C.S. M., c. C-280.

Judgment for plaintiff.

Note: This decision was affirmed by the Court of Appeal.

The case began: "Rozanne Kettunen was at a mud bog race sponsored by the Sicamous Firemen's Club, when a driver lost control of his vehicle, ran through a fence, and struck her. ... The day before the accident, Mrs. Kettunen signed her name to a document headed "RELEASE AND WAIVER OF LIABILITY AND INDEMNITY AGREEMENT." The Sicamous Firemen's Club brings this ... application for an order dismissing the plaintiffs' claims on the basis that the document operates to bar the action."

The court concluded that her signing the document did not bar her claim because it was not "short, easy to read" and was in fine print and there was "no effort made to bring to her attention the intended effect of the document." The court also found that the wording of the agreement did not cover the camping area, the area in which she was injured.

Kettunen, et al. v. Sicamous Firemen's Club et al.
http://www.courts.gov.bc.ca/
Supreme Court of British Columbia (In Chambers)
August 19, 1999

d.   *when the carrier does not adhere to the Warsaw Convention contained in the* Carriage By Air
     Act.

Nuvo Electronics Inc. v. London Assurance—the full case showing the complexity inherent in international trade—has among the many issues raised, the question of the effectiveness of a limited liability clause. Fifteen cartons containing integrated circuits valued at $1.4 million (U.S.) were bound for Toronto. They were sent from Seoul, Korea, arrived at the Korean Airlines Warehouse in San Francisco, but were never delivered by Air Canada to the carrier responsible for the final delivery in Toronto. The consignee sued, among others, its insurer and Air Canada.

With regard to the liability of Air Canada, the judge finds as a fact that Air Canada did not deliver the shipment to Emery Air Freight Corporation for delivery and thus Air Canada is responsible for the loss. The remaining issue was whether or not Air Canada could limit its liability under the terms of the Warsaw Convention, which is Schedule 1 to the *Carriage By Air Act*. The judge reviews articles of the Warsaw Convention, including:

> Article 9
> If the carrier accepts cargo without an air waybill having been made out, or if the air waybill does not contain all the particulars set out in Article 8 (a) to (i) inclusive and (q), the carrier shall not be entitled to avail himself of the provisions of this Convention which exclude or limit his liability.

> Article 11
> (1) The air waybill is prima facie evidence of the conclusion of the contract, of the receipt of the cargo and of the conditions of carriage.

Finding that the air waybill was missing a number of pieces of pertinent information—the name of the airport of departure, the name of the first carrier of the goods, whether the specified weight was pounds or kilograms, and the nature and quantity of the goods—the judge concluded Air Canada lost its ability to rely on the limited liability clause of the Convention.

Furthermore, Air Canada could lose its right to rely on the limited liability clause if the shipment were stolen by Air Canada employees in the course of their employment. In the words of the court:

> [para97] Much of the time at trial was devoted to the efforts of the parties opposite Air Canada to prove this shipment had been stolen by Air Canada employees and the efforts of Air Canada to defeat those allegations. ...

> [para103] In my view, the evidence is powerfully persuasive that this shipment of highly valuable computer components was either stolen by one or more Air Canada employees or at the very least with their complicity. ...

> [para105] ... In these circumstances, Article 25 precludes their carrier from availing itself of the limitation of liability provisions of the Convention.

Thus the plaintiff was entitled to judgment against both the insurance company and Air Canada.

Nuvo Electronics Inc. v. London Assurance
[2000] O.J. No. 2241 (Q.L.)
Ontario Superior Court of Justice
June 14, 2000

3. Equitable Remedies

Question

Can a party to a contract obtain an equitable remedy if he or she does not come with "clean hands"?

An insurance company terminated an insurance contract on the basis that it was obtained by a fraudulent misrepresentation. The person who made the fraudulent misrepresentation sued for the return of the premiums paid. After reviewing the facts, the arguments of the parties and the law, the court held in favour of the defendant insurer. The judge cited *Brophy v. North American Life Assurance Co.* (1902), 32 S.C.R. 261 for "perhaps the strongest language against the return of the premiums in any case" and quoted Taschereau J.:

> An interference, in the name of equity, to alleviate the offender's punishment by ordering the return of the premiums into his guilty hands would seem to me an inconsistency. The insured is not in a position to ask the assistance of the court, nor to invoke rules of equity the sole effect of which would be then to benefit the sole culprit. He has received no consideration from the company for the moneys he has paid, it is true, but he owes his loss to his own turpitude, and the court should have no pity upon him and no mercy for him, under any circumstances. I would apply to him the rule that he who has committed iniquity cannot claim equity.

Justice Pitt concludes: "... I believe that the authorities support the position of the insurer, and I also believe that it is the more principled and rational position."

Moscarelli v. Aetna Life Insurance Company of Canada
[1995] O.J. No. 1709 (Q.L.)
Ontario Court (General Division)
June 14, 1995

A. Specific Performance

Question

When is the equitable remedy of specific performance available?

 See *Semelhago v. Paramadevan* for the answer of the Supreme Court of Canada on p. 212.

B. Injunction

1267623 Ontario Inc. et al. *v.* Nexx Online, Inc.

[1999] O.J. No. 2246 (Q.L.)

ONTARIO SUPERIOR COURT OF JUSTICE

JUNE 14, 1999

Wilson J.: — This is a motion for an interlocutory injunction requiring that the defendant reactivate the plaintiff company's website. It is the plaintiffs' position that they rely upon the website and its advertising through bulk e-mail to carry on business. The plaintiffs through a third party were sending unsolicited bulk e-mail through the Internet at the rate of 200,000 e-mails per day. The defendant service provider warned the plaintiffs that if they did not cease sending the bulk e-mails through the third party, they would deactivate their website as contravening the parties' governing contract. The plaintiffs continued sending out bulk e-mails. The defendant disconnected the plaintiff's website. As the plaintiffs are unable to find another service provider that permits unsolicited bulk e-mails, they bring this motion seeking injunctive relief requiring that the website be reactivated.

This motion raises issues with respect to the recent but burgeoning use of the Internet communication services for commercial bulk e-mail advertising purposes, colloquially known amongst internet users as "spam". To determine whether an injunction should be granted, it will be necessary to examine the terms of the contract between the parties. This contract is governed by the rules of "Netiquette", which is defined as the growing body of acceptable, though as yet largely unwritten, etiquette with respect to conduct by users of the Internet.

THE TEST FOR GRANTING AN INJUNCTION

The authority of the court to provide interlocutory relief is found in s. 101 of the Courts of Justice Act, R.S.O. 1990, c. C.43:

101(1) In the Superior Court of Justice, an interlocutory injunction or mandatory order may be granted ... where it appears to a judge of the court to be just or convenient to do so.

The test in Canada for granting interlocutory relief was first set out by Lord Diplock in *American Cyanamid Co. v. Ethicon Ltd.*, [1975] A.C. 396 (H.L.), and has most recently been reaffirmed by the Supreme Court of Canada in *RJR-MacDonald Inc. v. Canada (Attorney General)*, [1994] 1 S.C.R. 311, 111 D.L.R. (4th) 385. In determining whether such an order should be made, it is necessary to consider three questions:

(1) Is there a serious question to be tried?

(2) Will the applicant suffer irreparable harm, which cannot be compensated by an award of damages, if the injunction is not granted?

(3) Which party will suffer the greater harm from granting or refusing the remedy pending a decision on the merits, i.e., where lies the balance of convenience?

FACTUAL BACKGROUND

[The judge reviews the business and relationship of the parties and the sequence of events that led to this lawsuit]. ...

THE TERMS OF THE CONTRACT

The plaintiffs allege that Nexx is in breach of the contract for having disconnected the beaverhome.com website, several months prior to the expiry of the service agreement between the parties. The full yearly fee of $352.51 had been paid in advance by the plaintiffs.

There is a factual dispute as to what was specifically discussed with respect to bulk e-mail prior to the contract being executed. The plaintiffs claim to have been told by Nexx before signing the contract that there were no provisions prohibiting the sending of bulk commercial e-mail. In sharp contrast, the president of Nexx ... [says the opposite].

Although several contractual issues were argued, in my view, there are two relevant provisions of the contract:

The Account Holder agrees to follow generally accepted "Netiquette" when sending e-mail messages or posting newsgroup messages ...

The undersigned Account Holder agrees to abide by the following provisions of this service contract and may have to agree to additional provisions from Nexx Online covering this agreement and/or any future services added to this agreement. If Account Holder refuses to accept any future provisions, Account Holder will have the option to cancel service and receive a pro-rated refund of any moneys pre-paid for this agreement. The pro-rated refund will be calculated after the normal monthly cost for the service has been deducted from any amounts pre-paid by Account Holder.

DOES UNSOLICITED BULK E-MAIL OFFEND THE RULES OF "NETIQUETTE"?

The governing contract does not specifically forbid bulk e-mail advertising. It does provide, however, that the "Account Holder agrees to follow generally accepted "Netiquette" when sending e-mail messages or posting newsgroup messages . . .." It is the position of the defendant that sending out unsolicited bulk e-mail is in breach of established rules of Netiquette, and hence the defendants were entitled to disconnect the plaintiffs' website services without a pro rata reimbursement of the prepaid balance of the contract. The plaintiffs argue the sending out of bulk e-mail through a third party is not a breach of Netiquette.

What then are the rules of Netiquette? It is acknowledged that there is no written Netiquette policy. It appears that a code is evolving based upon good neighbour principles for the orderly development of the Internet, and to prevent potential Internet abuse.

The defendant has provided copies of reports on bulk e-mail advertising that lead to the inevitable conclusion that the sending of unsolicited bulk commercial e-mail is considered an inappropriate and unacceptable use of the Internet by most users and service providers. Few if any Internet service providers allow unsolicited bulk e-mail. In the United States, several states have prohibited the practice or severely restricted its use. John Levine, author of *The Internet for Dummies*, has posted a paper entitled "Why is Spam Bad?" at http://spam.abuse.net/spambad.html, in which he summarizes six important problems with spam advertising and why it is considered unacceptable:

(1) the recipient pays far more, in time and trouble as well as money, than the sender does, unlike advertising through the postal service;

(2) the recipient must take the time to request removal from the mailing list, and most spammers claim to remove names on request but rarely do so;

(3) many spammers use intermediate systems without authorization to avoid blocks set up to avoid spam;

(4) many spam messages are deceptive and partially or entirely fraudulent;

(5) spammers often use false return addresses to avoid the cost of receiving responses;

(6) some forms of spam are illegal in various jurisdictions in the United States.

The complaints received by the defendant were included in the motion material. There is a consistent flavour to the responses. The complaints received by Nexx regarding the plaintiffs' unsolicited advertising e-mail were often intense and to the point of outrage. This negative public response from Internet users is an indication that unsolicited commercial bulk e-mail advertising is not an accepted Internet practice. Some of the complaints also pointed out apparently forged return addresses and e-mail headers on e-mail sent out by the plaintiffs: one had the return address "catholic.org", implying the existence of a religious affiliation, but was advertising the beaverhome.com website.

CASE LAW RELEVANT TO THE ISSUE OF "NETIQUETTE"

Not surprisingly, there are no Canadian cases on point defining rules of Netiquette or with respect to unsolicited bulk e-mail. However, several American cases have dealt with disputes over unsolicited bulk e-mail. ... [The judge reviews the U.S. decisions]. ...

The Internet is a potent legitimate means of advertising, selling on the Internet benefiting retailers and consumers alike. The use of the Internet is in its relative infancy. In the words of counsel, it is "an unruly beast". Or so it will certainly become without a foundation of good neighbour commercial principles. The unrestricted use of unsolicited bulk commercial e-mail appears to undermine the integrity and utility of the Internet system. Network systems become blocked. The user expends time and expense reviewing or deleting unwanted messages. Of fundamental importance is the distortion of the essentially personal nature of an e-mail address.

I conclude after reviewing the principles that emerge in the American case law, the excerpts from the literature provided, and the reaction of individual Internet users that unless a service provider specifically allows in the contract for unsolicited commercial bulk e-mail to be distributed, it appears clear that sending out unsolicited bulk e-mail for commercial advertising purposes is contrary to the emerging principles of Netiquette. This conclusion is further reinforced by the admission by the plaintiff that they are unable to find another service provider which will permit bulk e-mail advertising through a third party.

NEXX'S RIGHT TO ADD PROVISIONS TO THE CONTRACT

Although the contract does not include a specific provision against bulk commercial e-mail, it does permit Nexx to add terms to the contract with the requirement to reimburse for the balance owing under the contract if the client is not in agreement with the new term. There is no dispute between the parties that Nexx informed the plaintiffs that they were not permitted to send bulk e-mail advertising prior to terminating their website. By the terms of the contract, the defendants were entitled to add a term to the contract prohibiting unsolicited commercial bulk e-mail, upon payment of the prorated balance of the fees that were prepaid for the one-year term of the contract.

THE CONTRACT BETWEEN NEXX AND EXODUS

The contract between the defendant Nexx and Exodus, Nexx's service provider, is relevant in assessing irreparable harm and the balance of convenience as between the parties. The Nexx/Exodus contract specifically precludes the sending of unsolicited bulk advertising e-mail. The contract includes an "Online Conduct Policy", which begins:

> Customer [here, Nexx] will not, and will not permit any persons using Customer's online facilities (including but not limited to Customer's Web site(s) and transmission capabilities), to do any of the following:
> * Send Spam (unsolicited commercial messages or communications in any form).

The Nexx/Exodus contract also includes a clear "Anti-Spamming Policy Statement", ... [which is reproduced in full].

Both Nexx and Exodus received multiple complaints about the unsolicited bulk e-mails received from the plaintiff company. Exodus warned Nexx that the unsolicited bulk e-mail was prohibited by their anti-spamming policy. Exodus warned Nexx that the Nexx/Exodus contract would be enforced if Nexx did not take timely action to prevent another such occurrence. It is clear that if the injunction requested is granted, Nexx will be in breach of the terms of the Nexx/Exodus contract creating serious business risks including potential termination of services.

CONCLUSIONS

In addressing the questions with respect to the granting of an injunction I conclude as follows:

(1) Is there a serious question to be tried?

For the reasons previously given, I conclude that there is no serious question to be tried. Firstly, I conclude that sending unsolicited bulk commercial e-mail is in breach of the emerging principles of Netiquette, unless it is specifically permitted in the governing contract. As the rules of Netiquette govern the parties' contract, the plaintiff is in breach of its terms justifying disconnection of service. Secondly, in the alternative, Nexx is permitted to add terms to the contract precluding a Nexx client sending unsolicited bulk e-mail directly, or through a third party. If the plaintiffs do not concur with the new term, they are entitled to a rebate of the pro-rated balance of the contract price, and the defendant is entitled to disconnect service. The defendant has agreed to repay the prorated balance owing under the contract from April 5, 1999 to August 5, 1999.

(2) Will the applicant suffer irreparable harm, which cannot be compensated by an award of damages, if the injunction is not granted?

The applicant paid the sum of $352.51 for the contract. The applicant could simply enter into another agreement with a new web host service provider to end any harm. If the plaintiff is unable to locate another service provider that will permit commercial bulk e-mail, the conclusion with respect to breach of Netiquette is irrefutable.

(3) Which party will suffer the greater harm from granting or refusing the remedy pending a decision on the merits, i.e., where lies the balance of convenience?

Finally, the balance of convenience lies with the defendant. Had the plaintiff been permitted to continue sending out unsolicited bulk e-mail directing potential customers to the beaverhome.com website, Nexx would have risked having their Internet access cut off by Exodus. Neither plaintiff nor defendant could have carried on their business. The ripple effect to the 984 customers of Nexx which have websites hosted by Nexx cannot easily be assessed but is a relevant factor in considering the balance of convenience.

DISPOSITION

For the reasons given the request for an injunction is dismissed. As there are no Canadian cases dealing with Internet issues, and specifically unsolicited bulk commercial e-mail in the context of Netiquette, there should be no order as to costs of this motion.

Motion dismissed.

C. ACCOUNTING

 For the court's use of the equitable remedy of accounting see the case involving copyright infringement, *Society of Composers, Authors and Music Publishers of Canada v. 348803 Alberta Ltd. et al.*, p. 225.

D. QUANTUM MERUIT

 For the court's use of the equitable remedy of *quantum meruit* see *Hoffer v. Verdone*, p. 101.

4. DAMAGES

LIQUIDATED DAMAGES

Questions

Can the parties to a contract agree in the contract on the amount of damages to be paid in the event of a breach? Is such an agreement binding?

Lee **v.** *Skalbania*

SUPREME COURT OF BRITISH COLUMBIA
VANCOUVER REGISTRY NO. C872510
DECEMBER 21, 1987

Background facts: Lee and Skalbania entered into a contract for the sale of Lee's property at a price of $975,000, the completion date to be March 31, 1987 and the balance of the cash payment to be paid that day. The vendor Lee was to carry a second mortgage of $200,000. The contract also provided that Skalbania pay a deposit of $50,000 which, at the option of the vendor, would be "absolutely forfeited to the owner as liquidated damages" in the event of his breach. He did breach. He failed to tender the cash payment on the completion date, which was extended to April 1, 1987. Lee refused to grant a further extension of time, cancelled the agreement, and sold the property to another for the same price, but for cash. Lee now claims the $50,000 deposit held in trust.

Gow J.:—... The primary issue is whether the deposit of $50,000 was liquidated damages or a penalty.

The position of the defendant is aptly set out in the affidavits of Skalbania [in which he argues, among other things, that it would be unfair and unconscionable for the plaintiff to retain the deposit when she suffered no loss and in fact made a profit (by not taking a mortgage back)]. ...

Filed on behalf of the plaintiff on October 26, 1987 was an affidavit by one Banu Foroutan, a real estate sales person of Vancouver, who stated "that the usual practice in the real estate business is to obtain a minimum deposit on the sale of residential property of between 5% and 10% of the total purchase price".

...

I hold that the failure of the defendant to perform timeously was a breach of contract on his part which relieved the plaintiff of her obligations to perform under the contract but the contract survived for the purpose of enabling the plaintiff to pursue her remedies thereunder.

I find that she elected the remedy of cancellation of the contract and the forfeiture to her of the deposit as liquidated damages. That is, however, a finding in fact of what the plaintiff did. The question remains is she entitled to that remedy? The answer is "yes" if the $50,000 was a genuine pre-estimate of damages: the answer is "no" if it was a penalty. But even if the answer is a "penalty" the plaintiff will be deprived of the $50,000 only if it were unconscionable for her to retain that sum. *Dimensional Investments Ltd. v. R.,* [1968] S.C.R. 93.

In *Elsley v. J.G. Collins Insurance Agencies Ltd.,* (1978) 2 S.C.R. 916, Dickson J. (as he then was) said at p. 937:

It is now evident that the power to strike down a penalty clause is a blatant interference with freedom of contract and is designed for the sole purpose of providing relief against oppression for the party having to pay the stipulated sum. It has no place where there is no oppression. ...

Of course, if an agreed sum is a valid liquidated damages clause, the plaintiff is entitled at law to recover this sum regardless of the actual loss sustained.

The facts in *Hughes v. Lukuvka* (1970)–75 (BCCA) bear a striking similarity to the facts in this case.

The headnote reads:

Appellant had agreed to buy property for $59,500 and time was expressed to be of the essence; he paid a deposit of $5,000. ...

The judgment of the Court was given by McFarlane J.A. who concluded his reasons by citing a dictum of Lord Parmoor in *Dunlop Pneumatic Tyre Co. v. New Garage & Motor Co.,* 1915 A.C. 79 PC 101:

No abstract can be laid down without reference to the special facts of the particular case, but when competent parties by free contract are purporting to agree a sum as liquidated damages, there is no reason for refusing a wide limit of discretion. To justify interference there must be an extravagant disproportion between the agreed sum and *the amount of any damage capable of pre-estimate.*

The emphasis added is mine because McFarlane J.A. went on to say:

Applying these principles to the facts, I am of the opinion that the deposit of $5,000 should not be regarded as a penalty and that its retention by the respondent is not unconscionable.

In that case, the amount of the deposit was approximately 1/12 of the purchase price. In the instant case, the amount of deposit is approximately between 1/19 and 1/20.

Applying the principles discussed to the facts of this case, I find that the sum of $50,000 is not a penalty, but a more than reasonable pre-estimate of damage and, therefore, is liquidated damages. Even if I were in error in making that finding, and the sum was a penalty I would find that it was not unconscionable for the plaintiff to "retain" it.

Does it make any difference that the plaintiff was fortunate enough to re-sell for the same price? [Clearly not. At] the time when the agreement about liquidated damages is made, each party takes a risk, the vendor that the damages he may in fact suffer from failure on the part of the purchaser to complete will be very much greater, and the purchaser, that the vendor may not suffer any damage at all, or if he does suffer damage that damage is much less in amount than the amount stipulated as liquidated damages.

Nor does it matter that the plaintiff as vendor was to take a mortgage back of $200,000. First of all, that was an advantage to the defendant and a disadvantage to the plaintiff because she could not put that part of the price into her pocket. Secondly, even with respect to the cash balance of $775,000, the $50,000 was only 1/15. ...

Judgment for plaintiff.

When the purchaser missed the deadline for tendering the $500,000 for the property, the deadline was extended provided the purchaser pay, in addition to the $10,000 already given as a deposit, $150,000, all to be "treated as a deposit." The failure of the purchasers to meet the second deadline resulted in a struggle for the $160,000. In the words of the court:

> "Can the defendants retain the $160,000 as a deposit? Neither law nor equity mandates such an unjust result. … Such damage is measured by the injury suffered by the vendor but does not include any punitive element. …[There are no] special circumstances that would warrant a finding that the sum that was 31.25% of the total purchase price could qualify as a true deposit."

*** Porto v. DiDomizio ***
[1996] O.J. No. 22 (Q.L.)
Ontario Court of Justice (General Division)
January 9, 1996

DOCTRINE OF MITIGATION

The contract between Whitener and the Royal Winnipeg Ballet (RWB) allowed the company to terminate his employment upon 12 months notice. The company wrote to Whitener informing him that his employment with RWB would cease in one year and stated: "In order to allow you to devote your full efforts to seeking other employment opportunities, you will not be required to continue performing any of your employment duties effective immediately." The RWB continued to pay him for several months but stopped about a month after Whitener began work elsewhere. Whitener sued for salary for the balance of the notice year; he contended that he was still in the employ of RWB until the expiry of the notice period. His action failed; the notice period was the period within which he was required to try to find alternative employment to mitigate his loss.

The Manitoba Court of Appeal rejected Whitener's argument that the contract bargained away "the doctrine of mitigation":

[para6]   The doctrine of mitigation was explained in the House of Lords decision in *British Westinghouse Electric and Manufacturing Company, Limited v. Underground Electric Railways Company of London, Limited,* [1912] A.C. 673. Lord Haldane wrote (at p. 689):

> The fundamental basis [of damages for breach of contract] is … compensation for pecuniary loss naturally flowing from the breach; but this first principle is qualified by a second, which imposes on a plaintiff the duty of taking all reasonable steps to mitigate the loss consequent on the breach, and debars him from claiming any part of the damages which is due to his neglect to take such steps. In the words of James L.J. in *Dunkirk Colliery Co. v. Lever* [(1878), 9 Ch.D. 20 at p. 25],
>
> > "The person who has broken the contract is not to be exposed to additional cost by reason of the plaintiffs not doing what they ought to have done as reasonable men, and the plaintiffs not being under any obligation to do anything otherwise than in the ordinary course of business."
>
> As James L.J. indicates, this second principle does not impose on the plaintiff an obligation to take any steps which a reasonable and prudent man would not ordinarily take in the course of his business.
> …

[para7]   The doctrine was restated in more modern terms by the Supreme Court of Canada in an employment contracts decision, *Red Deer College v. Michaels,* [1976] 2 S.C.R. 324. Chief Justice Laskin began (at pp. 330-332):

> It is, of course, for a wronged plaintiff to prove his damages, and there is therefore a burden upon him to establish on a balance of probabilities what his loss is. The parameters of loss are governed by

legal principle. The primary rule in breach of contract cases, that a wronged plaintiff is entitled to be put in as good a position as he would have been if there had been proper performance by the defendant, is subject to the qualification that the defendant cannot be called upon to pay for avoidable losses which would result in an increase in the quantum of damages payable to the plaintiff. The reference in the case law to a "duty" to mitigate should be understood in this sense.

In short, a wronged plaintiff is entitled to recover damages for the losses he has suffered but the extent of those losses may depend upon whether he has taken reasonable steps to avoid their unreasonable accumulation. In *Payzu, Ltd. v. Saunders*, [[1919] 2 K.B. 581] at p. 589, Scrutton L.J. explained the matter in this way:

> Whether it be more correct to say that a plaintiff must minimize his damages, or to say that he can recover no more than he would have suffered if he had acted reasonably, because any further damages do not reasonably follow from the defendant's breach, the result is the same.

The appeal was dismissed by a unanimous court.

***

Whitener v. Royal Winnipeg Ballet
[1998] M.J. No. 530 (Q.L.)
Manitoba Court of Appeal
November 3, 1998

***

QUANTUM OF DAMAGES

Question

How does the court approach the problem of determining the amount of damages to be paid by the party found to be in breach of contract?

Parta Industries Ltd. *v.* Canadian Pacific Ltd. et al.

48 D.L.R. (3D) 463
BRITISH COLUMBIA SUPREME COURT
JULY 4, 1974

Summary of the facts from the law report, reprinted with permission of Canada Law Book Inc., 240 Edward Street, Aurora, Ontario L4G 3S9.

The defendant carriers agreed to ship from Montreal to British Columbia certain goods imported from Belgium, described as construction material. The bill of lading was marked "RUSH." The goods consisted of equipment essential to the plaintiff's plan to bring into operation a manufacturing plant. Owing to the derailment of three railway cars the goods were damaged, and as a result, the plaintiff had to reorder the goods from Belgium, and the opening of its plant was delayed for 105 days. [The plaintiffs sued] for damages caused by the delay. ...

Craig, J.:—The plaintiff commenced an action against the defendants (hereinafter referred to as "the defendants") claiming

(a) Special and general damages for breach of contract entered into between the Plaintiff and the Defendants on the l2th day of September 1969, by which contract the Defendants, common carriers, contracted to deliver goods for and to the Plaintiff, and did fail to do so in accordance with the terms, express and implied, of the said contract. Which failure caused financial loss to the Plaintiff.

(b) In the alternative, damages against the Defendants for negligence in the performance of the aforementioned contract, which negligence caused financial loss to the Plaintiff.

The defendants have denied the plaintiff's claim, generally, and have counterclaimed for the sum of $1,548.59 which, they allege, is the net amount owing to them after making financial adjustments between the parties relating to this incident....

Mr. Moran contends that the failure of the defendant to deliver the equipment in usable condition on or before September 19th, or within a reasonable time of this date, was a breach of the contract to "rush" delivery and that the plaintiff suffered damages totaling $129,705. He filed a schedule as ex. "4" which representatives of the plaintiff had prepared, showing how damages were calculated and what items were included. He submitted that these items of damages and the amounts claimed for these items are such damages:

(1) "…as may fairly and reasonable be considered as…arising naturally…", or at least,

(2) "…as may reasonable be supposed to have been in contemplation of both parties, at the time they made the contract, as the probable result of the breach of it."

citing *Hadley v. Baxendale* (1854), 9 Ex. 341, 156 E.R. 145, and the well-known judgment of Asquith, L.J., in *Victoria Laundry (Windsor) Ltd. v. Newman Industries Ltd.; Coulson & Co. Ltd. (Third Parties)*, [1949] 2 K.B. 528, [1949] 1 All E.R. 997. …

In the *Victoria Laundry (Windsor) Ltd. v. Newman Industries Ltd.* case, *supra*, Asquith, L.J., listed six propositions applicable to damages for breach of contract. His judgment has been referred to on numerous occasions. These propositions are as follows [at pp. 539-40]:

(1) It is well settled that the governing purpose of damages is to put the party whose rights have been violated in the same position, so far as money can do so, as if his rights had been observed: (*Sally Wertheim v. Chicoutimi Pulp Company*, [1911] A.C. 301). This purpose, if relentlessly pursued, would provide him with a complete indemnity for all loss *de facto* resulting from a particular breach, however improbable, however unpredictable. This, in contract at least, is recognized as too harsh a rule. Hence,

(2) In cases of breach of contract the aggrieved party is only entitled to recover such part of the loss actually resulting as was at the time of the contract reasonably foreseeable as liable to result from the breach.

(3) What was at that time reasonably so foreseeable depends on the knowledge then possessed by the parties or, at all events, by the party who later commits the breach.

(4) For this purpose, knowledge "possessed" is of two kinds; one imputed, the other actual. Everyone, as a reasonable person, is taken to know the "ordinary course of things" and consequently what loss is liable to result from a breach of contract in that ordinary course. This is the subject matter of the "first rule" in *Hadley v. Baxendale*. But to this knowledge, which a contract-breaker is assumed to possess whether he actually possesses it or not, there may have to be added in a particular case knowledge which he actually possesses, of special circumstances

outside the "ordinary course of things," of such a kind that a breach in those special circumstances would be liable to cause more loss. Such a case attracts the operation of the "second rule" so as to make additional loss also recoverable.

(5) In order to make the contract-breaker liable under either rule it is not necessary that he should actually have asked himself what loss is liable to result from a breach. As has often been pointed out, parties at the time of contracting contemplate not the breach of the contract, but its performance. It suffices that, if he had considered the question, he would as a reasonable man have concluded that the loss in question was liable to result (see certain observations of Lord du Parcq in the recent case of *A/B Karlshamms Oljefabriker v. Monarch Steamship Company Limited*, [1949] A.C. 196).

(6) Nor, finally, to make a particular loss recoverable, need it be proved that upon a given state of knowledge the defendant could, as a reasonable man, foresee that a breach must necessarily result in that loss. It is enough if he could foresee it was likely so to result. It is indeed enough, to borrow from the language of Lord du Parcq in the same case, at page 158, if the loss (or some factor without which it would not have occurred) is a "serious possibility" or a "real danger." For short, we have used the word "liable" to result. Possibly the colloquialism "on the cards" indicates the shade of meaning with some approach to accuracy.

In his judgment, also, Asquith, L.J., said that the case of *British Columbia Saw-Mill Co. v. Nettleship* (1868), L.R. 3 C.P. 499, annexed a rider to the principle laid in *Hadley v. Baxendale* to the effect

…that where knowledge of special circumstances is relied on as enhancing the damage recoverable that knowledge must have been brought home to the defendant at the time of the contract and in such circumstances that the defendant impliedly undertook to bear any special loss referable to a breach in those special circumstances. The knowledge which was lacking in that case on the part of the defendant was knowledge that the particular box of machinery negligently lost by the defendants was one without which the rest of the machinery could not be put together and would therefore be useless.

Having regard to the evidence in this case and the circumstances generally, I find that the only knowledge possessed by the defendant was that he was to "RUSH" delivery of 77 packages of "construction material." There is nothing in the contract to indicate the nature of the material, nor the use to which it was to be put. Certainly, there is nothing to indicate that it was to be used in a large manufacturing plant and that the plant could not operate without the equipment. In other words, the defendant did not have knowledge of the special circumstances of the situation which would bring into operation the second branch of the rule in *Hadley v. Baxendale*. That being so, what damages, if any, in this case should be considered as "…such as may fairly and reasonably be considered as…arising naturally i.e. according to the natural course of things from the breach of contract…"? In my opinion, the defendant could have reasonably foreseen on the facts which were known to it in this case that a delay in delivery, or a failure to deliver was liable to result in:

(a) a delay in actual construction;
(b) extra labour costs;
(c) interest;
(d) depreciation of equipment;

(e) additional overhead expenses;
(f) cost of repairing and replacing equipment.

While I think that the defendant could have reasonably foreseen a delay in construction, I do not think that the defendant could have reasonably foreseen a delay of 105 days. …

Questions

Is a contractor liable in damages to a subsequent purchaser if the building is defective? Can one recover for an economic loss when there is no injury to persons or damage to property?

Winnipeg Condominium Corporation No. 36 *v.* Bird Construction Co.

http://www.lexum.umontreal.ca/
SUPREME COURT OF CANADA
JANUARY 26, 1995

[1] La Forest J. — May a general contractor responsible for the construction of a building be held tortiously liable for negligence to a subsequent purchaser of the building, who is not in contractual privity with the contractor, for the cost of repairing defects in the building arising out of negligence in its construction? That is the issue that was posed by a motion for summary judgment and a motion to strike out a claim as disclosing no reasonable cause of action argued before Galanchuk J. of the Manitoba Court of Queen's Bench . … Galanchuk J. dismissed the motions, but the Court of Appeal of Manitoba allowed an appeal from this decision and struck out the claim against the contractor on the grounds that the damages sought were for economic loss, which were not recoverable in the circumstances, and hence that the claim did not disclose a reasonable cause of action.

[2] For reasons that will appear, I do not, with respect, share the views of the Court of Appeal; I agree with Galanchuk J. that the action should proceed to trial. …

FACTS

[3] On April 19, 1972, a Winnipeg land developer, Tuxedo Properties Co. Ltd. ("Tuxedo"), entered into a contract ("the General Contract") with a general contractor, Bird Construction Co. Ltd. ("Bird"), for the construction of a 15-storey, 94-unit apartment building. In the General Contract, Bird undertook to construct the building in accordance with plans and specifications prepared by the architectural firm of Smith Carter Partners ("Smith Carter"), with whom Tuxedo also had a contract. On June 5, 1972, Bird entered into a subcontract with a masonry subcontractor, Kornovski & Keller Masonry Ltd. ("Kornovski & Keller"), under which the latter undertook to perform the masonry portion of the work specified under the General Contract. …

[4] The building was initially built and used as an apartment block, but was converted into a condominium in October, 1978, when Winnipeg Condominium Corporation No. 36 ("the Condominium Corporation") became the registered owner of the land and building. …

[5] In 1982, the Board of Directors of the Condominium Corporation became concerned about the state of the exterior cladding of the building (consisting of 4-inch thick slabs of stone), which had been installed by the subcontractor, Kornovski & Keller. The directors observed that some of the mortar had broken away and that cracks were developing in the stone work. As a result of these concerns, the Condominium Corporation retained a firm of structural engineers and the original architects, Smith Carter, to inspect the building. The engineers and Smith Carter recommended some minor remedial work but offered the opinion that the stonework on the building was structurally sound. The remedial work, costing $8,100, was undertaken at the Condominium Corporation's expense in 1982.

[6] On May 8, 1989, a storey-high section of the cladding, approximately twenty feet in length, fell from the ninth storey level of the building to the ground below. The Condominium Corporation retained engineering consultants who conducted further inspections. Following these inspections, the Condominium Corporation had the entire cladding removed and replaced at a cost in excess of $1.5 million. …

ANALYSIS

[12] This case gives this Court the opportunity once again to address the question of recoverability in tort for economic loss. …

[13] Traditionally, the courts have characterized the costs incurred by a plaintiff in repairing a defective chattel or building as "economic loss" on the grounds that costs of those repairs do not arise from injury to persons or damage to property apart from the defective chattel or building itself; see *Rivtow Marine Ltd. v. Washington Iron Works*, [1974] S.C.R. 1189, at p. 1207. … Adopting this traditional characterization as a convenient starting point for my analysis, I observe that the losses claimed by the Condominium Corporation in the present case fall quite clearly under the category of economic loss. In their statement of claim, the Condominium Corporation claim damages in excess of $1.5 million from the respondent Bird, the subcon-

tractor Kornovski & Keller and the architects Smith Carter, representing the cost of repairing the building subsequent to the collapse of the exterior cladding on May 8, 1989. The Condominium Corporation is not claiming that anyone was injured by the collapsing exterior cladding or that the collapsing cladding damaged any of its other property. Rather, its claim is simply for the cost of repairing the allegedly defective masonry and putting the exterior of the building back into safe working condition. ...

[16] Proceeding on the assumption, then, that the losses claimed in this case are purely economic, the sole issue before this Court is whether the losses claimed by the Condominium Corporation are the type of economic losses that should be recoverable in tort. In coming to its conclusion that the losses claimed by the Condominium Corporation are not recoverable in tort, the Manitoba Court of Appeal, we saw, followed the reasoning of the House of Lords in *D & F Estates*. In that case, the House of Lords found that the cost of repairing a defect in a building is not recoverable in negligence by a successor in title against the original contractor in the absence of a contractual relationship or a special relationship of reliance. I should say that the Court of Appeal might well have come to the same conclusion on the basis of the majority opinion in *Rivtow*, supra, ...

[21] Huband J.A. found the reasoning in *D & F Estates* to be compelling and of strong persuasive authority ... [The judge critiques *D & F Estates*.] ...

[34] I conclude, therefore, that the *D&F Estates* decision is not of strong persuasive authority in the Canadian context. Accordingly, the question arising in this appeal must be resolved with reference to the test developed in *Anns* and *Kamloops*. I will now proceed, applying this test, to discuss whether the costs of repair claimed by the Condominium Corporation are the type of economic loss that should be recoverable in tort. [The first test:]

Was There a Sufficiently Close Relationship Between the Parties so that, in the Reasonable Contemplation of Bird, Carelessness on its Part Might Cause Damage to a Subsequent Purchaser of the Building such as the Condominium Corporation?

[35] ... Buildings are permanent structures that are commonly inhabited by many different persons over their useful life. By constructing the building negligently, contractors (or any other person responsible for the design and construction of a building) create a foreseeable danger that will threaten not only the original owner, but every inhabitant during the useful life of the building. As noted by the Supreme Court of South Carolina, in *Terlinde v. Neely*, 271 S.E. 2d 768 (1980), at p. 770:

> The key inquiry is foreseeability, not privity. In our mobile society, it is clearly foreseeable that more than the original purchaser will seek to enjoy the fruits of the builder's efforts. The plaintiffs, being a member of the class for which the home was constructed, are entitled to a duty of care in construction commensurate with industry standards. [...] By placing this product into the stream of commerce, the builder owes a duty of care to those who will use his product, so as to render him accountable for negligent workmanship.

[36] In my view, the reasonable likelihood that a defect in a building will cause injury to its inhabitants is also sufficient to ground a contractor's duty in tort to subsequent purchasers of the building for the cost of repairing the defect if that defect is discovered prior to any injury and if it poses a real and substantial danger to the inhabitants of the building. ...

[37] Apart from the logical force of holding contractors liable for the cost of repair of dangerous defects, there is also a strong underlying policy justification for imposing liability in these cases. Under the law as developed in *D&F Estates* and *Murphy*, the plaintiff who moves quickly and responsibly to fix a defect before it causes injury to persons or damage to property must do so at his or her own expense. By contrast, the plaintiff who, either intentionally or through neglect, allows a defect to develop into an accident may benefit at law from the costly and potentially tragic consequences. In my view, this legal doctrine is difficult to justify because it serves to encourage, rather than discourage, reckless and hazardous behaviour. Maintaining a bar against recoverability for the cost of repair of dangerous defects provides no incentive for plaintiffs to mitigate potential losses and tends to encourage economically inefficient behaviour. ...

[38] This conclusion is borne out by the facts of the present case, which fall squarely within the category of what I would define as a "real and substantial danger." ... The piece of cladding that fell from the building was a storey high, was made of 4"-thick Tyndall stone, and dropped nine storeys. Had this cladding landed on a person or on other property, it would unquestionably have caused serious injury or damage. Indeed, it was only by chance that the cladding fell in the middle of the night and caused no harm. In this light, I believe that the Condominium Corporation behaved responsibly, and as a reasonable home owner should, in having the building inspected and repaired immediately. Bird should not be insulated from liability simply because the current owner of the building acted quickly to alleviate the danger that Bird itself may well have helped to create. ...

[42] ... I note that the present case is distinguishable on a policy level from cases where the workmanship is merely shoddy or substandard but not dangerously defective. ... Accordingly, it is sufficient for present purposes to say that, if Bird is found negligent at trial, the Condominium Corporation would be entitled on this reasoning to recover the reasonable cost of putting the building into a non-dangerous state, but not the cost of any repairs that would serve merely to improve the quality, and not the safety, of the building.

[43] I conclude that the law in Canada has now progressed to the point where it can be said that contractors (as well as subcontractors, architects and engineers) who take part in the design and construction of a building will owe a duty in tort to subsequent purchasers of the building if it can be shown that it was foreseeable that a failure to take reasonable care in constructing the building would create defects that pose a substantial danger to the health and safety of the occupants. Where negligence is established and such defects manifest themselves before any damage to persons or property occurs, they should, in my view, be liable for the reasonable cost of repairing the defects and putting the building back into a non-dangerous state.

[The second step in the *Anns* case is]

Are There Any Considerations that Ought to Negate (a) the Scope of the Duty and (b) the Class of Persons to Whom it is Owed or (c) the Damages to which a Breach of it May Give Rise?

[44] There are two primary and interrelated concerns raised by the recognition of a contractor's duty in tort to subsequent

purchasers of buildings for the cost of repairing dangerous defects. The first is that warranties respecting quality of construction are primarily contractual in nature and cannot be easily defined or limited in tort. ...

[45] The second concern is that the recognition of such a duty interferes with the doctrine of caveat emptor. ...

[46] In my view, these concerns are both merely versions of the more general and traditional concern that allowing recovery for economic loss in tort will subject a defendant to what Cardozo C.J. in *Ultramares Corp. v. Touche*, 174 N.E. 441 (N.Y.C.A. 1931), at p. 444, called "liability in an indeterminate amount for an indeterminate time to an indeterminate class." In light of the fact that most buildings have a relatively long useful life, the concern is that a contractor will be subject potentially to an indeterminate amount of liability to an indeterminate number of successive owners over an indeterminate time period. The doctrines of privity of contract and caveat emptor provide courts with a useful mechanism for limiting liability in tort. But the problem, as I will now attempt to demonstrate, is that it is difficult to justify the employment of these doctrines in the tort context in any principled manner apart from their utility as mechanisms for limiting liability.

[The judge rejects each of these concerns and concludes:]

CONCLUSION

[54] I conclude, then, that no adequate policy considerations exist to negate a contractor's duty in tort to subsequent purchasers of a building to take reasonable care in constructing the building, and to ensure that the building does not contain defects that pose foreseeable and substantial danger to the health and safety of the occupants. In my view, the Manitoba Court of Appeal erred in deciding that Bird could not, in principle, be held liable in tort to the Condominium Corporation for the reasonable cost of repairing the defects and putting the building back into a non-dangerous state. These costs are recoverable economic loss under the law of tort in Canada. ...

[56] I would allow the appeal, reverse the decision of the Court of Appeal and make the following orders: that the losses alleged in the statement of claim, to the extent that they may be found to constitute pure economic loss flowing from the negligence of the respondent, be recoverable from the respondent, and that the order of the learned motions judge, that the within action proceed to trial against the respondent Bird Construction Co. Ltd. with respect to the remaining issues raised in the statement of claim, be reinstated. The appellant is entitled to its costs throughout.

Appeal allowed.

A woman injured in two automobile accidents had worked full time in a bakery co-owned with her husband, and approximately 40 hours a week at home. She appealed from the trial judge's award of damages which she argued were "inadequate." The Saskatchewan Court of Appeal held that she was entitled to an award of damages that would compensate her not only for loss of earning capacity, pain and suffering and loss of amenities, but also for the impairment of her housekeeping capacity. The court would take into account the cost of employing someone to provide the services she had performed, including the value of management.

Dean v. Fobel; MacDonald v. Fobel
Saskatchewan Court of Appeal
83 D.L.R. (4th) 385
August 27, 1991

Note: The Supreme Court of Canada refused leave to appeal. This "landmark" decision allowing compensation for lost "housekeeping capacity" has now been followed in numerous cases.[32]

- *P*ennzoil successfully sued Texaco for interfering with its planned merger with Getty Oil and was awarded $10.53 billion by a jury, then the largest award in U.S. history. Texaco subsequently filed for bankruptcy. Later the companies reached a settlement by which Texaco would agree to pay to Pennzoil the sum of $3 billion in cash.[33]

DIFFICULTIES IN ASSESSING QUANTUM OF DAMAGES

- *A* proprietor of a Tokyo hotel is seeking damages against the estates of some deceased businessmen. He alleges his business plummeted because of the executives having committed suicide in his hotel.[34]

- *A* dispensing error by a pharmacist in Vancouver resulted in a fatal dose of an anti-psychotic drug being given to a 94-year-old woman.

- *I*n Louisiana, a coroner deliberately dropped a dead baby to examine the results of a fall on her head. The information would help him as an expert witness in an infant mortality case.

5. CONTEMPT OF COURT

Question

Equitable remedies are one type of orders of the court. What can be done if a person ignores an order of the court?

Canadian Imperial Bank of Commerce *v.* Sayani

http://www.courts.gov.bc.ca/
THE SUPREME COURT OF BRITISH COLUMBIA
JUNE 7, 1996

[1] Hall, J: This is a contempt proceeding brought by the plaintiff against the defendant. The proceeding has its immediate origin in an order made by the Honourable Mr. Justice Vickers on September 27, 1995. The operative part of his order reads as follows:

> THIS COURT ORDERS that the defendant Zarina Sayani appear before this Court at a time and date to be appointed to show cause why she should not be held in contempt of this Honourable Court.

That order was entered on October 20, 1995.

[2] This matter came on for hearing on October 27, was continued on November 9 and ultimately concluded on February 14, 1996. There was extensive written material placed before the Court and the defendant, Mrs. Sayani, gave oral testimony.

[3] In the early 1980s, there were dealings between the plaintiff bank and the husband and brother-in-law of the defendant, Mrs. Sayani. Monies had been borrowed from the bank and in the 1980s the bank was owed hundreds of thousands by the husband and brother-in-law. There were attempts to collect by the bank and I believe a tentative settlement was reached but this did not endure. Attempts at realization were not successful and by 1994, the plaintiff bank was seeking to obtain a judgment against the defendant for about $635,000 based on a guarantee she had executed in March of 1982. I presume the bank felt there was then some likelihood of success in getting some funds from the defendant because as a result of her entering into a venture to manage the Georgian Court Hotel in the late 1980s, she was in receipt from time to time of substantial funds and it was anticipated that further funds would be coming from that venture. … [Her guarantee was to cover the indebtedness of the Sayani brothers against whom judgment was taken for $518,064.33. Their appeal was dismissed. Leave to appeal to the Supreme Court of Canada was refused.]

[6] Arising out of the Georgian Court Hotel management joint venture, in February of 1993, the defendant received through her private company something in the order of $1.7 million Canadian. This money was initially in the HongKong Bank in Vancouver but was immediately moved to a Swiss bank by the mechanism of two bank drafts. Thereafter, it was moved from one Swiss bank to another because the latter bank was one that Mrs. Sayani's family had dealt with during a time when she lived in Africa. I should observe here that I see nothing sinister or indeed particularly unusual about her placing funds in a Swiss bank account. That was a perfectly lawful thing to do so far as the evidence discloses. The name of the bank where the funds were ultimately lodged was the Habib Bank AG, Zurich, hereinafter called the Habib Bank. The funds remained in that bank from the spring of 1993 until the spring of 1995, drawing interest at a comparatively modest rate.

[7] Mrs. Sayani testified that in March of 1995, as a result of certain diagnostic tests done by her physician, she discovered that she might have a cancerous lesion on one of her kidneys. She says that this greatly alarmed her and caused her to fear for the future economic well-being of her daughters. She says that there is a custom in her culture whereby if a family member dies, then a sibling may well take over responsibility for the well-being of the children of the deceased sibling. Mrs. Sayani says that these concerns led to her decision in the third week of March of 1995 to transfer the funds in the Habib Bank to the direction of her brother. …

[8] On March 28, 1995, Habib Bank formally notified Mrs. Sayani by a letter sent to her West Vancouver residence that it had paid out the full amount of her accounts which stood at U.S. $1,408,623.04 to the order of her brother, Mr. Shiraz P. Chatur. … The bank made efforts in the summer of 1995 to execute on its judgment against Mrs. Sayani. There were applications before my colleagues Paris J. and Thackray J. On

July 27, 1995, Thackray J. ordered the defendant to deposit the sum of $750,000 in trust not later than August 8, 1995. This apparently was reckoned to be approximately the figure of the judgment of $668,000 odd dollars plus costs and interest that was owing to the bank. Nothing happened. Thereafter, Vickers J. made the order referred to supra.

[9] [Sayani appealed the judgment against her, but was still required to post security in the amount of $750,000.]

[10] As Blackburn J. observed in Skipworth's case (1873), 9 L.R. Q.B. 230, the phrase, contempt of court, can often mislead persons who are not lawyers to misapprehend its meaning. It is sometimes thought that a proceeding for contempt amounts to some process taken for the purpose of vindicating the personal dignity of judges or protecting them from personal insults as individuals. His Lordship observes that in essence contempt of court is a procedure to ensure that the course of justice is not sullied or interfered with. In Skipworth's case, there is a reference to a case in the time of Lord Cottenham, Lechmere Charlton's case, (1837) 40 E.R. 661, where Charlton, a barrister and M.P. had attempted to obstruct the course of justice in the Court of Chancery by what were said to be threatening letters he sent concerning proceedings he was involved in before a Master in Chancery. Mr. Charlton was ultimately committed to the Fleet prison by Lord Cottenham for contempt. In Charlton's case, there is reference to case law in the time of Lord Hardwicke in the century before, where attempted bribery of a judicial officer occurred and was dealt with under the contempt power. It is an ancient power given to superior courts to ensure that the course of justice is not obstructed. It probably has its origins in a species of the Royal Prerogative. ...

[13] In the case at bar, ... [a]ccording to Mrs. Sayani and her brother [now resident in Uganda] the funds that were originally in the Habib Bank have now been placed in some type of unspecified investment in India. Her brother asserts that he has unnamed partners in his business in an undisclosed location and says that essentially for business reasons, he is not prepared to disclose the whereabouts of the funds or the nature of what is being done with them. It is said that the funds are tied up for a term of years at a favourable rate of return and that it would have harmful economic consequences to the brother and the partners if their location and employment were disclosed. Mrs. Sayani professed no ability to get any further information from her brother. Mrs. Sayani said she was hopeful that some further funds to be generated from the Georgian Court Hotel management joint venture would soon accrue to her and that these could be utilized to pay off her obligations under the judgment held by the plaintiff bank. ...

[14] Chief Justice Lemuel Shaw once observed that the proper object of jurisprudence is for a court to take a set of facts, proven or admitted, and to declare what rights or obligations flow therefrom. Judges do that everyday. That is the chief aim and purpose of the judicial branch and without that, civil society could scarcely go on. Concomitant with that, if adjudications of courts could be ignored and set at naught by citizens, then society would cease to be orderly.

[15] I think I could properly observe that the evidence of Mrs. Sayani and the evidence emanating by way of affidavit from her brother ... may well be described as fantastic. Having listened carefully to her evidence and having considered all of the material placed before me, I simply say that I do not find her narrative believable. The funds are said to have mysteriously vanished into an unnamed venture in the Indian continent. ...

[16] Commencing in the year 1994, ... Mrs. Sayani could not have failed to appreciate that she stood increasingly in peril of having a judgment rendered against her for a substantial dollar amount. ... [W]hen she arranged for the movement of the funds, the likely hour of reckoning was near at hand. I have no doubt that her actions were a calculated effort to prevent the plaintiff from being able in future to realize on the fruits of its likely judgment. Apropos of the comments of Chief Justice Shaw adverted to above, it would be an exceedingly idle enterprise for courts to proceed to adjudicate questions of property rights between citizens if actions as transparently artificial as those disclosed here could be used to frustrate the normal course of justice.

[17] Counsel for the defendant points out correctly that mere failure to pay money is not generally a contempt of court. In connection with that argument, reference was made to a judgment of our Court of Appeal, in *The Royal Bank of Canada v. McLennan* (1918), 25 B.C.R. 183. However, Huddart J. (as she then was), noted in *Manolescu v. Manolescu* (1991), 31 R.F.L. (3d) 421 at p. 433:

> Wilful breach of a court order will always be a contempt of court. A deliberate refusal to pay money pursuant to a court order when one has the ability to pay will constitute a civil contempt of the court. It is also a private injury or wrong to the person who is the beneficiary of the order.

...

I believe likewise that this case involves much more than a simple failure to satisfy a judgment debt by paying money to a judgment creditor. As I perceive the circumstances, the activity of the defendant undertaken in the month of March 1995 was intentional activity designed to put beyond the reach of any creditor the money she then held on deposit in the Swiss bank. By simply transferring the asset to her brother, she erected an impenetrable and opaque wall between the funds and the plaintiff here. The purpose was to render nugatory any judgment that might be rendered against her, the likelihood of which judgment was becoming extremely imminent. This was conduct calculated and designed to interfere with the due administration of justice in this country and I have no hesitation in characterizing it as contempt. The suggestions concerning her wish to preserve the economic positions of family members is to me a feeble attempt to justify the unjustifiable. Her real purpose was to make sure these funds were put beyond the reach of any power of execution. People are entitled to order their affairs to protect themselves from personal liability for debt and to enhance their economic interests but transparent ruses of the sort disclosed here are to be discouraged. Having considered all of the evidence here, I am fully convinced that the activities undertaken by Mrs. Sayani in Spring, 1995 to put her assets beyond ken and reach of a potential creditor were a calculated course of activity designed to frustrate the course of justice. Her continuing refusal to take steps to satisfy the judgment are merely confirmatory evidence of what was her original intent and purpose. I find her actions to amount to a contempt of court. I leave it in the hands of counsel to decide when they wish to again bring on the case before me so that the question of penalty can be addressed.

See *MacMillan Bloedel Limited v. Simpson*, p. 36, for the meaning and consequences of failing to obey an injunction.

- *L*yndon LaRoche, a controversial political figure in the U.S. frequently cited for contempt of court, once ran for the U.S. presidency and was quoted as saying "It's a terrible inconvenience running a presidential campaign from prison."[35]

CRIMINAL CONTEMPT

- *A* witness, J. N., who refused to answer questions at a murder trial was sentenced to three years in prison for contempt of court. In his reasons for imposing such a severe sentence the judge said "… individuals like [J.N.] … must know, and all citizens must know, that if they are lawfully required to attend at a court and testify, they must testify. Otherwise, the whole fabric of our system will be torn apart, and this court is not prepared to allow that to happen. We must be stern in guarding all the requirements of the administration of justice." The sentenced was appealed. On appeal the sentence was reduced to the time served which was nine months.[36]

- *W*hen the bailiff told the 18-year-old (who had been arrested for driving without a licence) that he could not go into the courtroom wearing shorts, the accused walked in naked. Found in contempt of court, the judge gave him the Florida maximum — 179 days in jail.[37]

- *A*n inmate, protesting his transfer to a different jail, plugged the toilet in the cell directly above the courtroom so that the overflowing water would fall on the judge below. It was reported that the judge, to continue on with his cases, merely ordered a bailiff to hold an umbrella over his head. The inmate was charged with contempt of court, but the judge, after receiving an apology from the inmate, imposed no sentence.[38]

ENDNOTES

1. For a more detailed and, therefore, a more astonishing account, see *Harper's Magazine*, August 1995, p. 23 which printed an excerpt from "A Sprocket in Satan's Bulldozer: Confessions of an Investment Banker" issue number 6 of *Might*.

2. *The Lawyers Weekly*, May 24, 1991, p. 2.

3. See *The Vancouver Sun*, October 30, 2000, p. A9.

4. *Dudka v. Smilestone* [1994] N.S.J. No. 187 (Q.L.)

5. *Time*, August 7, 2000, p. 7.

6. For a more detailed account see *The Globe and Mail*, July 25, 2000, p. 1. The publishing industry is watching this King phenomenon carefully and subsequent updates of the story refer to King's "honour system." For example, see *Los Angeles Times*, August 1, 2000, reprinted August 3, 2000 in Edupage.

7. *The Vancouver Sun*, November 30, 2000, p. A15.

8. For a summary of *Lemmex v. Bernard* (July 12, 2000) see *The Lawyers Weekly*, August 25, 2000, p. 18.

9. For a summary of *Ross v. Alumni Computer Group Ltd.* see *The Lawyers Weekly*, August 18, 2000, p. 27.

10. For more information about e-signatures see *The Globe and Mail*, September 26, 2000 and *Business Week*, August 14, 2000, reprinted on Edupage. For an example of such statutes see Ontario's or Nova Scotia's *Electronic Commerce Act*.

11. *The Lawyers Weekly*, October 2, 1992, p. 17.

12. *Vancouver (City) v. Jefferson*, British Columbia Court of Appeal, June 14, 2000, [2000] B.C.J. No. 1194 (Q.L.)

13. For a more detailed account see *The Lawyers Weekly*, July 1, 1994, p. 30 for its summary of *Andres v. Andres* heard by Judge Stach of the Ontario Court General Division.

14. See *Lalonde v. Coleman*, 67 Man. R. (2d) 187 Manitoba Court of Queen's Bench, July 3, 1990.

15. For a more detailed account see *Newsweek*, April 22, 1996, p. 79.

16. Summarized from *The Lawyers Weekly*, July 1, 1988, p. 6.

17. *BG Checo International Ltd. v. B.C. Hydro and Power Authority,* 44 B.C.L.R. (2d) 145 B.C.C.A. March 21, 1990.

18. *The Lawyers Weekly*, February 12, 1993, pp. 1, 21, http://www.lexum.umontreal.ca/.

19. Reprinted with permission from *The Advocate* (published by the Vancouver Bar Association), Volume 46, (1988), Part 6, p. 986.

20. Summarized from *The Lawyers Weekly*, September 27, 1991, p. 24.

21. Summarized from *The Lawyers Weekly*, October 23, 1992, p. 24.

22. A more detailed account is given in *Newsweek*, March 25, 1985, p. 72.

23. Summarized from *The Globe and Mail*, December 29, 1993, p. A9.

24. *Time*, November 8, 1999, p. 13.

25. *Time*, November 8, 1999, p. 13.

26. A more detailed account is given in *The Vancouver Sun*, December 15, 1993, p. A16.

27. For a more detailed account, see MTV.com, November 15, 2000.

28. For a more detailed account see *Maclean's*, August 1, 1994, August 8, 1994, p. 11.

29. His latest album released in 1997 is called "Blue Moon Swamp." For a more detailed account see *Time Magazine*, June 23, 1997.

30. For a more detailed account see The *Hollywood Reporter,* December 30, 1997 to January 5, 1998, p. 9.

31. *Time*, June 19, 2000, p. 90.

32. *The Lawyers Weekly*, September 18, 1992, p. 3.

33. More detailed accounts of this case can be found in *The New York Times*. See, for example, December 20, 1987, p. 1.

34. *The Lawyers Weekly*, January 15, 1999, p. 2.

35. A more detailed account is given in *The Vancouver Sun*, October 29, 1992, p. A14.

36. See *The Lawyers Weekly*, August 19, 1994, p. 27 for an extract from *R. v. Deas*. The case was also reported and summarized in *The Lawyers Weekly*, July 15, 1994, p. 27. The accused was found guilty for the murder even without the testimony of J.N. For the ruling of the court of appeal see *The Lawyers Weekly*, March 17, 1995, p. 5 and March 24, 1995, p. 15.

37. See *The Lawyers Weekly*, August 26, 1994, p. 21 which ends the article with a quotation from the judge: "He said he was sorry, but I told him that wouldn't cut it."

38. *The Lawyers Weekly*, June 6, 1986.

V

COMMERCIAL TRANSACTIONS

A. SALE OF GOODS ACT

Questions

What types of contracts are covered by the Sale of Goods Act?
What contractual terms are implied by the statute?

---

1. SCOPE OF THE STATUTE

Mr. Gee and Mr. and Mrs. Pan, customers of White Spot restaurant, claimed they suffered botulism poisoning from food eaten at the restaurant. They sued the restaurant for breach of the implied term of the contract that the food was fit for purpose. The defendant argued that the contract was one for services and not goods and was not properly covered by the *Sale of Goods Act*. The first question the plaintiffs put before the court was whether or not the *Sale of Goods Act* applied to the purchase of a meal from a restaurant.

The B.C. Supreme Court had no binding precedent before it. The Justice reviewed cases from Canada, the United Kingdom and the United States and concluded that "an item on the menu offered for a fixed price is an offering of a finished product and is primarily an offering of the sale of goods and not primarily an offering of a sale of services." In answer to the second question as to what must the plaintiff prove to establish the liability of the defendant restaurant, the court answered that to establish an implied condition of reasonable fitness three requirements must be met:

"First, the goods in question must be of a kind in which the seller normally deals in the course of his business. ...

The second requirement is that the proposed use of the food is made known to the seller so as to show the plaintiff's reliance on the seller's skill and judgment...

The third requirement is that the contract is not for sale of a specified article under its patent or other trade name."

Applying the law as stated to the facts of the case, the court held for the plaintiffs. The defendants were liable under s. 18(a) of the *Sale of Goods Act* (the fit for purpose provision).

Furthermore, the facts supported a claim under s. 18(b), namely, the defendants were liable for breach of the implied condition that the goods were of merchantable quality.

The judge commented that fourteen other actions were pending against White Spot on similar allegations.

Gee v. White Spot, Pan et al. v. White Spot
32 D.L.R. (4th) 238
British Columbia Supreme Court
October 27, 1986

- Ms. Gough ordered a plate of deep-fried chicken wings at Red Robin Restaurant. When the piece of deep-fried chicken wing turned out to be a deep-fried chicken head, Ms. Gough promptly vomited. Having received no compensation, no apology, and suffering from food phobias after the incident, she sued.

  Her action was successful; the court rejected the argument of the defence that she had planted the chicken head.[1]

2. IMPLIED TERMS

A. THAT THE SELLER PASS GOOD TITLE

- The owner of a mobile home left it with a business outfit to lease it on his behalf. The owner's signature was forged on documents transferring title to another. "Title" of the mobile home passed through approximately eight different purchasers before it was returned to its rightful owner. Relying in part on the implied condition of good title in s. 13 of the *Ontario Sale of Goods Act*, the judge found a series of sellers in breach of contract.[2]

B. THAT THE GOODS BE FIT FOR PURPOSE; OF MERCHANTABLE QUALITY

Sigurdson et al. v. Hilcrest Service Ltd., Acklands Ltd., Third Party

73 D.L.R. (3D) 132
SASKATCHEWAN QUEEN'S BENCH
DECEMBER 21, 1976

Estey, J.:—This action arises out of a single vehicle accident in which the plaintiffs allege that they did suffer personal injuries. The said vehicle was owned by the plaintiff Mr. K.E. Sigurdson. The plaintiffs allege that the cause of the accident was a faulty brake hose installed on the vehicle in the defendant's garage. The defendant joined Acklands Limited as a third party as Acklands supplied the defendant with the two hydraulic brake hoses which the defendant through its employees installed on the said vehicle.

The plaintiff Karl Edward Sigurdson stated that he was on June 16, 1973, operating a 1963 Ford vehicle owned by him and had as passengers his wife Hannelore and his children Christopher and Michael. At approximately 4:30 p.m. on June 16, 1973, Mr. Sigurdson was approaching the intersection of Avenue H and 20th St. in the City of Saskatoon intending to make a right-hand turn onto 20th St. when he was confronted with a red stop-light at the said intersection. Mr. Sigurdson stated that pedestrians were crossing the intersection in front of his vehicle and when he applied the brakes they failed to operate.

He immediately swung his vehicle to the right hitting a power pole. Mr. Sigurdson stated that at the time of the accident his speed was 15 to 20 m.p.h. and that the brakes of the vehicle had up until the time of the accident been operating in a proper manner. The vehicle as a result of the accident was damaged beyond repair. A few days prior to May 1, 1973, Mr. Sigurdson took his vehicle to the defendant's service station for certain repairs as the defendants had previously serviced his vehicle. Exhibit P.10 dated May 1, 1973, is the invoice which Mr. Sigurdson received from the defendant covering the repairs and labour performed on his vehicle immediately prior to the said date. This exhibit shows that two brake hoses were on this occasion installed by the defendant on Mr. Sigurdson's vehicle. Mr. Sigurdson as a result of the accident had three teeth removed and now has a partial denture. His son the plaintiff Michael received minor scratches while the plaintiffs Christopher and Mrs. Hannelore Sigurdson received injuries to which I will later refer. Mr. Sigurdson stated that after receiving his vehicle from the defendant's garage on or about May 1, 1973, the brakes on the said vehicle did until the time of the accident operate in a proper manner and that from May 1, 1973, to the date of the accident he had travelled approximately 1,300 miles. Mr. Sigurdson takes the view that the cause of the brake failure was due to a faulty brake hose. Counsel agreed that the brake hose removed from Mr. Sigurdson's vehicle is ex. P.11 and that exs. P.12, 13, 14 and 15 which are portions of a brake hose were cut off P.11 for purpose of examination.

Professor C.M. Sargent, from the faculty of mechanical engineering at the University of Saskatchewan in Saskatoon, examined the said brake hose by means of cutting off portions and found therein at least two particles which were composed of what he described as a "glassy material". His opinion was that due to the operation of the motor vehicle these particles tended to work towards the outside of the brake hose permitting the brake fluid to escape. His evidence was that in order for a garage operator to discover the presence of these "glassy particles" the hose would have to be cut and thereby destroyed. ...

[After reviewing the reports of injuries suffered by the plaintiffs, the judge turned to the evidence of the defendant.]

Evidence on behalf of the defendant was given by Mr. A.P. Halseth who in May, 1973, was an officer of the defendant company and worked in the company's service station. Mr. Halseth admitted that just prior to May 1, 1973, Mr. Sigurdson's vehicle was in the defendant's service station and that the two new brake hoses were installed on the said vehicle. The said brake hoses were obtained by the defendant from the third party Acklands Limited which company had been a supplier to the defendant since 1958. Mr. Halseth stated that the defendant company relied on the third party to supply proper brake hoses. Exhibit D.3 is an invoice from the third party referring to two brake hoses. Mr. Halseth stated that after the accident he inspected the plaintiff's vehicle to determine the cause of brake failure. He filled the master brake cylinder with brake fluid but found there was no build-up of pressure and on examining one of the brake hoses which had been installed by the defendant he found that brake fluid was dripping from the brake hose in the location immediately adjacent to the male end of the hose. The witness stated that he has had considerable experience with brake hoses but does not know of a method of testing a brake hose for leaks prior to installation. Mr. Halseth stated that after installing new brake hoses he puts the fluid under pressure and inspects for leaks. The witness denied that any member of the defendant's staff did anything in the installation of the brake hose which contributed to the rupture of the hose.

The plaintiffs in their statement of claim allege that the cause of their injuries was the failure on the part of the defendant's employee or employees to properly service and repair the vehicle and failure to test and examine the repairs to the vehicle. The plaintiffs also allege the use of defective materials by the defendant in effecting the repairs. The statement of defence pleads the provisions of the *Contributory Negligence Act*, R.S.S. 1965, c.91, and in the alternative that if liability is found the responsibility for such injuries and damages rests with Acklands Limited as its supplier of automotive parts. The third party's statement of defence admits that the said party is engaged in the wholesale automotive parts business and did on or about May 1, 1973, sell and deliver to the defendant's place of business two brake hoses priced at $6.60. The third party also alleges that the hydraulic brake hoses were supplied to it by a firm know[n] as Echlin Limited and that if there was negligence in the "supply and manufacture of the said brake hose, it was the negligence of Echlin Limited the supplier and manufacturer". It should be

pointed out that at the time of the trial of the action the manufacturer of the said brake hoses was not a party to the action.

I will first deal with the actions of Mrs. Sigurdson and her son Christopher. My understanding of the law is that in order for these parties to succeed against the defendant they must establish negligence on the part of the defendant in the repair of the vehicle. I am satisfied from the evidence that one of the brake hoses installed by the defendant was defective in that it contained at least two foreign objects as determined by Professor Sargent and that due to the operation of the vehicle these objects moved causing a rupture in the hose which permitted brake fluid to escape. I am further of the view that the cause of the accident was brake failure caused by the escape of the brake fluid. If there be negligence on the part of the defendant it must be carelessness on the part of its employee or employees in the installation of the brake hose or in the installation of the brake hose which the defendant's employees knew or should have known was defective. From the evidence I am unable to find that there was any negligence in the installation of the brake hose. The evidence further established to my satisfaction that no inspection by an employee of the defendant of the brake hose prior to installation would have determined the defects other than that of cutting the hose as was done by Professor Sargent. Indeed the professor stated that he knew of no test which could be made in the garage which would determine the presence of foreign objects in the hose other than by the destruction of the hose. The question of the necessity for an inspection of the brake hose by the defendant is dealt with in *Charlesworth on Negligence*, 5th ed. (1971), para. 654, pp.405-6, when the author writes:

> A retailer is under no duty to examine goods for defects before resale, in the absence of circumstances suggesting that they might be defective, when he obtains them from a manufacturer of repute. ...

Placing the defendant in a position of a retailer I take the view that there were no circumstances in the present case which would suggest to an employee of the defendant that the brake hose was or might be defective when it was delivered to the defendant's place of business by the third party. Indeed there was, prior to installation of the brake hose, no test or examination which could be conducted by the defendant which would locate the foreign object short of destruction of the brake hose. Moreover, the operation of the vehicle from May 1st to June 16th suggests in itself that the actual installation of the brake hose was proper. There is therefore in my opinion no negligence on the part of the defendant in either the installation of the break hose or in the failure to inspect such hose prior to installation. As I have held that there is no negligence on the part of the defendant, I dismiss the actions of the plaintiffs Mrs. Sigurdson and her son Christopher.

The liability of the defendant towards the plaintiff Mr. Sigurdson involves other considerations. While I have already held that the defendant's employees were not guilty of negligence the defendant, in so far as the plaintiff Mr. Sigurdson is concerned, is faced with the provisions of the *Sale of Goods Act*, R.S.S. 1965, c. 388, s. 16, which reads:

16. Subject to the provisions of this Act and of any Act in that behalf there is no implied warranty or condition as to the quality of fitness for any particular purpose of goods supplied under a contract of sale except as follows:

1. Where the buyer expressly or by implication makes known to the seller the particular purpose for which the goods are required so as to show that the buyer relies on the seller's skill or judgment and the goods are of a description that it is in the course of the seller's business to supply, whether he be the manufacturer or not, there is an implied condition that the goods shall be reasonably fit for that purpose;

2. Where goods are bought by description from a seller who deals in goods of that description, whether he is the manufacturer or not, there is an implied condition that the goods shall be of merchantable quality:

    Provided that if the buyer has examined the goods there shall be no implied condition with regard to defects which such examination ought to have revealed;

3. An implied warranty or condition as to quality or fitness for a particular purpose may be annexed by usage of trade ...

Waddams in his text *Products Liability* (1974) suggests that even in the absence of negligence a repairer may be liable to the plaintiff Mr. Sigurdson for breach of the implied warranty as set out in said s. 16 when the author writes at pp. 18-9:

> However, insofar as the defect complained of is caused by defective materials supplied by the installer or repairer, there may be liability even in the absence of negligence for breach of an implied warranty that the materials used are reasonably fit.

The said author points out at p.76 of his text:

> ...liability for breach of the implied warranties is strict liability in the sense that it is no defence for the seller to show that he exercised reasonable care or that the defect in the goods was undiscoverable.

I am of the view on the facts of the present case that there was by virtue of the *Sale of Goods Act,* an implied warranty or condition that the brake hose would be "reasonably fit" for the purpose for which it was intended. I find that the said brake hose was not "reasonably fit" in that it contained foreign bodies which eventually caused a rupture and brake failure which failure was the cause of the accident.

The defendant's plea of contributory negligence appears to be based on Mr. Sigurdson's failure to keep a proper look-out. The plaintiff was in the situation described by Hodgins, J.A., in *Harding v. Edwards et al.,* [1929] 4 D.L.R. 598 at pp. 599-600, 64 O.L.R. 98 at p.102 [affd 1931] 2 D.L.R. 521, [1931] S.C.R. 167], when he wrote:

> ...hence I cannot convince myself that he was sufficiently recovered from the shock of the emergency to be judged by standards involving deliberation and opportunity for conscious decision, or by what is called by Lord Sumner "nice judgment, prompt decision:" *SS. "Singleton Abbey" v. SS. "Paludina",* [1927] A.C. 16, at p. 26.

The plaintiff when confronted with pedestrians in front of him and a failure of his foot-brakes was faced with an emergency and he chose to turn to his right. There was no time for a "conscious decision" to the effect that he should try the handbrake for by turning right he would hit a power pole. I do not think that contributory negligence attaches to the plaintiff on the facts of this case.

The question now arises as to the damages to which the plaintiff Mr. Sigurdson is entitled. Counsel for the parties agreed to special damages in the amount of $2,079.56. I therefore award to the plaintiff Mr. Sigurdson special damages in the amount of $2,079.56. I award the said plaintiff general damages in the amount of $2,000. The plaintiff Mr. Karl Sigurdson shall be entitled to his tax [sic] costs in this matter, such costs to be taxed in accordance with column 4 of the Queen's Bench tariff of costs. ...

The third party did not take an active part at the hearing. The reason being no doubt that it admitted selling two brake hoses to the defendant. My view is that the defendant may successfully recover from its supplier the third party for a breach of warranty, *i.e.,* that the brake hose was defective or not reasonably fit for the purpose for which it was intended. This point is dealt with by Waddams at p. 189 when the author writes:

> Although it is doubtful that one held liable for breach of warranty has a claim for contribution against the manufacturer of the defective goods as a joint tortfeasor, he may have a remedy against his own supplier (whether manufacturer or other distributor) for breach of implied warranty.

I therefore award judgment in favour of the defendant against the third party in the amount of the judgment recovered by the plaintiff against the defendant, together with the taxed costs paid by the defendant to the plaintiff.

Judgment for the plaintiff

A woman, shopping at Safeway, bought a 7-Up which she began to drink while the cashier packed her other groceries. The can contained a small dry cell battery which had made the fluid toxic. The woman suffered a severe burning of the lining of her mouth, throat and stomach. She sued Safeway for breach of contract, namely, breach of the implied term that the goods were fit for purpose. In the alternative, she sued the manufacturer and bottler and distributors of 7-Up for negligence.

Estrin v. Canada Safeway Ltd., 7-Up Vancouver Ltd., and Gray Beverage Co. Ltd. [3]

Note: Robert Gardner, the lawyer for the plaintiff, confirmed that this matter was settled out of court.

- **B**ridgestone/Firestone Inc., tire maker, will recall 6.5 million tires because of a manufacturing defect that resulted in the tires shredding apart. By early September 2000, 88 deaths had been attributed to the defective tires.[4]

- **W**hen Sharon McClelland of Newmarket, Ontario, took her first free-fall jump from an airplane, the parachute malfunctioned. Miraculously, she fell in a marshy area, landed flat on her back and was able to walk away. When she stood up she apologized to her skydiving instructor.[5]

- **A** California vintner had to recall its 1986 vintage and reseal more than 700,000 bottles of wine. The corks had been covered with a substance that had acted like glue.[6]

- **O**ne lawyer of the new Union of Consumers was quoted as saying "We drank champagne that day;" another, "It was a real holiday. It was a historic day in our country." The cause of the celebration? Ivan Sumkin won a lawsuit against the government store which sold him a defective microwave oven. It may appear to us as commonplace but his victory was hailed as a milestone in post-communist Russia.[7]

EXEMPTION CLAUSES IN CONTRACTS FOR THE SALE OF GOODS

"… TO THE MAXIMUM EXTENT PERMITTED BY APPLICABLE LAW, MICROSOFT DISCLAIMS ALL OTHER WARRANTIES, EITHER EXPRESS OR IMPLIED, INCLUDING BUT NOT LIMITED TO IMPLIED WARRANTIES OF MERCHANTABILITY AND FITNESS FOR A PARTICULAR PURPOSE, WITH RESPECT TO THE SOFTWARE, THE ACCOMPANYING PRODUCT MANUAL(S) AND WRITTEN MATERIALS, AND ANY ACCOMPANYING HARDWARE…"

From the license agreement accompanying the computer program EXCEL.

C. THAT THE GOODS MATCH THE DESCRIPTION

Coast Hotels Ltd. **v.** *Royal Doulton Canada Ltd.*

http://www.courts.gov.bc.ca/
SUPREME COURT OF BRITISH COLUMBIA
MAY 31, 2000

Martinson, J.:

INTRODUCTION

[1] This is a claim under s. 17 of the *Sale of Goods Act*, RS Chap. 410, alleging that porcelain tableware that was delivered to the plaintiff, Coast Hotels Limited ("Coast Hotels") by the defendant, Royal Doulton Canada Limited ("Royal Doulton") did not conform with the contractual description of the goods.

[2] In 1992 Coast Hotels decided to standardize and upgrade its catering tableware as part of a business plan to enhance the image of the hotels. It chose Royal Doulton's Jupiter pattern, a plain white, non-embossed pattern, for its tableware. Various Coast Hotels ordered that pattern from 1992 to 1995.

[3] In 1995 a person doing contract work for Coast Hotels noticed a difference between two cups she saw in the coffee shop at a Coast hotel. She showed them to the company president and the person involved in the purchase of the standardized tableware. They noticed that the backstamp on the

back of the cups was not the same. One, the kind they say they purchased, had the words "Royal Doulton" prominently displayed on the backstamp. The other had the word Capital prominently displayed on the backstamp. There were also subtle differences in colour and thickness.

[4] Coast Hotels considered the change to the backstamp to be significant since Royal Doulton name recognition on the tableware was crucial to the plan to enhance the image of the hotels.

[5] Royal Doulton agrees that at some point in 1992 or 1993 the backstamp on the hotelware china was changed by Royal Doulton (U.K.) to make Capital the prominent word instead of Royal Doulton. The word Capital was used because the Jupiter pattern is part of the Capital Collection. The collection represents the body shape.

[6] Coast Hotels were not advised of this change.

[7] After unsuccessfully trying to reach a settlement with Royal Doulton, Coast Hotels arranged an internal transfer to deal with the remaining Jupiter stock. A few hotels therefore con-

tinued to use the Jupiter pattern. It then chose a new brand, Steelite, and a white embossed pattern that was more expensive than the Royal Doulton Jupiter pattern for the rest of its hotels. It says that the Steelite pattern was the closest it could come to the attributes it considered in choosing the Royal Doulton Jupiter pattern. It wants damages for the difference in price between what it paid for the Steelite tableware and what it originally paid for the Royal Doulton Jupiter tableware, as well as the administrative costs of the change.

[8] Coast Hotels says this was a sale by description as provided for in s. 17 of the *Act*. That description was Royal Doulton Jupiter Pattern tableware with the Royal Doulton name prominently identified on the brand (backstamp). Coast Hotels argues that when the Capital brand was substituted, it did not get what it bargained for. This amounts to a breach of the condition that the goods will correspond with the description and entitles them to damages.

[9] Royal Doulton agrees that this was a sale by description but says that the description did not include the words on the backstamp. Rather, the description was Royal Doulton's porcelain hotelware of a plain white, non-embossed pattern in the Capital body shape. That is what Coast Hotels received. ...

ISSUES

[11] The following issues arise: ...
(b) What was the description of the tableware within the meaning of s. 17 of the Act?
(c) If so, was there a breach of the implied condition that the goods must correspond with the description?
(d) If so, what damages if any flow from that breach? ...

ANALYSIS ...

(b) What was the description of the tableware within the meaning of s. 17 of the *Act?*

[29] As noted, it is agreed that these were sales by description. Section 17 of the *Sale of Goods Act* says that in a contract for the sale of goods by description there is an implied condition that the goods must correspond with the description. The real question is whether the description included a backstamp with the words Royal Doulton prominently displayed, as in the sample provided.

[30] Royal Doulton argues that correspondence with a description is a matter concerned with the use of language to identify the subject matter of the contract. It says that while a sale may be both a sale by description and a sale by sample (s. 17(2)) the two concepts are conceptually distinct and no authority is provided for their merger. A description cannot be derived, in whole or in part, from a sample.

[31] Coast Hotels says that if samples are provided, the sample may be the best evidence of what the parties intended the contractual description of the goods to be. In particular, it says that where a brand or mark, which can only be understood visually, identifies goods, the description of the goods is incomplete without reference to the sample, which displays it. ... [The court reviews the meaning of "description".]

[34] A description does involve the use of language. However, the production of a sample during the course of the negotiations can be relevant to the common intention of the parties and contribute to the verbal description. The provision of a sample

provides a context in which the proper meaning of the contractual description is to be ascertained. ...

[35] In this case the documents exchanged between the parties refer to the Jupiter pattern and do not refer to the backstamp. However, Coast Hotels made it clear to Royal Doulton throughout that Royal Doulton name recognition was crucial. Royal Doulton emphasized the importance of that name recognition in its sales pitch and provided samples, which included the Royal Doulton name prominently displayed. I conclude that this led Coast Hotels to reasonably believe that the kind of tableware they would receive, based on the standing offer, was the Royal Doulton Jupiter pattern with the Royal Doulton name prominently identified on the backstamp.

(c) Was there a breach of the implied condition that the goods must correspond with the description?

[36] Any minor deviation from the contractual description of the goods may constitute a breach of the implied condition that the goods must correspond with the description: *Arcos Limited v. E.A. Ronaasen and Son*, [1933] A.C., 470, (H.L.): (at 474)

> ...If the article they have purchased is not in fact the article that has been delivered, they are entitled to reject it even though it is the commercial equivalent of that which they have bought.

[37] The substitution of prominence of the word "Capital" for "Royal Doulton" altered the kind of goods the plaintiff received. When looking at the backstamp with the words Royal Doulton prominently displayed, one knows that the product is a Royal Doulton product. That is not the case with the backstamp with the word Capital prominently displayed. One would have to read the very small print to learn that the product was a Royal Doulton product. ...

[39] The goods provided therefore did not correspond with the description. They were goods of a different kind.

(d) Damages

[40] Damages for breach of contract are intended to put the innocent party into the position s/he would have been in had the contract been performed. Where goods have been accepted, the breach of any condition to be fulfilled by the seller can only be treated as a breach of warranty and not as a ground for rejecting the goods and treating the contract as repudiated: s. 15(4), *Sale of Goods Act*.

[41] The plaintiff has the onus of showing that there were damages, that they resulted from the breach, and what the amount of the damage is. The measure of damages for breach of warranty is the estimated loss directly and naturally resulting in the ordinary course of events: s. 56(2) of the *Act*. This involves determining what the parties might reasonably contemplate as being a serious possibility of such breach: G.H.L. Fridman, Q.C., Sale of Goods in Canada, Fourth Edition, (Toronto: Carswell, 1995) at 390-391.

[42] Coast Hotels, as a result of the breaches, ended up without a standard set of tableware with brand name recognition that met their business plan to enhance the image of the hotels. They were therefore required to find and purchase new standardized china that met that need.

[43] Was the purchase of Steelite as that substitute reasonable? Mr. Anglesio [president of Coast Hotels] has extensive experience

in the hotel industry generally and in dealing with the purchase of tableware in particular. I accept his evidence that there was no reasonably comparable substitute for Royal Doulton Jupiter except Steelite that met the needs of Coast Hotels as originally expressed to Royal Doulton.

[44] ... Although the embossed Steelite was priced higher than Jupiter, it was the least costly product that met the upgrading requirements of Coast Hotels. The evidence of Mr. Anglesio was the only evidence presented on this point.

[45] The parties might reasonably contemplate, as being a se-rious possibility as a result of the breaches, the need to purchase a reasonable replacement brand of tableware. ...

[After reviewing the arguments regarding the damages suffered, the judge continued:]

[48] ... I conclude that the estimated loss directly and naturally resulting from the breaches in the ordinary course of events, including the administrative costs, is $20,000. ...

Judgment for the Plaintiff

B. Other Consumer Protection Legislation

- *L*abels on Batman products warn the buyer that the "Armor does not provide actual protection and cape does not enable wearer to fly."[8]

Competition Act R.S.C.

- *U*nited States of America v. Microsoft

   Microsoft was charged by the federal government and nineteen states with violating antitrust laws. In the first hearing on November 5, 1999, the U.S. District Judge Jackson made a finding of fact: Microsoft did dominate the personal computer software industry and had used its monopoly position in a way that hurt competitors, and thus the consumer.[9]

   In the second hearing on April 3, 2000, the judge applied the law to the facts and ruled that Microsoft's behaviour of maintaining its monopoly position by "anti-competitive means" had breached the U.S. antitrust law.[10]

   In his final order, Judge Jackson ordered the breakup of Microsoft and placed restrictions on its conduct during the appeal period. If the breakup is upheld on appeal, the restrictions last three years; if the breakup is overturned, the restrictions last ten years. The severity of the remedy is partly due to the judge finding Microsoft "untrustworthy" in modifying its behaviour.[11]

   Lawyers for Microsoft feel confident that the three-judge appeal court will overturn the lower court on all three areas: the finding of fact, the application of the law, and the remedy.[12]

   Microsoft sought and obtained a delay in the breakup of the company.[13]

- *T*o settle claims that they were engaged in illegal practices to eliminate competition and improperly raise prices in their distribution of Mr. Potato Head, Barbie, and other toys, Toys Я Us Inc., Mattel Inc., and Little Tikes Co. agreed to pay $50 million U.S. Toys Я Us also agreed to donate $9 million in toys for three years.[14]

- *A* routine raid on the offices of Coca-Cola Co. by European regulators may confirm suspicions that Coke has illegally granted incentives to retailers to shelve fewer rival colas.[15]

- *B*ecause of concerns of the Competition Bureau, Coca-Cola Co. announced it would not buy Cadbury Schweppes Plc operations in Canada. In its 18-month review, the Competition Bureau heard opposition not only from distributors of other soft drinks such as Pepsi and Canada Dry, but also from a group representing 1,800 hotels and restaurants.[16]

- *B*oth auction houses, Sotheby's and Christie's, will each pay $465 million to settle a lawsuit commenced by buyers and sellers who claimed the auction houses colluded to cease competing with one another.[17]

- *T*he selling of "pseudo-generic" drugs—name-brand drugs sold as generic drugs at a lower price by the big-name manufacturers—may be contrary to the *Competition Act*. A motions judge struck out a statement of claim by a generic drug manufacturer but the Ontario Court of Appeal has overturned the ruling.[18]

FOOD AND DRUG ACT R.S.C.

- *R*ay Williams, a butcher, was convicted of 10 counts under the *Food and Drug Act* for deceptive sales practices, including selling turkeys as free range when they were not, selling foreign beef as Canadian beef, and selling hamburger patties that contained pigs' hearts. With the public's loss of trust, Williams lost both his livelihood and his political position as a councillor in Saanich, British Columbia.[19]

BUSINESS PRACTICES ACT/TRADE PRACTICE ACT

Schryvers and Schryvers v. *Richport Ford Sales Limited et al.*

BRITISH COLUMBIA SUPREME COURT
VANCOUVER REGISTRY NO. C917060
MAY 18, 1993

Tysoe, J.: —On May 15, 1991 Mr. and Mrs. Schryvers acquired two vehicles from Richport Ford Sales Limited ("Richport Ford") through its salesperson, Mr. Stehr. They had intended to purchase the two vehicles in cash but the transactions were ultimately structured as leases with options to purchase. The aggregate amount payable by the Schryvers under the leases is greater than the sale prices of the vehicles plus a financing charge. ...

Did the lease transactions involve a deceptive or unconscionable act or practice in contravention of the Act? [*Trade Practice Act* R.S.B.C. 1979, c 406]

Section 22 of the Act authorizes the Court to grant relief in a case where a consumer has entered a consumer transaction involving a deceptive or unconscionable act or practice by the supplier of the goods. Section 3(1) of the Act states that a deceptive act or practice includes any representation or conduct that has the capability, tendency or effect of deceiving or misleading a person. Subsection (3) of s. 3 lists instances of deceptive acts or practices, including a representation that is such that a person could reasonably conclude that a price benefit or advantage exists when it does not (clause j) and the failure to state a material fact in making a representation which makes it deceptive or misleading (clause r).

Section 4 of the Act deals with unconscionable acts or practices. There is no statement as to what constitutes an unconscionable act or practice. Subsection (2) states that a court shall consider all of the surrounding circumstances and it lists five types of circumstances that should be considered (e.g., undue pressure). Mr. Schryvers was an experienced businessman who has been involved in the purchase of over 100 vehicles in the past [from Richport]. Although the Schryvers may have been getting tired by the end of the dealings, they were not forced to continue. It may be argued that it was unconscionable for the Schryvers to be persuaded to enter into leases when they were too tired to realize that they were leases. However, I believe that Mr. Schryvers did appreciate that he was entering into leases and

that he had second thoughts at a later time. In any event, it is clear that the Schryvers appreciated that they were entering into some kind of financing arrangement and I do not think that it would be unconscionable for the Schryvers to have entered into a financing arrangement by way of a lease with an option to purchase rather than a more conventional financing arrangement.

There is more merit in the claim that there was a deceptive act. In *Rushak v. Henneken* (1991), 84 D.L.R. (4th) 87 the B.C. Court of Appeal commented on the wide scope of the Act. ...

It is my view that Richport Ford committed deceptive acts with respect to the lease transactions in at least two respects. In view of the fact that Mr. and Mrs. Schryvers had indicated their intention to purchase the vehicle with cash, it was incumbent on Mr. Stehr to have properly explained the financial differences between a lease and a cash purchase. Mr. Stehr failed to state a material fact when he did not advise the Schryvers that the cost of acquiring the vehicles by way of the lease/options was greater than the cost of purchasing the vehicles in cash (after taking into account the savings on the taxes under the lease and the saving of interest by leaving their money in the bank). I believe that Mr. Stehr intentionally left the impression that there was a price advantage by acquiring the vehicles through lease/options when such an advantage did not exist. Even if the "guaranteed" price or the availability of the three options at the end of the terms of the leases represents a significant benefit, the Schryvers should have still been properly advised on the financial comparison so that they could decide whether they were prepared to pay the extra amount for this benefit.

The second deceptive act relates to the position of Richport Ford that the sale prices of the vehicles is no longer relevant when it has been decided that the transaction is to be structured as a lease/option. In the words of counsel for the Schryvers which were adopted by Mr. Stehr, it is like comparing apples to oranges because the transactions are so different. Whether this position is right or wrong, Richport Ford had an obligation to disclose its position to the Schryvers so they would be aware that the two types of transactions could not be compared. I have no doubt that, to the knowledge of Mr. Stehr, the Schryvers believed that the plan was equivalent to a method of financing the purchase of the vehicles in a manner that was advantageous to an outright purchase. Mr. Stehr had a duty to point out to the Schryvers that the two methods of acquisition were not comparable and that the negotiated sale prices would not be utilized for the purposes of applying the lease rate factors to determine the amounts payable under the leases. …

[After lengthy discussion and calculation of damages the court concluded] The total of the general damages in respect of both vehicles is $4,948.31 + $6,630.16 = $11,578.47.

The Schryvers also seek punitive damages in the amount of $10,000. Counsel for the Schryvers relied on the following passage from *Novak v. Zephyr Ford Truck Centre Ltd.* *(unreported, B.C.C.A., November 24, 1988, No. CA008534) at p. 7:

> Secondly, I wish to add that while the power of the court to award punitive damages should always be exercised with extreme caution and care, I note in this case that the learned trial judge found not only that there had been a deceptive trade practice, he also specifically found that upon this matter being questioned the defendant then adopted a series of stalling tactics which led to a heated confrontation and other unpleasantness. In those circumstances it seems to me that the learned trial judge had ample reason to make an award of punitive damages if he thought as he did, and we ought not to interfere.

Counsel for the Schryvers pointed to the fact that Mr. Schryvers complained about the leases well within the 15-day period during which Ford Credit would have allowed Richport Ford to cancel the assignment of the leases.

If the deceptive act committed by Richport Ford was restricted to a failure to properly explain the financial differences between a lease and a cash purchase, I may not be inclined to award punitive damages. However, I have also found that Richport Ford intentionally committed a deceptive act by structuring the leases without regard to the sale prices that were listed on the vehicles. Richport Ford received from the Schryvers and Ford Credit the following amounts (net of taxes) in comparison to the agreed sale prices (as adjusted to reflect the extended warranty, the undercoating and the freight and inspection charges):

	Amount Received	Sale Price
Explorer	$28,244	$26,080
Escort	$19,258	$15,220

Little wonder Richport Ford had a contest for the salesperson who could persuade the most customers to acquire their vehicles by way of a lease transaction. I consider the actions of Richport Ford to be sufficiently flagrant and high handed to warrant an award of punitive damages.

There must be a disincentive to suppliers in respect of intentionally deceptive trade practices. If no punitive damages are awarded for intentional violations of the legislation, suppliers will continue to conduct their businesses in a manner that involves deceptive trade prices because they will have nothing to lose. In this case I believe that the appropriate amount of punitive damages is the extra profit Richport Ford endeavoured to make as a result of its deceptive acts. I therefore award punitive damages against Richport Ford in the amount of $6,000.

CONCLUSION

I grant judgment against Richport Ford in the amount of $17,578.47 plus costs. …

*(In which a dealer said the truck had not sustained damages over $2,000, when it had sustained damages over $34,000.)

- *I*n a lawsuit against Celine Dion, her former drummer, Peter Barbeau, alleges that in her concerts Dion lip-synchs to tapes. Much like the Milli Vanilli scandal and class action suit of 1990 (when it was discovered that the group had lip-synched its songs and had not even sung the songs on its best-selling album), the Dion case fuels the call for laws requiring lip-sync concerts to be advertised as such.[20]

- *T*he Attorney General in Texas challenged a Volvo ad in which the car withstands the crush of a huge truck. It was learned that the car in the ad had been reinforced with steel or wood. Volvo agreed to run a newspaper ad correcting the false ad, to make no unproved claims and to pay the state $316,250 for the costs incurred investigating the matter.[21]

- *L*aidlaw Inc., a company based in Burlington, Ontario, agreed to pay $3 million to settle a consumer protection action commenced in California. The customers alleged that they were sent forms with removable stickers which said the forms should be signed for insurance purposes or as pledges not to dispose of hazardous waste in the companies' garbage bins. In fact, the forms were used by Laidlaw as long-term contracts. Customers who complained were told that they would have to continue with the company or pay a six-month service charge to cancel the contract.[22]

C. Priority of Creditors

Q u e s t i o n s

In contracts for loans the debtor promises to repay the creditor,
but if the creditor wants more than just the promise what else can he take as security?
What can this secured creditor do if the debtor doesn't pay?
How does the procedure work?

---

1. Secured Transactions

- *I*n 1985, the entertainer Michael Jackson paid about $45 million for songs written by the Beatles. These and others, including songs by Little Richard, are estimated to be worth as much as $200 million and provide him with a valuable asset to use when borrowing money.[23]

Personal Property Security Act

Q u e s t i o n

Who takes the asset given as security if the secured creditor fails to register his interest?

Giffen (Re)

http://www.lexum.umontreal.ca/
Supreme Court of Canada
February 12, 1998

---

[1] Iacobucci J. — The principal question raised by this appeal is whether s. 20(b)(i) of the *Personal Property Security Act*, S.B.C. 1989, c. 36 (*"PPSA"*), can render a lessor's unperfected security interest in personal property ineffective against the rights acquired in the property by the trustee in bankruptcy, which finds its authority under the *Bankruptcy and Insolvency Act*, R.S.C., 1985, c. B-3 (*"BIA"*). I conclude that s. 20(b)(i) operates, on the present facts, to defeat the unperfected security interest of the respondent Telecom Leasing Canada (TLC) Limited (the "lessor"), in favour of the interest acquired by the appellant R. West & Associates Inc. (the "trustee"). ...

FACTS

[3] On October 27, 1992, the lessor leased a 1993 Saturn car to the B.C. Telephone Company, which in turn leased the car to one of its employees, Carol Anne Giffen (the "bankrupt"). The bankrupt and her employer were parties to the agreement of lease entitled "Employee Agreement Personal Vehicle Lease Program/Flex Lease Program". The term of the lease was for more than one year. The lease gave the bankrupt the option of purchasing the vehicle from the lessor.

[4] Although the lessor was not a party to the agreement, it played an important role in the arrangement contemplated by the agreement. More specifically, the lessor received a deposit from the bankrupt, it fixed the lease rates, and it was entitled to receive payments directly from the lessee/bankrupt if her employer stopped paying her. Further, the lessor and the bankrupt were named as the owners of the vehicle in the registration and insurance documents relating to the vehicle; the lessor was described as the "lessor" and the bankrupt was described as the "lessee".

[5] The bankrupt made an assignment in bankruptcy on October 12, 1993. Neither the lessor nor the B.C. Telephone Company had registered financing statements under the *PPSA* in respect of their leases. The failure to register meant that the

lessor's security interest in the car was not perfected, as defined in the *PPSA*, at the time of the assignment in bankruptcy.
[6] The appellant was appointed as the trustee in bankruptcy. The lessor seized the vehicle and sold it with the trustee's consent; proceeds of $10,154.54 were held in trust by the lessor's counsel. The trustee subsequently brought a motion for an order that it was entitled to the proceeds of sale relying on s. 20(b)(i) of the *PPSA*. The lessor opposed the claim on the grounds that the bankrupt never owned the car and that the trustee could not have a better claim to the car than the bankrupt had.
[7] Hood J. of the Supreme Court of British Columbia held that, by virtue of s. 20(b)(i) of the *PPSA*, the unperfected security interest of the lessor was of no effect as against the trustee. Hood J. ordered that the proceeds from the sale of the vehicle be paid over to the trustee. The lessor appealed to the Court of Appeal for British Columbia ... [which] allowed the appeal and held that the proceeds properly belonged to the lessor [on the grounds] ... that s. 20(b)(i) cannot possibly have the effect of transferring title from the lessor, the true owner, to the trustee in bankruptcy because this would give the trustee greater proprietary rights in the car than the bankrupt enjoyed. ...

ISSUES

[23] There is one principal issue in the present appeal: can s. 20(b)(i) of the *PPSA* extinguish the lessor's right to the car in favour of the trustee's interest, or is the operation of s. 20(b)(i) limited by certain provisions of the *BIA*?
[24] In my view, this issue can be resolved through a normal reading of the relevant provisions of both the *PPSA* and the *BIA*, buttressed by the policy considerations supporting these provisions.

ANALYSIS

A. The Locus of Title Is Not Determinative

[25] At the outset, it is important to note that the Court of Appeal's holding in the present appeal rests on the principle that the "property of the bankrupt" shall vest in the trustee (s. 71(2) *BIA*) and that only the property of the bankrupt shall be distributed among the bankrupt's creditors (s. 67(1) *BIA*). In the opinion of the Court of Appeal, the bankrupt, as lessee, did not have a proprietary interest in the car, and since the trustee obtains its entitlements to the contents of the bankrupt's estate through the bankrupt, the trustee cannot assert a proprietary interest in the car. In my view, the Court of Appeal, with respect, erred fundamentally in focussing on the locus of title and in holding that the lessor's common law ownership interest prevailed despite the clear meaning of [the Personal Property Security Act] s. 20(b)(i).
[26] The Court of Appeal did not recognize that the provincial legislature, in enacting the *PPSA*, has set aside the traditional concepts of title and ownership to a certain extent. ....
[28] The Court of Appeal in the present appeal did not look past the traditional concepts of title and ownership. But this dispute cannot be resolved through the determination of who has title to the car because the dispute is one of priority to the car

and not ownership in it. It is in this context that the *PPSA* must be given its intended effect and it is to this question that I now wish to turn.

B. Definition of "Security Interest"

[29] The *PPSA* applies to "every transaction that in substance creates a security interest, without regard to its form and without regard to the person who has title to the collateral" (s. 2(1)(a)).
[30] Section 1 of the *PPSA* defines "security interest", in part, as "an interest in goods, chattel paper, a security, a document of title, an instrument, money or an intangible that secures payment or performance of an obligation". This definition is elaborated upon by paragraph 1(a)(iii) of the *PPSA*, which provides that "security interest" means the interest of "a lessor under a lease for a term of more than one year, <u>whether or not the interest secures payment or performance of an obligation</u>" (emphasis added). ...
[31] The elements of the definition of "security interest" explicitly include within the definition of "security interest" leases for a term of more than one year. The lessor's interest in the car is the reservation of title in the car; this interest, created by the lease agreement, falls within the ambit of the *PPSA*.

C. The Nature of the Lessor's Interest in the Car

[32] A security interest is valid and enforceable when it attaches to personal property. Section 12(1)(b) of the *PPSA* provides that a security interest "attaches" when the debtor acquires "rights in the collateral". Section 12(2) states explicitly that "a debtor has rights in goods leased to the debtor ... when he obtains possession of them in accordance with the lease". Thus, upon delivery of the car to the bankrupt, the lessor had a valid security interest in the car that could be asserted against the lessee and against a third party claiming a right in the car. However, the lessor's security interest remained vulnerable to the claims of third parties who obtain an interest in the car through the lessee including, trustees in bankruptcy. In order to protect its security interest from such claims, the lessor must therefore perfect its interest through registration of its interest (s. 25), or repossession of the collateral (s. 24). The lessor did not have possession of the car, and it did not register its security interest. Thus, prior to the bankruptcy, the lessor held an unperfected security interest in the car. This brings us to the *BIA*.

D. The Bankrupt's Interest in the Car Vests in the Trustee

[After reviewing the wording of the *PPSA* and the *BIA*, the judge concludes:]
[37] From the perspective of both the *PPSA* and the *BIA* the bankrupt, as lessee, can be described as having a proprietary interest in the car.

E. The Priority Contest and the Operation of Section 20(b)(i)
(i) <u>Purpose of Section 20(b)(i)</u>
[38] The Saskatchewan Court of Appeal explained the theory behind s. 20 of the Saskatchewan *PPSA in International Harvester* (at pp. 204-5). A person with an interest rooted in title

to property in the possession of another, once perfected, can, in the event of default by the debtor, look to the property ahead of all others to satisfy his claim. However, if that interest is not perfected, it is vulnerable, even though it is rooted in title to the goods (at p. 205):

> A third party may derive an interest in the same goods by virtue of some dealing with the person in possession of them, and ... he may become entitled to priority. That is, he may become entitled, ahead of the person holding the unperfected security interest, to look to the goods to satisfy his claim.

Public disclosure of the security interest is required to prevent innocent third parties from granting credit to the debtor or otherwise acquiring an interest in the collateral. ...

(ii) The Present Appeal and Section 20(b)(i)

[43] In the present appeal, the trustee's possessory interest in the car, acquired through the bankrupt under the authority of the *BIA*, comes into competition with the unperfected security interest of the lessor. Section 20(b)(i) of the *PPSA* states explicitly that a security interest in collateral "is not effective against a trustee in bankruptcy if the security interest is unperfected at the date of the bankruptcy". On a plain reading of s. 20(b)(i), the lessor's interest in the car is ineffective against the trustee.

[44] Section 20(b)(i) does not grant title or any other proprietary interest to the trustee, but it prevents the lessor from exercising rights against the trustee. Admittedly, the effect of s. 20(b)(i), on the present facts, is that the trustee ends up with full rights to the car when the bankrupt had only a right of use and possession. The Court of Appeal refused to accept this result. ...

[50] I accept that there is a principle which provides that a trustee in bankruptcy cannot obtain a greater interest to the goods than the bankrupt (beyond the context of a trust where the goods are not property of the bankrupt). However, s. 20(b)(i) itself modifies that principle. Cases decided prior to the Court of Appeal decision in the case on appeal have consistently accepted that s. 20(b)(i), or its equivalent, can give the trustee a greater interest in the disputed property than that enjoyed by the bankrupt. ...

[52] [In *International Harvester* the] court acknowledged that federal bankruptcy legislation provides that a trustee shall step into the shoes of the bankrupt and "as a general rule acquires no higher right in the property of the bankrupt than that which

the bankrupt enjoyed" (p. 200). The court then considered the policy considerations supporting the *PPSA* regime and the potential for mischief which arises in security transactions where title to property is separated from possession of that property. Provincial legislatures, faced with a policy choice involving the competing interests of the true owner and those of third parties dealing with the ostensible owner, have decided that the true owner must forfeit title, when faced with a competing interest, if she failed to register her interest as required. ...

[56] I agree with the decisions of the courts that have held that the principle that a trustee in bankruptcy cannot obtain greater rights to the property than the bankrupt had has been modified through the policy choices of the legislatures represented in s. 20(b)(i) of the *PPSA*, and its equivalents in other provinces.

F.   The Trustee Can Confer Clear Title

[57] Title could not defeat the trustee's claim under s. 20(b)(i) of the *PPSA*, but does the lessor's retention of title and the principle of *nemo dat quod non habet* [I cannot give what I do not have] prevent the trustee from selling the car, conferring clear title, and distributing its proceeds under the *BIA*? [The court answers "no"; the trustee can sell the car and confer good title.]

G.   The Federal Priority Scheme, Which Is Subject to the Rights of Secured Creditors, Is Not Disturbed

[60] ... [T]he *BIA* sets out a priority scheme for the division of the property of the bankrupt. ...

[61] ... Section 20(b)(i) of the *PPSA* does not offend the priorities set out in the *BIA*. ... [It] serves, on the present facts, to define the rights of the lessor and indicates that for the purpose of the bankruptcy, the lessor does not have the status of a secured creditor. ...

[65] ... It is trite to observe that the [*BIA*] is contingent on the provincial law of property for its operation....

CONCLUSION AND DISPOSITION

[73] In accordance with s. 20(b)(i), the lessor's unperfected security interest is ineffective against the possessory interest acquired by the trustee in bankruptcy. The trustee's interest in the car takes priority over that of the lessor; the trustee is therefore entitled to the proceeds of the car.

[74] For the foregoing reasons, I would therefore allow the appeal. ...

Unanimous

Q u e s t i o n

If the debtor is in default and the creditor seizes the asset, under what circumstances, if any, can the debtor be reinstated under the contract?

Glenn v. General Motors Acceptance Corporation of Canada

ONTARIO COURT OF JUSTICE (GENERAL DIVISION)
FILE NO. 5274/92
JULY 7, 1992

MacLeod, J.:

This is an application brought by Robert Glenn against Canadian Motors Acceptance Corporation of Canada Limited for the return of the applicant's 1990 Mercedes-Benz 500 SL automobile, and for compensations and damages, pre-judgment interest and costs.

On or about the 4th of June, 1992, the respondent, or its agents, repossessed the automobile which was the subject of a conditional sales contract between the applicant and the respondent. On June the 8th and 9th of 1992, Mr. Glenn tendered, or attempted to tender, upon the respondent the sum actually in arrears, pursuant to the conditional sales contract, plus a sum equal to the respondent's reasonable expenses of repossession, pursuant to section 66, subsection 2 of the *Personal Property Security Act*. To date, the respondent has refused to reinstate the security agreement and to return the vehicle to Mr. Glenn.

The issue for the court to determine, on this application, is the interpretation of section 66, subsection 2 of the *Personal Property Security Act*. In particular, that section states as follows:

Where the collateral is consumer goods, at any time before the secured party, under section 63, has disposed of the collateral or contracted for such disposition, or before the secured party under subsection 65(6) shall be deemed to have irrevocably elected to accept the collateral, the debtor may reinstate the security agreement by paying,

(a) the sum actually in arrears, exclusively of the operation of any other default which entitles the secured party to dispose of the collateral; and

(b) a sum equal to the reasonable expenses referred to in clause 63(1)(a) incurred by the secured party.

The section provides, in section (3), that this remedy may only be exercised once during the term of the security agreement, unless leave of the court is obtained.

The issue to be determined by me is whether or not Mr. Glenn can reinstate the security agreement by paying the arrears and the expenses due to the respondent, which is his position on the application. The respondent's position is that they are opposing the reinstatement of the security agreement in relation to the second part of clause 66(2)(a), which is:

...by curing any other default which entitles the secured party to dispose of the collateral...

Counsel for General Motors Acceptance Corporation refers, specifically, to two paragraphs of the terms of the conditional sales contract between Mr. Glenn and G.M.A.C. ...

...should the Seller [G.M.A.C.] deem itself insecure the unpaid balance of the Total Time price and all other amounts owing under this contract shall immediately become due and payable and the Seller take possession of the vehicle where it may be found, so long as repossession is done peacefully.

The second aspect of the contract referred to by counsel is paragraph 7, which states that:

You ... [shall] not ... permit to continue any charge, lien or encumbrance of any kind upon the vehicle, and shall not use it illegally or for hire.

The respondent's position on the application is that Mr. Glenn has caused the respondent to deem ... [itself] insecure and, secondly, that he has operated, or allowed the vehicle to be operated, illegally.

The cross-examination of Mr. Glenn satisfies me that, in fact, he allowed the motor vehicle licence plates, and registration of the vehicle, to expire in June of 1991. It is clear, from his evidence given on that examination, that he has allowed the vehicle to be operated on the roads and highways in Canada and the United States without it being legally licensed. In my view, that clearly is an illegal operation of the vehicle, entitling the respondent to repossess the vehicle and prevent reinstatement of the security agreement.

Secondly, the respondent alleges that Mr. Glenn ... [has caused G.M.A.C. to feel] insecure. I accept Mr. Glenn's counsel's submission that G.M.A.C. cannot, capriciously, or of its own volition, decide whenever it likes that a creditor is deemed insecure; but having had the full benefit of argument, and the examination of the parties in this case, I am satisfied that the respondent has made its case that Mr. Glenn is, in fact, [causing G.M.A.C. to feel] insecure. There is no reasonable prospect that he will maintain the currency of the contract. There is also a risk to the creditor of removal of the vehicle from the province of Ontario and a history, at least on one occasion, of refusing to advise the respondent of the actual location of the vehicle.

The cross-examination of Mr. Glenn indicates that there are extensive executions registered against him, totalling several hundred thousand dollars, and that he has no present means of income from his corporation, which was his principal business operation, being a numbered company operating "Bandito Video." He refused, on his cross-examination, to disclose his other sources of income.

The *Personal Property Security Act* has a clear legislative policy in favour of reinstatement of security agreements for consumer goods, such as a vehicle, if all of the expenses and amounts owing, "except for an acceleration clause," are paid by the debtor. This is a policy that has been implemented in subsection 2 of section 66 of the Act. Clearly, however, the creditor is not without remedy in a situation where they have established, to the satisfaction of the court, that the deemed insecurity provisions of the contract have, in fact, been met on a reasonableness basis. The creditor also has a remedy for illegal operation of this vehicle.

I find that the respondent, on the facts of this case, is entitled to refuse to reinstate the security agreement. Counsel have advised me there is no law on this section of the *Personal Property Security Act*. The legal argument was novel. I am dismissing Mr. Glenn's application for return of the vehicle, and I am making no award as to costs.

- *M*r. Martins bought a $47,000 Canon laser photocopier. He gave the seller a $25,000 cheque as a down payment. The cheque was returned NSF (not sufficient funds) three weeks after the buyer had taken possession of the copier.

  When the seller repossessed the machine, a piece of paper containing three $50 Canadian bills was discovered. In all, $24,240 in $20, $50, and $100 counterfeit bills had been made using the machine. Despite the arguments of the accused which included his allegation that he was merely testing the colour of the reproduction, he was found guilty and sentenced.[24]

- *T*hirty-six cartoons of Mickey Mouse were seized by a bank from a museum in Florida because of a creditor/debtor dispute.[25]

2. GUARANTEES

Q u e s t i o n s

Under what circumstances would a guarantor be relieved of his or her obligation?
Under what circumstances would a guarantor be obligated to honour his promise
even after the principal debtor and lender changed the terms?

Manulife Bank of Canada **v.** *Conlin*

http://www.lexum.umontreal.ca/
SUPREME COURT OF CANADA
OCTOBER 31, 1996

Background facts: In 1987 Manulife Bank of Canada lent $275,000 to Dina Conlin. The term of the contract was three years and the interest rate was 11.5% per annum. It was guaranteed by her husband John and a company, Conlin Engineering and Planning Limited. The contract contained a clause that the guarantors would be bound as principal debtors. Furthermore, the contract provided that the guarantors would be bound even if the bank and the principal debtor changed the terms of the agreement. The couple separated in 1989. In 1990 before the contract was to mature Dina and the bank changed the terms: the agreement was renewed for a further three-year term and the rate of interest was to be 13% per annum. In 1992 Dina defaulted on the mortgage. The case reached the Supreme Court of Canada on the issue of whether or not the guarantors were released from their promise to pay when the principal debtor and the bank agreed to extend the term of the mortgage and increase the interest rate without giving notice to the guarantors.

[1] CORY J. — I have read with great interest the clear and concise reasons of Justice Iacobucci [dissenting].... However, I must differ with his conclusion that by the terms of the guarantee, the respondent waived the equitable right of a guarantor to be released upon renewal of the mortgage loan with a different term and interest rates to which the guarantor did not consent.

THE POSITION OF A GUARANTOR AS DEFINED BY EQUITY AND THE COMMON LAW

[2] It has long been clear that a guarantor will be released from liability on the guarantee in circumstances where the creditor and the principal debtor agree to a material alteration of the terms of the contract of debt without the consent of the guarantor. The principle was enunciated by Cotton L.J. in *Holme v. Brunskill* (1878), 3 Q.B.D. 495 (C.A.), at pp. 505-6, in this way:

> The true rule in my opinion is, that if there is any agreement between the principals with reference to the contract guaranteed, the surety ought to be consulted, and ... if it is not self-evident that the alteration is unsubstantial, or one which cannot be prejudicial to the surety, the Court ... will hold that in such a case the surety himself must be the sole judge whether or not he will consent to remain liable notwithstanding the alteration, and that if he has not so consented he will be discharged.

This rule has been adopted in a number of Canadian cases. ...

[3] The basis for the rule is that any material alteration of the principal contract will result in a change of the terms upon which the surety was to become liable, which will, in turn, result in a change in the surety's risk. The rationale was set out in *The Law of Guarantee* (2nd ed. 1996) by Professor K.P. McGuinness in this way, at p. 534:

> The foundation of the rule in equity is certainly consistent with traditional thinking, but it is a fair question whether it is necessary to invoke the aid of equity at all in order to conclude that in a case where the principal contract is varied materially without the surety's consent, the surety is not liable for any subsequent default. Essentially, a specific or discrete guarantee (as opposed to an all accounts guarantee) is an undertaking by the surety against the risks arising from a particular contract with the principal. If that contract is varied so as to change the nature or extent of the risks arising under it, then the effect of the variation is not so much to cancel the liability of the surety as to remove the creditor from the scope of the protection that the guarantee affords. When so viewed, the foundation of the surety's defence appears in law rather than equity: it is not that the surety is no longer liable for the original contract as it is that the original contract for which the surety assumed liability has ceased to apply. In varying the principal contract without the consent of the surety, the creditor embarks upon a frolic of his own, and if misfortune occurs it occurs at the sole risk of the creditor. A law based approach to the defence is in certain respects attractive, because it moves the surety's right of defence in the case of material variation from the discretionary and therefore relatively unsettled realm of equity into the more absolute and certain realm of law. In any event, it is

clear quite certainly in equity and quite probably in law as well, that the material variation of the principal contract without the surety's consent (unless subsequently ratified by the surety) will result in the discharge of the surety from liability under the guarantee. ...

> To require a surety to maintain a guarantee ... [when the terms are changed] would be to allow the creditor and the principal to impose a guarantee upon the surety in respect of a new transaction. Such a power in the hands of the principal and creditor would amount to a radical departure from the principles of consensus and voluntary assumption of duty that form the basis of the law of contract.

THE RIGHT OF A GUARANTOR TO CONTRACT OUT OF THE PROTECTION PROVIDED BY THE COMMON LAW

[4] Generally, it is open to parties to make their own arrangements. It follows that a surety can contract out of the protection provided to a guarantor by the common law or equity. ...
[6] The issue as to whether a surety remains liable will be determined by interpreting the contract between the parties and determining the intention of the parties as demonstrated by the words of the contract and the events and circumstances surrounding the transaction as a whole.

PRINCIPLES OF INTERPRETATION

[7] In many if not most cases of guarantees ... the document is drawn by the lending institution on a standard form. The borrower and the guarantor have little or no part in the negotiation of the agreement. They have no choice but to comply with its terms if the loan is to be granted. Often the guarantors are family members with limited commercial experience. As a matter of accommodation for a family member or friend they sign the guarantee. Many guarantors are unsophisticated and vulnerable. Yet the guarantee extended as a favour may result in a financial tragedy for the guarantor. ...
[8] In my view, it is eminently fair that if there is any ambiguity in the terms used in the guarantee, the words of the documents should be construed against the party which drew it, by applying the *contra proferentem* rule. This is a sensible and satisfactory way of approaching the situation since the lending institutions that normally draft these agreements can readily amend their documents to ensure that they are free from ambiguity. The principle is supported by academic writers.
[9] G.H.L. Fridman, in his text *The Law of Contract in Canada* (3rd ed. 1994), at pp. 470-71, puts the position in this way:

> The *contra proferentem* rule is of great importance, especially where the clause being construed creates an exemption, exclusion or limitation of liability. ... Where the contract is ambiguous, the application of the *contra proferentem* rule ensures that the meaning least favourable to the author of the document prevails.

...
[14] I would note in passing that the guarantor in this case comes within the class of accommodation sureties.
[15] It follows that if there is a doubt or ambiguity as to the construction or meaning of the clauses binding the guarantor in this case, they must be strictly interpreted and resolved in favour of the guarantor. Further, as a result of the favoured po-

sition of guarantors, the clauses binding them must be strictly construed.

[16] Finally, when the guarantee clause is interpreted, it must be considered in the context of the entire transaction. This flows logically from the bank's position that the renewal agreement was an integral part of the original contract of guarantee. … It follows that fairness demands that the entire transaction be considered and this must include the terms and arrangements for the renewal agreement.

APPLICATION OF THE PRINCIPLES OF INTERPRETATION TO THE GUARANTEE AND RENEWAL AGREEMENT PRESENTED IN THIS CASE

[After reviewing the terms of the original guarantee, which contained the clause stating the guarantors would be considered principal debtors, the judge continued.]

THE EFFECT OF THE "PRINCIPAL DEBTOR OBLIGATION" SET OUT IN CLAUSE 34

[19] … If the guarantor is to be treated as a principal debtor and not as a guarantor, then the failure of the bank to notify the respondent of the renewal agreement and the new terms of the contract must release him from his obligations since he is not a party to the renewal. This conclusion does not require recourse to equitable rules regarding material variation of contracts of surety. It is simply apparent from the contract that a principal debtor must have notice of material changes and consent to them. Of course, a guarantor who, by virtue of a principal debtor clause, has a right to notice of material changes, may, by the terms of the contract, waive these rights. However, in the absence of a clear waiver of these rights, such a guarantor must be given notice of the material changes and, if he is to be bound, consent to them. …

[22] Even if it were thought that the principal debtor clause does not convert the guarantor into a principal debtor, the equitable or common law rules relieving the surety from liability where the contract has been materially altered by the creditor and the principal debtor without notice to the surety would apply, in the absence of an express agreement to the contrary. The question is whether in this case, either as principal debtor or as surety, the guarantor has expressly contracted out of the normal protections accorded to him. This question must be determined as a matter of interpretation of the clauses of the agreement, through consideration of the transaction as a whole, and the application of the appropriate rules of construction. … [After doing so the judge concludes.]

[32] It follows I find that the words used … [in the original contract] are sufficiently clear to conclude that the guarantor did not waive his equitable and common law rights either as a principal debtor or as a guarantor. The renewal agreement which was entered into without notice to, or the agreement of, the guarantor materially altered the provisions of the original loan agreement. The guarantor was thereby relieved of his obligation.

[33] If the wording of the two clauses should be found to be ambiguous, the *contra proferentem* rule must be applied against the bank. The wording of clause 34 binding the guarantor to variations in the event of an extension of the mortgage should not be applied to bind the guarantor to a renewal without notice since there is ambiguity as to whether clause 34 applies to renewals at all. In these circumstances as well, the guarantor should be relieved of liability.

DISPOSITION

[34] I would dismiss the appeal with costs.

…

[4–3]

Note: This case gives a very clear statement of the law with regard to a guarantor's liability when there is no clause purporting to extend that liability even when the lender and principle debtor change the terms. But this case is about a contract that contains such a clause and note well that four of the seven judges found *on the facts of this case* the bank had not made it clear to the guarantor that his liability was to survive changes in the terms. The banks are now aware of the cost of being unclear and some have rewritten their standard form documents. (See the following case) Therefore, read the contract with great care; if you do not want your liability as a guarantor (or as a principal debtor if such a clause is included) to extend past the first term of the contract, delete unwanted provisions.

Canadian Imperial Bank of Commerce **v.** *Shire*

[2000] B.C.J. No. 1938 (Q.L.)
British Columbia Court of Appeal
September 28, 2000

The risk to the Shires as guarantors was increased when the bank negotiated changes with other guarantors without the Shires' knowledge. On the wording of the guarantee, were the Shires relieved of their obligation to pay?

Esson J.A.: ...
[14] Paragraph (1) of the guarantees reads as follows:

> (1) Dealings by Bank. The Bank may increase, reduce, discontinue or otherwise vary the customer's credit, grant extensions of time or other indulgences, take and give up securities, abstain from taking, perfecting or registering securities, accept compositions, grant releases and discharges and otherwise deal with the customer and other parties (including other guarantors) and securities as the Bank may see fit. My obligation to pay under this Part 1 - Guarantee will not be limited or reduced as a result of the termination, invalidity or unenforceability of any right of the Bank against the customer or any other party (including other guarantors) or for any other cause whatever.

[22] Personal guarantees of Bank indebtedness often have harsh consequences. In many cases, they are entered into at the out-

set of a corporate venture in an atmosphere of optimism and are then forgotten about by the guarantors. While things go well, they are largely ignored by the Bank but they remain in its file available to be used when things go wrong. A guarantee unlimited in amount creates a particular risk for the guarantor. As Mr. Justice Taggart said in 1987, it may be that the law should limit the use of such guarantees. But the law today remains as it was then. Unless and until the law is changed, the only protection for individuals is to not execute an unlimited guarantee and to never lose sight of the fact that, whether limited or not, that potentially deadly weapon is in the Bank file.

[23] I conclude with reluctance that the trial judge erred in finding the guarantee unenforceable and thus in refusing to enforce the mortgage. The Bank is entitled to an order nisi of foreclosure proceeding. ... I would allow the appeal.

Unanimous

3. BUILDERS' LIENS

Central Supply Company (1972) *v.* *Modern Tile Supply Co.*

[1998] O.J. No. 4989 (Q.L.)
ONTARIO COURT OF JUSTICE (GENERAL DIVISION)
NOVEMBER 24, 1998

[1] Jenkins J.: — Central Supply Company (1972) Limited (Central Supply) brings this action against Modern Tile Supply Company Limited (Modern Tile), Ernesta Beltrame, John Grepley, Nora Grepley and 629763 Ontario Ltd., for the sum of $42,287.77, representing the value of floor covering, wall covering and curtains supplied to Modern Tile. ...

[2] Central Supply's claim against the individual defendants is pursuant to the trust provisions of s. 8 (1) and s. 13 of the Construction Lien Act.

[3] The claim against 629763 Ontario Ltd., as pleaded, were that John Grepley and Nora Grepley fraudulently [impoverished] Modern Tile by making lease payments to 629763 Ontario Ltd., which they controlled.

[4] The defendants admit that Central Supply is entitled to judgment against Modern Tile for the sum of $42,287.77.

[5] As of July 1997 Modern Tile is insolvent.

FACTUAL BACKGROUND ...

[7] Central Supply and Modern Tile enjoyed an excellent business relationship over many years. ...

[8] In 1990 and 1991 John Grepley testified that the combination of a recession and free trade hurt border cities such as Niagara Falls where they conducted their business. He was involved in a motor vehicle injury in July 1990 and missed a full year of work. Ernesta Beltrame, John Grepley and Nora Grepley took no wages or other benefits from Modern Tile in 1996 and continuing until July 1997 when they closed their business. The Grepleys survived on a small pension and assistance from their daughter. They estimated that they advanced approximately $100,000 into their business in the past few years to keep it in operation. ... Modern Tile in 1986 and 1987 commenced issuing NSF cheques to Central Supply. ...

[9] The floor covering, wall covering and curtains were al-

ways delivered by Central Supply to Modern Tiles' show room [not to Modern Tiles' customers.] ...

THE LAW

[The court reviews the work of the draft committee, the cases, and the wording of the relevant statutory provisions including Section 8.]

Section 8 (1) All amounts,

a) owing to a contractor or subcontractor, whether or not due or payable; or

b) received by a contractor or subcontractor, on account of the contract or subcontract price of an improvement constitute a trust fund for the benefit or the subcontractors and other persons who have supplied services or materials to the improvement who are owed amounts by the contractor or subcontractor

(2) The contractor or subcontractor is the trustee of the trust fund created by subsections (1) and the contractor or subcontractor shall not appropriate or convert any part of the fund to the contractor's or subcontractor's own use or to any use inconsistent with the trust until all subcontractors and other persons who supply services or materials to the improvement are paid all amounts related to the improvement owed to them by the contractor or subcontractor. 1983, c. 6, s. 8.

...

FINDINGS

[24] It is clear from the report of the Attorney General's Advisory Committee on the draft Construction Lien Act that the purpose

of defining "improvement," the purpose of the Act, "is to protect those who contribute their services or materials towards the making of an improvement to a premise. ... While the definition of improvement is broad, the committee attempted to draft it in such a way that it will be clear that the trust created by the Act applies only in a case of construction and building repair industries." ...

[28] In the present case, Modern Tile was simply a retail merchant selling floor and wall coverings and curtains from its store in Niagara Falls to customers who came to the store to pick up their ordered goods. Central Supply delivered the goods to the store and not to any of the ultimate purchasers. Central Supply was not interested in nor inquired as to the name of the ultimate purchasers or the location where the materials were supplied.

[29] It would have been relatively easy for Central Supply to determine the ultimate destination of their products by making arrangements with Modern Tile. ...

[31] If I were to find that the materials supplied by the plaintiff to Modern Tile was impressed with a s. 8(a) Trust, I would have to find that everything that Modern Tile purchased by way of supplies to be resold to customers would be impressed with a similar trust regardless of its ultimate destination or use.

[32] I find that Central Supply has failed to establish that the amount owing to it by Modern Tile constitutes a trust fund for its benefit. Therefore, its action against the individual defendants is dismissed.

[33] On consent a judgment will issue against Modern Tile ... for $42,287.77. ...

---

4. BANKRUPTCY

Questions

What is the purpose of bankruptcy law?
What does the court consider when a bankrupt applies to be discharged?

Bank of Montreal | v. | Giannotti

http://www.ontariocourts.on.ca/
COURT OF APPEAL FOR ONTARIO
NOVEMBER 10, 2000

Macpherson J.A.:

INTRODUCTION

[1] Most first-time bankrupts apply for a discharge approximately one year after they have been adjudged to be bankrupt. Pursuant to s.172 of the *Bankruptcy and Insolvency Act*, R.S.C. 1985, c.B-3, a judge sitting in bankruptcy court has a wide array of remedies at his or her disposal. Positive remedies which will provide some measure of relief to the bankrupt include an absolute discharge, a conditional discharge and a suspended discharge.

[2] A judge is entitled, under s.172, to refuse to make any type of discharge order. This appeal raises the issue of what type of circumstances and conduct would justify such an order.

A. Factual Background

[3] Peter Giannotti was a major real estate development player in the booming economy of the late 1980s. As a senior officer and directing mind of the Carlyle group of companies, he was involved in scores of construction projects. Some of the projects were of quite grand proportions. ... In Mr. Giannotti's words "those were the good old days."

[4] As the calendar turned from the 1980s to the 1990s, the good old days disappeared. ...

[5] Mr. Giannotti had provided personal guarantees to several institutional lenders. On May 7, 1998, one of those lenders, the Bank of Montreal, and the Ontario New Home Warranty Program petitioned Mr. Giannotti into bankruptcy. At that juncture, he owed almost 30 creditors somewhere between

$25,000,000 and $29,000,000, including $892,000 to the Bank of Montreal, $335,000 to the Ontario New Home Warranty Program and almost $19,000,000 to Montreal Trust.

[6] Just over a year later, Mr. Giannotti applied for a discharge. ...

B. Issue

[10] The sole issue in this appeal is whether the bankruptcy judge erred by not refusing the bankrupt's application for discharge.

C. Analysis

[11] There is no question that a principal purpose of the *Bankruptcy and Insolvency Act ("BIA")* is the rehabilitation of unfortunate debtors. As expressed by Houlden and Morawetz in their treatise, *Bankruptcy Law of Canada* (3rd ed., rev., Vol. 1, 1998) at p. 1-5:

> The Act permits an honest debtor, who has been unfortunate in business, to secure a discharge so that he or she can make a fresh start and resume his or her place in the business community.

[12] However, the rehabilitation of the debtor must be balanced with the interests of creditors who have lost money because of the bankrupt's conduct. This requirement of a balanced approach in discharge hearings was well articulated by Adams J. in *Re Goodman*, [1995] O.J. No.72 (Gen. Div.), at para. 1:

> The rehabilitative purpose of bankruptcy legislation is well understood. ... Individuals and society generally

benefit from a process by which the crushing burden of financial debt can be lifted, thereby permitting a bankrupt to resume the life of a useful and productive citizen. ... Equally important, however, is the integrity of the bankruptcy process itself. While the central purpose of the statute is to enable the honest but unfortunate debtor to make a fresh start, parity of treatment between debtors and fairness to creditors need to be kept in mind.

[13] Both Adams J. and Houlden and Morawetz use two adjectives to describe a debtor who should be entitled to the relief of a discharge – "unfortunate" and "honest". I have no doubt that Mr. Giannotti has been unfortunate. The downturn in the real estate market in the late 1980s and early 1990s ruined many developers. Mr. Giannotti, with millions of dollars in personal guarantees behind his companies, was one of them.

[14] However, I do not think that the adjective "honest" applies to the manner in which Mr. Giannotti conducted himself in this proceeding. My review of his testimony at the discharge hearing leads to the inevitable and overwhelming conclusion that Mr. Giannotti has not told the truth to his creditors, his trustee in bankruptcy, or the court at the discharge hearing. In *Re Miklos Gestetner and Phyllis Pearl Gestetner* (25 November 1996), (Ont. Gen. Div.) [unreported], Sharpe J. said, at para. 7:

> An honest but unfortunate debtor is entitled by the law to have a fresh financial start. The applicants may have been unfortunate, but I find that they have not been honest. In my view, they are not entitled to have the fresh start the law allows them unless they are prepared to be honest with their creditors and with the court. The court has an obligation to ensure that the integrity of the bankruptcy law is maintained. The applicants have refused to provide the court with the information required to make an appropriate judgment. In light of the evidence the applicants have offered and the level of disclosure they have made as to the true state of their financial affairs, I find that they are not entitled to discharges on any terms.

[15] I agree entirely with the philosophy manifest in this passage—a dishonest debtor, and a debtor unwilling to make full disclosure of his financial affairs, is entitled to *no* relief under the *BIA*. For several reasons, I find that every word of the above passage applies to Mr. Giannotti and, therefore, like the bankrupts in *Re Gestetner*, he was entitled to no relief at his discharge hearing. [The judge reviews in more detail the bankrupt's conduct.]

[16] First, Mr. Giannotti did not co-operate with his trustee in bankruptcy as the trustee sought to administer his estate. ...

[19] Second, Mr. Giannotti's conduct and evidence with respect to the Giannotti Family Trust was, and continues to be, completely unacceptable. ...

[21] Third, Mr. Giannotti was evasive and inconsistent with respect to funding for an office he used after he became bankrupt. ...

[22] Fourth, ... an income and expense statement ... [strains] belief. ...

[23] Fifth, it is clear that Mr. Giannotti engaged in at least one development venture after he was petitioned into bankruptcy. He admitted to the bankruptcy judge that the trustee had told him that he could not engage in business deals while he was an undischarged bankrupt. ...

[24] Sixth, I return to Adams J.'s observation in *Re Goodman* that there should be "parity of treatment between debtors and fairness to creditors" in the bankruptcy process. Mr. Giannotti owes more than $25,000,000 to almost 30 creditors. He has not paid one cent to the trustee for the benefit of those creditors. Yet, to cite but one example, after he became bankrupt he continued to be a member at the exclusive King Valley Golf Club where the annual membership is approximately $4500. This is hardly parity and fairness.

[25] The factors and conduct that I have summarized clearly placed Mr. Giannotti within s. 173 of the *BIA*. The bankruptcy judge could not have granted him an absolute discharge; his options were to grant either a suspended discharge or a conditional discharge, or to refuse to order any kind of discharge. The bankruptcy judge chose a combination of a suspended discharge and a conditional discharge.

[26] The case law establishes that a complete refusal of any type of discharge is an unusual order given the *BIA's* emphasis on rehabilitation of the debtor. In *Re Adelman*, Urquhart J. said that a refusal of discharge "is a harsh step ... which should be resorted to only in extraordinary cases". ... However, in this case, given Mr. Giannotti's conduct and testimony, a refusal of any kind of discharge was, in my view, required. Mr. Giannotti was simply too unco-operative, evasive and untruthful with both the trustee and the bankruptcy judge.

[27] The *BIA* seeks to provide relief to honest and unfortunate debtors. The word 'honest' introduces a strong element of integrity into the administration of the Act. In my view, a reasonable member of the public would seriously question the integrity of the *BIA* if Mr. Giannotti was given any form of relief at this juncture. He has not been honest with the trustee or the bankruptcy court. He is free to re-apply for a discharge, but he must co-operate with the trustee and make full disclosure of the relevant facts.

DISPOSITION

[28] I would allow the appeal. ...

Unanimous

- **O**range County, California, a symbol of wealth and conservative politics, declared bankruptcy after it lost more than $1.5 billion in high risk investments.[26]

  In 1998 the brokerage firm of Merrill Lynch & Co. agreed to pay Orange County $400 million to settle the allegation that its negligence caused the county's bankruptcy.[27]

- **T**he Finnish Communist Party filed for bankruptcy. Some of its $19.06 million U.S. debt was incurred by "share investments gone bad."[28]

• *A*fter the court decision finding Kim Basinger liable for $8.1 million for breach of contract, the actress declared bankruptcy, but the bankruptcy judge rejected her plan for paying her debts as being too vague.[29] It was reported that Ms. Basinger changed her bankruptcy petition, a change that necessitated her selling many of her assets.[30]

Q u e s t i o n

Can the debtor transfer his assets to protect them from the creditors?

The facts found by the court were that the owner of the car dealership transferred $40,000 to his wife on the eve of the insolvency of the dealership. In the words of the court:

> The issue raised by the applicant in these proceedings is whether the payment to Donna Hunt is void against the Trustee in that it constituted a "settlement" within the meaning of s. 91 of the Bankruptcy and Insolvency Act, R.S.C. 1985, B-3 (the "BIA").

The court reviews the relevant section of the *BIA* and its definition of "settlement":

> Section 91(1) of the BIA provides:
> 91.(1)Any settlement of property made within the period beginning on the day that is one year before the date of the initial bankruptcy event in respect of the settlor and ending on the date that the settlor became bankrupt, both dates included, is void against the trustee.
> "Settlement" includes a contract, covenant, transfer, gift and designation of beneficiary in an insurance contract, to the extent that the contract, covenant, transfer, gift or designation is gratuitous or made for merely nominal consideration.

The court concludes that the payment was made within the one year prohibited period and was a settlement. In regard to the wife's argument that she did not receive the money directly from the bankrupt dealership, the court remarks:

> ...[I]t is my view that in light of the plain language of s. 91, which is inclusive rather than exhaustive, and in view of the objective of fairness to creditors and to bankrupts which permeates the BIA, a gratuitous transfer of money from a bankrupt's estate to the spouse of the bankrupt within the prohibited period cannot be achieved with impunity. Accordingly, a two step transfer, by which the controlling mind and principal of a bankrupt company notionally transfers money from the bankrupt company to himself and then to his spouse, must of necessity be illegal and caught by s. 91. ...

Thus the court found the transfer void against the claim of the Trustee in bankruptcy.

Grandview Ford Lincoln Sales Ltd. (Re)
[2000] O.J. No. 3280 (Q.L.)
Ontario Superior Court
August 29, 2000

Question

Does the Bankruptcy and Insolvency Act *prohibit the debtor from preferring a creditor?*

The case begins as follows:

[1] Browne J.:— In this action the plaintiff seeks a declaration that a payment made to Teac Canada Ltd. by Medler-McKay Holdings Ltd. in the amount of $108,589.80 is fraudulent and void as against the Trustee as a preference pursuant to the provisions of s. 95 of the *Bankruptcy and Insolvency Act* and he seeks a judgment against the defendant in the amount of $108,589.80.

[2] Section 95 provides that every payment made by an insolvent person in favour of any creditor with a view to giving that creditor a preference over the other creditors shall, if the payment is within three months of bankruptcy, be deemed fraudulent and void as against the Trustee in the bankruptcy.

[3] Section 95(2) provides a presumption that where the payment has the effect of giving any creditor a preference over other creditors it shall be presumed in the absence of evidence to the contrary to have been made with a view to giving a preference. The subsection provides further that when the payment was made voluntarily or under pressure shall not be evidence admissible to support the transaction.

The judge applies the facts of the case to every requirement of these statutory provisions. He finds that Medler-McKay had breached the provisions by preferring its supplier, Teac Canada, by "paying-off" Teac so that in the future he might obtain credit and/or the supply of inventory for any new company created after the bankruptcy.

This decision was affirmed by the Court of Appeal.

Medler-McKay Holdings Ltd. (Trustee of) v. Teac Canada ltd.
[1994] O.J. No. 618 (Q.L.)
Ontario Court of Justice—General Division

• *C*an Shaq save the planet? Planet Hollywood filed for bankruptcy protection in 1999 and closed nine of its 32 theme restaurants. With Shaquille O'Neal, basketball star with the Los Angeles Lakers, becoming a shareholder the chain may not fold.[31]

5. FRAUDULENT CONVEYANCES ACT/FRAUDULENT PREFERENCE ACT

Questions

How can the family home be protected from creditors?
How angry can the court be when assets are moved to defraud creditors?

The matrimonial home, valued near $500,000, was registered in the name of Cheryl Hennessey. Three days before she was served with a claim against her arising from fraudulent stock manipulation on the Vancouver Stock Exchange, she conveyed the home to her husband Ian. The plaintiff, United Services Fund, which had lost $20 million in the stock fraud, obtained judgment against her for $3.25 million. While that case was under appeal, the United Services Fund commenced an action alleging that she had fraudulently conveyed the matrimonial home with the intent to thwart its enforcement of the judgment against her.

The court found that the conveyance of the home was a fraudulent conveyance made with fraudulent intent on the part of both Cheryl and her husband Ian. The house was sold and the proceeds used to purchase another house, which was also sold. As the plaintiff had the right to trace the proceeds of the sale, the court reviewed the disposition of the funds and found that they had, through the complex and "deceitful" efforts of Ian, been exhausted. The court granted a monetary judgment in substitution for an order setting aside the fraudulent conveyance.

The court also allowed the amendment of the Statement of Claim to include a claim for punitive damages. The judge, who had referred to the testimony of the defendants as "complete fabrication" and "a pack of lies," concluded:

> "I find that the conduct of the defendants in their participation in the fraudulent conveyance and their subsequent deceitful activities to deny the plaintiffs access to any assets to satisfy even a small portion of the judgment against Cheryl is conduct which merits punishment by an award of punitive damages in order to demonstrate to the defendants that the law will not tolerate conduct which willfully disregards the rights of others. ... There will be judgment against the plaintiffs for punitive damages in the amount of $100,000.
>
> The plaintiffs are not the only victims of the fraudulent activities of the defendants. By their fraudulent defence to this action they have perpetrated a fraud on counsel of the plaintiffs, on this court and on the public generally who have had to provide court facilities and court staff at the tax payers expense for a seven-day trial. There was no defence to the plaintiffs' action. The seven days of trial time could have been used for parties who have a legitimate court action. Cheryl and Ian came to court to defend a fraudulent conveyance action knowing the conveyance was fraudulent, failing to disclose relevant documents, and lying under oath. ... 'Oh, what a tangled web we weave, when first we practise to deceive.'

United Services Funds v. Hennessey
Ontario Court (General Division)
Summarized from The Lawyer's Weekly
September 2, 1994, p.11

Note: In 1997 the Court of Appeal upheld that the conveyance was fraudulent and that the court had the right to trace the funds, but it overturned the award of punitive damages.

In the Matter of: Babbitt and Paladin Inc., Gary Husbands and Excalibur Technologies Inc.

ONTARIO COURT (GENERAL DIVISION) IN BANKRUPTCY
TORONTO FILE NO: B274/92
NOVEMBER 26, 1992

Background facts: The plaintiff, Babbitt, had successfully sued Paladin Inc. and Gary Husbands, its majority shareholder. At the examination in aid of execution it was learned that the defendant Husbands had shut down Paladin and transferred all its assets to a newly created company, Excalibur Technologies Inc. The plaintiff then applied to have the transfer of assets set aside under the *Fraudulent Conveyances Act*. As a creditor of a corporation, the plaintiff used the oppression remedy under s. 248 of the *Ontario Business Corporations Act*.[32]

Carruthers, J. (given orally) ...

The basic issue concerns the fact that all the business and assets of Paladin, of which the defendant Husbands at all relevant times had the majority interest and was its sole operating mind, have ended up with a company known as Excalibur Technologies Inc. This company was the creation of Husbands and at all relevant times was also under his sole control and direction.

Essentially what happened was that Husbands shut down Paladin and started Excalibur, and in the process of doing so took all of the assets of Paladin, including 45 service contracts, all of the employees required to service those contracts and its goodwill and gave or transferred them, without cost, to Excalibur. As a result Paladin was left as an empty shell, thereby rendering the claims of outstanding creditors, and in particular the plaintiff, Cynthia Babbitt, unenforceable.

There appears to be no disagreement between counsel that all of the circumstances surrounding these dealings between Paladin and Excalibur, all of which are not disputed, give rise to a presumption in favour of the plaintiff against the validity of the transaction between Paladin and Excalibur. ...

In the course of testifying the defendant Husbands said without any reservation or qualification that a factor, if not the factor, in changing his business operations from Paladin to Excalibur was his inability to overcome what he described as being "a mountain of debt" that had been generated on behalf of Paladin. He testified that he could see "no way out of the situation" but to start a new business in the manner in which he did.

... As I said to counsel during argument, what Mr. Husbands had to say comes about as close to an admission that he intended to defeat or defraud Paladin's creditors as one could expect in a case of this kind.

Frankly I am surprised and concerned that any business man in this Province would not understand that what was done here is wrong. Surely Husbands had to know that one cannot by simply organizing a succession of new companies, utilizing new labels and transferring assets, without any consideration avoid the indebtedness of those left behind. That surely is a simply straightforward common sense basic principle. To permit what Husbands did would create havoc in the business and commercial world.

In my opinion the defendants have not succeeded at all in rebutting the presumption which the circumstances of this case give rise to. ...

[H]ad there been a claim for punitive damages, I would have most probably assessed punitive damages against the defendants. This is just absolutely a case in which we have someone who is virtually thumbing his nose at the Law and the rights of others, and abusing the processes of this Court in the process. It is very difficult for me to understand how anyone of his apparent intelligence can think that he is entitled to do what he has done and then come to this Court and say, it is right. And, I might add at this point, bring with him a strong attitude, as well, that it is wrong to criticize him for what he did.

While lots of people might do these things, it is rare that they would then try and justify them in a Court of Law. The whole thing is just an absolute waste of everyone's time, except of course for the defendants. I am sure they thought time was in their favour. ...

I have endorsed the record for oral reasons given, Judgment for the plaintiff against Paladin Inc., Gary Husbands and Excalibur Technologies Inc., for $31,339.85, and costs on a solicitor and client basis at $16,330. The liability of each of the parties, Paladin Inc., Gary Husbands and Excalibur Technologies Inc., is on a joint and several basis.

Judgment for the plaintiff

D. NEGOTIABLE INSTRUMENTS

Question

When can the drawer of the cheque say to the holder of the cheque "I don't want to pay you" and succeed in law?

Confederation Leasing Ltd. v. *Cana-Drain Services Inc. et al.*

[1994] O.J. No. 1660 (Q.L.)
ONTARIO COURT OF JUSTICE—GENERAL DIVISION
JULY 26, 1994

Background facts: The plaintiff purchased assets of a bank. The assets included the bank's accounts receivable, which were assigned to the plaintiff. Among these receivables was a promissory note given to the bank. The makers of the note resisted paying as promised on the basis of a misrepresentation made to them by the bank.

Wilson J.:—...

DEFENCE OF MISREPRESENTATION

[5] Confederation Leasing is a holder in due course under s. 55(1) of the *Bills of Exchange Act*, R.S.C. 1985, c.B-4 which states:

55(1) A holder in due course is a holder who has taken a bill, complete and regular on the face of it, under the following conditions, namely:

(a) that he became the holder of it before it was overdue and without notice that it had been previously dishonoured, if such was the fact;

(b) that he took the bill in good faith and for value, and that at the time the bill was negotiated to him he had no notice of any defect in the title of the person who negotiated it.

(2) In particular the title of a person who negotiates a bill is defective within the meaning of this Act when he obtained the bill, or the acceptance thereof, by fraud, duress or force and fear, or other unlawful means, or for an illegal consideration, or when he negotiates it in breach of faith, or under such circumstances as amount to a fraud.

[6] As endorsers of the promissory note, the defendants Persichilli and Cornacchia (P & C) [the makers of the note] are liable for the amount of the promissory note to a holder in due course, subject only to what are known as real or absolute defences. Section 132 of the Act states:

132. The endorser of a bill by endorsing it, subject to the effect of any express stipulation authorized by this Act,

(a) engages that on due presentment it shall be accepted and paid according to its tenor, and that if it is dishonoured he will compensate the holder or a subsequent endorser who is compelled to pay it, if the requisite proceedings on dishonour are duly taken;

(b) is precluded from denying to a holder in due course the genuineness and regularity in all respects of the drawer's signature and all previous endorsements; and

(c) is precluded from denying to his immediate or a subsequent endorsee that the bill was, at the time of his endorsement, a valid and subsisting bill, and that he had then a good title thereto.

[7] Defences on a bill of exchange, cheque or note fall into three categories: real or absolute defences, defects of title and personal defences. Real or absolute defences, available against even a holder in due course, include, for example, the inca-

pacity to incur contractual liability or forgery of a party's signature. No defence of this type has been raised here.

[8] A defect of title defence affects the title of a person owning or assigned the bill. Crawford and Falconbridge … *Banking and Bills of Exchange* (8th ed.) (Toronto: Canada Law Book, 1986), vol. 2, p. 1524] gives some examples. If a person obtains an instrument by fraud or undue influence, or for illegal consideration, his or her title to the instrument is defective: *Pacific Finance Acceptance Co. Ltd. v. Turgeon et al.* (1978), 93 D.L.R. (3d) 301 (B.C. Co. Ct.). The title defect may prevent a transferee or a signee from obtaining a good title.

[9] By way of contrast, a personal defence is a defence raising equities between the parties. They do not affect title to the instrument. These include contractual defences such as misrepresentation, or a right of set-off arising out of another transaction between the maker of the instrument and the payee of a note. According to Crawford and Falconbridge at p. 1524:

The [personal] defence may be good as between the two parties between whom it arises, that is, between immediate parties, but it is not available as against a remote party taking in good faith.

[10] In *Banque de la Societe, Generale de Belgique v. McKissock*, [1961] O.W.N. 121 (H.C.J.), the Court affirmed this principle. …

[11] If a transferee takes as holder in due course, the assignment is not affected by personal defences. Section 73 of the Bills of Exchange Act provides as follows:

73 The rights and powers of the holder of a bill are as follows:

(a) he may sue on the bill in his own name;

(b) where he is a holder in due course, he holds the bill free from any defect of title of prior parties, as well as from mere personal defences available to prior parties among themselves, and may enforce payment against all parties liable on the bill;

(c) where his title is defective, if he negotiates the bill to a holder in due course, that holder obtains a good and complete title to the bill; and

(d) where his title is defective, if he obtains payment of the bill the person who pays him in due course gets a valid discharge for the bill.

[12] As misrepresentation is a personal defence between the Bank and the defendants, the enforceability of the promissory note by Confederation as holder in due course is not affected. . .

[14] I therefore conclude that Confederation Leasing is a holder in due course and therefore is entitled to rely on the promissory note as endorsed. The defendants may well have a remedy against the Bank, but that is a matter for another day. …

• ***A*** British mail order firm received a cheque for £100 with an order for toys. Although the cheque was not completely filled out, the firm sent the order. The cheque had been forged—by the owner's seven-year-old son.[33]

The drawer of the cheque, Ierullo, left the payee blank because her business associate, Nicholls, said he did not know precisely with which supplier of goods he would be dealing. Nicholls subsequently fraudulently filled in the name of Rovan, a man to whom he owed money. Ierullo then sued for the return of the money. In the words of the court:

[18] A cheque is a bill drawn on a bank that is payable on demand. Cheques are covered by the *Bills of Exchange Act*, R.S.C. 1985, c. B-4, specifically s. 165. The first issue raised is whether the payee of a cheque can be a holder in due course of it. This issue has been one that has been controversial for more than 100 years. While the House of Lords purported to resolve the issue in 1926 in *R.E. Jones Ltd. v. Waring & Gillow, Ltd.*, [1926] A.C. 670 wherein it was decided that a payee could not be a holder in due course, that decision was not without its detractors and, in any event, has technically not been binding on Canadian courts for decades with the result that existing decisions in our courts have not always chosen to follow it.

[19] The authors of Crawford and Falconbridge, *Banking and Bills of Exchange*, 8th ed. (Toronto: Canada Law Book, 1986), at pp. 1476-77, offer a strong argument that the payee of a cheque should be considered as a holder in due course of it. They contend, and I respectfully agree with them, that this is particularly so in a case such as this where the cheque is written in blank form since such circumstances will generally mean that the person whose name subsequently appears as payee on the cheque will be a person unconnected to the payor. Such a person is consequently and reasonably to be considered a remote party to the bill and thus is someone who ought to take as a holder in due course and to be entitled to the protection that such a status affords. ...

[22] Section 55(1)(b) has three requirements that the defendant must satisfy. First, the defendant must take the bill in good faith. Secondly, he must take it for value. Thirdly, he must not have notice of any defect in the title of the person who negotiated it to him.

[The court found that the defendant satisfied all the requirements.] ...

[29] In the end result, therefore, the plaintiff's claim is dismissed.

Ierullo v. Rovan
Ontario Superior Court
[2000] O.J. No. 108 (Q.L.)
January 20, 2000

ENDNOTES

1. For a more detailed account see *The Vancouver Sun*, March 15, 1999, p. B4.

2. For a more detailed summary of *Deonanan v. Wingate* see *The Lawyers Weekly*, October 7, 1994, p. 37.

3. A more detailed account is given in *The Vancouver Sun*, November, 1979.

4. As of September 2000, the tires had been linked to 88 deaths in the U.S. For the continuing saga of the Firestone crisis see *Time Magazine*, August 21, 2000, p. 44; September 4, p. 22; September 11, p. 19; September 18, p. 32; *The Miami Herald*, September 13, 2000, p. C1. In a segment on *60 Minutes*, aired October 10, 2000, it was alleged that the company knew of "tread separation" accidents as early as 1992.

5. For a more detailed account see *The Vancouver Sun*, September 6, 1994, p. A6.

6. For a more detailed account see *The Maui News*, February 24, 1995, p. A2.

7. For a more detailed account see *The Vancouver Sun* , February 1992.

8. Adapted from *The Globe and Mail*, October 16, 1990, p. A18.

9. *The New York Times*, Nov. 10, 1999.
   http://www.nytimes.com/com/library/tech/99/11/biztech/articles/10soft.html

10. *The Vancouver Sun*, April 4, 2000, p. 1.

11. *The New York Times*, June 8, 2000, p. 1.

12. *Time Magazine,* June 19, 2000, p. 22.

13. *Time Magazine*, October 9, 2000, p. 9.

14. *The Vancouver Sun,* May 26, 1999, p. D6.

15. *The Vancouver Sun*, July 23, 1999, p. A7.

16. For a more detailed account see *The Vancouver Sun*, July 27, 2000, p. F3.

17. *The Vancouver Sun*, September 26, 2000.

18. For a more detailed account of *Apotex Inc. v. Hoffman La-Roche Limited* see *The Lawyers Weekly*, January 12, 2001, p. 1.

19. For a more detailed account see *Times Colonist*, June 22, 2000, p. 1.

20. *The Vancouver Sun*, October 12, 1999, p. A4.

21. A more detailed account is given in *The Vancouver Sun*, November 6, 1990.

22. Summarized from *The Globe and Mail*, January 11, 1991.

23. For a more detailed account see *Newsweek*, November 13, 1995, p. 60.

24. R. v. Martins, summarized from *The Lawyers Weekly*, August 25, 1989, p. 20.

25. See *Time Magazine*, July 24, 2000, p. 7.

26. For more detailed accounts see *Maclean's*, December 19, 1994, p. 30 and *The New York Times*, June 28, 1995, p. A7.

27. For a more detailed account see *The Vancouver Sun*, June 3, 1998, p. D15.

28. *The Globe and Mail*, November 16, 1992.

29. Summarized from *The Globe and Mail*, November 11, 1993, p. A13.

30. A more detailed account is given in *The Miami Herald*, December 29, 1993, p. 2A.

31. For a more detailed account see *The Vancouver Sun*, July 18, 2000, p. C8.

32. Summarized from *The Lawyers Weekly*, February 26, 1993, p. 21.

33. Summarized from *The Globe and Mail*, October 28, 1992, p. A28.

VI

THE LAW OF EMPLOYMENT AND AGENCY

A. EMPLOYMENT

1. THE DISTINCTION BETWEEN AN EMPLOYEE AND AN INDEPENDENT CONTRACTOR

Truong v. *British Columbia*

http://www.courts.gov.bc.ca/
COURT OF APPEAL FOR BRITISH COLUMBIA
SEPTEMBER 13, 1999

Hinds, J.:

INTRODUCTION

[1] This is an appeal from the judgment of Madam Justice D. Smith awarding Ms. Truong damages for her dismissal, without just cause or reasonable notice, from employment as a court interpreter. The learned judge found that the respondent was an employee of Court Services Branch (Court Services) rather than an independent contractor. ...

[2] The primary issue raised on this appeal is whether the trial judge erred in concluding that the respondent was an employee of Court Services rather than an independent contractor. ...

1. Review of the Law on the First Issue

[20] ... The determination whether a particular individual is a servant or employee, as contrasted with an independent contractor, must in every case be made on the evidence adduced before, and accepted by, the trier of fact.

[21] In earlier cases a single test—the presence or absence of control—was frequently the determinative factor of whether the case was one of master and servant or of independent contractor. As more complex business conditions arose, more complicated tests have been advocated for the determination of the relationship. ...

[22] In *Wiebe Door Services Ltd. v. Minister of National Revenue*, [1986] 3 C.F. 553, MacGuigan J. gave the reasons for judgment of the Federal Court of Appeal. ...[He] extensively re-

viewed the law with respect to the master and servant employment relationship as opposed to the relationship of independent contractors. He referred to and quoted from leading text writers. ...

[23] Mr. Justice MacGuigan summarized his review. ... He stated: Perhaps the best synthesis found in the authorities is that of Cooke J. in *Market Investigations, Ltd. v. Minister of Social Security*, [1968] 3 All E.R. 732 (Q.B.D.). ... The observations of Lord Wright, of Denning, L.J., and of the judges of the Supreme Court in the U.S.A. suggest that the fundamental test to be applied is this: "Is the person who has engaged himself to perform these services performing them as a person in business on his own account?" If the answer to that question is "yes", then the contract is a contract for services [as independent contractor]. If the answer is "no" then the contract is a contract of service [as employee]. No exhaustive list has been compiled and perhaps no exhaustive list can be compiled of considerations which are relevant in determining that question, nor can strict rules be laid down as to the relative weight which the various considerations should carry in particular cases. The most that can be said is that control will no doubt always have to be considered, although it can no longer be regarded as the sole determining factor: and that factors, which may be of importance, are such matters as whether the man performing the services provides his own equipment, whether he hires his own helpers, what degree of financial risk he takes, what degree of responsibility for investment and management he has, and whether and how far he has an opportunity of

profiting from sound management in the performance of his task. The application of the general test may be easier in a case where the person who engages himself to perform the services does so in the course of an already established business of his own; but this factor is not decisive, and a person who engages himself to perform services for another may well be an independent contractor even though he has not entered into the contract in the course of an existing business carried on by him. There is no escape for the Trial Judge, when confronted with such a problem, from carefully weighing all of the relevant factors, as outlined by Cooke J.

2. Review of the Reasons for Judgment on the First Issue
[The judge reviews the decision of the lower court and finds that in determining whether or not Truong was an employee or independent contractor, the trial judge followed precedents calling for an "examination of multiple criteria to determine the type of relationship that in fact exists between the parties".

The approach adopted meant that "[t]he totality of the relationship, not merely one aspect of it, must be carefully examined in deciding how the relationship of the parties is to be classified."

The judge then addresses the submissions of the appellants that the trial judge erred in underestimating the factors that indicate Truong was an independent contractor. After considering each factor named, the judge concludes:]

[37] ... There was evidence before Madam Justice Smith to support her findings and I am not prepared to disturb them. In my view she applied the correct legal tests to her findings and I am not persuaded that she erred in law in concluding that the respondent "had an employment relationship with Court Services". She was an employee and not an independent contractor.

[On this issue, the appeal is dismissed]   2–1

Note: This was not a unanimous decision. Judge Finch dissented, not because of disagreement with the factors to be considered but he concluded that the facts would place Truong in the category of independent contractor. If you are interested in reading about the factors he considered significant in deciding to dissent from the majority view, see the full dissent in the case.

> Unfortunately, Ms. Tanner's baby-sitter took more than just care of the baby. If the thieving baby-sitter were an employee, Tanner's insurance policy would not cover the loss from the thefts. If she were an independent contractor, the loss would be covered by the policy. Applying the control test and the business organization test, the judge concluded that the baby-sitter "more closely meets the definition of an independent contractor than of an employee. Her thefts are not excluded from coverage."
>
> ***Formosa Mutual Insurance Co. v. Tanner***
> *[1997] O.J. No. 2605 (Q.L.)*
> *Ontario Court of Justice (General Division)*
> *June 11, 1997*

2. TERMS OF THE EMPLOYMENT CONTRACT

Questions

When you say "yes" to a job offer, what are you promising your employer?
What is the employer promising you?
In a non-union job, if your contract is silent on the matter, what are the implied terms about dismissal?

- *T*he company's policy of requiring all job applicants and employees to submit to mandatory alcohol and drug testing and to disclose any present or past drug abuse was *prima facie* discriminatory and contrary to the Ontario Human Rights Code. However, it was found to be a bona fide occupational requirement as long as the employer "accommodated individual difference to the point of undue hardship."[1]

- *T*he following are the words of Justice Iacobucci of the Supreme Court of Canada in *Wallace v. United Grain Growers (UGG)* (p. 172) in his response to the argument that there is an implied term in employment contracts that an employee will be kept on indefinitely:

> [75] The appellant urged this Court to find that he could sue UGG either in contract or in tort for "bad faith discharge". With respect to the action in contract, he submitted that the Court should imply into the employment contract a term that the employee would not be fired except for cause or legitimate business reasons. I cannot accede to this submission. The law has long recognized the mutual right of both employers and employees to terminate an employment contract at any time provided there are no express provisions to the contrary. In *Farber v. Royal Trust*, [1997] 1 S.C.R. 846, Gonthier J., speaking for the Court, summarized the general contractual principles applicable to contracts of employment as follows, at p. 858:
>
>> In the context of an indeterminate employment contract, one party can resiliate the contract unilaterally. The resiliation is considered a dismissal if it originates with the employer and a resignation if it originates with the employee. If an employer dismisses an employee without cause, the employer must give the employee reasonable notice that the contract is about to be terminated or compensation in lieu thereof.
>
> [76] A requirement of "good faith" reasons for dismissal would, in effect, contravene these principles and deprive employers of the ability to determine the composition of their workforce. In the context of the accepted theories on the employment relationship, such a law would, in my opinion, be overly intrusive and inconsistent with established principles of employment law.

- *J*ohn Pulitzer, the U.S. publisher, in whose name the Pulitzer prize for journalism is awarded, fired several employees because of the way they ate soup.[2]

3. JUST CAUSE/WRONGFUL DISMISSAL

Durand was a long-time employee of the defendant of the Quaker Oats Company of Canada Ltd. One of the company's customers made it possible for employees of the company to take a "trade trip." Durand's superior, the regional manager, cancelled the trade trip, but Durand surreptitiously arranged for his wife and her friend to go. After the company learned what he had done and questioned him about it, it terminated his employment. He received the following letter:

Dear Sir:

This is to confirm that your employment with Quaker has been terminated for cause.

We have discussed with you in detail our concern, and have listened carefully to your comments on the matter.

It is clear that you have broken the bond of trust required between us.

You have breached specific provisions of our Conflict of Interest Rules. Further, you have committed an act of direct insubordination in order to derive personal gain.

Your conduct with regard to this matter leaves us no choice.

Yours truly,

Durand sued successfully for wrongful dismissal. The following are excerpts from the decision of the Court of Appeal, which reversed that decision and held, unanimously, that Durand had breached his employment contract, and was fired for just cause.

Locke, J.A. concludes:

"The evidence establishes clearly that there was secrecy, that there was insubordination, that there was a conflict of interest and that there had been an acquisition of a "perk" by Durand for his own or his family's personal advantage.

... In my opinion, on the facts and on the law there were substantial reasons for the executives of the Quaker Oats Company determining that the taking of the unauthorized trip had placed the company in a sense in hostage to a potential contractor for advertising and that the confidence that they would feel in Durand in handling advertising matters in the future could not be justified any longer.

I think that the express and implied terms of the contract of employment were breached and that the discharge was justified. I would correspondingly allow the appeal and dismiss the action.

Seaton J.A.: I agree.

Southin J.A.: Mr. Justice Locke has stated the facts and I agree with him that the appeal must be allowed. I would like to put my legal foundation for that opinion in my own words.

The appeal is from a judgment granting judgment for what is called wrongful dismissal. What such an action is usually, and is in this case, is an action for damages for breach of the implied term of a contract of employment which lacks an express term on the point that it can only be terminated by either side on reasonable notice, and that in itself leads to the action being founded on the proposition that the employer's act in not giving reasonable notice was itself a repudiation. But here the employer says that the employee repudiated and thus its notice of dismissal was in law an acceptance of that repudiation.

As my learned brother has referred to the implied term of the contract of employment, however one puts it, it is a promise by the employee that he will faithfully, honestly and diligently serve his employer. If he commits a fundamental breach of that term the employer is entitled to say "I have no further obligations to perform and that includes the obligation of giving you reasonable notice."

I approach the matter this way because, despite much of the language in the cases, contracts of service are not governed by any different legal principles from those governing all other contracts. (See on that point, *Laws V. London Chronicle [(Indicator Newspapers) Ltd.*, [1959] 1 W.L.R. 698, [1959] 2 All E.R. 285 (C.A.)]). What constitutes a fundamental breach of the implied term is not always easy to determine, but it must be determined objectively. It is not a question of the intention, necessarily or at all, of the employee—that is, did it ever occur to him that he was about to be in breach of an implied term is not material. It may well be in this case that the respondent never thought for a moment that anything that he was doing was in breach of the implied term of his contract of employment.

The learned judge below called what the respondent did deceptive, dishonest and bordering on insubordinate. Those terms are descriptive. They do not come, in my opinion, to grips with the issue. The gravamen of the appellant's case is that the respondent obtained for his wife and a friend from a supplier to the company, two tickets for a trip to Las Vegas worth about $800 each, without the knowledge of his superiors, and that is the kind of conduct that an employer can look upon as a fundamental breach because it exposes the employee to the importunings, possibly of the supplier, in connection with his duties.

Thus, in my view, that sort of thing, even if it did not occur to Mr. Durand (as I hope that it did not) that it was dishonest, is in fact a fundamental breach. Where, in my opinion, the learned judge erred was first, in not asking himself whether to do this thing was a fundamental breach and secondly, in considering that the company was under any legal obligation to choose a different way of dealing with this fundamental breach than the course it did choose. The company was under no obligation to choose any other course once there was a fundamental breach and for that, of course, I need only refer to *Port Arthur Shipbldg. Co. v. Arthurs*, [1969] S.C.R. 85, 70 D.L.R. (2d) 693 [Ont.]. I would therefore allow the appeal.

Seaton J.A.: The appeal is allowed. The action dismissed."

Durand v. The Quaker Oats Company of Canada Ltd.
45 B.C.L.R. (2d) 354
British Columbia Court of Appeal
February 21, 1990

Q u e s t i o n s

Who has the burden of proving there was just cause for dismissal?
What types of behaviour give the employer "just cause" for dismissing the employee
without notice or even pay in lieu of notice?

An e-mail message based on a vulgar monologue by Andrew Dice Clay was altered to refer to a co-worker and sent by the plaintiffs to other co-workers. When asked by their superior in several meetings about the distribution of the message, both lied about the extent of the distribution of the "joke" (which eventually did come to the attention of the worker ridiculed).

After reviewing the character of the message, the facts of its distribution, and the subsequent meetings with the plaintiffs, Justice Drost states:

"[22] In an action for wrongful dismissal, the onus is on the defendant employer to satisfy the Court, on a balance of probabilities, that just cause existed for the summary dismissal of the employee. ...

[23] Here, the onus is on the defendant to establish misconduct on the part of the dismissed employees which is serious enough to amount to a fundamental breach of their contracts of employment.

[24] MDA advances two grounds which it says establish cause. First, that the plaintiffs engaged in hurtful and malicious conduct toward a co-worker which so seriously affected the work environment that their termination was necessary to rehabilitate it. Second, that the plaintiffs were so dishonest in all their dealings with management during the investigation of the incident that they can no longer be trusted. ...

[26] The argument advanced by the defendant is that, by engaging in a "prank" which was intentionally hurtful and vicious, the plaintiffs have revealed character flaws that are so serious as to justify their dismissal. It is not only their conduct, but also the fact that they were capable of such conduct, which concerns the defendant.

[27] In order to determine whether the sending of the e-mail is, in itself, serious enough to amount to a fundamental breach of their employment contracts, some analysis of the law is required. ...

[Although the judge concluded that the prank ridiculed, demeaned and humiliated the worker, he concluded on this point:]

[34] Nonetheless, I am not persuaded that the conduct of the plaintiffs, so far as their involvement in the distribution of the e-mail message is concerned, is alone sufficient grounds for their summary dismissal. I am of the view that, standing alone, that conduct warranted a severe reprimand, but nothing more.

[35] However, such conduct, when combined with the plaintiffs' subsequent dishonesty during the investigation, does, in my opinion, clearly amount to just cause for dismissal.

[36] As I mentioned above, the plaintiffs must have recognized the seriousness of their conduct. Nonetheless, they continued to be evasive and dishonest through three meetings with their supervisor. The leading statement concerning dishonesty as a just cause can be found in the judgment of Hollinrake J.A. in *McPhillips v. British Columbia Ferry Corp.* (1994), 94 B.C.L.R. (2d) 1 C.A., at p. 6:

Dishonesty is always cause for dismissal because it is a breach of the condition of faithful service. It is the employer's choice whether to dismiss or forgive.

...

[41] I find that neither of the plaintiffs lived up to their implied duties of honesty or faithfulness.

[42] [The plaintiff] ... concedes that he lied to his employer and that fact, when taken together with his participation in the distribution of the offensive material, amounts to a breach of his implied duty of honesty and faithfulness and thus constitutes just cause for his dismissal.

[43] [The second plaintiff] ... is in an even worse position. He lied to his supervisor on at least three occasions. ... His dishonesty, when taken in conjunction with his earlier conduct, also gives rise to just cause for his dismissal.

[44] For those reasons, the plaintiffs' action is dismissed. ..."

Di Vito v. Macdonald Dettwiler & Assoc. Ltd.
Vancouver Registry No. C944l98
The Supreme Court of British Columbia
June 27, 1996

Stanley Scott Werle v. *SaskEnergy Incorporated*

SASK. QUEEN'S BENCH
FILE NO. 1215-003
JUNE 3, 1992

Kyle J.: The defendant, SaskEnergy Incorporated ("SaskEnergy"), conducted a search for a Vice-President of its Sales and Marketing Department in September of 1990. The plaintiff, Mr. Stanley Scott Werle, was the successful applicant. Fifty-one people had applied. SaskEnergy is a public utility which sells natural gas to residents of Saskatchewan. ...When Mr. Werle sought the position of Vice-President of Sales and Marketing Department, it was a new position and the advertisement described aspects both of sales and of marketing as being part of the job.

Mr. Werle sent an application letter with a resume attached. In the resume he detailed his background as a salesperson with Xerox. He had been most successful in that role, and he was hoping that the new job, if he got it, would entitle him to a salary at or near the $100,000 level which he had attained at Xerox. In his resume he outlined his level of education which was stated to be a Bachelor of Commerce (Marketing) from the University of Saskatchewan. In fact, Mr. Werle had tried for four years to get his Bachelor of Commerce, but he had never passed even one year and he had certainly never been granted a degree. Mr. Werle has advanced no explanation for this misrepresentation which he says was an error resulting from a failure to carry forward some qualifying words which appeared in an earlier version of the resume.

Mr. Werle was hired after a number of interviews and a newsletter announcing his hiring was sent to the 500 or so employees of the company. It mentioned a Bachelor of Commerce and he noticed it, but did nothing. After a month or two, the personnel department asked him for a record of his university training, either a statement of marks or a copy of the diploma. After some delay, he indicated that he could not find his diploma. The personnel officer said: "Didn't you have it framed?" and he answered: "I am not a plaque collector." ·

When the personnel officer's suspicions were aroused, she called the University and discovered the truth and advised her superiors.

Mr. Bill Baker, President of the company, testified that he had hired Mr. Werle because of his sales experience and background of education in marketing at the University of Saskatchewan. He says he would not have hired Mr. Werle had he known that he did not have a degree. When he found out that indeed he did not have the education, his concerns were twofold. First he felt that Mr. Werle could not do the marketing work he was, in part, hired to do. Secondly, he was concerned that they had hired someone who had lied about his credentials. He was disappointed by this turn of events. He liked Mr. Werle, although some doubts as to his ability in the planning area had started to surface. He says that to have someone in the company who would do such a thing was simply unacceptable. It was something that everyone would know about and it would be a terrible precedent or signal. Mr. Baker was most sympathetic with Mr. Werle. He respected the effort which Mr. Werle had made to get where he was, he respected the success he had achieved, and he liked his motivated style. He would have liked to have been a forgiving boss in these circumstances, and he toyed with the idea. He was, however, fully aware that his duty to the company was on a higher level and he felt that dismissal was required.

Mr. Werle's testimony was not convincing, not only could he not explain how the inaccuracy occurred, but when the newsletter announced that he had a degree, he did nothing and when personnel asked for his diploma he prevaricated. One can only conclude that he was living a lie, if not from the beginning when he filed the false resume, at least from the time of the newsletter. It is not surprising that the company would find this to be evidence of a lack of the integrity requisite in a vice-president. The fact that he allowed the error, as he called it, to continue is quite clearly consistent with the view that the original misrepresentation of his educational status was intentional, a conclusion which the company reached. I find that the company was fully entitled to conclude, as it did, that it had a dishonest employee. Its reluctance to fire him is understandable—his wife was expecting, he was remorseful, and he was a valuable employee, notwithstanding his shortfall in the marketing area. The transfer to a lower position as opposed to termination would, of course, have constituted constructive dismissal so his consent would be essential if that were to be done. Mr. Labas, President of a subsidiary of SaskEnergy, was really in charge of resolving the problem which had arisen. Against Mr. Baker's better judgment, he made an offer of a much reduced status for Mr. Werle, one which would have allowed him to regain the company's confidence. He did not accept the terms proposed and accordingly his employment was terminated for the cause referred to above.

That the company would dismiss a vice-president for what can only be described as fraud, is not surprising. Indeed, the willingness of the company to give Mr. Werle a second chance is surprising; it can only be related to a humane and forgiving nature on the part of the officers of the company. ...

There are no cases where an employee whose dishonesty was so clearly established has been found to have been wrongfully dismissed. The cases cited by Mr. Werle which raise the level of proof to a higher level than that of balance of probabilities, are not relevant here as I am in no doubt as to the dishonesty of Mr. Werle in respect of his credentials. His efforts to rationalize his behavior as presented at trial were not credible and they simply reinforce the impression of dishonesty which the events themselves had justified. His decision to bring this action was simply another example of his bad judgment. Accordingly, the action is dismissed and SaskEnergy is entitled to its costs.

[The plaintiff's action for wrongful dismissal is dismissed.]

Fletcher, an employee of the Bank of Nova Scotia, had a friend who became a customer of the bank. Subsequently, this friend and customer gave Fletcher all of her money as well as a power of attorney for her accounts. The bank dismissed Fletcher who then sued the bank for wrongful dismissal. The court held this dismissal was for just cause. "One of the basic principles stated in the Guidelines [for Business Conduct agreed to by new employees] is to maintain the integrity of the Bank. The perception of a bank employee accepting a substantial gift from an elderly customer brings the Bank's integrity into question."

Fletcher v. Bank of Nova Scotia
http://www.courts.gov.bc.ca/
Supreme Court of British Columbia
April 19, 2000

IN THE FOLLOWING CASES THE EMPLOYEE CHALLENGED THE EMPLOYER'S ALLEGATION OF JUST CAUSE FOR DISMISSAL. THE EMPLOYEE LOST.

- *K*ennedy had a co-worker punch his time card for him each morning. His employer told them to stop and warned that continuation of the practice could lead to Kennedy's dismissal. His continuation of the practice came to light on the day he called the company to say he wouldn't be in because of a car accident. Unfortunately his time card had already been punched by his faithful but uninformed co-worker.[3]

- *A* discreet surveillance by an outside security specialist documented that the cashier allowed her friends to take away items that were not paid for or were entered under an improper code.[4]

- *A* computer programmer, the only employee who "knew the answers, or the keys, or the passwords" was *suspended* because of his refusal to document his work and because of his responding to their requests "with derision, insubordination and laughter." The employee asked for a letter of termination, but he never was terminated in hopes that he would be cooperative. After he left voluntarily, the company had to hire additional programmers "to find out what were the keys to the kingdom." In his rather impassioned judgment the judge remarked "This is one of the simplest cases I have ever had to decide in eleven years as a judge. I can't believe this is before me."[5]

IN THE FOLLOWING CASES THE EMPLOYEE'S ACTION FOR WRONGFUL DISMISSAL WAS SUCCESSFUL.

- *M*r. Ditchburn was one of the best salesmen of an Ontario company for which he had worked for almost thirty years. Unfortunately, after dining and drinking with one of the company's most important customers, Ditchburn and the customer got into an argument which escalated into a physical fight. Ditchburn was fired and offered two months' salary. He sued for wrongful dismissal and won. The court found the fight was an isolated incident of bad judgment and not cause for dismissal.[6]

Q u e s t i o n

Would the conduct reported below be grounds for dismissal?

- *Y*ou are a spy who leaves the top-secret documents in your minivan while you go into a hockey game, and your briefcase is stolen.[7]

- *Y*ou are selling marijuana instead of TimBits at the drive-thru window at Tim Hortons.[8]

CONDONATION

Q u e s t i o n

What factors jeopardize the employer's ability to dismiss an employee without notice?

The employer argued that it was justified in dismissing the employee without notice because of a series of incidents, although not any one of them alone would justify dismissal. The court, after reviewing the incidents cited, found only three of significance: a late report, the inadequacy of that report, and the inadequacy of a second report. The judge held that even these collectively did not justify dismissal without notice and gave the following among the reasons:

"[22] ... While there was certainly room for improvement, the evaluations which have been produced indicate that Dr. Chen was a valuable employee who contributed to the organization.

[23] Secondly, in every year Dr. Chen received a pay increase ... [sometimes a significant increase].

[24] Thirdly, Dr. Chen had demonstrated a tendency to be delayed in completing work, but there is no evidence that it was through serious misconduct, habitual neglect of duty, incompetence, or conduct incompatible with his duties. Indeed, as was evident from the 1994 evaluation, it may have been attributable to his tendency to be so analytical that completing was a challenge.

[25] .... When criticized [about the first report], he improved it ... [His supervisor] demanded that Dr. Chen revise [the second report], yet did not give Dr. Chen an opportunity to do so before he was fired.

[26] The employer had never given any indication that the problems with quantity of work were sufficiently problematic to jeopardize employment. Given the history Dr. Chen had, even if I accept the defendant's position about late delivery, ... the defendant was not entitled to terminate without effective notice, identifying objective standards which Dr. Chen had to meet, how Dr. Chen had failed to meet these standards, warning Dr. Chen to meet those standards or his job would be in jeopardy and giving Dr. Chen a reasonable time to correct the performance issues.

[27] In dealing with the defence of cumulative effect as it relates to the quality of the work, one must consider the "condonation" factor ...

[28] The Court of Appeal has indicated that if an employer retains the employee for any considerable

time after discovery of the fault, the employer is considered to have condoned the fault, and the employer cannot afterwards dismiss for that fault without anything new. I agree that if there is further misconduct, the old offence may be put on the scale in determining just cause for dismissal. ...
[31] For all of the foregoing reasons, I find that the plaintiff was wrongfully dismissed. ..."
The judge found that 15 months constituted reasonable notice and rejected the employee's request for punitive damages and for an extension of the notice period in accordance with the principles established in *Wallace v. United Grain Growers Ltd.* [see p. 172].

Chen v. Toronto Hydro Electric Commission
[2000] O.J. No. 1182 (Q.L.)
Ontario Superior Court of Justice
January 28, 2000

CONSTRUCTIVE DISMISSAL

Question

Can an employee quit and still successfully sue for wrongful dismissal on the grounds that the employer had forced him or her to walk away because the employer had breached the employment contract?

Nethery v. Lindsey Morden Claim Services Limited

http://www.courts.gov.bc.ca/
SUPREME COURT OF BRITISH COLUMBIA
JANUARY 12, 1999

Davies, J.:-
[1] The plaintiff, Clyde Nethery, [employed as an insurance claims adjuster] alleges that he was wrongfully dismissed when his employer, the defendant, Lindsey Morden Claims Service Limited, refused to reimburse its customers for monies that it had obtained by improper billing.
[2] The facts of this case require a determination of whether an employee can require an employer to take specific remedial action to rectify the consequences of an allegedly improper act by that employer and whether if the employer fails to do so, the employee may treat that failure as a repudiation of the employment contract and obtain compensation for wrongful dismissal. As far as I am aware, no Canadian court has previously been required to determine that specific issue. ...

ISSUES

[56] Mr. Nethery submits that the evidence establishes that the defendant repudiated a fundamental term of his contract of employment by refusing to make restitution to the defendant's customers for the increased billings resulting from Mr. Skinner's [Mr. Nethery's immediate supervisor] fraudulent increase of the hours recorded by the Kamloops branch adjusters. He submits that the repudiation of the contract constitutes a constructive dismissal and that he is entitled [*inter alia*] to damages... .
[The court reviews the counter-arguments of the defendant.]
[62] These issues require an assessment of the credibility of Mr. Nethery and Mr. Skinner and answers to the following questions: ...
Were Mr. Skinner's billing practices fraudulent?
[After concluding that Mr. Skinner was not a credible witness and that Mr. Skinner's practice of inflating billings was fraudulent, the judge addressed the second question.]
Did Mr. Nethery's refusal to follow Mr. Skinner's directions justify dismissal for cause? ...
[78] Mr. Nethery candidly admitted to refusing to follow some of Mr. Skinner's directives. Although his conduct might in normal circumstances be considered to be insubordinate, in this case his dispute with Mr. Skinner which gave rise to the ignoring of some directives had its genesis in the .... memorandum [about] the inflated billing practices which Mr. Skinner was seeking to implement. Mr. Nethery rightly concluded that these

practices were contrary to corporate policy and unethical in the circumstances.

[79] I cannot accept that a refusal to follow directions which are contrary to established corporate policy and professionally un-ethical can be the foundation of a claim for the dismissal of an employee for cause. ...

Did the defendant repudiate its contract of employment with Mr. Nethery by refusing to make restitution for the inflated billings?

[85] In determining whether the defendant's conduct amounted to a repudiation of Mr. Nethery's contract of employment and as such constituted a wrongful constructive dismissal, I start with the proposition enunciated by Southin, J.A. in *Stein v. British Columbia (Housing Management Commission)* (1992), 65 B.C.L.R. (2d) 181 (B.C.C.A.) at page 185 that:

> ... an employer has a right to determine how his business shall be conducted. He may lay down any procedures he thinks advisable so long as they are neither contrary to law nor dishonest nor dangerous to the health of the employees and are within the ambit of the job for which any particular employee was hired. It is not for the em-ployee nor for the court to consider the wisdom of the procedures. The employer is the boss and it is an es-sential implied term of every employment contract that, subject to the limitations I have expressed, the employee must obey the orders given to him.

[86] I have determined that the billing practice instituted by Mr. Skinner was dishonest as being contrary to the existing rela-tionship between the defendant and its clients. Was it therefore open to Mr. Nethery not only to refuse to accept the practice, but also to demand restitution on behalf of the wronged clients? I have determined that in the circumstances of this case it was. ...

[88] At issue was the integrity and reputation not only of the de-fendant but also of Mr. Nethery who was in most cases the adjuster responsible for the work on the files which were over-

billed and also the manager of the branch which issued all the bills. I am satisfied that in those circumstances Mr. Nethery had a sufficient personal and professional stake in the propri-ety of the bills delivered to the defendant's clients to demand that the defendant take appropriate steps to compensate the clients for the overcharges. In my judgment, the defendant could ignore that reasonable and appropriate demand only at peril of being found to be in breach of a fundamental term of the employment contract between an insurance adjuster and his employer.

[89] In an industry where integrity and reputation are essential, it cannot be that one party to a contract can adversely affect the reputation of the other by its own dishonesty and lack of in-tegrity.

[90] I am satisfied that in the circumstances of this case the defendant repudiated its duty to act ethically, honestly and with integrity in dealing with its clients and that it was in breach of its reciprocal obligations to the plaintiff when it failed to do so. The defendant breached a fundamental term of its em-ployment contract with the plaintiff. Mr. Nethery was entitled to treat that breach as a constructive dismissal without justifi-cation. Mr. Nethery could reasonably infer from the defen-dant's support of Mr. Skinner's action as evidenced by a refusal to acknowledge wrongdoing and by Mr. Skinner's promotion in the defendant's ranks that the defendant did not consider itself bound by its own corporate billing policies or its stated eth-ical standards which were fundamental to Mr. Nethery's in-tegrity and good reputation.

What is the appropriate notice period and did the plaintiff fail to mitigate his losses?

[The judge reviews the arguments made and the precedents cited by the plaintiff and the defendant and concludes, with his reasons, that Mr. Nethery was entitled to eight month's notice and that he did not fail to mitigate his losses.]

Judgment for the plaintiff

After working for Xerox for twelve years, Shah resigned. He then sued his employer for wrongful dismissal. The trial judge found that Shah had been constructively dismissed; that the employer's treatment of him made his continued employment intolerable and such conduct was a repudiation of the employment relationship. Xerox appealed, arguing that the court could find an employee con-structively dismissed only if the terms of the employment were examined and it was found that the employer unilaterally changed a fundamental term of that contract. The Ontario Court of Appeal disagreed. It affirmed the decision of the trial judge:

"[7] In cases where an employer requires an employee to relocate or take on a different position as part of a restructuring, the court, obviously, must decide whether in doing so the employer has changed a fundamental term of the employment contract.

[8] In some cases, however, the employer's conduct amounts not just to a change in a specific term of the employment contract but to repudiation of the entire employment relationship. For example, in *Whiting v. Winnipeg River Brokenhead Community Futures Development Corp.* (1998) 159 D.L.R. (4th) 18 (Man. C.A.), the trial judge concluded that an employee had been con-structively dismissed because ... the employer had created a hostile and embarrassing work envi-ronment. The trial judge concluded that, "viewed objectively, the plaintiff's continued employment in such environment was no longer possible." This conclusion was upheld by the Manitoba Court of Appeal. ... The employer ... had by its conduct demonstrated an intention no longer to be bound by the contract.

[9] The case before us is similar. Xerox's treatment of Shah ... demonstrated that it no longer intended to be bound by the employment contract, and that it had, therefore, constructively dismissed Shah. ... [The judge reviews the evidence].

[10] On this evidence Cullity J. could reasonably find that Xerox had made Shah's position intolerable and had constructively dismissed him. That finding is entitled to deference in this court. We have not been persuaded that we should interfere with it.

[11] The appeal is therefore dismissed with costs."

Shah v. Xerox Canada Ltd.
http://www.ontariocourts.on.ca/
Ontario Court of Appeal
March 20, 2000

4. Damages for Wrongful Dismissal

Question

What factors does the court consider in determining what constitutes reasonable notice?

Wallace *v.* United Grain Growers

http://www.lexum.umontreal.ca/
Supreme Court of Canada
October 30, 1997

[1] Iacobucci J.: [For the majority]— This case involves both an appeal and a cross-appeal. The appeal is largely concerned with issues of compensation in a wrongful dismissal action, specifically, the existence of a fixed-term contract, the right to damages for mental distress, whether or not one can sue for "bad faith discharge", and the appropriate length of the period of reasonable notice. The cross-appeal raises an issue of bankruptcy law, namely, whether an undischarged bankrupt can maintain an action for wrongful dismissal in his or her own name.

1. FACTS

[2] In 1972, Public Press, a wholly owned subsidiary of the respondent, United Grain Growers Ltd. ("UGG"), decided to update its operations and seek a larger volume of commercial printing work. Don Logan was the marketing manager of the company's publishing and printing divisions at that time. For Logan, the key to achieving this increase in volume was to hire someone with an existing record of sales on a specialized piece of equipment known as a "Web" press.

[3] In April 1972, the appellant, Jack Wallace, met Logan to discuss the possibility of employment. Wallace had the type of experience that Logan sought, having worked approximately 25 years for a competitor that used the "Web" press. Wallace had become concerned over the unfair manner in which he and others were being treated by their employer. However, he ex-

pressed some reservation about jeopardizing his secure position at the company. Wallace explained to Logan that as he was 45 years of age, if he were to leave his current employer he would require a guarantee of job security. He also sought several assurances from Logan regarding fair treatment and remuneration. He received such assurances and was told by Logan that if he performed as expected, he could continue to work for Public Press until retirement.

[4] Wallace commenced employment with Public Press in June of 1972. He enjoyed great success at the company and was the top salesperson for each of the years he spent in its employ.

[5] On August 22, 1986, Wallace was summarily discharged ... [with no explanation]. In the days before the dismissal [he had been complimented on his work.]

[6] [Wallace was advised] ... that the main reason for his termination was his inability to perform his duties satisfactorily. Wallace's statement of claim alleging wrongful dismissal was issued on October 23, 1986. In its statement of defence, the respondent alleged that Wallace had been dismissed for cause. This allegation was maintained for over two years and was only withdrawn when the trial commenced on December 12, 1988.

[7] At the time of his dismissal Wallace was almost 59 years old. He had been employed by Public Press for 14 years. The termination of his employment and the allegations of cause created emotional difficulties for Wallace and he was forced to

seek psychiatric help. His attempts to find similar employment were largely unsuccessful.

[8] On September 26, 1985, Wallace made a voluntary assignment into personal bankruptcy....

[71] [After a lengthy review of the bankruptcy law the judge concludes], that the appellant can maintain an action for wrongful dismissal in his own name. I would therefore dismiss the cross-appeal and I now turn to the issues raised by the appeal. ...

[The court rejected several arguments put forward by the dismissed employee, Wallace, namely, that he had a fixed-term contract until retirement, that he could sue in contract for "bad faith discharge", that he could sue in tort for breach of a good faith or fair dealing obligation, and that punitive damages were warranted. Nevertheless, the court did award damages at the "high end of the scale" (by restoring the trial judge's award of damages in the amount of 24 months' salary in lieu of notice) given the criteria adopted by the court to determine the appropriate length of the notice period.]

[81] In determining what constitutes reasonable notice of termination, the courts have generally applied the principles articulated by McRuer C.J.H.C. in *Bardal v. Globe & Mail Ltd.* (1960), 24 D.L.R. (2d) 140 (Ont. H.C.), at p. 145:

> There can be no catalogue laid down as to what is reasonable notice in particular classes of cases. The reasonableness of the notice must be decided with reference to each particular case, having regard to the character of the employment, the length of service of the servant, the age of the servant and the availability of similar employment, having regard to the experience, training and qualifications of the servant.

[82] ... Applying these factors in the instant case, I concur with the trial judge's finding that in light of the appellant's advanced age, his 14-year tenure as the company's top salesman and his limited prospects for re-employment, a lengthy period of notice is warranted. I note, however, that *Bardal, supra,* does not state, nor has it been interpreted to imply, that the factors it enumerated were exhaustive. ... Canadian courts have added several additional factors to the *Bardal* list. ...

[83] One such factor that has often been considered is whether the dismissed employee had been induced to leave previous secure employment . ....

[84] Several cases have specifically examined the presence of a promise of job security. ...

[85] In my opinion, such inducements are properly included among the considerations which tend to lengthen the amount of notice required. ... The significance of the inducement in question will vary with the circumstances of the particular case and its effect, if any, on the notice period is a matter best left to the discretion of the trial judge. ...

[91] The contract of employment has many characteristics that set it apart from the ordinary commercial contract. ... [The judge discusses the power imbalance.]

[94] ... [F]or most people, work is one of the defining features of their lives. Accordingly, any change in a person's employment status is bound to have far-reaching repercussions. ...

[95] The point at which the employment relationship ruptures is the time when the employee is most vulnerable and hence, most in need of protection. In recognition of this need, the law ought to encourage conduct that minimizes the damage and dislocation (both economic and personal) that result from dis-

missal. ... I note that the loss of one's job is always a traumatic event. However, when termination is accompanied by acts of bad faith in the manner of discharge, the results can be especially devastating. In my opinion, to ensure that employees receive adequate protection, employers ought to be held to an obligation of good faith and fair dealing in the manner of dismissal, the breach of which will be compensated for by adding to the length of the notice period. ...

[98] The obligation of good faith and fair dealing is incapable of precise definition. However, at a minimum, I believe that in the course of dismissal employers ought to be candid, reasonable, honest and forthright with their employees and should refrain from engaging in conduct that is unfair or is in bad faith by being, for example, untruthful, misleading or unduly insensitive. ...

[The court reviews cases in which the employer showed egregious bad faith in the manner of dismissal.]

[103] It has long been accepted that a dismissed employee is not entitled to compensation for injuries flowing from the fact of the dismissal itself. ... although the loss of a job is very often the cause of injured feelings and emotional upset. ... However, where an employee can establish that an employer engaged in bad faith conduct or unfair dealing in the course of dismissal, injuries such as humiliation, embarrassment and damage to one's sense of self-worth and self-esteem might all be worthy of compensation depending upon the circumstances of the case. In these situations, compensation does not flow from the fact of dismissal itself, but rather from the manner in which the dismissal was effected by the employer.

[104] ... It is likely that the more unfair or in bad faith the manner of dismissal is the more this will have an effect on the ability of the dismissed employee to find new employment. However, in my view the intangible injuries are sufficient to merit compensation in and of themselves. I recognize that bad faith conduct which affects employment prospects may be worthy of considerably more compensation than that which does not, but in both cases damage has resulted that should be compensable. ...

[107] ... I note that there may be those who would say that this approach imposes an onerous obligation on employers. I would respond simply by saying that I fail to see how it can be onerous to treat people fairly, reasonably, and decently at a time of trauma and despair. In my view, the reasonable person would expect such treatment. So should the law. ...

6-3

DISSENT

The reasons of La Forest, L'Heureux-Dubé and McLachlin J.J. were delivered by

[111] McLachlin J. (dissenting in part) — I have read the reasons of Justice Iacobucci. While I agree with much of his reasons, my view of the law leads me to differ both in method and in result.

[112] As to method, I differ from Iacobucci J. in two respects. First, I am of the view that an award of damages for wrongful dismissal should be confined to factors relevant to the prospect of finding replacement employment. It follows that the notice period upon which such damages are based should only be increased for manner of dismissal if this impacts on the employee's prospects of re-employment. Secondly, I am of the view the law has evolved to permit recognition of an implied duty of good faith in termination of the employment. ...

Mitigation

Question

What is the doctrine of mitigation?
How can an employee wrongfully dismissed mitigate his losses?

Mifsud v. *MacMillan Bathurst Inc.*

63 D.L.R. (4th) 714; 70 O.R. (2d) 701
Ontario Court of Appeal
November 21, 1989

Background facts: The plaintiff Mifsud, having been employed by the defendant for 18 years, had been promoted; his last position was supervisor. He was later reassigned to a less responsible position but at the same rate of pay. Mifsud stayed in the new position for only a few days. After he left, he sued for wrongful dismissal. The lower court held that he had been constructively dismissed and awarded damages. The employer appealed the decision. It argued that even if Mifsud had been dismissed from his position as supervisor, he had a duty to take the new assignment as a way to mitigate his losses.

McKinlay J.A.:—The defendant, MacMillan Bathurst Inc., appeals a judgment in favour of the plaintiff, Frank George Michael Mifsud, awarding him the sum of $38,332.13 plus costs as a result of a finding that he was constructively dismissed from his position as a shift superintendent at the appellant's Etobicoke plant on September 4, 1984. This sum represents a notice period of 10 months. ...

Counsel for the appellant argues that where there is a constructive dismissal, but where the new assignments involve no subjection to degrading work or humiliating relationships, the employee is obliged to mitigate his loss by accepting the position that was offered to him, and to work out his period of reasonable notice in that position. ...

The doctrine of mitigation was concisely stated by Chief Justice Laskin in *Red Deer College v. Michaels* (1975), 57 D.L.R. (3d) 386 at p. 390, [1976] 2 S.C.R. 324, [1975] 5 W.W.R. 575 (S.C.C.):

The primary rule in breach of contract cases, that a wronged plaintiff is entitled to be put in as good a position as he would have been in if there had been proper performance by the defendant, is subject to the qualification that the defendant cannot be called upon to pay for avoidable losses which would result in an increase in the quantum of damages payable to the plaintiff. The reference in the case law to a "duty" to mitigate should be understood in this sense.

In short, a wronged plaintiff is entitled to recover damages for the losses he has suffered but the extent of those losses may depend upon *whether he has taken reasonable steps to avoid their unreasonable accumulation.*
(Emphasis added.)

There is no doubt that the duty of the plaintiff to take steps to mitigate his damages applies in all wrongful dismissal cases. The question is simply whether or not the steps taken by the plaintiff were reasonable.

When an employer wishes to dismiss an employee (other than for cause) the employer may choose either to give the employee reasonable notice of his termination date and require that he work out the notice period, or he may require the employee to leave immediately, thus rendering the employer liable for damages equal to the employee's remuneration and benefits for the reasonable notice period. If the employee leaves immediately, he is required to take reasonable steps to mitigate his loss and, barring any agreement to the contrary between the parties, any moneys earned in mitigation must be credited against his damages.

Is the situation substantially different when an employer does not wish to dismiss an employee but, being unsatisfied with his performance, or for some other valid reason, wishes to place him in a different position at the same salary? Why should it not be considered reasonable for the employee to mitigate his damages by working at the other position for the period of reasonable notice, or at least until he has found alternative employment which he accepts in mitigation?

The fact that the transfer to a new position may constitute in law a constructive dismissal does not eliminate the obligation of the employee to look at the new position offered and evaluate it as a means of mitigating damages. In all cases, comparison should be made to the contractual entitlement of the employer to give reasonable notice and leave the employee in his current position while a search is made for alternative employment. Where the salary offered is the same, where the working conditions are not substantially different or the work demeaning, and where the personal relationships involved are not acrimonious (as in this case) it is reasonable to expect the employee to accept the position offered in mitigation of damages during a reasonable notice period, or until he finds acceptable employment elsewhere.

It must be kept in mind, of course, that there are many situations where the facts would substantiate a constructive dismissal but where it would be patently unreasonable to expect an employee to accept continuing employment with the same employer in mitigation of his damages.

In this case, Mr. Mifsud improperly rejected the opportunity to mitigate his damages by maintaining an employed status from which to seek a preferable position elsewhere.

I would allow the appeal, replace the judgment of the trial judge with a judgment dismissing the plaintiff's claim, and allow the appellant its costs here and below.

Appeal allowed.

Note: The Supreme Court of Canada refused to hear an appeal.

Cox v. Robertson

http://www.courts.gov.bc.ca
BRITISH COLUMBIA COURT OF APPEAL
MARCH 25, 1999

Background facts: A "chair-side" or "head to head" dental assistant, who worked for the dentist for 18 years was dismissed with one month's notice. She worked during the notice period and when the dentist refused her claim for more notice, she sued for wrongful dismissal. The dentist then offered to re-employ her to mitigate her loss.

McEachern, C.J.B.C.:

DISCUSSION ...

[11] Probably the leading case on mitigation by re-employment is the judgment of this court in *Farquhar v. Butler Brothers Supplies Ltd.* [(1988), 23 B.C.L.R. (2d) 89 (B.C.C.A.),] ... where the Court stated ... that in mitigation of losses, an employee is only required to take such steps as a reasonable person would take. Each case, of course, will be different, but it is clear that while an employee may be under a duty to accept re-employment on a temporary basis in some circumstances, such obligation will arise infrequently because "[v]ery often the relationship ... will have become so frayed that a reasonable person would not expect both sides to work together again in harmony..." (per Lambert J.A., writing for the Court, at 94). ...

[13] It might be different if the offer of continued employment had been made during the currency of the notice period. At that time, the parties were still working together and a reasonable person might well conclude that if the offer had been made, she should have mitigated her damages by continuing to work "in harmony" with the defendant until she found new employment.

[14] Once the notice period expired, however, the plaintiff immediately demanded further compensation and the defendant responded most inadequately. The plaintiff then commenced this action, and only after that did the defendant offer further employment.

[15] It might also be different if the employment relationship had not been such a close and personal one. The plaintiff was obviously disappointed by the conduct of the defendant. Expecting her to work so closely with the person who had been unfair to her, particularly after he failed to respond adequately to her request for fair treatment, would be unreasonable.

[16] It might also be different if the offer of re-employment had been made before an action was commenced. In this respect, it is noted that the plaintiff did not rush to litigation. As Mr. Justice Donald mentioned in argument, it is almost amusing, and highly artificial, to say that these two persons should be expected to work closely and professionally together on the same mouths in the morning and then attend examinations for discovery in the afternoon and then continue to work harmoniously again the next day, all the while preparing for a summary trial.

[17] As the authorities suggest, a reasonable person might rightly think that in some cases, an employee should accept temporary employment in mitigation of damages. In such cases, the parties did not usually have to interact closely with each other. In this case, however, with the plaintiff and defendant always working side by side, the employment relationship could not have been closer. In my view, no reasonable person would conclude that a dental assistant in these circumstances should be expected to co-operate harmoniously with a dentist who had been unfair to her and to litigate with him at the same time. ...

[21] I would allow the appeal and award the plaintiff damages for 13 months less amounts already paid or earned during that period.

Unanimous

5. WRONGFUL RESIGNATION

Question

If you are not a member of a union and your employment contract is silent on the point, how much notice must you give your employer if you want to quit your job?

Systems Engineering and Automation Ltd. *v.* Power et al.

78 NFLD. & P.E.I.R. 65
NEWFOUNDLAND SUPREME COURT
OCTOBER 12, 1989

Wells, J.: The parties, I will refer to as SEA, Power, Guy and Avalon, respectively. SEA is a Newfoundland company, incorporated in 1983 and is a "high tech" supplier of services and hardware to other companies which require design, installation, and repair services for computer and control systems. Messrs. Power and Guy are technicians who were employed by SEA until May 7, 1987. Avalon was incorporated in May of 1987, and is owned by Messrs. Power and Guy.

SEA says that Messrs. Power and Guy, acting in concert, resigned from their employment on May 7, 1987 without notice and that in so doing they seriously prejudiced the work of SEA and caused it severe financial losses in the amount of $171,974.00.

...

Messrs. Power and Guy admit that they resigned without notice, however they say that SEA's demands upon them were such that their personal and family lives were being destroyed, and that they were justified in resigning without notice.

...

The evidence indicated that the resignation enraged the management of SEA. ...

The first issue is whether or not Messrs. Power and Guy were justified in leaving their employment without notice.

I have no doubt that their working conditions, which included long hours and the frustrations of working away from home, were difficult. Neither of them could have been expected to continue indefinitely to work these hours under these conditions. Nevertheless they were well aware that their particular jobs were important to their employer, and despite the frustrations which they felt, they must have known that to leave their employment without notice, would cause some difficulties and expense for SEA. Furthermore, nothing new or startling had taken place, for they had been working under similar conditions for months prior to May 7th.

[Their solicitor advised] that in the circumstances, they would have been justified in giving the minimum notice required by law.

It is agreed that there were no written contracts between the parties nor was their employment governed by a collective agreement. For these reasons it was argued that the *Labour Standards Act* applies, and I accept that argument as it applies to the minimum requirements.

Section 48 says:

Subject to sections 49 and 50, no employer or employee shall terminate a contract of service unless written notice of termination is given by or on behalf of the employer or employee, as the case may be, within the period set out in paragraph (a) or (b) of Section 51.

Section 51 says in its relevant parts:

The period of notice required to be given by the employer and employee under section 48 is

(a) one week, if the employee has been continuously employed by the employer for a period of one month or more but less than two years; and

(b) two weeks, if the employee has been continuously employed by the employer for a period of two years or more, ...

Accordingly I find as provided for in the Act, that Mr. Power should have given at least one week's notice and Mr. Guy, two.

[The Judge reviewed various projects on which the defendants were working at the time of their resignations to determine the extent of damages suffered by the plaintiffs because of their resigning without notice.]

In summary therefore, I am prepared to allow under the various headings of damage:

(a) $2,000.00 for lost profits from Marystown Shipyard Limited,

(b) $3,000.00 for additional expenses in completing projects on which Mr. Power might have been able to assist,

(c) $5,000.00 for additional expenses in completing projects on which Mr. Guy might have been able to assist.

    Total $10,000.00 ...

The evidence of Messrs. Power and Guy was to the effect that considerably more than $1,000.00 was owed to each of them, but they did not have records from which the amounts owing could be calculated. On a balance of probabilities, I am satisfied that they are owed at least $1,000.00 each, so that the sum of $2,000.00 should be deducted from the sum of $10,000.00 to which I have found the Plaintiff is entitled.

Judgment will therefore be entered for the plaintiff against the defendants jointly and severally in the amount of $8,000.00 together with prejudgment interest calculated from May 7, 1987. ...

Order accordingly.

6. Legislation to Protect Employees

A. Employment Standards Act

Rizzo and Rizzo Shoes Ltd. (Re:)

http://www.lexum.umontreal.ca/
Supreme Court of Canada
January 22, 1998

Background facts: When Rizzo and Rizzo Shoes Ltd. (Rizzo) was placed into bankruptcy, the employees lost their jobs. The Ministry of Labour delivered a proof of claim to the Trustee in Bankruptcy for severance pay owing to the former employees under the *Employment Standards Act*, but the claims were disallowed. A successful appeal to the Ontario Court (General Division) was overturned by the Court of Appeal.

Iacobucci, J.: ...

ISSUES

[17] This appeal raises one issue: does the termination of employment caused by the bankruptcy of an employer give rise to a claim provable in bankruptcy for termination pay and severance pay in accordance with the provision of the ESA [Employment Standards Act]?

5. Analysis

[18] The statutory obligation upon employers to provide both termination pay and severance pay is governed by ss. 40 and 40a of the ESA, respectively. ...

[20] At the heart of this conflict is an issue of statutory interpretation. Consistent with the findings of the Court of Appeal, the plain meaning of the words of the provisions here in question appears to restrict the obligation to pay termination and severance pay to those employers who have actively terminated the employment of their employees. At first blush, bankruptcy does not fit comfortably into this interpretation. However, with respect, I believe this analysis is incomplete.

[21] Although much has been written about the interpretation of legislation... Elmer Driedger in *Construction of Statutes* (2nd ed. 1983) best encapsulates the approach upon which I prefer to rely. He recognizes that statutory interpretation cannot be founded on the wording of the legislation alone. At p. 87 he states:

> Today there is only one principle or approach, namely, the words of an Act are to be read in their entire context and in their grammatical and ordinary sense harmoniously with the scheme of the Act, the object of the Act, and the intention of Parliament.

Recent cases ... have cited the above passage with approval. ...

[22] I also rely upon s. 10 of the Interpretation Act, R.S.O. 1980, c. 219, which provides that every Act "shall be deemed to be remedial" and directs that every Act shall "receive such fair, large and liberal construction and interpretation as will best ensure the attainment of the object of the Act according to its true intent, meaning and spirit".

[The court also relies on case law that supports the view that the Act should be interpreted to extend its protections to as many employees as possible] ...

[25] The objects of the termination and severance pay provisions themselves are also broadly premised upon the need to protect employees. Section 40 of the ESA requires employers to give their employees reasonable notice of termination based upon length of service. One of the primary purposes of this notice period is to provide employees with an opportunity to take preparatory measures and seek alternative employment. It follows that s. 40(7)(a), which provides for termination pay in lieu of notice when an employer has failed to give the required statutory notice, is intended to "cushion" employees against the adverse effects of economic dislocation likely to follow from the absence of an opportunity to search for alternative employment. ...

[27] In my opinion, the consequences or effects which result from the Court of Appeal's interpretation of ss. 40 and 40a of the ESA are incompatible with both the object of the Act and with the object of the termination and severance pay provisions themselves. It is a well established principle of statutory interpretation that the legislature does not intend to produce absurd consequences. ...

[28] The trial judge properly noted that, if the ESA termination and severance pay provisions do not apply in circumstances of bankruptcy, those employees "fortunate" enough to have been dismissed the day before a bankruptcy would be entitled to such payments, but those terminated on the day the bankruptcy becomes final would not be so entitled. In my view, the absurdity of this consequence is particularly evident in a unionized workplace where seniority is a factor in determining the order of lay-off. The more senior the employee, the larger the investment he or she has made in the employer and the greater the entitlement to termination and severance pay. However, it is the more senior personnel who are likely to be employed up until the time of the bankruptcy and who would thereby lose their entitlements to these payments. ...

[36] Finally, with regard to the scheme of the legislation, since the ESA is a mechanism for providing minimum benefits and standards to protect the interests of employees, it can be characterized as benefits-conferring legislation. As such, according

to several decisions of this Court, it ought to be interpreted in a broad and generous manner. Any doubt arising from difficulties of language should be resolved in favour of the claimant. ... It seems to me that, by limiting its analysis to the plain meaning of ss. 40 and 40a of the ESA, the Court of Appeal adopted an overly restrictive approach that is inconsistent with the scheme of the Act. ... [and] would undermine the object of the ESA, namely, to protect the interests of as many employees as possible. ...

[41] In my view, the impetus behind the termination of employment has no bearing upon the ability of the dismissed employee to cope with the sudden economic dislocation caused by unemployment. As all dismissed employees are equally in need of the protections provided by the ESA, any distinction between employees whose termination resulted from the bankruptcy of their employer and those who have been terminated for some other reason would be arbitrary and inequitable. Further, I believe that such an interpretation would defeat the true meaning, intent and spirit of the ESA. Therefore, I conclude that termination as a result of an employer's bankruptcy does give rise to an unsecured claim provable in bankruptcy pursuant to s. 121 of the BA for termination and severance pay in accordance with ss. 40 and 40a of the ESA. ...

Appeal allowed   Unanimous

B. Occupational Health and Safety Act

Mr. Dourchesne, an employee of Inco Mines for 30 years, operated a rock bolter—a machine that affixed screens to the walls and roofs in mines to prevent falling rock from injuring miners. The front of the bolter has the ability to move from side to side, up and down, and to rotate. Although "the how, under what circumstances and by what means Ray Courchesne met his untimely demise" was not the issue before the trial court, it was a fact that Mr. Courchesne had been crushed by the machine and the court convicted Inco, his employer, under the *Occupational Health and Safety Act* of Ontario. Two appeals later, the offences were two: failing to maintain equipment in good condition and failing to leave a guard to protect workers from a moving part in equipment. Each offence carried a fine of $250,000.

R. v. Inco Ltd.
http://www.ontariocourts.on.ca/
Ontario Court of Appeal
May 30, 2000

* *T*wenty-six men died by methane fire, carbon-monoxide poisoning and coal-dust explosion caused by concentrations of methane gas and coal dust in the Westray mines. Two managers of the mines face charges of criminal negligence and manslaughter, but the fault of the explosion was also attributed to the inspectors of the Department of Labour who failed to force the company to keep the mine safe.[9]

* *A* worker was crushed to death in a die-casting machine. The supervisor was unable to use a protection switch because the workers hung a spray gun on a wire that held the switch in an off position. The company, which knew its workers frequently blocked safety switches, was fined $200,000 under the Ontario *Occupational Health and Safety Act*.[10]

C. Human Rights Code

Tawney Meiorin had worked as a firefighter for three years when she fell 49.4 seconds short on a revised aerobic standard. She lost her job. She took legal action against her employer under the B.C. Human Rights Code for unjustifiable discrimination. The Supreme Court of Canada set out a three-point test for determining whether or not the employer's standard was a bona fide occupational requirement (BFOR). It held that an employer must establish that the standard is "rationally connected to the performance of the job"; that the employer adopted the standard in good faith; that the standard is legitimately necessary to accomplish the job.

The court found the government failed to show that the aerobics standard was a bona fide occupational requirement and ordered that the employee be reinstated.

B.C. (P.S. Empl. Rel. Comm.) v. BCGSEU
Supreme Court of Canada
Summarized from The Lawyers Weekly
Sept. 17, 1999, p. 1.

D. WORKPLACE SAFETY/WORKERS' COMPENSATION

▶▶ *See p. 25 for Pasiechnyk v. Saskatchewan (Workers' Compensation Board)*, a Supreme Court of Canada decision in which the history and purpose of the Workers Compensation legislation are reviewed and in which the issue of judicial review is addressed.

- *O*n the national day for honouring workers killed or injured on the job, government buildings fly flags at half staff. We have been advised by the Workers' Compensation Board that in British Columbia 147 fatal claims were accepted in 1999.

- *M*r. Ethier, angry with two co-workers, "saw red" and punched a metal filing cabinet with his fist. Off work for two months because of a fractured bone, he claimed workers' compensation but it was denied by the commission on the grounds that the injury was the result of a voluntary act or the result of gross negligence. The revisory board hearing the appeal rejected his claim; the appeals commission rejected his claim. Still arguing that the act could not be reasonably qualified as voluntary or the result of gross negligence, the worker has now appealed to the Quebec Superior Court.[11]

7. COLLECTIVE BARGAINING

INTERESTS DISPUTE

BARGAINING IN BAD FAITH

- *T*he Canada Labour Relations Board ruled that the owner of the Giant gold mine in Yellowknife had bargained in bad faith leading up to a May, 1992 strike action. The board ordered the company and union to negotiate a settlement within 30 days or face binding arbitration. The workers subsequently accepted an offer from the owner, Royal Oak Mines. The offer left some contentious issues to be negotiated by representatives from both sides or by a mediator if the two sides could not agree.[12] Labour peace came too late for some miners. Four months after the strike began, nine miners died in an explosion. A union member charged with murder was found guilty of nine counts of second-degree murder.

Strikes and Lockouts

U.F.C.W. Local 1518 v. KMart Canada Ltd.

http://www.lexum.umontreal.ca/
Supreme Court of Canada
September 9, 1999

[1] Cory J. — The peaceful distribution of leaflets accurately setting out the position of employees involved in a labour dispute with their employer would ordinarily be protected by the guarantee of freedom of expression provided by s. 2(b) of the *Canadian Charter of Rights and Freedoms*. It is conceded that a legislative restriction on picketing which prohibits members of a union from peacefully distributing such leaflets at separate and distinct divisions of their employer infringes s. 2(b) of the *Charter*. The question then arises, can that legislation be justified pursuant to s. 1 of the *Charter*? ...

[12] It must be emphasized that the only activity at issue in the present appeal is the peaceful distribution of leaflets at the secondary sites.

[13] In my opinion, the definition of "picketing" which would prohibit leafleting at secondary sites contained in s. 1(1) [now *Labour Relations Code*, of B.C.] is overly broad and infringes the guarantee of freedom of expression. It cannot be justified on the basis that it is necessary to achieve the legislative objective of minimizing the harmful effects to third parties which would result from others impeding access to premises or encouraging employees to break their contract of employment. ...

II. RELEVANT STATUTORY AND CONSTITUTIONAL PROVISIONS ...

[14] Canadian Charter of Rights and Freedoms
1. The *Canadian Charter of Rights and Freedoms* guarantees the rights and freedoms set out in it subject only to such reasonable limits prescribed by law as can be demonstrably justified in a free and democratic society.
2. Everyone has the following fundamental freedoms: ...
(b) freedom of thought, belief, opinion and expression, including freedom of the press and other media of communication;
Constitution Act, 1982
52. (1) The Constitution of Canada is the supreme law of Canada, and any law that is inconsistent with the provisions of the Constitution is, to the extent of the inconsistency, of no force or effect.

[28] The distribution and circulation of leaflets has for centuries been recognized as an effective and economical method of both providing information and assisting rational persuasion. It has long been used as a means to enlist support. ... Free expression on matters of public interest and the right to publicly disseminate news and information and to express opinions on matters of public interest were considered to be fundamental rights long before the enactment of the *Charter*. ...The distribution of leaflets and posters is typically less expensive and more readily available than other forms of expression. As a result, they are particularly important means of providing information and seeking support by the vulnerable and less powerful members of society. ...

[33] It is true that impugned legislation may infringe a *Charter* right or freedom by its purpose <u>or</u> its effects. ... [I]n my view, the operation of ss. 1, 65 and 67 of the Code has, at the very least, the <u>effect</u> of restricting consumer leafleting and thus infringes the appellant's freedom of expression. Consequently, the first constitutional question must be answered in the affirmative.

B. Section 1 of the Charter

[34] The aim of the analysis under s. 1 of the *Charter* is to determine whether the infringement of a *Charter* right or freedom can be justified in a free and democratic society. Following the test elaborated initially in *R. v. Oakes*, [1986] 1 S.C.R.103, ... it is incumbent on the respondent and the Attorney General as the parties seeking to uphold the restriction on a *Charter* freedom to show on a balance of probabilities that such an infringement can be justified. To satisfy this burden, they must demonstrate that the objective sought to be served by the legislative restriction is of sufficient importance to warrant overriding a constitutionally protected right or freedom. Only a significantly pressing and substantial objective can meet this requirement. They must also demonstrate that the legislative restriction is proportional to the objective sought by the legislature. In determining proportionality, three factors must be examined. First, the measure chosen must be rationally connected to the objective. Second, it must impair the guaranteed right or freedom as little as reasonably possible. And third, there must be proportionality between the importance of the objective and the deleterious effects of the restriction and between the deleterious and salutary effects of the measure. The analysis must be undertaken in the context of labour relations.
1 <u>Pressing and Substantial Objective</u> ...
[43] Consumer leafleting is very different from a picket line. It seeks to persuade members of the public to take a certain course of action. It does so through informed and rational discourse which is the very essence of freedom of expression. Leafleting does not trigger the "signal" effect inherent in picket lines and it certainly does not have the same coercive component. It does not in any significant manner impede access to or egress from premises. Although the enterprise which is the subject of the leaflet may experience some loss of revenue, that may very well result from the public being informed and persuaded by the leaflets not to support the enterprise. Consequently, the leafleting activity if properly conducted is not illegal at common law. In the absence of independently tortious activity, protection from economic harm resulting from peaceful persuasion, urging a lawful course of action, has not been accepted at common law as a protected legal right. See J. G. Fleming, *The Law of Torts* (9th ed. 1998), at pp. 765-77.

Significantly, the harmful effects that flow from leafleting do not differ from those which would result from a consumer boycott campaign conducted by permissible means. In fact it is well nigh impossible to distinguish between the situation whereby consumers are informed and persuaded not to buy through leafleting at the place of purchase, and the situation whereby the same consumers are informed and persuaded not to buy through leaflets delivered to the mailbox, newspaper advertising, internet mailing or billboards and posters. ...

(e) *Permissible Leafleting*

[56] In deciding whether the consumer leafleting activity in question is acceptable, it will be important to determine whether consumers are able to determine for themselves what course of action to take without being unduly disrupted by the message of the leaflets or the manner in which it was distributed. Consumers must retain the ability to choose either to stop and read the material or to ignore the leafleter and enter the neutral site unimpeded. ...

[58] ... [The judge reviews the content of the leaflet and the manner and effect of the activity of leafleting and finds that it] would normally constitute a valid exercise of freedom of expression carried out by lawful means. Yet it would be prohibited by the impugned legislation. It is against this background that the justification of the legislation under s. 1 of the *Charter* should be considered. The question is whether the complete prohibition of leafleting under the Code which violates the guaranteed right of freedom of expression can be justified under s. 1 of the *Charter*. ...

[60] The objective of the picketing restrictions must be read in concert with the overall purposes of the Code found at s. 2(1). ...

2. (1) The following are the purposes of this Code: ...

(c) to minimize the effects of labour disputes on persons who are not involved in the dispute;

(d) to promote conditions favourable to the orderly, constructive and expeditious settlement of disputes between employers and trade unions;

(e) to ensure that the public interest is protected during labour disputes. ...

[61] ... While a restriction on conventional picketing activity at neutral sites is rationally connected with the legislative objective, the restriction on leafleting activity is too broad. ....

(b) *Minimal Impairment* ...

[78] I have found that the definition of "picketing" at s. 1(1) of the Code is overbroad and catches more expressive conduct than is necessary to achieve the legislative objective. Accordingly, with regard to leafleting activity, the requirement of minimum impairment is not met. It is not necessary to proceed to the final stage of the proportionality analysis under s. 1 of the *Charter* because a "finding that the law impairs the right more than required contradicts the assertion that the infringement is proportionate" (*RJR-MacDonald*, at para. 175).

C. Conclusion and Remedy

[79] The definition of "picketing" ... [in] the Code infringes s. 2(b) of the *Charter* and is not a reasonable limit under s. 1. A violation of a protected freedom engages the application of s. 52 of the *Constitution Act*, 1982. That section requires the offensive legislation to be struck down "to the extent of the inconsistency". Following the principles of constitutional remedies stated in the case of *Schachter v. Canada* [1992] 2 S.C.R. 679, I would strike down the definition of "picketing" at s. 1 of the Code and suspend the declaration of invalidity for six months in order to allow the legislature to amend the provision to make it conform with the constitutional guarantee of freedom of expression as discussed in these reasons. ...

Appeal allowed   Unanimous

- *T*he 135,000 members of the Screen Actors Guild (SAG) and American Federation of Television & Radio Artists ended the longest labour dispute in the history of Hollywood by reaching a tentative settlement with commercial producers. The end of the six-month strike also ended the boom in Canada's commercial production industry. The Entertainment Industry Development Corp. estimated the Los Angeles area lost $275 million in "runaway productions," most of which came to Canada.[13] A day after the strike began, Tiger Woods, a member of SAG, refused to be in a Nike ad. He also spoke in favour of the union. However, months later he made a commercial for Buick in Kitchener, Ontario. The union fined him $100,000, half of which is suspended unless he takes part in another non-union shoot.[14]

- *I*n November of 1996, the baseball owners, in a 26-4 vote, ratified a new collective agreement. The approval of the contract by the owners and players ended a four-year fight during which the players went out on strike. The strike which began on August 12, 1994 lasted for 232 days and knocked out the World Series for the first time in 90 years. The strike was ended by a court order.[15]

- *M*r.Devries of Victoria, B.C. had tickets for a Canucks–L.A. Kings game in Vancouver. When the ferries quit running because of an illegal strike called by the B.C. Ferry and Marine Workers Union, he missed the game. He sued. He won.[16]

B. Agency

Questions

If you are acting as an agent, what are your obligations to your principal?

What are your duties as a fiduciary?

Ocean City Realty Ltd. *v.* A & M Holdings Ltd. et al.

36 D.L.R. (4TH) 94
BRITISH COLUMBIA COURT OF APPEAL
MARCH 5, 1987

I

Wallace J.A.:—The appellant appeals from a decision wherein the trial judge awarded the plaintiff a real estate commission earned in connection with the sale of real property in the City of Victoria.

II

Facts

The plaintiff, Ocean City Realty Ltd. (Ocean City), is a licensed real estate agency. The defendant, A & M Holdings Ltd. (A & M), was the owner of a commercial building in Victoria, British Columbia known as the Weiler Building.

At all material times Mrs. Patricia Forbes was a licensed real estate sales person employed by Ocean City.

In January of 1983, Mr. Holm Halbauer contacted Mrs. Forbes for assistance in locating a commercial building in downtown Victoria which he might be interested in purchasing.

Mrs. Forbes contacted the principals of A & M to inquire as to whether the Weiler Building might be for sale. She also inquired as to the sales commission A & M would be willing to pay.

Following a series of negotiations an interim agreement for the sale of the Weiler Building was concluded between A & M and Mr. Halbauer. It included a commission agreement between A & M and Ocean City whereby Ocean City was to receive 1.75% of the sale price of $5.2 million.

The trial judge found that at some point during the negotiations Mr. Halbauer advised Mrs. Forbes of his intention to proceed no further with the transaction unless Mrs. Forbes agreed to pay him, on completion of the sale, the sum of $46,000, representing approximately one-half of the total prospective commission. [Mrs. Forbes discussed this request with the agent at the office and it was decided that the money would be paid. Later] it was discovered by the solicitors for A & M that, prior to the conclusion of the agreement, Mrs. Forbes had made an arrangement with Halbauer whereby she agreed to rebate to him the sum of $46,000 from her portion of the commission to be paid to Ocean City. Up to that time A & M were unaware of that agreement.

A & M refused to pay the commission claimed by Ocean City with respect to the transaction. Ocean City brought this action against A & M for the commission. ...

III

Issues

The issues raised by this appeal are of narrow compass:

    (1) Is the real estate agent obliged to disclose to its principal the fact that it has agreed to rebate to the purchaser a portion of its real estate commission from the sale?

    (2) If it is under such an obligation what effect does such nondisclosure have upon its claim to the real estate commission?

IV

The trial judge in addressing these issues made the following remarks:

The relationship between a real estate agent and a person retaining him to sell property is a fiduciary and confidential one and the real estate agent's duty to his principal is to be construed strictly. The agent has a duty to obtain the highest price possible for his client and he has a duty to disclose all material facts which might affect the value of the property ...

In *Canada Permanent Trust Co. v. Christie* (1979), 16 B.C.L.R. 183, Mr. Justice Esson ... quoted with approval the following test [at pp. 185-6]:

"The onus is upon the agent to prove that the transaction was entered into after full and fair disclosure of all material circumstances and of everything known to him respecting the subject matter of the contract which could be likely to influence the conduct of his principal. The burden of proof that the transaction was a righteous one rests upon the agent, who is bound to produce clear affirmative proof that the parties were at arm's length, that the principal had the fullest information upon all material facts and that having this information he agreed to adopt what was done."

...

And further:

The authorities relied on by the defendant concern situations where the broker gained an advantage in the transaction and failed to disclose all material elements of the arrangement to his principal. In the case at bar the plaintiff says that no advantage was being sought by the broker and, indeed, Mrs. Forbes agreed to suffer a very considerable reduction in the anticipated commission in order, on her testimony, to secure the deal for the vendor and to permit the vendor to realize the full asking price ...

In the case at bar the legal duty of the agent, if she engaged herself in the subject of her arrangement with the defendant, was to find a buyer for the Weiler Building ready willing and able to pay the sum that the defendant had declared ... . The agent also had an obligation to avoid any conflict of interest with the defendant. In my view, the agreement to pay over to the purchaser a portion of the agent's commission on completion of the sale did not put the plaintiff into conflict with the defendant, as both the defendant and the plaintiff had the same interest to advance, that is to say, to complete the sale at the plaintiff's asking price. Obviously, the defendant had more to gain than did the plaintiff by the completion of the sale on the terms negotiated by the plaintiff.

In my opinion, the trial judge's interpretation of the obligation owed to a principal by its agent is too restrictive. The duty of disclosure is not confined to those instances where the agent has gained an advantage in the transaction or where the information might affect the value of the property, or where a conflict of interest exists. The agent certainly has a duty of full disclosure in such circumstances; they are commonly occurring circumstances which require full disclosure by the agent. However, they are not exhaustive.

The obligation of the agent to make full disclosure extends beyond these three categories and includes "everything known to him respecting the subject-matter of the contract which would be likely to influence the conduct of his principal" (*Canada Permanent Trust Co. v. Christie, supra*) or, as expressed in 1 Hals., 3rd ed., p.191, para. 443, everything which "...would be likely to operate upon the principal's judgment." In such cases the agent's failure to inform the principal would be material nondisclosure. ...

The test is an objective one to be determined by what a reasonable man in the position of the agent would consider, in the circumstances, would be likely to influence the conduct of his principal.

I would emphasize that the agent cannot arbitrarily decide what would likely influence the conduct of his principal and thus avoid the consequences of non-disclosure. If the information pertains to the transaction with respect to which the agent is engaged, any concern or doubt that the agent may have can be readily resolved by disclosure of all the facts to his principal. In the instant case the very withholding from the principal of the information concerning the payments to the purchaser of a portion of the commission could be evidence from which one might properly infer that the agent was aware that such circumstances would be a matter of concern to the principal.

One can readily appreciate that a vendor may wish not to enter into a complex sale arrangement which is subject to a variety of terms, such as vendor financing; a mortgage agreement; or a management agreement with a related company, unless that vendor was confident the purchaser was a person of integrity. ...

In the instant case the trial judge found that the agent justified her non-disclosure of the arrangement to pay the purchaser a percentage of the commission on the ground that she sought no advantage from the arrangement and indeed suffered a considerable reduction in her anticipated commission in order to secure the deal for the vendor and to permit the vendor to realize the full asking price for the property.

One may excuse a somewhat skeptical reaction to this altruistic rationale for non-disclosure of information by Mrs. Forbes. It ignores the fact that, if one accepts the premise that the arrangement was solely for the benefit of the principal, the agent would anticipate that the principal would approve of the agent's beneficence and proceed with the transaction. Accordingly, there would be no reason to withhold the information. ...

In the circumstances of this case, I find that the agent's nondisclosure was motivated by her desire to earn at least a portion of her commission and constituted a breach of her fiduciary duty to her principal and as a consequence she is not entitled to the commission claimed. ...

I would allow the appeal with costs here and below.

Unanimous

---

von Bismark | *v.* | *Sagl*

[2000] O.J. No. 2757 (Q.L.)
ONTARIO SUPERIOR COURT OF JUSTICE
JULY 14, 2000

[1] Eberhard J.:— The Plaintiff is a painter. She contracted with the Defendant to promote her artwork for the purpose of sale. The Defendant did not sell her work but the Plaintiff received what appeared to be the agreed asking price for two batches of 100 paintings each. The Defendant represented that an unnamed client was purchasing the paintings but she was keeping them herself. Further batches of paintings were delivered and kept by the Defendant until most were destroyed by fire at her premises.

... [The court finds as a fact that over 400 paintings were delivered to the defendant].

[10] The oral agreement called for [a sale price of $100 per painting for the first batch—due to the Defendant's representation that a modest initial price would augment exposure and result in an increase in value for subsequent batches]; $200 per painting for the second batch of 100. ...

[15] Bridgette Sagl is an accomplished, talented individual. She is articulate. In representing herself she demonstrated the

ability to marshal her evidence, formulate questions and responsive cross-examination, articulate her position with respect to the issues of the case and hold her own in unfamiliar circumstances with a competence not seen in many self represented litigants. Unfortunately, she appears to be completely dishonest. ...

[16] When I received the Defendant's written argument this conclusion was confirmed. ...

[17] Transcripts from an insurance examination of the Defendant were admitted both for the purpose of impeaching credibility [and] for the truth of their contents. These admissions, made in the context of a claim for insurance for the very paintings at issue in this proceeding, are her only statement in evidence as to the value of the paintings since the Defendant elected not to testify in these proceedings.

[18] The admissions are another demonstration that Ms. Sagl lies without flinching. ... This is consistent with her modus operandi. ... She told the Plaintiff that payments received for the first two batches were from the client she so often described in the United States as not only purchasing the paintings but maximizing their exposure for the ultimate goal of increased value. The ongoing delivery of paintings by von Bismark and the belief that the contract was being performed were fostered by the Defendant. ... All this was based on deceit, at all times hiding the fact from the painter, that the Defendant was hoarding the paintings unto herself and claiming ownership.

[19] Not only did this scheme artificially reduce the price per painting for the 200 paintings that were paid for, not only did it result in the paintings being lost by fire where they were hoarded by the Defendant in her basement, it also deprived von Bismark of her chance to be a recognized artist.

[20] The conduct of Bridgette Sagl and the results are despicable. ...

DAMAGES

[28] A possible means of compensation is fair market value of the paintings which the agent Defendant did not sell but converted to her own use. In this proceeding, the Defendant has repeatedly minimized the value of the paintings, however, in her own insurance claim where she purported to own the paintings, she demanded compensation of $207,750.00 for 300 of them.

[29] There is no direct evidence before me that the art is worth that figure ... Also, all participants acknowledged that fair market value is effected by the exposure of an artist's work in the marketplace. ... Von Bismark's work was prevented from such exposure by the conduct of the Defendant under the guise of an exclusive agency contract. ...

[31] In any event, I can give no weight to the evidence [of the defendant's witness, the source of the appraisal, who was] completely biased ... argumentative, evasive and disingenuous in every aspect of his testimony. Insofar as he addressed any relevant issue, I reject his evidence as entirely unreliable. ...

[34] Ultimately, I find the best evidence of the value of the paintings is what the Plaintiff agreed to sell them for. I recognize that her reason for accepting the lower value for early batches was because she was persuaded that she would thereby receive an exposure for her work that would enhance the value

of later sales. This was hardly accomplished with the paintings in Ms. Sagl's basement. However, for the 420 paintings herein, it was a price she agreed was fair. That value ... is $116,000. She has received $22,500. That leaves $83,500 due to her.

[35] Ms. Sagl is not entitled to commission.

[36] She did not promote to merit a commission. She did not sell to merit a commission. She hoodwinked the Plaintiff and sought thereby to acquire the paintings.

[37] In argument, counsel for the Plaintiff reviewed agency principles of performance, obedience and duty to account. He cited the fiduciary nature of the agency relationship. This manifests in the duty of disclosure by an agent who is in a position in which his own interest may effect [sic] the performance of his duty to the principal. "An important ... illustration of this is provided by the situation that arises where the agent himself purports to purchase the property he is engaged to sell on his principal's behalf." [Fridman's *Law of Agency* (5th edition) at page 153] Breach of such duty disentitles the agent to commission.

[38] Moreover, the obvious plan of the Defendant was to retain the Plaintiff's paintings and sell them at a profit ... to make these secret profits. Failure to account for all such profit, whatever it may have been thus far amounts "to a breach of [her] contract of agency and disentitles the agent to [her] commission." [Fridman's *Law of Agency* (5th edition) at page 156].

[39] I find that the Defendant owes the Plaintiff $83,500 for the paintings in damages for breach of contract and conversion. ...

INSURANCE ...

[43] I find that the obligation to insure [existed and] continued and was in effect when the fire destroyed the paintings in Ms. Sagl's possession.

[44] I find and declare that the Defendant holds in trust for the Plaintiff and all monies received or to be received from Chubb Insurance as a result of fire loss ... respecting paintings created by the Plaintiff and insured by the Defendant.

[45] Because there are other items insured under the same policy, any recovery may be pro rata. I declare that the Plaintiff has priority over Ms. Sagl for the amount of judgment awarded above together with interest as set out above.

PUNITIVE DAMAGES

[46] The Plaintiff has also claimed punitive damages.

[47] I find that such damages are rare but available in cases of breach of contract where the conduct complained of constitutes an independent actionable wrong. [*Vorvis v. Insurance Corporation of British Columbia* (1989), 58 D.L.R. (4th) 193 (Supreme Court of Canada)].

[48] I am satisfied that the conduct of the Defendant can and does constitute both a breach of contract and a breach of fiduciary duty. ...

[49] I am reminded of the adjectives appearing in cases where punitive damages are considered: outrageous, heinous, repugnant, malicious, vindictive, arrogant, insulting, harsh and reprehensible.

[50] If I have been too subtle to this point in my findings, let me correct that now. Bridgette Sagl was all of these in her treatment of Ruth von Bismark.

[51] It is not an instance where token punitive damages will suffice. It must be recognized that the damages for breach of contract and conversion based on the contract value of the paintings have been artificially reduced by the despicable scheme of the Defendant. Moreover, she denied Ruth von Bismark the satisfactions of her life's work.

[52] I grant the Plaintiff's claim for $50,000 in punitive damages together with pre-judgment post-judgment interest.

Question

What is the result if you sign on behalf of a company not in existence?

Szecket v. Huang

http://www.ontariocourts.on.ca/
ONTARIO COURT OF APPEAL
DECEMBER 10, 1998

[1] The issue raised by this appeal is whether Conant J. correctly applied s.21(1) of the Business Corporations Act, R.S.O. 1990, c.B.17 (the "OBCA") in finding that the appellant, Geoffrey Huang, was personally liable to the respondents, Alexander Szecket and Alberto Geddo, for the breach of a contract which the appellant, and others, entered into with the respondents "on behalf of a company to be formed", in circumstances where the company was not formed and the contract was not performed. It is the position of the appellant that under s.21(4) of the OBCA he was not bound by the contract. ...

[5] Dr. Szecket, a research scientist, and his associate, Mr. Geddo, a consulting engineer, developed a process, or technology, for the bonding of dissimilar metals called "Dynamic Bonding", for which Dr. Szecket held three patents. In the mid-1980s they lived, and were employed, in the Toronto area. About 1985 they were approached by Mr. Huang who represented that he was aware of specific opportunities in Taiwan for the development of the respondents' technology, including the financing required to do so. ..

[After three years of discussions, correspondence, visits and drafts, a licensing agreement was signed by Huang and others "acting on behalf of a company to be formed"] ...

[19] This appeal deals with a pre-incorporation contract. ...

ANALYSIS

Liability ...

[23] To provide the context for the discussion that follows, it is necessary to reproduce s.21 of the OBCA:

> 21(1) Except as provided in this section, a person who enters into an oral or written contract in the name of or on behalf of a corporation before it comes into existence is personally bound by the contract and is entitled to the benefits thereof.

> (2) A corporation may, within a reasonable time after it comes into existence, by any action or conduct signifying its intention to be bound thereby, adopt an oral or written contract made before it came into existence in its name or on its behalf, and upon such adoption,

> (a) the corporation is bound by the contract and is entitled to the benefits thereof as if the corporation had been in existence at the date of the contract and had been a party thereto; and

> (b) a person who purported to act in the name of or on behalf of the corporation ceases, except as provided in subsection (3), to be bound by or entitled to the benefits of the contract.

> (3) Except as provided in subsection (4), whether or not an oral or written contract made before the coming into existence of a corporation is adopted by the corporation, a party to the contract may apply to a court for an order fixing obligations under the contract as joint or joint and several or apportioning liability between the corporation and the person who purported to act in the name of or on behalf of the corporation, and, upon such application, the court may make any order it thinks fit.

> (4) If expressly so provided in the oral or written contract referred to in subsection (1), a person who purported to act in the name of or on behalf of the corporation before it came into existence is not in any event bound by the contract or entitled to the benefits thereof. ...

[24] Counsel for the appellant argued that the trial judge erred in failing to invoke s.21(4) to exclude the appellant from personal liability under s.21(1) on the evidence that Mr. Huang had expressed a clear intention not to assume personal liability for the obligations of the company to be incorporated ... [and that

a] guarantee was ultimately deleted from the draft of the agreement at the insistence of Mr. Huang and his associates, which they executed solely on behalf of the company to be incorporated. It was counsel's position that this satisfied the requirements of s.21(4) and relieved Mr. Huang of personal liability under s.21(1) when the company was not incorporated and the contract was not performed.

[25] Counsel for the respondents ... argued that s.21(4) requires that an express term be included in a pre-incorporation contract to limit the liability of a person signing it on behalf of a company to be formed. As there was no express term in the contract limiting the appellant's liability, this contract did not fall within the class of contracts contemplated by s.21(4), with the result that Conant J. [trial judge] correctly found Mr. Huang liable for the breach of the contract pursuant to s.21(1). In our view, the submission of counsel for the respondents is correct. .... [The court reviews the case law on that point.]

[31] ... Section 21(4) is clear and unambiguous. To limit the liability of a person who enters into a pre-incorporation contract, an express provision to that effect must be contained in the pre-incorporation contract. The contract in this appeal did not contain such an express provision. Whatever may have been the result of the negotiations between the parties preceding the execution of the contract about the personal responsibility of Mr. Huang for the obligations of the company to be incorporated, the contract itself contained no express provision relieving Mr. Huang from personal liability under s.21(1) if the company was not incorporated, or if it was incorporated, and failed to adopt the contract. Had he wished to avail himself of s.21(4), Mr. Huang could have sought the consent of the respondents to include an appropriate provision in the agreement. In the absence of such a provision, it follows, in our view, that Conant J. was correct in his application of s.21(1) to the circumstances of this appeal and his conclusion that Mr. Huang was personally liable for the breach of the contract. ...

RESULT

[39] [T]he appeal is dismissed with costs.

Unanimous

Note: In the provinces in which statute has not overruled the common law, a contract by a person on behalf of a company not yet in existence would be an agent contracting on behalf of a non-existing principal. The company would not be bound, nor would the person who signed on behalf of the company. By warranting the company was in existence, however, the person would be liable for "breach of the warranty of authority."

Q u e s t i o n

What remedy is available if an agent breaches a fiduciary duty?

Soulos v. Korkontzilas

FILE NO.: 24949
http://www.lexum.umontreal.ca/
SUPREME COURT OF CANADA
MAY 22, 1997

McLachlin, J., —

I

[1] This appeal requires this Court to determine whether a real estate agent who buys for himself property for which he has been negotiating on behalf of a client may be required to return the property to his client despite the fact that the client can show no loss. This raises the legal issue of whether a constructive trust over property may be imposed in the absence of enrichment of the defendant and corresponding deprivation of the plaintiff. In my view, this question should be answered in the affirmative.

II

[2] The appellant Mr. Korkontzilas is a real estate broker. The respondent, Mr. Soulos, was his client. In 1984, Mr. Korkontzilas found a commercial building which he thought might interest Mr. Soulos. Mr. Soulos was interested in purchasing the building. Mr. Korkontzilas entered into negotiations on behalf of Mr. Soulos. He offered $250,000. The vendor, Dominion Life, rejected the offer and tendered a counter-offer of $275,000. Mr. Soulos rejected the counter-offer but "signed it back" at $260,000 or $265,000. Dominion Life advised Mr. Korkontzilas that it would accept $265,000. Instead of conveying this information to Mr. Soulos as he should have, Mr. Korkontzilas arranged for his wife, Panagiota Goutsoulas, to purchase the property using the name Panagiot Goutsoulas. Panagiot Goutsoulas then transferred the property to Panagiota and Fotios Korkontzilas as joint tenants. Mr. Soulos asked what had happened to the property. Mr. Korkontzilas told him to "forget about it;" the vendor no longer wanted to sell it and

he would find him a better property. Mr. Soulos asked Mr. Korkontzilas whether he had had anything to do with the vendor's change of heart. Mr. Korkontzilas said he had not.

[3] In 1987 Mr. Soulos learned that Mr. Korkontzilas had purchased the property for himself. He brought an action against Mr. Korkontzilas to have the property conveyed to him, alleging breach of fiduciary duty giving rise to a constructive trust. He asserted that the property held special value to him because its tenant was his banker, and being one's banker's landlord was a source of prestige in the Greek community of which he was a member. However, Mr. Soulos abandoned his claim for damages because the market value of the property had, in fact, decreased from the time of the Korkontzilas purchase.

[4] The trial judge found that Mr. Korkontzilas had breached a duty of loyalty to Mr. Soulos, but held that a constructive trust was not an appropriate remedy because Mr. Korkontzilas had purchased the property at market value and hence had not been "enriched": (1991), 4 O.R. (3d) 51, 19 R.P.R. (2d) 205 (hereinafter cited to O.R.). The decision was reversed on appeal, Labrosse J.A. dissenting: (1995), 25 O.R. (3d) 257. …

[5] For the reasons that follow, I would dismiss the appeal. In my view, the doctrine of constructive trust applies and requires that Mr. Korkontzilas convey the property he wrongly acquired to Mr. Soulos. …

IV

[9] This brings us to the main issue on this appeal: what remedy, if any, does the law afford Mr. Soulos for Mr. Korkontzilas' breach of the duty of loyalty [as a fiduciary, by] acquiring the property in question for himself rather than passing the vendor's statement of the price it would accept on to his principal, Mr. Soulos? …

V

…

[17] The history of the law of constructive trust … suggests that the constructive trust is an ancient and eclectic institution imposed by law not only to remedy unjust enrichment, but to hold persons in different situations to high standards of trust and probity and prevent them from retaining property which in "good conscience" they should not be permitted to retain. This served the end, not only of doing justice in the case before the court, but of protecting relationships of trust and the institutions that depend on these relationships. These goals were accomplished by treating the person holding the property as a trustee of it for the wronged person's benefit, even though there was no true trust created by intention. In England, the trust thus created was thought of as a real or "institutional" trust. In the United States and recently in Canada, jurisprudence speaks of the availability of the constructive trust as a remedy; hence the remedial constructive trust. …

[The judge reviews English and Canadian jurisprudence and several scholarly articles.]

VI

…

[34] It thus emerges that a constructive trust may be imposed where good conscience so requires. The inquiry into good conscience is informed by the situations where constructive trusts

have been recognized in the past. It is also informed by the dual reasons for which constructive trusts have traditionally been imposed: to do justice between the parties and to maintain the integrity of institutions dependent on trust-like relationships. Finally, it is informed by the absence of an indication that a constructive trust would have an unfair or unjust effect on the defendant or third parties, matters which equity has always taken into account. Equitable remedies are flexible; their award is based on what is just in all the circumstances of the case. …

[43] I conclude that in Canada, under the broad umbrella of good conscience, constructive trusts are recognized both for wrongful acts like fraud and breach of duty of loyalty, as well as to remedy unjust enrichment and corresponding deprivation. While cases often involve both a wrongful act and unjust enrichment, constructive trusts may be imposed on either ground: where there is a wrongful act but no unjust enrichment and corresponding deprivation; or where there is an unconscionable unjust enrichment in the absence of a wrongful act, … Within these two broad categories, there is room for the law of constructive trust to develop and for greater precision to be attained, as time and experience may dictate. …

VII

[45] … Extrapolating from the cases where courts of equity have imposed constructive trusts for wrongful conduct, and from a discussion of the criteria considered in an essay by Roy Goode, "Property and Unjust Enrichment," in Andrew Burrows, ed., *Essays on the Law of Restitution* (1991), I would identify four conditions which generally should be satisfied:

(1) The defendant must have been under an equitable obligation, that is, an obligation of the type that courts of equity have enforced, in relation to the activities giving rise to the assets in his hands;

(2) The assets in the hands of the defendant must be shown to have resulted from deemed or actual agency activities of the defendant in breach of his equitable obligation to the plaintiff;

(3) The plaintiff must show a legitimate reason for seeking a proprietary remedy, either personal or related to the need to ensure that others like the defendant remain faithful to their duties and;

(4) There must be no factors which would render imposition of a constructive trust unjust in all the circumstances of the case; e.g., the interests of intervening creditors must be protected.

VIII

[46] Applying this test to the case before us, I conclude that Mr. Korkontzilas' breach of his duty of loyalty sufficed to engage the conscience of the court and support a finding of constructive trust for the following reasons. [The court reviews the facts that support the factors above.]

[50] But there is more. I agree with the Court of Appeal that a constructive trust is required in cases such as this to ensure that agents and others in positions of trust remain faithful to their duty of loyalty: see *Hodgkinson v. Simms,* supra, per La Forest J. If real estate agents are permitted to retain properties which they acquire for themselves in breach of a duty of loyalty to their clients provided they pay market value, the trust and confidence

which underpin the institution of real estate brokerage will be undermined. The message will be clear: real estate agents may breach their duties to their clients and the courts will do nothing about it, unless the client can show that the real estate agent made a profit. This will not do. Courts of equity have always been concerned to keep the person who acts on behalf of others to his ethical mark; this Court should continue in the same path. ...

[52] I conclude that a constructive trust should be imposed. I would dismiss the appeal and confirm the order of the Court of Appeal that the appellants convey the property to the respondent, subject to appropriate adjustments. The respondent is entitled to costs throughout.

Appeal dismissed.   *[5–2]*

ENDNOTES

1. For a review of the Ontario Court of Appeal's unanimous decision in *Entrop v. Imperial Oil Ltd.*, see *The Lawyers Weekly*, August 25, 2000, p. 20.

2. Adapted from *The Globe and Mail*, October 29, 1992, p. A20.

3. See *The Lawyers Weekly*, April 12, 1991, p. 16 for the summary of *Kennedy v. MTD Products Ltd.* of the Ontario Court (General Division).

4. See the unreported case *Murphy v. Canadian Tire Corp.*, Ontario Court of Justice (General Division Registry O. 25752, November 25, 1991).

5. *Kim v. Wray Energy Controls Ltd.*, Ontario Court (General Division) Toronto Region, June, 1992.

6. For a more detailed account see the summary of *Ditchburn v. Landis & Gyr Powers, Ltd.* in *The Lawyers Weekly*, October 27, 1995, p. 1; November 3, 1995, pp. 15, 16; July 10, 1998, p. 3.

7. For a more detailed account see *The Globe and Mail*, November 30, 1999, p. A1.

8. For a more detailed account see *The Lawyers Weekly*, July 21, 2000, p. 6.

9. For a more detailed account of the released report "The Westray Story: A Predictable Path to Disaster" see *The Globe and Mail*, December 2, 1997, p. 1.

10. For a more detailed account see *The Lawyers Weekly*, January 20, 1995, p. 16.

11. For a more detailed account see *The Lawyers Weekly*, February 11, 1994, p. 16.

12. For detailed accounts see *Maclean's*, January 30, 1995, p. 23; February 6, 1995, p. 11.

13. *The Vancouver Sun*, October 25, 2000, p. D1.

14. *The Vancouver Sun*, November 11, 2000, p. A20.

15. For the history of the negotiations and strike see *Maclean's*, August 8, 1994; October 24, 1994, p. 35; January 9, 1995, p. 28; February 6, 1995, p. 37; February 20, 1995; for news of the ratification, *The Vancouver Sun*, November 27, 1996, D1.

16. Summarized from *The Lawyers Weekly*, October 29, 1993, p. 12.

VII

BUSINESS ORGANIZATIONS

A. PARTNERSHIP

Q u e s t i o n s

What is the consequence to you of your partner being incompetent, negligent or dishonest?
What are the terms of the partnership agreement?
What is the consequence of a partner breaching the express or implied terms of that contract?

1. LIABILITY OF PARTNERS TO THIRD PARTIES

Victoria and Grey Trust Company v. *Crawford et al.*

(1986) 57 O.R. (2D) 484
ONTARIO HIGH COURT OF JUSTICE
NOVEMBER 12, 1986

Background facts: A partner in a law firm was acting on behalf of an estate which maintained a savings account at Victoria and Grey Trust Company, the plaintiff. The lawyer was given a cheque for $60,025.61 signed by the executrix of the estate and instructed to transfer the funds from the plaintiff Trust Company to a bank in California. Instead, without the knowledge of his partners, the lawyer destroyed that cheque and created another one on which he made himself the payee and forged the signature of the executrix. He negotiated the cheque at his bank, the Toronto-Dominion Bank in Orillia. The plaintiff trust company, having been told by the estate accountant that the account was being cleared out and knowing that the lawyer was a partner of the defendant firm, honoured the cheque. Later, when the fraud was discovered, the plaintiff trust company (pursuant to the *Bills of Exchange Act*) indemnified (paid back) the Estate because it had paid out on a forged cheque. In this case the trust company is suing the partnership to recover its loss.

Holland J. (orally): — This case involves a claim against partners carrying on the practice of law for the fraud of one of the partners. ...

The plaintiff relies on two sections of the *Partnerships Act*, R.S.O. 1980, c. 370. The defence is that, on the facts of this case, the sections do not apply and that a partnership is not liable for the independent fraud of one of its partners.

Section 11 of the Act reads as follows:

11. Where by any wrongful act or omission of a partner acting in the ordinary course of the business of the firm, or with the authority of his co-partners, loss or injury is caused to a person not being a partner of the firm, or any penalty is incurred, the firm is liable therefor to the same extent as the partner so acting or omitting to act.

Section 12 of the Act reads as follows:

12. In the following cases, namely,

    (a)   where one partner, acting within the scope of his apparent authority, receives the money or property of a third person and misapplies it…the firm is liable to make good the loss.

Dealing with s. 11, it is admitted that there was a wrongful act by a partner, that in acting for the estate and in receiving estate funds or property, Mr. Farr was acting in the ordinary course of the business of the firm, and that loss occurred. It is also agreed that the word "person" in the section includes a corporation. It is submitted, however, that the section does not apply because the "person" who sustained the loss — Victoria & Grey Trust Company — was not dealing with the firm.

Sections 11 and 12 of the Act fall under a heading which reads: "Relation of Partners to Persons Dealing with Them". This raises the point to what extent, in considering the meaning of a section, may or should I have reference to this heading. [The court reviews the Interpretation Act and texts and concludes the headings are not significant as they are not part of the legislation they are inserted after the bill has become law. The court also dismisses the argument that when the lawyer prepared the false cheque he was acting on his own and was not in the scope of his apparent authority.]

For the above reasons there will be judgment for the plaintiff against all defendants for $60,025.61 together with interest at 11% from April 1, 1982, the date upon which the money was replaced in the estate account, together with costs to be assessed.

I have endorsed the record as follows: "Oral Reasons. Judgment for $60,025.61 with interest at 11% from April 1, 1982, together with costs to be assessed."

Thank you, gentlemen.

Judgment for plaintiff.

---

2. Obligations of Partners to Each Other

Olson **v.** *Gullo*

Ontario Court of Justice
No. 32867/88 July 9, 1992

Boland J.: This action arises out of the purchase and sale of ninety acres of land situate in the Township of Georgina and involves claims for damages for breach of contract, breach of fiduciary duty and payment for unjust enrichment. …

It is the plaintiff's position that during the month of February, 1988, he and Gullo entered into an oral partnership agreement for the purpose of acquiring, developing and eventually disposing of the 1,000 acres situate on the west side of Woodbine Avenue. Gullo was to contribute his expertise as a real estate speculator and developer, and Olson was to provide his skills in marketing, promotion, public relations and financing. Olson further contends that it was also agreed that he and Gullo would contribute equal amounts of capital as required to purchase the various farms and they would share equally in the profits.

The defendants, on the other hand, flatly deny that there ever was any partnership agreement. They contend that at no time was there any relationship of trust, confidence and dependence created between the parties. …

The evidence also establishes that … unknown to Olson, in May of 1988, Gullo Enterprises Limited in Trust, entered into an agreement to purchase a ninety-acre farm, known as the Walshe Property, for approximately $20,000 an acre and, prior to closing, assigned the purchase agreement to Wesrow Estates Inc. at a profit of approximately $2,500,000. The Walshe farm was part of the 1,000 acres located on the west side of Woodbine Avenue in the Township of Georgina … . In September, 1988, Olson discovered that Gullo had secretly entered into agreements to purchase and sell the Walshe property at a considerable profit. He expressed his disappointment and anger to Gullo and his employment with [Gullo's company] Glacier Clear Marketing Inc. terminated the end of that month. This action was commenced November 4, 1988.

…

[The judge reviews the evidence]. …

There was a mountain of evidence to support a finding that in February, 1988, Gullo and Olson orally agreed to become equal partners in the purchase of farms within the 1,000 acre tract of land and they anticipated making a great deal of profit. Furthermore, all this evidence supports a finding that the Walshe property was to be purchased and held as partnership lands.

It follows that Gullo and Olson, as partners, were in a fiduciary relationship and each had a duty of the utmost good faith and loyalty to the other and to the partnership. Once the partnership was established, it was not possible for either partner to utilize a partnership opportunity or divert a maturing business opportunity for his exclusive personal gain. Gullo owed a fiduciary duty to disclose all material facts to Olson. The evidence establishes that at no time did Gullo advise Olson of the purchase and sale of the Walshe farm and he never asked Olson to pay his share of the purchase money. He surreptitiously planned to pocket the entire profit of approximately $2,500,000. By secretly purchasing the Walshe property for himself and not for the partnership, Gullo failed to meet the minimum standards the law imposes on a partner and I find this was a serious breach of the fiduciary duty he owed to Olson.

Having found that there was partnership agreement and that Gullo breached that agreement, as well as the fiduciary duty he owed to Olson, one is faced with the difficult issue in this trial which is the appropriate measure of damage to be awarded in these circumstances. Unquestionably Gullo was unjustly enriched as a result of the breach of his fiduciary duty to Olson. At the time the partnership was established, Gullo and Olson had agreed to divide the partnership profits equally. Certainly, Olson is entitled to at least fifty per cent of the profits from the sale of the ninety-acre parcel comprising the Walshe farm. The contentious issue is whether the court should prevent Gullo from retaining any of the proceeds of the sale, including those profits which he was entitled to under the partnership agreement.

Counsel for the defendants argue that should the court find that there was a partnership agreement, Olson is only entitled to his share of the profits in accordance with the terms of that agreement. Counsel for the plaintiff seeks judgment for the entire profit. …

I cannot agree with the defendants' position. I have given a great deal of consideration to the evidence heard during the trial and in my view this is not an appropriate disposition of the profit made on the sale of the Walshe property as there would be no penal aspect to the result. Gullo would receive precisely what he would have received if he had acted honestly and shared the proceeds equally with his partner, Olson. The result provides no disincentive. If this were the rule of law, a fiduciary could breach his trust hoping to hide the breach and after a lengthy trial retain his share of the secret profit. …

Gullo compounded his wrongful conduct by attempting to avoid this litigation by obstructing justice and contracting to kill Olson. He pleaded guilty to two charges of attempt [sic] murder and was sentenced to three years in the penitentiary on each charge to be served concurrently. He was punished for this conduct. However, he also threatened witnesses and police officers were required in the courtroom throughout the trial. The court must demonstrate that it will not tolerate this type of behaviour. …

In this case, the appropriate measure of damages is for Gullo to hand over to Olson the entire secret profit. The court is merely removing the millions of dollars secretly pocketed by Gullo and placing them in the pocket of the plaintiff. In my view this is preferable to encouraging fraudulent conduct and weakening our structures of trust.

For the above reasons there will be a declaration that Norman Olson and Antonio Gullo were partners with each entitled to one-half of the profits. The defendants hold fifty per cent of the profits on the purchase and sale of the Walshe farm in trust for the plaintiff. …

[Judgment for the plaintiff]

Note: On the issue of the proper way to distribute the profit, the decision of the trial judge was appealed. See below.

Olson **v.** *Gullo*

113 D.L.R. (4TH) 42
ONTARIO COURT OF APPEAL
MARCH 1994

Morden A.C.J.O.:—Antonia Gullo Jr., as administrator of the estate of Antonio Gullo Sr., deceased, and Gullo Enterprises Limited appeal from a judgment against them in favour of the plaintiff, Norman Olson, in the amount of $2,486,940. Mr. Olson cross-appeals, with leave, from the costs order in the judgment, seeking to have his costs awarded on a solicitor-and-client basis in place of the party-and-party basis awarded in the judgment. (Antonio Gullo Sr. died after the evidence at the trial was given. His son, Antonio Gullo Jr., was appointed administrator of his estate and an order to continue this proceeding has been granted.) [The judge reviews the basic facts as found by the trial judge and the court's decision.] For the reasons which I shall give, I have concluded, however, that it was contrary to principle and authority in the present case to deprive the defendants of their one-half share in the transaction in question.

The relevant fiduciary principle with which to begin the analysis is expressed in s. 29(1) of the *Partnerships Act*, R.S.O. 1990, c. P5, which reads:

29(1) Every partner *must account to the firm* for any benefit derived by the partner without the consent of the other partners from any transaction concerning the partnership or from any use by the partner of the partnership property, name or business connection. (Emphasis added.)

The same principle is expressed in s. 30 of the Act which reads:

30. If a partner, without the consent of the other partners, carries on a business of the same nature as and competing with that of the firm, the partner *must account for and pay over to the firm* all profits made by the partner in that business. (Emphasis added.)…

We must … begin our consideration with the basic premise that the profit in question is the property of the partnership, not of all the partners except the defaulting partner. To exclude the wrongdoer would be to effect a forfeiture of his or her interest in this partnership property. The point may be understood by considering a starker form of wrongdoing—a case where a partner misappropriates partnership funds for his own benefit. In such a case I am not aware of any principle or decision to the effect that not only must the partner account to the partnership for the money but must also suffer a forfeiture of his or her interest in it. In fact, the case law of which I am aware is to the contrary. …

[He then reviews a Supreme Court of Canada decision in *Sutton v. Forst* (1924) and a Massachusetts case *Shulkin v. Shulkin* (1938) which supported that position.]

I have not found any United States decision to the contrary. …

I have no doubt that stripping the wrongdoing partner of the whole of the profit, including his or her own share in it, is a strong disincentive to conduct which breaches the fiduciary obligation. Further, as a host of equity decisions have shown for at least two centuries, the fact that this would result in a windfall gain to the plaintiff cannot, in itself, be a valid objection to it.

I do not however, think that it can accurately be said that the defaulting partner does profit from his wrong when he receives his pre-ordained share of the profit. With respect to this share, the partner's conduct in the impugned transaction does not involve any breach of duty. Under the terms of the relationship, with respect to this share, it was expected that the partner would act in his own interest. To the extent that there is a dilemma, I resolve the issue, in accordance with what I consider to be the more appropriate principles and authorities, against the forfeiture of the wrongdoing partner's interest in the profit.

I mention, for the sake of completeness, that in awarding the penal remedy the trial judge appears to have taken into account very serious criminal conduct of Mr. Gullo related to this litigation. This conduct took place after the events giving rise to Mr. Olson's claim and Mr. Gullo was convicted and sentenced for it. In my view it is not relevant to the remedy and it is not submitted on Mr. Olson's behalf that it is.

I turn now to the cross-appeal respecting the basis on which the plaintiff's costs should be assessed … [I]n light of the variation of the judgment which I propose, I think that this is now an entirely proper case for the award of solicitor-and-client costs of the action. The plaintiff has been the victim of the breach of a fiduciary obligation and it is appropriate for the court to express its disapproval of the defendants' conduct: see *Maximillian v. M. Rash & Co.* (1987), 62. O.R. (2d) 206 … The criminal conduct referred to in the proceeding paragraph, which involved counselling to have Mr. Olson killed, is also relevant to this issue.

For the foregoing reasons I would allow the appeal, with costs, and vary the trial judgment to provide that the plaintiff recover one-half of the profit in question. …

I would allow the cross-appeal, without costs, and vary the costs order to provide that the plaintiff be awarded the costs of the action on a solicitor-and-client basis.

Appeal allowed; cross-appeal allowed.

Note: The Supreme Court of Canada refused to hear an appeal.

B. THE CORPORATION

Questions

When will the law not allow a person to rely on the priniciple that a company is a separate legal entity?

If a person chooses to use the corporate structure for carrying on business, can he or she avoid personal liability?

---

1. LIFTING THE CORPORATE VEIL

Lockharts Ltd. **v.** *Excalibur Holdings Ltd. et al.*

210 A.P.R. 181
NOVA SCOTIA SUPREME COURT
DECEMBER 14, 1987

Background facts: Mr. Harrison and his wife were the sole shareholders of two companies, Baron Developments Ltd. (Baron), a construction company, and Excalibur Holdings Ltd., (Excalibur), an investment company. Baron bought a piece of property under an Agreement for Sale from Clayton Developments Limited (Clayton) and began construction of a house. The plaintiff Lockharts Ltd. contracted with Baron to supply building materials. When Baron failed to pay its account, Lockharts Ltd. sued Baron and a default judgment was entered in favour of Lockharts Ltd. for $19,513.80 on March 14, 1986. Both Baron and Excalibur had notice of the judgment.

On June 24, 1986 Excalibur bought the land from Clayton and took an assignment from Baron of all Baron's interest in the land under the Agreement for Sale with the result that Excalibur had both legal and equitable interest in the property and Baron, the judgment debtor, no longer owned any property.

Davison, J.: ...

ISSUES: ...

[T]he plaintiff's submissions to me were:

(1) That the events which took place in June, 1986, constituted a fraudulent scheme designed to defeat the rights of the plaintiff under the judgment. Therefore, it is submitted I should ignore the separate corporate entity of Excalibur and grant an order declaring the judgment "binding upon... the assets and land of the defendant, Excalibur."

(2) That an order should issue declaring the judgment against Baron an encumbrance against the land known as lot 9-44 Grenadier Drive by reason of s. 18 of the *Registry Act*, R.S.N.S. 19967, c. 265, and the equitable interest of Baron in the land pursuant to the agreement of purchase and sale. ...

LIFTING THE CORPORATE VEIL

Since *Salomon v. Salomon & Co. Ltd.*, [1897] A.C. 22, it has been a clear principle of law that a company is an independent legal entity distinct from its shareholders. In this case the plaintiff asks me to "lift the corporate veil" on the grounds of fraud. The plaintiff says Mr. Harrison used Excalibur to strip the assets of Baron to avoid payment to the plaintiff of the amount of the judgment.

In England there have been signs that the firm principle of *Salomon* has been the subject of some erosion and the most often quoted comments are those of Lord Denning in *Littlewoods Mail Order Stores Ltd. v. McGregor*, [1969] 3 All E.R. 855, at 860:

> ... I decline to treat the Fork Company as a separate and independent entity. The doctrine laid down in *Salomon v. Salomon & Co. Ltd.* has to be watched very carefully. It has often been supposed to cast a veil over the personality of a limited company through which the courts cannot see. But that is not true. The courts can and often do draw aside the veil. They can, and often do, pull off the mask. They look to see what really lies behind. ... I think that we should look at the Fork Company and see it as it really is — the wholly-owned subsidiary of the taxpayers. It is the creature, the puppet, of the taxpayers in point of *fact*: and it should be so regarded in point of *law*.

The facts in *Jones v. Lipman* [1962] 1 W.L.R. 832, are similar to the facts before me. The defendant, Lipman, entered an agreement with the plaintiff to sell a parcel of land but before completion under the agreement Lipman transferred the land to a company the sole shareholders of which were Lipman and a clerk at the office of Lipman's solicitor. The court granted an order requiring both defendants to perform the agreement with the plaintiff. Mr. Justice Russell found that the company was a sham or "a mask which he (Lipman) holds before his face in an attempt to avoid recognition by the eye of equity."

In *Merchandise Transport Ltd. v. British Transport Commission*, [1962] 2 Q.B. 173, a transport company which owned vehicles applied for licences in the name of a subsidiary company because it feared it would be unsuccessful if the application was in its own name. The court refused to treat parent and subsidiary companies as independent bodies and decided the issue as if they were one commercial unit. ...

In Canada, the principle enunciated in *Salomon* is alive and well, but it is also clear that courts will disregard the corporate entity in certain circumstances including situations involving "fraud or improper conduct." Authors of texts on company law are fond of saying that the only consistent principle which has evolved is that in the *Salomon* case (see Gower, *The Principles of Modern Company Law* (3rd Ed.) p. 189). In my respectful opinion the courts have been equally consistent in clearly enunciating an exception to the basic principle by refusing to permit a corporate entity to be used for fraudulent or improper purposes. It is true that there has been inconsistency in the application of this exception but the existence of the exception has been recognized by all levels of Canadian Courts.

In his dissenting judgment in *Jodrey's Estate v. Province of Nova Scotia* (1980), 41 N.S.R. (2d) 181; 76 A.P.R. 181; 32 N.R. 275, Chief Justice Dickson was clearly of the view that the principle of *Salomon* has been rigidly applied in the Canadian Courts but also recognized the exception with these words at page 228 N.W.R., A.P.R.

> Generally speaking in the *absence of fraud or improper conduct* the courts cannot disregard the separate existence of a corporate entity: (emphasis added).

...

The Saskatchewan Court of Appeal in *Nedco v. Clark et al.* (1973) 43 D.L.R. (3d) 714, referred to *Toronto v. Famous Players Canadian Corp.*, [1936] 2 D.L.R. 129, as an illustration of how the Supreme Court of Canada has recognized "the right to pierce the corporate veil for a specific purpose." After reviewing a number of authorities, Chief Justice Culliton concluded at p. 721:

> ...while the principle laid down in *Salomon v. Salomon & Co. Ltd.*, supra, is and continues to be a fundamental feature of Canadian law, there are instances in which the court can and should lift the corporate veil, but whether it does so depends upon the facts in each particular case. Moreover, the fact that the court does lift the corporate veil for a specific purpose in no way destroys the recognition of the corporation as an independent and autonomous entity for all other purposes.

The recognition of the right by the Supreme Court of Canada is even more apparent since the dicta of Madame Justice Wilson in *Kosmopoulos v. Constitution Insurance Co. of Canada* (1987), 74 N.R. 360: 21 O.A.C. 4; 34 D.L.R. (4th) 208, at 213-214. ...

What can be drawn from the foregoing authorities? In my assessment, the fundamental principle enunciated in the *Salomon* case remains good law in Canada and "one man corporations" should be considered as separate entities from their major shareholder save for certain exceptional cases. A judge should not "lift the veil" simply because he believes it would be in the interest of "fairness" or of "justice." If that was the test the veil in Salomon case would have been lifted. On the other hand the courts have the power indeed the duty, to look behind the corporate structure and to ignore it if it is being used for fraudulent or improper purposes or as a "puppet" to the detriment of a third party.

One of the fundamental purposes of establishing a corporate existence is to limit the liability of the shareholders. In doing so, growth of commerce is encouraged by providing a vehicle by which monies can be invested with the knowledge that losses would be restricted to an amount usually equivalent to the extent of the investment.

The purpose of the corporate entity was not to defraud or mislead others including creditors and shareholders and in my opinion where a company is being used for this purpose the "veil" should be lifted and a remedy made available to the victims of such conduct.

In the case before me the plaintiff supplied materials to Baron when Baron had an equitable interest in the lands on which the building, for which the material was to be used, was to be constructed. After Baron defaulted in payment, the plaintiff secured a judgment which, if the agreement for purchase and sale had been completed, would have attached to Baron's legal interest in the land and dwelling. After the judgment was obtained no effort was made to complete under the purchase and sale agreement and the property was conveyed to Excalibur which, like Baron, is solely owned by the principal, Harrison. The sequence and nature of the documents and events raised a strong *prima facie* inference that the conveyance from Clayton Developments Limited to Excalibur was intended to defeat the rights of the plaintiff. It was incumbent upon the defendants to adduce evidence to rebut that inference. In my opinion, the defendants failed to meet that burden. The plaintiff has convinced me, on the balance of probabilities, having regard to the gravity of the finding (see *Hanes v. Wawanesa Mutual Ins. Co.*, [1963] S.C.R. 154, at 162) that Mr. Harrison made use of Excalibur for a fraudulent and improper purpose.

Mr. Harrison would have the court believe that the reason for having the conveyance in the name of Excalibur was because Excalibur could complete the construction; whereas Baron did not have financial resources to do so. I do not accept this evidence and it is not supported by any other evidence. ...

I was not convinced by the evidence that Baron could not have completed under the agreement of sale. There was no evidence of any attempts by Mr. Harrison to secure funds other than the two conversations he had with Mr. Lisson [the lender]. Even if Baron did not have the ability to secure funds by itself why couldn't Excalibur have guaranteed to loan Baron? This would have achieved the same result and would have permitted the agreement to have been completed as originally contemplated.

If the situation had been such that the agreement of purchase and sale had been completed before the judgment was entered and legal title conveyed from Baron to Excalibur after the entry of the judgment, that conveyance could have been set aside pursuant to the terms of the *Assignments and Preferences Act*, R.S.N.S. 1967, c.16. In effect, that is precisely what occurred in this case, except that title was retained in Clayton Developments Limited until the appropriate time.

In my opinion, the evidence clearly establishes that the corporate entities owned by Mr. Harrison were used as "puppets" to the detriment of the plaintiff and in that respect were used for fraudulent and improper purposes.

My conclusion is that the plaintiff is entitled to declaratory relief and that an order, declaring that the plaintiff's judgment against Baron is binding upon and forms a charge upon the interest of Excalibur on the lands referred to in the deed of conveyance from Clayton Developments Limited to Excalibur dated the 24th day of June 1986 should issue. ...

The plaintiff shall recover from the defendants its costs.

Judgment for plaintiff.

Property owned by Riverside Fisheries Ltd. of Windsor, Ontario was destroyed by fire. When the insurance company refused to compensate the company for its loss on the grounds that the fire was deliberately set, Riverside Fisheries Ltd. sued the insurance company.

The following are the concluding words of Judge Walsh of the Ontario Supreme Court. "There is no doubt whatsoever but that the fire was deliberately set, most probably the work of a professional arsonist. After a most careful and anxious scrutiny of all the facts and circumstances I find that the defendants have satisfied the onus imposed on them.

"Mr. Shulgan [counsel for the plaintiff], in a most novel argument, submitted that even if I should find, as I have, that the plaintiff Irving Goldhar was responsible for the fire, it should not prevent recovery by the corporate plaintiff, Riverside Fisheries Limited on the ground that it is a separate legal entity and its recovery should not be barred by the guilt or wrongdoing of Irving Goldhar, even though he is its president and principal shareholder.

"This submission is based by analogy to the recent decision of the Ontario Court of Appeal in *Higgins v. Orion Insurance Co.*, 50 O.R. (2d) 352, which held that arson on the part of one partner did not deprive a co-insured innocent partner from recovering from the insurer the loss actually sustained by him.

"A close perusal of the reasons of Robins J.A. in the Higgins case makes it abundantly clear that given the interwoven family business relationships here existent public policy considerations would never qualify Riverside as 'an innocent partner' as that term was used in that judgment.

"The plaintiffs' action is therefore dismissed. ..."

Riverside Fisheries Ltd. et al. v. Economical Mutual Insurance Co. et al.
(1986) 19 C.C.L.I. 130
Ontario Supreme Court

2. DUTIES OF A DIRECTOR

Q u e s t i o n s

What are your duties as a director and to whom are they owed?
What is the consequence of being in breach of those duties?

China Software Corp. **v.** *Leimbigler et al.*

(1989) 27 C.P.R. (3D) 215
SUPREME COURT OF BRITISH COLUMBIA
JUNE 15, 1989

Callaghan J.: — The plaintiff claims damages from the defendants, two of its former directors and shareholders, for breach of fiduciary duty in intentionally misleading the plaintiff as to the state and cost of completion of the TM (Tianma) Chinese Text Generator and Word Processor System in order to induce the plaintiff to sell the system to Malaspina College.

The Chinese text generation and word processing system is a system for generating and handling Chinese character text (Hanzi text). The system automatically converts text from the standard romanized form of Chinese (Pinyin) into Hanzi text . ...and permits the user to look up the English equivalent of a Chinese word, as well as the Chinese synonyms of a Chinese word, a useful feature for individuals who work with the Chinese language.

[By 1985 a group consisting of Dr. Leimbigler, a linguist, Mr. Slade, who had expertise in the computer field, Mr. Green a lawyer who could assist in raising venture capital and Kambeitz, who had computer equipment and the willingness to work on the project, formed a company, China Software Corporation, the plaintiff in this case. The development of the software system proceeded on schedule. Regular project review meetings were held. At one such meeting it was agreed that Leimbigler and Kambeitz should go to China and Japan to demonstrate the software system. On their return from the trip, Leimbigler reported to Green that neither Sony or NCR was interested in the system and that it would take another eight to ten months to complete the prototype at a cost of approximately $200,000 to $300,000. The information with regard to timing and cost was contrary to what he had led his partners to believe before the trip.

Later that month, in August of 1985, the company rejected an offer to purchase the system for $100,000 from International Geosystems Corporation. Within a few days Leimbigler advised that Malaspina College was prepared to offer $100,000 cash and urged acceptance. At the meetings in which the offer was discussed, Leimbigler again said the prototype could not be completed for another eight to ten months and would cost an additional $200,000 to $300,000 and that similar systems were being developed. Furthermore, Leimbigler and Kambeitz indicated they would abandon their work on the system if the sale was not completed. Green and Slade reluctantly concluded the company should accept the Malaspina offer.

Unknown to the company, Leimbigler and Kambeitz had surreptitiously negotiated an agreement with Malaspina College under which they would form a limited partnership which would benefit Leimbigler and Kambeitz. When Green learned of the

agreement, he demanded the disclosure of its contents to the company. Despite initial statements to mislead the company about the nature of the agreement and reluctance to disclose its contents, meetings were held at which the details of the agreement were disclosed and the parties negotiated an arrangement to resolve the matter. Malaspina rejected the arrangement.

The company later agreed to proceed with the sale without a satisfactory arrangement because it was clear that Leimbigler and Kambeitz would not complete the project. The College insisted that with the sale of the system the company execute a general release of Leimbigler, Kambeitz and Malaspina. The company agreed. Leimbigler and Kambeitz transferred their shares in the company back to the company and gave up their share of the $100,000 of the sale proceeds.

The system was soon sold to three men who sold it to International Geosystems Corporation. Malaspina received $150,000 cash and a promissory note for $150,000. Leimbigler and Kambeitz received $100,000 and 250,000 shares of International Geosystems Corporation valued at $2.00 a share.] ...

Clearly there was a fiduciary relationship. The defendants breached that relationship in order to obtain a more abundant award through the agreement entered into with Malaspina College.

Counsel for the defendants candidly acknowledges that the defendants likely have no defence on the merits since there are no extenuating circumstances sufficient to justify the defendants' positioning themselves as they did to take a corporate opportunity that belonged to China Software Corporation. The defence proceeded on the assumption that the two defendants were guilty of misrepresentation and non-disclosure in order to induce the sale by China Software to Malaspina College, as pleaded. Counsel submits, however, that the plaintiff gave these two defendants a full release and discharge in connection with a claim of breach of trust which was not induced by any fraud or misrepresentation and consequently cannot be set aside. ...

While the argument in many respects at first blush is inviting, it is clear that the plaintiff would not have consummated an agreement with Malaspina College if it had been aware of the ongoing interest of International Geosystems Corporation and Sony, all of which was kept from it by the secretive conduct of the defendants. Malaspina had no interest in keeping to itself the technology acquired but was desirous of marketing the system in order to recoup its $100,000 investment. The defendants' failure to divulge information of the interest of other parties, the representation (which was false) that it would take eight to ten months and $200,000 to $300,000 to complete the prototype, and the refusal of the defendants to work further on the project were the effectual causes of the sale to Malaspina. The plaintiff, because of the intractable position of Malaspina (it refused to purchase unless it and the two defendants Leimbigler and Kambeitz were provided with a final release and discharge), as well as the misrepresentation of the defendants, was left, because of the disparity in their positions, with little choice. To accede to the defendant's' argument would be tantamount to condoning the fraudulent misrepresentations perpetrated by the two defendants. The plaintiff was induced to grant the release as a result of non-disclosure of material information and because of the fraudulent misrepresentations already alluded to.

In dealing with the submission of the defendants that the final release was effective to bar the claim of the plaintiff because the release was not obtained by a fraud or misrepresentation on the part of the defendants, I need only point out that the release and sale were inextricably bound. If the defendants had divulged to the plaintiff that International Geosystems Corporation and Sony had shown great interest in the China Software System and if they had represented the true state of affairs as to the system's cost and completion time, the release would not have been executed, nor would the sale to Malaspina have been proceeded with.

There need not be misrepresentation with respect to the document itself. The releasor may be fully cognizant as to what he is signing but if the defendants, who are in a fiduciary position, have misrepresented the true state of affairs to which the release is directed, breaching their fiduciary duty and thereby inducing the plaintiff to execute the release, the release will be set aside: *Francis v. Dingman* (1983) 2. (4th) 244, 43 O.R. (2d) 641, 23 B.L.R. 234 (C.A.)

The release was obtained as a result of deliberate non-disclosure and fraudulent misrepresentations and, accordingly, is vitiated.

Considering the admissions or concessions made by counsel for the defendants, it hardly seems necessary for me to proceed to discuss the doctrine that company directors stand in a fiduciary relationship to the company they represent, in that they must:

(a) act honestly and in good faith and in the best interests of the company;
(b) disclose the nature and extent of any personal interest they have in a proposed contract, and
(c) disclose any and all conflicts.

These basic principles have been enshrined in ss. 142, 144 and 147 of the Company Act, R.S.B.C. 1979, c. 59.

It is of course a fundamental rule of equity that a person in a fiduciary capacity must not place himself in a position where his duty and personal interest conflict. The rule is clearly enunciated by Lord Herschell in *Bray v. Ford*, [1896] A.C. 44 (H.L.), at p. 51:

> It is an inflexible rule of a Court of Equity that a person in a fiduciary position, such as the respondent's, is not, unless otherwise expressly provided, entitled to make a profit; he is not allowed to put himself in a position where his interest and duty conflict. It does not appear to me that this rule is, as has been said, founded upon principles of morality. I regard it rather as based on the considera-

tion that, human nature being what it is, there is danger, in such circumstances, of the person holding a fiduciary position being swayed by interest rather than by duty, and thus prejudicing those whom he was bound to protect. It has, therefore, been deemed expedient to lay down this positive rule.

The leading Canadian case on fiduciary obligations is *Canadian Aero Service Ltd. v. O'Malley* (1973), 11 C.P.R. (2d) 206, 40 D.L.R. (3d) 371, [1974] S.C.R. 592. At p. 219, Laskin J. (as he then was), in discussing the fiduciary duties of directors, said:

> An examination of the case law in this Court and in the Courts of other like jurisdiction on the fiduciary duties of directors and senior officers shows the pervasiveness of a strict ethic in this area of the law. In my opinion, this ethic disqualifies a director or senior officer from usurping for himself or diverting to another person or company with whom or with which he is associated a maturing business opportunity which his company is actively pursuing; he is also precluded from so acting even after his resignation where the resignation may fairly be said to have been prompted or influenced by a wish to acquire for himself the opportunity sought by the company, or where it was his position with the company rather than a fresh initiative that led him to the opportunity which he later acquired.

After quoting from the judgment of Viscount Sankey and Lord Russell of Killowen in *Regal (Hastings), Ltd. v. Gulliver*, [1942] 1 All E.R. 378 (H.L), at pp. 381 and 389, he went on to say, at p. 220: "The reaping of a profit by a person at a company's expense while a director thereof is, of course, an adequate ground upon which to hold the director accountable." Further, at p. 221:

> What these decisions indicate is an updating of the equitable principle whose roots lie in the general standards that I have already mentioned, namely, loyalty, good faith and avoidance of a conflict of duty and self interest. Strict application against directors and senior management officials is simply recognition of the degree of control which their positions give them in corporate operations, a control which rises above day accountability to owning shareholders and which comes under some scrutiny only at annual general or at special meetings. It is a necessary supplement, in the public interest, of statutory regulation and accountability which themselves are, at one and the same time, an acknowledgment of the importance of the corporation in the life of the community and of the need to compel obedience by it and by its promoters, directors and managers to norms of exemplary behaviour.

The conduct of the two defendants falls far short of the conduct that one would expect of a director and employee and, in effect, was a stratagem concocted and developed in order to appropriate unto themselves a business opportunity which in fairness belonged to the plaintiff.

As a result of this breach there must be a disgorgement of profits. ...

Judgment accordingly.

3. Liability of Directors

Question

If the company structure is used for improper conduct, we have seen that the law will "lift the corporate veil." In what other ways might a director be found liable for a debt?

Petro-Canada supplied fuel and services to a company (1127388 Ontario Inc.) after it was given a personal guarantee from Satraj Singh Matharu, who represented himself as the president of the company. He was not the president of the company and the actual presidents (C. Jain until the day before Matharu signed the guarantee and then his son S. Jain) did not inform Petro-Canada of the true status of the parties. The agent for Petro-Canada alleges that if he had known the true state of affairs he would have "requested other security and guarantees" before agreeing to supply the fuel.

Petro-Canada sued for unpaid accounts. Both C. and S. Jain, defendants in the action, moved to have the claim against them dismissed as having no sustainable cause of action against them. The motion was dismissed. In the words of Judge E. Macdonald:

"[13] I conclude that this case is not so "open and shut" .... The undisputed chronology of events suggests, at the very least, that the Jain Defendants may be exposed to liability. Misrepresentation can occur as a result of silence, and an implied misrepresentation can give rise to actionable negligence.

[14] The themes of misrepresentation through silence and of implied misrepresentation have been considered in both *The Queen v. Cognos Inc.* (1993), 99 D.L.R. (4th) 626 (S.C.C.) and *Spinks v. Canada* (C.A.), [1996] 2 F.C. 563 (C.A.). In *Queen v. Cognos Inc.*, supra, the Supreme Court allowed an appeal in an action involving damages for negligent misrepresentation. The case concerned an appellant who was attempting, through an action in tort, to recover damages caused by alleged negligent misrepresentations articulated by the respondent's representative in a hiring interview. In that case ... Iacobucci J. stated that ... that negligent conduct by the representor may "[i]n some cases" include "the failure to divulge highly pertinent information." In *Spinks v. Canada* (C.A.), supra, a case involving a successful appeal from the dismissal of an action against an employer who had provided erroneous advice, Linden J.A., writing for a unanimous Federal Court of Appeal, said the following ... :

> It seems to me that where one party is advising another, the failure to divulge material information may be just as misleading as a positive misstatement. Missing information can be just as harmful as mistaken information. Both types of advice are equally erroneous. This is especially the case where, as here, the information in question is of a specialized nature, which is easily available to the advisor but not easily obtainable by the party being advised. In such a context, the duty of an advisor is to advise competently, accurately, and fully.

. . .

[16] It is also well settled that, as officers of 1127388, the Jain Defendants may be liable for their own "independent" tortious acts, especially if they made a misrepresentation in bad faith to a third-party in a special relationship with them, and that third-party relied on the misrepresentation to its own detriment. In *ADGA Systems International Ltd. v. Valcolm Limited.* (1999), 43 O.R. (3d) 101 (C.A.), a case concerning the liability of corporate officers and directors for acts done in furthering a corporate purpose, Carthy J.A. stated, at p. 107, that "[t]he consistent line of au-

thority in Canada holds simply that, in all events, officers, directors and employees of corporations are responsible for their tortious conduct even though that conduct was directed in a bona fide manner to the best interests of the company, always subject to the *Said v. Butt* exception." (See *Said v. Butt*, [1920] 3 K.B. 497 [in which it was held that if "a servant acting bona fide within the scope of his authority procures or causes a breach of contract between his employer and a third person, he does not thereby become liable to an action in tort at the suit of the person whose contract has thereby been broken"]). ...

Disposition

[19] In responding to the defendants' motion, Petro-Canada has adduced some evidence that falls inside the category of what may invoke personal liability on the part of the Jain Defendants. In fact, Petro-Canada has adduced some evidence that indicates that the Jain Defendants' silence may have constituted implied representations that were negligent, misleading, or fraudulent.

[20] For these reasons, I have endorsed the record that this motion is dismissed. ..."

Petro-Canada Inc. v. 1127388 Ontario Inc.
[2000] O.J. No. 2798 (Q.L.)
Ontario Superior Court of Justice
July 27, 2000

- *O*ral presentation to prospective purchasers has traditionally been a method of marketing the shares of a company embarking on its initial public offering. These "roadshows" are now on the Internet, forcing administrators responsible for preventing securities fraud to create policy and issue guidelines that will accommodate the new technological methods of marketing and will also protect buyers.[1]

4. Rights of the Shareholders

Relief from Oppression

Question

Do the statutes that provide for business corporations afford any protection to the shareholders?

Lee v. To

[1998] S.J. No. 347 (Q.L.)
Saskatchewan Court of Appeal
May 12, 1998

Tallis, J.A.:

[1] In this action, brought under s. 234 of The Business Corporations Act, R.S.S. 1978, c. B-10 (BCA), the appellants Tom Nghia Thach To and Sandra Sieu Hien To appeal from a judgment for $50,000 entered against them on June 27, 1997. In this judgment ... the respondents were granted relief under s. 234 on the grounds that "their rights as minority shareholders [in Rose Valley Grocery Ltd.] have been unfairly prejudiced and their interests have been unfairly disregarded by [appellants] within the meaning of s. 234 of the BCA." At the conclusion of the appellants' argument we affirmed this finding and only called upon the respondents to address the appropriateness of the remedy granted by the learned trial judge.

[2] Subsection 234(2) of the BCA empowers the Court, fol-

lowing a finding of "oppressive" conduct thereunder, to make an order "to rectify the matters complained of". ...

[3] The present controversy arises out of the respondents' decision to invest in a grocery business operated by the appellants at Rose Valley, Saskatchewan.

[4] In 1991, the respondents who were then resident in Hong Kong decided to apply under Canada's Immigrant Investment Program. They were approached by their sister-in-law (a personal friend of the appellants), to invest money in the appellants' grocery business at Rose Valley. With that the respondents contacted the appellants and sought assurances that the business was viable financially. Although requested financial statements were not provided at that time, the respondent Jimmy Lee testified that he relied on "Tom To's guarantee" that the grocery

business was financially stable and profitable, that he would be provided with a job with sufficient income to support his family when they came to Canada and that after a period of training under Mr. To, he would be fully involved in the management and day to day operations of the business.

[5] Rose Valley Grocery Ltd. was incorporated in August 1991 and the appellants became the sole shareholders, officers and directors, having been allotted 1267 shares in consideration of the transfer of the business to the company. Given the requirements of the Immigrant Investor Program, the respondents then purchased 621 of the appellant's shares, representing 49 percent of the issued capital stock of the company. They paid the appellants $75,000 cash. The appellants, as majority shareholders and the directors of the company, assumed the sole management of its business, pending the arrival of the respondents.

[6] In addition to the grocery business the appellants operated a restaurant in Rose Valley which occupied a significant amount of their time.

[7] Although this investment in the grocery business was made in 1991, the respondents did not move to Canada and Rose Valley until June of 1994. Unfortunately the parties did not get along in their business relationship. The respondent Jimmy Lee tried to determine the financial status of his investment but the appellants were not forthcoming with the information or relevant financial statements. In 1995 the parties terminated their relationship and the respondent left Rose Valley and commenced this application.

[The judge enters several pages of the trial judge's decision which summarized the situation and turns to the present issue of the appropriate remedy.]

[11] The appellants challenge the remedy ... [of $50,000 entered against them personally]. They contend that before any monetary judgment is awarded under s. 234, the court must conduct a full hearing to first value the assets of the corporation and then determine the value of the shares. ...

[13] In this case the learned trial judge was well aware of the approach frequently employed in cases of this kind. But trial of an issue to determine such matters was not a reasonable or practical approach. The evidence of each of the two chartered accountants who submitted affidavit evidence, one on behalf of each party, made it clear that the state of accounts between the respondents and the grocery business or the restaurant and grocery business could never be determined with accuracy. ... Given the intermingling of funds and the impossibility of reconstructing accurate records a remedy such as an accounting would serve no useful purpose.

[14] The essential question is whether an alternative remedy is available and appropriate in the circumstances of this case. Since we must focus on the potential scope of the remedies under s. 234 and their application to the circumstances of this case, we find it convenient to reproduce that section in material part:

234(1) A complainant may apply to a court for an order under this section.

(2) If ... the court is satisfied that in respect of a corporation or any of its affiliates: ...

(b) the business or affairs of the corporation or any of its affiliates are or have been carried on or conducted in a manner; or

(c) the powers of the directors of the corporation or any of its affiliates are or have been exercised in a manner;

that is oppressive or unfairly prejudicial to or that unfairly disregards the interests of any security holder, creditor, director or officer, the court may make an order to rectify the matters complained of.

(3) In connection with an application under this section, the court may make any interim or final order it thinks fit including, without limiting the generality of the foregoing:

[The court reviews the multitude of remedies granted to the court under s. 234 including:]

(g) an order directing a corporation, subject to subsection (6), or any other person, to pay to a security holder any part of the moneys paid by him for securities; ...

[16] As a starting point we observe that these statutory provisions mark a substantial departure from the traditional common law rules governing corporations. Under this provision minority shareholders are no longer faced with a "hands-off" approach with the courts being powerless to deal with the internal management of corporations. The Legislature had this object and purpose in mind when it passed such legislation. This purpose must be kept in mind when reviewing the appropriateness of a remedy ....

[18] In small closely held corporations the determination of an appropriate "oppression" remedy is frequently intertwined with the reasonable expectations of a minority shareholder. ...

[19] The "oppressive" conduct found in this case not only demonstrates the appellants' disregard of their legal obligations as directors, officers, and managers of the grocery company and its business, legally made possible by their majority shareholding, it also strikes at the very basic and most fundamental expectations of the respondents as shareholders. The failure of the appellants in one or another of their capacities to maintain basic records, coupled with their intermingling of money between the grocery company and their restaurant business, illustrates the extent to which they disregarded the interests and expectations of the respondents as minority shareholders. With this type of conduct, the respondents' interests as shareholders were in peril from the very beginning. The persistent failure or refusal of the appellants to produce relevant financial information to the respondents marked a continuation of this pattern of utter disregard of the interests of the respondents. The appellants, in their various capacities, simply paid no attention to the respondents' interests in the company and its business, but chose to ignore or treat their interests as of no importance. ... Indeed, they operated this grocery business as if it were a sole proprietorship, in complete disregard of its incorporation and of the fundamental objects and expectations of the share transaction by which they had transferred a 49 percent interest in the business to the respondents for $75,000.

[20] Since the usual remedies available to "rectify the matters complained of" such as accounting or winding up would have served no useful purpose in this case, the learned trial judge granted relief under s. 234(3)(g) but limited to ordering repay-

ment of $50,000, being two thirds of the original purchase price of the shares. ... He ordered the respondents to transfer their shares to the appellants upon payment, with the appellants then at liberty to continue and carry on the company as a sole proprietorship, or arrange a sale if so minded. This relief, which is case specific, was the only effective means available to rectify to some extent the unfair disregard of the interests of the respondents. [The judge reviews the case law supporting this remedy.]

[27] Given the circumstances of this case we decline to inter-

fere with the order directed against the appellants under s. 234(g). Furthermore, we would not interfere with the discretion exercised by the learned trial judge in discounting the amount payable by one-third of the original investment. ...

[29] In the result the within appeal is dismissed with costs. ...

Unanimous

B. DERIVATIVE ACTION

Question

What if the company has been wronged but the company through its directors won't sue?

Hercules Managements Ltd. v. Ernst & Young

Background facts of this Supreme Court of Canada case are given on p. 72 above. In short, investors allege that their investment loss was caused by the company auditors who prepared the annual financial statements. The Court dismissed their claims on policy grounds. It held that the statements were prepared for the shareholders as a collective body, not for the shareholders to make investment decisions, and that to hold otherwise would subject auditors to indeterminate liability. The following is the decision of Justice La Forest on the issue of whether or not the shareholders' action against the auditors hired by the company should properly be a derivative action.

La Forest, J.:—

... Does the rule in *Foss v. Harbottle* affect the appellants' action? ...

ISSUE 2: THE EFFECT OF THE RULE IN *FOSS V. HARBOTTLE*

[58] All the participants in this appeal—the appellants, the respondents, and the intervener—raised the issue of whether the appellants' claims in respect of the losses they suffered in their existing shareholdings through their alleged inability to oversee management of the corporations ought to have been brought as a derivative action in conformity with the rule in *Foss v. Harbottle* rather than as a series of individual actions. The issue was also raised and discussed in the courts below. In my opinion, a derivative action—commenced, as required, by an application under s. 232 of *the Manitoba Corporations Act*—would have been the proper method of proceeding with respect to this claim. Indeed, I would regard this simply as a corollary of the idea that the audited reports are provided to the shareholders as a group in order to allow them to take collective (as opposed to individual) decisions. Let me explain.

[59] The rule in *Foss v. Harbottle* provides that individual shareholders have no cause of action in law for any wrongs done to the corporation and that if an action is to be brought in respect of such losses, it must be brought either by the corporation itself (through management) or by way of a derivative action. The legal rationale behind the rule was eloquently set out by the English Court of Appeal in *Prudential Assurance Co. v. Newman Industries*

Ltd. (No. 2), [1982] 1 All E.R. 354, at p. 367, as follows:

> The rule [in *Foss v. Harbottle*] is the consequence of the fact that a corporation is a separate legal entity. Other consequences are limited liability and limited rights. The company is liable for its contracts and torts; the shareholder has no such liability. The company acquires causes of action for breaches of contract and for torts which damage the company. No cause of action vests in the shareholder. When the shareholder acquires a share he accepts the fact that the value of his investment follows the fortunes of the company and that he can only exercise his influence over the fortunes of the company by the exercise of his voting rights in general meeting. The law confers on him the right to ensure that the company observes the limitations of its memorandum of association and the right to ensure that other shareholders observe the rule, imposed on them by the articles of association. If it is right that the law has conferred or should in certain restricted circumstances confer further rights on a shareholder the scope and consequences of such further rights require careful consideration.

To these lucid comments, I would respectfully add that the rule is also sound from a policy perspective, inasmuch as it avoids the procedural hassle of a multiplicity of actions.

[60] The manner in which the rule in *Foss v. Harbottle*, supra, operates with respect to the appellants' claims can thus be demonstrated. As I have already explained, the appellants allege that they

were prevented from properly overseeing the management of the audited corporations because the respondents' audit reports painted a misleading picture of their financial state. They allege further that had they known the true situation, they would have intervened to avoid the eventuality of the corporations' going into receivership and the consequent loss of their equity. The difficulty with this submission, I have suggested, is that it fails to recognize that in supervising management, the shareholders must be seen to be acting as a body in respect of the corporation's interests rather than as individuals in respect of their own ends. In a manner of speaking, the shareholders assume what may be seen to be a "managerial role" when, as a collectivity, they oversee the activities of the directors and officers through resolutions adopted at shareholder meetings. In this capacity, they cannot properly be understood to be acting simply as individual holders of equity. Rather, their collective decisions are made in respect of the corporation itself. Any duty owed by auditors in re-spect of this aspect of the shareholders' functions, then, would be owed not to shareholders qua individuals, but rather to all shareholders as a group, acting in the interests of the corporation. And if the decisions taken by the collectivity of shareholders are in respect of the corporation's affairs, then the shareholders' reliance on negligently prepared audit reports in taking such decisions will result in a wrong to the corporation for which the shareholders cannot, as individuals, recover.

...

CONCLUSION

[64]. …With respect to the claim regarding the appellants' inability to oversee management properly, I would agree with the courts below that it ought to have been brought as a derivative action. …

[65] I would dismiss the appeal with costs.

C. WINDING-UP

Patheon Inc. v. *Global Pharm Inc.*

[2000] O.J. No. 2502 (Q.L.)
ONTARIO SUPERIOR COURT OF JUSTICE
JUNE 30, 2000

[1] Greer J.: — Patheon Inc., ("Patheon") has made an Application for an Order for the just and equitable winding up of Global Pharm Inc. ("Global Pharm") and its sale, by public auction, as a going concern. …

[2] Global Pharm's common shares are 52% owned by Junyk through #113, his holding company. Patheon, a public corporation, owns the other 48% common shares, as a result of a joint venture and partnership formed by it and Junyk in 1995. Patheon provides contract manufacturing and drug development services to the pharmaceutical and biotechnology markets. …

THE BREAKDOWN OF THE RELATIONSHIP

[3] Each of Patheon and Junyk seems to have had different expectations when they entered into the joint venture agreement. ….

[4] Junyk … says that Patheon is really trying to compete with Global Pharm, a step, which was not anticipated when they entered into the joint venture. Junyk says that the two companies, at first, did not compete because Patheon mainly dealt with the production of over-the-counter drugs, whereas Global Pharm concentrated more on prescription drugs, also known as "ethical" pharmaceuticals, and sterile manufacturing. … Junyk, in his Affidavit states that when the joint venture began, Patheon's business was 7% prescription drugs and 93% over-the-counter drugs, whereas Global Pharm's was 90% prescription and 10% over-the-counter.

[5] Given what has now happened between the parties, it is clear that their understandings were never ad idem. …

[8] On October 7, 1999, Patheon issued a press release announcing that it had made this Application to the Court, seeking a dissolution of Global Pharm because of their differences. In that press release, Patheon notes that it serves 16 of the world's largest 25 pharmaceutical companies, as well as a growing number of biotechnical companies. The mass of material placed before me makes it clear that the parties' have reached an impasse and require the Court to intervene in this shareholders' dispute. One of the difficulties facing the parties is the very different positions the parties are in, as shareholders. Patheon, as a public company, must account to the members of the public who own 43,000,000 or so shares of the company. I am told that one pension fund alone owns 18% of those outstanding shares. On the other hand, Junyk only has to account to himself, his bankers and P&U [Pharmacia & Upjohn Canada which he partly owns]. There is no doubt that Patheon is on an expansion plan to become bigger and larger and to provide more prescription drug manufacturing for distribution companies, as noted. Junyk, as I see it, wants [Global Pharm to] protect the markets it has. It does not want its joint venture partner to compete with it, as Junyk says that this was not intended when Global Pharm and Patheon entered into the Agreement. …

[14] The parties made certain attempts to negotiate a Buy/Sell Agreement on terms …

THE BUY/SELL DRAFT AGREEMENT

[17] On June 2, 1999, Junyk made an offer in writing to Patheon to acquire its 48% interest in Global Pharm. Junyk's offer was rejected but was countered by Patheon on June 10, 1999. No agreement was reached by the parties before this Application was launched.

[18] Junyk now takes the position that the parties had reached the terms of a Buy/Sell Shot/Gun Agreement. … Patheon, however, takes the position that no such agreement was ever reached. [The court finds there was no conclusive agreement.]

THE PROVISIONS OF THE OBCA

[20] The Court may, under s. 207(1)(b)(iv) of the Business Corporations Act, ... order that a corporation be wound up, where it is satisfied that it is just and equitable for some reason, other than the bankruptcy or insolvency of the corporation, that it should be wound up. Under s. 207(2) the Court may make such order under this section or under section 248 as it thinks fit. ...

[21] The Court ... may make whatever Order it deems "just and equitable". This gives the Court the right to grant a wide range of discretionary remedies, which are available to it in "oppression remedy" cases. ...

[22] ... It is clear that the parties no longer trust one another, have lost confidence in the other's ability to deal fairly, and can no longer act compatibly in their business relationship. In many respects, there is deadlock in the operation of the company.

ANALYSIS ...

[25] Should the Court then order a public auction of Global Pharm or order that a Buy/Sell Shot/Gun take place between the parties? ...

[26] Patheon's position is that a public auction is the only fair way to deal with it. ...

[27] On the other hand, [Junyk's] ... position is that the Court should take the least intrusive solution to the problem, which should be as consistent as possible with the reasonable expectations of the parties. In that regard, Junyk says, the Buy/Sell Shot/Gun approach is the appropriate one to take. Such a remedy was ordered ... in *Classic Organ Co. v. Artisan Organ Ltd.* ... [which followed] Madam Justice Southin in *Safrik v. Ocean Fisheries Ltd.* ... where she said that there is no better way for a person to put a fair value on what he or she owns than to agree upon a price for which they would be prepared either to buy or to sell.

[28] Junyk takes the position that a public auction would be damaging to Global Pharm and any public party interested in bidding for it would want to carry out extensive due diligence of Global Pharm's business and would thereby obtain competitive information.

[29] In fact, Junyk points to the fact that Patheon, in its publicity about this lawsuit, did say that it intended to be a bidder at that public auction. Various trade publications have published stories about the lawsuit and Patheon's position of wanting to acquire the balance of the shares, which it does not already own. Such publicity, says Junyk, will preclude other parties from coming forward.

CONCLUSION

[30] Having weighed and balanced the massive affidavit evidence before me and taken into account the case law as noted above, I conclude that the least intrusive and fairest way to make a just and equitable decision is to impose a Buy/Sell Shot/Gun agreement on the parties. I made no finding that oppression has occurred. The dispute between these parties is not the classic oppression, which we so often see in the courts. The shareholders have simply very differing views on how the future of Global Pharm shall unfold. ... The evidence before me is that the parties almost reached an agreement, and were close to terms, when the negotiations ceased. I have found that no final agreement was ever reached. I am of the view, however, that public auction of Global Pharm would not necessarily bring the parties the best possible price. Who other than these two parties knows better what the value is than they do?

[31] The Buy/Sell Shot/Gun shall be subject to the following terms:

1. Patheon shall have 30 days from the date of this Order, within which to make whatever further due diligence it sees fit to perform. On the 30th day from the date of this Order, or earlier if it wishes, Patheon shall make an offer to purchase all of Junyk's/113's shares, both common and preferred at whatever price it is prepared to pay.

2. With such an Offer, Patheon shall outline what terms it is prepared to make to Junyk, if the Offer is accepted, to effect his termination of employment from Global Pharm. Such terms shall not be less than what Patheon, as I understand it, had earlier offered to Junyk.

3. Junyk shall have 30 days from the date of such Offer, to either accept the Offer or reject it. If Junyk rejects the Offer, he shall then have an obligation to buy from Patheon at the same price on a pro rata basis, the shares owned by Patheon.

If the parties cannot otherwise agree on Costs, I may be spoken to.

D. RIGHTS REGARDING THE AGM

Yves Michaud, a shareholder of both the Royal Bank and the National Bank of Canada, wanted some shareholders' proposals to be included in the annual information circular and put to a vote at the annual general meeting. Among the proposals was one to limit the salaries of bank executives to twenty times the salary of the average employee; a move that would cause some top salaries to plummet. The banks resisted. The issue, pressed to the Quebec Court of Appeal, was decided in favour of Michaud, in favour of certain "inalienable" rights of the shareholders. In his review of this case, Mr. Seeman said this was the first time "that a publicly traded Canadian company has been compelled to vote on shareholder proposals relating to corporate governance at their annual meeting."

Michaud v. National Bank of Canada
Summarized from The Lawyers Weekly
January 31, 1997, p. 32

Note: The proposals were defeated.[2]

ENDNOTES

1. For a discussion of securities regulation of Internet presentations see the article by Vishva V. Ramlall in *The Lawyers Weekly*, August 18, 2000, p. 14.

2. *The Lawyers Weekly*, October 31, 1997, p. 2.

VIII
PROPERTY

A. PERSONAL PROPERTY

Who gets the ring?

"Resolution of this question, I think, involves a choice between conflicting authorities. The plaintiff [he] relies upon *Cohen v. Sellar*, [1926] 1 K.B. 536. At p. 548, McCardie J. defined the law on this topic, in the following words:

> If the engagement to marry be dissolved by mutual consent, then in the absence of agreement to the contrary, the engagement ring and like gifts must, I think, be returned by each party to the other.

The defendant [she] relies upon *Vezina v. Blais*, [1953] C.S. 48 (P.Q.S.C.). Mr. Wilson contends that the law on this topic is described by Collins J. at p. 49, in the following words:

> ... [An engagement ring is] an outright gift by the [donor] to the [recipient]. ... It [becomes] the absolute property of the [recipient] upon ... acceptance of it.

I apply the principle of law stated in Cohen. I think Cohen contains an accurate statement of the current law in this province. That principle was not referred to in *Vezina*. And in any event, in my opinion, the principle expressed in Cohen is more in harmony with contemporary notions of matrimonial property dispute resolution. I am persuaded that an analysis founded upon principles of commercial and contract law are more sound, than an analysis founded upon principles of gift."

Hitchcox v. Harper
Victoria Registry No. 96/3296
Supreme Court of British Columbia
August 21, 1996

Question

Finders keepers?

Weitzner v. Herman et al.

[2000] O.J. No. 906 (Q.L.)
ONTARIO SUPERIOR COURT OF JUSTICE
MARCH 15, 2000

Who gets the coins and the $130,000 in cash that was hidden in the basement? The estate of the deceased Mr. Weitzner, the former owner of the house? His widow? The present owner who purchased the house from the widow? Or the demolition contractor who found the money when he was razing the house?

After reviewing all the evidence, the court found, on the balance of probabilities, that Mr. Weitzner, who used part of the house as an office, hid the money, but who gets it?

McDermid J.:—

[6] The basic and ancient principle of law that governs in such situations is that the finder of a chattel acquires a good title to it as against all but the true owner or one enjoying a superior title: *Armory v. Delamirie* (1722), I Stra. 505. However, as with most legal principles, there are exceptions to the rule.

[7] In this case, the Gansevles defendants claim to be entitled to the money because they enjoyed salvage rights in connection with the demolition of the building ... [The judge reviews the testimony of the witnesses.]

[9] ... I find there was no agreement that Mr. Gansevles or his corporation would enjoy salvage rights to the property, other than to some items upon which he did agree specifically with Mr. Herman [the present owner]. ... Nor do I find on the evidence before me that the Gansevles defendants have established a custom of their trade to support their position.

[10] Mr. Nowak submits on behalf of Mr. and Mrs. Herman that

(a) The inclusion of the clause "Purchaser accepts properties in as is condition" in the agreement of purchase and sale includes the money.

(b) The conveyance of the realty carried the money with it.

(c) If not, then the agreement between the Hermans and the plaintiff with respect to certain chattels evidenced by a bill of sale conveying "all chattels in personal residence", entitles them to the money.

(d) The plaintiff was unaware of the existence of the money and therefore was unable to exercise the degree of control over it necessary to constitute her the owner of it.

(e) The plaintiff "abandoned" her house and everything in it, including the money.

[11] It is clear to me that neither the plaintiff nor the Hermans knew that there was money hidden in a fire extinguisher when they executed the agreement of purchase and sale. Therefore, the possibility of its being included in the transaction was not in the contemplation of either side when the agreement of purchase and sale was signed, or when the bill of sale and deed were delivered. In my opinion, the words "as is" in the agreement of purchase and sale were meant to refer to the condition of the properties and were included for the plaintiff's protection in order to negate any implied warranty as to their quality or fitness for any particular purpose. In fact, there were environmental concerns arising from the use of the lands as a scrap yard and concerns about the cost of complying with the relevant environmental standards, against which protection was sought for the plaintiff by the inclusion of these words. They were not meant to pass title to any chattels. Nor does s. 15 of the Conveyancing and Law of Property Act R.S.O. 1990, Ch. 90 assist the defendants because it does not refer to or include chattels. It would be absurd to conclude that anyone would be prepared to sell property zoned for commercial and industrial use comprising 8 discrete lots and 2 buildings for $163,500 and at the same time to relinquish title to an alleged $130,000, even if there were some concerns relating to environmental problems.

[12] With respect to the legal effect of the bill of sale, again it is my opinion that the parties, being unaware of the existence of the money or even of the fire extinguisher [in which the money was hidden], had no intention that the money should pass to Mr. and Mrs. Herman. In other words, while there may have been delivery of "all chattels in personal residence", there was no delivery in law of the money: *Merry v. Green* (1841), 7 M. & W. 623. Nor in my opinion does the issue of abandonment arise in these circumstances.

[13] [The court reviews all the evidence that supports the finding that the money was hidden by Mr. Weitzner and passes under his will to his widow; that there was no legal foundation for concluding the money was passed to the Hermans with the sale of the house]. ...

[14] Having found that the money belongs to the plaintiff, I must now decide how much money actually was found and whether Mr. Gansevles took some of it, as alleged by Mr. and Mrs. Herman. [The judge reviews the testimony of the defendants with regard to their words and actions after the money was found and concludes]:

[20] ... I find that the found money totalled $130,000 and that Mr. Herman is unable to account satisfactorily for what happened to a substantial amount of it. ...

[22] ... Mrs. Weitzner shall have judgment against Wilbert Dalton Herman and Jean Elaine Herman for $130,000. ...

- *A* U.S. federal appeals court ruled that Spain still owned the wrecks of two frigates that sunk off the coast of the state of Virginia in 1750 and 1802 respectively. Citing a 1902 treaty between the U.S. and Spain, the court ruled that Spain owned the wrecks of the vessels because it did not explicitly abandon its ownership.[1]

B. REAL PROPERTY

1. LEGAL INTERESTS IN LAND

Q u e s t i o n

When a person buys property, what is included, what is one getting?

The Minister of Finance of Manitoba, pursuant to the Manitoba *Retail Sales Tax*, submitted a tax bill of $1,375,387 to Air Canada in respect of aircraft, aircraft engines and parts consumed and services, meals and liquor consumed in and over the Province of Manitoba. One of the arguments by Air Canada in its appeal from the assessment of the Minister of Finance was that the Province of Manitoba did not have the power to tax aircraft in the airspace over the Province. Justice Morse considering this issue wrote:

> The respondent in the present case relied on the hoary maxim: *Cujus est solum ejus est usque ad coelum and ad inferos* ("Whoever owns the soil owns all that lies above it to the sky and to the centre of the earth"). However, in my view, there has never been in England or Canada any interpretation of this maxim requiring me to hold that the owner of the land does, in fact, own or have the right to possession of the airspace above his land to the sky. I adopt the following statement made by Mr. Richardson in the article to which I have referred (at p. 134):
>
> > 1. It has not been necessary for an English court to give literal effect to the maxim *cujus est solum, ejus est usque ad coelum*, and no court has done so...
>
> In my view, the effect of the maxim goes no further than to protect the owner or occupier of land in his enjoyment of the land and to prevent anyone else from acquiring any title or exclusive right to the space above the land which would limit the landowner or occupier in making whatever proper use he can on his land. And in Fleming, *The Law of Torts*, 4th ed. (1971), the following is stated (at pp. 43-4):
>
> > The extent of ownership and possession of superincumbent air-space has become a topic of considerable controversy since the advent of air navigation. Much play has been made of the maxim *cujus est solum ejus est usque ad coelum*, but the 'fanciful phrase' of dubious ancestry has never been accepted in its literal meaning of conferring unlimited rights into the infinity of space over land. The cases in which it has been invoked establish no wider proposition than that the air above the surface is subject to dominion in so far as the use of space is necessary for the proper enjoyment of the surface.
>
> The appeal was allowed.

Re Air Canada and the Queen in Right of Manitoba
77 D.L.R. (3d) 68
Manitoba Queen's Bench
February 18, 1977

The further appeal by the Province of Manitoba to the Manitoba Court of Appeal was allowed in part, but on the issue of ownership of the airspace the Court of Appeal agreed with the Queen's Bench. About the maxim, argued even in the Court of Appeal, Justice Monnin said:

> The Latin phrase, much more picturesque than the English, speaks of 'up to heaven and down to hell'. ... The maxim cannot go further than direct the owner or occupier of land in his enjoyment of the land and also to prevent anyone else from acquiring any title or exclusive right to the space above such land so as to limit a person to whatever proper use he can make of his land. Further than that it cannot go. Academic writers and modern jurisprudence reject its literal application. So must I in this age of jet aircrafts, satellites, supersonic Concordes, orbital travel and visits to the moon. The sooner the maxim is laid to rest, the better it will be.

Re the Queen in Right of Manitoba and Air Canada
86 D.L.R. (3d) 631
Manitoba Court of Appeal
January 19 and February 16, 1978

Note: This decision was affirmed by the Supreme Court of Canada.

Meconi v. Crichton

[2000] O.J. No. 2457 (Q.L.)
ONTARIO SUPERIOR COURT
JUNE 19, 2000

Jenkins J.:— . . .

[15] It is conceded by both parties that the cedar hedge planted by the plaintiff's wife in 1991 is located about two feet onto the defendants' property. ...

[16] ... Mrs. Meconi mistakenly or negligently planted the hedge on the defendant's property.

[17] I also find that the error was discovered in 1994 by Mr. Collavino [the owner of the adjoining property] and the plaintiff when they saw the "R" plan prepared for Mr. Collavino's severance application. At that time, Mr. Collavino told Mrs. Meconi that she should move the trees. Later, when the severance was approved, he offered to sell half of the lot to the plaintiff which would have solved the encroachment problem.

[18] After he sold the lot, he spoke to the purchaser, Mr. Pare, about the encroachment and he told Mrs. Meconi that Mr. Pare would let her move the hedge. The hedge was not moved and I find that the lot was subsequently sold to Mr. and Mrs. Crichton who had no notice of the Meconis' claim to the hedge. When Mr. and Mrs. Crichton bought the property, they got a survey from Mr. Pare that showed that the hedge was on their property and they believed that they owned it. I find that they were justified in that belief.

[19] Ordinarily this action would be governed by the operation of s. 15 of the Conveyancing and Law of Property Act R.S.O. (1990) ch. c.34 which provides that every conveyance of land includes all trees and hedges belonging to such land. The plaintiff, however, argues that in the circumstances of this case, the trees do not belong to the lands sold to the defendants. As a result, the plaintiff alleges that he is entitled to a lien on the defendants' land for the value of the hedge pursuant to s. 37(1) of the Conveyancing and Law of Property Act.

[20] This argument is based on the plaintiff's contention that he and his wife had an honest but mistaken belief that they were planting the trees on their property and they made a bona fide error when they located the hedge on the defendants' land.

[21] The defendants deny that the plaintiff had an honest belief that the trees were planted on his property and even if he did, he abandoned any claim he had for compensation when he failed to move the hedge.

[22] In *Olson v. Olson* (1996), 6 R.P.R. (3d) 107 Platana J. held ... .

> The onus is on the plaintiff either to establish a gift or to establish his entitlement under s. 37 of the Conveyancing and Law Property Act.

Then at p. 119 he held that:

> Case law has subsequently established that s. 37(1) requires an honest belief on the part of the person claiming ownership that the land is his or her own.

[23] Accepting those principles and applying them to this case, I find that the plaintiff has failed to satisfy me that he had an honest belief that the hedge was planted on his property. I find that as Mr. Collavino said at the trial, the plaintiff's family and friends were simply "digging holes and flopping trees in." They did not take any steps to locate the property line and if they ran a string between two stakes, it was for the purpose of planting the trees in a straight line and had nothing to do with the lot line.

[24] An honest belief must be based on fact or logic. In this case there was a surveyor's iron bar in the ground near the plaintiff's house and either a stake or a second iron bar at the rear of the property. It would not have been difficult for the plaintiff to locate the lot line if he had made the effort. In fact, his wife, family and friends simply planted the trees in a convenient location.

[25] If, however, I am wrong about the plaintiff's belief as to the location of the lot line, I find that any claim the plaintiff may have had to the trees or their value was abandoned by him when he failed to move the trees or purchase half of the lot.

[26] The plaintiff knew the trees were on Mr. Collavino's property, he knew Mr. Collavino intended to sell the lot and he knew Mr. Collavino wanted him to move the trees or buy half the lot. He chose to do nothing.

[27] The plaintiff sat by and watched Mr. Pare build a house on the lot and sell it to the Crichtons. He still did nothing. He took no action until the Crichtons decided to erect a fence.

[28] I am satisfied that he, not only demonstrated an intention to abandon the trees, but he carried that intention into effect when he stood by and watched while the property was developed and sold to uninformed third parties.

DAMAGES

[29] In case this matter goes to a higher court, I am obliged to assess the plaintiff's damages. The cost to replace this hedge has been estimated by various landscapers and an arbourist at between $5,000 and $11,500.

[30] I find that to replace the hedge with a cedar hedge that would provide privacy and meld with the other cedar trees on the plaintiff's property would cost $6,000 and I assess the plaintiff's damages at that amount. My assessment is based on $300 per tree for 15 trees for a total of $4,500 plus $1,500 for planting and a guarantee.

JUDGMENT

[31] The defendants shall have Judgment dismissing the plaintiff's action. ...

Question

In Canada, can one obtain title to land without a formal transfer or bequest in a will?

VARIATIONS OF WILLS

Sawchuk v. *MacKenzie Estate*

[2000] B.C.J. No. 29 (Q.L.)
BRITISH COLUMBIA COURT OF APPEAL
JANUARY 11, 2000

[1] Mackenzie J.A.:— The issue on this appeal is whether the amount of $500,000 awarded to the appellant by the trial judge from the estate of the testatrix in substitution for a legacy of $10,000 has made adequate, just and equitable provision for the appellant pursuant to the Wills Variation Act, R.S.B.C. 1996, c. 490. For the reasons that follow I would allow the appeal and increase the appellant's provision to $1 million.

[2] The testatrix, Cathlene MacKenzie, was the widow of William Ross MacKenzie ("MacKenzie"), who died in 1960. The estate of the testatrix was $4 million. The testatrix's will left only $10,000 to the appellant Corrine Sawchuk, her daughter and only child. ...

[6] The court's jurisdiction to make provision for the appellant is stated in the Wills Variation Act, s. 2 as follows:

2 Despite any law or statute to the contrary, if a testator dies leaving a will that does not, in the court's opinion, make adequate provision for the proper maintenance and support of the testator's wife, husband or children, the court may, in its discretion, in an action by or on behalf of the wife, husband or children, order that the provision that it thinks adequate, just and equitable in the circumstances to be made out of the testator's estate for the wife, husband or children.

[7] As persons entitled to claim relief under the Act are limited to spouses and children of a testator, the appellant is the only person with a statutory claim against this estate.

The moral duty of a judicious parent

[8] The classic statement of the test for relief is that of Duff J. for the Supreme Court of Canada in *Walker v. McDermott*, [1931] S.C.R. 94 recently affirmed by *Tataryn v. Tataryn*, [1994] 2 S.C.R. 807 (S.C.C.) at p. 817:

> What constitutes "proper maintenance and support" is a question to be determined with reference to a variety of circumstances. It cannot be limited to the bare necessities of existence. For the purpose of arriving at a conclusion, the court on whom devolves the responsibility of giving effect to the statute, would naturally proceed from the point of view of the judicious father of a family seeking to discharge both his marital and his parental duty; and would of course (looking at the matter from that point of view), consider the situation of the child, wife or husband, and the standard of living to which, having regard to this and the other circumstances, reference ought to be had.

[9] McLachlin J. in Tataryn commented at p. 817:

> *Walker v. McDermott* may be seen as recognizing that the Act's ambit extended beyond need and maintenance. As Amighetti, supra, puts it (at p. 36), "the award in *Walker v. McDermott* can be supported only on the basis that the court interpreted the Act as a vehicle for redistribution of the capital of the estate".

[10] Spouses and dependent children have the most pressing claims on an estate. However, claims of independent adult children are also entitled to recognition depending on the size of the estate and the nature and extent of other claims under the Act. After addressing claims of spouses and dependent children in *Tataryn*, McLachlin J. added at pp. 822-823:

> .... While the moral claim of independent adult children may be more tenuous, a large body of case law exists suggesting that, if the size of the estate permits and in the absence of circumstances which negate the existence of such an obligation, some provision for such children should be made ...

[11] The court is required to apply a judicious parent standard in determining the extent to which the estate should be redistributed in favour of an adult daughter, who is independent but in economic circumstances far less comfortable than those of her late mother.

[12] The trial judge summarized his conclusions in these terms at p. 14:

> While it cannot be said the plaintiff is destitute, she can hardly be classed as living comfortably. Given the considerations set out in *Tataryn*, the meagre lifestyle of the plaintiff and the wealth of her mother militates in favour of a considerable variation although the lack of dependants or health problems for the plaintiff are factors militating against a substantial variation. While it is a fact the plaintiff made no contribution to the estate or the care of her mother, it cannot be overlooked that the solid foundation of the estate originated with her husband, includ-

ing the house he transferred into the name of the testatrix shortly before his death. That property had a value at her death of $1,900,000, $1,750,000 of which was land value. This represents approximately 20% of the total estate.

> As for the submission of a lack of contribution to the care of the testatrix, that, in my view, was the result of the unpleasant nature of the testatrix and the shabby manner in which she treated her daughter. Efforts made by the plaintiff were met with suspicion, criticism, slander and anger. The plaintiff and her husband were insulted, criticised, insulted and accused of theft. The plaintiff could hardly be expected to insist in efforts to care for her mother under these circumstances.

> Balancing the testamentary autonomy of the testatrix against what I conclude is her failure to meet her moral obligation to her daughter and the court's need to provide an adequate, just and reasonable amount for the plaintiff, I conclude that the appropriate decision is to vary the Will to provide the plaintiff with $500,000, to be shared rateably.

[13] In my view the issue comes down to whether $500,000 is adequate to provide the appellant with a standard of living that a judicious parent would consider appropriate having regard to the size of the estate and the testatrix's own standard of living.

[14] The testatrix disapproved of the appellant for reasons that the trial judge found were not justified. His findings are not disputed on this appeal. ...

[16] A judicious parent, viewing this background objectively, would recognize a moral obligation to make amends for the unfair and excessively critical treatment of the appellant and the false aspersion cast on the appellant from the grave. These are reasons to make the provision for the appellant a generous one. However, ... the Wills Variation Act is not intended as a means of awarding compensation for family abuse. The primary consideration is provision of an appropriate standard of living for the appellant. The estate is large and the provision for her by a judicious parent should be accommodated without excluding other claims that the testatrix reasonably had in contemplation. In my view the claims of all the respondents are entitled to that recognition even though none of them have status to claim under the Act.

[The judge reviews the financial situation of the daughter and the cost of living in Vancouver.]

[17] ... Keeping in mind that this Court is directed to exercise an independent discretion in the matter, I would vary the provision from that awarded by the trial judge to $1 million. In my view that amount would strike a reasonable balance between the moral obligation of the testatrix to the appellant, which the testatrix has disregarded, and her testamentary autonomy to designate other beneficiaries. I agree with the trial judge that the incidence of the provision for the appellant should fall rateably on the residuary beneficiaries. ...

[24] I would allow the appeal and increase the legacy to the appellant to $1 million.

Unanimous

TENANCY IN COMMON AND JOINT TENANCY

Questions

If a person decides to co-own property with another, should he or she buy as a joint tenant or as a tenant in common?

What is the significance of the difference?

Caluori v. Caluori

ONTARIO COURT OF JUSTICE
COURT FILE NO. 59859/92
JULY 16, 1992

Rutherford, J.: The applicant [Mrs.], a dependant within the meaning of s. 57 of the *Succession Law Reform Act* R.S.O. 1990, Chapter S. 26, seeks relief by way of proper support from the estate of her late husband, pursuant to s. 58 of the Act.

It is clear from the evidence that this 72 year old widow is not destitute. Her monthly income from all sources will be between $1,200 and $1,700 a month depending on how this application is determined. The real issue concerns the house in which she and her husband lived since 1964. It was their matrimonial home for all those years and the house in which the applicant insisted on maintaining and caring for her late husband during his declining years. He was not well in his last 6 years and required close care and attention in his final year or two. The applicant expresses a strong, emotional attachment to the home saying she wants to die there, as did her husband.

The marriage was the second for each of them. It lasted almost 20 years and the Caluoris were close. They shared the burdens and benefits of life equally. Their financial contribution to their overall situation was roughly equal.

When the Caluoris purchased the house in question at 1284 Lambeth Walk in the City of Nepean, they took title to it as joint tenants, having discussed the mutual objective they had at that time of having the house left to the survivor of the two. Sometime later, without disclosing it to his wife, the late Mr. Caluori obviously changed his mind about that mutual objective and conveyed his interest in the home to himself in a deed to uses, thus creating a tenancy in common. Then, in a will created at about the same time, he left his entire estate to the children of his first marriage, making no provision for the applicant. The respondent as executor of the will, seeks an order by way of counter application to sell the house and divide the proceeds between the estate and the applicant. The house is worth about $130,000 and if sold, the applicant would receive approximately $60,000 for her own use. This would be her sole asset, apart from savings of about $15,000 and pension and old age security income of about $1,200 per month.

In assessing the applicant's claim that she has not been adequately provided for, I have evaluated the evidence against the criteria set out in s.62 of the *Succession Law Reform Act*. In particular, I have considered the 19 year, close, caring relationship between the applicant and her late husband; the length of time

they lived in the house in question; the applicant's expectation which was reciprocal as far as she knew, that the house was jointly owned and she and her late husband each intended the survivor to have it; the relatively equal sharing and contributing the applicant and her late husband had and made to their financial circumstances; and of course, the contextual circumstances including the applicant's assets, means and other legal recourse for support together with the estate of the applicant's late husband and his testamentary wishes.

I am guided by the views expressed in such cases as *Re Davies v. Davies* (1980) 27 O.R. 98 and *Re Dentinger* [1981] 128 D.L.R. (3d) 613, holding that "proper support" as contemplated by s. 58 of the *Succession Law Reform Act* includes more than necessities of life and may extend to non-essentials and even luxuries. The difference between "adequate support" and "adequate proper support" involves consideration of the life-style of the parties, such that the support is fitting or appropriate to the circumstances.

In *Re Mannion* (1984) 45 O.R. (3d) 339, Dubin J.A. (now Chief Justice of Ontario) said at page 342 concerning s. 58:

> The new statute being remedial, it should be given a broad and liberal interpretation...

When I balance the evidence as applied to the criteria in s.62 and apply the s. 58 formula of "adequate provision for the proper support of the applicant," I am driven to the conclusion that her proper support must include being able to live in the house at 1284 Lambeth Walk for as long as she wishes. It is the matrimonial home, her home for the last 18 years and one, in a neighborhood, to which she attaches a strong emotional tie. The applicant shuns apartment life as "living in a tomb" and in my view, is entitled, by the legislation, to stay where she is.

I appreciate that the half-interest in the house is the only asset in the estate, apart from a few items of personal property of relatively small economic value, but the beneficiaries under the will are the next generation and all good things come to those who wait, especially each in their proper turn.

Accordingly, under the authority of subsection 58(1) of the *Succession Law Reform Act*, it is the order of the Court that the respondent as executor and trustee of the Will of Eugene Caluori hold the interest of the estate in the house at 1284

Lambeth Walk, more particularly described in the Deed of Land registered as instrument no. 671288 in the Registry Office for the Registry Division of Ottawa on May 30, 1975, in trust for the benefit of the applicant and for her use as long as she wishes to live in that house. Upon her death or upon her no longer residing in the house, the estate's interest therein shall be disposed of as directed in the will. While the applicant re-sides in the house, she will be responsible for maintaining it and will bear all the expenses necessary therefor.

Because there are no other liquid assets in the estate, I make no order as to costs in this application. The counter-application for sale of the estate's interest in the house is dismissed and no costs are awarded in relation to it either.

Q u e s t i o n

What if co-owners disagree as to the management of the property?

Peters v. *Peters*

[2000] O.J. No. 1849 (Q.L.)
ONTARIO SUPERIOR COURT OF JUSTICE
MAY 8, 2000

[1] Platana J.:— In October 1962 Donald Benjamin Peters and Ruth Baumbach Peters acquired parcel 23762, being summer resort location EB2073 in the Township of McGeorge, District of Kenora. That is a summer cottage property in the beautiful area of Lake of the Woods.

[2] In October of 1986, they transferred the property to their three sons, Kent, Randall and Jeffrey, each as to an undivided one third interest. At the time of the transfer there can be no doubt but that the parents anticipated that their three sons, to-gether with their families, would continue to enjoy the property as a family residence.

[3] Such is not the case. After a few years of jointly enjoying the property, within one year of their mother's death, difficulties arose between the three. These difficulties centred around the scheduling of times when each was entitled to occupy the property during the summer months, the payment of bills re-lating to the property, and disputes over the maintenance, up-keep and capital improvements which were necessary. ...

[The judge reviews the specifics of the difficulties of the co-ownership, the arguments of both sides and several cases on point.]

[25] The decision cited by both counsel which is most directly on point is that of *Fellows v. Lunkenheimer*, [1998] O.J. No. 4923. ... At paragraph eight, Justice McWilliam noted a situa-tion which is virtually identical to one of the major issues in this case when he stated:

> The central problem in jointly owned premises is when each owner gets to use the property and for how long.

[26] Justice McWilliam ... [notes]:

> From a review of the case law, it appears that there was a limited discretion to be exercised in an application under the Partition Act where the parties were not hus-band and wife.

[27] In referring to the decision in *Moss v. Zorn* Justice McWilliam refers to the headnote which indicates:

> The alternative to an order for sale is partition. Maintaining the status quo is not an alternative avail-able under the Act.

After reviewing the relevant legislation and legal principles, Justice McWilliam determined that there was not sufficient conduct in that case which could be described as vexatious or malicious which would justify the use of the limited dis-cretion in refusing the order.

[28] In my view, the circumstances before me are the same. There can be no doubt in my view that the respondent [brother Kent] is still in a position where he is willing to come to an accommodation in terms of structuring a schedule for the use of the property, and for the payment of bills and maintenance. However, as much as I might consider the position of the Applicants to be personally unreasonable, the evidentiary back-ground is such that it indicates that they are not taking this ac-tion for any vexatious or oppressive reason, but because the family situation has deteriorated to the fact where it is no longer possible for them to operate as joint owners. In this case, par-tition of vacation time is not a solution which I believe would accomplish anything. The relationship between these three brothers, at least as it relates to this cottage property, has now reached the point where all three of them agree that it would be virtually impossible for them to continue as joint owners in the absence of being able to come to some very funda-mental agreements as to how this property can be jointly oc-cupied. They have not been able to do so for a period of several years, and I see no basis in the evidence to suggest that there would be any change in the future.

[29] Accordingly, there will be an order for sale of this property. ...

RESTRICTIVE COVENANTS

- *T*he court concluded that the covenant was not intended to run with the land, but was merely a personal covenant that would not bind subsequent purchasers. Therefore, when a buyer allowed his taxes to be in arrears—by over $700,000—and bought the property back in a tax sale, he defeated the restrictive covenant.[2]

- *I*n California, Mr. Liebaert, a lawyer, is suing a land developer on the grounds that his civil rights have been violated by the developer's policy to exclude certain persons. What, in this case, is the excluded class? Lawyers.

2. REMEDIES FOR BREACH OF CONTRACT

SPECIFIC PERFORMANCE AND DAMAGES IN LIEU THEREOF

Semelhago *v.* Paramadevan

http://www.lexum.umontreal.ca/
SUPREME COURT OF CANADA
JUNE 20, 1996

...

[2] The judgment of Sopinka, Gonthier, Cory, McLachlin, Iacobucci and Major JJ. was delivered by Sopinka, J.:—This appeal concerns the principles that apply in awarding damages in lieu of specific performance. The appellant vendor refused to close a transaction for the sale of residential property to the respondent purchaser. The latter sued for specific performance and, in the alternative, damages in lieu thereof. At the commencement of the trial, the respondent elected the latter. Subsequent to the date fixed for closing, property values rose. If the closing date is the date on which damages are assessed, the respondent would not recover the increase in the value of the property he agreed to purchase. If, however, damages are assessed as of the date of trial, the question is whether the respondent is entitled to recover not only this increase but also to retain the increase in value of the residence which the respondent owned at the time of the agreement of purchase and sale and which was not sold as a result of the aborted transaction. ...

III. ISSUE

[9] What principles apply to the assessment of damages in lieu of specific performance and, further, how do those principles apply to the facts of this case?

IV. ANALYSIS

...
[11] A party who is entitled to specific performance is entitled to elect damages in lieu thereof. ...

[Judge Sopinka continues to reason that if the plaintiff seeks specific performance the acceptance of the breach is delayed. If the plaintiff subsequently elects damages in lieu of specific performance the amount awarded needs to be the amount necessary for the plaintiff to purchase the asset.]

[18] I therefore conclude that, in the circumstances of this case, the appropriate date for the assessment of damages is the date of trial as found by the trial judge. Technically speaking, the date of assessment should be the date of judgment. That is the date upon which specific performance is ordered. For practical purposes, however, the evidence that is adduced which is relevant to enable damages to be assessed will be as of the date of trial. It is not usually possible to predict the date of judgment when the evidence is given.

[19] The difference between the contract price and the value "given close to trial" as found by the trial judge is $120,000. I would not deduct from this amount the increase in value of the respondent's residence which he retained when the deal did not close. If the respondent had received a decree of specific performance, he would have had the property contracted for and retained the amount of the rise in value of his own property. Damages are to be substituted for the decree of specific performance. I see no basis for deductions that are not related to the value of the property which was the subject of the contract. To make such deductions would depart from the principle that damages are to be a true equivalent of specific performance.

[20] This approach may appear to be overly generous to the respondent in this case and other like cases and may be seen as a windfall. In my opinion, this criticism is valid if the property agreed to be purchased is not unique. While at one time the common law regarded every piece of real estate to be unique, with the progress of modern real estate development this is no longer the case. Residential, business and industrial properties are all mass produced much in the same way as other consumer products. If a deal falls through for one property, another is frequently, though not always, readily available.

[21] It is no longer appropriate, therefore, to maintain a distinction in the approach to specific performance as between realty and personalty. It cannot be assumed that damages for

breach of contract for the purchase and sale of real estate will be an inadequate remedy in all cases. The common law recognized that the distinction might not be valid when the land had no peculiar or special value. ...

Specific performance should, therefore, not be granted as a matter of course absent evidence that the property is unique to the extent that its substitute would not be readily available. The guideline proposed by Estey J. in *Asamera Oil Corp. v. Seal Oil & General Corp.,* [1979] 1 S.C.R. 633, with respect to contracts involving chattels is equally applicable to real property. At p. 668, Estey J. stated:

> Before a plaintiff can rely on a claim to specific performance so as to insulate himself from the consequences of failing to procure alternate property in mitigation of his losses, some fair, real and substantial justification for his claim to performance must be found.

A similar position has been taken by the British Columbia Supreme Court in *McNabb v. Smith* (1981), 124 D.L.R. (3d) 547, at p. 551.

[23] The trial judge was of the view in this case that the property was not unique. She stated that, "It was a building lot under construction which would be interchangeable in all likelihood with any number of others." Notwithstanding this observation, she felt constrained by authority to find that specific performance was an appropriate remedy. While I would be inclined to agree with the trial judge as to the inappropriateness of an order for specific performance, both parties were content to present the case on the basis that the respondent was entitled to specific performance. The case was dealt with on this basis by the Court of Appeal. In the circumstances, this Court should abide by the manner in which the case has been presented by the parties and decided in the courts below. In future cases, under similar circumstances, a trial judge will not be constrained to find that specific performance is an appropriate remedy. ...

DISPOSITION

[27] In the result, the appeal is dismissed with costs.

Appeal dismissed with costs.

---

3. THE LANDLORD/TENANT RELATIONSHIP

Minto Developments Inc. **v.** *Nuttall, et al.*

[1993] O.J. No. 2543 (Q.L.)
ONTARIO COURT OF JUSTICE—GENERAL DIVISION
AMENDED REASONS FOR JUDGMENT JANUARY 24, 1994

[1] Binks J.:—The applicant is a landlord and the respondent Sue Nuttall (Carter) is the tenant of Unit 18 of an 18 unit townhouse at 83 Woodridge Crescent, in the City of Nepean. On June 21st, 1993 the respondent Legault's reticulated python which is between 13 and 20 feet long and 4 to 6 inches wide appeared at the window of Unit 18 where children were sitting below, creating alarm in the area. The police were summoned, along with City by-law officials at which time various constrictor snakes, tarantulas and lizards were found in Unit 18. The applicant commenced this application and obtained an interim injunction removing the pythons, boa constrictors and similar animals by an order of McWilliam J. dated July 2nd, 1993.

[2] In her application for a lease, the respondent Nuttall (Carter) stated that only she and her sister Mary Carter would be occupying the premises. Minto entered into a lease with Nuttall (Carter) dated March 21st, 1992 which stipulated in part that only two adults might occupy the subject premises being the respondents Sue Nuttall and Mary Carter and this was set out in the application for lease.

[3] The lease was dated March 21st, 1992 and was extended on a month to month basis by the parties and stipulated *inter alia*:

  (i) the subject premises will be used and occupied by the respondent Nuttall and one adult in her immediate family;

  (ii) the subject premises will only be used for the purposes of a private dwelling and residence;

  (iii) the tenant will not do or permit to be done any act on the subject premises that will be deemed by the landlord to be a nuisance or that will cause disturbance or inconvenience to any other tenant of the building;

  (iv) the tenant shall not alter or caused to be altered the lock on any entry door or affix a night latch upon any entry door to the subject premises without the landlord's written consent;

  (v) the tenant cannot assign or sublet the subject premises without the landlord's consent, which consent shall not be arbitrarily withheld;

  (vi) no tenant shall do, or permit anything to be done in said premises or bring or keep anything therein which will in any way ... obstruct or interfere with the rights of other tenants, or in any way injure or annoy them, or conflict with ... any statute or municipal by-law;

  (vii) tenants, their families, guests, visitors and servants shall not make or permit ... do anything that will annoy or disturb or interfere in any way with other tenants or those having business with them.

  (vii) "NO DOGS OR PETS ALLOWED" clause—at the end of the lease in bold letters.

[4] In December, 1992 the respondent Nuttall allowed a third adult the respondent Todd Legault to occupy the premises

without the applicant's knowledge or consent, contrary to paragraphs 6 and 11 of the lease.

[5] When she signed the lease Sue Nuttall indicated her intention was to house only cats in the premises. The intention of the respondent Legault was substantially different. His intention was set out in his employment resume when he stated "in the future I hope to have one of the largest and healthiest collection of reptiles in the country."

...

[7] As a result of his intention the respondent Legault brought the following animals into the subject premises:

> one (1) reticulate python
> one (1) Burmese python
> two (2) royal pythons
> one (1) carpet python
> two (2) rainbow boa constrictors
> one (1) Mexican boa constrictor
> one (1) Columbia boa constrictor
> one (1) Kenyan sand boa constrictor
> one (1) corn snake
> one (1) Californian king snake
> one (1) yellow anaconda
> one (1) African house snake
> one (1) rose hair tarantula
> one (1) Mexican brow tarantula
> one (1) nile monitor lizard
> one (1) savannah monitor lizard
> one (1) tokay gecko lizard
> one (1) gold tegu lizard

...

[9] Legault looks after the snakes and because they are tropical, the bedroom where they are kept is quite warm, warm enough that Legault finds it necessary from time to time to open the window when he is in the bedroom tending to the reptiles. On June 21st, 1993 Legault left the bedroom window part way open (1 inch) and a reticulate python between 13 and 20 feet long and 4 to 6 inches wide called "Taipan" crawled onto a terrarium (which is really an aquarium with sand in it and a lid on top) housing other snakes and opened the window while no one occupied the premises.

[10] There are conflicting versions of what happened that evening. ... [The judge finds the reptile collection was contrary to a city by-law, and a breach of a by-law was a breach of the lease, an illegal act constituting grounds for termination under the *Landlord and Tenant Act*.]

[20] The respondent Legault has already tried to persuade the neighbourhood to adopt his view regarding the subject of constrictor snakes, tarantulas and lizards by an open invitation to discuss the issue, but only a twelve year old took him up on his invitation because the neighbours are just "set in their ways" according to Legault. The respondent Legault also tried to allay the neighbourhood's fears by approaching the *Ottawa Sun* and co-operating in an article appearing therein on June 24th,

1993 in that paper. Unfortunately, the article did nothing to stop the alarm in the neighbourhood. ...

[21] As a result of the respondent Legault using the subject premises as a zoo for exotic animals the respondents have breached paragraphs 6, 25K and 25M of the lease by not using them solely as a private dwelling and residence and have thereby caused a disturbance, annoyance, interference and inconvenience to their neighbouring tenants who fear for their safety and that of their children. ...

[25] Pursuant to a recent amendment to the Act, Section 107 (6) and 108 of the *Landlord and Tenant Act* permits eviction of a tenant or removal of a pet only when the presence of the pet constitutes a breach of s. 107 (1). [For example, by interfering with the enjoyment of the property or by being inherently dangerous.] ...

[28] The court has already ruled that the fear of an animal is sufficient to constitute a substantial interference with the neighbours' enjoyment of their premises. ...

[30] The evidence shows that the Legault animals belonged to dangerous species. There is no evidence regarding the individual specimens' temperament involved in this case but there need not be. The *Landlord and Tenant Act* refers to inherently dangerous species that interfere with a reasonable enjoyment of property, both without regard to the nature of the individual specimen. This follows the common law which holds that the nature of the species is to see if it is inherently dangerous, and disregards the fact whether the particular specimen was not tame.

> If a person wakes up in the middle of the night and finds an escaping tiger on top of his bed and suffers a heart attack, it would be nothing to the point that the intentions of the tiger were quite amiable. ... It is not, in my judgment, practicable to introduce conceptions of *mens rea* and malevolence in the case of animals. *Behrens v. Bertram Mills Circus Ltd.* [1957] 2 Q.B. 1 at 17-18 cited in *Lewis v. Oeming* (1983) 24 C.C. L.T. 81, at 95 (Alta T.D.).

[31] In Fleming, *The Law of Torts* 345 (5th ed, 1977) it is stated that classification of a particular species is dangerous is a matter of law for the court and it does not depend on the nature of the particular specimen. ...

[35] On the basis of all of the evidence, it is appropriate therefore to issue an order:

(a) terminating the tenancy agreement between the applicant and the respondent Sue Nuttall dated March 21st, 1992 as extended on a month-to-month basis;

(b) a writ of possession in favour of the applicant with respect to the subject premises to issue;

(c) an order requiring the respondents to remove the boa constrictors, pythons, tarantulas and monitor lizards from the subject premises within 15 days of the date of this order.

[36] There shall also be a declaration that Todd Legault is not entitled to occupy Unit 18, of 83 Woodridge Crescent, in the City of Nepean, and an order prohibiting him from residing there. ...

Pinheiro *v.* *Bowes*

[1994] O.J. No. 115 (Q.L.)
ONTARIO COURT OF JUSTICE—GENERAL DIVISION
JANUARY 7, 1994

[1] Killeen J.:— This application by the landlord under s. 113 of the *Landlord and Tenant Act*, R.S.O. 1990, c.L.7 has been narrowed down, by agreement, to one issue, namely, whether a contractual provision as to notice of termination may override s. 80(1) of the Act.

THE AGREED FACTS

[2] The parties entered a lease which contained … [a provision that] a monthly tenancy may be terminated by giving written notice to terminate on or before the last day of one month of the tenancy to be effective on the last day of the following month of the tenancy.

[3] It is acknowledged that … the tenant stayed in the premises for some time and, on October 27, 1993, served a written notice purporting to terminate the tenancy as of November 30, 1993. In doing so, the tenant thought that she was lawfully complying with the one-month notice proviso set out in paragraph 19(d) of the lease.

[4] If the tenant was entitled to rely on paragraph 19(d), then, of course, she owes nothing further to the landlord. If, however, that clause cannot be relied upon, then the tenant owes the landlord one additional month's rent by virtue of s. 99 of the Act.

THE RESOLUTION OF THE NOTICE ISSUE

[5] The parties acknowledge that two provisions of the Act must be considered in deciding the central issue of this case. These sections are as follows:

> 80.-(1) This Part applies to tenancies of residential premises and tenancy agreements despite any other Act or Parts I, II, or III of this Act and despite any agreement or waiver to the contrary except as specifically provided in this Part.

> 99.-(1) A notice to terminate a monthly tenancy shall be given not less than sixty days before the date the ter-

mination is specified to be effective and shall be specified to be effective on the last day of a month of the tenancy.

[6] Mr. Schlemmer, for the tenant, argues that s. 99 … does not bind the tenant in this case because of the express provision in the lease which permits termination on notice for the lesser period of 30 days.

[7] Mr. Schnurr, on the other hand, argues that s. 80(1), in clear and unambiguous language, invalidates the shorter one-month notice period in the lease for all purposes and, in combination with s. 99(1), effectively requires the tenant, or landlord, to give 60 days notice. …

[9] … [S]. 80(1) … seems to be crystal clear in its intent. Section 80 (1) says, in explicit terms, that every provision of Part IV applies to all residential tenancy agreements and that this is so "despite any agreement or waiver to the contrary except as specifically provided in this Part." (Emphasis added.)

[10] I can identify no ambiguity in s. 80(1) and the parties acknowledge that there is nothing in Part IV which permits any agreement or waiver to the contrary.

[11] I must express some discomfiture at permitting a landlord to rely on the statutorily-created invalidation of that landlord's own lease proviso but it is not for a judge to run rough-shod over a statute in an effort to protect a tenant. …

[13] Judges must accept statutes as they find them if they are clear and unambiguous and catch the factual situation under consideration.

[14] In my view, while s. 99 was largely created to protect tenants, it cannot be said to be contrary to public policy to enforce it in favour of a landlord. Section 99 provides a broadly-gauged protective rule for landlord-tenant relationships and must be enforced as it plainly reads and provides. On its face, it invalidates the lease proviso in issue and makes the tenant liable for one month's additional rent. …

4. MORTGAGES

Question

What is the relationship between the mortgagee and the mortgagor?

Bayshore Trust Company v. *Assam*

ONTARIO COURT OF JUSTICE
No. 75510/90
APRIL 9, 1992

Background facts: Mr. Assam granted a mortgage in favour of Bayshore Trust Company for a loan of $210,000 for a one-year term, interest at 14%. It was renewed for a further one-year term with interest at 14.5%. Assam fell into arrears. He consented to judgment against him for $241,667.06 and agreed to deliver possession of the mortgaged property. However, the court has to address Assam's counterclaim.

MacDonald, J: ...

Mr. Assam alleges that the plaintiffs caused him to suffer economic loss by reason of granting him the mortgage. Mr. Assam states that the monthly obligations for service of the mortgage were so high as to make it impossible for him to meet these obligations. ... The monthly mortgage obligation was in fact significantly more than Mr. Assam's monthly income on a net basis, and he alleges that Bayshore, with this information in hand, ought not to have granted him the mortgage in question. It was also known to Bayshore Trust that a second and third mortgage were being postponed by the placement of the first mortgage with Bayshore on the property in question. The second and third mortgages were privately held. Mr. Assam also suggested that he was induced into the transaction by Bayshore and its agents. ...

Mr. Assam alleges that the activities of Bayshore induced him into a situation of financial disaster and it is on this basis that his counterclaim is based. Mr. Christopher gave evidence. He was very familiar with all aspects of the transaction as it related to Mr. Assam. Mr. Christopher struck me as a straightforward witness who tried to accommodate Mr. Assam as much as possible. Mr. Christopher advised me that Bayshore Trust is what is known as an "equity lender;" that is to say that Bayshore Trust assesses a prospective borrower on the basis of the equity of the property in question. Bayshore loans up to 70% of the value of the property, and in Mr. Assam's case, the loans extended to Mr. Assam by Bayshore never exceeded 70% of the value of the property in question. Mr. Christopher indicated to me that the application form does make enquiries about the level of one's income, but the only consideration in respect of the decision to extend funds is based on the equity in the property. ...

The issue is whether or not Bayshore Trust, an equity lender, owes a fiduciary duty of care to the borrower, Mr. Assam? If Bayshore Trust is found to have a fiduciary duty of care, then the court would have to address the question of damages that may arise from any breach of this duty.

It is well settled that as a general rule, a mortgagee is not in a fiduciary relationship with the mortgagor. In the absence of evidence of special circumstances upon which to base a fiduciary duty, the relationship between the parties is purely one of a lender and a borrower or debtor and creditor.

The Supreme Court of Canada considered the test to be applied to determine whether a fiduciary relationship had arisen in *Lac Minerals Ltd. v. International Corona Resources Ltd.*, [1989] 2 S.C.R. 574. Mr. Justice Sopinka was of the opinion a fiduciary obligation is one that arises out of a fiduciary rela-

tionship. He concluded that there was no precise test, but that certain characteristics were so frequently found in relationships which had been found to be fiduciary, that they served as a guide. He quoted with approval the enumeration of those characteristics by Madam Justice Wilson in *Frame v. Smith*, [1978] 2 S.C.R. 99 at pp. 135 and 136. They are as follows:

1) The fiduciary has scope for the exercise of some discretion or power.

2) The fiduciary can unilaterally exercise that power or discretion so as to affect the beneficiary's legal or practical interests.

3) The beneficiary is peculiarly vulnerable to or at the mercy of the fiduciary holding the discretion or power.

Mr. Justice Sopinka pointed out that a fiduciary relationship could exist even though not all of the above characteristics were present. However, he stated that the third, that of dependency or vulnerability, was indispensable.

In *Northland Bank v. 230720 Alberta Ltd.* [1990] A.J. No. 838, the defendant debtors sought to establish a fiduciary relationship between themselves and the plaintiff creditor. ... The Alberta Court of Queen's Bench held that it was a straightforward case of a lender-borrower with no "special circumstances" to create a fiduciary relationship of any kind. The court stated as follows:

> It is not a defense for a borrower to say that the lender knew or should have known that he did not have the ability to repay the loan so the lender should not have made it.
>
> The wisdom of a lender in giving a loan is not a defense to why the loan should not be repaid. Poor business decisions belong in a court of business, not a court of law.

...

The three characteristics to establish a fiduciary relationship are not disclosed in the evidence before me. I do not find that Mr. Assam was vulnerable or dependent upon Bayshore Trust. He was an educated person who understood the extent of the obligation he was undertaking. He had legal counsel. The relationship between him and Bayshore was that of a lender and a borrower. There was a lot of contact between Mr. Assam and Bayshore Trust and its agents, particularly over his inability to make monthly payments, but I cannot find that Bayshore had any duty of a fiduciary nature to Mr. Assam. It is not appropriate to transform the relationship of a lender and a borrower into a fiduciary relationship. I cannot find that Bayshore exercised a dominating influence over Mr. Assam and there is nothing in the evidence that would bring me to the conclusion that Bayshore went beyond a normal business relationship so as to place itself in the position of a fiduciary. The counterclaim against both defendants is, therefore, dismissed. ...

TERMS

> To complete a real estate transaction, a borrower, through a series of transactions, ended up obligated to pay a total of $2,113,660 plus monthly interest on a mortgage debt of $1,556,830. The borrower defaulted on the loan. The lender began foreclosure proceedings. The borrower argued that the rate of interest was contrary to s. 347(2) of the *Criminal Code* which prohibits a rate of interest that exceeds 60%. The judge, in a chambers hearing, held for the borrower.
>
> The B.C. Court of Appeal dismissed the appeal by the lender and concluded that in this case the effective rate of interest was 148.29%.
>
> **Kebet Holdings Ltd. v. 351173 B.C. Ltd.**
> *Summarized from* The Lawyers Weekly
> *January 29, 1993, p. 27*

S. 8 OF THE INTEREST ACT

Citizens Bank of Canada v. *Babich*

http://www.courts.gov.bc.ca/
SUPREME COURT OF BRITISH COLUMBIA
JUNE 20, 2000

Master Joyce:

[1] On May 15, 2000 I granted the petitioner an order nisi of foreclosure but reserved judgment with respect to the amount required to redeem and the amount of the judgment. The issue is the rate of interest payable from November 23, 1999, being seven days before the maturity date of December 1, 1999.

[2] The mortgage was granted May 14, 1996 and had a maturity date of May 15, 1997. The mortgage interest rate stated at paragraph 5 of the first page of the mortgage was 7.00% per annum calculated semi-yearly not in advance. However, the mortgage also contained "additional or modified terms" that were set out in an attached schedule. One of those terms provided as follows:

> 1.1(l) "Mortgage Rate" means the annual rate described as the "Interest Rate" in item 5(b) of the Mortgage Form calculated at the end of each Interest Calculation Period, not in advance, provided that the Mortgage Rate shall be adjusted seven (7) days prior to the Balance Due Date to become the Toronto-Dominion Bank Prime Rate plus five (5%) percent per annum compounded monthly not in advance. This adjusted rate shall continue in effect until such time as the Principal and all other amounts outstanding hereunder are paid in full or, alternatively, until the Mortgage is renewed. ...

[3] The mortgage was subsequently renewed on three occasions. ...

[4] The renewal letters, which were signed by the Babichs, contained the following condition:

> This Agreement shall, without prejudice to the present state of the Mortgage account, be read and construed with the Mortgage, and be treated as a part thereof and the Mortgage and all covenants and terms whatsoever therein shall continue in force and effect and be applicable to this Agreement except herein provided. ...

[5] The mortgage matured on December 1, 1999 without having been renewed. The mortgagee claims interest pursuant to paragraph 1.1(l) of the modified terms at prime plus 5% which it says is equivalent to 12% per annum. Mr. Babich submits that interest should be calculated at 7% per annum, the rate set out in the renewal letter. In *TD Trust Co. v. Guinness* (1995) 12 B.C.L.R. (3d) 102 (S.C.) Tysoe J. dealt with a similar mortgage

provision and held that it offended s. 8 of the *Interest Act* and was unenforceable. . . .

[6] At paras. [16] and [17] Tysoe J. said:

[16] ... A provision in a mortgage increasing the interest rate one week prior to the maturity date of the mortgage is a device similar to the device of forgiving interest in the event of timely payment of the mortgage monies. Strictly speaking, the increase in the interest rate is not triggered by a default. However, the effect of the provision is to charge a higher interest rate on the mortgage monies if they are not paid by the maturity date.

[17] The authorities establish that in considering s.8 the Court should not restrict itself to the form of the provision in the mortgage and should look to its substance. In this case the substance of the provision is clearly to extract a higher rate of interest if the mortgage was not repaid by its maturity date. It is apparent on the face that the wording of the provision was an attempt to avoid s.8 and no other explanation to justify the provision was offered. Section 8 cannot be avoided by clever devices if the substance of the provision has the effect of increasing the interest rate in the case of default. In this case, the substance of the interest provision violates s.8 and is unenforceable. (emphasis added)

[7] Section 8(1) of the *Interest Act* provides as follows:

(1) No fine, penalty or rate of interest shall be stipulated for, taken, reserved or exacted on any arrears of principal or interest secured by mortgage on real property that has the effect of increasing the charge on the arrears beyond the rate of interest payable on principal money not in arrears.

[8] Mr. Justice Tysoe recognized that there may be circumstances in which an increase in the mortgage interest rate during the term of the mortgage might not offend s.8. At paras. [20] and [21] his Lordship said this:

[20] Where does one draw the line in deciding whether an interest provision contravenes s.8? This is an obvi-

ous question and it was asked in the hearing before Master Bolton in the Raintree case. He said that he did not have to decide the point because he was satisfied that the provision before him was on the wrong side of the line. In my view, the line should be drawn between interest provisions which are intended to extract a higher rate of interest in the event of default and interest provisions which have a legitimate commercial purpose. The true intent may be obfuscated by clever devices by ingenuous lawyers and it will be the function of the Court to determine the true intent.

[21] An example of an interest provision which could pose difficulty for the Court is one in a mortgage having a two year term that stipulates interest at 12 percent for the first year of a mortgage and 24 percent for the second year and after maturity. The true intent of the provision may be in violation of s.8 if, for instance, the mortgagor had only wanted the loan for one year and it was anticipated that the high interest rate after the end of the first year would force the mortgagor to repay the mortgage if possible and that the mortgagor would not be able to pay the monthly payments with the increased interest rate in the second year. On the other hand, the provision could have a legitimate commercial purpose if, for instance, the mortgagor wanted the loan for two years and the mortgagee was only prepared to make the loan for more than one year if the interest rate was substantially increased after the end of the first year. The Court would have to determine the true intent of the provision in order to decide whether, in substance, it violates s.8.

[The court, after reviewing the arguments of the mortgagee:] ... [13] In my opinion the provision in this case falls on the wrong side of the line. In my view the true intent of this provision is simply to extract a higher rate of interest in the event of default and I conclude that it contravenes s.8 of the *Interest Act* and is unenforceable. Interest is therefore to be calculated at 7.000% per annum. Counsel for the petitioner is to provide a new summary accounting using that interest rate.

C. INTELLECTUAL PROPERTY

1. COPYRIGHT

Questions

Who owns copyright?
What can be the subject of copyright?

Gould Estate v. *Stoddart Publishing Co.*

[1998] O.J. No. 1894 (Q.L.)
COURT OF APPEAL FOR ONTARIO
MAY 6, 1998

Finlayson J.A.:—This is an appeal from two summary judgments of the Honourable Mr. Justice Lederman dismissing Action No. 95-CQ-62384 (the "photograph action") and the other dismissing Action No. 95-CU-92931 (the "words action"). The motions judge held that there was no basis in law for either action.

The two actions concern a book entitled "Glenn Gould: Some Portraits of the Artist as a Young Man" that was published by the respondent Stoddart Publishing Co. Limited ("Stoddart") in 1995 without the consent of or compensation to the appellants, the Estate of Glenn Gould and Glenn Gould Limited. The book contains photographs of the late Glenn Gould taken by the late Jock Carroll with captions and an accompanying narrative written by Carroll. ...The photographs were taken and the interviews conducted for the purposes of an article that Carroll was to write and submit to Weekend Magazine for publication. The article headed "I Don't Think I'm At All Eccentric" was in fact published. It contains nine photographs of Gould and a narrative that contains many quotations attributed to Gould.

At issue in this appeal is whether the respondent Carroll was entitled, for his own exclusive benefit, to later exploit commercially the photographs he took of Gould in 1956 and to use his notes and tapes of his interviews at that time to write other articles on Gould notwithstanding that such later use of the photographs and interviews had never been discussed with or agreed to by Gould or his successors or assigns.

The appellants submit that the respondents' use of the photographs and what the appellants describe as "transcriptions" in the book in 1995 for a purpose different from that ever discussed with or agreed to by Gould constitute:

(a) a breach of contract;

(b) a tortious misappropriation of Gould's personality; and

(c) a breach of copyright.

...

THE FACTS

The late Glenn Gould was a world-famous concert and recording pianist who died in 1982. ... In 1956, the late Jock Carroll was a freelance writer associated with Weekend Magazine as a writer and photographer. Carroll died on August 4, 1995.

In the early spring of 1956, Gould's agent, Walter Homburger, approached Carroll to enquire whether Carroll would be interested in interviewing Gould and taking photographs of him for a story in Weekend Magazine. Carroll, after consultation with his editor at Weekend Magazine, agreed.

Gould and Carroll met on several occasions for interviews and picture taking. ... During these occasions, Carroll took approximately 400 photographs of Gould and made notes and

audio tape recordings of numerous interviews. Carroll retained all the photographs, notes and tape recordings. ...

ANALYSIS

[The judge finds no evidence to support the contention that there was a contract between Carroll and Weekend Magazine on the one hand and Gould on the other.] ...

Gould clearly consented to the photographs being taken and to the continuing interviews by Carroll. There was no contract between them, express or implied. The only issue is whether Gould or his agent imposed any limitation on that consent. On this record there was none. Indeed, it is common to all the evidence that there was no discussion whatsoever of any conditions to the consent. While all parties expected that an article in Weekend Magazine would come of this association, there was no suggestion by anyone that the material obtained from it was limited to this one article. At no time was any suggestion made that Carroll was to deliver up to Gould the negatives of his film, the audio tapes or his notes.

It is conceded that in 1995 Carroll was the owner of the copyright in all 400 of the photographs taken in 1956 and, for reasons that I will develop, it is clear that he also owned the copyright in the captions under the photographs and the accompanying text in the impugned book. Accordingly, prior to entering into publishing arrangements with the respondent Stoddart Publishing, Carroll had exclusive proprietary rights in the photographs and he became the exclusive owner of the copyright in the text and captions to the photographs by virtue of being the author. In these circumstances, it would appear to me that the onus is upon Gould and those who now represent him to show that the copyright in all the photographs, tape recordings and notes was retained by Gould or, at the very least, that Carroll's copyrights expired once the article in question was published in Weekend Magazine. As I have discussed above, there is no evidence on the record that Gould or his agent placed any limitation on his consent given in 1956.

Despite the concession with respect to copyright in the photographs, I find it necessary to refer briefly to the subject because it places in context the suggestion that there was an implied restriction placed by Gould on the use that Carroll could make of the photographs. Under the Copyright Act, R.S.C. 1985, c. C-42, copyright subsists in a photograph for 50 years from the end of the year of the first making of the original negative (or photograph if there is no negative) from which the photograph was directly or indirectly derived. The owner of the original negative, or photograph as the case may be, is deemed to be the author and the first owner of the copyright: see s. 10(2). Today it is taken for granted that photography is an art, although the proof of a truly "artistic" character is no longer required for copyright protection. The technical labour involved in producing a photograph is sufficient to accord it copyright protection. ...

It is evident from this record that Gould did not have a copyright with respect to his oral utterances or in the "transcriptions" of them, to use the appellants' phrase. To the contrary, Carroll as the author of the text and captions in the book was the owner of the copyright in the very written material the appellants are attempting to suppress. ...

Once it is established that Carroll owned the unrestricted copyright in the photographs and the written material in the book, there is nothing else to decide. Section 5(1) of the Copyright Act provides that "copyright shall subsist in Canada, for the term hereafter mentioned, in every original literary, dramatic, musical and artistic work". Carroll created the portraits that are the artistic subject-matter of the book in question and he was the author of the captions and text that supported and explained them. When this book was published, Carroll had obtained an assignment of whatever rights Weekend Magazine enjoyed as publisher of the original article in 1956. Accordingly, it was Carroll, and Carroll alone who was the owner of all relevant copyright and he was the only person entitled to publish the book sought to be suppressed. ...

As must be evident from my approach to this case, I am not persuaded that I should analyze the facts of this case in the context of a claim for misappropriation of personality. I am satisfied that it can be disposed of on conventional intellectual property lines and there is no necessity to explore any

balance between privacy rights and the public's interest in a prominent Canadian. However, I cannot leave the matter without commenting on the efforts of the appellants to seek the moral high ground by asserting that Carroll was exploiting the artistic genius of another at no cost to himself. This misdescribes the legal issues. We are not concerned about Gould's musical or artistic works but with Carroll's literary and artistic work. The book of portraits is Carroll's creation, not Gould's. He was and now his heirs are the owners of this literary and artistic creation and it is his estate that is entitled to protection from the appellants who contributed nothing to the book. Not only did the appellants not create the book, they were incapable of doing so. Carroll had the photographs, the tapes and his notes of his interviews with Gould. He was the only person who could have reached back in his memory and recreated the scenes where he first met Gould. The results are captivating. The book provides a compelling insight into the character of a musical genius. In protecting Carroll's artistic creation, the law permits the public to benefit from an insight into Gould's early years to which it would otherwise be denied.

For these reasons, I would dismiss the appeal with costs.

Unanimous

Note: The Supreme Court of Canada refused to hear an appeal.

- *B*arbara Hager, who wrote a biography of Shania Twain based on her interviews with the singer, sued ECW Press Ltd., who used substantial quotes from Hager's book. The Federal Court Trial Division ruled in favour of Hager by following a 1900 case heard by the House of Lords, which held that written copy of interviews belongs to the reporter.[3]

Q u e s t i o n

What tests do the courts use to determine who owns copyright when the work was a collaborative effort?

Singer Sarah McLachlan was a defendant in an action by Darryl Neudorf, her former drummer, who alleged that he was denied proper compensation as a co-author, and thus co-owner of copyright, of her hit songs "Vox," "Strange World," "Steaming," and "Sad Clown." The following excerpts focus on what the court determined was necessary for a person to successfully claim coauthorship.

"THE TEST FOR JOINT AUTHORSHIP

[14] Section 2 of the Copyright Act, R.S.C. 1985, c. C-42 (the "Act") defines a "work of joint authorship," as follows: ... a work produced by the collaboration of two or more authors in which the contribution of one author is not distinct from the contribution of the other author or authors[.]

...

[18] ... [A]uthorship has two basic requirements: originality, and expression.

[19]....[The judge quotes from a 1916 English case] "The word 'original' does not in this con-

nection mean that the work must be the expression of original or inventive thought. Copyright Acts are not concerned with the originality of ideas, but with the expression of thought... . The originality which is required relates to the expression of the thought. But the Act does not require that the expression must be in an original or novel form, but that the work must not be copied from another work—that it should originate from the author." ...

[37]... I think it is now well-established by the body of law in Canada and England, and for that matter in the United States, that to satisfy the test for joint authorship a putative joint author must contribute original expression, not merely ideas, to the creation of the work. ...

[39] Indeed, the notion that a joint author need not have been the originator of the ideas embodied in the work is completely consistent with the rule that copyright does not exist in ideas. As long as the claimant contributes original expression to the work, he may be a joint author, regardless of the source of the ideas being expressed. Applying this principle to the instant case, even if McLachlan was the one who came up with all of the ideas for the songs, this in itself would not be fatal to the plaintiff's claim of joint authorship. The test, as discussed above, is not whether the plaintiff came up with the ideas for the songs, but whether he gave the ideas original expression. ...

[40] The case law also provides that the contribution of joint authors to the work need not be equal. ...

[43] However, even though the contribution of one joint author need not be equal to that of the other joint authors, it appears that the contribution of each joint author must nevertheless be significant or substantial. ...

[68] There is a dearth of Canadian law on the meaning of the word "collaboration" in s. 2 of the Act. However, the Canadian and English authorities have interpreted the statutory definitions of joint authorship to require a common design. ...

[71] ....[I]n my opinion, the authorities, at the very least, have settled that to satisfy the test for joint authorship a putative joint author must establish that he has made a contribution of significant original expression to the work at the time of its creation, and that he has done so pursuant to a common design (or, in other words, some form of shared intent). ...

[93] In my opinion, the common law definition of joint authorship, the statutory definitions of joint authorship in Canada, England and the United States, and the judicial interpretation of the statutory definitions all confirm that mutual intent is a prerequisite for a finding of collaboration. ...

[96] In the result, I find that the test for joint authorship that should be applied to the facts in the instant case is, as follows: (i) Did the plaintiff contribute significant original expression to the songs? If yes, (ii) Did each of the plaintiff and McLachlan intend that their contributions be merged into a unitary whole? If yes, (iii) Did each of the plaintiff and McLachlan intend the other to be a joint author of the songs?

[After an exhaustive review of the creation of each of the songs, the judge concluded:]

SUMMARY

[231] The plaintiff has proven that he made a contribution of original expression to the verse vocal melody in the song "Steaming." However, he has failed to satisfy the test for joint authorship because he did not prove a mutual intent to co-author this song with McLachlan. The plaintiff has failed to prove that he contributed original expression to "Vox," "Sad Clown" or "Strange World." Accordingly, his claim to co-ownership of copyright in the songs must be dismissed. As well, his unjust enrichment claim must be dismissed. However, he is entitled to judgment against Nettwerk for its failure to pay him the outstanding balance for the services he performed on Solace."

Neudorf v. Nettwerk Productions Ltd. et al.
http://www.courts.gov.bc.ca/
Supreme Court of British Columbia
December 12, 1999

Question

What are the risks when the artist is paid to do the job but ownership of copyright is not made clear?

Cselko Associates Inc. and Ernie Cselko v. Zellers Inc. and Display Industries of Canada (Eastern) Ltd.

ONTARIO COURT OF JUSTICE
COURT FILE No. 33515/88Q
JULY 10, 1992

Hawkins, J:—This is a motion by the defendant Zellers to dismiss the plaintiffs' action. The plaintiff Cselko is a commercial illustrator who carries on his business through the vehicle of the corporate plaintiff of which he is sole proprietor.

Zellers is a retail merchant and the defendant Display Industries of Canada (Eastern) Limited (Display Ltd.) is a commercial art broker.

Zellers developed an advertising and merchandising gimmick which they named "Zeddy Bear." They had some commercial illustrations done of Zeddy with which they were not entirely satisfied. They retained Display Ltd. to find them an illustrator to do some drawings of Zeddy in various activity poses. Display Ltd. engaged Cselko on behalf of Zellers, to do drawings. Zellers had no direct contact with Cselko. Zellers' end of the transaction was handled entirely through Display Ltd. and in particular by the late Mr. James Renwick, Sr.

It was made known to Cselko that the illustrations he was commissioned to do were going to be used by Zellers for advertising purposes. No limitation on the use to which Zellers could put the illustrations was ever discussed. The plaintiff billed Display Ltd. by means of invoices which contained no limitations or copyright warnings. He was paid approximately $16,000.00 for his work.

Zellers used the illustrations in connection with usual advertising, packaging and promotional material (e.g. a colouring book) and has even reproduced some of the drawings to be sold in frames.

The plaintiff, after he discovered the extent to which his drawings were being put, registered his copyright in them. He now sues for substantial damages for breach of copyright and injunctive relief.

There is only one issue in this law suit—what limitations on use, if any, are to be implied in the circumstances of this case.

There was, as I have already noted, no limitation discussed. The plaintiff asserts that "advertising" and "packaging" are different and that art sold for use in advertising does not encompass packaging. It is clear from his cross-examination that he did not make this view known to Mr. Renwick.

In his affidavit the plaintiff alleges as follows in paragraph 2(b):

> I negotiate fees for my artwork based on the complexity of the artwork, the extent of the use required by the client and the duration of the use. Payment may be negotiated in the form of a royalty arrangement or straight fees or both. The use of artwork on packaging for products requires a special contractual relationship and special remuneration to the artist, as packaging normally has a long shelf life of many years.

... [The court reviews affidavit evidence on the industry practice. Some of the affidavits state that the artist negotiates separate fees for each of the various uses to which his work is put; others, in support of Zellers, say that the artist assigns all rights to the client unless he expressly limits the use of his work. The court holds that the plaintiff's version is not supported by the evidence and that he assigned his rights without restriction.]

THE COPYRIGHT ACT PROBLEM

Section 13(4) of the *Copyright Act* R.S.C. Ch. C-42 provides "the owner of the copyright in any work may assign the right ... and may grant any interest in the work by licence but no assignment or grant is valid unless it is in writing ...."

It has been held that a licence to use may be implied by the conduct of the parties and need not be in writing. *Howard Drabble Ltd. v. Hycolith Manufacturing Company* (1928), 44 T.L.R. 264 (Ch.Div.). See also Fox *Copyright* (2nd edition) 298 ff.

Judgment may issue dismissing the plaintiff's claim against both defendants. ...

[Plaintiff's claim dismissed]

• *A*round Christmas one movie seems to dominate the TV selections —*It's a Wonderful Life* with Donna Reed and Jimmy Stewart. The theme is appropriate to the season, but the more important factor affecting its availability is the price — the stations are paying no royalties to the creators because the copyright lapsed.[4]

PARODY

Compagnie Generale des Establissements Michelin-Michelin & Cie.	***v.***	***National Automobile, Aerospace, Transportation and General Workers Union of Canada (CAW-Canada)***

[1997] 2 F.C. 306
FEDERAL COURT

Teitelbaum J.:

...

As I stated briefly above, the defendant CAW conducted an organizing campaign at Michelin Canada's plants in Nova Scotia in February and March 1994. The defendant CAW distributed 2,500 leaflets to Michelin workers outside the factory gates at the three Nova Scotia Michelin Canada plants. ... The top right hand corner of the leaflet displays the CAW logo, a mark with the letters "CAW' and "TCA" separated by a stratified maple leaf and the word "Canada" underneath a thinly drawn line. The contentious portion of the leaflet depicts a broadly smiling "Bibendum," arms crossed, with his foot raised, seemingly ready to crush underfoot an unsuspecting Michelin worker. In the same leaflet, another worker safely out of the reach of "Bibendum's" looming foot has raised a finger of warning and informs his blithe colleague, "Bob, you better move before he squashes you!" Bob, the worker in imminent danger of "Bibendum's" boot has apparently resisted the blandishments of the union since a caption coming from his mouth reads, "Naw, I'm going to wait and see what happens". Below the roughly drawn figures of the workers is the following plea in bold letters, "Don't wait until it's too late! Because the job you save may be your own. Sign today for a better tomorrow." The leaflet also gives the phone number for the CAW office in Granton. Defendant Wark, the defendant CAW's organizer for Nova Scotia, admitted that he had photocopied and prepared the leaflet with the offending "Bibendum" figure in the CAW office.

The leaflet was also reproduced as a poster and displayed on the windows of CAW offices in Granton, Waterville and Bridgewater. ...

As I have ruled that the defendants have reproduced a substantial part of the plaintiff's work and thus infringed the copyright, the burden now shifts to the defendants to prove that they fall under an exception to copyright infringement. Like the plaintiff in regards to the *Trade-marks Act,* the defendants have offered a novel argument and radical interpretation of the law. In this case, the defendants argue that parody is a form of "criticism" under paragraph 27(2)(a. 1), the relevant exception to copyright infringement.

Paragraph 27(2)(a.1) reads:

27.—

(2) The following acts do not constitute an infringement of copyright:

    (a.1) any fair dealing with any work for the purposes of criticism, review or newspaper summary, if

        (i) the source, and

        (ii) the author's name, if given in the source, are mentioned.

Parody is not explicitly discussed in the *Copyright Act. ...* [The judge reviews the case law cited.] I am not satisfied that these cases are applicable to the current matter. ... Under the *Copyright Act,* "criticism" is not synonymous with parody. Criticism requires analysis and judgment of a work that sheds on the original. Parody is defined in the *Collins Dictionary of the English Language* (2nd ed., London: Collins, 1986) as "a musical, literary or other composition that mimics the style of another composer, author, etc. in a humorous or satirical way." ... In the Canadian and Commonwealth courts, parody has never been held to figure as criticism although the term criticism is not confined to "literary criticism."

The defendants have added a twist to this usual reasoning by urging the Court to consider in line with the recent decision of the American Supreme Court in *Luther R. Campbell a.k.a. Luke Skywalker v. Acuff-Rose Music, Inc.,* 114 S. Ct. 1164 (1994), (hereinafter *Acuff-Rose)* that parody is a form of "criticism", under paragraph 27(2)(a.1). ...

... In *Acuff-Rose,* the defendant [2 Live Crew] had used the characteristic bass riff and opening line from Roy Orbison's classic rock song, *Pretty Woman* in its own rap song with new lewd and crude lyrics and distinctive rap background motifs. Justice Souter writing for the Court held at page 1173 that the Court of Appeals had erred in overstating the parodist's commercial motive to deny the fairness of the use... : " The rap version of *Pretty Woman* could still qualify as a parody or critique of the romantic fantasy embodied in the original song and could be considered an exception to copyright infringement as fair use for the purpose of criticism under section 107 of the

American statute. The United States Supreme Court remanded the case to the trial level to reconsider the rap version of *Pretty Woman* against all of the factors for "fair use" in section 107.

While the American case is most fascinating from both a cultural and legal perspective, I have not found it to be persuasive authority in the context of Canada's particular copyright regime. Chief Justice Laskin in *Morgentaler v. The Queen*, [1976] 1 .C.R. 616, held at page 629 that a court should be prudent in applying American precedents to the Canadian context and should take into consideration the particular rules of each system of law: "they do not carry any authority beyond persuasiveness according to their relevance in the light of context, with due regard to the obvious differences that exist." American decisions are only persuasive to the extent that the laws in both jurisdictions are similar: ... [The judge examines the differences between the American and Canadian copyright provisions.] I cannot accept that I should give the word "criticism" such a large meaning that it includes parody. In doing so, I would be creating a new exception to the copyright infringement, a step that only Parliament would have the jurisdiction to do. ...

Thus, I hold, in line with the prevailing Canadian authorities, that parody does not exist as criticism, an exception to acts of copyright infringement. And even if I were to follow the American authority in *Acuff-Rose* and state that parody exists as a fair dealing exception to infringement, the defendants would have failed under the two secondary elements of paragraph 27(2)(a. 1). First, the defendants did not mention the source and author's name of the original on their "Bibendum" leaflets and poster. This is condition of the fair dealing exception. ...

In addition, the defendants did not treat the original work in a fair manner, a further requirement of the "fair dealing" exception. The defendants argued that as a parody, their work could not be held to treat the copyright in a kid glove fashion. Parody has to bite and in some way batter the reputation of the original. However, once again, the defendants have sought to dilute the usual rules of the fair dealing exception and defeat the wording of paragraph 27(2)(a. 1) simply by labelling the "Bibendum" posters and leaflets a parody. It is not enough that because it is a parody, there is no need to mention the source. Now the defendants would have the Court rule that by the mere fact of the parody label, the defendants are permitted to forego treating the plaintiff's copyright in a fair manner, a requirement for all the existing exceptions like criticism, review and summary. To accept the defendants' submissions on parody would be akin to making the parody label the last refuge of the scoundrel since the Court would have to do away with two of the usual strictures of paragraph 27(2)(a.1): mentioning the source and fair treatment.

(V) CONCLUSIONS ON COPYRIGHT

I am not prepared to take the two leaps of faith urged by the defendants. The first is that parody is synonymous with criticism. The second is that the defendants can dispense with the need to mention the source and fair treatment because of the peculiar nature of parody with its implicit acknowledgment of the source. My role is not to create legislation but to apply the existing rules crafted by Parliament. ...

Note: This decision was appealed, but the Federal Court advised that the parties filed Notices of Discontinuance.[5]

MORAL RIGHTS

Q u e s t i o n

What rights remain with a creator, even if he has assigned or sold his copyright?

- *T*he artist, Walt Spitzmiller, was commissioned by L.L.Bean, Inc. to illustrate the cover of its mail-order catalogue with a hunting scene. He painted a rough hunter with his Labrador retriever. The released cover showed a clean-shaven hunter with a "preppified pooch."

  Spitzmiller sued the company, *inter alia*, for copyright infringement and breach of contract. He asked for the destruction of the altered copies and damages equal to the total fall catalogue earnings. Spitzmiller's lawyer is quoted as saying "It's a good thing the dog can't sue."[6]

- *M*r. Biesinger of Utah sells copies of the movie, *Titanic*, in which he has cut the "profanity, nudity or violence." Paramount Pictures has requested he stop this practice and they are closely watching his activities. Would this editing be an infringement of moral rights if it happened in Canada?[7]

INFRINGEMENT

Q u e s t i o n s

What are the consequences of infringing copyright?
In an action for damages, how much should the infringer have to pay to
the copyright owner?

Society of Composers, Authors and Music Publishers of Canada   *v.*   348803 Alberta Ltd. et al.

REPORT OF REFERENCE: AS TO THE AMOUNT OF DAMAGES, INTEREST AND COSTS OWING BY THE DEFENDANT TO THE
PLAINTIFF FOR THE PERIOD 01 JANUARY 1994 TO 09 JANUARY 1997.
http://www.fja-cmf.gc.ca/en/cf/1997/recents/html/
FEDERAL COURT OF CANADA
JULY 3, 1997

John A. Hargrave, Prothonotary, :
This Reference, pursuant to the designation of the Administrator of the Court, 12 March 1997, to determine the profits, damages, interest and costs owing by 348803 Alberta Ltd. and Damir Zoranic to the Society of Composers, Authors and Music Publishers of Canada (the "Society of Composers") arises out of the Plaintiff's action claiming an accounting and various other relief for the use of copyright music, including royalties payable in accordance with the applicable tariffs set out from time to time in the Supplement to the *Canada Gazette*. The claim for relief is based on a Judgment obtained by the Society of Composers, in default of defence, on 20 February 1997.

The Reference took place at Vancouver, BC, on the afternoon of 24 June, 1997. The Defendants, who are now in the position of judgment debtors, with profits, damages, interest and costs payable to the Plaintiff to be determined by this reference, all as set out in Federal Court rules 500 through 507, have had ample notice from time to time of these proceedings, including the present reference. No one attended to represent the Defendants.

APPLICABLE TARIFFS

The Society of Composers is the only performing rights society authorized by the Copyright Board of Canada to issue licences and to collect licence fees from parties wishing to perform copyright musical works in public in Canada. The tariffs and fees are authorized by Section 67 through Section 67.2 of the *Copyright Act*, R.S.C. 1985, Chapter C-42. The Copyright Board publishes, each year, in the *Canada Gazette*, a statement of the royalties which the Society of Composers may collect. These are in the form of tariffs. The relevant tariff, in this instance, is Tariff 18, applicable to recorded music for dancing. In the present instance the applicable tariffs are those of 13 August 1994, for the 1994 year, 11 March 1995 for 1995, and 21 September 1996 for 1996. the Plaintiff's evidence establishes the Defendants' establishment is still in operation, but not that it presently plays recorded music. Thus there is no claim for 1997.

APPROACH TO ASSESSMENT

The relief sought in this case involves the determination of a royalty or licence fee as damages, the portion of net profits to go to the Society of Composers and exemplary damages.

Damages
Where it is customary to licence the use of a work, music in this instance, damages may be measured on the basis of the usual royalty or licence fee. The licence fees for music are calculated using given figures and rates from the Copyright Board Tariffs and various statistics as to the operation of the licensee. Where a licence fee alone is inadequate recompense, general damages at large may be in order: *Hay v. Sloan* (1957) 27 C.P.R. 132 at 140 (Ont. H.C.).

Profits
Recompense does not necessarily end with damages, but may also, in a copyright infringement matter, at a court's discretion, include an accounting of profit. This is touched on indirectly in section 34 (1.01) of the *Copyright Act*, in the context of an accounting, and is specifically provided for in section 35 (1) of the Act. I have treated damages and profits not as alternative, but as cumulative relief.

[He reviews arguments that it should be damages or profits in the alternative, but concludes that the *Canadian Copyright Act* clearly allows both.]

An award of profits is, in a sense, an equitable approach, although one that by recognition in the Copyright Act has become a legal remedy to be applied equitably. It is a determination of the Defendants' gain by reason of wrongful use of the Plaintiff's property, an amount which is awarded to the Plaintiff. ... One must, however, in the present instance, keep in mind that the award of profit is based on a default judgment specifying profit as a remedy: the outcome might well have been different had the Defendants appeared.

Estimating Licence Fees and Profits

By reason of the absence of representation on behalf of the Defendants, and the fact that there has been no access to the Defendants' records, an accurate calculation of the licence fees owing and of profits is not possible. Therefore I must calculate the licence fees and profits as best I can: see for example *Performing Rights of Canada Ltd. v. 497227 Ontario Ltd.* [and others].

In summary, it is not improper to calculate damages and profit in a rough and ready manner, particularly if the necessity to do so is the result of omissions on the part of defendants to attend and to protect their interests by providing appropriate information and documents.

Material Tendered by the Plaintiff

[After reviewing the material supplied by plaintiff he moves to the calculations.]

CALCULATION OF LICENCE FEES

… To summarize, I have calculated the licence fee for the full years 1994 through 1996 as though the lounge operated between four and seven days a week at the basic licence fee, together with a premium of 160% for the 150 patron capacity over the basic 100 patrons.

The calculations are as follows:

1994 $334.93 × 260% =	$	868.40
1995 $347.34 × 260% =		903.08
1996 $359.72 × 260% =		935.27
Total		$2,706.75
GST @ 7%		193.72
TOTAL		$2,900.47

CALCULATION OF AWARD OF PROFITS

As I noted earlier, an award in the nature of profits derived from infringement is an equitable approach, made into a legal remedy by section 35(1) of the *Copyright Act*. It is the confiscation of and transfer to the Plaintiff of the portion of profits made by the Defendants through their unauthorized use of the Plaintiff's works. I have decided to recommend this transfer of profit, in addition to damages, for an award merely of the usual licence fee and of the court's tariff based costs for legal expenses does not adequately reimburse the Plaintiff for the time and trouble it has taken to enforce its rights. It is thus proper to transfer a portion of the profit. The more difficult conclusion to reach is the value of the Plaintiff's music to the Defendants.

Mr. Justice Holmes of the Supreme Court of the United States recognized the inherent value of music in a restaurant setting in a 1917 case, *Victor Herbert v. Shanley Company*, reported (1917) 61 Law. Ed. 511. The case involved infringement of Mr. Herbert's "Sweethearts" by a live performance in a Broadway restaurant. The Defendant argued that there was no infringement because diners paid nothing at the door, but only for their food and drink. A portion of the final paragraph of the reasons is worth reading:

> The defendants' performances are not eleemosynary. They are part of a total for which the public pays, and the fact that the price of the whole is attributed to a par-

ticular item which those present are [595] expected to order is not important. It is true that the music is not the sole object, but neither is the food, which probably could be got cheaper elsewhere. The object is a repast in surroundings that to people, having limited powers of conversation, or disliking the rival noise, give a luxurious pleasure not to be had from eating a silent meal. If music did not pay, it would be given up. If it pays, it pays out of the public's pocket. Whether it pays or not, the purpose of employing it is profit, and that is enough. (page 514).

It matters not that the Defendants had no specific charge, for example a cover charge at the door, for the music at their establishment. Music adds an ambiance to such establishments. The music added a value to the Defendants' operation, otherwise they would have given up playing music. Just what the value of the music might be I must now arrive at in a rough and ready manner.

Earlier in this report I referred to ratios of profit to statutory licence fees derived from four references in which the plaintiffs were either The Performing Rights Organization of Canada Ltd. or, as in the present instance, The Society of Composers, Authors and Music Publishers of Canada. I also noted the circumstances in each of those four cases were analogous to those in the present instance, with obvious differences in the facts cancelling out each other.

To simplify the calculation I have revised the average ratio from 18.38 to 18. Thus the portion of the net profit which I have attributed to music and which I recommend as an award of profit to the Plaintiff is 18 times the licence fee in each year:

1994 - 18 × $868.40 =	$15,631.20
1995 - 18 × $903.08 =	$16,255.44
1996 - 18 × $935.27 =	$16,834.86
Total	$48,721.50

PRE-JUDGMENT INTEREST

[Pre-judgment interest on the license fees: $355.16; on the profits $3,239.84.]

EXEMPLARY DAMAGES

In its Statement of Claim the Society of Composers asks for exemplary damages. Exemplary damages, also referred to as punitive damages, are not compensatory, but rather are to punish and must be sufficient to act as a deterrent.

[The court reviews the case law in which punitive damages were awarded.]

In the present instance, I am of the view that there ought to be punitive damages for a number of reasons. First, the material shows that the Plaintiff visited the premises of the Defendants five times, over a period of 4 years, to ask them to voluntarily pay the required licence fee. Second, the Society of Composers provided the licence fee forms to the Defendants on a number of occasions. Third, the Society of Composers and subsequently their lawyers, sent some dozen letters to the Defendants, ranging from form letters enclosing the licence forms, through follow up letters, letters explaining what steps they would take if the licence fees were not paid, and finally, a letter from their lawyers not long before the present action was commenced, all of which appear to have been ignored. Fourth, at one point the affidavit of material indicates that the Defendant, Damir Zoranic, had thrown the licence application material in the garbage and subsequently said that he had no intention of paying the licence fees. Finally, the Defendants had ample notice of the present proceedings and yet chose to ignore them, thus putting the Plaintiff to additional expense. I would also observe that while many establishments using music for which the Society of Composers collects a royalty, pay the required fee, a number of others do not and thus an award of exemplary damages in this instance might act as a deterrent to those who use others' music without payment.

In view of the substantial recommended award of profit to the Plaintiff, I have tempered what would otherwise be a larger exemplary award. However exemplary damages are in order as a caution to those who would capitalize by using another's property and then not only ignore requests for properly payable licence fees, but also ignore a copyright holder's rights in a willful and flagrant manner, or to those whose conduct is un-cooperative and disdainful. I therefore recommend exemplary damages in the amount of $5,000.

TAXATION OF BILL OF COSTS

… . A copy of the bill of costs is attached as Schedule A. I recommend that it be allowed as presented at $ 2,808.80.

CONCLUSION

I recommend to the Court that the Plaintiff be awarded:

1. Licence fees, including GST	$2,900.47
2. Interest on licence fees	355.16
3. Net profit attributable to use of Plaintiff's music	48,721.50
4. Interest on net profits	3,239.84
5. Exemplary damages	5,000.00
6. Costs and disbursements	2,808.80
Total	$63,025.77

This amount should be payable jointly and severally by the Defendants.

I thank Counsel for the Plaintiff for good material and a complete presentation.

Q u e s t i o n

Can infringement of copyright lead to a criminal conviction?

R. *v.* J.P.M.

C.A.C. No. 121549
NOVA SCOTIA COURT OF APPEAL
MARCH 29, 1996

Roscoe, J.A.:—This is an appeal by a young offender from convictions entered by Judge Atton on three counts of distributing infringing copies of computer software contrary to s. 42(l)(c) of the *Copyright Act,* R.S. 1985, c.C-42, which is as follows:

42. (1) Every person who knowingly

(c) distributes infringing copies of any work in which copyright subsists either for the purpose of trade or to such an extent as to affect prejudicially the owner of the copyright, is guilty of an offence and liable

(d) on conviction on indictment, to a fine not exceeding one million dollars or to imprisonment for a term not exceeding five years or to both.

Other provisions of the *Copyright Act* relevant to this matter are:

2. In this Act,

"literary" work includes tables, compilations, translations and computer programs; "telecommunication" means any transmission of signs, signals, writing, images or sounds or intelligence of any nature by wire, radio, visual, optical or other electromagnetic system …

…

Since computer programs are expressly protected by the *Act* as literary works, and the owners of the copyrights have the sole right to communicate the work to the public by telecommunication, there can be no doubt that the appellant created infringing copies of the software by placing them on the bulletin board in such a way that they were available to be used and copied …

It is also clear that when he accessed his computer by modem from his friends' homes and downloaded the programs onto their computers, he was "distributing" the infringing copies.

Furthermore, by … providing the software to assist in the downloading by modem by those users, the appellant was also distributing, that is giving out, or sharing the infringing copies. Although it is suggested that the programs were "scrambled" so that they could not be copied or downloaded by the callers, the evidence accepted by the trial judge was that they were "packaged" or "compressed" for efficient [transmission]. …

Appeal dismissed.

Piracy Cases

- *T*he Recording Industry Association of America (RIAA*) filed a lawsuit alleging copyright violation against the software firm Napster, which provides a free computer program that allows a person to send digital music (in the form of MP3 files) over the Internet. The court rejected Napster's first-round argument that it was exempt from liability under the "safe harbor" provisions of the U.S. *Digital Millennium Copyright Act*, which protects Internet service providers (ISPs) from liability for illegal material on their systems.[8]

   In the meantime, Bertelsmann AG, one of the members of the RIAA, has settled out of court with Napster (and offered to buy 15% of Napster) but others proceeded with the lawsuit.[9]

   The U.S. Circuit Court of Appeals ordered Napster to stop allowing the free swap of copyrighted songs among its estimated 50 million users. Napster will appeal.[10]

   Subsequently, Napster offered to pay the record companies $1 billion. They rejected the offer.[11]

- *M*etallica, the heavy-metal band, also sued Napster for music piracy as well as several universities that Metallica claims could "block this insidious and ongoing thievery scheme."[12] Smashing Pumpkins, however, did use Napster. Upset with Virgin Records, it released its album, *Machina II/The Friends and Enemies of Modern Music*, free online. Will this prompt Virgin Records to sue Smashing Pumpkins for infringing the company's copyright?[13]

- *E*ric Corley, who published software that cracked the encryption code on DVD files, allowing widespread piracy of DVD movies, was found by the court to be in violation of the 1998 U.S. *Digital Millennium Copyright Act*, which prohibits the creation and publication of software to break encryption programs.[14] The law that emerges to find a just course between the interests of the consumer, distributors, and artists will also affect other such enterprises (e.g., Gnutella and Freenet, other music exchange sites, as well as Swapoo, which allows users to share copyrighted video games.)[15]

- *M*P3.com, a service that allows users to download CDs, settled with record companies (including Time Warner, EMI, Sony, and BMG). Robertson, the founder and CEO of MP3.com, will pay the record companies $100 million, and will get a licence to run My.MP3.com thereby developing a legal digital delivery system.[16]

   The judge commented that some Internet companies "may have a misconception that, because their technology is somewhat novel, they are somehow immune from the ordinary application of the laws of the United States, including copyright law. ... [T]he law's domain knows no such limits."[17]

   Later MP3 settled with Seagram Co.'s Universal Music Group. MP3.com agreed to pay $53.4 million to Universal and to pay royalties for the right to use music from Universal artists.[18]

- *T*he Chiffons (composers of "He's So Fine") sued George Harrison for "My Sweet Lord." Harrison lost the case even though the infringement was found to be done unconsciously.[19]

- *A* U.S. court stopped the sale of rapper Biz Markie's album "I Need a Haircut" because of Markie's unauthorized "sampling" of music from Gilbert O'Sullivan's song "Alone Again (Naturally)." Sampling, using pieces of old songs to create new music, had not been tested in the court; hereafter, the record companies may insist that every sample used be authorized.[20]

- *A* U.S. Superior Court Judge in Los Angeles ruled that Ms. Cynthia Plaster Caster was entitled to the return of her plaster mouldings of the genitalia of famous male rock stars.[21]

- *D*o not try to market a book on *Seinfeld* trivia without permission. Castle Rock Entertainment, the producer and copyright owner of the *Seinfeld* series, was granted a permanent injunction and was awarded U.S.$403,000 for the infringement.[22]

- **W**imzie, Horace, Jonas, and Loulou—the puppets created by the Cinar Corporation—look too much like Muppets, is according to the Jim Henson Company.[23]

LICENSING

- **I**n 1989 Bill Gates, the chairman of Microsoft, incorporated Interactive Home Systems to acquire the electronic rights to photos and works of art. The company, now Corbis Corp. [Corbis = woven basket, Lat.] turns photographic negatives into electronic images. CEO Doug Rowan stated the objective of the company was to "capture the entire human experience throughout history." The licensing agreements are nonexclusive. The company operates from Bellevue, Washington, and employs photographers, photo editors, art historians, and copyright lawyers.[24]

2. BREACH OF CONFIDENCE / TRADE SECRET

Question

What does the plaintiff have to prove in order to win an action against a defendant on the grounds that the defendant breached a confidence?

Cadbury Schweppes Inc. **v.** *FBI Foods Ltd.*

http://www.lexum.umontreal.ca/
SUPREME COURT OF CANADA
JANUARY 28, 1999

[1] Binnie, J. — Clamato juice is a confection of tomato juice and clam broth. By the early 1980s it had developed a market in Canada about 10 times the size of its market in the United States, where it originated. To a significant extent, its success in Canada is attributed to the efforts of the appellants [FBI] and their predecessors, who manufactured Clamato juice at plants in Vancouver and eastern Ontario under licence from the respondents [Cadbury]. The respondents terminated the licence effective April 15, 1983. The courts below concluded that thereafter the appellants misused confidential information related to the Clamato recipe obtained during the licence period to continue to manufacture a rival tomato-based drink, which they called Caesar Cocktail. Liability for breach of confidence is no longer contested. This appeal requires us to consider appropriate remedies for breach of confidence in a commercial context. ...

ANALYSIS

[19] Equity, as a court of conscience, directs itself to the behaviour of the person who has come into possession of information that is in fact confidential, and was accepted on that basis, either expressly or by implication. Equity will pursue the information into the hands of a third party who receives it with the knowledge that it was communicated in breach of confidence (or afterwards acquires notice of that fact even if innocent at the time of acquisition) and impose its remedies. It is worth emphasizing that this is a case of third party liability. The appellants did not receive the confidence from the respondents, but from the now defunct Caesar Canning [which contracted with FBI]. The receipt, however, was burdened with the knowledge that its use was to be confined to the purpose for which the information was provided, namely the manufacture of Clamato under licence.

[20] ... In *Lac Minerals* [[1989] 2 S.C.R. 574] it was suggested that the action for breach of confidence should be characterized as a *sui generis* hybrid that springs from multiple roots in equity and the common law. ...

[24] The result of *Lac Minerals* is to confirm jurisdiction in the courts in a breach of confidence action to grant a remedy dictated by the facts of the case rather than strict jurisdictional or doctrinal considerations. ... There is much to be said for the majority view [in *Lac Minerals*] that, if a ground of liability is established, then the remedy that follows should be the one that is most appropriate on the facts of the case rather than one derived from history or over-categorization. ...

A. Significance of the "Sui Generis" Characterization ...

[28] Reference to anything as "*sui generis*" tends to create a frisson of apprehension or uncertainty amongst lawyers until the jurisprudence about a particular subject matter is further developed. I do not think such apprehension would be justified here. The *sui generis* concept was adopted to recognize the flexibility that has been shown by courts in the past to uphold confidentiality and in crafting remedies for its protection. ...

B. Relationship Between Breach of Confidence and Fiduciary Duty

[29] The respondents at trial pleaded breach of fiduciary duty. The law takes a hard line against faithless fiduciaries. ...

[30] Even prior to *Lac Minerals* the Court expressed the view that the policy objectives underlying fiduciary relationships did not generally apply to business entities dealing at arm's length. ... [The court finds no fiduciary relationship nor a fiduciary duty.]

C.   Relevance of the Licence and Tolling Agreements ...

[37] ...The contract cannot reasonably be read as negating the duty of confidence imposed by law. ...

D.   Relevance of Respondents' Argument Based on an Alleged "Proprietary" Interest in the Information ...

[41] The respondents' characterization of confidential information as property is controversial. Traditionally, courts here and in other common law jurisdictions have been at pains to emphasize that the action is rooted in the relationship of confidence rather than the legal characteristics of the information confided. ...

[48] ... Breach of confidentiality is the gravamen of the complaint. When it comes to a remedy, ... equity, with its emphasis on flexibility, keeps its options open. It would be contrary to the authorities in this Court already mentioned to allow the choice of remedy to be driven by a label ("property") rather than a case-by-case balancing of the equities. ... Application of the label "property" in this context would add nothing except confusion to the task of weighing the policy objectives furthered by a particular remedy and the particular facts of each case. ...

E.   Relevance of Tort ...

[51] ... In these circumstances, tort principles do not carry us any closer to the solution.

F.   Relevance of Detriment

[52] La Forest J. said in *Lac Minerals* that if the plaintiff is able to establish that the defendant made an unauthorized use of the information <u>to the detriment</u> of the party communicating it, the cause of action is complete ...

[54] The concept of detriment need not be explored on this occasion because ... the parties had agreed prior to trial that any evidence regarding losses allegedly suffered by the plaintiff would be deferred to a post-trial reference. ...

G.   Relevance of Lord Cairns' Act 1858 to Jurisdiction to Award Financial Compensation ...

[61] Equity, like the common law, is capable of ongoing growth and development . ... In my view, therefore, having regard to the evolution of equitable principles apparent in the case law, we should clearly affirm that, in this country, the authority to award financial compensation for breach of confidence is inherent in the exercise of general equitable jurisdiction and does not depend on the niceties of *Lord Cairns' Act* or its statutory successors. This conclusion is fed, as well, by the *sui generis* nature of the action. The objective in a breach of confidence case is to put the confider in as good a position as it would have been in but for the breach. To that end, the Court has ample jurisdiction to fashion appropriate relief out of the full gamut of available remedies, including appropriate financial compensation.

H.   The Subject Matter of the Compensation

[62] In the present case, the trial judge found, and the Court of Appeal agreed, that the Clamato formula ... was worthy of protection, but what, in dollar terms, did its misuse cost the respondents? ...

[64] The applicable concept of restoration was set out in the reasons of McLachlin J. in *Canson Enterprises* [1991] 3 S.C.R. 534]. ...

> In summary, compensation is an equitable monetary remedy which is available when the equitable remedies of restitution and account are not appropriate. By analogy with restitution, <u>it attempts to restore to the plaintiff what has been lost as a result of the breach; i.e., the plaintiff's lost opportunity</u>. The plaintiff's actual loss as a consequence of the breach is to be assessed with the full benefit of hindsight. Foreseeability is not a concern in assessing compensation, but it is essential that the losses made good are only those which, on a common sense view of causation, were caused by the breach. [Emphasis added.]

The concept of the "lost opportunity" is particularly apt here. ...

J.   The Trial Judge Found the Confidential Information to be "Nothing Very Special"...

K.   The Springboard Doctrine

[67] The trial judge acknowledged that the breached confidences had acted as a "springboard" to enable the appellants to bring Caesar Cocktail to market 12 months earlier than would otherwise have been the case. ...

[74] In my view, the key to the assessment of equitable compensation in this case is the expected duration of the respondents' "lost opportunity", i.e., the economic advantage they would have enjoyed after the cancellation of the licence "but for" the breach.

L.   Award of a Permanent Injunction ...

[87] ... An injunction in the circumstances of the present case would inflict competitive damage on the appellants in 1999 far beyond what is necessary to "restore" the respondents to the competitive position they would have enjoyed "but for" the breach. ...

M.   The Measure of Financial Compensation

[90] The respondents, thus denied an injunction, must look entirely to dollars and cents for their restoration.

[The court, accepting the finding that the appellants' misuse of information gave them a 12-month "head start," then outlines factors to be considered by the referee responsible for determining the proper dollar amount that will constitute fair restitution.]

DISPOSITION OF THE APPEAL

[101] The appeal is therefore allowed.

Unanimous

• *A* U.S. court ordered Walt Disney Co. to pay $360 million to All Pro Sports Camps Inc. and its owners for, *inter alia*, theft of trade secrets and breach of confidence. The owners of the company, N. Stracick and E. Russell (a Canadian architect), presented their ideas for a sports complex to the company's representatives. Soon after the company rejected their scheme it announced it would build just such a complex. Lawyers for Disney, announcing they would appeal the decision, said, "the notion that we had to steal this idea is utterly preposterous."[25]

Questions

What can I take when I leave the company?
When is it know-how and not a trade secret?

In the high-stakes business of drug manufacturing, time, secrecy and ownership are of essence. By agreement the employee promises not to disclose confidential information and agrees that inventions are the property of the employer. When Jagroop Dahiya, the biochemist who invented a process for the manufacture of an anti-cholesterol drug left Apotex Fermention Inc. for Novopharm Ltd. he took information. Was the information confidential information belonging to the company or general knowledge? Justice Monnin, in a 148-page decision, found it was a confidential trade secret and awarded the plaintiff $3.7 million.

Apotex Fermentation Inc. v. Novopharm Ltd.
Summarized from The Lawyers Weekly
September 22, 1995, p. 20 and October 6, 1995, p. 13

---

3. PASSING OFF

Questions

Why is the tort of passing-off significant in protecting a person's intellectual property?
What is its relationship to the law of trade marks?

Eli Lilly & Co. Inc. et al. v. Novopharm Ltd., Apotex Inc. and Nu-Pharm Inc.

http://www.fja.gc.ca
FEDERAL COURT OF APPEAL
DECEMBER 19, 2000

Background facts: The patent protection period expired for the well-known drug Prozac. Manufacturers of generic drugs began manufacturing a look-alike pill. The manufacturers of Prozac alleged that because the pills had the size, shape, and colour of the original, the generic manufacturers were liable for, among other things, the tort of passing-off. Their action failed in the Federal Court Trial Division after forty-two hearing days over a period of five months.

Desjardins J.A.:
[1] The appellants seek to reverse a judgment of the Trial Division dismissing their claims that the respondents had passed off their generic fluoxetine hydrochloride capsules as the ap-

pellants' Prozac brand fluoxetine hydrochloride capsules. ...
[15] The trial judge summed up the issue before her in the following manner:

> The issue is whether or not the capsule appearance of the Lilly fluoxetine is distinctive as an indication of trade source or provenance, and whether the use of a similar capsule appearance by the defendants would result in a likelihood of confusion.

...

II—ISSUES

[27] The key issue in this appeal is whether the trial judge applied and, if she did, whether she correctly applied the decision of the Supreme Court of Canada in *Ciba-Geigy Canada Ltd. v. Apotex Inc.* [[1992] 3 S.C.R. 120] and the rules of passing-off. ...

IV—ANALYSIS

[30] My analysis must, therefore, begin with an examination of the decision of the Supreme Court of Canada in the *Ciba-Geigy* case.

(a) The Ciba-Geigy decision . . .

[34] In the course of his analysis, Gonthier J. reviewed the general principles of passing-off developed by the courts as early as 1842 in *Perry v. Truefitt* (1842), 6 Beav. 66, 49 E.R. 749 where it was stated:

> ... no man is entitled to represent his goods as being the goods of another man.

[35] He confirmed the three necessary components of a passing-off action as being: (1) the existence of goodwill or reputation attached, in the mind of the purchasing public, to goods or services which, by association with the get-up, have become distinctive specifically of the plaintiff's goods and services, (2) deception of the public due to a misrepresentation leading or likely to lead the public to believe that the goods and services of one person are those of the plaintiff, and (3) actual or potential damage to the plaintiff. ...
[47] The *Ciba-Geigy* decision stands, in my view, for two propositions. The first is that the target clientele or the relevant universe in the pharmaceutical field encompasses the patient. ...
[48] The second proposition which *Ciba-Geigy* stands for is that the general rules in a passing-off action apply to the prescription drug market without any difference or exception. This means that similarities in shape, size and colour of a capsule may be found a passing-off action if the three necessary components are met. ...
[49] While Gonthier J. gave a long description of the state of affairs in the pharmaceutical field, I cannot conclude, as the appellants suggest, that the Supreme Court of Canada is of the view that the appearance of a prescription drug constitutes in every case a trade-mark right. Each case must be demonstrated by relevant evidence.

(b) Application of the Ciba-Geigy decision to the judgment appealed from

[50] The trial judge characterized the *Ciba-Geigy* case as "of vital importance to the present litigation". She did not ignore

it. The real question before us is whether she applied it correctly. I will first consider whether she correctly defined the relevant universe. I will then deal with her application of the passing-off action.
(i) Relevant universe
[51] The dispute between the parties concerns the extent to which potential patients and members of the general public are to be included as the target clientele in a passing-off action in the field of prescription drugs. ...
[53] ... After a review of ... four studies, she concluded:

> Overall, the survey results show very little evidence to support a claim of association between capsule colours being the same and capsule source being the same, very little evidence of an association between the Prozac name and the actual colours of the Prozac capsule, and very little evidence of an association between the capsule colours green and pale yellow and the Prozac name.

[54] Therefore, whether the relevant universe was a narrow one, as submitted by the appellants, or a larger one, including the potential patients, makes no difference in the case at bar. The conclusion the trial judge arrived at is the same. Her finding of fact does not reveal any "palpable and overriding error".
...
(ii) Paragraph 7(b) of the *Trade-marks Act*
[55] With respect to appearance or get-up, the appellants claim they have given to their capsules a specific trade dress which is a distinguishing feature of their goods, and that their goods are known on the market and have acquired a reputation by reason of that distinguishing feature. . . . By adopting those same colours, they say, the respondents have created a situation which is likely to cause confusion.
[56] The trial judge found, as a fact, that the appellants had not proven that the capsule appearance had acquired the requisite reputation in the market place as a distinguishing feature of their product. She concluded that many of the consumers ... will associate the capsule's appearance with the character of the medicine and not its trade source or provenance. She added:

> [...] Those consumers will not be confused by the defendants' products being of similar appearance to that of the plaintiff.

[57] Her fact finding is not one that warrants our intervention.
(iii) "Significant" likelihood of confusion ...
[61] It is clear that in making her determination, the trial judge correctly directed herself to the question of whether the evidence established that there was a likelihood of confusion that surpassed the *de minimis* standard.
[62] I conclude on the whole that the trial judge did not misdirect herself in the law and that it was open to her, as a trier of fact, to conclude that the appellants had not met the requirements of the passing-off action. ...

CONCLUSION

[84] Having concluded that it was open to the trial judge to dismiss the action in passing-off, I would dismiss these appeals with costs.

Unanimous

Institute National des Appellations d'Origine des Vins & Eaux-de-Vie *v.* Andres Wines Ltd.

40 D.L.R.(4TH) 239
ONTARIO SUPREME COURT
JULY 2, 1987

Dupont J.:

INTRODUCTION

The plaintiffs seek injunctive relief restraining the defendants from using the appellation "Champagne" in the manufacture and sale of their products; they also seek damages for loss of sales, diminution of their market, and depreciation of goodwill allegedly resulting from the defendants' use of the appellation "Champagne." ...[T]hey base their claim for injunctive relief upon the common law action of passing off.

The plaintiff, L'Institut National des Appellations d'Origine des Vins et Eaux-de-Vie (I.N.A.O.), is a national organization established by French law; its primary duty is to regulate the areas and conditions of production and sale of wines and spirits bearing controlled appellations of origin. Its co-plaintiffs are companies incorporated under the laws of the Republic of France and carry on business as producers of wine in geographically designated areas located in that part of France described as the Champagne District.

The defendants are companies duly incorporated in Canada who for many years have been producing, advertising and selling sparkling and still wines under various names, some of which incorporate the word "champagne"; in particular, "Canadian Champagne." ...

CANADIAN CASE-LAW

The Ontario Court of Appeal had occasion to deal with the law of passing off, in *Orkin Exterminating Co. Inc. v. Pestco Co. of Canada Ltd. et al.* (1985), 5 C.P.R. (3d) 433, 50 O.R. (2s) 726, 19 D.L.R. (4th) 90. ... [in which it] did consider the general nature of the tort of passing off and clearly stated that, in its view, misrepresentation leading to confusion was a requisite element of the action. Quoting from *Spalding v. Gamage*, Morden J.A. wrote (p. 442 C.P.R., P. 735 O.R., p. 99 D.L.R.: "A fundamental principle upon which the tort of passing off is based is that 'nobody has any right to represent his goods...as the goods... of somebody else'." Later on, he explained (p. 450 C.P.R., p. 744 O.R., p. 108 D.L.R.): "In this kind of case I think that the main consideration should be the likelihood of confusion with consequential injury to the plaintiff."

The Supreme Court of Canada has also approved of the principle that misrepresentation is the underlying basis for an action in passing off. ...

The absence of confusion was considered critical by the Supreme Court because of its conception of the basis of the tort (pp. 15-6 C.P.R., p. 175 D.L.R.):

> ...the passing-off rule is founded upon the tort of deceit, and while the original requirement of an intent to deceive died out in the mid-1800's there remains the re-

quirement, at the very least, that confusion in the minds of the public be a likely consequence by reason of the sale...by the defendant of a product not that of the plaintiff's making, under the guise or implication that it was the plaintiff's product or the equivalent.

In its judgment the Supreme Court of Canada quoted and approved of the following passage which defines the nature of passing off (pp. 13-4 C.P.R., p. 173 D.L.R.):

> It consists of the making of some false representation to the public...likely to induce them to believe that the goods...of another are those of the plaintiff...The test laid down in such cases has been whether... the defendant's conduct results in a false representation, which is likely to cause confusion or deception, even though he has no such intention. (Prosser, *The Law of Torts*, 4th ed.)

This test is found, in various formulations, throughout reported cases. There seems no doubt that for both the House of Lords in England and the Supreme Court in Canada, a necessary, constitutive element of the tort of passing of, the very thing which causes damage to the plaintiff's goodwill, is the defendant's misrepresentation of its product which is likely to cause confusion in the public's mind between the defendant's goods and those of the plaintiff. Although the misrepresentation may take a variety of different forms, as indeed it does in each particular case, it must nevertheless exist and be established through admissible evidence by the plaintiff in order for the plaintiff to succeed in an action for passing off. In a sense "passing off" is a synonym for "misrepresentation" or "false description."

CONCLUSION

A detailed consideration of the evidence brought before the court has led me to conclude that Canadian champagne is a distinct Canadian product not likely to be confused or even compared with French champagne. This conclusion is based on the following evidence: the many years during which the defendant wine producers marketed Canadian champagne in Ontario; the manner in which the defendants' products are labelled, with the word "Canadian" displayed as prominently as the word "champagne," in compliance with government directives, so as to clearly identify the products as Canadian; the way the Canadian product has, for many years, been physically separated from French champagnes in L.C.B.O. stores and listed separately by them as well as by restaurants on their wine lists; the vast body of evidence confirming that Canadian champagne has attained a reputation of its own in Ontario.

The evidence further establishes that the Ontario public concerned with or interested in wines, as purchasers or otherwise, have not been misled and do not confuse the French and the

Canadian products. The purchaser who is completely ignorant about wine and wishes to purchase a bottle of champagne for a special occasion will very likely realize the difference between the two products either by the clear labelling of both, or the difference in listing and physical location at the L.C.B.O. stores, or, finally, by the vast price differential between the products.

The evidence indicates quite clearly that the high regard and reputation of French champagne has not been affected by Ontario sales of Canadian champagne and remains well established in this province. This is supported by evidence illustrating the constantly growing sales of French champagne notwithstanding its dramatic price increases, while the price of Canadian champagne, by comparison, has remained basically stable.

...

This court has concluded, for the reasons detailed throughout this judgment, that the plaintiffs have not established the defendants' misrepresentation and have therefore failed to prove all the elements which constitute the tort of passing off.

The Plaintiff's claim is dismissed.

Note: The appeal from this decision was dismissed by the Ontario Court of Appeal and the Supreme Court of Canada refused to hear a further appeal.

- *W*alt Disney Productions successfully enjoined the West Edmonton Mall from using the name "Fantasyland" for its indoor amusement park,[26] but did not succeed in obtaining an injunction and damages against Fantasyland Hotel for passing off its hotel as "being licensed by, associated with or having the approval of Walt Disney."[27] This latter decision was upheld by the Federal Court of Appeal in February 2000.

4. TRADE MARK

Question

What constitutes infringement of one's trade mark?

Ethical Funds Inc. *v.* *Mackenzie Financial Corporation*

http://www.fja.gc.ca
FEDERAL COURT OF CANADA—TRIAL DIVISION
FEBRUARY 23, 2000

Gibson, J.: ... .

THE PARTIES

[5] Ethical Funds is a company duly incorporated pursuant to the laws of Canada which promotes and manages a family of 12 "socially responsible" mutual funds known as the Ethical Funds. The first word in the name of each of Ethical Funds' "family" of funds is "Ethical".

[6] Ethical Funds is the owner of registered trademarks ETHICAL GROWTH FUND, ETHICAL and ETHICAL FUNDS. Each is registered for use in Canada in association with financial and investment services, namely the operation and management of mutual funds.

[7] Mackenzie is the third largest mutual fund company in Canada. It is the largest fund company selling its mutual funds through independent dealers. ...

BACKGROUND

[9] On the 30th of November, 1999, Mackenzie filed a preliminary prospectus for a new fund in the family of Universal funds, Universal Ethical Opportunities Fund (the "Universal Ethical Fund"). In early January of 2000, Mackenzie launched the Universal Ethical Fund. ...

[10] ... Mackenzie refused to comply with the "cease and desist" demands [of Ethical Funds]. In the result, Ethical Funds filed a statement of claim ... Ethical Funds claims for: a declaration that Mackenzie has adopted and used its registered trademarks and has passed off its wares, services and business as the wares, services and business of Ethical Funds; an interim, interlocutory and permanent injunction in the terms of the injunction here being sought on an interim basis; delivery up to the plaintiff of all materials bearing the registered trademarks; damages or an accounting of Mackenzie's profits as Ethical Funds may elect; and costs.

[11] On the 15th of February, 2000 Mackenzie filed its statement of defence together with a counterclaim. In its counterclaim, Mackenzie seeks an order pursuant to section 57 of the *Trade-marks Act* that Ethical Funds' registered trademarks here at issue be expunged.

THE ISSUE

[12] The issue before the Court on this application is simply stated: whether or not the plaintiff is entitled to an interim injunction in the terms sought or in a variation of those terms.

THE TEST FOR ISSUANCE OF AN INTERIM INJUNCTION

[13] In *R.J.R.-Macdonald Inc. v. Canada (Attorney-General)* [1994] 1 S.C.R. 311, the Supreme Court of Canada consolidated the guidance for lower courts on applications for interlocutory injunctions. I am satisfied that the guidance applies equally on applications such as this for interim injunctions.

[14] At page 334, Justices Sopinka and Cory, for the Court, wrote:

Metropolitan Stores adopted a three-stage test for courts to apply when considering an application for either a stay or an interlocutory injunction. First, a preliminary assessment must be made of the merits of the case to ensure that there is a serious question to be tried. Secondly, it must be determined whether the applicant would suffer irreparable harm if the application were refused. Finally, an assessment must be made as to which of the parties would suffer greater harm from the granting or refusal of the remedy pending a decision on the merits.

[15] At pages 337-8, the Court wrote:

What then are the indicators of "a serious question to be tried"? There are no specific requirements which must be met in order to satisfy this test. The threshold is a low one. The judge on the application must make a preliminary assessment of the merits of the case. ...

Once satisfied that the application is neither vexatious nor frivolous, the motions judge should proceed to consider the second and third tests, even if of the opinion that the plaintiff is unlikely to succeed at trial. A prolonged examination of the merits is generally neither necessary nor desirable. [emphasis added]

...

[17] ...[T]he Court went on to consider the second test, that is to say, "irreparable harm". It wrote:

At this stage the only issue to be decided is whether a refusal to grant relief could so adversely affect the applicants' own interests that the harm could not be remedied if the eventual decision on the merits does not accord with the result of the interlocutory application.

"Irreparable" refers to the nature of the harm suffered rather than its magnitude. It is harm which either cannot be quantified in monetary terms or which cannot be cured, usually because one party cannot collect damages from the other. [emphasis added]

[18] Finally, at pages 342-3, the Court wrote:

The third test to be applied ... was described by Beetz J. in *Metropolitan Stores* at p. 129 as: "a determination of

which of the two parties will suffer the greater harm from the granting or refusal of an interlocutory injunction, pending a decision on the merits". ...

The factors which must be considered in assessing the "balance of inconvenience" are numerous and will vary in each individual case. ...

ANALYSIS

[20] In *Fournier Pharma Inc. v. Apotex Inc.*, (1999), 1 C.P.R. (4th) 344 (F.C.T.D). Madame Justice Tremblay-Lamer, in considering an application for an interim injunction, wrote ... :

It has been said many times by this Court, that interim injunctions are a rare and exceptional remedy. As stated in *The Kun Shoulder Rest*:

... Both the Rules and the particular nature of an application for an interim injunction require that the applicant demonstrate an urgency of such importance that there is no alternative way to proceed in order to counter the harm that might or is actually occurring.

I am satisfied that the urgency requirement is demonstrated here. The RRSP season, this year January 1, to February 29, is indicated by the evidence before me to provide a unique annual opportunity for marketers of mutual funds such as Ethical Funds and Mackenzie.

[21] While the threshold to establish a serious issue for trial is low, the threshold for establishing irreparable harm is much higher. Madame Justice Tremblay-Lamer adopted the following passage from the reasons of our colleague Mr. Justice Dubé in *Merck Frosst Canada Inc. v. Canada (Minister of Health)* (1997), 74 C.P.R. (3d) 460 (F.C.T.D):

... [It] is not for the motion judge to go very deeply into the merits of the case. Thus, the threshold of serious issue is very low: the motion judge merely has to decide whether or not there is some merit in the sense that it is not frivolous. However, the threshold of irreparable harm is very high. An injunction is an extraordinary remedy. It is discretionary. The Court ought not to grant it merely to favour one side at the expense of another in what is obviously an on-going battle ...

...

[22] Further, I note that the Federal Court of Appeal cautioned ... that the evidence of irreparable harm must be "clear and not speculative". ...

[26] I am satisfied that, against the low threshold on the question of triable issue, the issue of whether or not "Ethical" is the exclusive property of Ethical Funds or is a generic term in the context of the market in which Ethical Funds and Mackenzie operate is an issue for trial and not one that should be determined on an application such as this. The registration of a trade-mark is *prima facie* evidence of its validity. I adopt the conclusion of Mr. Justice Dubé in *Tele-Direct (Publications) Inc. v. American Business Information Inc.* (1994), 58 C.P.R. (3d) 10 (F.C.T.D) where he wrote at pages 12 and 13:

There is undoubtedly a serious question to be tried. Section 7 of the *Trade-marks Act* provides that no person shall direct public attention to his services in such a way as to cause confusion, or pass off other services for those requested. Section 19 stipulates that the registration of a trade-mark, unless shown to be invalid, gives to the owner the exclusive right to its use throughout Canada. Section 20 provides that the right of the owner of a registered trade-mark shall be deemed to be infringed by a person not entitled to its use. And s. 22 dictates that no person shall use a trade-mark so as to depreciate the value of the goodwill attached thereto.

[27] I reach a different conclusion on the issue of irreparable harm. The harm to Ethical Funds if Mackenzie is allowed to continue to market its Universal Ethical Opportunities Fund lies in loss of sales, possible confusion between Ethical Funds' family of funds and Mackenzie's new fund and through depreciation of the value of the goodwill attached to Ethical Funds' "Ethical" marks.... Further, there can be no doubt that Mackenzie is a substantial corporation and that damages assessed would be recoverable. Indeed, in an affidavit of [an officer of Mackenzie] ... attests that Mackenzie's income from the first year of operation of Universal Ethical Opportunities

Fund would not be substantial and would be well within the ability of Mackenzie to satisfy an award. [He] further undertakes on behalf of Mackenzie to "... keep a careful account of all sales of units of this fund" and indicates that Mackenzie "... is willing to expedite this matter to an early trial date, well before next year's RRSP season."

[28] On the evidence before me, against an appropriately high threshold for determination of irreparable harm on an application such as this, I simply am not satisfied that Ethical Funds has met that threshold.

[29] Having reached the conclusion that I have with respect to irreparable harm, it is not necessary for me to go further to consider the issue of balance of convenience. However, very briefly, if I were required to do so I would conclude that the balance of convenience in this matter lies in favour of Ethical Funds. ...

CONCLUSION

[32] Based upon the foregoing considerations and analysis, this application for an interim injunction was dismissed on the 22nd of February, 2000. ...

- *T*he owners of The Loose Moose Tap & Grill failed to obtain an interlocutory injunction to restrain the owners of the restaurant, The Spruce Goose Brewing Co., from commencing operations. The court did not find the words in the name of the new restaurant so similar as to create confusion in the minds of the public; but in the event confusion was established at trial, the court refused to grant the injunction on the grounds that The Spruce Goose would suffer more if the injunction were granted than The Loose Moose would suffer if the injunction were not granted.[28]

- *I*n Newark, New Jersey, the proprietor called his business "Dom Knows Pizza." Domino's Pizza Corporation was not amused and sued for trade mark infringement.[29]

- *I*n 1990, the proprietor of a tavern decorated with velvet paintings named his bar "Velvet Elvis" and registered the trademark. He argued the bar celebrates the phenomenon of velvet oil paintings, not Elvis. Nevertheless, Elvis Presley Enterprises Inc. was successful in its court action to stop him from using the name "Velvet Elvis."

- *H*ormel Foods Corporation, the makers of Spam, a pressed meat product, has demanded that the e-mail distributor Cyber Promotions Inc. not use a picture of a can of Spam at its Web site. Hormel Foods would be pleased that people not use the term "spamming" for wholesale distribution of junk e-mail.[30]

- *H*ogg Wyld Ltd. and Oink, Inc. of New Mexico, manufacturers of jeans to fit large women, were unsuccessfully sued by Jordache Enterprises for using a mark that included the name "Lardashe."[31]

Question

Can you use your competitor's trademark in comparison advertising?

Future Shop Ltd. *v.* *A. & B. Sound Ltd.*

[1994] 8 W.W.R. 376
BRITISH COLUMBIA SUPREME COURT
APRIL 14, 1994

MacKenzie J.:—The plaintiffs (hereinafter referred to as "Future Shop") apply for an interlocutory injunction to restrain the defendants (hereinafter referred to as "A. & B. Sound") from referring to Future Shop trademarks in comparative advertising. The parties are each engaged in the retail sale of commercial electronic products. Future Shop operates nationwide in Canada with a few outlets in the United States. A. & B. Sound's outlets are confined to British Columbia and Alberta. Future Shop's sales overall are substantially greater than sales of A. & B. Sound but both have annual sales in excess of $100,000,000.

"The Future Shop" is a registered trademark of Future Shop; the plaintiffs have also applied for registration of "Future Shop" and "Future Shop Ltd." For the purposes of this application, A. & B. Sound concedes that all three names are trademarked and they are treated as interchangeable hereafter.

The complaint before me relates to the use by A. & B. Sound of the Future Shop trademark in comparative advertisements of A. & B. Sound. For the purposes of this application, the ads are otherwise accepted as fair and accurate. ...

Future Shop claims that A. & B. Sound's use of its trademark name is in violation of its trademark rights pursuant to s. 19 and s. 22(1) of the *Trade Marks Act*, R.S.C. 1985, c.T-13. Future Shop also relies on the definition of "use" in s. 2 of the statute and the "deemed use" provision of s.4.

For ease of reference, s. 19 and s. 22(l) are as follows:

Rights conferred by registration

19. Subject to sections 21 and 32, the registration of a trade-mark in respect of any wares or services, unless shown to be invalid, gives to the owner of the trade-mark the exclusive right to the use throughout Canada of the trade-mark in respect of those wares or services.

Depreciation of goodwill

22.(1) No person shall use a trade-mark registered by another person in a manner that is likely to have the effect of depreciating the value of the goodwill attaching thereto.

The authorities establish a two-part test for interlocutory injunctive relief which may be conveniently summarized as, first, a threshold question whether there is "a fair issue to be tried" and, if the applicant satisfies the threshold test, secondly whether the balance of convenience favours granting the relief. ...

"FAIR QUESTION TO BE TRIED"

The proposition pressed most strenuously by Mr. Dyer on behalf of Future Shop was that the use of the Future Shop name in a comparative ad was "likely to depreciate the value of the goodwill attaching" to the Trademark in breach of s. 22(l). This section was first interpreted by Thurlow J. in *Clairol International Corp. v. Thomas Supply & Equipment Co.*, [1968] 2 Ex. C.R. 552. ...

There is no provision similar to s. 22 in any other jurisdiction and it is capable of a sweeping ambit. Thurlow J. notes that it could be interpreted to extend to comparative price lists identified by trademarks displayed in a poster by a shopkeeper on his counter. He concludes that s. 22 was not intended "to forbid legitimate comparisons or criticisms of that kind." There is no difference in principle between a counter display of comparative prices and a newspaper, radio or T.V. advertisement containing the same information. ...

The question, depending on the evidence in any particular case, is whether the use of the competitor's trademark is for a purpose which stresses the similarities or the differences with the trademarked competition. If the purpose is to stress the similarities, the value of the goodwill associated with the trademark is appropriated in a manner contrary to the intent of s. 22. If use stresses the differences with the trademark, then the use is for the purpose of distancing the trademarked ware or service and 22 is not offended. ...

... In my view, the *Clairol* decision supports the position of A. & B. Sound that their fair and accurate comparative price ads do not offend s. 22(l) of the *Trade Marks Act*. ...

... The broad construction [of s. 22] pressed by Future Shop would preclude comparative pricing, at least of services, and prohibit comparative price ads of a type that are commonplace in contemporary retail advertising of price-sensitive products, among grocery stores for example. For that reason, I share the reservations of the merits of a broad interpretation of s. 22 expressed by Thurlow and Reed JJ. I doubt that an expansive interpretation will ultimately prevail. But at the present stage of the evolution of the jurisprudence, I cannot say that the position advanced by Future Shop is untenable. Accordingly, I conclude that Future Shop's position raises a "fair issue to be tried" and Future Shop has met the threshold test.

...

BALANCE OF CONVENIENCE

[The court reviews the case law.]

Future Shop contends that it will suffer harm that cannot be compensated for in damages if the injunction is not granted. It submits that the potential damage to its reputation is unquantifiable and cannot be adequately repaired by an award of damages.

The parties are large retailers of consumer items where price competition is intense. A. & B. Sound pursues a strategy of seeking to attract customers by highlighting its low prices in comparison with those of its competitors by ads which, for the purposes of this application, are assumed to be otherwise fair and accurate. An injunction would deprive A. & B. Sound of that option, at least with respect to Future Shop, and likely work to its disadvantage in the battle for market share. Consumers face a bewildering array of products and prices; comparative information helps them to make better choices. The public has an interest in comparative advertising, providing it is fair an accurate. I think that the impact upon the market share of the parties from either granting or refusing an injunction is difficult to measure but equally imponderable either way. ...

As discussed above, Future Shop's case is arguable but weak. The dispute involves two large and, I think, essentially responsible retailers engaged in a hotly contested struggle for market share. To the extent there is a status quo, refusal of the injunction will best maintain the status quo until all the issues between the parties can be thoroughly canvassed at trial. I conclude that the balance of convenience favours refusing this injunction.

This application has been argued against a background of advertisements by each side which have been challenged by the other as false and deceptive. Each has responded to this criticism by modifying its advertising. Some of those modifications have been confirmed by solicitors' undertakings. Irritants still remain and criticism continues, but the parties seem to have made considerable progress in resolving their differences. Future Shop fears a repetition, at a sensitive time in the marketing year, of an ad similar to the so-called "Pinocchio" ad of A. & B. Sound which portrayed Future Shop with a long liar's nose. A. & B. Sound has agreed not to repeat the Pinocchio ad but has not ruled out ads of a similar nature in the future. The Pinocchio ad was offensive and Future Shop's indignation and desire to avoid any repetition is understandable. In a struggle for customers, emotions can run high even for large, sophisticated retailers. It appears to me that the Pinocchio ad was probably an over-reaction to any provocation present in Future Shop ads. The parties ought not to let emotion overcome good judgment. There are limits to legitimate advertising and the courts of necessity will determine those limits if the issues are pressed. But limits set by the courts are unlikely to be as satisfactory to either side as limits which they devise themselves as experienced retailers and agree to respect. The progress which the parties have made to date suggests that they ought to be able to complete the process.

The application for an interlocutory injunction on the terms argued before me is denied.

Application dismissed.

- *T*he ad showed two pies. One had a bottom crust inverted over the bottom crust. It looked silly. It was labelled "Maple Leaf" with the words "their idea of a top crust." Robin Hood's pie had a proper "lattice-work" top. Maple Leaf applied for an injunction. It argued that the ads were false and misleading. The court found that the balance of convenience favoured Maple Leaf and granted the injunction.[32]

Question

Could I make an agreement with my competitor about the use of my trademark in comparative advertising?

Eveready Canada v. *Duracell Canada Inc.*

64 C.P.R. (3D) 348
ONTARIO COURT (GENERAL DIVISION)
NOVEMBER 9, 1995

Lane J. (orally)—This motion involves a dispute over whether the defendant is in breach of obligations under the *Trade-marks Act*, R.S.C. 1985, c. T-13, and under an agreement between the parties, in broadcasting a T.V. commercial in which it makes a ~~~m that its batteries are superior to the batteries of the plaintiff.

advertisement in question is called "Staying Alive." It is TV commercial of 30 seconds in length. There is a ~~~ng of a superscript which reads "The Copper Top ll" which is agreed to be a claim for superiority of the defendant's product over all other batteries and therefore, clearly over the batteries of the plaintiff.

The theme of superiority is also carried through the imagery of the commercial. The commercial shows a party going on. The partygoers are in costume. A unicorn, which has the defendant's battery strapped to his back and is therefore powered by it, outdances all other dancers until at the last, he dances with a masked dancer in a blue dress. He dances vigorously, she dances more languorously. She collapsed in a heap, her mask falls away revealing a pink bunny whose eyes close as she expires. The unicorn then dances up the stairs.

There was some debate over whether or not the pink bunny was actually dead or not, but I regard this as a somewhat esoteric debate. The implication is very clear that the battery of the defendant powering the unicorn is far superior to the battery of the plaintiff powering the pink bunny.

These parties both have pink bunnies as trade marks. It is conceded by Mr. Skea [Vice-President of Marketing for the defendant] in giving his evidence this afternoon that the pink bunny in the commercial is intended to represent the plaintiff's trade mark pink bunny. The bunny is, however, not dressed in the fashion that is characteristic of the plaintiff's bunny in that it is not beating a drum and it is not wearing sun-glasses. This, however, does not seem to be a distinction with a lot of difference for the present since, as I say, it is conceded that the pink bunny is intended to represent the plaintiffs trade mark. Having seen the commercial myself in court, I would not have any doubt that it would be so recognized by at least a good many consumers.

Now the fact that these parties both have pink bunnies, albeit differently got up, has apparently led to some confusion in the past and in order to minimize that confusion the parties have entered into an agreement, one clause of which is of some importance in this litigation. That is an agreement of January 10, 1992, which recites the background of the use of pink bunnies by each of them, defines the plaintiff's pink bunny as one that wears sun-glasses, carries a drum bearing an Eveready trade mark and shoes known as flip-flops and the defendant's bunny as a pink bunny with and without a drum. There are also drawings of these bunnies attached.

The agreement requires the parties to exercise good faith efforts to avoid confusion between the two bunnies and then in para. 5 provides as follows:

> The parties agree that neither party will use the other's bunny, or a bunny confusingly similar thereto, in comparative advertising unless the advertising party makes an unambiguous and truthful claim that the advertiser's brand possesses service-life superiority.

Also of importance in the litigation is s. 52(l) of the *Competition Act*, R.S.C. 1985, c. C-34, which reads as follows:

> 52(l)   No person shall, for the purpose of promoting, directly or indirectly, the supply or use of a product or for the purpose of promoting, directly or indirectly, any business interest, by any means whatever,
>
> > (b) make a representation to the public in the form of a statement, warranty or guarantee of the performance, efficacy or length of life of a product that is not based on an adequate and proper test thereof, the proof of which lies on the person making the representation;

The plaintiff submits that there is a serious issue to be tried here as to the right of the defendant to broadcast this commercial. In the first place, it says that claim for superiority is contrary to s. 52 just read because, the defendant does not have in its possession any testing of the plaintiff's product that can support the claim of superiority.

[The judge reviews the evidence of tests and of improvements in the products made by the companies.]

I think from a technical point of view the defendant would have trouble meeting the test of s. 52 because it has done no testing of its own on the latest batteries and I think it is stretching the section somewhat to suggest that the defendant can justify its advertisement by seizing, after the event, on the plaintiff's testing. The intent of the section is clearly that no one shall put a commercial of this sort out into the stream of commerce without doing testing himself in advance to ensure that the claim that is being made is true.

I am also of the view that the differences that are demonstrated by the plaintiffs evidence of testing may well, as the plaintiff's witness suggests in his affidavit, fall into the category of differences that are not statistically or commercially significant.

I conclude that there is a serious issue to be tried as to whether in the last 15 days while this commercial has been aired, the necessary proof of superiority existed and whether the claim is indeed a truthful one within the meaning of the agreement between the parties. Having concluded there is a serious issue to be tried, I turn to the balance of convenience and the question of irreparable harm.

[The court concludes that both would suffer loss of sales.]

The plaintiff argues that the commercial directly attacks its trade mark bunny and denigrates it. Although, as I have noted, the dying bunny is not wearing sun-glasses nor is she beating a drum, it is admitted that it is intended to depict the plaintiffs bunny trade mark and, as I have said, it so appears to me.

The defendant responds that the agreement allows the use of the plaintiff's trade mark by the defendant in a comparative advertisement making an unambiguous and truthful claim and accordingly, the use of the trade mark cannot form the basis for a lawsuit. I have already mentioned that I think there is a serious issue about whether or not the claim is a truthful one. But there is a further point and that is, that having considered the nature of this agreement, I cannot accept that these two enormous business enterprises with the huge investments that each has, on the evidence, in their respective trade marks, intended to subject their trade marks to visual humiliation at the hands of the other party in comparative advertising. It makes no commercial sense to think that these parties had the intention of putting their trade marks at that kind of risk. And it is not essential in giving full meaning to the language of the clause, to take it that far. It makes commercial sense to read the clause as allowing the fair depiction of the other side's trade mark so as to make clear who is the target of the superiority claim. But it seems to me that a very serious issue exists as to the fairness of the treatment of the plaintiff's trade mark by the defendant within the context of the activity permitted under the agreement cl. 5.

For these reasons, I have concluded that the potential damage to the plaintiff is in a different realm than the potential damage to the defendant. The loss of sales is one thing. Damage which may be long lasting or even permanent to a valuable trade mark is another thing altogether. For these reasons, I find that the balance of convenience favours the plaintiff.

Accordingly, the motion for an injunction will be adjourned but upon terms that the advertisement is withdrawn during the term of the adjournment.

Motion adjourned.

Q u e s t i o n

What kind of evidence can be introduced to defend against a claim of passing-off or trade mark infringement?

Tony the Tiger v. Esso Tiger: The plaintiffs alleged passing-off and trademark infringement by the Esso Tiger. The defendant pleaded that TONY THE TIGER has coexisted with the ESSO TIGER for 30 years in 17 countries. When the plaintiffs refused to produce evidence relating to the co-existence claim, the Senior Master ordered them to do so. This action is an appeal to the court to determine whether evidence of co-existence without confusion in other countries may be relevant to the passing-off and trade-mark infringement claims asserted by the plaintiff. ...

[The judge reviews the law and the history of the company's use of their tigers.]

"It is apparent from this summary that the focus of the plaintiffs' claims is damages for activities of the defendant within Canada. But that does not mean that the defendant is compelled to answer only with respect to Canada; the defendant had the option to put into issue a history of co-existence without confusion in other countries.

"For the foregoing reasons, I answer the first question of law in the affirmative. Co-existence without confusion outside Canada is relevant. ...

"... On the basis of the above review, I cannot find that it is plain and obvious that co-existence without confusion in other countries over a prolonged period of time does not disclose a defence to a claim based on passing-off and trade-mark infringement. I agree with the defendant's counsel that, at best the plaintiffs have shown that such evidence was, historically, viewed with some hesitation, but that such evidence is currently, more likely considered relevant, particularly if the issue is raised in the pleadings. The test is the likelihood of confusion. The burden of proof is on the plaintiff to prove that there is a likelihood. If, as alleged by the plaintiffs, there was a hiatus of many years in Canada, co-existence without confusion in other countries may be significant on the issue of likelihood of confusion in Canada. Where the issue is the tendency of similar marks to cause confusion, experience in similar market places, at least at this stage, is *prima facie* relevant."

Kellogg Co. et al. v. Imperial Oil Ltd.
136 D.L.R. (4th) 686
Ontario Court (General Division)
April 30, 1996

Note: This cat-fight is also being fought south of the border where the U.S. Supreme Court agreed with the lower court that Kellogg did not wait too long before taking action against Exxon Mobil Corp. for infringing trademark. Therefore, Kellogg's lawsuit can proceed in Texas.[33]

- *A* U.S. court ruled that AT&T could use the phrase "You have mail" in the action by AOL, which uses that phrase in its e-mail service, on the grounds that the terms are generic.[34]

- *T*he British owner of the television characters, Teletubbies, has filed suit against Wal-Mart for producing and selling Bubbly Chubbies, which the owner of Teletubbies alleges infringes its intellectual property rights. Stay tuned.[35]

Q u e s t i o n

What are the dangers of licensing?

- *T*he fact that brand-name clothes, makeup, underwear, etc. may not be made by the designers is "fashion's dirty little secret." Calvin Klein has sued Warnaco, the company that makes, markets, and distributes the "Calvin Klein" jeans and underwear, for damaging his brand name by affixing the Calvin Klein label to designs he has not approved and by selling his wares to discount stores.[36]

DOMAIN NAMES

Q u e s t i o n

What laws and regulatory bodies are prohibiting cybersquatters from misusing trademarks?

- *M*adonna evicted a cybersquatter from the address madonna.com with a ruling of the World Intellectual Property Organization (WIPO). WIPO is the UN agency that operates an arbitration system for ordering the transfer of domain names when the person who registered the name had no trademark right and no legitimate interest in the name. Other complainants who received a favourable ruling include Christian Dior, Microsoft, Julia Roberts, and Nike. Sting lost his application on the grounds that "sting" was a common English word.[37]

- *H*arvard University sued for the right to use its name in its Internet address after Michael Rhys attempted to sell Harvard 65 domain names relating to Harvard University and Radcliffe for $325,000. The action is taken under the U.S. *Anticybersquatting Consumer Protection Act* aimed to stop such "cybersquatting" or "cyber-piracy," the practice of people registering trademarks or names of celebrities, established corporations, or products as domain names with the intention of selling them for a profit.[38]

5. PATENT

Q u e s t i o n

What is patentable?

President and Fellows of Harvard College v. Commissioner of Patents

http://www.fja.gc.ca
FEDERAL COURT OF APPEAL
AUGUST 3, 2000

Rothstein J.A.:

OVERVIEW

[1] The issue in this appeal is the patentability of genetically altered non-human mammals for use in carcinogenicity studies. ... The Commissioner of Patents found that the appellant was not entitled to be granted a patent covering these claims. ... [An appeal was dismissed]....

OBJECTIVES OF PATENT CLAIMS . . .

[3] ... The objective of the appellant is to produce animals with a susceptibility to cancer for purposes of animal carcinogenicity studies. ...

[4] The technology by which a cancer-prone mouse is produced is described in the Commissioner's decision. An activated oncogene sequence (oncogene) is a gene which makes a mouse more susceptible to cancer. A plasmid (a carrier) is constructed containing the oncogene. The plasmid is injected into a fertilized mouse egg (preferably while it is at the one-cell (zygote) stage and generally not later than the eight-cell stage). The injected egg is then transferred into a female "host" mouse and allowed to develop to term. The reason for injecting the oncogene preferably into the zygote is to ensure, to the extent the oncogene is taken up, that it will affect all the cells of the mouse which develop from the zygote. If the resulting mouse is found to have all of its cells affected by the oncogene, it is called a "founder" mouse. The founder mouse is then mated with an uninjected mouse. In accordance with Mendelian inheritance of single loci, 50% of the offspring will be found to have all their cells affected by the oncogene.

[5] The appellant seeks to protect the product of this process, that is, the founder mammal and the offspring whose cells are affected by the oncogene. In this decision, for ease of reference, the product ... will be referred to as a transgenic non-human mammal or an oncomouse. ...

ANALYSIS

1. The Patent Act
(a) Object and Purpose of the *Patent Act*
[24] Some insight into the appropriate approach to interpreting the *Patent Act* may be derived from a consideration of the object and purpose of the legislation.
[25] A patent protects an invention. When a patent for an invention is granted, the patentee is given the "exclusive right, privilege and liberty of making, constructing and using the invention and selling it to others to be used" for a period specified in the *Patent Act*: 17 years from the date on which the patent is issued for patent applications filed before October 1, 1989, as in this case, or 20 years from the date of the filing of

a patent application filed on or after October 1, 1989. The 17 or 20 year terms are intended to enable the inventor to exploit the invention free from competition for that period. The purpose is to permit the recovery of research and development investment necessary to produce the invention and a return on that investment to the inventor, commensurate with the value purchasers place on the invention. The intention is to provide an incentive for the creation of processes or products which are new, useful and unobvious. Without patent protection, as soon as a product implementing a new idea is marketed, others could copy it and compete with the original inventor without having to have made the initial research and development investment. Competitors who did not have to cover such costs could drive prices down to such a level that the original inventor could not recoup the research and development investment made, let alone a return on that investment, thereby discouraging the creation of inventions.

[26] In return for the 17 or 20 year period of protection from competition, the patentee is required to make full disclosure of the invention. In its recent decision in *Cadbury-Schweppes v. FBI Foods* [1999] 1 S.C.R. 142], the Supreme Court of Canada described the "bargain that lies at the heart of patent protection":

> A patent is a statutory monopoly which is given in exchange for a full and complete disclosure by the patentee of his or her invention... Accordingly, at least one of the policy objectives underlying the statutory remedies available to a patent owner is to make disclosure more attractive, and thus hasten the availability of useful knowledge in the public sphere in the public interest.

Thus, the object of the *Patent Act* is to promote the development of inventions in a manner that benefits both the inventor and the public.
(b) The Requirement that an Invention be New, Useful and Unobvious
[27] ... "Invention" is defined in section 2 of the *Patent Act*:

> 2. In this Act, except as otherwise provided, "invention" means any new and useful art, process, machine, manufacture or composition of matter, or any new and useful improvement in any art, process, machine, manufacture or composition of matter.

[28] Under section 28.3 of the *Patent Act* the subject matter of a patent claim must not have been obvious to persons skilled in the art or science. ...
(d) Policy Considerations
[30] There was considerable fanfare in this appeal that significant policy questions are at stake ... To the extent the appeal gives rise to policy questions, they are to be addressed by Parliament and not the Court.
(e) Supreme Court Observations on Patentability of Life Forms

...

[32] The Supreme Court ... has instructed that where the issue is the patentability of a form of life involving new technology, a cautious approach to the scope of pronouncements by the courts must be adopted.

2. Patentability of the Oncomouse ...

[34] I conclude that the oncomouse is both unobvious and a new and useful "composition of matter". Therefore it is an "invention" within the meaning of that term in section 2 of the *Patent Act*. ...

[35] In *Chakrabarty, Diamond, Commissioner of Patents and Trademarks v. Chakrabarty*, [(1980) 206 U.S.P.Q. 193] . . ., in dealing with the term "composition of matter" Chief Justice Burger . . .[stated]:

> ... "composition of matter" has been construed consistent with its common usage to include "all compositions of two or more substances and ... all composite articles, whether they be the results of chemical union, or of mechanical mixture, or whether they be gases, fluids, powders, or solids."

.... [The court reviews the process of injecting a plasmid with DNA into a fertilized mouse egg to show that the founder oncomouse and its offspring are composition of matter.]

[43] ... [Nothing in the term "composition of matter" suggests that living things are excluded from the definition. ...

[46] The definition of "invention" in the *Patent Act* does not expressly exclude discoveries that follow the laws of nature. It would thus appear that the reason creations or discoveries that <u>only</u> follow the laws of nature do not meet the requirements of patentability is because they are not considered new and unobvious. Rather, such creations or discoveries are considered to have existed and only to have been uncovered by man. Something more is required for patentability, namely, a non-naturally occurring "composition of matter" arising from the application of inventiveness or ingenuity. ...

[49] In my opinion, the oncomouse must be considered to be the result of both ingenuity and the laws of nature ...

[51] ... The question is ... whether the oncomouse described in the patent claims would exist in nature. Clearly it would not. ...

[53] Having regard to section 40 of the *Patent Act, supra*, on a straightforward interpretation of the term "composition of matter" and taking into account the roles of ingenuity and the laws of nature, there is no reason in law why the product, in this case the oncomouse, is not patentable ...

THE INTERVENOR'S SUBMISSIONS

[107] The Canadian Environmental Law Association was granted intervenor status in this appeal. ...

[114] The intervenor then makes a number of public interest arguments ...

[115] ... In this type of case, the Court is not the forum for a public policy debate. ...

[118] I have already indicated that, in my respectful view, the words of the *Patent Act* do not exclude living things. It is Parliament and not the Court that defines the limits of patentability. ... If anyone is of the opinion that the scope of patentability should be narrowed, it is open to that person to ask Parliament to do so.

SCOPE OF CLAIMS

[119] [The court agrees to accept claims as drawn, that is, covering all non-human mammals and all oncogenes.] ...

THE IMPLICATION FOR HUMAN BEINGS

[125] A final question is whether the *Patent Act* could be extended to cover human beings. ...For example, on a theoretical level, could a person whose genome has been modified by the addition of an engineered gene in order to eliminate or suppress a genetic predisposition to a disease be the subject matter of a patent?

[126] Strictly, the question does not arise here ...

[127] The answer is clearly that the *Patent Act* cannot be extended to cover human beings. Patenting is a form of ownership of property. Ownership concepts cannot be extended to human beings. There are undoubtedly other bases for so concluding, but one is surely section 7 of the *Charter of Rights and Freedoms* which protects liberty. There is, therefore, no concern by including non-human mammals under the definition of "invention" in the *Patent Act*, that there is any implication that a human being would be patentable in the way that the oncomouse is. ...

CONCLUSION

[129] The appeal will be allowed . . . and the matter will be remitted to the Commissioner of Patents with the direction to grant a patent ....

2–1

- *T*he deciphering of human DNA requires delineating 3.1 billion biochemical "letters." While some scientists are trying to patent sequences, the scientists involved in the international Human Genome Project are racing to put all their findings on the Internet—sometimes within 24 hours of decoding a sequence—so that the information will be available free to the people of the world.[39]

6. INDUSTRIAL DESIGN

- *U*nder the *Industrial Design Act*, electronic icons like those used on computer screens and cell phones are registrable as long as they meet the requirements of the Act.[40]

• **M**irabai Art Glass of Ontario asked the court for an interlocutory injunction against Paradise Designs of Vancouver to stop it from selling designer toilet plungers, a popular Christmas present. The request was refused.[41]

7. REMEDIES

INJUNCTION

 See *Ethical Funds Inc. v. Mackenzie Financial Corporation*, p. 234, for a discussion of the legal tests for granting an injunction.

The heirs of Lucy Maud Montgomery, the author of "Anne of Green Gables," were awarded damages and granted an injunction prohibiting Avonlea Tradition Inc. (Avonlea) from selling merchandise connected to the characters of the book. Avonlea was a party to a licence agreement but failed to pay royalties almost from the time of the agreement because of the president of Avonlea's "irrational yet firm view that the respondents did not deserve payment of royalties as it was she who was exerting all of the effort and work."

Applying a three-part test set out in *RJR MacDonald Inc. v. Canada* (1994) 54 C.P.R. (3d) 114, the Ontario Court of Appeal dismissed Avonlea's motion to stay part of the injunction until the hearing of its appeal from the trial court. First, Avonlea failed to present a serious issue for adjudication as it reiterated arguments advanced at trial. Second, the company did not show it would suffer irreparable harm because it already had long-standing financial difficulties. Third, "and perhaps most importantly," the balance of convenience did not favour Avonlea. On the contrary it favoured the respondents. The respondents state that the appellant's long-standing and ongoing failure to pay royalties has impaired the ability of other licensees to fairly compete in the market place and has undermined the Authority's licensing program. Several licensees have threatened to discontinue paying royalties if the appellant is permitted to continue operating its business without paying royalties.

Anne of Green Gables Licensing Authority Inc. v. Avonlea Traditions Inc.
http://www.ontariocourts.on.ca/
Ontario Court of Appeal
April 4, 2000

ANTON PILLER ORDER

Q u e s t i o n

What is an Anton Piller Order and what do the courts require before granting one?

Profekta International Inc. **v.** *Mai*

http//www.fja-cmf.gc.ca
FEDERAL COURT TRIAL DIVISION
AUGUST 29, 1996.

McKeown J.: The plaintiff seeks an Anton Piller order on an *ex parte* and *in camera* basis, for the detention, custody and preservation of copies of video-cassette taped programs allegedly in the control of the defendant and allegedly infringing the plaintiff's rights as the exclusive Canadian licensee for those programs.

THE FACTS

The plaintiff filed a statement of claim on September 22, 1995. The plaintiff's statement of claim alleges that: 1) the defendant has knowingly infringed copyright in video-cassette taped programs owned by Television Broadcasts Limited of Hong Kong; 2) it is the exclusive Canadian licensee for the programs and as such possesses an interest protected pursuant to the provisions of the *Copyright Act*, R.S.C., 1985, c. C-42 (the Act) and the plaintiff licenses retail video stores to rent the programs to the public, and; 3) the defendant, who operates a retail store, rents out the programs on video-cassette tapes without the plaintiff's permission in violation of the Act.

[Although the plaintiff requested an affidavit of documents—and video-cassette tapes are "documents" within the meaning of the Federal Court Rules [C.R.C., c. 663]—the defendant has twice failed to give an accurate listing. The plaintiff knows they are inaccurate because the plaintiff's investigator has rented offending videos from the defendant's store.]

The plaintiff has brought this motion for an Anton Piller order in part on the basis [of] the defendant's failure to provide an accurate and complete affidavit of documents, despite having been expressly asked. ...

ANALYSIS

An Anton Piller order is a remedy which should be granted in only the rarest of circumstances as it confers on the moving party a search and seizure power which runs contrary to the principles of private property and trespass. Accordingly, an Anton Piller order must only be granted where the moving party has satisfied a burdensome test. As was enunciated in the original case dealing with such an order, *Anton Piller K.G. v. Manufacturing Processes Ltd.*, [1976] R.P.C. 719 (C.A.), the moving party must first demonstrate that it has an extremely strong *prima facie* case; secondly, that the potential for damage is very serious, and; thirdly, there must be clear evidence that the other party has in its possession incriminating documents or things, and that there is a real possibility that the other party may destroy such material before any application *inter partes* can be made. Furthermore, in my view, after an action has been commenced, I must be satisfied that it is appropriate to proceed in the absence of the other party.

I will indicate at the outset of these reasons that I am satisfied that the plaintiff has demonstrated that there is an extremely strong *prima facie* case. The plaintiff provided

documentary evidence of its interest in the copyright which subsists in these programs through an exclusive licensing agreement with the owners of the copyright. There is no evidence that the defendant has any authority to rent video-cassette tapes of the programs to the public. Thus, there is a serious issue to be tried. Furthermore, the potential for damage is very serious and there is clear evidence that the defendant has in her possession video-cassette tapes which she rents out without the plaintiff's permission in violation of the Act and I am satisfied that there is a real possibility that the defendant may destroy the tapes before any application *inter partes* can be made.

Practically speaking, so that these orders have their intended effect, Anton Piller orders are most often sought on an *ex parte* basis. This is to ensure the element of surprise in the sense that, as the defending party is not given notice of the order, there is no opportunity for the offending documents or things to be destroyed or removed. In addition, Anton Piller orders are, generally speaking, sought either before or at the onset of court proceedings as it is at this point that the plaintiff becomes aware that such an order is necessary. This particular motion is unusual in the sense of its timing. The plaintiff brings this motion midway through the proceedings, after the usual discovery process has begun. Because the matter is so far advanced, both parties are represented by counsel. It is because this motion is brought *ex parte* and because of its timing that it poses difficulties which in my view had to be addressed by counsel for the plaintiff.

[The judge reviews the case law including *Yousif v. Salama* in which an Anton Piller order was granted. He quotes Lord Denning for the majority and Justice Donaldson for a very strong dissent.] ...

In my view, as was the case in *EMI Ltd.* and in *Yousif*, there is compelling evidence that if the defendant were provided with notice of this motion, the plaintiff's litigation will be "unfairly and improperly frustrated." The plaintiff has, through the affidavit of its private investigator, provided this Court with compelling evidence that there is a probability, and more than a possibility, that were the defendant to be given notice of this motion, the evidence being sought would disappear. I must state, however, that I come to this conclusion reluctantly as I am loathe to proceed in any matter where there is legal counsel, without providing counsel with the opportunity to be heard.

The second issue which counsel for the plaintiff addressed was whether seeking an Anton Piller order is appropriate at this stage of the proceedings, where the parties have already begun the ordinary discovery process. The Federal Court Rules provide for discovery between parties through the exchange of affidavits of documents and in the case at bar, the parties have, at least in form, complied with this requirement. The plaintiff is not satisfied with the affidavit of documents provided by the defendant, and has tendered to the Court, evidence that the affidavit of documents is deficient. In these circumstances, I am faced with two applicable Federal Court Rules. First, there is Rule 453. ... Under ordinary circumstances, where a party is dissatisfied with an affidavit of documents, Rule 453 provides the appropriate course of action. Upon motion for an order under that Rule, the opposing parties would be afforded the opportunity to satisfy the Court as to whether or not the affidavit of documents at issue is accurate.

However, in the present circumstances, there is also Rule 470, under which Rule the plaintiff in the case at bar moves, which contemplates that this Court may make, *inter alia*, an order such as an Anton Piller order, for the detention, custody and preservation of property. In this case, the plaintiff is relying on the allegedly inaccurate affidavit of documents as the evidence that an Anton Piller order is required. Rather than seek to obtain an order requiring an accurate affidavit of documents, the plaintiff has chosen the more extreme route of being granted the power to enter onto the defendant's premises and seize those documents which it alleges are present there and which are not listed on the affidavit of documents. To proceed in this manner is to circumvent the ordinary discovery process in a major way. Counsel for the plaintiff has cited authority for the proposition that Anton Piller orders may be granted long after the proceedings between the parties have commenced and advanced. ...

... Thus, the plaintiff in this case had the choice of which Rule under which to proceed and it chose Rule 470; the only limitation on proceeding in that manner is, of course, that the plaintiff must meet the stringent test that is applicable to the granting of Anton Piller orders. ... To use Mr. Justice Sharpe's words, quoted above, the plaintiff must demonstrate that this is a case where there is "compelling evidence that the defendant is bent on flouting the process of the court by refusing to abide by the ordinary procedure of discovery." In my view, the affidavit evidence of the plaintiff's private investigator provides this compelling evidence. The defendant has twice remitted an affidavit of documents to the plaintiff, each of which, on the evidence presented to this Court, is inaccurate; the private investigator's evidence is that he has rented seven programs which properly should have been disclosed, but have not been. The defendant has been given two opportunities to comply with this Court's Rules, and I am satisfied on the evidence that she has failed to do so. ... [I]n my view, this is one of the rare cases where the evidence demonstrates that the ordinary discovery process will not have its intended effect and an Anton Piller order is appropriate. It should be noted that the courts are careful to ensure that Anton Piller orders are not used as tools for fishing expeditions. I am satisfied, in light of the private investigator's evidence with respect to his having rented seven allegedly infringing videos, that the plaintiff is not seeking this motion as part of a fishing expedition. On the evidence, I draw the inference that there are additional allegedly infringing video-cassette tapes at the defendant's retail premises.

In my view, the plaintiff has met the three parts of the test for an Anton Piller order. In addition, the plaintiff has satisfied me that this motion should be done on an *ex parte* basis and that it is a remedy which is available at this point in the proceedings. For these reasons, an Anton Piller order is granted.

Oakley, Inc. v. *Jane Doe*

[2000] F.C.J. No. 1388 (Q.L.)
FEDERAL COURT OF CANADA—TRIAL DIVISION
AUGUST 29, 2000

[1] Pelletier J. (Reasons for Order, orally):— Seema and Jatinder Gupta's business took a turn for the worse on November 13, 1999. A team of lawyers and investigators representing various copyright and trade-mark holders showed up armed with a number of "rolling" Anton Piller Orders and seized a significant portion of their inventory. When the Guptas took stock of the wads of paper left with them by the team, they found nine Statements of Claim, nine Anton Piller Orders and nine Notices of Motion for the review of the execution of the Anton Piller Orders. They did not appear on the return of the Motion and allowed the Statements of Claim to be noted for default. They might not have done so had they ... known that a claim for judgments totalling some $42,750 would be made against them.

[2] When this matter came on before me on May 11, 2000, I issued directions dealing with the judgment which I was prepared to sign. Representations were received from counsel for the plaintiffs as a result of which a hearing was held. The issue in that hearing was whether nominal damages are still nominal damages if they are assessed nine times over. Specifically, each of the plaintiffs sought nominal damages for infringement in the amount of $3,000 and costs of $1,750 for the review of the execution of the Anton Piller Order and entry of default judgment. Simple arithmetic (4,750 x 9) leads to the conclusion

that the Guptas' potential exposure was $42,750. This is not a number which leaps to the lips when lawyers gather to discuss nominal damages. ...

[The court reviews the provisions of the Trade-marks Act and the Copyright Act and the case law relevant to the issue of multiple applications for nominal damages.]

[12] If one accepts that a conventional award of $3,000 for all claims by one plaintiff is fair, is it less fair if the same claim is advanced by multiple plaintiffs at the same time? This effectively amounts to asking whether the method of enforcement should affect the quantum of damages. If each plaintiff were to enforce its rights individually on successive days, it would be no defence for the defendant to say that the damages sought by the ninth plaintiff were excessive because of amounts paid to the first plaintiff. The number of plaintiffs involved in a particular enforcement action may be relevant to the question of costs but logically should be irrelevant to the question of damages.

[13] In the result, I conclude that if one is satisfied that a conventional damage award of $3,000 is a fair resolution of all claims which a single plaintiff could raise arising from the infringement of its marks or works, then it is not made less fair by being advanced by a number of plaintiffs at once. The fact

that there are multiple plaintiffs is a result of the defendant's conduct, not the plaintiffs'.

[The court then reviews the cases and tariffs regarding costs] ...

[21] In the end result, I would order that the costs and damages in this matter would be as follows:

Damages	$ 3,000
Costs of review motion	500
Costs of default judgment	250
	$ 3,750

Having arrived at this point, I wish to point out certain limiting factors.

[22] These conclusions ... are subject to review in the event of representations being made by defendants at some point in time .... [and are] subject to being displaced by evidence of actual damages.

[24] Finally, given that none of the material served upon defendants under the current practice would alert them to the quantum of the claim for damages and costs to be advanced against them, it would be appropriate for plaintiffs to bring to the attention of defendants the possibility of a judgment against them in this amount for each order obtained. ... This is not to say that the award of damages is contingent upon such notice being given but that a judge's concerns about the fairness of the cumulative effect of such awards might be allayed by the fact of notice having been given.

[25] In the end result, judgment and order will issue in favour of the plaintiff against the defendants in the amount of $3,000 for damages and $750 for costs. These reasons apply equally to the other plaintiffs on whose behalf orders were served upon the defendants ...

CONTEMPT OF COURT

- *I*n its Statement of Claim, Apple Computer alleged that the defendants were importing, assembling and selling computers that contained programs for which Apple owned the copyright. It also alleged that the defendants used a computer case and symbols that would confuse the public. Apple was awarded an interlocutory injunction. The defendants continued to import and assemble the Apple clones. Apple then returned to court for a contempt of court ruling.

  The court found the defendants were in contempt of court, and fined Minitronics of Canada, O.S. Micro Systems and Comtex Micro System $1,000, $10,000 and $20,000 respectively. The court further fined Lam of Minitronics $1,000, Lam, Lieu and Wu of Micro Systems and Comtex, $5,000 each and ruled that they would be sent to jail unless they paid the fines, apologized to the court, conducted themselves properly for a year and posted a $100,000 performance bond. Lam of Minitronics had to pay Apple's legal costs up to the morning on which he entered a guilty plea; the other defendants had to pay costs of $60,000.[42]

D. INSURANCE

Question

Insurance law requires uberrima fides, *"the most abundant good faith; absolute and perfect candor"[43] on the part of the insured. What are the consequences if the insured does not provide all of the material facts to the insurer?*

Lachman Estate	*v.*	*Norwich Union Life Insurance Co. (Canada)*

[1998] O.J. No. 2211 (Q.L.)
ONTARIO COURT (GENERAL DIVISION)
MAY 28, 1998

Himel J.: — This case involves a claim by the estate of the deceased, Mala Devi Lachman, for payment of the proceeds of a life insurance policy issued by the defendant Norwich Union Life Insurance Company (Canada). The defendant has denied the request for payment of the proceeds to the estate.

THE FACTS

In June of 1994, Mala Devi Lachman (hereinafter referred to as "Lachman") took out a policy of insurance on her own life from Norwich Union Life Insurance Company (Canada). The policy issued on July 12, 1994 was a term life policy which provided for a payment of $400,000 on death and the beneficiary named was Mr. Terry Tombran [a man whom she believed would provide a business opportunity]. Tombran took out a policy at the same time of $400,000 on his own life and named as his beneficiaries his wife, children, sister-in-law and Ms. Lachman. On November 14, 1994, Ms. Lachman was murdered and Tombran has since been convicted of the murder. A claim was made by the family of Lachman and Norwich has refused payment. An action was brought by the estate of Lachman. ...

[C]ounsel for the defendant [Ms. Tough] relies on s. 183 of the Insurance Act and submits that the contract may be voidable by the insurer for misrepresentations which need not be fraudulent and that negligent or innocent misrepresentations are sufficient. ... The Supreme Court of Canada [in *Coronation Insurance Co. v. Taku Air Transport Ltd.*, [1991] 3 S.C.R. 622 ... cited Lord Mansfield's comments on the duty of disclosure in an insurance contract in *Carter v. Boehm* (1766) ... and held that if the insured fails even inadvertently to fulfil the duty to communicate all relevant facts to the insurer; then the policy would be void. ... Cory J. described the principle of insurance law that an insured when applying for insurance has a heavy burden to make full and complete disclosure of material facts:

> The *ubberima fides* doctrine is a longstanding tenet of insurance law which holds parties to an insurance contract to a standard of utmost good faith in their dealing. It places a heavy burden on those seeking insurance coverage to make full and complete disclosure of all relevant information when applying for a policy.

In *Lloyd's London, Non-Marine Underwriters v. National Armoured Ltd.* (1996), 142 D.L.R. (4th) 506 (Ont. Gen. Div.), Sharpe J.... [referring to *Coronation Insurance* held]:

> The rationale for this rule is the disparity in access to information. The insured has superior knowledge of the relevant facts and the law imposes upon that party the duty to be open and honest. As already noted, this rule has been a feature of insurance law for over 200 years.
> ...

DECISION

There are essentially two issues before me: (1) whether there were material misrepresentations made by the deceased Ms. Lachman such that the insurance policy is void; and (2) if it is not void, whether the estate of the deceased Ms. Lachman may claim successfully where the beneficiary designated under the policy is disentitled as a result of a criminal act.

(1)   The issue of misrepresentations

In order for a claim for life insurance to be considered on its merits, it is necessary to show that the policy is a valid and enforceable contract. A contract may be void *ab initio* as a result of misrepresentations if the complaining party was induced to enter the contract based upon false information.

In particular, with contracts of life insurance, there is a duty upon the party seeking the insurance to make true and full representation of facts which are material to the insurance risk. What is material to the life insurance risk must be assessed from the insurer's perspective and the test is an objective rather than subjective test. That is why it must be demonstrated by the insurer that the underwriting guidelines of the insurer "must be in reasonable conformity with the ordinary standards for measuring insurable risks applied by insurers in general". Materiality, therefore, must be tested in the context of a "reasonable insurer"...

Whether the misrepresentations are fraudulent or innocent does not become an issue where the policy has not been in force for two years during the lifetime of the insured. The motive or intention of the insured is not relevant as long as the misrepresentations are of a fact known to the insured which could be regarded by a reasonable insurer as material to the risk.

In the case before me, there is evidence called by the insurer of misrepresentations as to occupation, length of occupation and the relationship of the insured and the beneficiary designated which facts the witnesses ... have described as material to the risk. ...

We will never know why Ms. Lachman purchased life insurance which designated Tombran as the sole beneficiary or why she made the misrepresentations to the agent on the questions of occupation, duration of occupation and relationship. Regardless of her intentions, innocent as they may have been, it is obvious she knew these facts to be untrue. There is no suggestion that she did not understand what she was signing when she completed the application for insurance. That application was also attached to the policy which provided her with a second opportunity to correct any errors in the application form. In fact, there was evidence that she had completed a Grade 12 education in Guyana, taken a secretarial course and could read and write English.

As a result, I am satisfied that the defendant has succeeded in proving that material misrepresentations were made well within the two-year period following the issuance of the policy. Accordingly, the policy is void. The policy being repudiated by the insurer is rescinded. In the circumstances, the premiums paid by Ms. Lachman should be refunded to her estate.

(2)   The issue of entitlement by the estate to the proceeds of insurance

Having determined that the contract is void, it is not necessary for the purposes of the result of this case to deal with the entitlement issue. [However, the court reviews the law and rejects the estate's contention that it] stands in the shoes of the insured who owned the policy. Respectfully, I disagree with that analysis. Much as it might have pleased Ms. Lachman to know that her family would enjoy the benefits of the proceeds of the policy, she did not name them as alternative beneficiaries to Mr. Tombran. Nowhere, in fact, are they mentioned. Although the court sympathizes with the plight of Ms. Lachman's family which has suffered a tragic loss, the court is not able to rewrite the terms of the contract of insurance. ...

In the result, judgment is granted in favour of the defendant Norwich Union Life Insurance Company (Canada). The policy of insurance on the life of Mala Devi Lachman is void due to material misrepresentations made in the application for insurance. The contract having been rescinded, the plaintiff is entitled to a refund of the premiums paid under that policy ...

Action dismissed.

Below are other instances in which the insurance contracts were rescinded because of the misrepresentations or deceit of the insured.

- *H*uang Chun-ming of Taipei had his friends chop off one of his hands with a samurai sword in his effort to defraud an insurance company and collect funds to pay his gambling debts. His day job: insurance salesman.[44]

- *A* man failed to disclose to the insurer a medical history that suggested serious illness. He was diagnosed as having colon cancer the day after the policy was delivered.[45]

- *M*r. Chan failed to tell the insurer that he intended to kill his wife two days after the policy was obtained.[46]

Q u e s t i o n s

Does the insurance company owe a duty of good faith to its insured?
What if the insurance company refuses to pay without evidence of wrongdoing?

Whiten *v.* Pilot Insurance Company *et al.*

http://www.ontariocourts.on.ca/
COURT OF APPEAL FOR ONTARIO
FEBRUARY 5, 1999

Laskin, J.A. (Dissenting in Part):

[1] Pilot Insurance Company appeals a punitive damages award of $1,000,000, the largest award in Canada against an insurer for dealing in bad faith with a claim by one of its insureds.

[2] ... [A] fire destroyed the Whitens' home and all of their belongings. Daphne Whiten claimed for the fire loss under her insurance policy, but Pilot refused to pay. Pilot alleged arson, even though it had opinions from its adjuster, its expert engineer, an investigative agency retained by it and the fire chief that the fire was accidental. Pilot maintained its defence of arson throughout a four week trial before Matlow J. and a jury, although it now concedes that the evidence unequivocally shows the fire was accidental. ...

[4] I would not give effect to Pilot's submissions. In my opinion, Pilot's breach of its obligation of good faith was an independent actionable wrong for which punitive damages could be awarded. Pilot's conduct was so reprehensible that a punitive award was justified; and the amount of the award is supportable in the light of the deference to be accorded to the jury's assessment, the extent of Pilot's reprehensible conduct, the need to deter this kind of conduct and the need to impose a fine that is more than a licence fee. Therefore, I would dismiss the appeal... .

[The court reviews the night of the fire, the numerous investigations into the cause of the fire, and Pilot's shabby treatment of the Whitens.]....

First Issue: Was Daphne Whiten Entitled to an Award of Punitive Damages?

[21] Punitive damages are awarded, not to compensate the plaintiff, but to punish the defendant and to deter the defendant and others from acting in an outrageous or reprehensible manner. Cory J. discussed these general principles in *Hill v. Church of Scientology of Toronto*, ...

> Punitive damages bear no relation to what the plaintiff should receive by way of compensation. ... It is the means by which the jury or judge expresses its outrage at the egregious conduct of the defendant. They are in the nature of a fine which is meant to act as a deterrent to the defendant and to others from acting in this manner. It is important to emphasize that punitive damages should only be awarded in those circumstances where the combined award of general and aggravated damages would be insufficient to achieve the goal of punishment and deterrence.

[22] For an award of punitive damages to be made, two requirements must be met: first, the defendant must have committed an independent or separate actionable wrong causing damage to the plaintiff; and second, the defendant's conduct must be sufficiently "harsh, vindictive, reprehensible and malicious" or "so malicious, oppressive and high-handed that it offends the court's sense of decency." Pilot submits that neither requirement has been met in this case.

[23] The first requirement, that of an independent actionable wrong, emerges from the judgment of the Supreme Court of Canada in *Vorvis v. Insurance Corporation of British Columbia*, a wrongful dismissal case. In *Vorvis*, McIntyre J. acknowledged that punitive damages may be awarded in breach of contract cases although he cautioned that such awards would be rare. He wrote:

... Punishment may not be imposed in a civilized community without a justification in law. The only basis for the imposition of such punishment must be a finding of the commission of an actionable wrong which caused the injury complained of by the plaintiff.

[24] The requirement of an independent actionable wrong was affirmed in *Wallace v. United Grain Growers Ltd.* and has been consistently applied by provincial appellate courts since *Vorvis*. Pilot submits that it did not commit an independent actionable wrong because it simply breached its contract of insurance with Daphne Whiten. Pilot acknowledges that an implied term of that contract was to deal with Daphne Whiten's claim in good faith. But, Pilot argues, even a breach of its covenant to act in good faith is no more than a breach of its contractual obligation, not an independent actionable wrong as *Vorvis* requires. Pilot submits that to sustain an award of punitive damages what would have been required was the commission of a separate tort, such as defamation or deceit, neither of which was pleaded or made out in this case.

[25] I do not agree with this submission. A contract of insurance between an insurer and its insured is one of utmost good faith. Although the insurer is not a fiduciary, it holds a position of power over an insured; conversely, the insured is in a vulnerable position, entirely dependent on the insurer when a loss occurs. For these reasons, in every insurance contract an insurer has an implied obligation to deal with the claims of its insureds in good faith. That obligation to act in good faith is separate from the insurer's obligation to compensate its insured for a loss covered by the policy. An action for dealing with an insurance claim in bad faith is different from an action on the policy for damages for the insured loss. In other words, breach of an insurer's obligation to act in good faith is a separate or independent wrong from the wrong for which compensation is paid.

[26] *Vorvis* requires an independent actionable wrong, not an independent actionable tort. ...

[27] If *Vorvis* makes it necessary ... I would be prepared to hold that an insured has a duty in tort of good faith towards its insureds... .

[28] A strong argument can be made for finding that the relationship between insurer and insured is of sufficient proximity to give rise to a concurrent duty in tort alongside the insurer's implied contractual obligation to act in good faith. However, I do not think that it is necessary to go this far because I am satisfied that an insurer's breach of the implied term of the insurance contract to act in good faith meets the *Vorvis* requirement of an independent actionable wrong.

[29] Pilot also submits that even if acting in bad faith is an independent actionable wrong, its conduct was not reprehensible enough or high-handed enough to attract an award of punitive damages. This submission has no merit whatsoever. There was overwhelming evidence in this case from which the jury could reasonably conclude that Pilot's handling of the Whitens' claim was so malicious or vindictive or so reprehensible or high-handed that an award of punitive damages was warranted. In summary, the evidence overwhelmingly shows that Pilot handled the Whitens' claim unfairly and in bad faith; that it deliberately ignored any opinion, even of its own adjuster and its own experts, that would oblige it to comply with its contractual obligation to pay the claim; and, that it abused its financial position and contrived an arson defence to avoid payment of the claim or, at least, to force a significant compromise. [The court enumerates the insurer's actions that evidence its bad faith in dealing with the Whitens]...

[30] In the face of this evidence, an award of punitive damages was fully justified. I would not give effect to this ground of appeal.

Second Issue: Is the Award of $1,000,000 Excessive?

[31] [Judge Laskin considers Pilot's submissions and concludes that the award of punitive damages of $1,000,000 is not unreasonable.]

[49] ... I would dismiss the appeal with costs.

[50] ... [Finlayson, J.A., with Catzman J. concurring, found for the plaintiff, but concluded the award of punitive damages was excessive and set aside the award of $1,000,000 and substituted $100,000.]

[Punitive damages reduced to $100,000] 2–1

Note: The Supreme Court of Canada has heard the appeal. The decision has not yet been released.

BELOW ARE OTHER INSTANCES IN WHICH THE INSURED ALLEGED BAD FAITH ON THE PART OF THE INSURANCE COMPANIES.

- *I*n *McIsaac v. Sunlife Assurance Company of Canada*, the B.C. Court of Appeal upheld the trial court's decision that improper refusal of an insurance company to pay money owing under a disability insurance policy warranted an award of aggravated damages because the subject matter of such contracts is to provide peace of mind and freedom from distress.[47]

- *A* Hamilton lawyer began 66 court actions against insurance companies and individual claims adjusters hired by the insurance companies, for unlawfully withholding insurance money. In most cases he sought aggravated, exemplary, and punitive damages. An adjuster argued that there was a term of good faith in the contract between the insurance company and the insured, but he, the adjuster, had no contract with the insured.

The court answered that the company is liable in contract and the adjuster can be liable as "duty of good faith has an independent and concurrent existence arising out of the principles of tort."[48]

What if the insurer negligently fails to ascertain the needs of the person buying insurance?

- *W*hen 227 tonnes of chocolate bars were found in "one big lump" when they reached their destination in Trinidad, the sender successfully sued the carrier, as well as the insurance agent, because the agent failed to provide the proper insurance to cover the sender's business needs.[49]

ENDNOTES

1. For a more detailed account see *The Vancouver Sun*, October 17, 2000, p. A14.

2. For a review of *Saskatchewan Wheat Pool v. 1037619 Ontario Inc.*, see *The Lawyers Weekly*, July 14, 2000, p. 9.

3. For a more detailed account see *The Lawyers Weekly*, September 10, 1999, p. 9.

4. Summarized from *The Globe and Mail*, July 1, 1993, p. A9.

5. This case was followed for years in *The Lawyers Weekly*. The U.S. case involving 2 Live Crew's use of Roy Orbison's 1964 song, "Oh, Pretty Woman," was also covered by *Time magazine*, December 13, 1993, p. 93.

6. A more detailed account is given in *Newsweek*, March 16, 1987, p. 53.

7. For a more detailed account see *Playback*, November 2, 1998.

8. Summarized from: *Wired News*, February 17, 2000; reprinted by Edupage; *Time*, April 3, 2000, p. 66; and *The Globe and Mail*, July 4, 2000, p. 8. This article also lists the members of the RIAA: Seagram Co. Ltd.'s Universal Music; Bertelsmann AG's BMG; Sony Corp.'s Sony Music; and Time Warner Inc.'s Warner Music Group. The latter is merging with EMI Group Plc.

9. *The Vancouver Sun*, November 1, 2000, p. A14.

10. *The Vancouver Sun*, February 13, 2001.

11. *The Globe and Mail*, February 23, 2001, paragraph B7.

12. Summarized from *Cnet*, April 13, 2000, reprinted by Edupage.

13. *The Vancouver Sun*, September 21, 2000, p. E5.

14. Summarized from the *Wall Street Journal*, August 18, 2000, reprinted by Edupage.

15. Summarized from *USA Today*, August 4, 2000, reprinted by Edupage.

16. *Time*, June 26, 2000, p. 31.

17. *The Illinois State Journal-Register*, September 7, 2000, p. 28.

18. *The New York Times*, 15 November, 2000, reprinted by Edupage.

19. *The Lawyers Weekly*, July 28, 1989.

20. A more detailed account is given in *Newsweek*, January 6, 1992, p. 55.

21. Summarized from *The Globe and Mail*, April 28, 1993, p. A7.

22. *Playback*, April 5, 1999, p. 15.

23. *Playback*, April 5, 1999, p. 17.

24. For a more detailed account see *Newsweek*, June 24, 1996, p. 89.

25. For a more detailed account see *The Vancouver Sun*, August 12, 2000, p. A3.

26. For a summary of *Walt Disney Productions v. Triple Five Corp.*, see *The Lawyers Weekly*, July 24, 1992, p. 3.

27. See *The Lawyers Weekly*, October 14, 1994, p. 33 regarding the dismissal of the appeal, June 7, 1996, p. 12.

28. See *697234 Ontario Inc. carrying on business as The Loose Moose Tap & Grill v. The Spruce Goose Brewing Co.* (1991) 38 C.P.R. (3d) 449, Federal Court Trial Division, November 7, 1991.

29. For a more detailed account see *The Lawyers Weekly*, June 25, 1993, p. 23.

30. Received by e-mail from Edupage, *USA Today*, June 3, 1997.

31. *The Lawyers Weekly*, Jeffrey Miller, December 16, 1988.

32. For a summary of *Maple Leaf Foods Inc. v. Robin Hood Multifoods Inc.* see *The Lawyers Weekly*, November 4, 1994, p. 28.

33. For a more detailed account see *The Globe and Mail*, October 17, 2000, p. B13.

34. Summarized from the *Wall Street Journal*, August 17, 1999, reprinted by Edupage.

35. *The Lawyers Weekly*, April 16, 1999, p. 2.

36. For a more detailed account see *Time*, June 12, 2000, p. 25.

37. For a more detailed account see *The Globe and Mail*, October 17, 2000.

38. Summarized from the *Boston Globe*, December 8, 1999, reprinted by Edupage.

39. For a more detailed account of the historical significance of this accomplishment and the rivalry between the public and private sector see *Time*, July 3, 2000, pp. 12–24.

40. For a discussion of those requirements see *The Lawyers Weekly*, November 17, 2000, p. 14.

41. For a more detailed account see *The Ottawa Citizen*.

42. A more detailed account is given in *The Vancouver Sun,* March 19, 1988, p. 1, D12.

43. From *Black's Law Dictionary*: "the most abundant good faith; absolute and perfect candor or openness and honesty; the absence of any concealment or deception, however slight."

44. For a more detailed account, see *The Vancouver Sun*, August 19, 2000, p. A2.

45. For a more detailed account, see a summary of *Pusateri's Ltd. v. Prudential of America Life Insurance Co. (Canada)* in *The Lawyers Weekly,* June 4, 1999, p. 16.

46. For a more detailed account, see coverage of *Chan Estate v. Allstate Life Insurance Co. of Canada* in *The Lawyers Weekly*, February 5, 1999, pp. 16, 20.

47. See *McIsaac v. Sunlife Assurance Company of Canada,* British Columbia Court of Appeal, http://www.courts.gov.bc.ca/ April 30, 1999.

48. See *Spiers v. Zurich Insurance Co.*[1999] O.J. No. 3683 (Q.L.), Ontario Superior Court of Justice, September 16, 1999.

49. For a summary of *1013799 Ontario Limited v. Kent Line International Limited*, see *The Lawyers Weekly,* September 8, 2000, p. 22.